S0-CBI-300

Child Care Administration

Child Care Administration

JUDITH W. SEAVER

CAROL A. CARTWRIGHT

Wadsworth Publishing Company
Belmont, California
A Division of Wadsworth, Inc.

To our husbands, Leigh and Phil,
and to our children, Burleigh, Barton, Cathie, Steve, and Susan

Education Editor: Miriam Nathanson
Production: Mary Forkner, Publication Alternatives
Text and Cover Design: Gary A. Head
Copy Editor: Jonas Weisel
Illustrator: Pamela Manley

Printed in the United States of America
1 2 3 4 5 6 7 8 9 10—90 89 88 87 86

ISBN 0-534-03681-3

Library of Congress Cataloging-in-Publication Data

Seaver, Judith W.
Child care administration.

Bibliography: p.
Includes index.
1. Day care centers—United States—Administration.
2. Education, Preschool—United States—Philosophy.
3. Child care workers—United States. I. Cartwright, Carol A. II. Title.
HV854.C37 1986 362.7′12 85-17961
ISBN 0-534-03681-3

Contents

Preface

Because increasing numbers of women with young children are working, there is an urgent need to prepare professionals for administrative and leadership roles to care for those children. Educational institutions are recognizing this need and planning courses and programs accordingly. We are beyond the question of "should we have child care?" We have it. We are now concerned with questions of how to provide child care with quality for families with diverse needs. *Child Care Administration* is a comprehensive book that has been written to fill these needs.

Child care takes many forms—from informal, private arrangements with relatives and neighbors to organized child care programs staffed by professionals and operated by agencies or community groups. In *Child Care Administration* we describe this comprehensive range of services and discuss the issues that support as well as discourage child care. About half the book's content deals with practical management and administrative information, and the other half deals with information about child care programs. A unique feature of the book is the decision-making approach to designing programs for children from infancy through early adolescence. The application of this decision-making process is seen in the numerous examples in the different child care programs presented.

Some theoretical material is included in this book because we believe that those who work in child care need the information to guide their day-to-day decisions. We realize that this may cause concern for some students and instructors, but child care cannot depend on a "bag-of-tricks" approach and just enough administrative skill and information to get through the next crisis. The field of child care will strengthen as its workers and leaders gain a solid understanding of developmental theory and research results to use in decision making. Although the theoretical material is challenging and sometimes difficult, it can and should be mastered. To present the material in a more readable and interesting way, we have included many examples from our experiences and those of colleagues to help make the ideas come alive. We hope we have conveyed both the challenge and the excitement that comes from knowing that the work you do has a sophisticated foundation to draw on.

This book is organized in four parts. In Part I, Looking at Child Care, Chapter 1 traces the history of child care and discusses its influences on current policies and practices. Chapter 2 presents the foundations for planning programs by describing three viewpoints of human development—maturationist, behaviorist, and cognitive. A daily care pattern that includes eight activity blocks as the basic structure of all programs is also presented.

In Part II we move from the "why" to the

"how to do it." We integrate the daily care pattern and the universal program components of staffing (Chapter 3), environmental design (Chapter 4), materials and equipment (Chapter 5), and evaluation (Chapter 6) with practical examples from each developmental viewpoint. The *process* of making program design decisions is illustrated as well as the resulting procedures and practices. This presentation captures and conveys the essence of the *child's experience* within each of three programs—maturationist, behaviorist, and cognitive.

Chapters 3–6 illustrate three fully developed program plans (one for each developmental perspective) and serve as general guides to preparing the implementation sections of a program plan. The chapters may be read and used in two ways.

1. *As a General Guide.* Read the discussion sections on staffing, environmental design, materials and equipment, and evaluation. Compare the maturationist, behaviorist, and cognitive examples to help you understand the nature of the program components and the various ways to implement them. Pay particular attention to how different theoretical assumptions result in different practices. Follow through by consulting the resources that are given for each of the universal program components.

2. *As Exemplary Plans.* The examples of practice and the discussion of decision-criteria for each of the three developmental programs are, in fact, cohesive program plans. By reading selectively and using the headings, you can isolate and individually study the components of maturationist, behaviorist, or cognitive programs. For example, you could work through the chapters reading only what appears under the behaviorist heading one time and then read through again for the other perspectives. The extensive resource lists provide an opportunity to gain depth in any of the three approaches.

   The examples in each of the plans are drawn from actual child care programs and represent what you might find if you observe a program in action.

Part III, Understanding Types of Programs, includes three chapters covering unique aspects of programs serving different groups of children. Infant care (Chapter 7), school-age care (Chapter 8) and family day care programs (Chapter 9) are described. The daily care pattern is a common thread among the chapters in Parts II and III.

Part IV, Making Programs Work, provides comprehensive coverage of the technical aspects of administering child care programs. Part IV begins with a general look at program management (Chapter 10) and continues with in-depth presentations on personnel (Chapter 11), budgets and funding (Chapter 12), regulations and legal matters (Chapter 13), parent roles (Chapter 14), and community and professional resources (Chapter 15).

Between the two of us, we have a great deal of experience. We have been teachers of young children in public and nonpublic school settings and research assistants in model programs such as Head Start. We have been college instructors specializing in early childhood methods and child care management courses as well as in graduate level courses dealing with policy issues and research. We have supervised students in internships in child care programs. We have conducted workshops for child care staff in programs for infants, preschoolers, and school-age children. Each of us has served in a leadership role on boards of directors for child care organizations, and we consult for state and federal agencies. Finally, we are both working mothers, and between us (and our five children) we have probably used just about every type of child care available. We have personal experience with the advantages and disadvantages of in-home care, family day care, center-based care, cooperative arrangements with neighbors, and, recently, older children responsible for their own care for brief periods after school. There is a reason for the ring of truth in this book—we have been there and know what it takes to make choices and make programs work!

We are grateful to the following reviewers for their many valuable comments and suggestions: Lucy J. Bell, Riverside City College; Louise D. Dean, Los Angeles Valley College; Barbara Harkness, San Bernardino Valley College; Nancy Hensel, University of Redlands; Sandra M. Long, Indiana University and International Graduate School; Deanna Radeloff, Bowling Green State University; Carol Sharpe, Bakersfield College; Mary Knox Weir, Long Beach City College; and Naomi Ziphin, Los Medanos College.

Throughout the preparation and production of this book, we have had some extraordinary support. Those who deserve special applause and appreciation for their competence, persistence, and good humor are Carolyn Harbolis and Ruth Kilhofer for typing the original manuscript; Becky Young and Karen Bruno for proofreading and tracking a thousand details; Leigh Seaver, Phil and Cathie Cartwright, and Carol Phillips for proofreading and index preparation; and Jonas Weisel for special editing. Mary Forkner and her staff at Publication Alternatives did a superb job in managing the production of the book; we value the good working relationship that she provided during the final months of publication.

Child care is a people-intense activity. Those who seek information and practical skills for work in child care do so primarily to increase their personal effectiveness in providing care for children. This book is for those people—for those who want to keep the *child* in child care and provide quality programs.

J. W. Seaver

C. A. Cartwright

Part I

Looking at Child Care

1

Child Care: Past and Present

Introduction

Child care: What is it? Who does it serve? Why do we need it? There are no easy answers.

To the uninitiated, the term *child care* is often confusing. The general public usually hears about this area only when the media reports on such problems as bureaucratic regulations, menial tasks, low wages, and fiscal crises. Even to the initiated, such as parents or staff members, the essence of child care is hard to pinpoint.

To get a better idea of what child care means today, we'll begin this book with a complete working definition, including the various features that constitute a typical program. In this field, as in many others, understanding the history helps to clarify the present situation. Following the definition, therefore, we'll devote the remainder of the chapter to a look back at how the two major historical traditions of child care—day care and early education—grew separately and in some cases merged. We'll start by outlining the history of the movements, reviewing the key events and people that marked their progress. As we'll see, elements from each movement gradually contributed to a new form of care program. In the 1960s Head Start, a prominent experiment in combining these traditions, indicated both the successes and the difficulties to be encountered in this combination. We'll look at Head Start in this light and try to define a number of basic terms that describe the level of care and the aim of modern child care programming.

Defining Child Care

There is no single accepted definition of what constitutes a child care program. Many definitions really describe only the setting or ages served or tend to reflect a point of view about the purpose of child care. Consider the following common definitions:

Center-based care for preschoolers Care of a preschooler (two and a half to five years) in a group setting for extended periods of the day

Family day care homes Care of a child in the home of another family. Generally serves no more than six children between the ages of six months and fourteen years

Infant care Care of an infant (birth to approximately two and a half years) by someone other than the child's mother. Care may be given in home or center setting with specific restrictions on infant-caregiver ratio

School-age care Care of a school-aged child (five to fourteen years) during hours when school is not in session. May be center- or home-based, with hours of care varying according to school schedules and other community activities available

Most child care can be looked at in this way, but the type of child care practiced at any facil-

Infants and toddlers are the newest participants in formal child care programs. Most very young children are cared for in private homes rather than in groups in center programs. (Courtesy of U.S. Department of Housing and Urban Development, Washington, DC.)

ity is actually made up of much more. Let's look at the full range of features that must be considered when spelling out how one program differs from another.

Age

Child care serves children from birth to age fourteen. Birth is an obvious beginning point for substitute care to be needed by parents. Fourteen is generally considered as the age beyond which children are firmly entered into adolescence and are not likely to seek out or benefit from a child care program. Other forms of activity and supervision seem better for teenagers.

Setting

Child care is defined as care that takes place outside the child's own home. It is, by definition, a care experience that involves separating children from their homes. The family day care home is considered to most closely approximate the physical characteristics of a home.

Preschool children, ages three to five are found in all types of child care programs. (Photo by Dick Swartz; courtesy of Department of Health and Human Services, Washington, D.C.)

Size of Group

Child care implies a group of children. Child care implies that the care group is larger and different in age composition from that experienced by the child in his or her own home with siblings. This difference in group may or may not hold for all children. At a minimum, child care is experienced in groups that do not naturally occur as sibling groups and are subject to frequent change in membership.

Time

Child care is care offered for part of a twenty-four-hour period. It usually takes place regularly on a daily basis or to fit a parent's shift schedule or working days. If the child spends long periods of time with adults other than the parent, that child care is referred to as *extended care*. Periods as short as two hours may be child care; eight or nine hours a day is clearly ex-

Center-based programs offer a wide range of activities and services. Publicly or privately funded, center programs may serve children from infancy through school age. (Courtesy of U.S. Department of Housing and Urban Development, Washington, DC.)

tended care. The longer a child spends in care, the more varied and complex the care services required.

Purpose

Child care is needed first and foremost for reasons of protection and safety. When parents are absent, young children cannot be left alone with reasonable assurance that they will be physically safe and able to cope with daily routines such as meals, naps, and toileting. Adult supervision is needed for these activities. Yet, it is a mistake to assume that all young children need from substitute caregivers is physical care. Children need understanding, affection, love, stimulation, and a host of related humanizing interactions with others. Time is growth and development for young children. The most important purpose of child care is to aid in facilitating children's development, and this means providing a substitute for or supplement to parental involvement in the development of the child.

Sponsorship

Child care programs that operate for profit are called proprietary. Parents' fees must cover the entire cost of care provided and allow for a margin of profit. Many privately run programs operated by churches, institutions, and individuals are nonprofit. Fees can be quite low or very high depending on the services provided. Various governmental jurisdictions may license privately run centers; city and/or state codes may apply. Centers may have to meet labor, industry, health board, and fire codes. Enforcement and inspection is not uniform from locality to locality, and regulations vary widely in substance and rigor.

Child care programs that receive public funds are subject to budget monitoring by sponsoring and funding agencies. Fees charged to parents are often low, indicating that care is subsidized. Sliding fee scales have been used in some states to more evenly allocate the actual cost of care. Various governmental jurisdictions license publicly funded centers. Centers must meet local applicable codes as well as any codes of the funding agencies. Regulations for publicly funded centers may be more comprehensive than those for privately run centers.

Caregivers

An adult or several adults other than the parents or relatives of the children involved comprise the staff of the child care center or the family day care home. Child care is substitute parental care. The implication is that someone

Using their homes and neighborhood resources, family day care mothers care for small mixed-age groups of children. Homes are often unregulated and many arrangements for care are private agreements between parent and day care mother. (Courtesy of U.S. Department of Health and Human Services, Washington, DC.)

Programs for school-age children can operate before and after school and during vacations. Concern is mounting for the large number of latchkey children who appear to have little formal supervision during nonschool hours. (Courtesy of U.S. Department of Housing and Urban Development, Washington, DC.)

other than a person intimately knowledgeable about the family values is assuming temporary responsibility for the care of the child while a parent is otherwise occupied. As part of the child care experience, children build strong ties with adults other than their parents and may be exposed to frequent changes in caregivers. Child care brings a special meaning to the terms *caring* and *caregiver*. The terms *teaching* and *teacher* and *parent* and *parenting* have universal meaning. The list of tasks and responsibilities unique to each role is relatively easy to determine. The spheres of influence of teacher and parent relate to differences in goals and reponsibilities. Despite the blurring of lines between home and school, it is still possible to clearly differentiate parenting from teaching. *Caring* and *caregiver* are newly minted terms to capture the essence of a relationship that is not universally recognized and accepted. The tasks and responsibilities of the caregiver overlap considerably with those of both teacher and parent.

Caregivers are involved with the total development of children. They work actively to ensure progress and growth and assume responsibility for, yet never control, the course of the child's development. It is the prerogative of the parent to determine the nature of the child's development. The role of the caregiver is to nur-

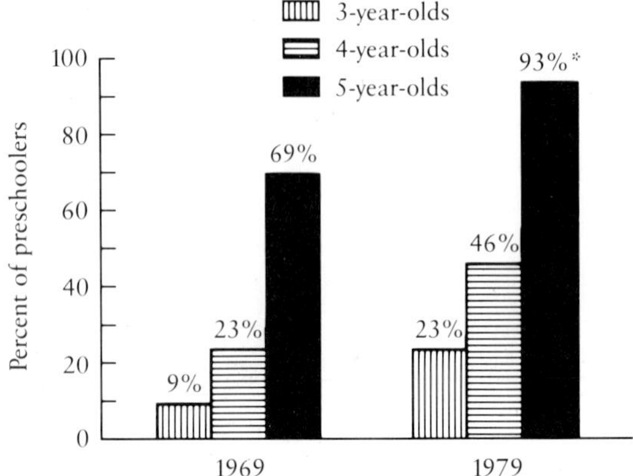

Figure 1.1 Preschool enrollment. (From "School-Enrollment-Social and Economic Characteristics of Students: October 1979." *Current Population Reports,* Series P-20 (360), by U.S. Bureau of the Census, 1981, Washington, DC: U.S. Department of Commerce.)

ture the child toward that course by working in harmony with the parent. Children, of course, affect their own development in many ways and provide yet another variable in the work of the caregiver.

Caregiving is special. It is what sets child care apart from education and keeps it distinct from parenting. Caregivers substitute for parents, enlarging but not duplicating the child's experiences with loving and concerned adults. In the most positive sense, caregivers provide modern day extended families for young children. Both parents and caregivers now generally recognize the importance of cooperative efforts in preserving the strengths of each other's practices for the ultimate good of the child.

Today's Composite Model

Although there are fewer young children today than a decade ago, more children attend some kind of child care program than ever before (see Figure 1.1). One large reason for this change is the increased number of mothers of young children who have entered the work force. Between 1970 and 1980 the number of working mothers with children aged less than six increased by 50.5%; those with children aged six to seventeen increased 31.9% (Bureau of Labor Statistics, 1980).

In the past, distinctions were made between child care programs that tried to meet parents' needs for extended care (day care) and programs that purported to meet children's educational or developmental needs (nursery, preschool, or kindergarten). The 1960s, however, brought heightened research and analysis of young children. Researchers studied the capacity of young children to learn, their responsiveness to improved conditions, and many different but effective curriculum approaches. At the same time working parents began to seek quality early educational experiences for their children. With these two influences, the former artificial distinctions began to blur. Today child care progams can draw upon the varied traditions of past practices as a rich resource for contemporary needs. The following section explores those traditions in more detail.

Two Child Care Movements

Historically, there have been two distinct and divergent child care movements, namely, day care and early education. *Day care* has generally referred to those facilities that offer full-day programs for young children whose parents must work outside the home. The *early education* movement has consisted of kindergartens and nursery schools.

Day care was originally designed to provide just for the health and safety of young children while their parents were absent. There was no intentional educational program. Day care has had a heritage of sponsorship by philanthropic or charitable organizations or support by government welfare. The early education movement, on the other hand, grew among the middle and upper classes who wanted social and learning experiences for their children. A great emphasis was placed on the application of educational theories.

These general trends have had important consequences for present-day programs. They have helped to delineate the social position of women as workers and mothers, the importance we place on our children's development, the type of educational approach we adopt, and the source of financial support.

Day Care

Throughout history, young children have alternately been viewed either as the hope of the future and citizens of tomorrow or as the salvation of the present, the extra pair of hands, the extra wages that could mean survival for the larger family unit as it struggled to maintain itself economically. America has prided itself on being a country that is child oriented, a country that values children and allows them a prolonged period of dependence before entrance into adult society. A natural outgrowth of America's child-centeredness would seem to be a child care system that supports child development directly as well as indirectly through supports to the family. However, American child care does not fit this utopian dream. Digging into the history of day care reveals interesting and sometimes startling gaps in the levels of service and types of care provided for children.

We can actually approach day care's history through two historical perspectives. In the first we'll see how interest in day care has fluctuated with society's notions of the proper behavior of mothers in the home and the work world. In the second perspective we'll consider how day care has evolved as the provider of funding has changed.

Economic Role of Women

Far from being a product of our nation's concern for its children, day care in the United States is tied to the economic role of women. Women carry the major responsibility in our society for bearing and rearing children. Perhaps this will change, but for the two centuries of our nation's existence, we have glorified the home, hearth, and mother love. Women, however, are also adults who may have skills or financial needs that compel them to participate in the work force. Many of these women have young children and family responsibilities. The provision of day care services has been aligned very closely to changing societal attitudes about women participating in the work force.

From the early 1800s, women were expected to remain in the home caring for their children. Immigrant status, marginal skills of husbands, and to a small extent, personal wishes caused many women to seek employment outside the home. Philanthropic groups provided day care to protect the children of working mothers. Near the end of this period, as immigration was slowing and family economic conditions were stabilizing, women returned to their homes, and day care services were provided only for women and children whose economic conditions were very dire.

World War II changed the direction of day care, at least for a short time. The need for women to work in factories required dependable care for their children. Day care services expanded rapidly and were generally of high quality. The end of the war, however, put an end to this, and day care once again contracted to a service provided for women and children in economic and social difficulties, becoming part of a constellation of social services provided by society for indigent families. So pervasive was the attitude that women belonged at home with their children, that many women were encouraged by social workers and welfare stipends to remain out of the work force while their children were young.

The years following World War II were characterized by a return to the notions that women belonged at home with their children and that mother love and care were the best possible nurturants for child development. This period was particularly characterized by the strength of conviction about the mother as the primary caregiver. Women did continue to work for reasons of personal and professional desire as well as economic necessity, but their needs were often ignored. Child care for most middle-class women was a problem that just didn't exist in the collective mind of society. Women from lower classes were either paid to stay home through AFDC (*A*id to *F*amilies with *D*ependent Children) or provided with day care that would enable them to work and join the ranks of the marginally poor.

The late 1960s heralded a time of ferment and dissent concerning the role women were to play in society. Many questioned the unthinking acceptance of previous attitudes toward women as child-rearers and nonessential members of the work force. As women pushed for equality and opportunity, they precipitated changes in attitudes toward child care. Child care's horizons are widening now as a direct result of the changing attitudes toward women and women's opportunities for increased participation in the work force at all social levels.

In the future the economic role of women will undoubtedly affect the quality and scope of child care programming. One obvious result of changes in attitudes toward working mothers and increased levels of participation in the work force by women is a demand to expand child care services. Funding for these programs may or may not be publicly provided. Many women are not eligible to use the child care services now available because, among other things, they earn too much money. Private child care programs may increase or child care may be provided as a public service available for all children, much like the public schools. Along with the need for efficiency and availability of services will come increased pressures for definable content in programs and for quality care that goes beyond provision of safe, physical care of the child. Child care that is available on a choice basis for all working mothers will result in a sweeping change in clientele. All children, from all levels of society, will be served, and the effect on child care programming will be profound.

Major Events in Day Care History

The history of day care has been punctuated by social and political events that illustrate the changing focus of societal interest in day care. Looking at these events along a time line illustrates the cumulative impact of events on the changing emphasis in child care programming. Figure 1.2 shows events that are generally thought to have shaped the direction and character of day care services. Day care services and public opinion regarding such services have gone in and out of public favor, but we see over time a steadily increasing favorable response in both absolute numbers of day care services and general public acceptance of day care.

Four distinct but somewhat overlapping eras emerge when day care events are viewed from a historical perspective: the charity era, the social welfare era, the federal era, and the new initiatives era. Each era is named for the type of support given to day care. Overall the history has been dominated by subsidies, first from charities and later from government. The weight of this longstanding external aid as well as the more recent beginnings of private enterprise have helped to shape society's image of day care and the actual nature of day care programs themselves.

Charity Era. The first era of day care events revolved around philanthropic and charitable efforts to provide day care services for children of the needy. Such efforts were community-based and zealously implemented. During this time, from 1828 to 1900, day care established itself as a credible cause for do-gooders—those who provided the care hoped to do the children some good and save them from harm. Programs provided physical care for children, and forms of service evolved in a relatively unpressured and unchecked fashion. Evaluation of the quality of care rested in the minds and hearts of the charitable ladies who sponsored day care services.

Social Welfare Era. Next came the social welfare era. It began around the turn of the century with the establishment of regulations and standards for the level of care and appropriateness of facilities. Sponsorship of day care gradually shifted from charitable organizations to local agencies and government groups. Day care became part of a relief effort, or welfare, that was organized and provided by communities and states and delivered through more formal channels than church groups and community associations. For instance, day care services were implemented under the Works Progress Administration (WPA) and the Community Facilities Act (Lanham Act) during the 1930s and 1940s. These agencies gave federal money to the states for specific, short-term puposes. The money was given without directives or guidelines to control the programs being underwritten.

Although day care expanded its clientele briefly during the depression and the war years, the pervasive image of day care as a welfare service of the states was not diminished. Following the war years, day care became firmly entrenched as a social welfare service for individuals who were outside the economic and social mainstream of society. Except for the experience of the war years, day care programs continued to emphasize physical care. The social welfare era established day care as part of the organized, bureaucratized, and institutionalized social welfare system.

Federal Era. Head Start, a federally funded program for disadvantaged children, began in 1965. Although it is not a part of day care's history, Head Start marks the beginning of the federal era of child care, when the federal government began to assume responsibility for welfare services and, more importantly, began to accept a role as leader and initiator in the provision of services for young children. Now the money came with strings attached—guidelines and regulations for the recipient programs. The Federal Interagency Day Care Requirements (FIDCR) in 1968 were a first step in sharing concerns and control over day care services between state and federal levels. (In 1979 these were renamed Health, Education and Welfare Day Care Requirements, or HEWDCR.) The vetoed Comprehensive Child Development Act of 1971 coalesced child care advocates and focused public attention squarely on the existing strengths and weaknesses of the current and proposed day care system. Various bills during this period provided expanded federal food and nutrition subsidies for day care.

The Social Security Act of 1975, the successor of the Social Security Acts of 1935 and 1967, grouping all social services together for purposes of federal funding, reiterated day care's position as a piece of the federal social service pie.

The federal era of day care can be viewed as a logical extension of the more narrowly focused eras of day care in the past. Money and program regulations continued to be targeted at low-income and socially disadvantaged individuals. Being part of the welfare system had two effects on day care programming: The federal government controlled a major portion of the funds available for day care services, and the government was in a position as a leader of opinion and a financier to initiate novel and broader means of delivering day care.

Concern for the mother-child relationship formed a consistent thread of purpose throughout the various stages of day care's connection with state and federal welfare. Changes in day care programming must build from the legacy that day care has inherited from its long association as a program for welfare recipients. Table 1.1 (p. 12) summarizes this legacy.

New Initiatives Era. In the 1980s the pendulum has swung again and there has been a new shifting of responsibility for day care back to-

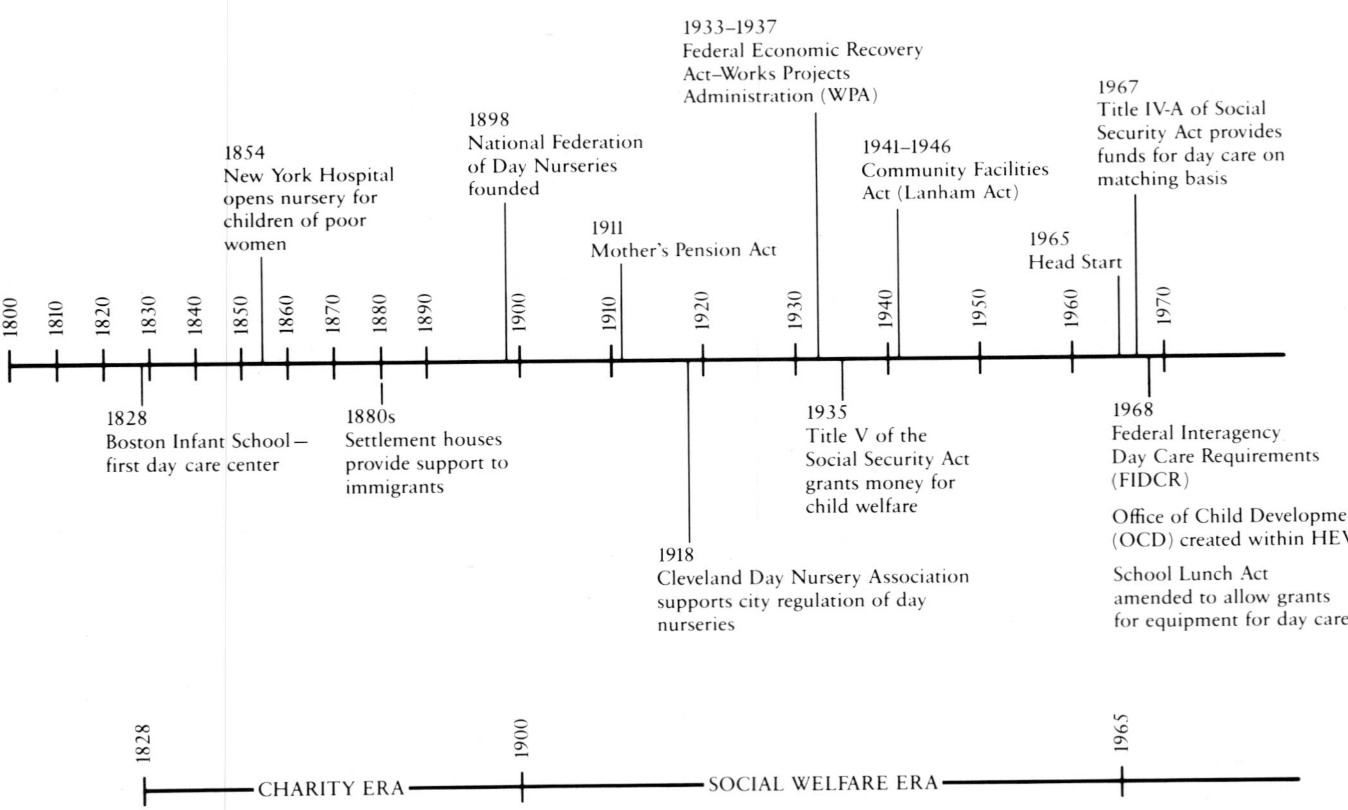

Figure 1.2 Major events in day care's history.

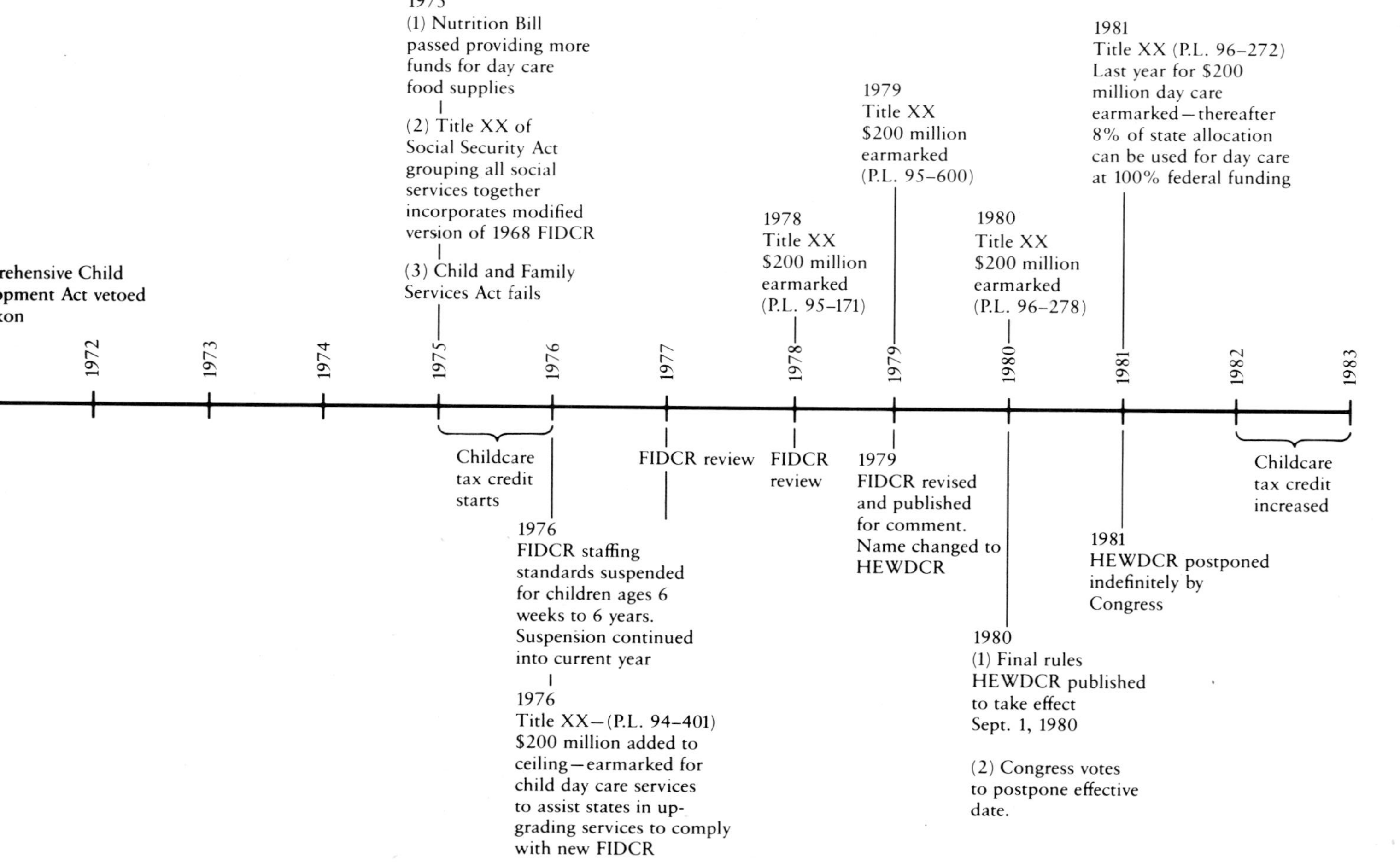

Figure 1.2 Major events in day care's history (*continued*).

Table 1.1. Day Care's Social Trend Legacy

Date	
Early 1800s	Day care provided shelter for children and exerted proper influences on their development.
1840s–1870s	Hygiene and sanitation were stressed as important to the physical well-being of children. Many day nurseries were supported as charities.
1870s–1900	Philanthropic day care for children of the poor became a venerable institution. Settlement houses "Americanized" the children of recent immigrants as they worked to make their way into the mainstream of economic life.
1900–1920	Professionals began to view day care as a social service tied to maternal difficulties in caring for children for reasons of work or unfitness. Local and state agencies moved to establish standards and regulations for day nurseries.
1920–1940	Home care of children by mother was considered best; day care served families who deviated from this social norm. WPA nurseries of the depression were considered temporary programs to "nurture" children. The Social Security Act provided public money for child services through Department of Welfare.
1940–1945	Women worked in factories during the war years. Day care was considered necessary to support the war effort and for a short period became part of the patriotic national war effort.
1945–1960	Home care of children was once again the norm. Families who deviated from this norm were considered to be victims of some social pathology. Day care was firmly entrenched in public opinion as a welfare service.
1960–1970	Public atitudes toward day care began to change. The feminist movement challenged the notion that mothers were the only ones capable of quality child care. Perhaps consumers of child care were not social deviants after all! Psychological research strongly suggested that the early years of life were important foundations for later development. Day care was increasingly viewed as an opportuity to provide developmental as well as custodial care.
1970–1980	The growing demand for day care and the drop in public school enrollments have shaken the monopoly welfare has historically had on the provision of day care services. Working parents of all economic levels view child care as a necessary purchasable service. For the first time, there are visible private-sector alternatives to publicly subsidized care.

ward local control, and in some cases, even to private enterprise.

By 1981, with the postponement of the implementation of the HEWDCR, the federal government signaled it was out of the business of regulating day care. States were to become the locus of regulatory control. Under the Reagan administration, Title XX became a block grant to states meaning that day care had to "compete" for a share of social service funds with other state Title XX services. It could be argued that these two events have merely shifted day care from a federal to a state program. This is true. Yet, such a simplistic interpretation masks the reality of state control. There is no uniformity amongst the fifty states and assorted jurisdictions concerning day care regulation and funding. Bureaucracies, resources, priorities, grass roots support and local consciousness of children's plight vary from state to state. Without the fiscal and regulatory federal glue, day care is a collection of single jigsaw pieces that may not even belong to the same large picture.

What can we expect in the future? Diversity and local responsiveness of programming, not chaos, will result from state efforts. While it may take the child care community and children's advocates time to adjust, ultimately day care programs will be controlled closer to home. Local and regional differences that are emerging are a sign of strength based on the input of consumers of care. The federal era served its purpose in building a foundation for future practices.

Another contribution to diversity in child care is the Child and Dependent Care Tax Credit. Begun in 1975–76 and recently expanded in 1982–83, the tax credit allows working parents to recover some of the costs of child care associated with working. The tax credit in effect extends federal child care subsidies to middle-class parents but does not restrict the kind of child care option they may choose. Once again, a federal act is promoting consumer choice and diversity.

A related part of the tax code permits employers certain tax breaks related to establishing child care programs for employees. In Chapter 12 we describe the growth of numerous types of employer-sponsored child care options and fringe benefits. The combination of business financial support and the strong interests of women employees promises to move employer-sponsorship of child care forward. The business sector will probably provide significant leadership in establishing not only child care programs but also changes in "work life" that will make parenting and working more compatible.

Child care has also become a business in its own right. No longer is it unthinkable to operate a child care program for profit. We accept child care as a service that parents are willing and increasingly able to pay for. National chains with satellite programs in many cities are proving that acceptable care at reasonable prices can be provided.

The debate over the role of public schools in child care continues too. But, no longer is the debate over absolute control or no control. Public schools can be expected in the future to be one of many locations and/or sponsors of child care programs. Care programs for school-age children are frequently school-based. Public schools will be increasingly responsive to parents' child care needs and public education will begin to actively seek partnership and cooperation with child care programs.

Day care thus has evolved from a charity-based effort to a government-sponsored service and finally to a locally controlled program. Each change has brought a difference to the value placed on child care, a different image of those who require child care, and new approaches to the actual care provided.

Early Education

The early education child care movement has a more succinct and contemporary history than that of day care. From the beginning, early education programs for young children were distinguishable from day care programs for two basic reasons:

1. The length of time spent by children in the program differed greatly, with day care children spending five to nine hours a day and children in early education programs spending two and a half to three hours a day.
2. The socioeconomic class of the children differed, with day care children generally from lower-class families while children in early education programs generally came from middle- to upper-class families.

At no time did the programs of the early education movement threaten the mother-child bond thought to be so critical to healthy development. Early education programs were supplements and supports to mother and home in their child-rearing.

In the early education movement, two distinct but related forms of programs evolved. The kindergarten movement served five-year-olds; the nursery school–play group movement served three- and four-year-olds. There were important differences between these two programs, other than the ages of children served, but there were also important similarities in purpose.

The Kindergarten Movement

Kindergarten programs emphasized play and social activities to promote sharing and cooperation. Some emphasized content, with units or themes on familiar ideas and activities, such as community helpers, circuses, and pets, that appealed to the kindergartener. Other forms of kindergarten programs fostered development of such skills as learning color names, alphabet letters, and number names that would be useful for success in later grades. Later this emphasis on content was called *readiness*. Kindergarten programs were eclectic, drawing support from a number of theoretical and philosophical traditions. In one degree or another, all kindergarten programs were concerned with the overall development of the child, the social-emotional health of the child and the acquisition of content through informal teaching and instruction.

Kindergartens flourished. Many became connected with the public schools, although it was not until recently that kindergarten became almost universally available through the public school system. Despite its eventual connection to the public schools, kindergarten did not begin as a downward extension of the elementary school curriculum. Kindergarten began as a unique program for young children, which advocated a special curriculum and specialized training for kindergarten teachers. Even after the association with the public schools became formalized, kindergartens continued to maintain a programmatic uniqueness that set them apart from the mainstream goals and practices of the elementary school.

Kindergartens occupy a particular position in the history of the early education movement. They continue to serve only five-year-olds. They have increasingly become connected with the public schools. They have maintained their uniqueness within the public school system, having exerted considerable influence on the organization and goals of the lower primary grades. Nevertheless, kindergartens have assimilated much of the philosophy of the public schools. Whereas first grade used to be the first step in twelve years of public education, kindergarten is now the first step for most children. The term *preschool* is reserved for those programs, nursery school and play group, that serve young children before they enter public school.

The kindergarten movement stimulated professional thinking concerning the needs of young children and the kinds of activities that could form an integrated curriculum for young children. Kindergarten professionals were instrumental in organizing university and college training programs to provide special training for those who wanted to work with young children. These professionals led the way in translating the best of current psychological theory into classroom practices and lobbying for planned programs for five-year-olds. The kindergarten movement greatly influenced prevailing attitudes toward the education of young children and the public financing of that education. Kindergarten programs are different from child care programs in purpose, organization, and general sponsorship, but child care has reaped many of the benefits of the change in public opinion that the kindergarten movement was responsible for seeding.

The Nursery School–Play Group Movement

Paralleling the momentum of the kindergarten movement was a second early education movement: the nursery school–play group movement. Nursery schools and play groups provided opportunities for social interaction and play for three- and four-year-old children of the middle classes. Nursery schools were supported by fees from parents and organized and run by women whose training almost always emphasized experience with their own children. Settings were in church basements, homes, or other familiar neighborhood locations. Play groups were informal versions of nursery schools, organized by mothers. Some were merely scheduled babysitting services in which children rotated to play in each other's homes. Many play groups were formally organized by groups of mothers who set up and stocked nursery school classrooms and took turns teaching the children.

Nursery school curriculums, like kindergarten programs, emphasized social-emotional development and the encouragement of play as the child's way of learning about the world. Play and the rehearsal of reality were considered to be all important. Another important influence on nursery school programs was the establishment of model nursery school programs at many universities and colleges as part of the expanding child study movement within psychology. Laboratory nursery schools evidenced the best of current educational practice woven in with serious observational study and documentation of children's overall development. Nursery schools have traditionally, then, been associated with efforts to understand and influence the development of children.

During the years preceding Head Start in 1965, attendance at nursery school was an accepted part of the childhood experience of most advantaged children. The nursery school program provided a warm supportive emotional climate and provided the child with many choices of activities and experiences.

Merging Basic Care and Educational Programs

The home situation of the advantaged child attending nursery school or kindergarten was considered to be of high quality; therefore, these programs were an addition to the home and what the home provided the child. The nursery school and kindergarten movement focused on extending the home by providing educational experiences for the child. On the other hand, the clientele of day care, not having the advantage of a similar quality home situation, was considered to be lacking important fundamental experiences and attention. Day care focused more intensely on remediating the deficits of the home by providing essential services.

The "hidden curriculum" of the middle class home divided the two child care movements. The effect of the nursery school and kindergarten movements was to exaggerate the difference in program between day care and early education. Each child care movement had carved out a specific territory and clientele.

As we said earlier, in the mid-1960s this situation changed as day care programs merged with programs in early education. This merger took place because elements from each movement were necessary to forge new types of child care that would meet the needs of all socioeconomic classes. Educational researchers, social planners, teachers, and parents began to realize that children from all homes might benefit from the basic care provided in day care and from the educational experiences of kindergarten and nursery school. The combination of these elements led to approaches known as developmental programming. Let's see what this means.

Analyzing the forms of day care programs that prospered under welfare's jurisdiction leads to the conclusion that one form of care, custodial care, predominated throughout all three eras. *Custodial care* refers to the physical care of children for the purpose of protection from immediate or future harm. Custodial care programs provided safe and clean settings for children. They were not, however, noted for systematic attention to the provision of developmentally appropriate and stimulating activities and experiences. We have used the term *basic care* throughout this book to refer to those aspects of physical care that are an essential part of child care practices. Basic care practices are the foundation for all other activities. Custodial care, in contrast, was a total program goal. The term is often used derogatorily to refer to practices that are deemed minimal care.

Another form of day care program that emerged from the welfare tradition can be termed *comprehensive.* Less numerous and more costly and difficult to coordinate, comprehensive care programs added a wide range of supplemental support services to basic care. This increased the impact and, to some, was evidence of welfare's intervention in the family's right to rear its children.

Educational programming is the acquisition of skills and information through systematically planned and sequenced activities. Education builds cultural competence but does not fully address the issue of personal competence and the child's position in the larger society.

Developmental programming includes both basic care and educational programming as well as other components, such as parental involvement and health, that positively influence the development of children. Developmental programming is not accomplished by the mere addition of educational components. To add educational components to custodial programs minimizes the important role that basic care plays in the daily care of young children. To equate development with education loses sight of critical, yet subtle differences in the goals and purposes of each. A relationship exists among the three types of programming (basic care, and educational and developmental programming).

Developmental care programs have appeared in isolated instances sporadically throughout day care's history. They depended on the training and vision of individual staff and welfare agency personnel who saw the opportunity day care provided to affect positively the quality and direction of young children's development. These early versions of developmental day care programs earned the label "developmental" for a number of reasons: A period of time was designated for educational activities, a staff member was certified as a teacher, or materials were purchased for educational games and activities. In general, however, no systematic effort was made to design the entire program around developmental goals for children; all too often "facilitating development" was confused with collections of educational activities.

True developmental programs involve a qualitative reorganization of the basic design of day care programs. Their primary purpose is aiding development through the coordination of home and program for the long-term benefit of the child. Such programs have the support of growing numbers of parents, child care personnel, and welfare and educational professionals.

In the mid-sixties an enormous educational experiment called Head Start showed the potential for developmental programming. We'll look at it in the next section.

Head Start—A New Direction in Programming

The education that the young child received in programs of the early education movement was essentially nonacademic and noncompetitive. It was not until the advent of Head Start in 1965 that education for the young child was considered an academic experience that could directly facilitate the young child's performance in later school grades. Head Start was a watershed program in that it represented a federally funded effort in which services were designated for and delivered directly to children. In the past, federal funds for programs for young children were available primarily as an offshoot of programs designed for adults, such as job training programs for working mothers.

Programming Practices

Head Start began in the summer of 1965. It was hastily organized amid much enthusiasm, fanfare, and hopes for success. Head Start was planned as a comprehensive program for young disadvantaged children to include educational experiences, health and nutrition services, parent involvement, community involvement, and social-psychological services. In organization and scope of service, Head Start was comparable to social welfare programs. The critical difference between Head Start and welfare services for young children was emphasis on education. The educational program was the heart of the Head Start experience.

The Head Start programs of the first summer and most of the later year-round programs were essentially transplanted versions of the socialization programs that had traditionally been provided for advantaged children in nursery schools, play groups, and kindergartens. The early education child care programs were borrowed wholesale by Head Start because of (1) lack of time initially to design and operate anything else; (2) lack of information regarding the educational characteristics of the population of young children Head Start was to serve; and (3) the unavailability of any tested or fully developed alternatives.

As Head Start matured and funding stabilized, opportunities arose to develop and implement a number of different curriculum models that were deemed more compatible with the clientele Head Start programs served and the purposes Head Start was to achieve. As long as Head Start programs met the general objectives and observed administrative and funding guidelines, local sponsors and developers could experiment with diverse curriculum plans, rationales, philosophies, and teaching strategies.

A number of interesting and provocative curriculum approaches were developed under the sponsorship of Head Start during this period. Many program models were developed by researchers who translated various developmental theories into educational practices for young children. Many models were locally designed programs tailored to the ethnic or cultural characteristics of particular communities. Other program models concentrated on techniques

In the mid-1960s the federal government initiated Head Start, a program for preschool disadvantaged children that was designed to give them a "leg-up" or head start as they entered public school and competed with more advantaged peers. (Courtesy of U.S. Department of Health and Human Services, Washington, DC.)

purported to improve the academic performance of disadvantaged children. As program models proliferated, comparisons between various approaches were almost impossible to make, because no systematic data bases or mechanisms for sharing program materials were operating.

Follow Through and Planned Variation

In the late 1960s, concern mounted that Head Start was not enough—not intense enough or long-lasting enough to impact children's performance in public school. Follow Through was piloted in 1967 through the Office of Education (OE) to extend the planned-program experiences of disadvantaged young children through the early primary grades. Follow Through was designed from the beginning as a Planned Vari-

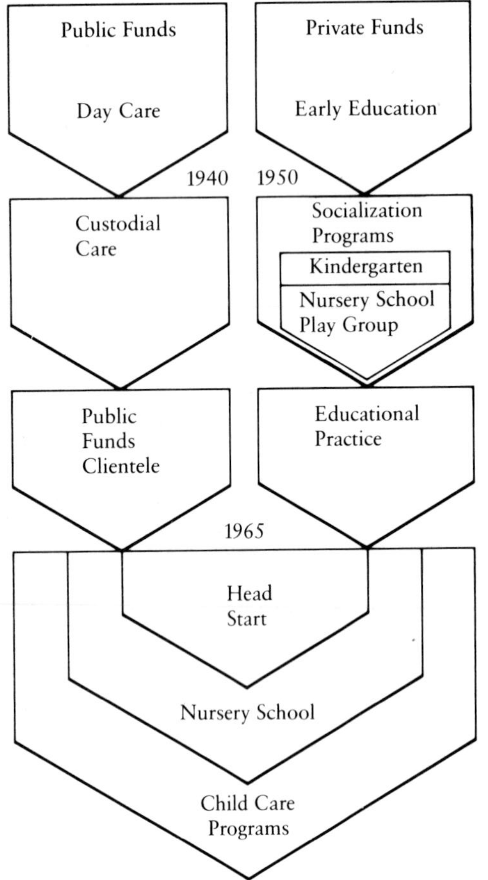

Figure 1.3 Two child care movements: The merging of purpose and program.

ation experiment, which meant that a few selected program models would be field tested, documented, and compared.

The intent of the Planned Variation approach in Follow Through (and the subsequent Planned Variation Study in Head Start) was not to identify the best program model; rather, Planned Variation was an effort to document, compare, and identify features and characteristics of different programs related to outcomes for a selected group of program models. Head Start fostered diversity of program development. Follow Through legitimized program diversity, and Planned Variation in Follow Through and Head Start sought to capture the knowledge and experience such program diversity produced.

Epilogue of Head Start and Follow Through

Head Start continues to operate. The administration of Head Start by the Department of Health and Human Services ensures that education will remain an important component of the program but that continued emphasis will be placed on upgrading and delivering the comprehensive services that are part of the basic Head Start concept. Head Start programs today are characterized by serious efforts to refine and improve the quality of the service provided and to extend the program to more eligible children. Program innovation is generally a locally directed effort with strong in-service programs, staff training, and delineation of local program objectives and goals.

Follow Through is no longer operating. From the beginning, Follow Through depended for its existence on the cooperation of local school districts and program developers. When federal sponsorship ended, many districts chose not to purchase program monitoring services from the respective program developers, but rather to continue implementing the model program with district resources. Thus, many "second-cousin" versions of Follow Through programs can be found in public school classrooms today.

The Implications of Head Start for Child Care Programming

Head Start drew together three critical components of the two disparate child care movements that existed in this country (see Figure 1.3). From the early education movement, Head Start drew both educational practices and the general concept that the early years of childhood are important foundation years for later learning. From the day care movement, Head Start drew a clientele of children and families and, inadvertently at the beginning, all the cultural bias regarding the reason for and treatment of the social condition of disadvantage. Head Start did not use day care social service funds, but did parallel the day care movement in the use of federal funds to provide programs at the local level. Federal sponsorship created for Head Start a conceptual and financial momentum similar to the social momentum that had carried day care from the social welfare era to the federal era.

Examination of the full impact of Head Start on child care programming must focus on the cumulative impact of three components present in the two child care movements prior to Head Start. Under the aegis of Head Start these three components and the diverging directions of the two child care movements became firmly merged:

1. *Funding* Public funds were used in Head Start to provide *educational* programs for young children.
2. *Clientele* Educational programs were provided for a clientele that previously had not had access to such experiences.
3. *Educational Practices* Public funding and the needs of a different clientele spurred the adoption, subsequent modification, and later rapid development of different programming practices for young children.

Summary

Child care is not a fad of the 1980s. It is not a whitewashed old welfare program revived to dazzle for a few years, sparked by the momentum of women entering the labor force and increased public acceptance of educational programs for young children. Child care is here to stay. It is an integral part of American child-rearing customs. It is simultaneously a widespread practice and a publicly debated issue. As a practice, child care is growing rapidly. As an issue, child care has attracted both more critics and more supporters than ever before. Child care exists in an environment of public opinion, professional knowledge, and parental needs unlike any other program or human service. Issues in child care reflect concerns that have emerged over time in response to different interpretations of past practice and research evidence.

No single definition of child care can describe every kind of facility. Each program is actually made up of its own way of delineating the age of children enrolled, the setting provided, the size of the enrollment, time of the sessions, purpose of the care, type of sponsorship, and the caregivers who work with the children.

Modern child care programs are derived from two separate historical movements: day care and early education. Day care originated as a service to provide full-day custodial care for the children of working-class parents. As a result its history has been linked with society's own changing ideas of the suitable role of mothers in the home and at work. Financial support for day care has progressed from charities to community welfare to government welfare and finally to state sources and, sometimes, individual consumers. The two forms of early education, kindergarten and nursery school, were developed for the children of middle- and upper-class families. They occupied only a portion of the day and were intended to supplement the social and educational experiences available in the home. In the 1960s child care facilities began to combine these two services in developmental programming. Head Start was one large-scale social experiment in this combination.

Child care today is many different philosophies, programs, facilities, and funding sources. Programs range from marginal care to sophisticated educational programs and supplemental health and social services. The definition of a quality child care program is obviously a relative judgment, but nevertheless the image of quality child care has haunted all who seek to explain child care as consumers, providers, or supporters. Thus, while child care is a dynamic contemporary activity, it represents no single vision to the observer attempting to understand quality child care in practice.

As an issue, child care is debated from political platforms, in professional circles, and in private gatherings. Politicians as well as early childhood professionals and laypersons have opinions regarding child care. Child care may provide care for some children, serve some parents, use only a small portion of public tax dollars or be funded privately, but it affects the lives of every citizen in some way. Why such a universal concern for child care? The answer is simple. Child care touches the very structure of our society—family. If the debate over child care is polarized, the two sides center their arguments on the family. For proponents, child care is a mechanism for supporting the family in its tasks of child-rearing. For opponents, child care usurps family responsibilities and threatens the family's existence.

But this is a simplistic conceptualization of the issues involved in child care since it ignores the context surrounding the issues; namely, child care exists and is currently being practiced, regardless of the issues. Only the most idealistic and naive individuals believe that child care can be argued away, legislatively abolished or otherwise prohibited. Child care will not disappear. In fact it appears to be flourishing. We need to admit that child care exists and acknowledge that not all child care is quality care, and we must work to support quality child care programs for all who must or who choose to use child care.

Resources

Abt Associates. (1979). *Children at the center: Final report of the national day care study* (Vol. 1). Cambridge, MA: Abt Associates.

Anderson, R., & Shane, H. (Eds.). (1971). *As the twig is bent: Readings in early childhood education.* Boston: Houghton Mifflin.

Appropriateness of the Federal Interagency Day Care Requirements. (1978). Washington, DC: USDHEW, Office of the Assistant Secretary for Planning and Evaluation.

Aries, P. (1962). *Centuries of childhood: A social history of family life.* New York: Knopf.

Auerbach, S. (Ed.). (1975). *Rationale for child care services: Programs vs. politics.* (Vol. 1). New York: Human Sciences Press.

Auleta, M. (Ed.). (1967). *Foundations of early childhood education: Readings.* New York: Random House.

Bane, M. J., Lein, L., O'Donnell, L., Stueve, C. A., & Wells, B. (1980). Child care arrangements of working parents. *Special labor force reports,* (233), 50–56.

Beller, E. K. (1971). Adult care interaction and personalized day care. In E. H. Grotbeg (Ed.), *Day care: Resources for decision.* Washington, DC: Office of Economic Opportunity.

Belsky, J. (1977, September 23). *An ecological analysis of unknowns in the day care equation.* Invited address presented at Conference on Day Care and the Family, Auburn University, Auburn, Alabama.

Belsky, J., & Steinberg, L. (1978). The effects of day care: A critical review. *Child Development, 49,* 929–949.

Bergstrom, J. M., & Dicker, D. L. (1977). *The evaluation of existing interagency day care requirements: Day care for the school-age child.* Washington, DC: USDHEW, Office of the Assistant Secretary for Planning and Evaluation.

Bergstrom, J. M., & Morgan, G. (1975). *Issues in the design of a delivery system for day care and child development services to children and their families.* Washington, DC: Day Care and Child Development Council of America.

Boguslawski, D. B. (1966). *Guide for establishing and operating day care centers for young children.* New York: Child Welfare League of America.

Braun, S. J., & Edwards, E. P. (1972). *History and theory of early childhood education.* Washington, DC: Charles A. Jones.

Breitbart, V. (1974). *The day care book.* New York: Knopf.

Bremmer, R. H. (Ed.). (1971, 1974). *Children and youth in America: A documentary history* (Vols. 2 & 3). Cambridge, MA: Harvard University Press.

Caldwell, B. M. (1971). Day care: Pariah to prodigy. *Bulletin of the American Association for Teacher Education,* 24, 2.

Chapman, J. E., & Lazar, J. B. (1971). *A review of the present status and future needs in day care research.* Washington, DC: George Washington University, Social Research Group.

Child and Family Services Act. (1975). Joint Hearings on S. 626 and M.R. 2966.

Clarke-Stewart, A. (1977). *Child care in the family.* New York: Academic Press.

Cohen, D. J. (1974). *Day care 3: Serving preschool children* [DHEW Publication No. (OHD) 74-1057]. Washington, DC: USDHEW-OHD-OCD.

Combs, A. W., Avila, D. L., & Purkey, W. W. (1971). *Helping relationships: Basic concepts for the helping professions.* Boston: Allyn & Bacon.

Community solutions for child care. (1979). Washington, DC: National Manpower Institute.

Emlen, A. C. (1973). Slogans, slots, and slander: The myth of day care need. *American Journal of Orthopsychiatry, 43*(1), 23–26.

Evans, E. D. (1971; 2d ed. 1975). *Contemporary influences in early childhood education.* New York: Holt, Rinehart & Winston.

Fein, G. G., & Clarke-Stewart, A. (1973). *Day care in context.* New York: Wiley.

Fosburg, S. (1981). *Family day care in the United States: Summary of findings. Final report of the national day care home study* (Vol. 1) [DHHS Pub. No. (OHDS) 80-30282] Washington, DC: U.S. Dept. of Health & Human Services, ACYF.

Frost, J. L. (Ed.). (1968). *Early childhood education rediscovered—Readings.* New York: Holt, Rinehart & Winston.

Frost, J. L. (Ed.). (1973). *Revisiting early education—Readings.* New York: Holt, Rinehart & Winston.

Goldman, K. S., & Lewis, M. (1976). *Child care and public policy: A care study.* Princeton, NJ: Educational Testing Service.

Goldsmith, C. (1972). *Better day care for the young child.* Washington, DC: National Association for the Education of Young Children.

Goodlad, J. I., Klein, M. F., & Novotney, J. M. (1973). *Early schooling in the United States.* New York: McGraw-Hill.

Gordon, Ira (1972). *Early childhood education* (Seventy-first Yearbook of the National Society for the Study of Education, Part II). Chicago: University of Chicago Press.

Greenblatt, B. (1977). *Responsibility for child care.* San Francisco, Jossey-Bass.

Grotberg, E. (Ed.). (1971). *Day care: Resources for decision.* Washington, DC: Office of Economic Opportunity.

Haskins, R. (1979). Day care and public policy. *Urban and Social Change Review, 12,* 3–10.

HEW Day Care Requirements—Final Rules. (HEWDCR) (1980). *Federal Register, 45*(55), 17870–17855.

Hill, C. R. (1977). *The child care market: A review of evidence and implications for federal policy.* Washington, DC: USDHEW, Office of the Assistant Secretary for Planning and Evaluation.

How to start a day care center. Washington, DC: Day Care Council of America, 1981.

Jones, L. W. (1980). Who knows? Who cares? *Journal of the Institute for Socio-economic Studies, 5*(9), 55–62.

Kamerman, S. B., & Hayes, C. D. (Eds.) (1982). *Families that work: Children in a changing world.* Washington, DC: National Academy Press.

Kamerman, S. B., & Kahn, A. J. (1976). *Social services in the United States: Policies and programs.* Philadelphia: Temple University Press.

Keyserling, M. D. (1972). *Windows on day care.* New York: National Council on Jewish Women.

Larson, M. A. (1975). *Federal policy for preschool services: Assumptions and evidences.* Menlo Park, CA: Stanford Research Institute.

Levine, J. A. (1978). Day care and the public schools. Newton, MA: Education Development Center.

Levine, J. A. (1979). Day care and the public schools: Current models and future directions. *Urban and Social Change Review, 12*(1), 17–21.

Levitan, S. A., & Alderman, K. C. (1975). *Child care & ABC's too.* Baltimore: Johns Hopkins University Press.

Margolin, E. (1974). *Socio-cultural elements in early childhood education.* New York: Macmillan.

National Elementary School Principal (Theme Issue-Early Childhood Education), 1971, *51*(1), 8–116.

National Research Council. (1976). *Toward a national policy for children and families.* Washington, DC: National Academy of Sciences.

Parker, R. K., & Knitzer, J. (1972). *Day care and preschool services: Trends and issues.* Atlanta: Avatar Press.

Perspectives on working women: A data book. (1980). (Bulletin 2080). Washington, DC: Department of Labor, Bureau of Labor Statistics.

Peters, D. L. (1980). Social science and social policy and the care of young children: Head Start and after. *Journal of Applied Developmental Psychology. 1,* 7–27.

Policy issues in day care: Summaries of 21 papers. (1977). Washington, DC: U.S. Department of Health, Education, and Welfare.

Prescott, E., & David, T. G. (1976). *Concept paper on the effects of the physical environment on day care.* Pasadena, CA: Pacific Oaks College. (ERIC Document Reproduction Service No. ED 156 356)

Prescott, E., & Jones, E. (1969). *Patterns of teacher behavior in preschool programs.* Pasadena, CA: Pacific Oaks College. (ERIC Document Reproduction Service No. ED 075 092)

Prescott, E., Milich, C. & Jones, E. (1972). *The "politics" of day care* (Vol. 1). *Day care as a child-rearing environment* (Vol. 2). Washington, DC: National Association for the Education of Young Children.

Rivlin, A. (1978). *Child care and preschool: Options for federal support.* Washington, DC: Congressional Budget Office.

Roby, P. (Ed.). (1973). *Child care—Who cares?* New York: Basic Books.

Rosenberg, M. E. (1972). *Early childhood education: Perspectives on the federal and Office of Education roles.* Menlo Park, CA: Stanford Research Institute. (ERIC Document Reproduction Service No. ED 066 621)

Ruopp, R., O'Farrell, B., Warner, D., Rowe, M., & Friedman, R. *A day-care guide for administrators, teachers, and parents.* Cambridge, MA: MIT Press.

School Enrollment—Social and Economic Characteristics of Students: October 1979. (1981). *Current Population Reports,* Series P-20 (360). Washington, DC: Department of Commerce, Bureau of the Census, 1981.

Seaberg, D. I. (1974). *The four faces of teaching: The role of the teacher in humanizing education.* Pacific Palisades, CA: Goodyear.

Senn, M. J. E. (1977). *Speaking out for America's children.* New Haven, CT: Yale University Press.

Smith, R. E. (1979). *Women in the labor force in 1990.* Washington, DC: Urban Institute.

Steiner, G. Y. (1976). *The children's cause.* Washington, DC: Brookings Institution.

Steinfels, M. D. (1973). *Who's minding the children? The History and Politics of Day Care in America.* New York: Simon & Schuster.

Takanishi-Knowles, R. (1974). *Federal involvement in early childhood education (1933–1973): The need for historical perspectives.* Los Angeles: University of California at Los Angeles, Department of Education. (ERIC Document Reproduction Service No. Ed 097 969)

U.S. Bureau of Labor Statistics. (1980). *Special labor force reports.*

U.S. Bureau of the Census. (1976). Daytime Care of Children: October 1974 and February 1975. *Current Population Reports,* Series P-20 (298). Washington, DC: U.S. Government Printing Office.

U.S. Senate, Committee on Finance. (1977). *Child care—Data and materials.* Washington, DC: U.S. Government Printing Office.

Waldman, E., Grossman, A. S., Haygie, H., & Johnson, B. L. (1979). Working mothers in the 1970s: A look at the statistics. *Special Labor Force Reports (233), 39–48.*

Weber, E. (1969). *The kindergarten: Its encounter with educational thought in America.* New York: Teachers College Press.

White, S. H., Day, M. C., Freeman, P. K., Hantman, S. A., & Messenger, K. P. (1973). *Federal programs for young children: Review and recommendations* (3 volumes). Washington, DC: U.S. Department of Health, Education, and Welfare.

Working mothers and their children. (1981). *Monthly Labor Review, 104*(5), 49–54.

Zigler, E., & Valentine, J. (Eds.). (1979). *Project Head Start: A legacy of the war on poverty.* New York: Free Press.

Zigler, E. F., Kagan, S. L., & Klugman, E. (Eds.). (1983). *Children, families and government: Perspectives on American social policy.* New York: Cambridge University Press.

2

Foundations for Designing Child Care Programs

Introduction

Every child care program has the potential to provide children with a supportive developmental experience. It is true, though, that child care programs see quality experiences for children in different ways, and regrettably, many programs fail to provide appropriate experiences for children. Parents, program personnel, and sponsors face the tasks of advocating, managing, and monitoring child care programs. Few guidelines exist for ensuring quality programs in any particular local situation.

Similarities do exist among child care programs. All programs must provide basic care. All programs have long periods of time during which children and staff have opportunities to pursue interests and activities. Certain components such as staff, equipment, facility, and environment are universal features of all programs. And, finally, all programs operate with an implicit or explicit viewpoint that undergirds both daily and long-term goals and activities. These components form a general structure for program description and design.

Approaches to the design of a particular child care program can begin from many different perspectives. It is possible to start with the children attending a program, then establish needs, specify goals and describe child characteristics, and finally, design a program that maximizes the development of the children. Still other child care programs are planned using a framework of regulations, with special locally desired program features added after all required factors have been taken care of. Still another approach is to begin the planning process with parents or staff, or a combination of input from the two groups. The resulting program encompasses parental values, staff capabilities, philosophies, and many other local variations for program activities. Designing a program at the local level requires an enormous amount of coordinated effort from all persons involved—agencies, staff, parents, and children. Each group has some legitimate right to influence decisions about the experiences that will be provided in the program.

The following chapter looks at two elements that help to form the bedrock of any child care program: program framework and developmental viewpoint. This choice of foundations comes from an analysis of certain components and their relationship to each other. Deciding on one's own interpretation of these factors is one sound method of designing a program.

We begin by outlining a model for a program framework. The model consists of a time schedule, called a daily care pattern, and descriptions of how the program will provide basic care and an educational curriculum. Finally, we explore three developmental viewpoints—maturationist, behaviorist, and cognitive—from which the designer must choose to form the theoretical basis for the program.

Child care programs must attend to children's developmental needs as well as their basic physical care and safety. (Courtesy of U.S. Department of Housing and Urban Development, Washington, DC.)

Constructing a Program Framework

Our general framework for the design of child care programs is based on the fact that any such program must first deliver basic care services. Concern for the logistics of scheduling, coordination, legal factors, and staffing must come first. When children are away from home and under the care and protection of someone other than a parent or legal guardian, concern must be first and foremost for safety and physical well-being. This section describes a *daily care pattern,* which is a model timetable for activities, and indicates how these activities satisfy the requirements for both basic care and curriculum.

Daily Care Pattern

Child care program designers must recognize that the experiences of children are the *primary units* of program planning. Follow a child through a day in child care and you will see eight units that represent the range of experiences possible for any child of any age in any type of child care program. These eight units are the primary building blocks of child care program design; they are arrival, breakfast, morning activity, snacks, lunch, rest, afternoon activity, and departure. Every child care program is made up of some combination of these primary building blocks.

Each of the eight units has both a basic care and a curriculum component. Some are more one than the other.

The Basic Care Component Basic care requirements are determined by children's physical care needs and the regulatory demands that determine the form and substance of staff activities and children's experiences—for example, napping, toileting, brushing teeth.

The Curriculum Component Curriculum opportunities are found in activity periods that have few regulatory restraints and are relatively independent of children's physical care routines—for example, story time, outdoor play, table games, easel painting. The curriculum component includes educational activities deliberately planned to enhance development and skill acquisition.

The model we describe involves looking at the mix of basic care requirements and curriculum opportunities for each activity block. The generalized model of the daily care pattern shown in Figure 2.1 helps ensure an adequate level of protective care for children throughout the day without ignoring the obligation to nurture their development.

Two of the eight units are combined in our model. Snack appears twice as an activity occurring during each of the major activity periods. We use the term *activity* as a general label intended to include the many formally planned and informal curriculum activities that programs choose to implement during these time blocks.

We believe that all child care programs can be reduced to these eight building blocks. All child care programs share the common bond of a daily care pattern that incorporates both basic care requirements and curriculum opportunities. While care for infants *looks* very different from school-age care and family day care homes *look* different from child care centers, in reality each is a specialized variation of the daily care pattern. Program designers will see several advantages to using the daily care pattern.

1. *It's easy* The daily care pattern is easy to understand and easy to use. The model is simple and straightforward, and it fits with the child care practices with which most people are familiar.
2. *It's neutral* No single philosophy is favored. The simple unit blocks and the idea of a basic and developmental (curricular) balance of care are compatible with any program philosophy in any local situation.
3. *It's flexible* The daily care pattern can be embellished to fit whatever level of sophistication and complexity a program designer desires. The model provides the bare bones design framework for a simple program, or it can be the foundation for a highly developed multifaceted program. As programs grow in size or directors wish to extend features, the model can accommodate.
4. *It works* The model works because children come first. The daily care pattern continuously focuses the program planner on "what's happening to children" and forces all decisions about program to be made in light of the basic and developmental balance of care children must receive. It works because the principles of the model are accessible to all child care workers. It helps both novice and trained early childhood professionals to organize thoughts and programming decisions in a systematic way. Whatever the level of local resources, the model is a way to integrate those resources to form a quality care program for children.

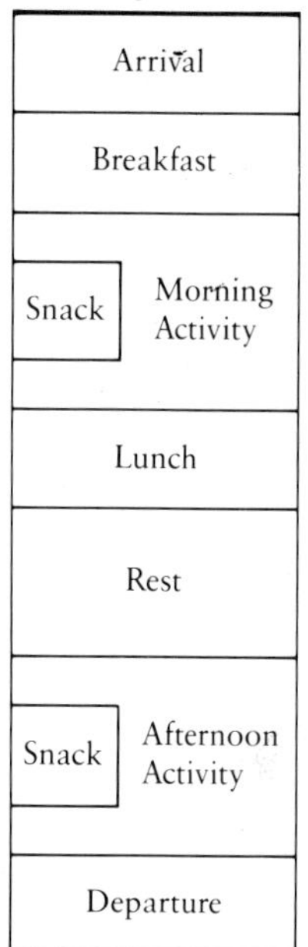

Figure 2.1 Daily care pattern.

To illustrate how program design proceeds from these eight units, we will use a daily care pattern typical of a preschool center-based program. Daily care patterns for infants, school-age children, and family child care situations are variations and are presented in subsequent chapters.

Basic Care Component

Basic care includes cleaning toilets, hugging lonely children, and capping electrical outlets. It is tedious and routine, repetitious, and sometimes messy work. Most staff perform basic care without even thinking twice—such tasks as counting the children on the field trip bus, wiping runny noses and dirty bottoms, and reassuring children who are scared or tired.

Many of the regulations and on-site inspec-

Figure 2.2 Basic care within the daily care pattern.

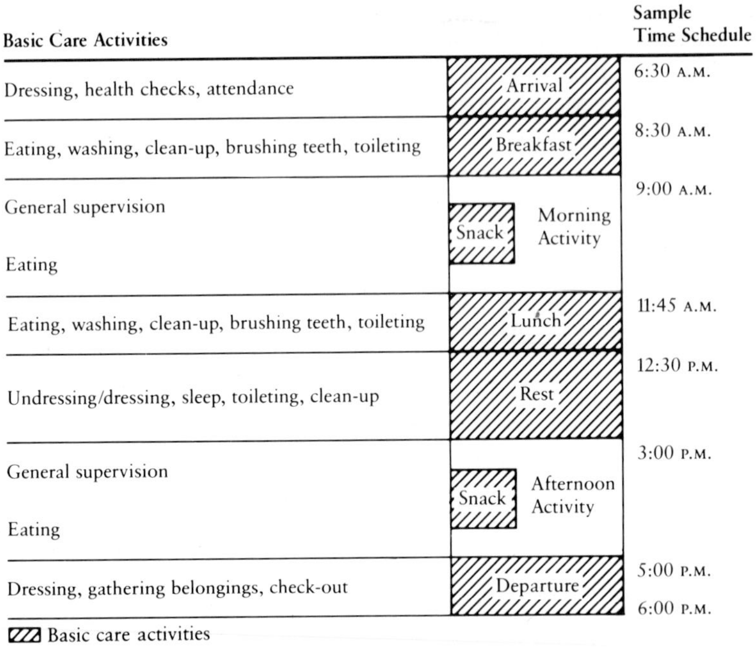

Basic Care Activities		Sample Time Schedule
Dressing, health checks, attendance	Arrival	6:30 A.M.
Eating, washing, clean-up, brushing teeth, toileting	Breakfast	8:30 A.M.
General supervision Eating	Snack / Morning Activity	9:00 A.M.
Eating, washing, clean-up, brushing teeth, toileting	Lunch	11:45 A.M.
Undressing/dressing, sleep, toileting, clean-up	Rest	12:30 P.M.
General supervision Eating	Snack / Afternoon Activity	3:00 P.M.
Dressing, gathering belongings, check-out	Departure	5:00 P.M. 6:00 P.M.

▨ Basic care activities

tions for child care programs emphasize basic requirements such as temperature of the water in the dishwasher, fire drill procedures and exits, and nutritional balance of the meals served.

Parents often express concern for children's safety and ask staff for information about children's activities: "Did he take a nap today?" "I hope she had a good run outside today." or "How did she get so wet—was it play or an accident?"

Improper basic care has given child care a bad reputation. When basic care is inadequate, children suffer, and this has caused child care programs to be seen as incubators for disease and social stress. Because of this, rigorous regulatory attention to safety and protective features of child care has often overshadowed other aspects of care. Inspectors and program staff can spend inordinate amounts of time dealing with physical plant problems. Meeting basic care requirements can sometimes drain program and staff resources so much that little energy is left to use for curriculum activities for children.

Creative activity plans will always have to take second place to eating, sleeping, and other care routines. Children must be fed during the period of time they are at the center. When a center is open for eleven hours, meals include breakfast, a midmorning snack, lunch, and an afternoon snack. Meals for large groups of children require appropriate eating areas, food preparation facilities, and sanitation routines. Young children require some period of rest or quiet to break up long periods of activity. Provision must be made in the daily schedule and in the physical layout of the center to provide for rest and nap times. Toileting, hand washing, and brushing teeth must be planned into the schedule, and bathroom facilities must be accessible to children.

The activities listed in Figure 2.2 provide some common examples of basic care that make it easy to understand why child care programs seem heavily oriented toward basic care—large parts of the day are devoted to physical care activities. It is equally clear that there are certain predictable uninterrupted periods in the day when program activities can take precedence. Six time blocks in the daily care pattern (arrival, breakfast, lunch, rest, snacks, and departure) are primarily basic care activities. All schedules in this chapter are intended only as examples; different time periods may be assigned to meet the individual program's needs.

The final form and details of the basic care component of any particular child care program will depend on input from several sources. The following list identifies six general factors that must be considered by local program designers. For each of these factors, some common contributing items are identified as examples of the influences on planning basic care. The list is not exhaustive, but that of the local designers should be.

Local designers should assess fully those factors applicable to their situation. Everything identified should be recorded under the most appropriate category label. Items in the resulting list can then be rank-ordered to show how important each is in planning the program. The actual details of basic care can be determined from this list.

Operational Requirements

- Hours facility available—hours care needed
- Conditions of sharing physical plant with church or other group
- Parking problems for late-afternoon child pick-ups
- Amount of money available

Legal Requirements

- Applicable local codes
- Regulatory requirements

Coordination of Services

- Access to state-provided dietician
- County health nurse availability
- Mid-day transportation to public school kindergarten
- Eligible services (USDA—Child Care Feeding, and so on)

Staff Competencies

- Experience with young children in extended care situations
- First aid knowledge
- Need for volunteers and temporary workers in early A.M. hours

Child Characteristics

- Ages of children
- Handicaps and/or disabilities

Parental Concerns

- Traditional foods served at meals
- Second-language role models
- Opening of center by 6 A.M.

Curriculum Component

Young children learn and grow by doing. Play, activity, movement, involvement, touching, testing, tasting, and much more—this is the stuff of growth and development. The term *curriculum* is used to designate activities deliberately selected and systematically implemented by staff. Both the casual observer and the seasoned professional recognize that virtually any experience or thing can become the raw material for growth and development. Scrounged junk or fancy toys, spontaneous play or a sit-down lesson can all fuel a child's curiosity and become vehicles for growth. Yet, placing children and materials together does not automatically produce growth. The task of the caregiver in child care programs is to match maturing minds and bodies with ever increasing skills and challenges to create learning opportunities.

Many people are attracted to child care positions because they love children and achieve satisfaction from helping children. These staff members see themselves as "good" with chil-

Figure 2.3 Curriculum opportunities within the daily care pattern.

Curriculum Activities		Sample Time Schedule
Puzzles, groups for games, books, and stories	Arrival	6:30 A.M.
	Breakfast	8:30 A.M.
Opening Play and activity lessons, groups times, free play, interest centers, and so on	Snack / Morning Activity	9:00 A.M.
	Lunch	11:45 A.M.
Music Quiet games Stories	Rest	12:30 P.M.
Table games Group and individual activities Outdoor play	Snack / Afternoon Activity	3:00 P.M.
Puzzles, books, and stories	Departure	5:00 P.M. 6:00 P.M.

(hatched) Primary opportunity for planned curriculum

(dotted) Secondary opportunity for planned curriculum

dren. Long on experience with young children and perhaps short on advanced education or specialized training, these staff members form the majority and the backbone of program staffs. Through intuition, experience and commitment, these staff members plan and supervise the experiences of children in their care. The activities that are provided by staff beyond basic care are, in the broadest sense, the curriculum.

Regulations for child care programs rarely require specific activities for children. General guidelines, such as the following, usually allow wide interpretation:

- Materials appropriate to the ages or developmental levels of the child should be provided.
- There should be a sufficient supply of materials for the number of children present.
- Provisions should be made for large motor activities and outdoor play.
- Children with handicaps should be provided with suitable equipment and activities.

Often the regulations governing program activities are so vague (or nonexistent) that each child care program is essentially left to its own devices to select and implement appropriate activities.

The units designated as morning activity and afternoon activity are the primary opportunities a program has to implement a planned curriculum (see Figure 2.3). The two activity blocks account for large portions of the time a child spends in a child care program. The example given in Figure 2.3 shows two and three-quarters hours in the morning activity block and two hours in the afternoon activity block. The serving of snacks during each activity period is not a significant interruption.

Three basic care blocks are supplementary opportunities for curriculum: arrival, departure, and rest. Often arrival and departure times are staggered so that some groups of children are present as others are arriving and leaving; because of this, programs may choose to plan curriculum activities during these times. Rest takes many forms. Music, storytelling, and quiet table games are examples of curriculum-related activities that can occur as part of a rest period.

Every local program should make a determined effort to fully identify both available resources and the constraints within which it must work. Taken together, these factors provide a way to estimate the depth and breadth possible for local curriculum design. Lack of money, strong parental input, highly trained or untrained staff are all examples of single factors that will influence the final character of the local program. Examples of factors that affect a curriculum program at the local level are shown in the following list. Each child care program should set realistic goals in designing curriculum opportunities consistent with available resources.

Operational Requirements

- Money available for supplies and equipment
- Appropriateness of space in facility
- Ease of operation of activities within particular setting

Parents

- Personal biases and values
- Family child-rearing practices and cultural traditions
- Likelihood of parental/home support
- Channels of communication available for exchange of information

Staff

- Personal biases, attitudes, and habits
- Skills and training in planning activities
- Knowledge/information background
- Commitment to curriculum efforts
- Number of staff, volunteers, and so on

General

- Strength of status quo—reluctance to depart from familiar paths
- Local support services and professional resources in community
- Funding source or agency reactions to programming practices

The daily care pattern is a blueprint for program design. The architect and master builder is the program director who coordinates the planning energies of all interested groups and translates the plan into practice. The program director's viewpoint on children's development and related philosophical ideas determines the character of daily activities in the program.

In the following section we'll discuss three viewpoints on child development. The choice of developmental viewpoint should be compatible with the director's personal views and amenable to all the individuals who participate in the program.

Every activity block in the daily care pattern, whether part of basic care or a curriculum opportunity, requires the program director to prescribe a set of practices for staff and children. This set of practices becomes the method and the means through which the daily care pattern is set in action.

Choosing a Developmental Viewpoint

Planning and implementing a child care program is a complex decision-making process that must proceed from some intellectual foundation and be guided by some organizing framework. Developmental theory provides both the foundation and the framework for making program decisions.

The three major developmental viewpoints that influence child care program design are the maturationist, the behaviorist, and the cognitive. *Maturationists* believe that children are born with inherited patterns of behavior that become evident as the child grows up. *Behaviorists* believe the environment determines development and shapes destiny. *Cognitive theorists* believe that exercise of intelligence can shape destiny. These three viewpoints, any one of which can be the basis for deriving programming practices in child care, are widely accepted as the dominant viewpoints underlying most of the work that has been done in early childhood programming during the last fifteen years.

We suggest that you recognize the existence of these several viewpoints while favoring a particular theoretical foundation in your own work with children. Those who do not admit other viewpoints exist are unrealistic. We advocate a *pluralistic position* that acknowledges the many helpful concepts found in each viewpoint. Such a position encourages you to make an informed choice of a particular, single viewpoint as your foundation for decision making in program design.

Consistency of Philosophy, Theory, and Practice

The hierarchical nature of the relationship between philosophy, developmental theory, and program practice is not widely recognized. A *philosophy* is commonly regarded as a perspective on the world and the nature of humans (Langer, 1969). A *developmental theory* is a set of related principles that explain or predict the course of growth over time (Reese and Overton, 1970); early childhood professionals are most familiar with developmental theories and principles of learning that apply from infancy to adolescence. A *program practice* is a set of activities that are deliberately constructed to foster in children development in the cognitive, socioemotional, and psychomotor domains. A kind of linkage relates philosophy to theory to practice. However, in real life, the connections often seem blurred, and resulting programs sometimes lack this conceptual consistency.

Often philosophy is an unknown or implicit part of the philosophy-theory-practice linkage for those who design and implement child care programs. Philosophy is part of a person's belief or value system. It is part of an unspoken foundation for behavior. When asked, we describe general aims and goals for development. What we often fail to mention is that the choice of which specific goals and aims is a function of our personal values.

Child care program designers' beliefs about children, caregiving, and learning make a difference in how they behave with children and how they expect others in the program to behave. Even unstated beliefs influence directors and staff. To think about a child care program only in terms of materials, activities, and tasks ignores the comprehensive influence of each individual's personal belief system.

From Theory to Practice

The need for consistency between theory and practice is well recognized by professionals. Theory is typically used to justify particular programming practices, indicating that practice or action preceded a search for an explanation. Or theory is used to derive practice, indicating that practice is an *outgrowth* of explanations in the theory. We believe that program practices should arise in the latter way—that is, *derived from theory*. This process is illustrated in Figure 2.4.

First look at the top of the figure at the theoretical assumptions. The developmental viewpoint, or philosophy, of the designer will determine what kind of assumptions he or she has at the start. Specifically, the philosophy will dictate how the designer would answer the following three questions, which correspond to the three assumptions:

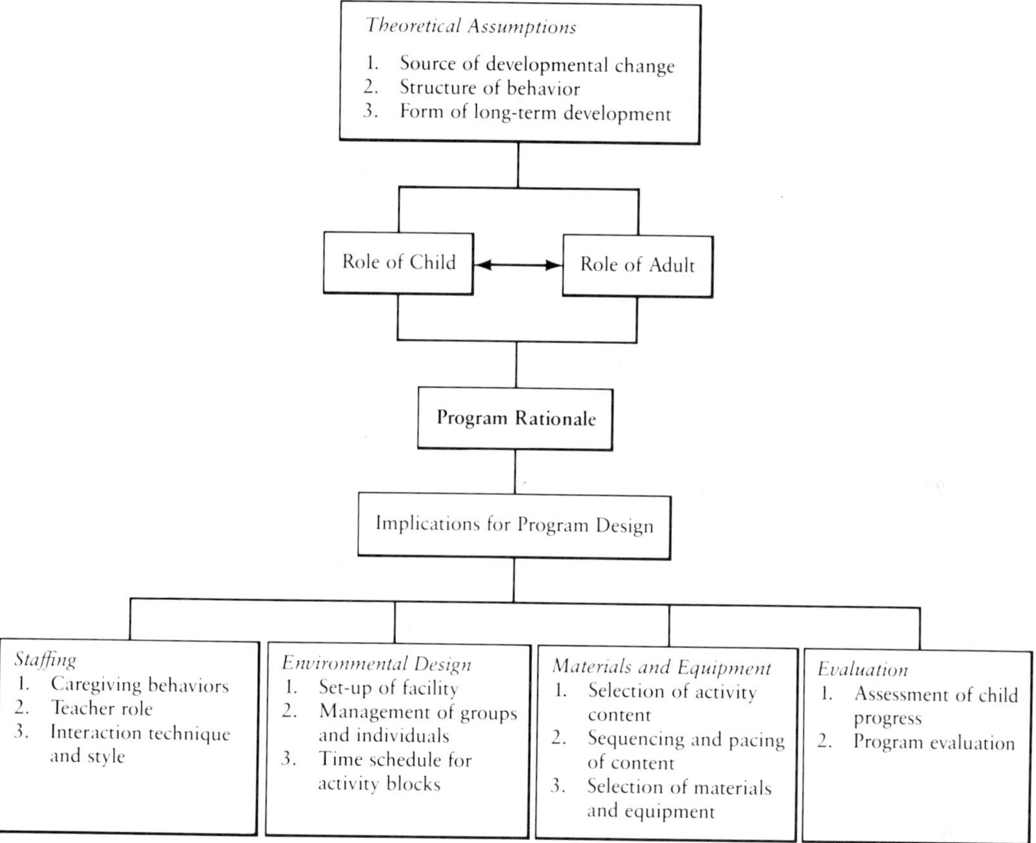

Figure 2.4 General theory-to-practice derivation process.

1. Where does behavior come from? The answer to this describes the *source of developmental change.*
2. What is the basic behavioral unit? The answer describes the *structure of behavior.*
3. What are the developmental goals? The answer describes the *form of long-term development.*

Each of the three developmental viewpoints answers these questions in a different way, and each provides a unique basis on which to build program decisions.

Since program designers are concerned ultimately with the experiences children will have in the child care program, they also have assumptions about the respective roles of the child and the adult in the developmental process. This assumption, therefore, appears next in the figure.

The designer's formulations of the theoretical assumptions provide the material for a *program rationale,* which is a written statement of the principles underlying the program. The program rationale makes explicit and public the philosophical and theoretical viewpoint that is the basis for program services and activities. It describes in language meaningful to the staff, parents, and local community why and how the program seeks to support children's development.

With the program rationale in hand, the designer can begin to devise an approach to the four major components of a program: staffing, environmental design, materials and equipment, and evaluation.

In the remainder of this chapter we'll explore the three developmental viewpoints by examining, in turn, each of the elements of Figure 2.4 that were just described. This gives you a consistent, orderly way to distinguish the viewpoints.

Deriving practice from theory does not guarantee that identical programs will result for all who start with the same theory. However, the planning process can result in different practices that are all consistent with a theory base. Caregiving cannot be based on blind faith about the efficiency or effectiveness of an approach, or on intuition, or on the momentum of an idea that is currently on the bandwagon. As architects of child care programs, directors can use conceptually consistent theories and program practices as a basis for their decision making and for implementing program practices.

For purposes of clarity and example, the three developmental viewpoints—behaviorist, cognitive, and maturationist—are described here as if each were a discrete, self-contained hierarchy of philosophy, theory, and practice. Treated this way, the principles and assumptions of each hierarchy become clear. Using similar formats allows child care program designers to survey the three viewpoints and consider where there is overlap. The terminology used in the research literature varies somewhat. We have chosen some commonly used terms that are familiar to most readers.

The Maturationist Viewpoint

Maturationists believe that children come equipped with innate, predetermined patterns of behavior—a genetic blueprint, as it were—that unfold with age. Certain characteristic patterns and behaviors go with certain ages. The use of age as an indicator that on the average certain behaviors are present is widespread. For example, children are thought ready for preschool at age three, ready for first grade and reading at age six, and ready to vote, drink alcoholic beverages, or go to war at ages eighteen to twenty-one. It is from the maturationist viewpoint that much of the popular and folk wisdom about the rituals and routines of child growth and development derives. For example,

> "He's gotten such a big ego from playing sports."
> "Don't worry—it's just a stage. She'll outgrow it and be on to something different soon."
> "You can't expect thin, wiry kids to sit still long."
> "Five's are so sunny. What a joy after all that aggressive four-year-old talk."

Philosophy

A maturationist believes that children are products of their biology. Development is paced by internal, regulatory mechanisms. The impetus for development is internal and governed by heredity. The related psychoanalytic view of humankind is concerned primarily with inner feelings and thoughts.

To the maturationist, each child possesses an organic individuality that becomes apparent as time passes and physiological maturation takes place. Heredity, as activated by physical growth, prepares the child to relate in new ways to environmental surroundings. Without this organically distilled readiness, the child is not capable of practicing newer and more complex forms of behavior.

Theoretical Assumptions

At least three theories have been articulated within the maturationist world view. Arnold Gesell's nativist theory emphasizes the whole child and sees developmental change occurring as a result of the natural unfolding and maturing of physiological structures. Ages are comparable with route markers along the predictable highway of development. Each age is characterized by certain personality patterns and skill accomplishments. Children move from one stage to another at their points of *readiness*. Gesell emphasizes a genetically programmed sequence of developmental stages. Originally formulated in the 1940s, the basic premises of Gesell's work, especially the use of age-related descriptive behavior patterns, permeates child development textbooks and early childhood curriculum practices.

Sigmund Freud's psychoanalytic theory postulates a stage structure that is related to the maturation of the child's age and reality comprehension. This is paralleled by the movement of the child through predicted stages of psychosocial development. Theoretical constructs of personality development, emotions, and self-concept are central ideas in understanding the development of the child. Freud hypothesizes a primary role for feelings and emotions that have a biological basis. He constructs a developmental sequence based almost entirely on the resolution of internal conflict at various stages.

Among neo-Freudians—those who have drawn from and extended Freud's original work—is Erik Erikson, whose theoretical work focuses on the socialization process as the mediator for personality development. Each of his eight stages of man is characterized by particular behavior patterns that involve psychosocial crises that must be resolved before the next higher stage can be reached. More detail on Erikson's work is included in the developmental theory section of Chapter 9 since it is with school-age children that his work appears to be most helpful for program designers.

Source of Behavior. Behavior comes from within. Heredity determines the shape of development. Environment is a nutrient for growth. Physiological maturation activates structures that already have taken shape within the child. Change occurs through a combination of physiological maturation and availability of raw materials in the environment. Readiness is the transition state. A developmental crisis offers maximum opportunity for growth through conflict resolution because readiness is at its peak then. Developmental tasks are environmental situations that encourage behavior.

Structure of Behavior. Behaviors are emerging patterns in which, at some point, there is change of such quality, magnitude, and permanence that past patterns drop from the child's repertoire. Emerging patterns show rhythmic fluctuations with periods of equilibrium (consolidation and organization) alternating with periods of disequilibrium (breakdown). It is helpful to think of these stages as occurring in a spiral that gradually encompasses a broader and more complex range of behaviors. These behavior changes are so consistent and predictable that each age is almost like a personality. Full descriptions of the patterns characteristic of each age show that four categories of behavior are typically used: physical motor, adaptive, language, and personal-social. The age-stage description for any given age serves as the basis for developmental expectations for an average child at that chronological age. Table 2.1 displays descriptors in the four categories of behavior for children aged three, four, and five.

Form of Long-Term Development. For the maturationist, the goal of development is adulthood. Rate and speed vary for each individual, but everyone passes through a specific sequence of stages. Maturation is time-based change and certain aspects of physiology cannot be recaptured. Timing is critical. Developmental progress occurs in two general time periods:

Optimum Period Fairly long period in which general physiological structures are in readiness for broad range of age-related developmental tasks.

Critical Period Specific time period in which physiological structures are present; passage of time will qualitatively change physiology since some structures will disappear or be radically altered.

Table 2.1. Developmental Characteristics of Preschool Children

Category of Behavior	Three-Year-Old	Four-Year-Old	Five-Year-Old
Physical Motor	Walks alone up stairs alternating feet May jump from bottom step Rides tricycle and can turn wide corners Can walk on tiptoe Stands on one foot—momentary balance	Climbs ladders and trees Expert rider of tricycle Can run on tiptoe Hops on one foot "One-footed" skip	Runs lightly on toes Dances to music Skips using feet alternately Can stand on one foot 8 to 10 seconds Can hop 2 to 3 yards on each foot
Adaptive	Copies circle Imitates cross Paints with large brush on easel Cuts with scissors	Copies cross Matches four primary colors correctly Draws a man with head and legs, sometimes trunk or features Counts three objects correctly and answers how many	Copies square Copies triangle Names four primary colors Writes a few letters spontaneously Counts fingers on one hand with index finger of other
Language	Gives full name and sex Uses plurals and pronouns Carries on simple conversations and verbalizes past experiences Asks many questions beginning "What?" "Where?" and "Who?"	Gives connected account of recent events and experiences Gives age Listens to and tells long stories, sometimes confusing fact and fantasy Can tell names of siblings	Gives name and address Asks meaning of abstract words Knows ages of siblings Loves stories and acts them out in detail later Names penny, nickel, and dime
Personal-Social	Pours well from pitcher Puts on shoes Undresses with supervision Unbuttons front and side buttons Willing to share	Dresses and undresses with little supervision General behavior self-willed and out of bounds Understands taking turns Needs other children to play with	Undresses and dresses alone Serial domestic and dramatic play Plans and builds constructively Chooses own friends Comforts playmates in distress

According to psychoanalytic theory, which is part of the maturationist viewpoint, the goal of development is also adulthood—the change from a pleasure-seeking child to a reality-oriented, self-controlled adult.

Role of the Child. Children initiate their own activities, choosing what they will do, when, and for how long. A fair degree of freedom is accorded the child because it is assumed that children gravitate naturally toward activities that are most appropriate for their level of development.

Role of the Adult. Responsibilities of adults are to become familiar with age-related behavior and experience and to ensure that appropriate materials and activities are available for each child. Using a clinical teaching style, adults observe and respond to child-initiated activities. Teachable moments occur when adults can use children's spontaneous activities as a basis for formal learning. Adults strive to promote self-esteem and the easy expression of feelings. The adult "operates around" the child—that is, provides a warm, stimulating, nurturant environment in which development flourishes.

Implications for Program Design

Program practices derived from these theoretical views concern the stage-patterned process of development and the healthy resolution of conflicts. The following list describes basic implications of the maturationist viewpoint for staffing, environmental design, materials and equipment, and evaluation. The subcategories within each of these areas are described in more detail in Chapters 3–6.

Staffing

- *Caregiving Behaviors* Adult "operates around" the child, providing a rich, warm, stimulating environment that will foster growth and learning. The child is free to grow and develop within very broad limits.
- *Teacher Role* The teacher sets the stage by selecting and arranging the environment. Teacher behaviors are focused on linking child with activities that are developmentally appropriate. Teacher always looks for the "teachable moment" when developmental readiness and interest peak.
- *Interaction Technique and Style* Adults are spontaneous and patient, striving to stimulate play activity in harmony with children's developmental stages. Through verbal interchanges adults help children connect with environmental opportunities and resolve social situations.

Environmental Design

- *Setup of Facility* Space is arranged to be attractive, inviting, and appealing. It must provide enough different spaces for different types of activities to occur simultaneously.
- *Management of Groups and Individuals* Heterogeneous groups based loosely on ages or stages of development provide for exchange of play ideas. Consistent statements of limits and redirection are used to help children achieve self-discipline.
- *Time Schedule for Activity Blocks* Time schedule is flexible and activities fluid to exploit the rhythms of children's interests and needs.

Materials and Equipment

- *Selection of Activity Content* Any content is appropriate if it reflects the familiar environment and experiences of children. Objectives are stated in terms of developmental norms.
- *Sequencing and Pacing of Content* Planning is organized around units and broad themes. Activities and ideas are integrated and multipurposeful.
- *Selection of Materials and Equipment* Materials and equipment are chosen to allow many modes of expression. They are based on age, ability, and developmental needs of children. A rich assortment is essential.

Evaluation

- *Assessment of Child Progress* The purpose of assessment is to obtain a picture of the whole child in terms of developmental norms. Naturalistic observation is desired since it gives information about behavior in context.
- *Program Evaluation* The program is a success if the child's development proceeds according to normative standards. Factors within the child set the boundaries of developmental potential.

Applying the Maturationist Viewpoint

One of the most appealing features of the maturationist viewpoint is that the basic descriptive information about development is very accessible. The theory itself is easy to understand and it is relatively easy to find instances of theory in practice in programs with young children. Similarly, those looking for a foundation for program design will find that much of what they observe children doing in a variety of settings fits neatly with age-stage descriptors and personality phases. In general, this viewpoint looks like an easy, comfortable one to implement.

Beware! It is entirely too easy for adults charged with responsibility for young children

Can you see the possibilities here to introduce the concepts of balance and weight distribution? This may be a teachable moment, but it could go by without being recognized unless the caregiver is highly skilled in the maturationist approach. (Courtesy of U.S. Department of Health and Human Services, Washington, DC.)

to abdicate responsibility for outcomes. At one level, since heredity determines development, the questions of "why bother?" and "can I really make any difference?" must be confronted. Even with satisfactory answers to these questions, there is still the difficulty of prescribing and monitoring adult behaviors in the program. Clinical teaching, guiding, supervising free play, and staying alert for "teachable moments" are all nonspecific tasks for which there are no clear right or wrong procedures. It is all too common for untrained staff to try to fake their responses to these tasks. Program designers tend to underestimate the difficulty of providing a nurturant environment. Setting up and then orchestrating reasonable degrees of consistency among staff across all program practices is a formidable challenge for the program director.

The Behaviorist Viewpoint

Behaviorists believe the environment is the key. Environment determines development and shapes destiny. "At the core of this perspective is the thesis that *man grows to be what he is made to be by his environment*" (Langer, 1969, p. 4). The young child is thought of as a blank slate to be written upon by environmental events or as a mirror, reflecting in individual behavior events from a larger sphere of general experience. To the behaviorist, the child acquires and stores information and switches behaviors in methodical fashion. This has led some to use the label *mechanistic* to describe how behaviors are established.

Philosophy

A behaviorist believes that a child is a product of the environment. The child is viewed as passive, reactive, and receptive; he or she has response capabilities that environmental conditions will form into behaviors. When a child is viewed as a product of environment, development occurs as patterns of behavior are acquired from the environment.

Behaviorists are optimists. Since control takes place through environmental manipulation, behaviors can be constructed and changed. Development can be directed or altered in preselected ways. Behaviorism sets forth the mechanisms of learning independent of content. Culture and content provide the raw material of learning but do not alter the basic processes of learning that are thought to be widely applicable. The specifics that are learned are a result of choices by the program designer and caregiver.

Theoretical Assumptions

Theories derived from the behaviorist world view ignore emotionality, feelings, and inner states and focus instead on overt and visible behaviors. These behaviors are described in a body of laws. Such theories concentrate on prediction and description of the mechanisms of learning. They use operational definitions, precise methodology, and controlled systematic observation of outcomes.

Theorists such as Skinner, Bijou, and Baer take a fundamental approach to development, presupposing that the conditioned reflex is the underlying mechanism. Respondent and operant conditioning are further explanations for the acquisition and modification of behavior. Another approach in the behaviorist tradition is social-learning theory. Postulating the mechanisms of identification and modeling, social-learning theory concentrates on acquisition and modification of social behavior. Bandura and Gewirtz have written extensively to explain the social-learning approach, which some feel has made behaviorism more flexible and more compatible with certain observable "realities" of development. Recent work by Mahoney describes the contribution of thinking or cognitions within the behaviorist framework.

Source of Behavior. Environment provides the blueprint of knowledge, skills, and social and moral rules of culture from which behavior is drawn. Behaviors are established as a result of the consequences or reinforcing events that a child experiences from the environment. Behaviors can be established through planned reinforcement or happenstance.

Structure of Behavior. The basic form of behavior is the *stimulus-response (S-R) unit.* Over time, theorists have emphasized different components of this unit. Most current theorists deal primarily with an expanded unit of behavior S-R-R. Reinforcement, the final R, is the application of consequences to increase the frequency or strength of a response (the first R). Examples of these different emphases are as follows:

S – R
↑ (arrow under S)
Classical conditioning, conditioned reflex (Pavlov)—a response already under control of a stimulus is put under control of another stimulus through association. *Example:* A hungry baby sucks when a nipple is placed in its mouth. Through association the baby comes to suck upon seeing a bottle.

S – R
↑ (arrow under the link)
Emphasis on the link (Thorndike)—habit formation is promoted through drill and repetition strengthening and quickening responses. *Example:* A child's correct pronunciation of a friend's name is strengthened by the friend's responding when the correct name is used.

S – R – R
↑ (arrow under final R)
Operant conditioning (Skinner)—previous random response is put under stimulus control by using reinforcement as a consequence of response. *Example:* A child is given social praise each time he or she uses the potty. The frequency of the child's potty use increases.

Operant conditioning is the tool through which behavior can be managed. Program practices derived from behaviorist theory are generally based on the S-R-R operant-conditioning unit as the means with which desired learning outcomes can be achieved. Learning is observable, countable, measurable; in short, developmental change can be quantified. Behavior can be structured in several ways: (1) child can perform an increasing number of different S-R units; (2) child uses chains of S-R units to form complex behaviors; (3) child can perform several S-R units simultaneously; (4) child increases in skill of response in an S-R unit. For

These children are having a structured lesson emphasizing color and shape recognition and matching. Children are praised for correct naming of shapes and colors. (Courtesy of U.S. Department of Agriculture, Washington, DC.)

the behaviorist, development is an accumulation, in linear fashion, of new skills. A response is established when reinforcement is keyed to performance; hence, learning is operant.

Form of Long-Term Development. The initial behavior of the child is conceived to be random and purposeless. Environment provides the reinforcing structure for the child's behavior. Ultimately, the child becomes a product of the special stimulus situations and reinforcing elements of his or her particular environment. Every child's reinforcement history is different. Every individual represents a unique, very personal developmental pattern. The goal of long-term development is behavioral competence for the individual within the parameters of his or her daily environment.

Role of the Child. Children are seen as responders to their environment. They react to stimuli, absorb information, and are reinforced for certain behaviors. When children do these things, they are said to have learned. Heredity may set some limits on the capacity of children to respond to stimulation, but it is not thought to alter the basic S-R behavior mechanism.

Development is perceived to be lagging if the child's skills are inadequate to meet environmental expectations of competence. This may be explained as resulting from inadequate S-R connections or from a lack of effective reinforcers in the environment to establish behaviors.

Role of the Adult. Children's behavior is a function of adult behavior. If a child lacks competence, it is because the adults in the environment have failed to keep reinforcements high and to keep the environment salient. One could say that the adult "operates on" the child. It is the adult who specifies the desired changes that the child undergoes, arranges the activities that result in these changes, and reinforces the changes. Teachers and caregivers in this viewpoint have sometimes been referred to as "environmental engineers."

Implications for Program Design

Behaviorism sets forth the basic mechanisms of learning independent of content. Program practice derived from behaviorist theory is built on the assumption that the curriculum planner should decide what the child is to learn. Judgment and personal values are critical in determining the content of learning and the nature of the experiences in which the child participates. The following list describes the behaviorist perspective on program design.

Staffing

- *Caregiving Behaviors* Adult "operates on" the child, using reinforcement to establish behaviors and build a positive climate for learning.
- *Teacher Role* The teacher plans and controls all parts of the learning environment. Through deliberate stimulation and purposeful reinforcement, children master special skills and subject content.
- *Interaction Technique and Style* Adults are in charge and highly goal directed. Activities are formal, well scheduled, and confidently and positively managed.

Environmental Design

- *Setup of Facility* The environment is structured to focus attention and avoid conflicts and distractions.
- *Management of Groups and Individuals* Children are put in small ability groups to promote teacher contact and direction. Principles of behavior modification are used to prevent and control deviant behavior.
- *Time Schedule for Activity Blocks* Time is tightly scheduled with a brisk pace often evident. Timetables are precise, and some activities are routinely required of all children.

Materials and Equipment

- *Selection of Activity Content* Decisions about content and objectives are determined by analyzing what children in the group need to function competently in their environment.
- *Sequencing and Pacing of Content* Sequences of objectives are built by carefully analyzing tasks to identify small units of behavior. Adults plan by systematically ordering tasks from simple to complex levels.
- *Selection of Materials and Equipment* Materials and equipment must allow adults to control the stimuli and cues in the learning environment.

Evaluation

- *Assessment of Child Progress* Precise assessments are essential to diagnose and prescribe instructional levels and tasks. Systematic quantitative procedures are used.
- *Program Evaluation* The program is a success if children have accomplished established objectives and are prepared to enter the next level of instruction. Teachers are accountable for children's success.

Applying the Behaviorist Viewpoint

Supporters of the behaviorist viewpoint as a basis for child care programming emphasize the positive aspects of control over daily practices. The methodology of behaviorist caregiving and teaching is precise and systematic. Most staff can quickly acquire the skills of direct teaching and reinforcing behavior. Behaviorism is a positive approach. It focuses on desired behaviors and liberal use of reward, reinforcement, and praise. It produces results that are observable and immediate. Children are treated as individuals who are capable of learning. Teaching and caregiving efforts can be specifically directed toward skills that children need for daily activities. Task analysis techniques allow adults to pinpoint behaviors and build skills or solve problems effectively.

Some find behaviorism a sterile approach to learning, inferring that such complete adult control of the environment extinguishes spontaneity and exploratory activities for children. Detractors generally believe that somehow children have some effect on the course of their own development and they are not quite passive reactors. Others feel that thinking is too complex to be reduced to S-R explanations of any sort. Some do not want the bother or the responsibility of always being accountable and in charge of learning.

At issue is the fundamental belief of behaviorists that environment determines all. Those who do not embrace that belief will not be comfortable with the principles of behaviorism as a foundation for programming practice. Whether one can sporadically and selectively use behaviorist principles is also in question. Can adults "turn on" and "turn off" environmental management of behavior using the techniques for short periods or special tasks? Are children confused by this?

The Cognitive Viewpoint

Think and then act. The key to the cognitive perspective is understanding the power a person has over his or her destiny through the exercise of intelligence. "At the heart of this view is the autogenetic thesis that *man develops to be what he makes himself by his own actions*" (Langer, 1969, p. 7). Through the dynamic interaction of heredity and environment every person creates himself or herself. Through will and effort one can transcend the limits of innate capacity and immediate environment—a person as an organism has the power to develop from within, not according to a genetic blueprint or environmental dictates, but according to self-organization. Other terms for this perspective are *organismic, interactionist,* or *cognitive comprehensive.*

Philosophy

Cognitivists believe that children are more than a simple sum of parts—the contributions of heredity and environment. The cognitive view recognizes both the frontiers and limits of environment and heredity and postulates a role for humans that maximizes free will and self-determinism. Philosophically, education is seen as a vehicle to enhance human powers of self-organization.

Humans are perceived as naturally and spontaneously active. Life itself creates the impetus for growth. The implication of this world view is that development occurs when a person's self-organization is matched or challenged by experiential events. The cognitive perspective is essentially focused on one's intellectual powers as the means and method of development.

Some see the cognitive or organismic perspective as a middle ground between the behaviorist and maturationist views, integrating in a balanced way their different positions regarding the contributions of environment and heredity. Appealing as this notion is, it should be flatly rejected. Behaviorist, cognitive, and maturationist perspectives do not fall neatly in line on a continuum between environment and heredity. The dynamic participation of the individual in his own development makes the cognitive perspective distinctly more complex than a simple combination of environment and heredity.

Theoretical Assumptions

Theories derived from the cognitive viewpoint tend to focus on the processes people use to organize themselves and the ways in which people come to know themselves in relation to the world. These theories use stages to indicate successive levels of organization at given points of development. A stage, then, refers to a level of internal organization that is qualitatively different and discontinuous from all other previous stages. Children and adults, just by differences in age, have had different amounts and opportunities for experience. Children and adults function at different stage levels. Thus, children are expected to be qualitatively different (more primitive) from adults. Age is a good indicator of experience for descriptive purposes, but age itself does not *cause* behaviors.

The theory widely discussed in the child development literature that adheres to the cognitive viewpoint is Jean Piaget's theory of cognitive development. Essentially a theory of the growth of intelligence, Piagetian theory postulates a set of biologically based processes through which the child comes to know the world. These processes are stage-independent. Piagetian theory also describes a series of stages that are considered universal and always occur in the same sequence. Each stage is characterized by a particular level of mental operations.

Kohlberg has described a developmental view drawn from the work of several cognitive theorists. Specifically, he states "the cognitive-developmental or interactional view is based on the premise that the cognitive and affective structures which education should nourish are natural emergents from the interaction between the child and the environment under conditions where such interaction is allowed or fostered" (1968, p. 1015). Kohlberg's work has been focused on the growth of moral judgment to illustrate his cognitive developmental principles. He outlined a series of stages that consider the development of morality within a strong cognitive framework.

Piaget's theoretical ideas are the most fully developed and widely disseminated of all the cognitive theorists. The following presentation of theoretical principles is drawn primarily from Piaget's work. It is useful to know, however, that many other positions are being explored within the cognitive perspective; much of the work has been stimulated by ongoing attempts to interpret Piaget's ideas for program application. Piaget's theory of cognitive growth uses a specific vocabulary to define processes and stages. Child care program designers will find that familiarity with this vocabulary will help them grasp the underlying theoretical principles.

Source of Behavior. Development comes from within. Children are seen as intrinsically active. Piaget believes that maturation, environment, social experience, and equilibration contribute to children's attempts to organize and structure their world. *Equilibration* is the state between what is known and what is yet to be understood. Children are continually engaged in transactions with the world, setting in motion complex interactions between their present mental organization and their activities. Piaget uses a specific terminology to describe the process through which new developmental behaviors are generated and equilibration is maintained.

The process is termed *adaptation,* and the parts are called *assimilation* and *accommodation.* New experiences that can be fitted into previously existing ways of knowing or thinking are assimilated. Experiences that do not fit and that cause changes in ways of thinking or knowing are accommodated. Both assimilation and accommodation are modes of adaptation. Our natural tendency to maintain internal balance (equilibration) helps regulate the pace at which new organizational structures are formed.

Structure of Behavior. Through progressive reconstruction in the process of adaptation, schemas are formed. *Schemas* are complex ways of behaving or of organizing thoughts and information. New schemas arise when simpler schematic structures prove to be inadequate. Schemas may be temporary or permanent. The content of schemas is specific for an individual according to his or her experiential interactions.

Stages, however, are theoretical explanations of qualitatively different levels of mental organization. The order of stages is always the same and irreversible. The growth of intelligence can be viewed as a flight of stairs that a person mentally mounts in stages (see Figure 2.5).

For instance, from ages two to four children are egocentric. They use themselves as the standard and are unable to take the viewpoint of other people. They judge things on face value; categorize only a single characteristic and cannot classify with several aspects of an object simultaneously. Their conceptualization is dominated by perceptions. As Sigel describes: "[the child] is not able to incorporate the variety of characteristics of an object into a single classification. He can grasp such ideas as men and

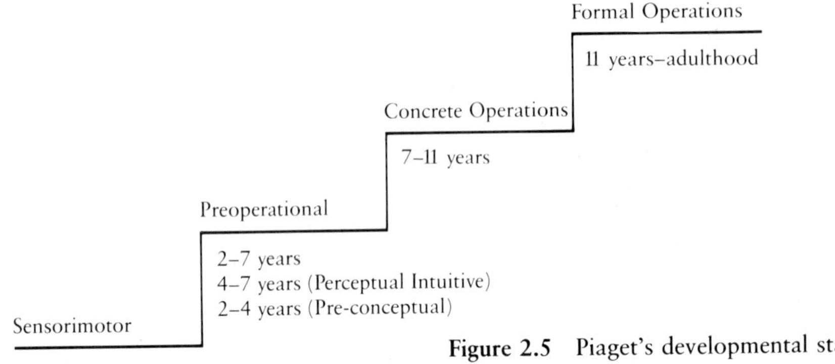

Figure 2.5 Piaget's developmental stages.

women being classified as people, or that potatoes and apples are food . . . but he cannot employ two attributes of the same object, that is, break up a group of apples along the multiple dimensions of big red apples and small green apples" (1964, p. 218).

From ages four to seven, children experience increased symbolic functioning. They are better able to understand the meaning of similarity and classification. Sigel continues: "It is now possible for him to see relationships such as 'Mrs. Smith is the mother of John,' as a result of the ability to perceive relations as well as to compare and order items" (1964, p. 219).

An example for the sensorimotor stage appears in Chapter 8; Chapter 9 includes an example of the concrete operations stage.

Form of Long-Term Development. The course of development is toward higher order stages. New ways of thinking become dominant and submerge previous patterns. The goal of development is competence in dealing with the world—that is, handling abstractions and competently solving problems.

Role of the Child. The child is seen as a fundamentally different thinker than the adult. Actively involved in situations to promote assimilation and accommodation, the child functions as a mental manipulator. Development for the child is not viewed as something that can be accelerated or denied. The child will construct mental processes to whatever degree demanded by comfortable survival in the environment.

Role of the Adult. The cognitive view sees a teacher or caregiver as "operating with" a child. The adult follows a "wait-challenge-wait" procedure, which allows the child to accumulate experience at a given level until the level is established. The teacher or caregiver arranges activities that challenge current levels and stretch the child to higher levels, and then the adult waits for that new level to become stable. Child and adult have complementary roles in this situation. Each alternates between passive and active roles in the process of development.

Implications for Program Design

Program practices built from cognitive theory generally have two basic assumptions: (1) the child progresses through a sequential series of stages of mental development that must be taken into account when planning programs; and (2) active participation by the child through construction and organization of experiences is necessary for development. These implications are presented in the following list:

Sorting and classifying information are two common tasks in a cognitively based program. (Courtesy of U.S. Department of Health and Human Services, Washington, DC.)

Staffing

- *Caregiving Behaviors* Adult "operates with" the child, encouraging children to become actively involved with people and activities.
- *Teacher Role* The teacher orchestrates the environment in order to give children practice in the generation of ideas that will alter concept formation and build cognitive structure.
- *Interaction Technique and Style* Adults focus on thinking processes as evidenced in children's on-going activities. Through open-ended and challenging questions adults help to cognitively structure children's activities.

Environmental Design

- *Setup of Facility* Activity areas are clearly marked. Placement of materials conveys a sense of conceptual order.
- *Management of Groups and Individuals* Grouping is not essential but is often done for convenience or convergence of interest. The goal of discipline is for children to plan for and be responsible for their own behavior.
- *Time Schedule for Activity Blocks* Predictable routines and schedules are used to give children experiences with temporal order. Activities are paced to allow children time to anticipate and to explore consequences.

Materials and Equipment

- *Selection of Activity Content* Any subject matter can be used as a means to build cognitive abilities and basic thinking processes. Language is emphasized because it is a primary tool for thought.
- *Sequencing and Pacing of Content* Concrete to representational sequences are used. Activities are planned to challenge current levels of thinking without creating frustration.
- *Selection of Materials and Equipment* Materials and equipment are chosen for their potential for children to explore, construct and become absorbed in them.

Evaluation

- *Assessment of Child Progress* Samples of skill in problem-solving situations are used to reach conclusions about children's thinking abilities.
- *Program Evaluation* The program is a success if the children's thinking skills change qualitatively over time. Progress is a function of teach-

ers' skills in involving the children in interactions with their environment.

Applying the Cognitive Viewpoint

Many supporters of this viewpoint feel that good thinking skills provide a child with a strong organizer for all other aspects of development. They believe that facilitating processes of thought rather than fixing on "right" answers is a desirable mode of teaching. Children can be helped to help themselves. The active, interactive role prescribed for children by cognitive theorists appeals to many professionals who work with children.

Child care program designers will find that using a cognitive viewpoint can provide a challenging situation for staff members as they are stimulated to devise ways in which everyday experiences can become "mind stretchers" for children. Piaget's stages provide a clear framework within which staff can judge the predominant thinking levels of children.

In contrast, some program designers find that, while a cognitive viewpoint appears reasonable as a basis for program rationale, it is too abstract for staff to deal with on a daily basis. Without intensive training and extensive guidance the majority of the staff may feel uncomfortable with the resulting curriculum. They may be able to carry out specific plans but may not be facile in making spontaneous responses consistent with the theory. Through actions and words, staff may communicate a need to put more emphasis on physical motor activities and social emotional aspects of play and may simply ignore cognitive concerns when interacting with children. At the theory level, many have expressed concern that Piagetian theory is not truly applicable to education. They believe that it was not developed as a tool for teaching and that it is cumbersome to interpret. Further, since the theory does not support the idea of intervention or acceleration, further questions are raised about its usefulness for building curriculum. However, for those who wish to base child care program practices on cognitive theory, there is a considerable body of documented curriculum work upon which to draw. Despite Piaget's original intentions, American practitioners have charted new courses in program design that are based on his stages in processes of thinking.

Avoiding an Eclectic Approach

Different world views and theory families exist because many people believe many different things about the nature and course of development. Exploring the details of these differences and resolving the many contradictions and similarities among theorists has created a continuing dialogue among developmental theorists. No grand, all-encompassing theory is in sight. The child care program designer confronts the need to choose one from among the existing viewpoints. These perspectives remain distinct, separate entities because:

- There is a fundamental lack of communication among them. Each interprets facts and events differently. This is reflected in the unique vocabulary that has grown up around each viewpoint.
- The subject matter of the viewpoint and related theory families do not overlap completely. Each theorist looks at only those events that appear most salient, and these selected events are not common to all theories.
- The proposed rules of process and change are different.

Trying to compare viewpoints is like trying to compare apples and oranges. Our brief overview of each viewpoint in the preceding sections only highlights the differences among viewpoints. "Different world views have different criteria for determining the truth of propositions, and therefore a synthesis that mixes world views also mixes truth criteria" (Reese &

Overton, 1970, p. 121). Child care program designers should strive to choose and work within the *one* viewpoint that is most compatible with their personal beliefs and skills.

Eclecticism, or choosing what is best from several sources, is intuitively appealing since it seems to allow for the use of a broad range of methods and materials in working with young children. Too often, though, eclecticism results in a "bag of tricks" approach—a relatively disconnected accumulation of "things to do." We would like to distinguish carefully between the flexibility that is possible in a single hierarchy and the eclecticism that is composed of methods from various theories. Only when a single rationale serves as the foundation for program decisions is the character of program practice likely to be similar across decisions. Interpretive decisions regarding program practice come from thoughtful analysis and finding the match between the program practices and the theory base.

Eclecticism is not all bad. One reason that different world views and theories exist at all is because different explanations of development seem more appropriate at one point in the life span than others. For example, to some, infant development is best explained by a mechanistic or behaviorist model while adolescent development seems more amenable to explanation with Erikson's "Stages of Man." Perhaps certain subjects are learned through behaviorist processes and others through cognitive reasoning processes.

Any child care program is, in the final analysis, an individual's interpretation of the link between theory and practice. Multiple relationships between theory and practice can and do exist in programs that have been drawn from the same theory base. Different program designers have different interpretations of the links between theory and practice. Considerable latitude exists for interpretations, and child care program designers enjoy considerable flexibility in decision making.

Summary

The foundation for any child care program consists of a program framework and a choice of developmental viewpoint.

One model for a program framework is a daily care pattern, or a timetable for the day's activities. This schedule follows the eight units of the child's daily experience: arrival, breakfast, morning activity, snacks, lunch, rest, afternoon activity, and departure. Each unit has a basic care and a curriculum component.

The designer of a child care program must choose from among three major developmental viewpoints—maturationist, behaviorist, and cognitive. Working from a philosophy, the designer examines the theoretical assumptions that underlie the chosen viewpoint and writes a program rationale. This will provide the reasoning behind choices concerning staffing, environmental design, materials and equipment, and evaluation.

The maturationist viewpoint holds that children are born with certain internal patterns of behavior that become apparent with age. According to the behaviorist viewpoint, the environment determines a child's development. Cognitive theory says that children create themselves through their own will and effort and are not limited by their heredity or environment.

If the child care program is to have consistency, a program designer has to choose a single viewpoint, not take parts from several viewpoints. Within a viewpoint, however, the designer can find a flexible approach that suits his or her own particular needs.

Resources

General

Ausubel, D. P., & Sullivan, E. V. (1970). *Theory and problems of child development.* New York: Grune & Stratton.

Baldwin, A. L. (1967). *Theories of child development.* New York: Wiley.

Cowles, M. (1971). Four views of learning and development. *Educational Leadership, 28,* 90–95.

Crain, W. C. (1980). *Theories of development: Concepts and application.* Englewood Cliffs, NJ: Prentice-Hall.

Early childhood education: How to select and evaluate materials. (1972). (Educational Product Report, No. 42). New York: Educational Products Information Exchange Institute.

Goldhaber, D. (1979). Does the changing view of early experience imply a changing view of early development? In L. G. Katz (Ed.), *Current topics in early childhood education: Vol. II.* Norwood, NJ: Ablex.

Langer, J. (1969). *Theories of development.* New York: Holt, Rinehart & Winston.

McCandless, B. R., & Evans, E. D. (1973). *Children and youth: Psychosocial development.* Hinsdale, IL: Dryden Press.

Reese, H. W., & Overton, W. F. (1970). Models of development and theories of development. In L. R. Goulet & P. B. Baltes (Eds.), *Life-span developmental psychology* (pp. 115–145). New York: Academic Press.

Rohwer, W. D., Ammon, P. R., & Cramer, P. (1974). *Understanding intellectual development.* Hinsdale, IL.: Dryden Press.

Sears, R. R. (1975). Your ancients revisited: A history of child development. In E. M. Hetherington (Ed.), *Review of child development research* (Vol. 5). Chicago: University of Chicago Press.

Seaver, J. W., & Cartwright, C. A. (1977). A pluralistic foundation for training early childhood professionals. *Curriculum Inquiry, 7* (4), 305–329.

Senn, M. J. E. (1975). Insights on the child development movement in the United States. *Monographs of the Society for Research in Child Development, 40,* nos. 3 and 4 (Serial No. 161).

Stone, L. J., & Church, J. (1972). Some representative theoretical orientations in developmental psychology. In W. R. Looft (Ed.), *Developmental psychology: A book of readings.* Hinsdale, IL: Dryden Press.

Watson, R. I. (1965). *Psychology of the child* (2nd ed.). New York: Wiley.

Maturation Theory

Ames, L. B., Gillespie, C., Haines, J., & Ilg, F. (1979). *The Gesell Institute's child from one to six: Evaluating the behavior of the preschool child.* New York: Harper & Row.

Biber, B., & Franklin, M. B. (1967). The relevance of developmental and psychodynamic concepts to the education of the preschool child. In J. Hellmuth (Ed.), *The disadvantaged child* (Vol. 1). New York: Brunner/Mazel.

Brown, J. A. C. (1961). *Freud and the post-Freudians.* Baltimore: Penguin Books.

Erikson, E. H. (1963). *Childhood and society* (2nd ed.). New York: Norton.

Erikson, E. H. (1968). *Identity: Youth and crisis.* New York: Norton.

Fraiberg, S. H. (1959). *The magic years.* New York: Scribner's.

Gesell, A., & Amatruda, C. S. (1965). *Developmental diagnosis* (2nd ed.). New York: Harper & Row.

Gesell, A., Ilg, F. L., & Ames, L. B. (1974). *Infant and child in the culture of today* (rev. ed.). New York: Harper & Row.

Havighurst, R. J. (1964). *Developmental tasks and education* (2nd ed.). New York: McKay.

Highberger, R., & Schramm, C. (1976). *Child development for day care workers.* Boston: Houghton Mifflin.

Ilg, F. L., & Ames, L. B. (1955). *Child behavior.* New York: Harper & Row.

Isaacs, S. (1972). *Social development in young children* (2nd ed.). New York: Schocken Books.

McCandless, B. R. (1969). Childhood socialization. In D. A. Goslin (Ed.), *Handbook of socialization theory and research.* Chicago: Rand McNally.

Miller, D. R. (1969). Psychoanalytic theory of development: A re-evaluation. In D. A. Goslin (Ed.), *Handbook of socialization theory and research.* Chicago: Rand McNally.

Murphy, L. B. (1937). *Social behavior and child personality.* New York: Columbia University Press.

Smart, M. S., & Smart, R. C. (1973). *Infants.* New York: Macmillan.

Smart, M. S., & Smart, R. C. (1973). *Preschool children.* New York: Macmillan.

Spock, Benjamin (1976). *Baby and child care.* New York: Pocket Books.

Stone, J., & Church, J. (1964). *Childhood and adolescence.* New York: Random House.

White, B. L. (1975). *The first three years of life.* Englewood Cliffs, NJ: Prentice-Hall.

Behaviorist Theory

Bandura, A. (1969). Social-learning theory identificatory processes. In D. A. Goslin (Ed.), *Handbook of socialization theory and research.* Chicago: Rand McNally.

Bandura, A. (1974). Behavior theory and the models of man. *American Psychologist, 29,* 816–820.

Bijou, S. W., & Baer, D. M. (1961). *Child development* (Vol. 1): *A systematic and empirical theory.* New York: Appleton-Century-Crofts.

Engelmann, S. (1969). *Preventing failure in the primary grades.* Chicago: Science Research Associates.

Gewirtz, J. L. (1968). Mechanisms of social learning: Some roles of stimulation and behavior in early human development. In D. A. Goslin (Ed.), *Handbook of socialization theory and research.* Chicago: Rand McNally.

Mahoney, M. J. (1974). *Cognition and behavior modification.* Cambridge, MA: Ballinger.

Risley, T. R., & Baer, D. M. (1973). Operant behavior modification: The deliberate development of behavior. In B. M. Caldwell & H. N. Ricciuti (Eds.), *Review of child development research* (Vol. 3). Chicago: University of Chicago Press.

Skinner, B. F. (1953). *Science and human behavior.* New York: Macmillan.

Skinner, B. F. (1972). *Beyond freedom and dignity.* New York: Knopf.

Cognitive Theory

Almy, M. (1966). *Young children's thinking.* New York: Teachers College Press.

Brearly, M., & Hitchfield, E. (1969). *A guide to reading Piaget.* New York: Schocken.

Bruner, J. S. (1964). The course of cognitive growth. *American Psychologist, 19,* 1–15.

Bruner, J., Olver, R. R., & Greenfield, P. M. (1966). *Studies in cognitive growth.* New York: Wiley.

Elkind, D., & Flavell, J. H. (Eds.). (1969). *Studies in cognitive development* (Essays in honor of Jean Piaget). New York: Oxford University Press.

Feldman, D. H. (1980). *Beyond universals in cognitive development.* Norwood, NJ: Ablex.

Flavell, J. H. (1963). *The developmental psychology of Jean Piaget:* Princeton, NJ: Van Nostrand.

Honstead, C. (1968). The developmental theory of Jean Piaget. In J. L. Frost (Ed.), *Early childhood education rediscovered.* New York: Holt, Rinehart & Winston.

Inhelder, B., & Piaget, J. (1958). *The growth of logical thinking from childhood to adolescence.* New York: Basic Books.

Kagan, J. (1971). *Change and continuity in infancy.* New York: Wiley.

Kohlberg, L. (1968). Early education. A cognitive-developmental view. *Child Development, 39,* 1013–1062.

Kohlberg, L. (1969). Stage and sequence: The cognitive-developmental approach to socialization. In D. A. Goslin (Ed.), *Handbook of socialization theory and research.* Chicago: Rand McNally.

Kohlberg, L., & Mayer, R. (1972). Development as the aim of education. *Harvard Educational Review, 42*(4), 449–496.

Saunders, R., & Bingham-Newman, A. M. (1984). *Piagetian perspective for preschools: A thinking book for teachers.* Englewood Cliffs, NJ: Prentice-Hall.

Sigel, I. E. (1964). The attainment of concepts. In M. L. Hoffman & L. W. Hoffman (Eds.), *Review of child development research* (Vol. 1). New York: Russell Sage Foundation, 209–248.

Vygotsky, L. S. (1962). *Thought and language.* Cambridge, MA: MIT Press.

Weikart, D. P. (1972). Relationship of curriculum, teaching and learning. In J. C. Stanley (Ed.), *Preschool programs for the disadvantaged: Five experimental approaches to early childhood education.* Baltimore: Johns Hopkins University Press.

Part II

Planning a Program

3

Staffing Roles

Introduction

What do child care staff do all day? What is it about staff behavior that makes or breaks a program? This chapter examines staff behaviors and analyzes the skills and knowledge that characterize child care staffs in programs based on each of the three developmental viewpoints. Staff provide caregiving, have a teaching role, and exhibit interaction techniques and styles that are the basis for the intimate relationship that grows between child and adult. Our main interest is looking at differences in staff behavior from maturationist, behaviorist, and cognitive programs.

Child care staff need guidelines and examples for interacting with children. Staff are the daily interpreters of the program. Staff behavior should be consistent across all staff members and appropriate for each situation. By helping staff identify the links between program philosophy and their own behaviors, directors maximize the impact of the program for children.

We subdivided the program component on staffing into three parts to describe the full range of the adult-child relationship. In practice, each of these parts often merge, but since we want to illustrate the theory-to-practice model, it is helpful to consider each separately.

1. *Caregiving Behaviors* All adult behaviors in a child care program are caregiving behaviors. This category describes the general nature of the adult role with children. Each developmental viewpoint places emphasis on particular adult behaviors, sets up a specific orientation for adult behaviors, and points toward differing general goals for adults in their interactions with children in a program setting.

   The clearest illustrations of caregiving behaviors are seen in the following activity blocks of basic care: arrival, departure, breakfast, lunch, snacks, and rest. Every program establishes routines for these activities, and staff follow common procedures for transitions between these and other activities. Caregiving *routines and transitions* are part of the basic care of a program, but they also can reflect the developmental viewpoint of the program. How staff handle caregiving routines and transitions sets an *affective climate* for the program and establishes comfort and security for the children's *physical protection.* The affective climate, or emotional tone of a program, is strongly influenced by the sensitivity, responsiveness, warmth, and overt concern that staff demonstrates while performing caregiving behaviors. Routines and transitions give staff numerous predictable and spontaneous opportunities to interact and build personal relationships with children. All of these caregiving contacts reflect the personal style of staff and should reflect the developmental viewpoint of the program.

2. *Teacher Role* We define teaching behaviors as *deliberate behaviors* that have the goal of promoting learning and supporting development. This artificial distinction between caregiving and teaching is useful for illustration purposes and does not necessarily imply that teaching is a more

important adult behavior than caregiving. Teacher role includes the *functions* of the teacher as an agent of the developmental program. It also includes the *decision process for curriculum planning* that characterizes the adult's behavior when functioning as a teacher in the program.

The daily care pattern has two large blocks of time for curriculum opportunities—a morning and an afternoon activity block. During these periods the teaching aspects of adult behaviors predominate. During these two extended time periods program planners implement core curriculum plans based on their chosen developmental viewpoint. Arrival, rest, and departure offer supplemental opportunities for curriculum implementation. Less formal aspects of the appropriate teaching behaviors may be in evidence at these times. Teachers working from different viewpoints have clearly different functions in the classroom and engage in different decisions about curriculum planning and implementation.

3. *Interaction Technique and Style* There is more to caregiving and teacher role than the simple sum of the parts. Whenever we see early childhood professionals "in action" with children, it is obvious that individual staff personality traits interact with curriculum plans. The result is an interaction that is a blend of individual style and program technique. We cannot presume to identify the many nuances of personality traits and assess the relative desirability of some traits versus others. By singling out this part of staff behavior, we want to capture the *dynamics of the adult-child relationship* that evolves.

Caregiving Behaviors

The term *caregiving* implies dependency—the dependency of a child upon adults. It is an emotional term, too, since it concerns adult responsibility for the welfare of young children. Children are deeply dependent upon adults for physical care, protection, and the provision of a comforting environment. Caregiving permeates all activities in a child care program. Children must be "taken care of." The need for caregiving is so basic that program staff often overlook it and pay little attention to the details of caregiving tasks. However, the cumulative impact upon children and program goals is great.

Most of the contact children have with staff in a program will come during routines and transition times—the basic care blocks of arrival, departure, breakfast, lunch, snack, rest, and transitions between activities. Staff responses during these periods of caregiving will be spontaneous and highly personal. The natural inclinations, training experiences, and personal beliefs that staff have about children will surface.

Caregiving cannot be forgotten or relegated to the bottom of the list of concerns about staff skills. Selecting staff whose beliefs are in harmony with the developmental viewpoint of a program is critical. Many programs give candidates for staff positions tests or even trial work periods during which the director or a hiring committee tries to assess how competent and capable the person is with existing program practices. Generally, what is being assessed is the "informal" or caregiving behavior of the staff candidate. Very little can be done to alter the general pattern of caregiving behaviors that result from personal beliefs about children's development.

Fully designed programs for young children establish specific guides for routines and transitions. These may not always correspond to specific activity blocks in the daily schedule. Typically, these are staff caregiving behaviors that all staff may need to perform at one time or another (for example, toileting, caring for minor injuries, lining up, cleaning up, and taking naps). Through observation of staff and review of curriculum documents, the program director should identify those caregiving behaviors that are repeated frequently. In our description, we use the terms *routines* and *transitions* somewhat interchangeably, because in daily practice the distinctions between the two are often blurred. For example, morning snack could be considered a routine because it happens everyday. Cleaning up after snack, getting coats on,

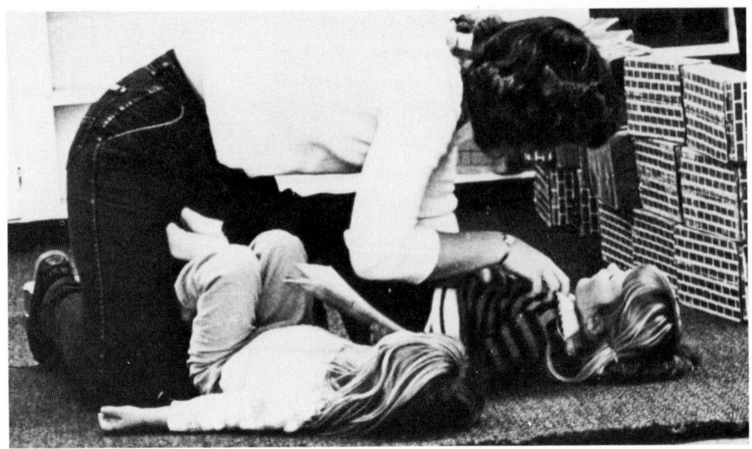

When selecting staff, we want to know how a person performs outside the curriculum plan, without the lesson script or the props of toys and materials. (College of Human Development, Department of Individual and Family Studies, Pennsylvania State University; used with permission.)

and going outside for play are transitions that follow snack time. It would be awkward in planning and in practice to firmly separate the snack routine and the getting-ready-to-go-outside transition.

When preparing program guidelines for routines and transitions, directors should consider five points:

1. Develop written guidelines only for those routines and transitions that are vital parts of your program. Ignore lining up if it's rarely done; include toileting even if it seems incidental—it's unavoidable with small children!
2. Be as loose or manicured, rigorous or informal as you expect the staff to be in implementing these guides. The format for your guidelines will convey a message as important as the content.
3. Solicit and use staff help in preparing written procedures. Consider ways to incorporate guideline preparation in in-service or training plans for staff.
4. Strive for procedures that match the developmental viewpoint of the program. Review theoretical and program resources. Arrange for third-party review, if possible.
5. Incorporate final routine and transition guidelines in staff appraisal procedures for selecting new staff, supervising current staff, and planning in-service training.

The next three subsections describe in detail the process of deriving caregiving behaviors appropriate for each of the three developmental viewpoints. All programs, regardless of perspective, aim to provide healthy, affective climates and safe physical conditions. Within this broad goal, each developmental viewpoint focuses selectively on some components more than others. The program descriptions highlight these differences. The program examples are drawn from actual events in programs ascribing to different theoretical views.

Maturationist Program

In the maturation program the adult "operates around" the child, helping to create a rich, warm, stimulating environment that is essential for development. Using information about the norms of development for given ages, program staff prepare an atmosphere in which the child can negotiate freely. The implications for caregiving routines and transitions are considerable.

First, staff are always available and ready to help when children encounter difficulties. Staff need to know children individually in order to judge just when to help and how long to let the child try. The program values experiences that promote self-confidence and socialization (while the child's health and safety are protected).

Caregivers may stage routines so that children can achieve independence and self-direction. Although staff may sometimes "tuck in" help, verbal directions, or demonstration of skills, routines basically proceed at the child's pace and competence level. Children are encouraged to undertake routines and transitions in individual ways.

The program environment is relaxed and friendly. Getting to know you better and trying things out are very important for staff and children. Staff may spend time in conversation with one child at a time, or may quietly observe the activities of one child over a period of time. Children come to feel comfortable with many adults in the program and use them as resources for help when playing. Through timely assistance the staff seek to encourage children to trust them to set comfortable limits on the boundaries of play and exploration.

EXAMPLES

Cleaning Up. Cleaning up can be a big part of a maturation program, partly because the potential for creative mess, extensive construction, and imaginative use of materials is so great. Cleaning up is a responsible act and a socializing act that children are encouraged to consider as a meaningful activity. Adults help children clean up in several ways. One is by talking about the need for cleanup—putting back for another day, making materials available for other children, the satisfaction to be drawn from order and closure of an activity—in a motivational pep talk for cleanup. Adults participate in cleanup—sharing the effort, modeling efficient means, and socializing. Cleanup is a boundary, or a limit on exploration that serves to give children a sense of mastery over their own environment. Cleanup might happen this way:

> *Spills and Messes.* During the course of the day spills and messes are to be expected. Cleanup kits and tools are available and placed at strategic locations around the room. Children are expected to use these materials to wipe up juice spills, clean up around the water table, and clean up around the house corner or art area.

Smelling | *Tasting* | *Seeing*
Yeasty | Sweet | Color
Burned | Sour | Shape
Buttery | Salty | Size
| Bitter |

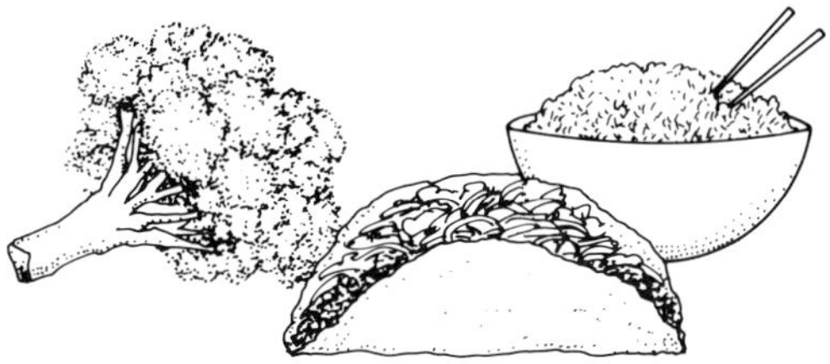

Hearing | *Feeling*
Crunch | Weight
Snap | Texture
Tear apart | Temperature

Figure 3.1 Food experiences.

> *Daily Cleanup.* At the end of play sessions children work together to clean up the room. The last children playing in an area are responsible for picking it up. Shelves, books, and storage containers are accessible at child height, near areas of material use, and usually picture-coded to help children identify contents. Teachers help with cleanup. As children finish in their play area they help with general room cleanup. Often songs accompany the cleanup, and everyone gathers together as the job is completed.

Experiencing Foods. Snacks are important for the young child. Snacks, like meals, are useful learning experiences. Maturationist programs are likely to stress the social aspects of eating (good company and acceptable eating habits). Food is seen as a material worth exploring with the senses (see Figure 3.1). Stress is on exploring food and relating these special foods to everyday eating experiences.

Pitcher and Ames (1975, 194–208) urge programs to serve a variety of foods in place of the usual juice and crackers. They point out that frequently children prepare and serve snacks as part of their morning or afternoon activity, and they suggest that programs experiment as follows:

1. Eat a food raw and then cooked. Explore the differences with fingers, tongue, and words.
2. Eat a food whole and in pieces. Try chopping, grating, or shredding with different foods.
3. Juice a food. What can you use the leftover pulp for?

Behaviorist Program

To the behaviorist, environment shapes the child. Caregiving routines and transitions are viewed as opportunities for adults to "operate on" children, using systematic reinforcement to establish or sustain desired behavior patterns.

Caregiving routines are planned and scheduled. Staff and children recognize and follow set procedures for these routines. Routines give the child a sense of constancy and provide continuing opportunities for behavior practice. Liberal use of praise during routines and transitions helps to build a positive climate for all subsequent learning and performance.

Extended positive reinforcing environments accomplish three objectives:

1. Children come to accept and value reinforcement from adults. External motivation is to spur children to monitor their behavior in many different kinds of situations.
2. Systematic use of specific reinforcement or patterns of reinforcement works to improve the quality levels of children's behavioral performance. Simply put, extra practice leads to more skillful behaviors.
3. A positive reinforcement climate promotes self-concept, self-esteem, and self-confidence. Children come to expect to be "able to do it" when put in learning situations.

Caregiving routines and transitions are opportunities for staff to work on general work habits rather than specific content skills. Listening, persevering, following directions, paying attention, and delaying gratification are examples of critical skills that are necessary for mastering academic lessons. Alert staff can take seemingly incidental tasks and activities and build in child behaviors that contribute to success during formal lessons.

Routines and transitions in a behaviorist program are also important breaks and pace changes for both children and staff. These are times in which behavioral objectives and reinforcement schedules are less obvious.

EXAMPLES

Sequencing Snacks. The snack procedure is efficient and organized. Children are cued to perform the steps in sequence. The task is set up so children can master each part. Success is easy to observe. Adults can praise good performance.

Snack is scheduled for 10:15 to 10:30 A.M. following the first few work periods. After snack children go outside for thirty minutes of vigorous play. Snack is an occasion to learn simple social skills and to learn how to handle food. Equipment is child-sized, procedures are routine, and praise is abundant.

1. Children leave work groups and proceed to snack area. Each child locates his or her name and sits at that place at the table.
2. When all children are present at a table, the child who has a stack of napkins in front of his or her place gets up and distributes them. When this child sits down, the children put the napkins on their lap.
3. Next, a child passes out cups.
4. The teacher initiates pouring juice. As each child pours his or her own juice, the teacher comments on the child's success. The teacher helps with pouring as needed.
5. Snack is passed on a plate after all the juice is poured. A number sign in the middle of the table tells the children how many items to take—for example, six cherries, two cookies, four apple slices. Each child counts aloud as he or she takes the snack. The teacher and other children may count with the child.
6. When all are served, the teacher begins to eat. The children follow. The conversation is liberally sprinkled with positive comments about eating behavior and morning work.
7. When all are finished, the children gather their own paper trash, proceed in a line to the trash

Cubbies for clothes have name tags with animal pictures.

Activity board indicates room area where child should go first.

An objective for Sarah is to follow directions. She wears a reinforcement card that allows teachers to reinforce her appropriate behaviors and keeps her reminded of her good progress.

Figure 3.2 Arrival—Cueing in the day.

can, and then as a group to the play area to go outside to play.

Arrival. Arrival in the morning may look like a casual event, but in a behaviorist program considerable thought has gone into setting up the environment to cue and signal the child. The predictability and ease of the routine help the children make the transition from home to school and from parent to teacher (see Figure 3.2).

Cognitive Program

In cognitive programs for young children the adult "operates with" children, encouraging them to become actively involved with people and activities. The general aim of adult behavior is to facilitate the child's emergence from the sensorimotor stage into the preoperational stage of cognitive development. Adults help provide motivation and general language facility to enable the child to actively manipulate and use experiences.

Caregiving routines and transitions can provide numerous opportunities for incidental learning experiences. But cognitive theory does not offer much guidance for handling the logistics of basic care routines and activity transitions. A well-trained adult can adapt aspects of cognitive teaching strategies to caregiving routines, but such adaptation usually depends on the skill of the adult to respond spontaneously to children within a cognitive framework. This skill level is characteristic of experienced teachers who are well-versed in cognitive theory and adept at a variety of related teaching strategies. Child care programs can expect that a few, but not all, staff will be committed and experienced enough to carry this off. During all but the morning and afternoon curriculum activity blocks in the daily care pattern, cognitive programs may closely resemble maturationist programs. In overall caregiving behaviors, differences between cognitive and maturationist programs may be only a matter of degree of emphasis. The cognitive program may place slightly more weight on thinking processes than on social-emotional and physical needs.

Program designers can help staff to incorporate cognitive teaching strategies into caregiving routines in several ways: (1) by providing specific information and training experiences to build staff skill in cognitive teaching strategies; (2) by pinpointing specific caregiving routines as points of extension for cognitive principles, and then developing detailed protocols for staff for these routines; and (3) by providing staff with role models—other staff who can take the lead in putting these cognitive protocols into action. (A *protocol* is a statement of procedures that serves as a guide for staff to follow when implementing lessons or routines. It gives staff the essential cognitive elements that should be present in the interaction.) But program designers should remember that cognitive programs can operate effectively only if the morning and afternoon curriculum activity blocks are tightly designed.

EXAMPLES

Eating Cognitively. Social interactions and opportunities for incidental learning abound at lunchtime. These ideas for lunchtime conversations highlight how simple experiences can be "cognitively upgraded" through the staff's adept use of language and action:

- The concepts of on and off are explained through use and placement of napkins on and off laps, utensils on and off plates, and hands on and off table.
- Food is frequently cut or served in different size pieces. For instance, children may be asked to take a big piece and a little piece of broccoli. Cookies of two sizes are another good example.
- The concepts of first, second, and last are emphasized and related to the order in which various foods are served and eaten.
- Throughout mealtime there is discussion about milk glasses being full and empty. Teachers ask children to describe their own glasses and then find a glass that is the opposite.
- Conversation centers around past and future events and activities. This gives children opportunities to think about temporal order and chronological sequences.

Departure and Putting the Day in Perspective. By helping children remember the events of the day, staff builds a sense of time and seriation of events for children. Rehearsal of activities and linking products to past activities help children to solidify and hold onto the "thoughts" of the day. This preparation for sharing one's day with parents is an important bridge between program and home that language can help smooth over.

- As children gather their things, teachers help them remember activities in which they participated.
- A picture of lunch or snack foods served may be displayed and children's attention directed to this along with discussion of how they liked the foods.
- As children put outer clothing on, teachers may ask about weather in the morning versus the afternoon, and if the same clothing is still needed.
- Teachers use questions to help children recall playmates and particular events of the day.

Lining Up. This transition between activities should not be ignored as an opportunity. It can involve seriation, or arranging according to some succession, if children line up according to size (smallest to biggest, tallest to shortest, or youngest to oldest). Classification can be discussed if children line up by characteristic (blue shoes, black shoes, brown shoes, and so on; children with hats, children without hats). Lining up can also be a time for body awareness as children relate clothing to specific parts of body (hat-head, shoes-feet, mittens-hands).

Teacher Role

Adults teach so that children will learn. Teaching means that decisions have been made about what children will learn (content and/or method) and that adults are prepared to engage in behaviors to promote children's learning. Teaching requires formal preparation and planning. Teaching implies that an outcome (change) will occur. Evaluation is the means to measure that change and is intimately connected with the goals of teaching.

In school, teaching occurs as adults and children work on mastery of the three Rs and other subjects. But in child care programs the term *teaching* is used loosely and there is no clear-cut agreement on what content adults and children should work on. Staff may be called teachers, supervisors, caregivers, or leaders regardless of their purpose or function in the program. Labels for staff are not really important. What is important is the recognition that certain caregiving behaviors to implement a chosen developmental viewpoint are, in fact, teaching behaviors. Three assumptions about teaching in child care programs are appropriate:

1. Teaching is a planned, organized way of interacting with children, derived from theoretical assumptions about children's development and intended to produce change (growth or learning) in children's behavior.
2. Depending upon the chosen developmental viewpoint for the program, a particular decision process will be appropriate for planning and implementing curriculum.
3. Teaching behaviors are a subset of caregiving. At certain points in the program day, individual staff will have teacher roles in which their teaching behaviors dominate their interactions with children.

The morning and afternoon activity blocks in the daily care pattern are the primary periods when child care staff are likely to be assigned teaching roles. These curriculum opportunity activity blocks closely resemble periods in other early childhood programs when teaching roles predominate for staff. Teaching roles are difficult to sustain over the extended child care schedule. Children would find such exposure exhausting. Child care programs retain a certain uniqueness in the balance that staff must maintain between caregiving and teaching behaviors.

Maturationist Program

Maturationist teachers "set the stage" by choosing and arranging the environment. They try to match children with activities that are developmentally appropriate, and they stay alert for the "teachable moment" when developmental readiness and interest coincide.

To the maturationist, teaching is an art, not a science. On a minute-to-minute, hour-to-hour basis it is impossible to predict what a teacher should do to facilitate children's growth and development in the program. Attempts to categorize the maturation-based teaching role have resulted in a number of commonly used labels. For example:

Clinical teaching style Adult responds to the perceived needs and conditions of the situation and child.

Nonstandard pedagogy Adult relies on general principles and exemplars as basis for formulating personal teaching behaviors.

Case study approach Adult considers each child's current developmental stage and responds individually.

Teachers' behaviors are always directed to individuals. Teachers select materials, arrange environments, and make provisions for activities—all as part of their primary role of "stage setter." Once the environment is set, the teacher moves to the background, functioning as a participatory observer. Look for teachers on the floor playing games, tucked in a corner reading to a child, or off in the closet retrieving the makings for playdough. Children and their play activities dominate the scene.

The maturationist teaching role:

1. allows and abides by children's choice of activities.
2. encourages children to use equipment and materials in exploratory ways.
3. accepts and supports response attempts.
4. uses ongoing child activities as basis for spontaneous learning.
5. provides information when asked.

Despite appearances, this teaching role is hard work and an easy one to botch. Many programs have simply disintegrated into chaos in the pursuit of free play. Three qualities distinguish the successful maturation teacher:

1. *Mentally Prepared* This teacher really knows the developmental norms for children—the age and stage descriptions and the patterns of physical, emotional, social, and intellectual growth—and understands the cyclical nature of equilibrium and disequilibrium. Every child this teacher works with adds to his or her personal core of developmental information, giving the teacher new examples and experiences.
2. *Alert* When "on the floor" with children, the teacher acts like an all-seeing, all-hearing video camera. Much of this information is also retained—written down later or mentally stored—to compare with a child's behavior in the future. The teacher is generally responsible for monitoring the activities of several children simultaneously. He or she is always searching for "teachable moments" when the child will need to be supported through verbal and physical behaviors that will sustain and perhaps extend the experience. In a real sense the teacher becomes part of the nurturing environment that facilitates the natural unfolding of the child.
3. *Tough* Stamina, patience, and tolerance are demanded in large quantities. Staying alert is exhausting, especially when there is not clear evidence of success. The tasks never end and can be hard to escape in nonworking hours. The sensitivity and intuition needed to function in this teacher role can render adults incapable of distancing themselves from their jobs. To a large extent individual personality becomes part of the teaching role and leaves adults vulnerable to burnout.

The maturation teaching role is a popular choice for child care program planners. The requirements can be mastered by staff of varying educational backgrounds, and its flexibility in response to children is very appealing. In addition, program designers and staff will find a wealth of resources to use for information about children's developmental stages and the provision of age-appropriate environments and materials. What is lacking for this teaching role are systematic and objective means for evaluating the quality of teaching performance and child outcomes. Just because it is fun, feels good, and works okay doesn't mean it's worthwhile. Maturationist programs are difficult to assess, and many program designers do not make the effort.

EXAMPLES

Verbal Techniques at Different Ages. Perhaps the most versatile tool a maturation teacher has is voice. What the teacher says and when he or she says it can help a child extend play or understand how to manipulate a material. Training for maturation teachers often emphasizes general principles for verbal techniques with children, with these techniques tailored to specific developmental ages. Certain qualities of behavior characteristic of each age make certain teacher techniques potentially more useful during those periods. For example (Pitcher & Ames, 1975, pp. 194–208):

Two	Be concrete and repetitive. Use lots of demonstrations and gestures.
Two and A Half	Avoid "no" questions. Avoid giving choices. Choose specific words thoughtfully.
Three	Get involved in two-way conversations.

	Use size (big), novelty, and surprise as motivators.
Three and A Half	Go to extremes by using loud and soft voices.
	Whisper.
Four	Use words that involve love and humor.
	Use negatives.

Teachers. What do teachers do in a maturation-based program? We asked a few and then cross-checked their lists through observation.

1. *During arrival* "I try to welcome every child a special way, a hug, a comment about their clothes, and maybe a toy they've brought in. I want to connect, let them know they're welcome and wanted here."
2. *During breakfast* "We talk about home—what happened at night. I note tiredness, upsets, if any, who's real hungry. We share a lot of good times at breakfast."
3. *During morning activity* "This is my busy time. I'm on the floor constantly. Always alert, watching, aware of the rhythm of activities, the flow of the children. I replenish supplies if necessary, lend a hand, comment on actions and activities. I guess you would say I keep my hands at the pulse of group. I always know where everyone is and how things are going."
4. *During lunch* "This is a busy time. I serve food, help children cut and eat. We talk about the food, how to eat it, what it's like. Sometimes we talk about the morning's activities. I'm the role model."
5. *During rest* "I catch up on anecdotal notes. Write letters to parents. Maybe talk with the other adults about the children, new projects, etc."
6. *During afternoon activity* "We're more likely to be outdoors or doing quiet table games in the afternoon. I can sit down a little here watching children run outdoors or indoors with a small group game. Sometimes I attract children like a magnet if I have music or story activities. I'm more aware of how children work in groups, who they are with during these afternoon activities."
7. *During departure* "I key on parents at departure. I try to help parents connect with children, talk about the day's activities and give the parent some openings for talking with child. Everyone's tired now. I mediate, smooth over, pull together for everyone. It's hard. I'm tired, too."

Behaviorist Program

Teachers in behaviorist programs have been called technicians, engineers, and, not so kindly, manipulators. The formal teaching strategies that characterize the behaviorist program require teachers to exert control over the immediate learning environment of the lesson. Nothing is left to chance. Lessons are premeditated—even scripted. Teachers control and arrange stimulus conditions so that the desired response has a high probability of occurring. They carefully sequence content and tasks and pinpoint instruction on specific skills. They are responsible for selecting materials and pacing presentations. And reinforcement is used to manage the group and reward individuals.

General behaviorist teaching strategy involves developing objectives and delivering instruction as follows:

1. Initiate children's activities.
2. Provide continuous direction and guidance (verbal and nonverbal).
3. Monitor child's performance and products to ensure acceptable results.
4. Use rewards and praise in systematic manner.
5. Stress using materials or giving responses in prescribed ways.
6. Require child to follow set plan of activities.
7. Evaluate results.
8. Restate objectives and recycle as needed.

The basic unit of behavior, the S-R-R operant conditioning unit, which was described in Chapter 2, is a useful device to illustrate differences in teaching emphases among behaviorist programs (see Figure 3.3). Following this model, the differences fall into four general types, as described in the following list. All use the same principles of learning in devising formal instructional plans, and all are valid interpretations of behaviorist principles for instruc-

Figure 3.3 Four types of behaviorist programs based on the S-R-R unit.

tional settings. However, each program places a different value on particular subjects or skills leading to differing weights on some parts of learning processes over others.

Stimulus—Direct Teaching Programs that choose to emphasize the acquisition of academic information and subject content tend to force instructional strategies on the teacher's control and presentation of stimuli. What teachers do, what they say, and how they handle responses receives careful attention.

Response—Task Analysis Programs that state goals related to skill development or task mastery of necessity place considerable weight on the analysis of skill component tasks. Complex behaviors are broken down into simpler behaviors and sequenced. Through diagnosis of entry behaviors, instruction is keyed to children's skill levels. Objectives and performance assessment are based on the hierarchy of skills in the task analysis.

Reinforcement—Token Economy A few programs need elaborate and/or extensive systems for reinforcing behavior. This may be because of the range of situations in which goal behaviors can occur, the number of adults involved in reinforcing, or the need to alter patterns of reinforcement over long periods of time. Tokens are small objects that through various techniques come to substitute for more obvious reinforcers such as praise, hugs, or even food and toys. In programs with token economies children accumulate tokens under the prevailing rules and exchange them for rewards.

S-R-R—Responsive Environment Specially designed materials and careful room arrangements have become important teaching strategies for some behaviorist programs. These responsive materials are self-correcting and self-reinforcing (or "autotelic"). Because of their design features children get feedback about their responses from using the materials. A fuller discussion of responsive materials appears in the materials and equipment section of this chapter.

Program designers who choose a behaviorist perspective will find that teacher training and instructional design are relatively straightforward tasks. Staff can quickly be trained as "reinforcers" for caregiving routines and transitions. Many commercial sources supply plans for formal, direct teaching lessons and task analysis of skills. Teaching objectives are clear-cut and child success very obvious. This kind of teaching is rewarding for staff.

Elaborate reorganization of the program is not always necessary; if programs wish to extend teaching strategies to all staff levels for all activities, some conditions must be met. Staff in these situations must be committed to the behaviorist point of view—implementation of this depth requires all staff to breathe and think S-R-R. Some staff may be quite amenable to the positive caregiving routines and a few scheduled lessons but may draw the line at such tight management of their own behavior.

EXAMPLES

Task Analysis. An analysis of how to use scissors results in a task analysis that might be used by a child care staff as part of the routine teaching during craft activities. The plan is to work individually with children on mastery of this skill. The task analysis is given in Figure 3.4. A procedure for using questioning in lessons is given in Box 3.1.

This task analysis is used regularly by a kindergarten teacher in teaching and recording her students' use of scissors.*

Scissor cutting checklist:
Behavior criteria

Yes	*No*	*Sometimes*	
___	___	___	1. Child places thumb and second finger in correct scissor holes.
___	___	___	2. Child uses first finger as a lever to guide scissor opening and closing.
___	___	___	3. Child opens and shuts scissors repeatedly.
___	___	___	4. Child holds arm (elbow) tightly to the body.
___	___	___	5. Child places scissors perpendicular to the paper.
___	___	___	6. Child holds paper in the opposite hand, firmly, at the top of the paper. Not near the cutting line.
___	___	___	7. Child makes cutting motions in succession. One scissor opening and closing. Ex. cutting fringe.
___	___	___	8. Child moves scissors ahead into the paper, making 2-3 openings and closings.
___	___	___	9. Child cuts on lines through a 4″ × 8″ paper strip.
___	___	___	10. Child cuts longer straight lines.
___	___	___	11. Child cuts across an 8″ × 10″ paper in an X shape, making four triangles.
___	___	___	12. Child cuts straight lines of large shapes: triangle, rectangle, and square. The shapes fill the paper.
___	___	___	13. Child cuts out a large circle shape.

* We thank Jeanne Wenzel for providing this sample task analysis.

Figure 3.4 Task analysis—Using scissors. From *Activities, Guidelines, and Resources for Teachers of Special Learners* (p. 90) by C. A. Cartwright, G. P. Cartwright, M. Ward, and S. Willoughby-Herb, 1981, Belmont, CA: Wadsworth, Inc.

Cognitive Program

The cognitive viewpoint has an active role for children that allows them to interact with their environment in ways that are compatible with their mental levels. Teachers can function as mediators or arrangers of the environment; that is, through their actions, teachers can increase the likelihood the child will be able to interact in ways that further concept formation and build cognitive structures. Cognitive theory states that the complementary processes of assimilation and accommodation (together called adaptation) are the means through which the child gains control over new information. The teacher tries to make the distance between old and new information close enough for the child to handle, great enough to appeal and encourage further exploration, and tense enough to stimulate the formulation of new processes.

In order to function as teachers in a cognitive-based program, staff must:

Box 3.1 Behaviorist Questioning Strategy

Questioning allows the teacher to aim the child's behavior toward a given goal—for example, being able to state how another might feel or identifying the missing part.

Often questioning alone will be effective in producing the desired behavior. At other times, children will not respond correctly to the question. What should teachers do then? They could, of course, tell the child the correct answer, and at times this is necessary. Then the child can simply imitate the provided answer.

Another correction technique, however, is to provide the child with a prompt for the answer. This technique is more desirable since it engages the child in more advanced problem-solving behaviors. In fact, the teacher should start with a minimal prompt, adding stronger prompts until the child finally can answer the question. If the child cannot answer the question after several prompts, the teacher should provide the answer.

It is wise to plan ahead when using a questioning strategy, so that prompts will be available. Let's look at the following example.

Objective

Solves problems involving memory of a fact. In this case, the child is to remember that a toy teddy bear is hidden in the mouth of a large cardboard lion. The bear is hidden as the children watch at the beginning of a fifteen-minute lesson. Questioning is used at the end of the lesson to encourage the children to recall the fact.

Questioning plan

1. Primary question: "Do you remember where the bear is? Come whisper the answer to me." (Since the children whisper the answer, they all are forced to recall the fact independently of their peers.)
2. Prompts (minimal to maximal):
   a. "Think back to the beginning of our lesson. I picked up the bear and what did I do with it?"
   b. "Think of how big the bear is." (Teacher demonstrates its size with hands.) "Where could I have put it?"
   c. "Could I have put it in something?"
   d. Teacher points to the correct side of room. "Did I put it somewhere over here?"
   e. Teacher narrows the location through hand movements. "I put it near here, do you remember now?"
   f. Teacher again uses hand motions to narrow the vicinity. "I put it inside something over here. Do you remember?"

Source: From *Individualizing Early Education For Handicapped Children* (pp. 80–81) by J. T. Neisworth, S. J. Willoughby-Herb, S. Bagnato, C. A. Cartwright, and K. Laub, 1980, Germantown, MD: Aspen Systems Corporation; reprinted with permission.

1. master cognitive-stage development knowledge.
2. understand cognitive structuring processes and be sensitive to situations in which "stretching" can be encouraged.
3. be aware of each child's current cognitive skills and developmental momentum.

Teachers working within this viewpoint must invest considerable personal time mastering the details of cognitive theory. Knowing the theoretical assumptions, stage descriptions, and knowledge and process structures is essential. Many resources are available for this purpose and teachers will find that the task is manageable. If the background information necessary for cognitive-based teaching seems somewhat forbidding at first, it may be because many staff will have had no prior exposure to this information. Teachers who master the material have good reason to feel proud of their accomplishment. The following comment bears out this view.

> A teacher stopped me in the hall to remark, "Now that I have experimented in my classroom with some of Piaget's intellectual tasks, never again will I look at children in quite the same way—and the change is for the better." Her comment re-

flected my own feelings because it's heady stuff to become a student of Piaget's work. Suddenly one finds it necessary to be an astute observer of children's behavior; a critical listener of their speech; an assessor of their thinking abilities; a stimulus for provoking their thought; and, indeed, a player of a half dozen other roles, frequently all at once. Moreover, many long-valued teaching techniques appear trite and totally inappropriate in light of one's new knowledge about children. (Smart, 1970, p. 13)

The cognitive teaching role:

1. follows up children's initiatives with expansive or directed experiences.
2. permits children to structure situations to fit their mental level.
3. uses questions to clue or guide children in tasks.
4. organizes situations to reduce uncertainty and perplexity.
5. provides situations that help children experiment.

Teachers set the environment so that discovery learning will occur. Sociodramatic play helps children consider the possibilities of different roles and actions they might try. Teachers in a cognitive program can assume different relationships with children as they attempt to promote the child's interaction and generation of ideas. All lessons and materials are planned around a cognitive framework. Three teaching strategies frequently coexist in cognitive programs.

1. *Direct teaching* (*Teacher* > *Child*) For specific lessons or periods of time the cognitive teacher may choose to assume a role in which he or she makes a larger contribution to an interaction than the child. Through direct teaching, the teacher can give feedback and channel children's actions in ways he or she knows will be informative to the child. This is not an instruction situation organized around correct answers.
2. *Induce discovery* (*Child* > *Teacher*) A rich, stimulating environment that beckons the child to experiment and investigate is the basis for discovery. In discovery teaching situations the child creates the structure for the lesson; the teacher, however, has rehearsed several discovery scenarios beforehand and will be both verbally and materially prepared to follow the child wherever he or she leads.
3. *Manipulate environment* (*Child* = *Teacher*) Judicious choice and timely presentation of materials allow the teacher to pace the child's environmental experimentation. Materials may be responsive and give child immediate feedback. Or, teachers may interject themselves in a child's discovery work and verbally direct the child toward certain findings. This teaching strategy falls midway between direct teaching and inducing discovery.

EXAMPLES

Concept Web—Planning Strategy. Figure 3.5 is an example of a planning document that a teacher could prepare before working with children. The activity/concept web allows the teacher to rehearse mentally the discovery scenarios that a child may follow when working with materials in the classroom. In this example the teacher has recently set up the house corner with money, food containers, shopping bags, and other items about marketing. The questioning strategy is the plan for a direct teaching lesson in which the teacher will ask the children to think about going to the grocery store to buy food for later snack preparation. This type of teacher preparation is easily done by small groups of teachers and is excellent in-service training for teachers in cognitive programs.

Interaction Technique and Style

Beyond specialized training and written planning for curriculum, staff working in a program pick up a "bag of tricks" or "quick responses" that enable them to respond to situations as they occur. These seemingly unplanned staff behaviors should begin to form patterns that complement the formal curriculum components of the program. When individual staff style and desired program techniques blend consistently,

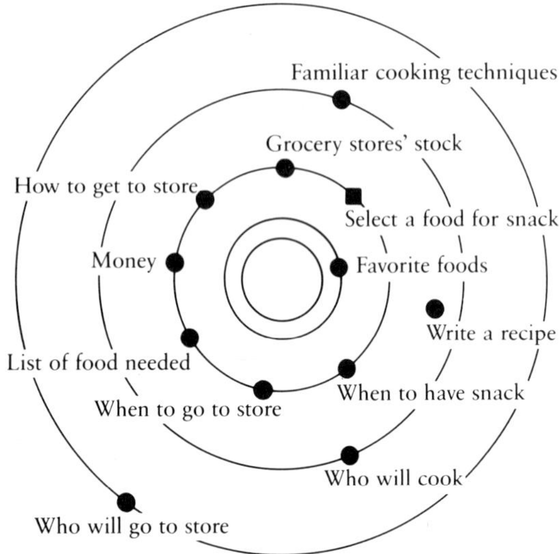

Figure 3.5 Planning strategies—Activity/concept web: Children will generate a list of possible foods. Teachers can record suggestions with pictures. For each food, discussions about appeal, availability, and practicality of preparation will give the teacher plenty of opportunities to ask questions and guide children's observations. The concentric rings are intended to convey how cognitive programs seek to provide children with experiences that extend and enlarge upon familiar thoughts and activities.

the depth of implementation of a chosen developmental viewpoint is considerably extended. Every adult-child interaction becomes an opportunity to enrich the experiences of children in the program. Children and adults act, look, and feel very differently in maturation, behaviorist, and cognitive programs.

Maturationist Program

Talking to children and using words to label objects, actions, and feelings are the most frequent techniques used by adults in a maturation program. Adults must be spontaneous. Any activity, any material, and virtually any social situation can become a point of departure for children, as long as it is appropriate to the children's developmental stage. Through the adult's guidance and suggestions children become aware of opportunities within their environment and learn to resolve social situations.

EXAMPLES

A Pocketful of Small Talk. Adults help children connect with ongoing activities through talking. General descriptive comments as well as social talk are considered appropriate. The purpose is to help children feel comfortable with language as a mode of expression and a tool for communication. For example:

"I'm cleaning out Wilbur's cage. [Wilbur is a guinea pig.] We'll put Wilbur in this smaller cage for awhile. Could you do that? It's hard to scrape out all these chips in his cage. Maybe I'll use a small whisk broom. That would help me get the chips in the corners."

"The colors in your painting are so bright. I like the way you have stripes going right to the corners."

"Your baby looks very sleepy. You gave her such a long bath. She's very clean. Yes, I think she'd like a stroll. Can I help you get the carriage?"

"I saw the astronauts on TV, too, last night. Their spaceship is called a shuttle. Your Lego ship looks very much like the shuttle."

"Kira, you and David have been building with sand for a long time. Where does this road go? . . . Oh, I see. You have all the wild animals in the jungle and the zoo-hunters have to come down this road to get them for the zoo."

Socializing the Child. The child-directed environment of the maturation program can lead to numerous social crises as children learn to adjust to each other and practice their rudimentary social skills. For example, children grab toys and spit at and hit each other. Adults in a maturation-based program often mediate disputes and disagreements that arise in the course of play and routine activities. The aim of adult behaviors is to preserve the children's dignity, protect the welfare of all involved, and exercise developing social skills. Some crises involve an individual child and these require adult help too. For example, children may lose their boots or mittens, spill food on themselves, or have a temper tantrum.

Behaviorist Program

In behaviorist programs adults are in charge and highly goal-directed. Through posture, voice, and confident demeanor caregivers lead children through predictably scheduled activities. Adults take the initiative, keeping activities flowing and children on task. Adults are always alert, looking for child behaviors that approximate or meet predetermined objectives and then reinforcing those behaviors according to each child's needs. During formal lessons, a snappy pace, teacher-led dialogue of questions and responses, close physical seating and monitoring, and frequent adult-child eye contact all serve to keep each child focused on the teacher and the task. Adults maintain a high profile in a behaviorist program. An example of a structured, teacher-directed formal lesson is given in Box 3.2. Read through the lesson script. It prescribes a series of questions and responses, along with gestures, that leaves no doubt as to who is in control of the lesson situation.

EXAMPLES

A Pocketful of Reinforcers. Examples of ways to praise are as follows:

Praising Words and Phrases

Good.	That shows a great deal of work.
That's right.	You really pay attention.
Excellent.	You should show this to your parents.
That's clever.	I like that.
Exactly.	Show the class your picture.
Fine answer.	That's interesting.
Good job.	See how well Joan is working.
Good thinking.	Jimmy got right down to work after recess; he's going to finish on time.
Great.	Let's all give John a round of applause.
	That was very kind of you.

Facial Expressions

Smiling	Looking interested
Winking	Laughing
Nodding up and down	

Nearness

Walking among students	Joining the class at recess
Sitting in their group	Eating with the children

Physical Contact

Touching	Stroking arm
Patting head, shoulder, or back	Shaking hand
Hugging	Holding hand
Holding on lap	

Source: From *Teaching: A Course in Applied Psychology,* by W. C. Becker, S. Engelmann, and D. R. Thomas. © 1971, Science Research Associates, Inc. Reprinted by permission of the publisher.

Cognitive Program

Adults in cognitively based programs focus on thinking processes that are part of children's ongoing activities. As a result, *questions* are an important tool for interaction between children and adults. Well-timed questions can stimulate children's thinking and be a point of departure for further child exploration. Similar results can be obtained through demonstration and action on the part of the adult if care is taken not to suggest a single correct answer or method.

The general pattern of interactions follows a wait-challenge-wait sequence with the adult creating a challenge only when children's activi-

Box 3.2 A Formal Lesson

Praise the children for correct responses. Correct mistakes immediately.

Lesson 51

TASK 1 Actions

Here's the first action game.

a. Point to a boy. Everybody, he will stand up. Say the whole thing about what he will do. Signal. *He will stand up.*
b. Is he standing up now? Signal. *No.*
c. What is he doing now? Signal. *Sitting down.* What will he do? Signal. *Stand up.*
d. __________, do it. The boy is to stand up. What is he doing now? Signal. *Standing up.*
e. What was he doing before he stood up? Signal. *Sitting down.* Sit down.

Here's the next action.

f. Everybody, let's all touch the floor. Signal. Touch the floor. Keep on touching it.
g. Point to a boy. Look at him. What is he doing? Signal. *Touching the floor.* Say the whole thing. Signal. *He is touching the floor.*
h. Point to a girl. Look at her. What is she doing? Signal. *Touching the floor.* Say the whole thing. Signal. *She is touching the floor.*
i. Look at me. What am I doing? Signal. *Touching the floor.* Say the whole thing. Signal. *You are touching the floor.*
j. Point to two children. Look at them. What are they doing? Signal. *Touching the floor.* Say the whole thing. Signal. *They are touching the floor.*
k. Point to everybody. What are we doing? Signal. *Touching the floor.* Say the whole thing. Signal. *We are touching the floor.*

TASK 2 From—To

Get ready for some actions.

a. Everybody, move your finger from your elbow. Get ready. Signal. Wait.
b. Everybody, move your finger from your ear. Get ready. Signal. Wait.
c. Everybody, move your finger from your ankle. Get ready. Signal. Wait.
d. Repeat *a* through *c* until all responses are firm.
e. Everybody, move your finger from your back. Get ready. Signal. Wait. How did you just move your finger? Signal. *From my back.* Say the whole thing about how you moved your finger. Signal. *I moved my finger from my back.* Repeat *e* until all children can make the statement.

Source: From *Distar® Language II,* Teacher Presentation Book "B," by Siegfried Engelmann and Jean Osborn. © 1977, 1970, Science Research Associates, Inc. Reprinted by permission of the publisher.

ties seem to profit from adult involvement of some sort. Adults accept and use whatever child responses and activities are occurring as reasonable bases for interactions.

EXAMPLES

A Pocketful of Questions. There are no absolute right answers or wrong ways to think. Adults use questions to suggest possibilities to stretch imaginations and to give structure to activities. Since language is a tool for thinking, most interactions stress language as a point of connection between adult and child. For example:

Open-ended questions (no simple yes or no answers)

"How did you build this city?"

Box 3.3 Seriation

Graduated materials provide opportunities for children to develop the concept of seriation—ordering objects in different ways, by size, color, texture, height, length, and so on.

Aligning shoes and stockings

9 pairs of shoes ranging from baby size to adult male size
9 pairs of stockings ranging from baby size to adult male size

1. Present the shoes and stockings to the children. With each size ask: *What person would be able to wear this size of shoes or stockings?* Establish these sizes.
2. Place the pairs of footwear in random order along a line in front of the children. Ask one child to remove the largest pair of shoes in the line and start a new line with them. Instruct another child to choose the largest pair of stockings and place it on the largest pair of shoes. Continue this matching procedure until all the children have participated and all of the stockings are matched with corresponding pairs of shoes.
3. Separate the shoes and stockings into parallel lines, matching the stockings with the shoes in the order of largest to smallest sizes.
4. In the shoe line, rearrange all the pairs and then point to one pair of shoes in the line, instructing a child to choose the matching pair of stockings. Each child should have a turn to match stockings with shoes.
5. Move across the room and ask individual children to bring specific pairs of stockings and shoes at your request and place them in a paper bag. Continue the procedure of asking for particular sizes of shoes or stockings until all shoes and stockings are inside the bag.

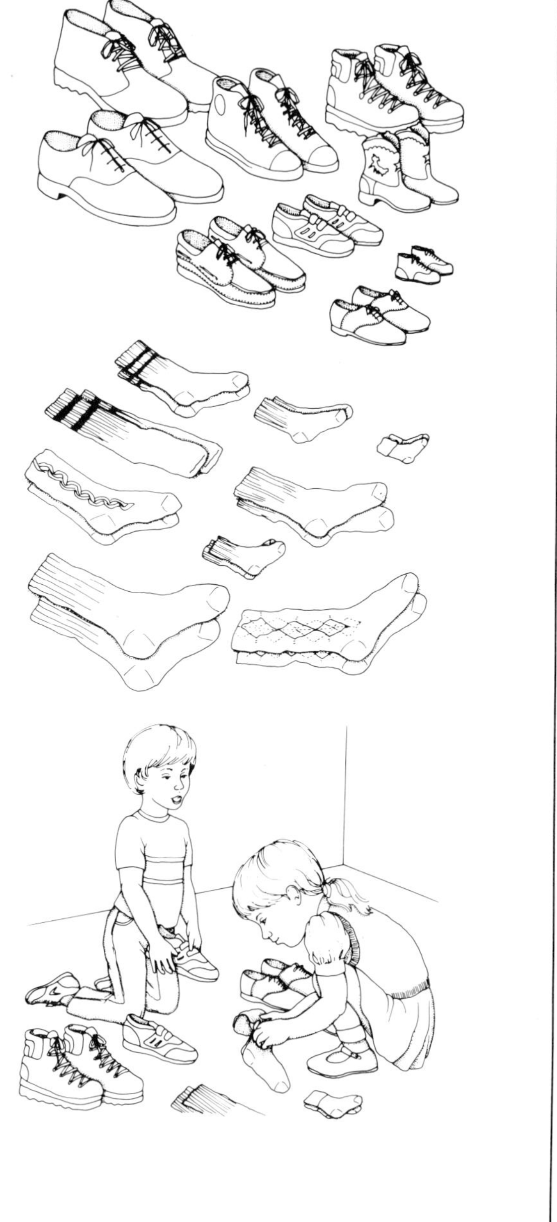

Source: From *A Teachers' Guide to Cognitive Tasks for Preschool* (pp. 23–24) by O. W. Cahoon, 1974, Provo, UT: Brigham Young University Press.

"What did you do when you found this game?"

Inviting questions (appeal to senses, aesthetics)
"Tell me about your morning?"
"How do you feel about your picture?"

Detail questions (require recall and organization of previous knowledge)
"What vegetables did you eat today?"
"What are some objects in your room at home that are round?"

Adaptive questions (encourage transfer of knowledge from one situation to another)

"How did you put the game away last time?"

"What other things can you mix or stir with a paddle?"

Assessment questions (encourage judgments, evaluations, or predictions)

"What do you think will happen next?"

"What else do we need to do to finish this job?"

Seriation. For the adult, turning everyday common events into "thinking" opportunities is a challenge. *Seriation* is the act of arranging things in a series or succession. In the example in Box 3.3, lining up shoes becomes a visual and physical exploration of size differences. The formal lesson on size illustrates how teachers can use any response as a starting point for thinking about the concept.

Summary

Child care staff provide appropriate caregiving behaviors, fulfill a teaching role, and participate in the program so that their personal styles interact with the program's technique. Each of the developmental viewpoints interprets these parts of the staffing responsibility differently.

Caregiving behavior refers to the general nature of adult participation in the program, especially during the basic care routines and transitions. The teacher role includes the adult's deliberate behaviors aimed at supporting development, particularly during the morning and afternoon activity blocks. During the day, caregivers continually interact with children in unplanned ways, blending their individual styles with the program's prescribed technique.

Maturationists' caregiving consists of using their knowledge of developmental norms to create a stimulating environment appropriate for the children's levels. In behaviorist programs caregivers use planned and scheduled routines to reinforce desired behavior patterns. Caregiving in cognitive programs includes encouraging children to become socially involved with people and activities.

The teacher role in maturationist programs is a matter of "setting the stage" for learning and keeping alert for "teachable moments." Teachers in behaviorist programs systematically control every aspect of the learning situation—initiating activities, selecting materials, monitoring performance, pacing presentations, and rewarding behavior. Cognitive theory teachers try to create situations that will stretch the children's thinking processes.

For maturationists interaction of program technique and caregiver style means relying on one's spontaneity and alertness to recognize opportunities for learning. In behaviorist programs interaction follows the program's schedule and pace; teachers stay watchful for chances to add reinforcement. Adults in cognitive programs use well-timed questions or demonstrations to guide children's activities toward new learning.

Good child care programs have good staffs. The qualities that make a good staff are not elusive. Caregiving, teaching, and interaction technique and style are critical elements of staff responsibility. How consistently these responsibilities are performed according to the program's stated developmental viewpoint directly affects the quality of children's care experiences. Careful analysis of the links between developmental viewpoint and staff practice will help program planners train and guide staff members.

Resources

Becker, W., Engelmann, S., & Thomas, D. (1971). *Teaching: A course in applied psychology.* Chicago: Science Research Associates.

Beller, E. K. (1971). Adult-child interaction and personalized day care. In E. H. Grotberg (Ed.), *Day care: Resources in decisions* (pp. 229–264). Washington, DC: Office of Economic Opportunity.

Bos, B. (1983). *Before the basics: Creating conversations with children.* Roseville, CA: Turn the Page Press.

Cahoon, O. W. (1974). *A teacher's guide to cognitive tasks for preschool.* Provo, UT: Brigham Young University Press.

Cartwright, C. A., Cartwright, G. P., Ward, M., & Willoughby-Herb, S. (1981). *Activities, guidelines and resources for teachers of special learners.* Belmont, CA: Wadsworth.

Cazden, C. B. (1970). Children's questions: Their forms, functions, and roles in education. *Young Children,* March, 202–219.

Evans, D., McMahon, L., & Cranstown, Y. (1980). *Working with under fives.* Ypsilanti, MI: High/Scope Press.

Hart, B. (1982). So that teachers can teach: Assigning roles and responsibilities. *Topics in Early Childhood Special Education, 2* (1), 1–8.

Jones, E., & Prescott, E. (1978). *Dimensions of teaching: Learning environments II. Focus on day care.* Pasadena, CA: Pacific Oaks College.

Joyce, B., & Weil, M. (1972). *Models of teaching.* Englewood Cliffs, NJ: Prentice-Hall.

Neisworth, J. T., Willoughby-Herb, S. J., Bagnato, S., Cartwright, C. A., & Laub, K. (1980). *Individualizing early education for handicapped children.* Germantown, MD: Aspen Systems.

Pitcher, E. G., & Ames, L. B. (1975). *The guidance nursery school* (rev. ed.). New York: Harper & Row.

Prescott, E., & Jones, E. (1969). *Patterns of teacher behavior in preschool programs.* Pasadena, CA: Pacific Oaks College. (ERIC Document Reproduction Service No. ED 075 092)

Prescott, E., Jones, E., with Kritchevsky, S. (1972). *Day care as a child-rearing environment: Vol. 11.* Washington, DC: National Association for the Education of Young Children.

Seaver, J. W., & Cartwright, C. A. (1976). *Early childhood student teaching.* University Park, PA: Pennsylvania State University, College of Education. (ERIC Document Reproduction Service No. ED 130 759)

Simmons, B. M., Whitfield, E. L., & Layton, J. R. (1980). The preparation of early childhood teachers: Philosophical and empirical foundations. In D. R. Range, J. R. Layton, & D. L. Roubinek (Eds.), *Aspects of early childhood education: Theory to research to practice.* New York: Academic Press.

Smart, M. (1970). What Piaget suggests to classroom teachers. In I. J. Athey & D. O. Rubadeau (Eds.), *Educational implications of Piaget's theory* (pp. 13–18). Waltham, MA: Xerox Publishing.

Stone, J. G. (1978). *A guide to discipline* (rev. ed.). Washington, DC: National Association for the Education of Young Children.

Warren, R. M. (1977). *Caring: Supporting children's growth.* Washington, DC: National Association for the Education of Young Children.

Weikart, D. P., Rogers, L., Adcock, C., & McClelland, D. (1971). *The cognitively oriented curriculum.* Washington, DC: National Association for the Education of Young Children.

4

Environmental Design

Introduction

People are particularly concerned with the quality of child care environments because of the long periods of time that some children spend in programs. Environments have the potential to contribute to the learning experiences of young children and to help staff members structure their conduct as they offer their caregiving and instruction. On the one hand, environments can be passive determiners of behaviors, subtly fostering or inhibiting behavior according to the context and space provided. On the other hand, items in the environment can also function to actively encourage or discourage behaviors.

In the past approaches to environmental design were haphazard and reflected the general lack of awareness of environment's powerful role. Many suggestions were based on factors of attractiveness and appeal (the interior decorating approach) or analysis of activity requirements (the efficiency approach). Traditionally, too, the child care environment was thought to consist only of the classroom's physical arrangement, the daily schedule, and the selection of durable materials and equipment.

More recently, however, we have come to see that the thoughtful arrangement of materials and space actually sets the stage for the implementation of program plans. Certain instructional environments are most appropriate for particular program goals. Planners must pay attention to such things as grouping, schedules, and space arrangement because they reflect the program's underlying theoretical assumptions.

We have also realized that the environmental setting as a context for behavior is a two-dimensional concept. It encompasses both the physical features of the environment and its usage patterns. Children's behavior in a program setting is shaped and influenced by the structure that the environment provides. High shelves restrict the availability of material. Open space areas allow expansive movement. Sitting on a chair involves different attention behavior than sitting cross-legged on a rug. Planned settings give children opportunities for behaviors that are consistent with program plans.

In this chapter we'll first look, briefly, at the environmental factors that must be faced in similar ways by all programs. Then we'll examine three broad areas of an environmental design that vary according to the program's theoretical viewpoint: setup of facility, management of groups and individuals, and time schedules for activity blocks. After defining these areas, we'll see how our three viewpoints differ in their treatment of each.

Common Environmental Concerns

All programs, regardless of developmental viewpoint, must be equally concerned about some factors of the environmental design.

These factors include physical features, regulations, use limits, private spaces, and outdoor space.

1. *Physical Features* The physical parts of the environment can directly affect children's comfort and safety. For instance, environmental conditions of light and noise levels can disturb or support children's behavior. The volume of space available, textures of surfaces, relationship of indoor space to outdoor space, and window and door access are also thought to affect children's behavior. Architects, developmental psychologists, and educators have begun to systematically study these conditions so they can establish guidelines for environmental design.
2. *Regulations* Regulatory requirements for child care programs frequently impose standards about the physical features of the environment. Zoning and facility specifications such as building and occupancy codes can impact environmental conditions for programs. Programs can also expect that fire, health, and safety codes will define specific features of the environment and perhaps require modification of the facility or adjustment of space usage patterns. Such codes are legal requirements, which are subject to inspection. In general, regulations and codes impose restrictions on facility setup and usage patterns for the protection and comfort of children.
3. *Use Limits* A serious and challenging problem facing program planners and staff is the lack of options in facility selection. Most programs use donated or rented space. Few programs have the luxury of designing a facility from scratch. In addition, programs that obtain reasonable existing space may be subject to occupancy conditions that preclude full use of the facility. It is not unheard of for painting to be prohibited or restricted to outdoor areas, for nails and tape on walls to be banned, or for programs to be required not to use particular doors except in emergency conditions. Some programs must pack up everything on the weekend when community halls and churches revert to their primary functions. Unfortunate indeed is the program that must pack up daily.
4. *Private Spaces* Because of the long days that many children spend in child care settings, the provision of private spaces for children is necessary and important. In fact, allowances for privacy are considered as indicators of quality in programs. Prescott and her colleagues (1972) included a measure of privacy in their Day Care Environmental Inventory. They measured privacy using a continuum of seclusion-intrusion factors. They counted the following features: insulated units (protected areas for small groups), hide areas (cozy places for one or two children), and softness measures such as overstuffed pillows, rugs, or soft bean-bag chairs to measure seclusion and intrusion. They found that quality environments included many provisions for privacy.

   Others suggest that children need private spaces in the child care setting in order to have a break from high levels of stimulation. Researchers have even cautioned that some children may react in aggressive and disruptive ways when faced with excessive stimulation.

   For example, Sheehan and Day (1975) observed that chaotic and frantic child behaviors were associated with centers lacking private spaces for children.
5. *Outdoor Space* Outdoor play space can be considered as an extension of indoor space and thus, subject to the same theoretically derived design criteria. However, outdoor play is primarily used as exercise and relief for most programs. Staff supervise and maintain consistent interactions with children but contact is usually incidental. In addition, outdoor play areas may be very limited for some programs. There may be little money available to build elaborate outdoor extensions of indoor program activities. Many programs must use public recreation facilities or nearby parks and playgrounds. Generally speaking, outdoor space will not be a high priority for program designers.

   Outdoor space and equipment must be safe for children. Familiar playground equipment such as slides, jungle gyms, seesaws, and swings require alert staff supervision. Placement of these items can create difficulties if children move about the activity area. Surfaces such as asphalt and gravel are potential problems; bark chips, sand, and softer "giving" surfaces help prevent injuries. If programs must use outdoor areas with traditional equipment and surfaces, staff should establish supervision procedures and enforce limits to prevent accidents.

Outdoor play areas provide important developmental opportunities for young children. (Courtesy of U.S. Department of Health and Human Services, Washington, DC.)

Imaginative, multilevel play structures or playscapes have been built recently for playgrounds. Local talent and materials can often duplicate these structures at low cost. G. Ellison (1974) suggests that one outdoor structure can and should offer the child:

- choice
- variation in levels and shapes
- a place for group interaction
- opportunity for fantasy play
- physical exercise
- flexibility
- an element of risk and challenge
- durability
- variation in surface and texture

Program-Specific Environmental Concerns

Recently, program planners, staff, architects, and child development specialists have come to understand and explore relationships between various environmental features and children's behaviors. From this work, the definition of environment as a behavior setting has come to include the physical setup of a facility, the management of groups and movement of children within the setting, and the timing of movement across several settings for different activity patterns.

1. *Setup of Facility* Once the necessary materials and equipment have been purchased, begged, or borrowed, the space must be arranged and set up. Deciding where to put things is closely related to the stated goals for children's behavior in the program. The *physical arrangement of space and contents* needs to facilitate desired behaviors. If children are expected to be neat and tidy, the program must provide child-accessible storage areas. If children are expected to work quietly in small groups, the facility should have meeting and work areas designed for small groups and removed from distractions. If exploratory play is called for, then easily cleaned spaces for paint, water, sand, and other materials must be provided.

   The eight units of the daily care pattern inevitably lead to the need for some spaces to do double duty. Nap or rest time may use the same space that was used in morning activity period for music and dance. Lunch and snacks may occupy tables that at other times hold art projects or become spaces for small groups to do workbook activities. In addition to the obvious need for double duty spaces, programs must consider the space requirements of movement from one activity to another. How does physical setup promote orderly transitions? The *functional expectations of space*, therefore, include movement patterns as well as use requirements.

2. *Management of Groups and Individuals* Programs for children tend to group children as a way of managing their activities and movement. *Grouping patterns* add another dimension to environment—social density. Grouping is often a function of the capacity of space to accommodate expected behaviors. When handled thoughtfully, grouping can help to target instruction or stimulate child-to-child interaction. Groups actually become features of the program environment and are very real and immediate to the children involved.

   Discipline modes can be positive or negative, internal or external. Environment puts passive, external limits on children's behaviors. In general, environment can encourage positive management by forestalling undesired behaviors. Often staff set additional limits and handle deviant behavior. Self-discipline within boundaries judged to be environmentally appropriate is the overall goal in child care programs. In this sense, self-discipline is a management tool that is practiced within environmental contexts. Program settings can be designed to give children opportunities to practice self-discipline by regulating the available behavioral options.
3. *Time Schedule for Activity Blocks* Time is structure and order. It is the *activity scheduling pattern*. Programs use time in different ways to organize activities and implement goals. Several decisions related to time are made in conjunction with the daily care pattern. The length of the program day and the number of days a week a program operates are time decisions. These decisions are frequently a function of client needs and cost factors. More directly related to children's experiences in the program are the decisions about the activity blocks within the daily care pattern. How long is the morning activity period? How much time should be allowed for lunch? For rest? Length of daily activity periods is a function of practical considerations and a particular developmental viewpoint.

   Similarly, the *pacing of activities* is a direct reflection of program goals. Should activities go quickly, slowly, or at whatever pace evolves? How concerned should staff be for keeping to a schedule? Development is change and change occurs over time. Different time schedules and activity pacing for programs have their roots in the different expectations of the maturationist, behaviorist, and cognitive viewpoints.

Setup of Facility

Setting up the program environment involves the actual placement of materials and equipment for expected activity functions. Through physical arrangement of space and contents, pathways and activity areas are created. Both are important determiners of children's behavior and should be consistent with program goals.

Activity areas are minisettings within the larger program environment. They are defined by specific materials and actual physical (or suggested) boundaries. When setting up activity areas, program planners need to consider:

1. The expected behaviors of the activity; depending on the potential for mess and the need for isolation from distraction, the planner can select central or peripheral locations.
2. The capacity of the activity area and the number of children likely to be involved simultaneously; capacity and optimum number of participants should match.
3. Traffic pattern to and from the activity area and how the activity area is positioned relative to the overall pathways in the classroom.
4. The storage needs and accessibility requirements for materials and equipment.

In order to plan the setup of a facility, program planners need to generate two kinds of planning documents. First, they need a blueprint drawing of the space available for arrangement. Scale drawings or close approximations are most helpful. Permanent fixtures, doors, windows, and built-in furniture should be drawn in and hallways and passages should be indicated. A separate drawing can show each self-contained space available. When the draw-

Table 4.1 An Activity and Capacity Plot

Time	Enrollment	Activity	Capacity	Assessment
8:30–9:00	15	Breakfast	20	Plenty of space for all children.
9:00–10:45	25	Morning Activity Available activity areas Blocks area Art area Table games House corner Sand table Story corner Total capacity	 7 4 5 6 5 8 35	Activity space exceeds enrollment. Careful monitoring of children's interests and movement patterns will determine if excess capacity allows children reasonable choices.
10:45–11:15	25	Morning Activity Snack Music/Story	 20 15	Since only 20 children can be seated for snack, this schedule provides for two simultaneous group activities.

ings are finished, planners need to make multiple copies.

Second, planners need a list of activities and enrollment figures for all periods of the day. This is easily accomplished by using the daily care pattern and indicating enrollment figures at half-hour intervals. Then for the same half-hour intervals, the planners list all the activities that will be available at that time. This allows the program planner to plot the capacity and kind of activities available by the number of children enrolled. At any time every child should have an "activity place." If the program gives children choices of activities, then sufficient extra "activity places" must be made available to make that choice a reality. Table 4.1 gives some examples of plotting activities.

The activity and capacity plot will vary for every program. It is essential, however, that this plot accurately record the activities that are available in the overall program plan. The first step in designing an environment to facilitate program goals is to make sure that every child has a place in a program-desired activity. Sufficient activity capacity is a must.

Let's imagine you are a program planner who needs to plan daily activities for a child care program. Once you have written an activity and capacity plot, you can begin to locate space for activities. Make a separate drawing for each half-hour period to correspond to the activity capacity plot. Now tentatively locate each activity. Arrange the drawings in time sequence. The drawings should tell you, for each half-hour, what space has been allocated to each activity and how many children are likely to be using that space. Use this sequence of drawings to identify spaces that must do double duty. Adjust space areas to allow for minor changes in capacity needs throughout the day. Check to be sure that double-duty uses are compatible in terms of storage and accessibility requirements as well as isolation requirements.

Make two checks before completing the layout. Assume you are a child in the program and "mentally visualize" your day; trace on the drawings the pathways and transition routes of activity changes. Ask yourself if the environmental plan provides the programmatically "correct" amount of closure or openness. Trace

Firefighter play. The addition of fire hats to the block area has stimulated a lively cooperative play situation. If interest persists, teachers may add bells, hoses, or other clothing items to extend the play fantasy. (Courtesy of U.S. Department of Health and Human Services, Washington, DC.)

the daily paths of other children to be sure. Adjust activity area locations if necessary. As a second check, "walk" your way through the program as a staff member. Ask staff to visualize themselves moving about the planned environment. Criteria for pathways and activity area relationships for each developmental perspective are given in the following program examples. Make adjustments as necessary and finalize a "best use" layout for each room and major hallway of the facility. This design procedure may seem tedious and repetitive and perhaps somewhat abstract since it is based on plans rather than actually moving physical objects or observing natural traffic flows in a program. But environmental setup should be derived from theoretical principles and connected to the daily schedule of activities. What comes naturally is not guaranteed to foster program goals.

Maturationist Program

The maturation program environment is rich, appealing, and varied. Large quantities of many different materials are desirable. Interest centers and activity areas are defined by equipment and materials. Clearly marked areas exist for activities. There must be sufficient space for different types of activities to occur simultaneously.

Physical arrangements are made with calculated care to enhance children's sense of freedom and mobility. All materials are displayed so that they are convenient and attractive. Children have lots of opportunity to handle their environment. Everything is within sight and easy reach. Returning materials is an important part of the program and is a way to maintain accessibility.

Maturationists conceive of activity areas having three components:

1. *Materials and Storage* A sufficient quantity and variety of materials along with child-managed storage. All materials for area *must* be in area for focused, intense play activities to occur.
2. *Work Space or Play Area* A defined area where materials can be used. A rug, table, or taped area on floor are possibilities. The size of work space must be compatible with amount of material available *and* number of children desired in area at any one time.
3. *Display and Attraction* Place to advertise the area, to suggest potential play possibilities, and to record or display products of children in area.

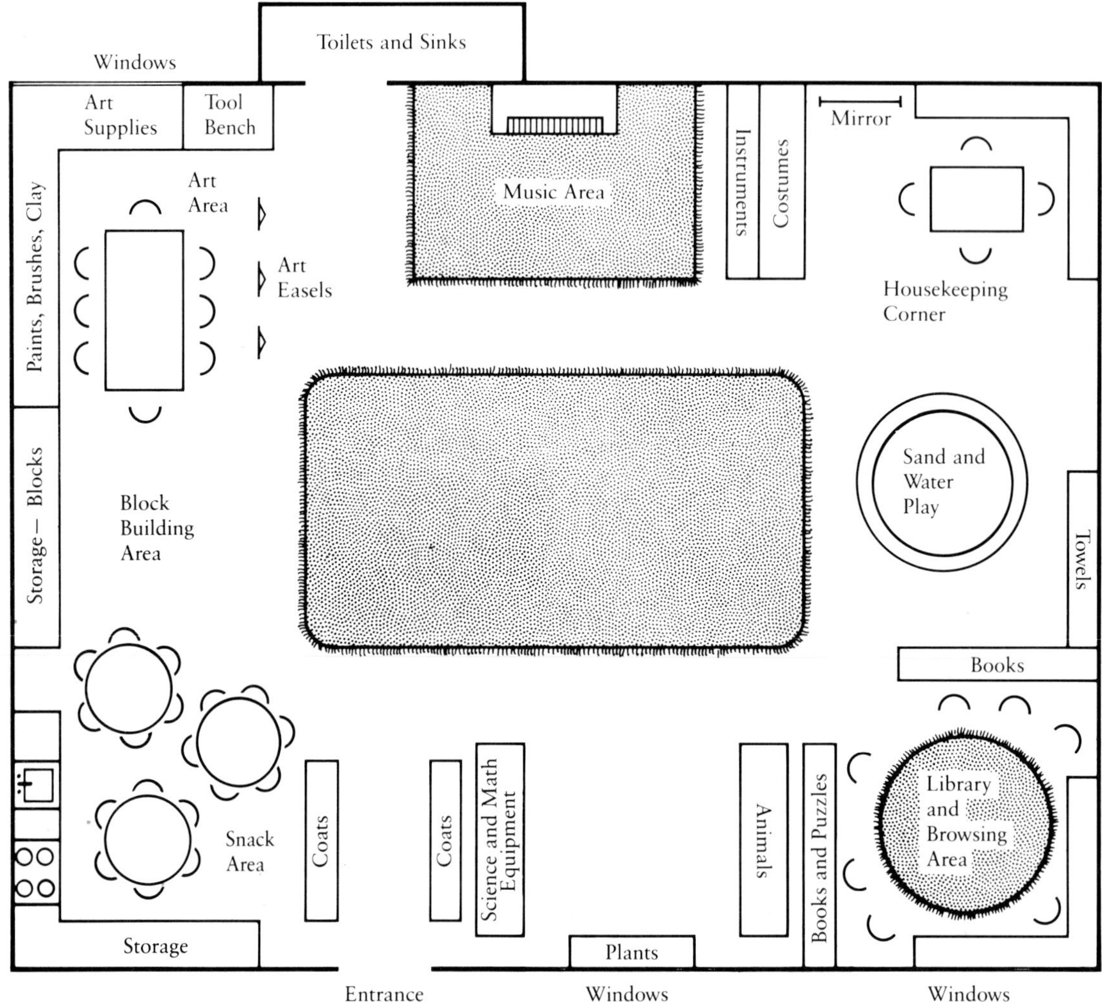

Figure 4.1 Room layout for maturationist program.

The environment is large, roomy, and easy to move around in. Areas for large group meetings and indoor active play are available. Work areas are convenient to one another. Circulation paths lead children easily from one area to another. A main pathway unifies and links all activities. Few physical or visual boundaries exist in the room. It is considered important for children to observe other children's play.

EXAMPLES

Activity areas are numerous and fill up the space. Children have ample choices among activity areas. The environment encourages free play. Figure 4.1 illustrates a typical room layout. Imagine as you look at the layout the following activities set up in addition to the usual selection of materials.

Art area Fat, colored chalks at the easel. Clay and different sizes of round dowels for rolling and punching at the art table.

Music area Bells and triangles on the rug in front of the piano.

Housekeeping area An extra supply of men's hats, ties, shoes, and coats in response to observations yesterday of great interest among the children in their father's activities.

Sand and water play Many sizes of empty bottles, cups, and tubes. Later some blue food coloring will be added to water in a large pail so children can observe the mixing process.

Library Three or four books about daddies are placed on prominent display on the table.

Science A large, brightly colored sign is placed near a gerbil's cage where some newborn gerbils are just starting to move around.

Snack Corn muffins and milk for snack today. Mixing bowls, baking pans, ingredients, and the recipe are set out to interest some helpers.

Blocks Small traffic signs are added to the block equipment. In recent days a group has been constructing roads and taking trips. One child has asked for masking tape to mark lines on the floor for roads, and that is available also today.

Pathways allow children to move freely, spending as much or as little time as they wish in any area. Teachers move slowly around the room, staying alert to all activities. Low shelves and lack of dividers provide good sight-lines.

Let's look at the movements of one child, Nora Age 4, during the morning activity period (see Figure 4.2). Once Nora takes care of her coat and gear, she moves to the center of the room. The central, circular arrangement of activity areas allows easy access and choice. Follow the dotted line as Nora inspects the instruments in the music area (1), makes several clay worms and snakes in the art area (2), briefly helps to stir the corn muffins (3), goes back to the art area to protect her work and put things away (4), walks around the central part of the room and pauses to watch the block play (5). After some time, Nora moves to sit in the housekeeping area (6), where she becomes involved in pretend muffin making, all the while keeping watch on the vigorous, noisy block play.

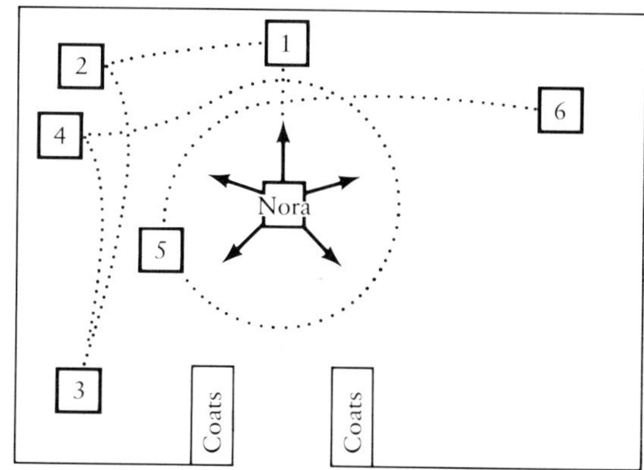

Figure 4.2 Pathway options in a maturationist program.

Imagine similar pathways drawn on this figure for each child in the program and for each teacher. Clearly, environmental design is promoting usage patterns consistent with maturationist principles.

Behaviorist Program

The behaviorist environment is arranged to focus attention and avoid conflicts and distractions. Privacy and enclosure are needed for group lessons. Moveable dividers and high shelves help restrict sight-lines and minimize distraction. Closed structure directs the child to activities. Often provision is made for individual work or testing. Reinforcement areas for token exchange are separate. Time-out areas are designated (see Figure 4.3).

Few materials are visible. Since activities are not generally available by choice, items need not be child-sized or easily accessible. The setting is clean, orderly, uncluttered, and suitable for focused work. Teachers decide which mate-

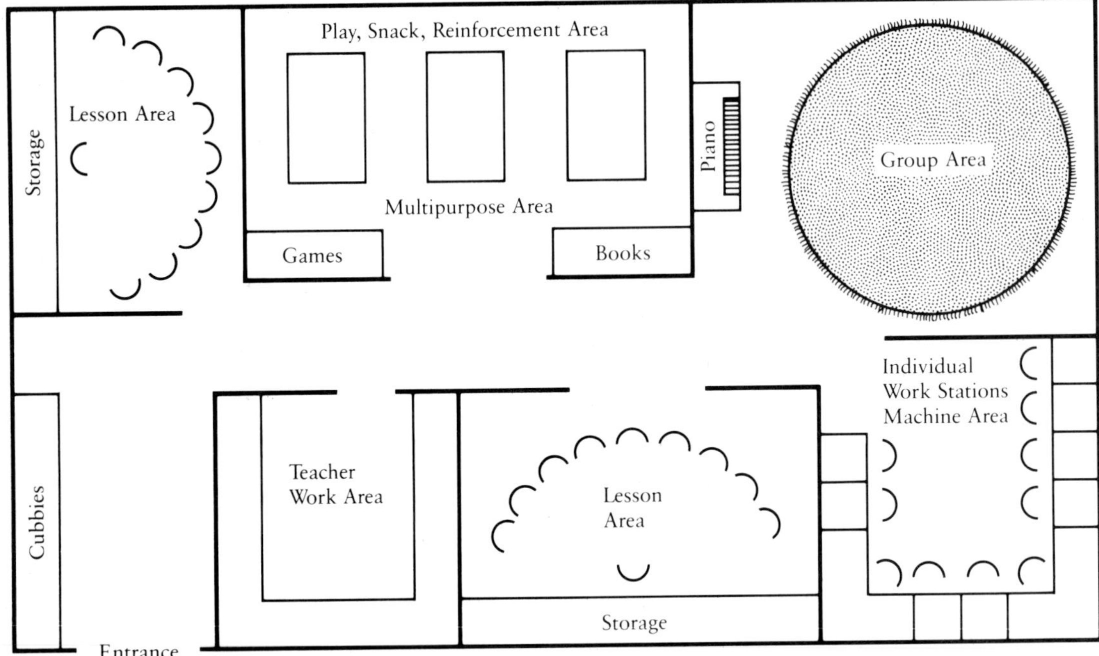

Figure 4.3 Room layout for behaviorist program.

rials will be out. Teacher may prescribe materials that are programmed or autotelic for children.

EXAMPLES

Activity areas are interchangeable since each will be similarly equipped. Storage is closed and arranged for teacher convenience. Spaces are rarely changed. Lesson content changes, but general teaching strategies and instructional devices do not. Special areas may be set aside for educational machines and for large-group instruction.

The room layout in Figure 4.3 illustrates the characteristic containment features of a behaviorist program. The lesson areas and individual work area are models of how environmental design can be used to focus behavior. The size of the teacher work area indicates the amount of record-keeping needed to implement the program. All the less controlled activities are relegated to one multipurpose area of the room. This gives children a very clear message as to when to differentiate their own behavior. Similarly, the group area is used for meetings, music, and games—all activities requiring similar responsive behaviors from children.

Pathways lead to specific, enclosed areas. Children's movement is further structured by no-option traffic patterns. In Figure 4.4 we can follow Colin through a morning activity period. He stops at the teacher's station to pick up his morning schedule (1), then goes to a lesson area for a language lesson (2), immediately followed by drill work with a head set and tape recorder (3). Music and movement (4) provide a change of pace, followed by a math lesson (5) and finally snack and games (6).

Colin's movement pattern keeps him in focused groups, on-task, and oriented toward teachers all morning. The behaviorist program environment is a continual reminder of the purposes and principles of the program.

Cognitive Program

Activity areas are carefully defined. Within areas, space and materials are arranged to demonstrate orderly relationships. Over time, areas change gradually, giving children the opportunity to cope with change slowly. Because too many materials can be confusing, teachers make selections and reduce competition among items.

Areas are somewhat restricted. Children are encouraged to stay with activities awhile. Areas may be for special interests or used for formal activities. Seating and work arrangements are comfortable. Storage is nearby. Items are displayed and available for child use. Other items are available through the teacher as needed to fit developmental growth.

EXAMPLES

Activity areas are a blend of the open maturation areas and the more formal restricted work areas of a behaviorist program. Enough material is available, and distractions from adjacent activities are minimized somewhat to promote exploration and perseverance of activity. The room layout in Figure 4.5 shows how these areas work together to support cognitive program activities. The first three areas are in the quieter end of the room; the latter four are in the busier end of the room.

Group meeting A place for teacher-guided discussions, presentations, and planning sessions. The area is oriented away from the room activities to help children focus their attention.

Work area Space for lessons and projects. Also doubles as eating area.

Science Materials and work space for observation and science fact-finding. Both work area and science area are good places for table games, manipulative activities, puzzles, and so on.

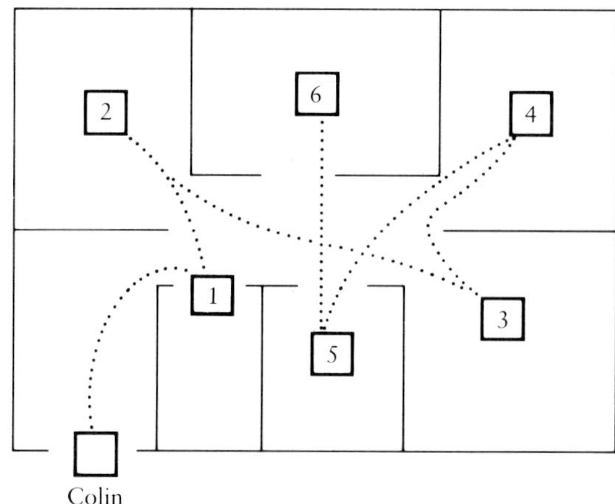

Figure 4.4 Pathway options in a behaviorist program.

Project Area Space and storage for special projects and longer term activities.

Art Space for small-group and individual work.

Blocks Rug helps define space. Block storage is organized to promote sorting and matching.

Housekeeping Room within the room to give sense of cohesiveness to area.

While multiple routes to activities are possible, children move about the room with a sense of purpose. Access to some areas is controlled. Teachers are positioned to guide and stimulate children's activity.

Henry, age 5, shows a typical movement pattern for morning activity period. (See Figure 4.6). At group meeting (1) Henry makes some choices about his morning's activities. He wants to continue with the box city that is rising in the special projects area (2). After a long period of time he is called to participate in a small group in the work area (3). He then is asked to select house or block area (4). When the signal is given, he joins other children for snack (5).

Henry's pathway is a mix of self-selection and teacher guidance. He spends most of his morning in closely monitored activities with constant access to or attention from a teacher. Henry's teachers mediate his movements and

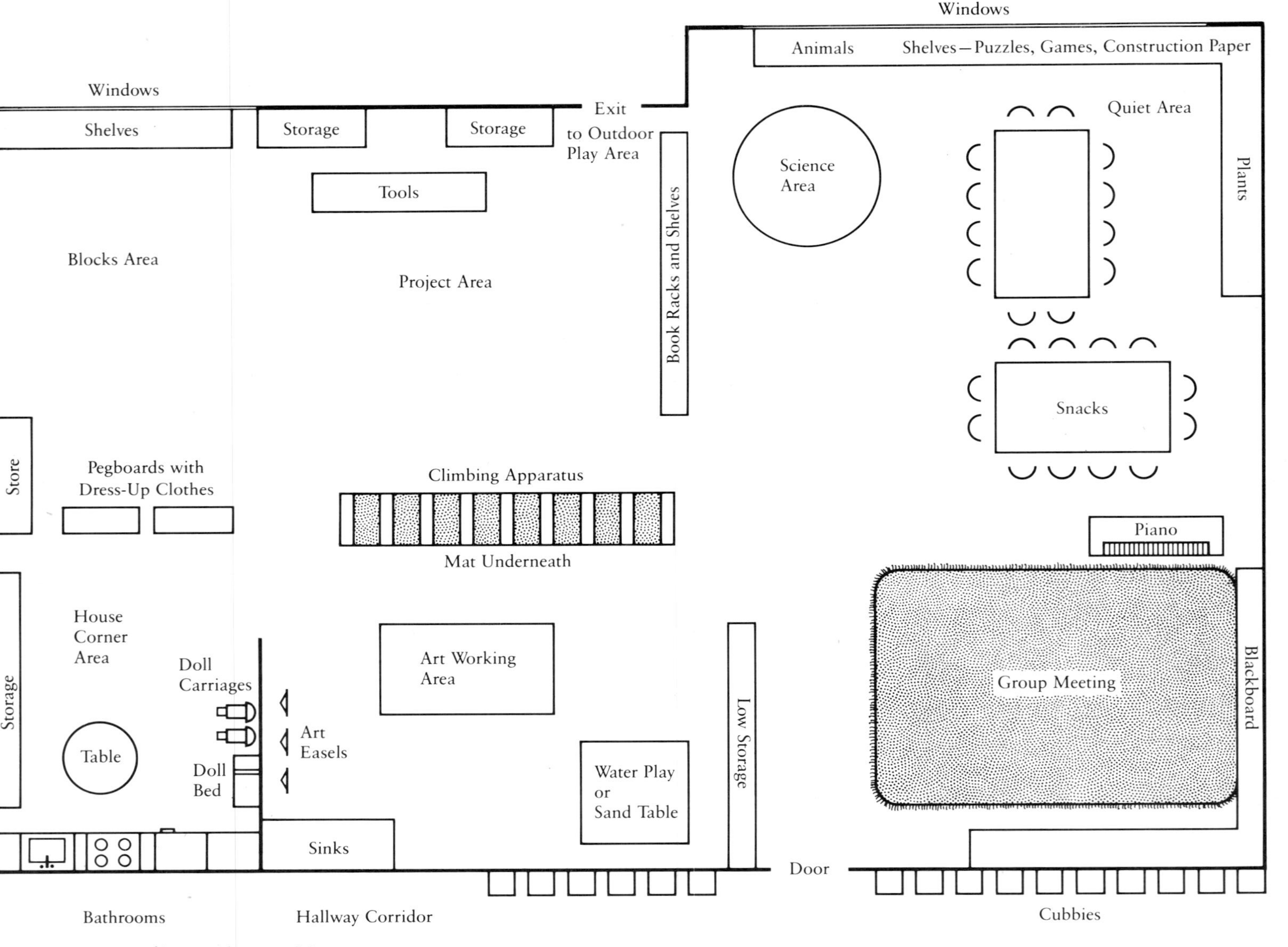

Figure 4.5 Room layout for cognitive program.

interaction with materials and people, a critical characteristic of cognitive program environmental design.

Management of Groups and Individuals

Programs vary on how children come to be members of small groups, how much interaction is encouraged among group members, the purpose of groups within the curriculum, and in the duration and scheduling of group activity periods relative to individual activity periods. Grouping patterns reflect the interaction opportunities that program environments allow.

Discipline techniques are needed to keep children's behavior goal-directed and within the limits of desired program plans. Environment is a powerful tool to encourage acceptable behaviors; it can limit situations in which deviant behaviors can occur. However, even the most carefully designed environments, the most alert teachers, and the most absorbing materials cannot prevent occasional instances of unacceptable behavior. Each developmental perspective views deviant behavior differently and handles such behavior through varying combinations of environmental and teacher control.

Maturationist Program

Grouping is not a vital part of a maturation program; social interaction is. Groups are fluid and temporary. They form and dissolve easily. Children come to mean a lot to each other as friends and playmates, but their relationships are not formally extended for any instructional purposes.

Discipline techniques are important. The environment of the program gives freedom and opportunity. Since young children are socially immature, numerous conflicts arise as they go about the serious business of play. Conflict, however, is actually desired because it gives children experience with social consequences and practice resolving conflicts. Adults may offer consistent descriptions of limits to help children achieve self-discipline. Teacher statements and responses to deviant behavior are nonjudgmental and aimed to help children label their feelings and redirect their actions.

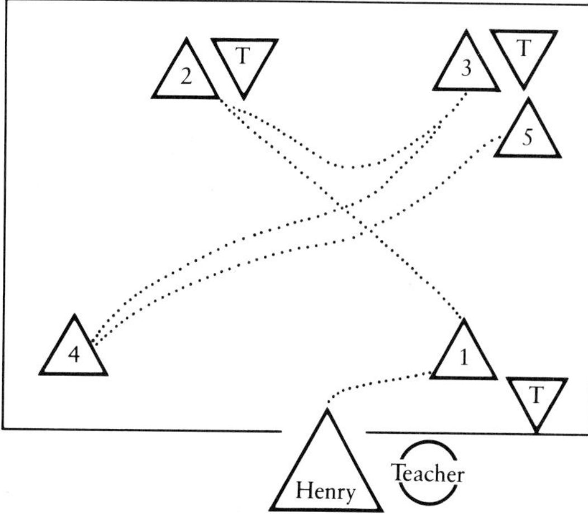

Figure 4.6 Pathway options in a cognitive program.

EXAMPLES

Grouping Patterns

Individual Children move in and out of small groups to play individually. At certain ages children prefer solitary play or to play alone but next to someone else. Self-directed play is always a major element of free choice activities.

Small Group This type of grouping allows cross-fertilization and exchange of play ideas to happen spontaneously during play; interest groups may be specially formed for trips or projects.

Large Group Multiage, familylike groups are formed for some activities. Large groups are used for films, stories, or shows where children are not expected to have to respond or compete for attention.

Criteria for Small-Group Management. The teacher chooses materials that are likely to suggest a variety of activities for children but will not invite chaotic and destructive activity. He or she needs to have or to provide the following:

1. Inviting arrangement of materials and activities
2. Selection of materials keyed to children's expressed interests
3. Sufficient materials for size of group
4. Free access to activity for children
5. Variety of skill levels accommodated by activities
6. Opportunities for peer interaction

Handling Unacceptable Behavior. Let's look at two examples of a maturationist teacher's handling of problem behaviors.

Aggression Sean and Billy have been building garages for their racing cars in the block area. Sean hits Billy with a small block. Billy cries and kicks Sean's garage. Sean starts crying. The teacher squats down and puts his arms around the two boys to comfort them and help them stop crying. "You boys seem to have a problem. [He checks Billy's arm where he was hit.] Let me help you put your garage together while we talk about it. Sean, show me how this wall was built." Sean starts to put blocks together. Billy says, "He hit me" and starts wailing again. The teacher says, "Sean, what made you mad? Can you use words to tell me how you felt when you hit Billy?" Sean says, "No, I was just mad. He put a block on my garage. I didn't want it there." The teacher says, "Tell Billy that. That's a good way to say it. We want to use words and not hit. Words help the other person know what's wrong."

Wetting Sarah wets her pants while playing with puzzles. The teacher notices a puddle on the floor. The teacher says, "Sarah, I'll watch your puzzle while you go to the bathroom." Sarah says, "I don't need to go." Steps in puddle. The teacher says, "Sarah, I'll go with you. You won't be comfortable in wet pants. I'll help you change. Then we can wipe the floor." [Points to puddle.] Sarah says, "I'll take the puzzle with me."

Note that in both instances the teacher avoids labeling the children as bad. Through redirection and close guidance he or she strives to get the children to initiate appropriate behaviors.

Behaviorist Program

Groups are an important part of the program curricula. Small ability groups, which are teacher-directed, promote teacher contact and allow instruction to be efficiently presented. Groups are usually homogeneous and based on children's performance skill levels.

Teachers may apply principles of behavior modification to control deviant behavior.

EXAMPLES

Grouping Patterns

Individual Children work individually on learning machines or in programmed texts. Diagnostic and prescriptive work is done individually.

Small Group This arrangement may be formed for most instructional purposes. Children are grouped according to skill levels.

Large Group Some activities, such as music, may be done in large groups. Children spend little time in large groups.

Criteria for Small Group Management. Teachers make provisions before and during the lesson to keep the children focused on them as the directors of learning. To do this, they must attend to the following:

1. Clear, precise instructions and/or demonstration for task
2. Provision of all necessary materials
3. Controlled environment or setting from group
4. Provision for variance in work rates (time)
5. Reasonable avoidance of interruptions

Handling Unacceptable Behavior. Behaviorist programs focus on positive or desired behaviors. These behaviors are stated in objectives. As children learn new behaviors, they pass through various approximations of the desired behavior. Through systematic reinforcement, behavior is shaped to the desired objective. Unacceptable behavior is behavior not related to objectives, disruptive of classroom processes, or physically threatening. Behaviorist programs use specific techniques, such as the following, to handle these unacceptable behaviors.

Time-Out Child is removed from a situation where reinforcement is available. The place (room or corner) where the child is put is considered neutral. For instance, Derek's cookie snatching during snack is disruptive. He is removed from the social situation of snack at a table with other children and placed at a far table. When the others have finished snack, he can return to the snack table to finish his snack.

Extinction The removal of a reinforcer following a behavior. This decreases the likelihood of the behavior persisting. For instance, when John shouts out answers instead of raising his hand to be called upon, the teacher does not respond in any way to him.

Negative Reinforcement A response is reinforced by taking away an aversive stimulus. For instance, Nadia does not like to be scolded and hurried when dressing. She responds by dawdling and taking an incredibly long time to dress. At school whenever she needs to dress to go outside, her teacher does not scold and nag. Nadia is left to dress at her own pace and asked to come outside when she is ready to play.

Behaviorist programs *do not* advocate using punishment. Defined as the presentation of an aversive stimulus after a response, punishment may or may not reduce the rate of the response. We mention punishment only to help you distinguish it from negative reinforcement.

Cognitive Program

Grouping is sometimes used to further program goals and activities. Since children are stimulated by the activities of others, temporary grouping may be done when interests and skill levels converge. During role play children form groups in which members may have very specific duties. Formal instruction is done with small groups of children who are closely matched in cognitive skill levels.

Discipline techniques are directed toward helping children label, understand, and identify the consequences of their behavior. Teachers help children analyze their actions and are actively involved in helping children find alternative behaviors when similar situations occur.

EXAMPLES

Grouping Patterns

Individual Most activity is individually directed; children choose, pursue, and learn activities as interest and personal involvement dictate.

Small Group This arrangement is occasionally formed for instructional purposes. Interest groups and play groups may form spontaneously during activity periods.

Large Group Meetings, sharing, and discussion are frequently held in large groups. Children experience different requirements for self-control in larger groups.

Criteria for Small Group Management. Teachers structure situations so that children can explore and approach problems in their own style, and they set up the environment to induce appropriate child behaviors. Teachers must allow for the following:

1. Orientation of child to task by use of appropriate language level and labels
2. Provision of all necessary materials
3. Controlled environment or setting for group
4. Provision for variance in conceptual ability to master task (teacher questions)
5. Reasonable avoidance of interruptions

Handling Unacceptable Behavior. Cognitive theory does not address itself to handling problem behavior. Kamii and DeVries, who have translated Piaget's theory into a curriculum for young children suggest two principles: "Avoid sanctioning the child's behavior when possible. When negative sanctions are unavoidable, use reciprocity sanctions." (1977, p. 380)

They go on with more suggestions:

> In a situation where a child is disrupting a group the teacher should remember an additional principle—express an opinion as just one of the many possible opinions by saying, "That noise bothers me. Does it bother anyone else?" Peer pressure is more desirable than adult pressure in promoting autonomy because with peers the child is on an equal footing. Hopefully, the child will be able to see the disapproval not only of the teacher but also of the other children. When the teacher encourages other children to sanction acts of disruption, the group may eventually take the initiative in telling noisy children to be quiet. Then, if necessary, the teacher can support the peer sanction by commenting to the disruptive child that the others have asked him not to bother them. (p. 381)

Time Schedule for Activity Blocks

The daily care pattern sets overall program schedules. Depending on some interpretations of developmental viewpoint, length of activity periods vary from program to program. Shorter or longer time periods are a function of the internal pacing of activities that each program may wish to use. Most of the variations among maturationist, behaviorist, and cognitive programs show up as differences in the activity scheduling and pacing that occurs during the long morning and afternoon activity blocks.

Maturationist Program

The curriculum activity blocks of a maturation program schedule are characterized by long stretches of time during which children choose and pursue activities. The schedule is flexible and may vary somewhat from day to day to fit children's interests. Time to sit and look at things is built into the schedule. Internal clocks set the pace; rhythms correspond to children's needs.

EXAMPLES

See the *maturationist program time schedule* in Figure 4.7. Meals and snacks punctuate long periods of activity in this maturation program. There is little need to meet time deadlines. Getting kindergarten children off to school in the afternoon is the only firm time commitment. The schedule serves as a guide, not a determiner of the sequence of daily activities. Children's interests and activities dictate actual time periods. This schedule is a responsive tool that helps staff nurture children's development in the maturationist tradition. From this schedule we can get only a general idea of what any particular child is doing at various points in the day. Other factors, besides time, determine children's daily experiences in the program.

Behaviorist Program

Rules and time govern activities in a behaviorist classroom. The highly regulated, briskly paced schedule is the same every day. The time periods are set and precisely timed; some activities are required of all students. Teachers must have an awareness of the time needed for the interaction and duration of activities.

EXAMPLES

See the *behaviorist program time schedule* in Figure 4.8. Every minute of a child's day in this program is accounted for. We know from looking at this schedule what every child in the program is doing during most time periods of the day. The sequence of short, designated time slots carries out the brisk, deliberate pacing desired in behaviorist programs. Teachers must assume the burden of meeting the time schedule.

Daily Care Pattern

Description	Period	Time
Children arrive and are greeted; health checks are performed	Arrival	6:30–8:00 A.M.
Hello time—greeting, sharing, discussion of activities available	Breakfast	8:00–8:30 A.M.
Free play—Children move about room and choose activities. Snack table opens at 10:00, and children come as they like. This large block of time allows for sustained involvement.	Morning Activity	8:30–11:30 A.M.
	Snack	9:00–11:00
Outdoor play in all but the most inclement weather		11:00–11:30
Lunch cleanup and bathroom; kindergartners go to public school; others get ready for nap	Lunch	11:30 A.M.–12:15 P.M.
Naps	Rest	12:15–2:45 P.M.
Group activity—story or music	Afternoon Activity	2:45–5:00 P.M.
Outdoor play	Snack	
Quiet activities, table games, individual projects		
Center closes. Staff member stays until last child is picked up	Departure	5:00–6:00 P.M.

Figure 4.7 Sample daily schedule for a maturationist program.

Cognitive Program

Invariance in routine gives children a sense of predictability. The daily routine is the chief means of implementing curriculum in the temporal area. Length of activities can vary. Individual activity period is the longest segment so children can pursue choices. Children are encouraged to plan ahead. Activities are paced to allow children time to anticipate and explore consequences. Tempo is slow and contemplative.

EXAMPLES

See the *cognitive program time schedule* in Figure 4.9. This schedule provides a sequence of clearly differentiated time periods, yet still preserves elements of choice for children during the activity periods. Close attention to transition points between time periods will further focus children's awareness of the passing of time and the consequent changes in activity. In a cognitive program time becomes a structuring element, but not an inflexible determiner of activ-

	Daily Care Pattern	
	Arrival	6:30–8:00 A.M.
	Breakfast	8:00–8:30 A.M.
Cleanup and toileting 9:00– 9:15 Group circle time 9:15– 9:30 Instruction period #1 9:30– 9:45 Instruction period #2 9:45–10:15 Toileting and recess 10:15–10:30 Snack 10:30–10:45 Instruction period #3 10:45–11:00 Instruction period #4 11:00–11:30 Activity period	Snack Morning Activity	8:30–9:00 A.M.
Eat Toileting and cleanup	Lunch	11:30 A.M.–12:00 P.M. 12:00–12:30 P.M.
Quiet group games Rest	Rest	12:30–1:00 P.M. 1:00–3:00 P.M.
3:00– 3:45 Toileting and recess 3:45– 4:15 Activity period Individual instruction 4:15– 4:30 Snack 4:30– 5:00 Music	Snack Afternoon Activity	
Quiet group games	Departure	5:00–6:00 P.M.

Figure 4.8 Sample daily schedule for a behaviorist program.

ity. From this schedule we can identify certain points (group meeting, small group, for example) when we know what an individual child is doing. The balance of the day's activities are the result of program elements other than time of day.

Summary

The environmental design of a child care program contributes to the children's learning experience. Program designers have come to realize, too, that the room layout and its materials play a significant role in the implementation of a particular developmental viewpoint. Environmental design includes both the environment's physical features and its usage patterns.

All programs, regardless of developmental viewpoint, must be equally concerned about such environmental factors as physical features, regulations, use limits, private spaces, and outdoor space. Other factors—such as facility setup, management of groups and individuals, and time schedules for activity blocks—are handled differently according to the underlying program philosophy.

The setup of a facility includes both the ac-

Daily Care Pattern

Activities	Pattern	Time
Arrival, quiet individual play	Arrival	6:30–8:30 A.M.
	Breakfast	8:30–9:00 A.M.
9:00– 9:20 Group meeting and planning time 9:20–10:30 Center activities (snack at 10:00) 10:30–11:00 Outdoor play 11:00–12:00 Small group activities	Snack / Morning Activity	9:00–11:00 A.M.
Cleanup, toileting, eating	Lunch	12:00 P.M.–1:00 P.M.
Naps	Rest	1:00–3:00 P.M.
3:00– 4:00 Quiet games, storytelling, music, puppets (snack available), individual work sessions 4:00– 4:30 Outdoor play 4:30– 5:00 Cleanup, group meeting	Snack / Afternoon Activity	3:00–5:00 P.M.
	Departure	5:00–5:30 P.M.

Figure 4.9 Sample daily schedule for a cognitive program.

tual physical arrangement of space as well as the arrangement's use as reflected in movement patterns. To design an appropriate setup, planners may want to draw a room layout and fill out an activity and capacity plot. Management of children requires decisions about how groups will be formed and how discipline will be managed by adults and communicated to children. Time schedules for activities vary in the scheduling of activities and the pacing of the day's routine.

In a maturationist program the facility setup is varied, accessible, and arranged to enhance the children's sense of mobility. Behaviorist setups have few visible or accessible materials and are designed to focus attention and restrict distraction. Setups in cognitive programs show a selection of materials and are planned to help children see orderly relationships among their activities.

Maturationists allow children to form or dissolve their own groups naturally, and adults respond to arising conflicts by helping children label their feelings and redirect their actions. In behaviorist programs small groups are formed for instruction, and behavior modification techniques, such as time-out, are used for control of unacceptable behaviors. Cognitive programs may use groups when interests converge; adults discipline by helping children analyze their actions.

Time schedules in maturationist programs

are flexible and provide long stretches when children choose their own activities. Behaviorists have precisely timed and briskly paced schedules. Cognitive programs follow predictable schedules, but allow lengthy periods for individual activity.

Through careful analysis of physical layout and usage patterns program planners can considerably extend the depth of implementation of a particular developmental viewpoint. The practical details of environmental design factors offer an interesting and often unexploited opportunity to magnify program impact. Both staff and children benefit from playing, working, and caring in circumstances specifically tailored to support program goals.

Resources

Abramson, P. (1971). *Schools for early childhood.* New York: Educational Facilities Laboratories.

Alger, H. (1984). Transitions: Alternatives to manipulative management techniques. *Young Children, 39* (6), 16–25.

Baas, A. M. (1972). Early childhood facilities. *Educational Facilities Review Series,* November, 9, 1–12. (ERIC Document Reproduction Service No. ED 070 138)

Barker, R. G., & Wright, H. F. (1954). *Midwest and its children: The psychology of a midwestern town.* Evanston, IL: Row, Peterson and Company.

Bartholomew, R., McCord, S., Reynolds, H., & Steen, H. (1973). *Child care centers: Indoor lighting—Outdoor playspace.* New York: Child Welfare League of America.

Berk, L. E. (1971). Effects of variations in the nursery school setting on environmental constraints and children's modes of adaptation. *Child Development, 42,* 839–869.

Cohen, U. (1979). *Recommendations for child play areas.* Milwaukee, WI: Center for Architecture and Urban Planning Research, University of Wisconsin.

Doke, L. A. (1975). The organization of day care environments: Formal versus informal activities. *Child Care Quarterly,* 4 (3), 216–222.

Doke, L. A., & Risley, T. R. (1972). The organization of day care environments: Required versus optional activities. *Journal of Applied Behavior Analysis, 5,* 405–420.

Drawbaugh, C. C. (1984). *Time and its use: A self-management guide for teachers.* New York: Teachers College Press.

Educational Facilities Laboratory. (1972). *Found spaces and equipment for children's centers.* New York: EFL.

Ellison, G. (1974). *Play structures.* Pasadena, CA: Pacific Oaks College.

Friedberg, M. P. (1969). *Playgrounds for city children.* Washington, DC: Association for Childhood Education International.

Frost, J. L., & Klein, B. L. (1979). *Children's play and playgrounds.* Boston, MA: Allyn and Bacon.

Getting started. (1974). Austin, TX: National Educational Laboratory Publishers.

Gewirtz, J. L. (1968). On designing the functional environment of the child to facilitate behavioral development. In L. L. Dittman (Ed.), *Early child cares: The new perspectives.* New York: Atherton Press.

Haase, R. W. (1969). *Designing the child development center.* Washington, DC: Project Head Start.

Honig, A. S. (1985). Compliance, control, and discipline: Part I. *Young Children, 40* (2), 50–58.

Honig, A. S. (1985). Compliance, control, and discipline: Part II, *Young Children, 40* (3), 47–52.

Kamii, C., & DeVries, R. (1977). Piaget in early education. In M. C. Day & R. K. Parker (Eds.), *The preschool in action: Exploring early childhood programs* (pp. 363–420). (rev. ed.). Boston: Allyn and Bacon.

Kamii, C. K. (1971). Evaluation of learning in preschool education: Socio-emotional, perceptual-motor, cognitive development. In B. S. Bloom, J. T. Hastings, & G. F. Madaus (Eds.), *Handbook on formative and summative evaluation of student learning* (pp. 281–344). New York: McGraw-Hill.

Krantz, P., & Risley, T. R. (1972). *The organization of group care environments: Behavioral ecology in the classroom.* Lawrence, KA: University of Kansas. (ERIC Document Reproduction Service No. ED 078 915)

Kritchevsky, S., Prescott, E., & Walling, L. (1969). *Planning environments for young children: Physical space.* Washington, DC: National Association for the Education of Young Children.

Kruvant, C., & Redish, G. (1976). *The effects on children of the organization and the design of the day care physical environment: Appropriateness of the federal interagency day care requirements.* Washington, DC: Associates for Renewal in Education.

Larson, C. (Ed.). (1965). *Schools environment research: Environmental evaluations.* Ann Arbor: University of Michigan.

LeLaurin, K., & Risley, T. R. (1972). The organization of day-care environments: "Zone" versus "man-to-man" staff assignments. *Journal of Applied Behavior Analysis, 5,* 225–232.

Loeffler, M. H. (1967). *The prepared environment and its relationship to learning.* Oklahoma City, OK: Casady School. (ERIC Document Reproduction Service No. ED 028 624)

Lovell, P., & Harms, T. (1985). How can playgrounds be improved? A rating scale. *Young Children, 40* (3), 3–8.

Marzollo, J., & Lloyd, J. (1972). *Learning through play.* New York: Harper and Row.

Miller, C. S. (1984). Building self-control: Discipline for young children. *Young Children, 40* (1), 15–19.

Moore, G. T. (1979). *Recommendations for child care centers.* Milwaukee, WI: Center for Architecture and Urban Planning Research, University of Wisconsin.

Moore, G., Cohen, U., & McGinty, T. (1979). *Planning and design guidelines: Childcare centers and outdoor play environments.* Milwaukee, WI: Center for Architecture and Urban Planning Research, University of Wisconsin.

Olds, A. R. (1982). Planning a developmentally optimal day care center. *Day Care Journal, 1* (1), 16–24.

Osmon, F. (1973). *Patterns for designing children's centers.* New York: Educational Facilities Laboratories.

Phase IV early childhood planning kit. (1974). Edison, NJ: Childcraft.

Prescott, E. (1981). Relations between physical setting and adult/child behavior in day care. In S. Kilmer (Ed.), *Advances in early education and day care: Vol. 2.* Greenwich, CT: JAI Press.

Prescott, E., & David, T. G. (1976). *Concept paper on the effects of the physical environment on day care.* Pasadena, CA: Pacific Oaks College. (ERIC Document Reproduction Service No. ED 156 356)

Prescott, E., Jones, E., & Kritchevsky, S. (1972). *Day care as a child-rearing environment: Vol. II.* Washington, DC: National Association for the Education of Young Children.

Ridgway, L., & Lawton, I. (1969). *Family grouping in the primary school* (2nd ed.). New York: Agathon.

Sanoff, H. (1982). *Planning outdoor play.* Atlanta: Humanics.

Sanoff, H., Sanoff, J., & Hensley, A. (1979). *Learning environments for children* (2nd ed.). Raleigh, NC: North Carolina State University.

Setting up the classroom. (1974). Austin, TX: National Educational Laboratory Publishers.

Shure, M. B., & Spivak, G. (1979). Interpersonal cognitive problem solving and primary prevention programming for preschool and kindergarten children. *Journal of Clinical Child Psychology, 2,* 89–94.

Stone, J. G. (1978). *A guide to discipline.* Washington, DC: National Association for the Education of Young Children.

Taylor, A., & Vlastros, G. (1974). *School zone: Learning environments for children.* New York: Van Nostrand Reinhold.

Waligura, R. I. (1971). *Environmental criteria: MR preschool day care facility.* College Station, TX: School of Architecture, Texas A & M University.

5

Materials and Equipment

Introduction

Programs for young children have lots of "stuff"—from child-size chairs and tables to gerbils and crayons. Every program for young children gathers and builds a collection of items that the program designer thinks are necessary for program activities. Staff recognize that materials and equipment are a significant means for implementing program practices. Many items are present in large numbers because the staff discovered over the years that they work. Children find them appealing and use them frequently. Furthermore, traditional materials such as blocks and clay evoke behaviors and activities considered to be appropriate for young children.

Tradition alone, however, is too vague a reason to use as a guideline for selecting activities and equipment. We need some specific criteria for the selection of materials and equipment. If materials and equipment are, in fact, a vital tool for implementing a program's developmental viewpoint, then it stands to reason that programs with different viewpoints will need different selections of materials and equipment. Many of the so-called standard materials and equipment for nursery schools work because they fit the needs of a traditional maturation-based program. They are not automatically valid for cognitive or behaviorist programs. We need to consider three general points: selection of activity content, sequencing and pacing of content, and selection of materials and equipment.

1. *Selection of Activity Content* We define *activity content* broadly to be the experiences and information children are exposed to in the program. It is a critical indicator of the developmental viewpoint of the program. Whether children have math experiences, learn about the planets, or experience the feel of working with mud is indicative of the emphasis program planners place on specific content areas. To be practical, a program must concentrate the information load of activities so that staff are prepared to handle children's behaviors and have the necessary materials on hand. *Selection of content* areas for program emphasis, therefore, must be a part of program planning.

   The daily care pattern shows two activity periods—morning and afternoon—during which curriculum opportunities predominate. Activities and experiences provided during these times will reflect the major content emphasis of the program. Those content areas thought to be most important by program planners will receive formal attention during these activity periods. Planners may *specify objectives* for selected content areas. Secondary curriculum opportunity periods—arrival, rest, and departure—provide additional times when small groups of children may be available for program activities. These are usually informal extensions of events occurring in the dominant activity periods.
2. *Sequencing and Pacing of Content* Once the planners have determined the information con-

tent and experience opportunities of activities, implementation with children requires that the planners *organize content and objectives* for the activities. Activities must be chunked and strung together. Planners and staff decide what comes first or last and what goes with what. Each developmental viewpoint sets forth a particular time line for growth and change. Activity sequencing and *planning goals* should be patterned after the theoretical time line.

3. *Selection of Materials and Equipment* Actually equipping a classroom or supplying a program with materials is exciting business. A wealth of commercial material is available. Also much can be constructed from scratch. *Criteria for selection* of materials and equipment are both general and specific. All programs require safe, durable, and reasonably priced items.

   Materials and equipment are the most visible indicators of program philosophy. The activities and physical objects selected by program staff are the tools through which curriculum decisions are implemented. While any piece of material or equipment is potentially useful, certain items will complement more closely the learning and developmental requirements of particular program situations. Well-selected materials and equipment support staff caregiving and teaching efforts. Activity content, sequencing, and selection criteria for materials and equipment items are decisions that will be addressed differently by maturationist, behaviorist, and cognitive programs.

Because many child care programs find Montessori materials and activities appealing, we are including a section about Montessori. The section analyzes the characteristics of Montessori materials and discusses the contributions these materials and activities can make to programs derived from the three developmental viewpoints.

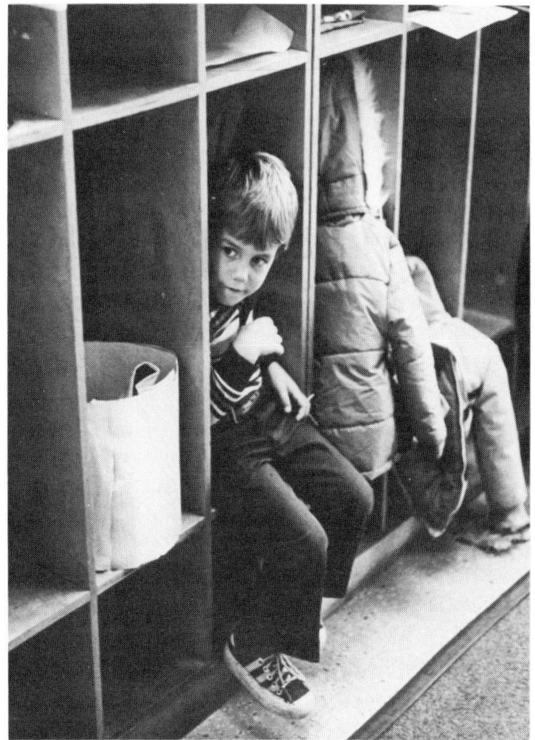

Over the years certain items have come to be almost standard features in classrooms for young children. For example, few programs are without blocks, clay, puzzles, or cubbies for children's personal belongings. (College of Human Development, Department of Individual and Family Studies, The Pennsylvania State University; used with permission.)

Selection of Activity Content

All programs for young children aim to help children learn more about their world. Over time children become more adept and skillful in dealing with the demands of their environment as they use the knowledge they have gained through program activities. The activity content choices that programs make reflect both the program's developmental viewpoint and any specific cultural or environment conditions that may affect the program's clientele. In programs for young children, activity and content are linked—each drawing on the other. It is difficult, if not impossible, to talk about content for young children without placing it within the framework of an activity. For example:

Content	*Activity*
Knowledge of mass	Clay or mud play
Math	Counting juice cups
Reading	Drill on beginning consonant sounds

Some programs determine the nature of the activities that will be emphasized and then fill in content. Others choose content and then utilize whatever activities occur as a means of presenting content.

Curriculum

Curriculum is the educational term typically used to label the activity content of a program. It implies that some systematic decision process based on specific guidelines was used to select activity content. Programs with behaviorist, cognitive, or maturation viewpoints use different decision criteria for the selection of activity content. The general framework within which these decisions are made is a two-step interaction between focus and balance.

Curriculum focus points include:

Topics Subject content, facts, or information
Skills Abilities, performances
Experiences Participation, demonstration, or observation

Curriculum activities balance points are:

Formal ⟷ Informal
Planned ⟷ Incidental
Structured ⟷ Unstructured

Curriculum decisions are made by linking focus and balance for individual activities to build an overall pattern of program activities. Patterns of curriculum decisions are different for each of the three developmental viewpoints. In a maturationist program planners focus on topics and experiences through informal, incidental, and unstructured activities. This deliberate imbalance directly reflects the maturationist view that children learn through interest and experience. The behaviorist view that children can be taught by adults is reflected in a deliberate focus on topics and skills implemented through formal, planned, and structured curriculum activities. Again, this is a deliberate imbalance that accurately mirrors behaviorist principles. Skills and experience are emphasized in a cognitive program through informal, structured and unstructured activities. Teachers work to challenge and stimulate children's thinking by providing structured, exploration situations. Thus, in a cognitive program there is a selective balance in curriculum activities that appropriately use cognitive principles.

Play

For most of us play is practically synonymous with young children. The free play period and play in general are integral parts of all maturationist programs. Behaviorists have a more academic, structured definition of play but are likely to use play as a reinforcer or reward in programs for young children. Cognitive programs view play as an intellectual exercise and believe sociodramatic play to be an important activity for children. Play is a child's work. People who work with young children may differ on the role of play in a planned program, but most would agree with the following statement:

> To the young child, play is life itself. Play fills mind and body, mentality, emotionability, and physical being. A child engrossed in play is inventive, free, and happy. Through the variety and depth of play, the child learns and grows. It is serious business, it is his world. (Evans, 1974, p. 267)

Types of play appropriate to various ages are described in Table 5.1. More information is given in the listings under "Play" in the Resources Section.

Table 5.1 Types of Play

Age	Imitation	Exploration	Testing	Construction	Social Adults	Social Children
2	own and other's acts	real objects	run throw large motor activities	objects as symbols	peeking funny-faces chase hide retrieval acting vertigo nonsense nursery	exploration
3	identifications with parents of objects as toys	manipulations tools	climb hop balance march hang	toys dyads	story rhyme central person	hiding testing choral games
4	personifications anticipations	matching games puzzles secrets surprises visits natures		plurals imaginary characters	role-reversals story-reversals story-participation puppets	imaginary monsters associative play central persons turns friends and enemies choral-verbal games
5	exaggerations mimicry	territories	vehicle speed	cities	conversations hunts lotto	surrogate prisoners conversations pastimes hide and seek

Source: Adapted from B. Sutton-Smith, (1970), p. 26.

Maturationist Program

The theme of the maturation curriculum is life experiences. Sometimes termed a "folk" curriculum, this plan places heavy emphasis on ideas and activities familiar to children from their everyday life. Activity content promotes social interaction and is culturally relevant for the particular group. Teachers teach from what is happening. Hands-on, concrete experiences; role rehearsal through dress-up, fantasy play, and play-acting; and sensitivity to the needs and feelings of others are the ingredients for growth in all developmental areas. Activities incorporate these aspects as staff are alert for subtle, visible signs of behavior and language that signal children are ready to change. Staff encourages children's exposure to new activities at times of developmental readiness. Staff organize events into themes that contain overlapping content and experience.

The interests and needs of individual children will be reflected in their choice of activities. Teachers determine objectives for children that are consistent with developmental norms and with their expressed modes of play. Through play experiences children have the opportunity to consolidate developmental gains and rehearse through role-play experiences from their daily lives.

EXAMPLES

Familiar activities for a maturation-based program, which are usually appealing and child-oriented, represent what are considered to be the traditional curriculum activities for young

Box 5.1 Activity Possibilities for a Maturationist Program

Dig a hole in his or her own backyard spot, big enough to sit in.
Prepare a small garden.
Rock in a hammock.
Make a tent under the dining room table or picnic table, or between two trees.
Use a hose.
Paint with water outside using a big brush.
Catch fireflies.
Draw with chalk on the sidewalk.
Fingerpaint on oilcloth.
Cut out pictures from magazines to paste on paper.
Use wrapping paper, ribbons and glue to make collages.
Prepare a rainy-day box.
Play in a sandbox in the shade.
Use a sprinkler.
Blow bubbles.
Enjoy feeding time at the zoo.
Take a quick trip to a museum; stop first at the museum shop for two or three postcards and go on a picture hunt.
Go on a picnic.
Make popsicles.
Go to the library for a basketful of books.
Play with a big beach ball.
Build with woodscraps.
Eat a breakfast picnic out on the grass.
Have backwards meals (dessert first).
Prepare a menu, help buy the food and prepare the meal.
Make a fruit salad.
Make a mud pie.
Watch a storm with you.
Take a bubble bath outside.
Go barefoot and even naked.
Have some time alone with you.
Enjoy old plastic bottles for pouring and squirting.
Watch ants at work.
Collect worms.
Use a trash can lid for water for the birds.
Read and be read to, again and again and again.

Source: From *Newsletter,* Washington, DC: St. Columba's Nursery School, May 1983; used with permission.

children. At any time children have a choice of activities ranging from quiet to active, messy to neat, and manipulative to passive. Almost all activities have a social component. Some examples are in the following list.

Life Experience Activities

Cleaning	Mud play
Washing	Sand play
Dress-up corner	Water play
Construction play	Easels and paint
Riding, walking	Seasonal dressing
Reading, story telling	Caring for animals
Trips	Housekeeping
Music	Sports
Cooking	Theater play

Other possibilities are in Box 5.1.

Unit themes are used to help children put together related ideas, activities, and experiences. Chosen to fit children's current interests or exposure to events, themes give teachers a framework for selecting materials and equipment. Teachers may plan field trips and visits to help children extend the theme beyond the classroom. Activity areas are set up and teachers are primed to follow up on children's theme-related behaviors as they occur. An example of a theme on "Friends" is in Box 5.2.

Objectives are stated in broad terms and incorporate many aspects of children's behavior: social, emotional, physical, and mental. Short-term objectives guide staff in working consistently together on specific goals for individual children. Long-term objectives provide general guidelines for interacting with children across several activities. Short- and long-term objectives frequently focus on smoothing out developmental "rough spots."

Box 5.2 Unit Theme on Friends

The theme of friends was sparked, perhaps, by close friendships or special friends among the children. Perhaps some children have had friends visiting from out of town. The activities and materials listed here will be provided as teachers feel situations require. For example: The Anglund story about friends may prompt a discussion at story or snack time about, "Who are my friends?" Teachers may write down children's comments. Later empty picture frames might be used to stimulate drawing of a friend's pictures with comments added as captions. Photographs and magazine pictures may be added to the friend's picture gallery. In time, more stories, discussions, trips, and collections will be related to the theme of friends. Children's interests and teacher's preparedness to respond will delineate the range of theme activities.

Activities

- Making pictures of friends
- Telling stories about friends
- Writing a letter to a friend
- Visiting neighborhood friends
- Visiting a nursing home to make friends

Materials

- Books on friends in book corner or stories at storytime about friends
- Pictures of activities friends do together
- Pictures that children bring showing friends

Books

Anglund, J. W. (1968). *A friend is someone who likes you.* New York: Harcourt.
DeRegniers, B. S. (1964). *May I bring a friend?* New York: Atheneum.
Minarik, E. H. (1960). *Little bear's friend.* New York: Harper.

Sample Objectives

Program objective

Program will foster positive self-concept.
Children will develop independence in self-care routines.

Long-term objectives

Tim will accept help from children and adults.
Pete will share and cooperate when asked.

Short-term individual child objectives

Sandy will eat snack when hungry.
Tim will feel comfortable leaving the center for field trips.

Behaviorist Program

Most programs based on behaviorist principles choose to emphasize academic subjects and social skills necessary for learning. This activity content is considered to be essential for children to function competently in their environment. Behaviorist programs teach specific content and train for skill mastery. Activities are formal, planned, structured lessons in math and reading (content and readiness skills). Social skills are emphasized during lessons and caregiving routines.

Individual learning prescriptions or contracts are devised for each child. Objectives are precise, specifying exact child behaviors and the acceptable evidence of success.

EXAMPLES

Social skills of learning are important to success now and in later school situations. So important are these skills that specific curriculum plans and activity procedures are devised to ensure that children master them. Table 5.2 shows social skills and recommended times and places for practicing them. Programs may also teach skills such as the following:

Table 5.2 Social Skills and Practice Times for a Behaviorist Program

PROGRAM SEGMENT	SKILLS
	Language Skills
Activity period, in motor area	Reads these sight words: *stop, exit, up,* and *down.*
Activity period/art	Listens to and follows a sequence of three instructions.
	Social and Self-care Skills
Snack	Identifies foods from the four basic food groups.
Greetings/dismissal	Buttons and unbuttons small buttons independently.
	Motor Skills
Free play at art table	Cuts out pictures following a general shape
	Cognitive Skills
Circle time, e.g., order characters in a story based on size, voice, etc.	Orders objects on basis of degree of specific physical characteristics

Source: From *Individualized early education for handicapped children* (p. 103) by J. T. Neisworth, S. J. Willoughby-Herb, S. J. Bagnato, C. A. Cartwright, and K. W. Laub, 1980, Rockville, MD: Aspen Systems Corporation; reprinted with permission.

1. Child will maintain eye contact with instructor.
2. Child will raise hand to speak in a group situation.
3. Child will respond when asked a question.

Academic skills and content for young children are primarily readiness and foundation skills in reading and math. The following example shows a small sample of the scope and detail of a curriculum plan taken from a behaviorist-based program. This set of objectives at the five-year-old level from the HICOMP Curriculum (1977) are for mathematical problem-solving:

Uses number names when asked "How many (objects) are here?" (objects up to ten)
Uses number names when asked to describe situations.
Understands and uses concepts *more* and *less.*
Adds objects to a group when asked to make that group "larger."
Takes away objects from a group when asked to make that group "smaller."

Source: Willoughby-Herb, S. J., and Neisworth, J. T. *The HICOMP Preschool Curriculum.* Columbus, Ohio: Charles Merrill, 1983; used with permission.

Objectives must be stated precisely so the teacher knows exactly when the expected behavior is accomplished. A precise objective states:

Who will perform.
What they will do, using verbs that describe observable actions—cut, count, write, say, and so on. It does not say what they will feel, imagine, dream, or think.
How specifics of the action are to be accomplished. This is often expressed with both a descriptive statement and a quantitative standard for acceptable performance.
When the conditions for performance are approximate, including equipment, range of problems, and special provisions if any.

Cognitive Program

Cognitive programs emphasize skills and abilities rather than subject topics. Experiences are used to give children opportunities for involvement. Much of what occurs in the child's familiar environment can be successfully utilized as activity content in a cognitive program. Many cognitive programs *look* very similar to maturation programs. The same activities that facilitate free play are also useful for exploration and discovery if handled appropriately by the adults in charge. Whereas the maturation teacher will allow children to pursue play ideas, the cognitive teacher will interpret questions and perhaps redirect activities to maximize the intellectual challenges of the situation. The following situation is indicative of how teachers transform activities to highlight their cognitive potential.

Maturation Activity	*Cognitive Potential*
Dress-up—clown clothes: As part of circus theme children have been making faces, doing clown jumps, and dressing in clown hats.	Teacher would help child carry the pretend play further by asking planning questions (What can you do to be funny? Where is the clown going? Does this clown have a story to tell?) and by helping the child evaluate his or her actions (How do people know you are a clown? Do you think people need clowns? Why?).

Language is considered an important tool for thought. Children's activities are always accompanied by language labeling. Adults help children use words to identify, organize, and evaluate the information and actions that are part of each experience.

Objectives for children are derived from cognitive skill principles, not subjects. Staff will find that general sets of objectives can govern their work with children in teaching as well as caregiving activities.

EXAMPLES

Weikart, Rogers, Adcock, and McClelland (1971) developed a *planning framework* for a cognitively derived curriculum that illustrates the use of generalized principles and nonspecificity of content. The focus in the planning process is on skills and thought processes, not specific content such as math or geography. The framework shown in Figure 5.1 provides a "mental" structure for the teacher when selecting activity content and formulating working objectives for children. The statements in Figure 5.1 illustrate the type of objective used in cognitive programs. Objective statements are a means for staff to translate theoretical stage assumptions into statements that use language, terms, and examples familiar to them. The process of planning children's activities from the objective statements in Figure 5.1 will give staff practice in the application of cognitive principles to daily classroom activities.

The *cognitive potential* of activities resulting from materials and equipment selected for the program must be apparent to staff. For example, common materials in the large muscle play area can be analyzed for cognitive potential (see Box 5.3). This prior analysis activity prepares the teacher and generates ideas for other equipment that could be added at later dates.

Sequencing and Pacing of Content

Curriculum is sequence as well as activity content. The sequencing of content and objectives is based upon theoretical assumptions about the pace of developmental progress. Program content and activities are sequenced according to fairly specific guidelines regarding order and timing. There are distinctive differences among the maturation, behaviorist, and cognitive viewpoints on the issue of sequencing.

Sequencing involves planning and requires program planners and staff to consider short- and long-term goals when organizing content and objectives. Planning goals form the basis for program evaluation and need to accurately summarize daily, weekly, and monthly progress of children.

Maturationist Program

In the maturation program the sequencing of content and objectives helps to keep the program on course throughout the year. Much of the activity and content in the program is spontaneous on-going child activities. Broad themes and long-term planning goals are essential to bring some cohesion to the efforts of all in-

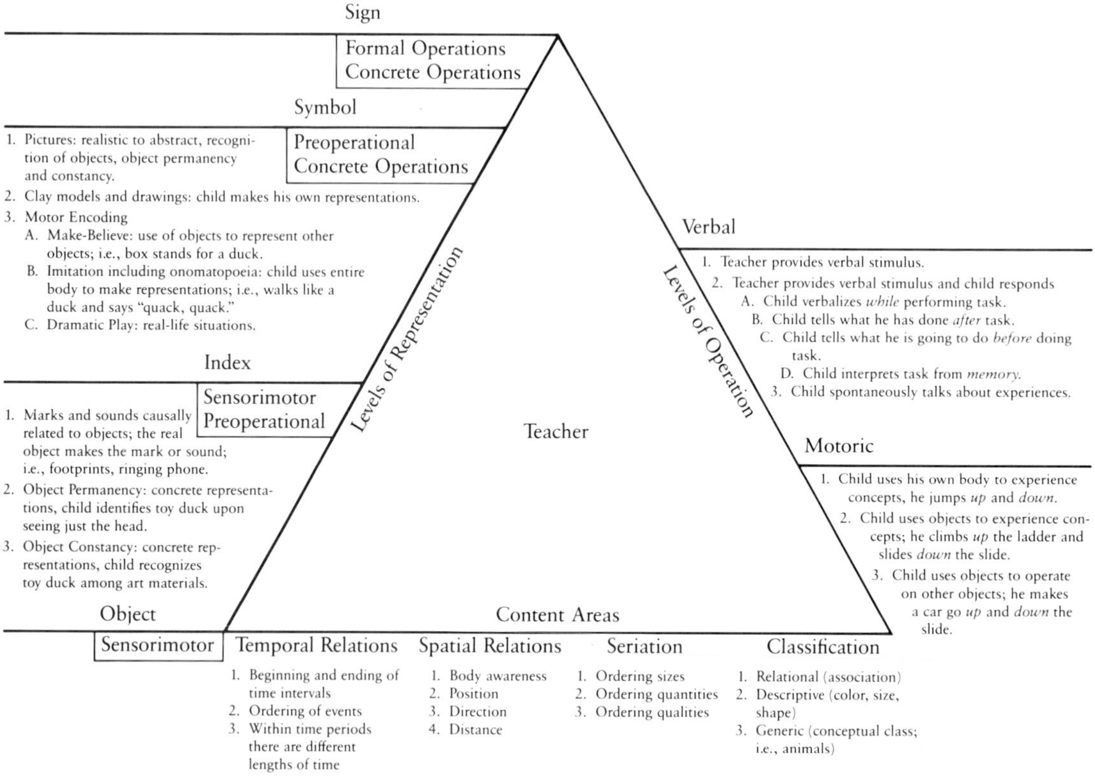

Sign

Formal Operations
Concrete Operations

Symbol

Preoperational
Concrete Operations

1. Pictures: realistic to abstract, recognition of objects, object permanency and constancy.
2. Clay models and drawings: child makes his own representations.
3. Motor Encoding
   A. Make-Believe: use of objects to represent other objects; i.e., box stands for a duck.
   B. Imitation including onomatopoeia: child uses entire body to make representations; i.e., walks like a duck and says "quack, quack."
   C. Dramatic Play: real-life situations.

Index

Sensorimotor
Preoperational

1. Marks and sounds causally related to objects; the real object makes the mark or sound; i.e., footprints, ringing phone.
2. Object Permanency: concrete representations, child identifies toy duck upon seeing just the head.
3. Object Constancy: concrete representations, child recognizes toy duck among art materials.

Object

Sensorimotor

Levels of Representation

Teacher

Levels of Operation

Verbal

1. Teacher provides verbal stimulus.
2. Teacher provides verbal stimulus and child responds
   A. Child verbalizes *while* performing task.
   B. Child tells what he has done *after* task.
   C. Child tells what he is going to do *before* doing task.
   D. Child interprets task from *memory*.
3. Child spontaneously talks about experiences.

Motoric

1. Child uses his own body to experience concepts, he jumps *up* and *down*.
2. Child uses objects to experience concepts; he climbs *up* the ladder and slides *down* the slide.
3. Child uses objects to operate on other objects; he makes a car go *up* and *down* the slide.

Content Areas

Temporal Relations
1. Beginning and ending of time intervals
2. Ordering of events
3. Within time periods there are different lengths of time

Spatial Relations
1. Body awareness
2. Position
3. Direction
4. Distance

Seriation
1. Ordering sizes
2. Ordering quantities
3. Ordering qualities

Classification
1. Relational (association)
2. Descriptive (color, size, shape)
3. Generic (conceptual class; i.e., animals)

Figure 5.1 Planning framework for a cognitive curriculum. (From *The Cognitively Oriented Curriculum* (p. 35) D. P. Weikart, C. Adcock, L. Rogers, and D. McClelland, 1971, Washington, DC: National Association for the Education of Young Children; Urbana, IL: ERIC/EECE.)

volved. On the basis of a chosen theme the caregivers may add new materials to activity areas within the room and make plans to relate snacks, stories, trips, and special projects to the theme. How and when these theme activities are introduced will depend on the responsiveness and interest of children in the program at the time.

In general, activities blend into one another. One activity just seems to lead to another. This is sequencing at the most abstract level. It requires comprehensive planning and considerable intuition from those in closest contact with the children.

EXAMPLES

Calendar themes organize children's activities around the seasonal and holiday events of the year. Through personal involvement in activities mirroring the behavior of adults, children gain information about the events of their world and can practice responses. Holidays

Box 5.3 Analyzing material in the large muscle play area for cognitive potential.

Equipment	Activities	Verbal Ideas
Wagons	Filling Pulling Riding	What to put in? What happens? Why haul cargo? What makes it go?
Small wooden trucks and cars	Motor mimicking Making trips Crashing Getting fixed	Where? How long to get there? How to get ready?
Climbing frame	Climbing Hanging Dangling Stretching Balancing	How did you get to the top? What have you done with your legs? Arms? Knees? Can you get down the same way you got up?

Materials for Future Activities

1. Cargo for wagons (heavy stones, styro blocks)
2. Tape to mark roads on floor
3. Stop signs and other road signs
4. Costumes

with their rituals and emotional significance are salient events for children. They provide a rich, naturally occurring flow of interest and activity for the program. For example:

Calendar Themes

September	Fall
October	Halloween
November	Thanksgiving Giving and sharing
December	Christmas and Hanukkah
January	Winter New Year
February	Valentine's Day Presidents' birthdays

March	Weather, wind, and kites
April	Spring flowers
May	May Day

Behaviorist Program

Sequencing is a critical ingredient of behaviorist programs. The success or failure of instruction is directly related to the hierarchies of objectives formulated to plan and evaluate children's performance. Activities proceed from simple to complex in small steps and with each step near the child's present performance level. So vital is sequencing in implementing program goals that sequences exist within sequences.

The activities of individual children are sequenced according to their current performance levels on various tasks. Once an entry point is diagnosed, children proceed through a strictly ordered sequence of skill development tasks leading to desired behavior acquisition and acceptable performance levels.

Content—math, reading, and related readiness skills—is analyzed and broken into discrete bits, which are then ordered from simple to complex. These content hierarchies are the basis for instruction. Planners arrange learning episodes in order. Caregivers use signal systems to maintain attention and to establish response patterns and cues. Instructional sequences are patterned or programmed.

EXAMPLES

Children's activities are planned and closely regulated. Each activity concludes with an assessment of performance that will be the basis for determining the next day's activities. Children who are working on identical objectives may be grouped for instruction. Teachers must have detailed recording systems to keep track of activities and make daily prescriptions for all children in the group. The following example is a list of the times and activities prescribed for a four-year-old child during a morning activity:

Job 1, 9:30 A.M.	Play shape-matching game with Judy (staff).
Job 2, 9:45 A.M.	Join Owen and Mary for practice with rhyming words with Bob (staff).
Job 3, 10:05 A.M.	Large muscle activity on outdoor obstacle course with Judy (staff).
10:25 A.M.	If objectives accomplished in all jobs, go to free play area.

Cognitive Program

Sequencing in a cognitive program follows the general progression of Piagetian stages from sensorimotor to formal operations. The basic principle for sequencing is that a child moves from sensory-based experiences through nonverbal, intuitive periods to increasingly verbal, complex abstractions of experiences. Children move from active manipulation of concrete materials to verbal and symbolic representation of their thoughts and actions.

On a daily basis the chunking of content and exact order of experiences cannot be precisely determined. Activities are planned to challenge current levels of thinking without creating frustration. Global ideas and specific facts are juxtaposed as children explore materials and experiences. Just as children construct their cognitive structures through active involvement, so do they construct idiosyncratic sequences of activities and ideas in the process. Other than the general principles of stage progression, teachers have few specific guidelines for sequencing.

Curriculum planning begins with teachers tracking and recording children's current activities and strategies. Using this information, teachers plan activities consistent with current behaviors. Teachers then instigate problems that challenge the child's current abilities. Numerous opportunities to consolidate new skills or understandings follow. Optimum sequencing patterns balance times of consistency, challenge, and consolidation parallel to the wait-challenge-wait teaching strategy.

EXAMPLES

Classification skill is developed during the early school years. As children mature mentally, their ability to classify and the level of representation and response mode changes, moving from concrete to abstract, nonverbal to verbal. No child would proceed directly from concrete to transitional to representational in three short steps. All would need many and varied experiences at each step. Our example illustrates activities typical of what many children would experience at each step (see Box 5.4).

Selection of Materials and Equipment

What materials and equipment should programs buy, beg, borrow, or build? What are reasonable criteria for selection? Materials and equipment are capital investments for programs. Well-chosen, durable items will become a permanent core collection for program activities. Good items stimulate children and staff and provide visible evidence of goals for the program. Rarely, however, do programs have enough money to buy everything all at once. Long-range purchase plans are necessary and should reflect the curriculum goals of the program.

Basic *equipment* for programs can set the tone for all other activities. Facilities need storage, seating, and work surfaces. Quantities sufficient to allow the program to run smoothly are necessary. Equipment that can do double duty is efficient and cost-effective only if transition time and appearance do not pose problems. Some programs need more furniture than others. Formal lessons require chairs, blackboards, and work surfaces. Exploratory activities require work surfaces, cleanup facilities, display and drying areas, and storage bins. In short, like everything else, the amount and kind of furniture a program needs varies according to the activities emphasized in the program's developmental plan and any regulations that may apply. The following lists give a few examples of basic equipment necessary for all programs and some examples of additional equipment that can often be found in typical maturation, behaviorist, and cognitive programs. Note that these lists are not exhaustive.

Basic Equipment Items

Child-sized chairs
Adult chairs
Cubbies, coat racks
Bookcases
Storage cabinets and bins
Work tables with wipeable surfaces
Blackboard
Corkboards or bulletin boards
Sink

Maturation Equipment

Cooking equipment
Blocks
Easels, paint
Rug, floor cushions
Baby cradle, dolls

Behaviorist Equipment

Film projector, screen
Room dividers, movable partitions
Desks, individual workspaces
Child-sized carrels
Shelves for individual assignments and work storage

Cognitive Equipment

Puppet stage
Science material
Sandbox
Blocks and storage area
Sorting games
Measuring equipment

General *materials* are those small items that programs gather to use in lessons or make accessible to children during activity periods. The distinction between material and equipment is mainly one of size and purpose. Equipment generally refers to furniture and large, durable items that are capital investments for a program. Materials are smaller, curriculum-related items that are changed or replaced periodically as children's activities or lessons require. Some materials appear in all types of programs, others are more likely to appear in one type of

Box 5.4 Activity Sequence in a Cognitive Program

The activity sequence here illustrates a simple construction activity that is accompanied by a recording process designed to capture critical elements of the thought processes involved. A concrete activity is linked to nonverbal indicators of symbolic representation.

Source: High Scope Resource, (Sample Activity Sequence), pp. 22–23, Ypsilanti, MI: High Scope Press, 600 N. River Street 48197; used with permission.

Worktime

Cut out these shapes and make your picture

Use this page to make your picture

Representation

Color in a box for each shape you used

■								
▲								
●								
▬								

Teacher's check

Homework Page

Dear Parents!
Please help your child count the number of different shapes on the graph
Write the number beside each shape

■								Number
▲								
●								
▬								

Find some things in your house that are different shapes.

● What are circles? ______________________

____

■ What are squares? ______________________

____

▲ What are triangles? ______________________

____

Parent's check

Box 5.5 General Criteria for Materials and Equipment

Safety Avoid sharp edged, small breakable parts, and rough finishes. Check to be sure painted surfaces are nontoxic. Moving parts should work smoothly and not offer hazards for small fingers. Children use toys for many purposes, often far-removed from the designers' original intent. Check to see that toys are safe for alternative uses.

Durability Materials and equipment should be designed and manufactured for sustained, hard use. Continued use should not dim the appeal or attractiveness of an item. Basic program equipment is a heavy capital investment. Expect to get many years use if you originally buy top quality goods.

Quantity Learning to share and cooperate are universal to growing up and functioning in a group. But children have a right to expect sufficient quantities of materials so that "working for a turn" and "making do" are not dominant activities. Sufficient quantity is a function of number of children *and* desired activities for the program. Multipurpose materials can help stretch program equipment dollars.

Appropriateness Ages of children served and program purposes are the best guides for selecting appropriate materials and equipment. Infants and toddlers require different toys than five-year-olds. An intensive academic-oriented program needs vastly different equipment than an open, free play-oriented program.

program than in others. *Supplies* are consumable materials and must be renewed or replaced periodically. Three types of materials are of interest to program planners: raw materials, program-prepared materials, and commercially prepared materials.

Raw materials are ones that have no particular inherent instructional or learning features. Children and/or teachers must transform raw materials into curriculum-appropriate materials. Maturation and cognitive programs are likely to find that the creativity and involvement unleashed by raw materials blends well with program goals. Behaviorist programs will find little use for such materials unless teachers incorporate the materials into existing instructional plans.

Program-prepared materials rely on teacher ingenuity and effort to turn available resources into instructionally relevant materials. Maturation programs may use local talent to construct play structures and large equipment, but generally children are allowed to use materials as they wish without teacher modification. Behaviorist programs rely on tightly scripted lessons with fewer concrete props. Worksheets, drill experiences, and repetitive exercises require considerable planning effort and must be carefully developed. Cognitive programs benefit greatly from program-prepared materials. Many games and challenging semistructured materials can be made cost-effectively by teachers.

Commercially prepared materials are available as idea banks, kits, and total curriculum plans. Such products are useful because they provide prepared objectives, fully described teaching strategies, and collections of materials and ideas ready for immediate use. Time-consuming staff planning work can be eliminated through judicious selection of commercial material. But these materials are not cheap, and they may inhibit staff engagement, especially if by providing staff with a ready-made guide for the program curriculum you have limited their opportunities to become involved with program goals.

Wisely used, commercial materials are invaluable for programs. Idea books and curriculum activity plans help maturationist teachers broaden their horizons and expand the range of offerings in the classroom environment. Programmed materials allow the behaviorist teacher to focus on in-class teaching strategies and invest time in child assessment and evaluation record-keeping. Cognitive games, puzzles, and lessons provide examples for teachers trying to master cognitive theory and translate principles into practice.

Program planners should seek an acceptable balance of purchased and homemade equipment and materials. Box 5.5 presents general criteria for selecting materials and equipment. A list of material and equipment suppliers is given in Appendix B.

Maturationist Program

Free play or play of the child's choice is the primary activity in a maturation program. Materials and equipment must be open, unstructured, and multipurpose. Consumable supplies and raw materials are important, because they allow children the greatest latitude for exploration and creativity. Teachers rotate and replenish materials. Variety and novelty are essential to sustain the appeal of the environment.

Materials must be available in rich supply to promote creative use. Planners consider developmental needs when selecting material and equipment. Children need to be able to find materials that meet their current developmental needs as well as allow them to reach out for higher-order developmental skills. Materials and equipment should also support social interaction by encouraging group play and pretend play.

EXAMPLES

Common Materials. The tried and tested materials for young children are essential. These materials invite social interaction and role play. Some age-appropriate examples are shown in Table 5.3.

Found Materials. Maturation teachers stockpile and collect the strangest things. Examples of free and found materials are milk cartons, plastic bottles, boxes, tubes, and wallpaper sample books.

Table 5.3 Common Materials and Equipment

Age Group	Housekeeping	Creative Art and Books
6 months–1 year	Soft dolls	
1 year–2 years	Add: Doll bed Doll blankets Doll mattress Unbreakable doll Wooden telephone	Large crayons Hard books Cloth books Records Record player
2 years–3 years	Add: Simple doll clothes Doll carriage Childsize furniture: sink, stove, etc., pots & pans Aprons	Add: Books
3-year-olds	Add: Ironing board, iron Rocking chair Broom, dustpan	Add: Easels Paints Brushes Blunt scissors
4-year-olds	Add: Chest of drawers Washbasin Clothesline & pins Basket Aprons, ties, etc. Childsize bed, cradle, carriage, wardrobe	Add: Clay
5-year-olds	Add: Indian Tepee	

Source: From *Criteria for Selecting Play Equipment for Early Childhood Education: A Reference Book* (pp. 36–37), 1981, New York: Community Playthings; used with permission.

Behaviorist Program

Formal instruction is emphasized in behaviorist programs. Materials and equipment are selected to meet the needs of the curriculum plan, to minimize distraction and focus children's attention on the teacher. Materials are structured, and specific results or products are expected.

Box 5.6 Sample Materials to Teach Dressing in a Behaviorist Program

These dolls are cute but would be rejected in behaviorist programs because the buttons, snaps, zippers, and laces require too many skills for dressing the dolls.

These dressing frames are preferred because they allow for practice on one skill at a time.

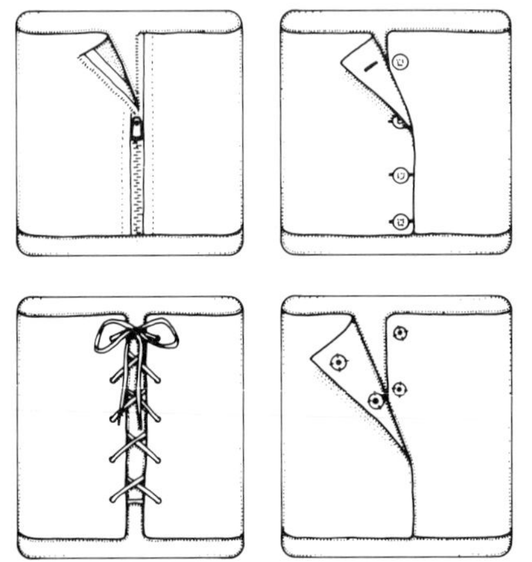

These vests are also appropriate since they provide for sequencing with smaller buttons and more buttons. Children begin with one large button and work to being able to manage the five small buttons.

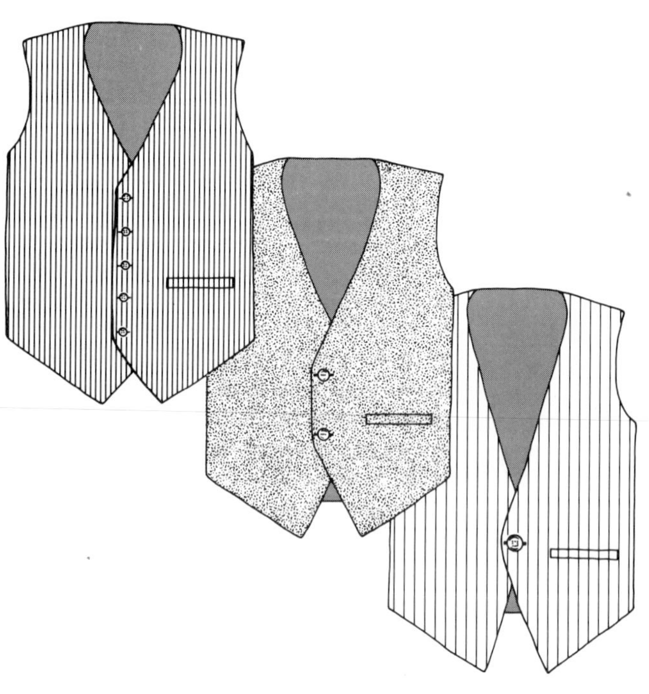

Children typically do not have uncontrolled access to materials. Task-directed materials that will help children meet learning objectives may be made available for short practice periods. Such materials will be autotelic or self-correcting so the child's behavior is structured towards a correct response. Commercially prepared curricula are often preferred; programmed materials are used to ensure desired instructional presentation.

EXAMPLES

Planners prefer materials that are self-correcting and that do not have distracting parts (for example, pictorial scenes just to make them look pretty but that do not contribute to the task). These principles are illustrated in the sample materials shown in Box 5.6.

Cognitive Program

Materials and equipment must help children abstract and organize their work. Materials should allow construction and involvement without any specific products indicated. Complex materials that encourage children to explore and test and have a high absorption potential are preferred. Considered to be the best are materials meeting these criteria but having relatively simple attributes that are easy for children to identify and work with.

EXAMPLES

Blocks have high complexity-absorption potential and encourage construction but have simple attributes of size, shape, and weight (see Box 5.7).

Montessori Materials

Working in her native Italy at the turn of the century, Dr. Maria Montessori developed a system of education for young children. The philosophy and methods she developed are a unique blend of cognitive and behaviorist principles. Montessori published extensively and traveled widely to disseminate her work. In the United States some interest in her system was aroused in the 1910s, but it faded. In the mid-1950s, under the leadership of Nancy McCormick Rambusch, Montessori's method received renewed attention. In the Montessori method all aspects of the program are prescribed. Prospective teachers complete special training programs for Montessori certification.

An integral part of the prepared environment of Montessori classrooms is a collection of materials and equipment that have greatly impressed childhood professionals with the quality and design concepts embedded in the materials. While it is *not* a Montessori recommended practice, many of these materials have been used apart from other Montessori practices. Montessori materials and their derivatives are widely used in many child care programs.

Material Characteristics

Montessori materials have several special attributes:

1. Materials are scaled physically and conceptually to children. They are lightweight and proportional; movable furnishings are child-sized.
2. Materials are autotelic, or self-correcting, providing children with continuous evidence of correctness of performance. Children are involved within limits. The hand is the chief teacher, or children learn by doing, and repetition of actions is essential.
3. Materials are sequential, focusing on one skill at a time; the skills then become touchstones for future reference.
4. Materials are intrinsically motivating and capitalize on children's purposefulness and desire to do meaningful work.
5. The prepared environment possesses a certain order, which disposes the child to develop at his or her own speed.

Materials are grouped into three divisions. The following list shows these divisions and of-

Box 5.7 Using Blocks in a Cognitive Program

Block Shapes

Blocks of different sizes and shapes in sufficient quantities can be used to construct almost any structure children wish. Special shaped blocks such as ramps, columns, and arches greatly increase the potential complexity of block structures.

Source: Association for Childhood Education International, 11141 Georgia Ave, Suite 200, Wheaton, MD 20902; used with permission.

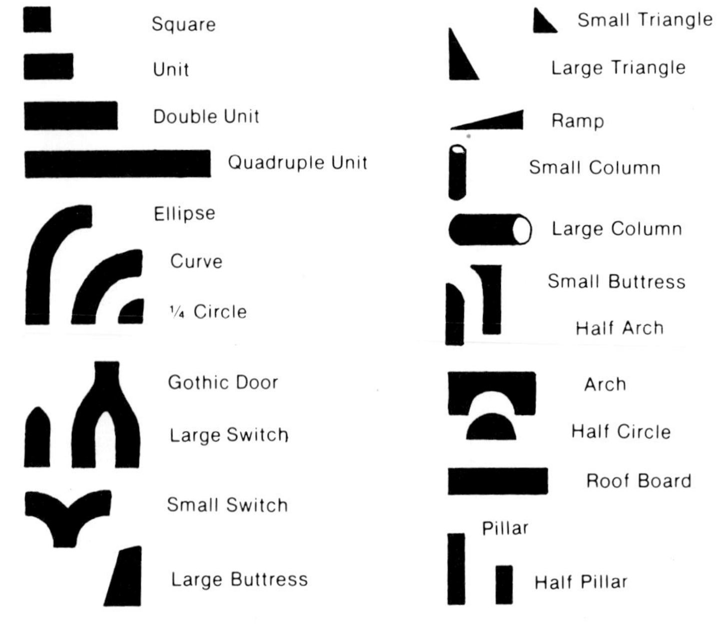

fers some examples:

1. *Practical Life Exercises* These are for the youngest children. They are based on a child's natural activities, but are structured into a regular sequence of action.

Scrubbing the table	Using dressing frames
Pouring	Polishing the mirror

2. *Sensorial Materials* These are used by all children. They help the child isolate one defining quality (for example, sound, weight, color) and understand sensorial impressions.

Brown stair	Cylinder block
Red rods	Knobless cylinder
Color chips	Baric tablets
Sound boxes	Bells
Geometric solids	Smelling jars

3. *Academic Materials* These are used at the child's moment of readiness.

Sandpaper letters	Spindle boxes
Movable alphabet	Red and blue rods
Command cards	Golden bead
Metal Insets	Bank game

Block Words

The words listed below can be learned through play. How? By using them naturally in conversations with your child as he plays with his blocks. "Which block is taller? Which one is behind you? Which block is round?"

Size Words

Big, bigger, biggest
Little, littler, littlest
Small, smaller, smallest
Short, shorter, shortest
Tall, taller, tallest
Long, longer, longest
Thin, thinner, thinnest
Fat, fatter, fattest

Shape Words

Circle
Ball
Cylinder
Round
Square, cube
Rectangle
Triangle
Pyramid

Position Words

On top of
On the bottom
Under
Behind
In the middle
Next to
In between
In front of
Left
Right
On
In
Inside
Outside

Source: P. 75 from *Learning Through Play*. Copyright © 1972, by J. Marzollo and J. Lloyd. Reprinted by permission of Harper & Row Publishers, Inc.

Contributions to Developmentally Based Programs

Montessori materials and activities can be adapted for use in programs based on all three developmental viewpoints. This is due in part to the rather eclectic mix of theories in the basic Montessori philosophy as well as the general quality and appeal of the materials themselves. We do not recommend that programs hire a trained Montessori teacher and set up a "Montessori Program" within a program. We consider that to be an inappropriate mixing of theoretical views. What we do recommend is that interested programs and staff take from the Montessori philosophy those ideas and materials that fit with their program viewpoint. Some extensions are suggested in the following list. Many more are possible by giving careful thought to the interaction of material and program teaching strategies.

1. *Maturation programs* Montessori's notion of purposeful work is compatible with the maturationist concept that play is work and serious business. Practical life exercises are very structured

versions of naturally occurring house play and water play. Maturation teachers can use the practical life exercises and procedures to guide them (not the children) in providing opportunities and role-modeling play behaviors.

2. *Behaviorist programs* The Montessori use of prescribed procedures for teacher demonstration and child use of materials fits the behaviorist emphasis on controlling the learning environment. The autotelic nature of the materials is compatible with feedback and reinforcement provisions required in behaviorist programs. However, children in Montessori programs have some choice of material and can work at their own pace. Behaviorist programs using Montessori materials would need to select materials for children and monitor pace and sequence of use to conform with overall program practices.
3. *Cognitive programs* Sensorial materials invite child involvement and manipulation. Children can "discover" the inherent sequences and relationships. Used without the Montessori-teacher demonstration, these materials are well matched to cognitive program goals. Academic materials are similarly well suited to cognitive programs.

Summary

Child care programs generally have a great number of physical objects that are used for teaching and play. Because each of these items evokes particular behaviors and requires certain teacher interaction, programs need specific criteria for choosing materials and equipment appropriate for their developmental viewpoint.

There are three parts to the process of compiling materials and equipment for a program: selection of activity content, sequencing and pacing of content, and selection of materials and equipment. Activity content is the experience and information to which children are exposed in a program. This content may be called curriculum, and in most programs it includes play. Sequencing requires that planners decide what comes first, second, and so on, and determine the program's goals. The actual physical objects selected by staff are the tools by which the curriculum is implemented. Basic equipment include the larger items, while materials usually refer to smaller items. The latter are further divided into raw materials, program-prepared materials, and commercially prepared materials.

Activities in a maturationist program are based on familiar experiences from everyday life. Behaviorist activities teach specific social and academic skills. Cognitive programs explore play with questions and redirect activity to maximize the intellectual challenges.

Sequencing is organized in maturationist programs by building spontaneous activities around broad themes. Behaviorists adhere to a strict sequence in which children's skills are initially diagnosed and then the children proceed in a learning plan from simple to complex learning experiences. Sequencing in cognitive programs follows the appropriate stages of cognitive development.

Maturationists choose materials that are unstructured, multipurpose, and apt to invite social interaction. Materials in a behaviorist program are highly structured and intended to meet curriculum needs and minimize distraction. Cognitive planners seek materials that absorb children, help them with their work, and yet are easy for children to identify.

Montessori materials or their derivatives may be used in a child care program based on any developmental viewpoint. These materials are scaled to children, self-correcting, sequential, and intrinsically motivating.

Resources

General Materials and Equipment

Case, R. (1979). Gearing the demands of instruction to the developmental capacities of the learner. *Review of Educational Research,* Winter, 59–89.

Community Playthings. (1981). *Criteria for selecting play equipment for early childhood education: A reference book.* Rifton, NY: Community Playthings.

Croft, D. J., & Hess, R. (1975). *An activities handbook for teachers of young children* (2nd ed.). Boston: Houghton Mifflin.

Dittmann, L. (Ed.). (1970). *Curriculum is what happens: Planning is the key.* Washington, DC: National Association for the Education of Young Children.

Educational Facilities Laboratory. (1972). *Found spaces and equipment for children's centers.* New York: EFL.

Educational Products Information Exchange Institute. (1972). *Early childhood education: How to select and evaluate materials* (Educational Product Report No. 42). New York: Educational Products Information Exchange Institute.

Equipment and supplies no. 9. Washington, DC: Project Head Start Series, Office of Economic Opportunity.

Kaban, B. (1979). *Choosing toys for children from birth to five.* New York: Schocken.

Mager, R. F. (1975). *Preparing instructional objectives.* Belmont, CA: Fearon.

Marzollo, J., & Lloyd, J. (1972). *Learning through play.* New York: Harper & Row.

Motor activities for preschool children. (1981). Austin, TX: National Educational Laboratory Publishers.

Neisworth, J. T., Willoughby-Herb, S. J., Bagnato, S. J., Cartwright, C. A., & Laub, K. W. (1980). *Individualized early education for handicapped children.* Germantown, MD: Aspen Systems.

Newson, J., & Newson, E. (1979). *Toys and playthings.* New York: Pantheon Books.

Quilitch, M. R., & Risley, T. R. (1973). The effects of play materials on social play. *Journal of Applied Behavior Analysis, 6,* 573–578.

Regan, E. M., & Harris, M. M. (1980). *To learn/To think.* New York: Teachers College Press.

Seefeldt, C. (Ed.). (1976). *Curriculum for the preschool-primary child: A review of the research.* Columbus, OH: Charles E. Merrill.

Sunderlin, S. (Ed.). (1968). *Equipment and supplies.* Washington, DC: Association for Childhood Education International.

Van Alstyne, D. (1976). *Play behavior and choice of preschool children* (2nd ed.). New York: Arno Press.

Weikart, D. P., Rogers, L., Adcock, C., & McClelland, D. (1971). *The Cognitively oriented curriculum: A framework for preschool teachers.* Washington, DC: National Association for the Education of Young Children.

Play Materials

Almy, M. (Ed.). (1968). *Early childhood play.* New York: Selected Academic Readings.

Arnaud, S. (1974). Some functions of play in the educative process. *Childhood Education,* 72–78.

Avedon, E., & Sutton-Smith, B. (1971). *The study of games.* New York: John Wiley.

Biber, B. (1971). The role of play. In R. R. Anderson & H. G. Shane (Eds.), *As the twig is bent.* Boston: Houghton Mifflin.

Biber, B., Shapiro, E., Urekens, D., & Gilkeson, E. (1971). *Promoting cognitive growth: A developmental interaction point of view.* Washington, DC: National Association for the Education of Young Children.

Caplan, F., & Caplan, T. (1973). *The power of play.* New York: Anchor Press.

Curry, N. E., & Arnaud, S. H. (1974). Cognitive implications in children's spontaneous role play. *Theory Into Practice Journal, 13* (4), 273–277.

Engstrom, G. (Ed.). (1971). *Play: The child strives toward self-realization.* Washington, DC: NAEYC.

Evans, M. W. (1974). Play is life itself. *Theory Into Practice, 13* (4), 267–272.

Fowler, W. (1971). On the value of both play and structure in early education. *Young Children, 27,* 24–26.

Frank, L. K. (1968). Play is valid. *Childhood Education,* March, 433–440.

Herron, R. E., & Sutton-Smith, B. (1971). *Child's play.* New York: John Wiley.

Piaget, J. (1962). *Play, dreams and imitation in childhood.* New York: Norton.

Piers, M. W. (Ed.). (1972). *Play and development.* New York: Norton.

Simpson, D. M., & Alderson, D. M. (1968). *Creative play in the infant school.* London: Pitman.

Singer, J. (1973). *The child's world of make believe.* New York: Academic Press.

Smilansky, S. (1968). *The effects of sociodramatic play on disadvantaged preschool children.* New York: John Wiley.

Sponseller, D. (Ed.). (1974). *Play as a learning medium.* Washington, DC: National Association for the Education of Young Children.

Sutton-Smith, B. (1966). Piaget on play: A critique. *Psychological Review, 173* (1), 104–110.

Sutton-Smith, B. A. (1970). A descriptive account of four modes of children's play between one and five years. Columbia University. (ERIC Document Reproduction Service No. ED 049 833)

Yawkey, T. D., & Pellegrini, A. D. (Eds.). (1984). *Child's play: Developmental and applied.* Hillsdale, NJ: Erlbaum.

Montessori Materials

Frost, J. L. (Ed.). (1968). The rediscovery of Montessori. *Early Childhood Education Rediscovered: Readings* (pp. 69–128). New York: Holt, Rinehart and Winston.

Lorton, M. B. (1972). *Workjobs.* Menlo Park, CA: Addison-Wesley.

McCarrick, Sister A. (Ed.). (1972). *Montessori matters* (rev. ed.). Cincinnati, OH: Sisters of Notre Dame deNamur.

Montessori, M. (1964). *The Montessori method.* New York: Schocken Books.

Montessori, M. (1966). *The secret of childhood.* New York: Ballantine.

Neubert, A. B. (1973). *A way of learning: A Montessori manual* (rev. ed.). Cincinnati, OH: Xavier University Press.

Orem, R. C., & Stevens, G. L. (1970). *American Montessori manual.* College Park, MD: Mafex Associates.

Standing, E. M. (1971). *The Montessori revolution in education.* New York: Schocken.

Wolf, A. D. (n.d.). *Commentary for set of forty-eight slides describing Montessori materials.* Altoona, PA: Penn-Mont Academy.

6

Evaluation

Introduction

Evaluation offers us knowledge and understanding of program effects and outcomes. It provides a systematic source of information for effective decision making. Yet few local child care programs use evaluation procedures systematically. Most programs use evaluation only when required by sponsors or to answer simple questions about children or program practices for specific reasons such as parent conferences. Some directors think evaluation is a complex technical subject that is hard to master and best avoided since results may be negative or perhaps not worth the effort.

In some sense, however, we all evaluate most of the time—even though we often do so in a haphazard manner. We form opinions, make judgments, and decide on courses of action that we think will lead to desired outcomes. We are pleased by what we think are our successes and disappointed by our apparent failures. When asked to justify why our service should continue or explain why we do things the way we do, we manage to give reasons.

Opportunities for evaluation include:

- Determining whether children are healthy enough to participate in program activities
- Measuring children's skill levels to select appropriate activities and materials
- Estimating how much help a child needs in self-care routines (dressing, feeding, washing)
- Describing a child's progress over time in the program
- Assessing the degree to which staff carry out program activities as planned
- Comparing curriculum plans with actual daily events
- Finding out how satisfied parents, community, and sponsors are with the program
- Showing how children benefit from participation in the program

Each of these situations calls for valid evaluation information specific to the local program. Another kind of evaluation consists of large-scale research studies and surveys and complex statistical treatment of data for the purpose of comparing different programs. Although we believe both kinds of evaluation are important, we will stress evaluation procedures that are useful to the local program director. The director's evaluation tasks are to identify information needs, choose appropriate information-gathering procedures, organize or collect information, interpret information, and apply findings.

The usual treatment of evaluation is filled with technical concepts taken from the fields of testing and measurement, statistics, and research design. All of these are necessary and appropriate if you want to perform large-scale evaluations for other researchers and policy-makers. If you are interested in these concepts, you will want to consult several of the excellent resources we have listed at the end of the chapter.

Our focus is on those things that a program director can do to improve the availability and quality of information about the local program and the children it serves. Our aim is to make certain evaluation techniques accessible to program directors since they often do not have extensive training in evaluation. We believe most program directors recognize the value of being well informed and are interested in implementing some basic evaluation procedures.

Evaluation should not be an afterthought, nor should it be a difficult forbidding task to be avoided at all costs. Evaluation in good program design is part of a feedback loop that provides the program director with information that is useful for improving the program. It answers the question, "How well are we doing in relation to what we want to be doing?" When evaluation is part of the design process and produces information that is related to program quality, it becomes a powerful and accessible tool for managing the program.

Evaluation has two basic components: information and judgment. Information may be numerical or qualitative, and it may come from tests or observations. To be useful for evaluation purposes, information needs to be objective and reliable. Judgments are needed at two points in the evaluation process. Initially, a program designer must decide what to evaluate. This involves specifying behaviors and goals and selecting a procedure to collect objective and reliable information about the behaviors and goals. The second judgment point concerns interpreting and using the information that is collected. The program designer draws conclusions about the information and decides on possible uses and interpretations of the findings.

At least two different kinds of evaluation are needed in local programs. One focuses on the characteristics, activities, and progress of individual *children*. The other concerns the operation and outcomes of the *program*. Specific evaluation activities will differ among maturationist, behaviorist, and cognitive programs.

1. *Assessment of Children* What happens to children in a child care program is of paramount importance to program planners, staff, and parents. Evaluation data enable judgments to be made about the impact of program experiences on children and the changes in children's behaviors that can be attributed to program efforts. Assessment data on children are useful only if the *purpose and need* for the evaluation data are related to the activities of the program. The *procedures and techniques* for assessment are selected to produce information that will enable program staff and parents to judge how the changes in child behavior are related to program goals and objectives. The planned activities and teaching behaviors that are the focal points of the morning and afternoon activity periods of the daily care pattern have specific child objectives for each of the three developmental viewpoints.
2. *Program Evaluation* Many kinds of program activities constitute program evaluation. Programs have numerous parts and consist of a great many simultaneous processes, all of which are directed toward common program goals as described in the rationale statement. It is helpful to think of program evaluation as having two overall objectives: formative evaluation and summative evaluation. The procedures used in formative and summative evaluation may be quite similar, but the purposes and uses of the information that is collected are very different. *Formative evaluation* is for fine tuning or tinkering with the program. Procedures are short term, results are immediate, and changes and revisions can be made quickly. *Summative evaluation* seeks to look at broader aspects of the program, usually over a longer period of time. Summative evaluation information is used to answer questions about the effects of the program or to make judgments about the value of the program effort.

Assessment of Children

Assessment of children is a technical term used to refer to all those things we do to learn about children's characteristics, activities, and progress toward goals. Sometimes these assessment activities are formal and involve systematic ob-

Adults who work with children need to watch for interesting behaviors and then capture them on anecdotal records for future reference. (College of Human Development, Department of Individual and Family Studies, The Pennsylvania State University; used with permission.)

servation, testing, or ratings in terms of specified criteria. Other times we rely on feelings, casual observation, or intuition. In either case, the systematic recording of information about children can substantially improve the program director's ability to plan appropriate activities and to know their results.

Purpose and Need

There are two major purposes for the assessment of children. The first is to describe children's abilities. Such descriptions are important for parent conferences in which staff are called upon to tell parents what goes on in the program and how children are doing. Program sponsors are also interested in descriptive information about children's activities. The second purpose is diagnostic. By this we mean an assessment of children on standards related to program goals. Diagnostic assessment is used for identifying children's needs and for planning program activities that match these needs. During diagnostic assessment children with special needs may be identified and referral for additional testing may be indicated.

Procedures and Techniques

For both descriptive and diagnostic purposes the key to child assessment is systematic observation—the direct observation of behaviors of interest and the recording of that observation information. Through observation of young children's behavior we can reasonably infer skill levels. Not until children are older can we directly ask and expect accurate self-reports. Formal testing (for example, multiple-choice tests or other written exercises) is not appropriate for young children. Recording observations on prepared forms serves to limit observations to only those behaviors of interest. Deciding in advance what aspects of the child's behavior are salient is a way to make observation both valid and efficient.

The general approach to systematic observation is:

1. to identify the domain of behavior of interest; for example, social interaction, skill in manipulating materials, or large motor skills;
2. to specify in advance a set of behaviors that exemplify the domain of interest and can be observed directly;

3. to prepare a format for recording information about the specific behaviors or activities; and
4. to write directions for the observer describing how and when to observe and how to use the form to record information.

The value of following this four-step approach is that it produces observational data that are replicable. In other words, the techniques can be taught to other observers who can observe the same activities and produce consistent descriptions of what happened. Thus the observations are not biased by preformed opinions and important behaviors will not go unnoticed. A program director and staff can have confidence in the results of such observation when describing a child's performance and using that information to plan for the child.

Among the many different techniques for conducting systematic observation, anecdotal records, checklists, rating scales, and structured interviews are particularly useful for early childhood programs. Each has unique characteristics, and all of them can be adapted to assessing a wide variety of behaviors.

Anecdotal Records Factual descriptions of events and happenings in the everyday lives of children. They are "word pictures." A typical anecdotal record describes behavior in context—the time and place as well as the actions and dialogue. An anecdotal record may result from observing a single child or a small group of children during a certain period of time. Observers record *all* behaviors. By having a record of all behaviors, staff gain understanding or provide explanation for a specific behavior. A collection of these anecdotal records shows patterns of behaviors. Staff may schedule anecdotal record observation to ensure that all children are observed frequently. Or they may target certain activity areas to observe. Or they may record all instances of a particular behavior for a given child.

Checklists Lists of statements describing a performance or a product. They are useful in situations where an observer wants to record whether a particular behavior was demonstrated. For each performance or product listed, the observer makes a yes-no judgment. Checklists differ from anecdotal records in that checklists contain statements of behaviors that can be anticipated (and therefore can be listed on the form), whereas anecdotal records are best used for recording spontaneous streams of behavior. Checklists are efficient to use since much of the recording has been done in advance and the observer needs only to check or tally to indicate a behavior was performed. In addition, since checklists are prepared in advance, the observer is watching for only certain behaviors and can easily limit the observation to a specific purpose.

Rating Scales Graduated measures for assessing behavior levels. These move beyond checklists and require a judgment about the quality or degree of a behavior rather than a simple yes-no decision about whether the behavior occurred. For this reason, each item is accompanied by a scale that presents qualitatively different levels of performance (for example, poor, average, good, and excellent). A typical rating scale has between three and seven rating positions, and each rating point should be clearly defined.

Structured Interviews Planned interactions with children. Interviews occur when an observer works directly with a child, presenting tasks and following a script to elicit behaviors of interest. Children's actions and responses are recorded as the interview progresses. A structured interview allows an observer to isolate a task and observe children's performance under common conditions. The tasks may not be ones that children would engage in spontaneously, or they may be behaviors for which observers want to probe additional responses.

An important consideration is the way in which the results of observations are interpreted. Some techniques, called *norm-referenced* tools, yield information that is designed to assess a child relative to norms for children of the same age. They are particularly useful in judging whether a child is making normal progress compared to other children. Others, called *criterion-referenced* tools, assess children on their progress toward goals and objectives rather than against the performance of other children. Their value is their emphasis on individual task performance.

Maturationist Program

Observers in maturationist programs are trying to obtain a picture of the whole child in terms of developmental norms. Anecdotal records, therefore, are the preferred observation tool for maturation programs. These records give staff the opportunity to include all behavior and events that seem relevant in an episode. Staff take their cues from children's activities and interests. Anecdotal records provide full "word pictures" of the individual children. The process is time consuming, but the anecdotal records serve to keep staff attentive and sensitive to nuances and subtleties of children's behavior. Staff may keep file cards or note sheets in every room to jot down events as they occur. Later, during breaks or planning periods, records may be fleshed out from these jottings.

Writing anecdotal records is an art. Through choice of words and structure of event reporting, staff can learn to convey the "feel" of a situation without introducing interpretation or judgment. One anecdotal record is never enough. Several records of similar instances are needed to begin to identify patterns of behavior and to interpret meaning. Often a collection of anecdotal records will be used to prepare a developmental report or complete a developmentally based checklist for children in a maturation program.

EXAMPLES

An anecdotal record might look like Figure 6.1.

An anecdotal record summary form is given in Figure 6.2

```
Name: Pete Brock              Date:3/18/85

Observer: C. Jones            Time:12:50 AM

Incident: Pete and Larry were swinging.
Pete was pushing Larry. Larry said,
"You're pushing too high." Pete said,
"No, you're just a scaredy-cat." Larry
started to cry and said, "Stop pushing
me." Pete said, "Scaredy-cat, scaredy-
cat." Then some other children came and
asked Pete to play ball. He went away
with them. Larry continued crying for
several minutes.
```

Figure 6.1 Anecdotal record. (From *Developing observation skills* (2nd ed.) (p. 117) by C. A. Cartwright and G. P. Cartwright, 1984, New York: McGraw-Hill; used with permission.)

Behaviorist Program

Behaviorist programs generally use checklists to assess children's skill levels. Item statements on the checklists reflect detailed task analysis of the steps in a behavior sequence. Statements are clear, direct, and very precise. Since checklists rely on systematic quantitative techniques, little observer discretion is required to perform an observation. Information obtained from observations is keyed to instructional activities, helping staff pinpoint a child's progress.

EXAMPLES

Two examples of checklists useful for behaviorist programs are given in Box 6.1.

Cognitive Program

Structured interviews are often used to assess children's problem-solving behavior. The observer utilizes materials and tasks similar to ones used in everyday lessons. Through guided questioning the observer can probe children's responses, challenge their thinking, and seek to understand the level of their cognitive functioning.

Carefully prepared checklists with statements keyed to the cognitive potential of daily activities can also be useful assessment tools. In general, child assessment for cognitive programs is complex. It requires rather sophisti-

ANECDOTAL SUMMARY RECORD

Directions: To be completed quarterly based on all anecdotal records written during that period.

OBSERVATION SUMMARY

Child's name: ______________________

Term: ______________________

Reported by: ______________________

Child's age	
School attendance	
Special considerations for health	
Coordination Large motor Small motor	
Verbal skills	
Reaction to routines Toileting Juice Rest Lunch	
Social interaction Child-child Child-teacher Child-other adult	
Interests and abilities How child uses special skills Attention span	
Emotional behavior What frustrates child Reaction to frustration Fears	
Summary	

Figure 6.2 Anecdotal record summary.

Box 6.1 Behaviorist Checklists

Record for Frequency of Behavior

Date: *from April 1 to April 5*

Name: *Tom Lipsitt*

Observer: *T. Bradley*

Description of Behavior: *Hitting—any deliberate physical contact made with the hands to another child*

Days	Tallies	Total
1	~~IIII~~ III	8
2	~~IIII~~ ~~IIII~~ II	12
3	~~IIII~~ IIII	9
4	~~IIII~~ ~~IIII~~ II	12
5	~~IIII~~ I	6

Average per day = *9.4 hitting behavior per day for the week*

Fine Motor Skills Checklist

Date: ______

Name: ______

Observer: ______

Directions: Place an X in the *Yes* column if the behavior is observed; place an X in the *No* column if the behavior is not observed.

	Yes	No
1. Touches forefingers together on first trial	____	____
2. Makes a stack of two small blocks	____	____
3. Makes a stack of four small blocks	____	____
4. Makes a stack of eight small blocks	____	____
5. Dumps object out of small container without dropping container	____	____
6. Holds pencil to make a mark on paper	____	____
7. Uses pincer grasp to pick up small object	____	____
8. Passes small object from one hand to the other without dropping object	____	____

Source: From *Developing observation skills* (2nd ed.) (pp. 68, 86) C. A. Cartwright and G. P. Cartwright, 1984, New York: McGraw-Hill; used with permission.

Box 6.2 Excerpt from the High/Scope Child Observation Record Preschool and Kindergarten

Sample

Child's Name ______________________________

Teacher's Name ______________________________

Date of Observation Period ______________________________
week/month/year

I. INTENSIVE FIVE-DAY OBSERVATION

PLANNING TIME

Item 1: Expression of Choices and Plans (Circle one)

0. Child gives *no* indication of having choices or *plans* in mind, stands around idly or follows the teacher around, not making any decisions of his own 0
1. Child *looks at or touches materials* in the room and/or moves toward an area or material. However, there is no other communication to the teacher of a plan 1
2. Child *intentionally communicates* choice to the teacher by pointing to, walking over to, or naming an area, material, or child, but the teacher *has to "recognize"* the plan....... 2
3. *With* a lot of prompting from teacher, child communicates *what* he is going to do 3
4. *Without* a lot of prompting from teacher, child communicates *how* he will carry out his plan 4
5. *With* a lot of prompting from teacher, child communicates *how* he will carry out his plan 5
6. *Without* a lot of prompting from teacher, child communicates *how* he will carry out his plan 6

Item 4: Problem-Solving with Materials (Circle one)

0. Child seems to *never or seldom perceive* problems 0
1. Child *perceives* problems, but *seldom confronts* them......................... 1
2. Child makes *one attempt* to solve a problem, but gives up if she does not succeed 2
3. Child tries to solve a problem in a *second,* different *way* if her first attempt is unsuccessful................................ 3
4. Child makes *more than two attempts* to solve a problem 4

Item 6: Diversity of Activities and Contacts (Circle all that apply)

Over the course of a week, the child:

1. incorporates a number of different *materials* in her activities....................... 1
2. works in two or more *areas* of the classroom 2
3. interacts with three or more *children*...... 3
4. accepts interactions with more than one regular classroom *staff* person 4

Source: From *Young children in action* (pp. 326–327) by M. Hohmann, B. Banet, and D. P. Weikart, 1979, Ypsilanti, MI: High/Scope Press, 600 North River St., Ypsilanti, MI 48197–2898.

cated systematic observation tools, and observer time must be invested in one-on-one interaction with the child.

EXAMPLES

Some of the questioning strategies used for teaching can be used for assessment by keeping a record of children's responses. Another type of checklist for use in cognitive programs is given in Box 6.2.

Program Evaluation

Program evaluation is the systematic gathering of information about the operations and outcomes of programs. The unit of evaluation is the program, not an individual child. As such this type of evaluation addresses questions such as whether there is a need for the program, whether the program is implemented as planned, and whether the program makes an impact on children's development. These are scary questions to ask, and to the program director struggling to keep a program operational, the answers may seem threatening. Equally, program evaluation may appear to be nonessential, and many program directors can be reluctant to take time and energies away from daily tasks.

Despite these apparent drawbacks, the information produced by program evaluations is exactly what is required to make effective management possible and to build community support for programs. The results of evaluations allow program directors to know, among other things, how much demand there is for program services, whether the program is designed appropriately to meet that demand, whether program staff are carrying out the program as designed, whether costs of program operations are excessive, and whether children benefit in any way from participation in the program. Far from being threatening, these kinds of data provide reassurance that program decisions are sound.

Program evaluations are designed for specific purposes. No two evaluations are alike. For that reason we cannot compile here a list of all possible evaluation objectives or techniques. The purpose of this section is to introduce some common terms and concepts used in program evaluations. Most program evaluations are conducted by local program personnel in collaboration with special consultants and technical experts. Program directors should be familiar with the general approaches to program evaluation so they can initiate evaluation activities and contribute to carrying them out.

All program evaluations can be divided into two general kinds, formative and summative. Formative evaluation is any systematic data gathering about the operations of an on-going program for the purpose of providing feedback to the program staff to improve the program. It is often conducted by local personnel in the spirit of "How are we doing?" and "How can we do better?" Summative evaluation is usually conducted at critical decision points for a program, such as when the program is under review for refunding by sponsors or external scrutiny of operating conditions. The purpose of summative evaluation is to obtain a measure of the overall worth of the program and the extent to which its outcomes satisfy its objectives. Summative evaluation is often conducted by people external to the program to avoid the appearance of conflict of interest. Frequently, summative evaluation involves comparison of several programs.

Within the general framework of formative and summative evaluation there are many distinct types of evaluation activity. Program directors will find the need periodically to use several of the following types of evaluation.

Management Evaluation Monitoring of program activities to ensure that they comply with regulations, follow established practices, and are managed efficiently. Assessment of staff performance is a type of management evaluation.

Cost Evaluation Assessment of program's effectiveness in terms of the outcomes per dollar spent. Cost-effectiveness techniques are often used to estimate the cost per child served. These techniques are useful in identifying whether the program as a whole or some aspects of it cost more than they are worth and provide a basis for directors to make programs more cost efficient.

Impact Evaluation Form of summative evaluation measuring changes in children that could be attributed to program participation. To be valid, impact evaluations usually require large samples, control groups, and sophisticated data analysis strategies. Outside funding and technical consultants are also necessary. A local program may be one of several programs included in an impact evaluation.

Needs Assessment Gathering of information about the demand for program services. It may include estimation of the number of children needing care, pattern of days and hours for which care is needed, and any special conditions required for care. Needs assessment is usually required in applications for grants to fund special projects. Decisions about program start-up and operating parameters are often made based on needs assessment findings.

Program Analysis Assessment of the extent to which programs are carried out as designed. For most local programs this is the heart of program evaluation. It is a formative evaluation activity that is well within the capabilities of local personnel and one that has the potential to provide valuable information regarding daily operation. It typically involves careful observation of staff behavior, analyses of curriculum activities, and assessment of the appropriateness of materials and equipment. The result of program analysis is the identification of aspects of program operation that may be discrepant from the intentions of overall program design. Feedback to the program director allows intervention through staff training and supervision to fine-tune activities to match program goals.

The basic tools of program evaluation apply to any program. Regardless of developmental viewpoint, the fundamental questions of program evaluation remain the same: What needs does the program serve? How well is the program implemented? How efficient is the program? And, what are its effects?

Evaluation is an important part of managing programs. General strategies are not difficult to learn. Nevertheless, the subject is complex enough to require fuller treatment than we can give here. We urge you to seek out specialized study in evaluation and to familiarize yourself with the excellent resources listed at the end of this chapter.

Summary

Evaluation offers child care programs a way to judge how well they are doing. Generally, evaluations have two components: information, which may be numerical or qualitative, and judgment which involves first deciding what to evaluate and then determining how to interpret and use the collected information. The two broad categories of evaluation are assessment of children and program evaluation.

The first category evaluates the behavior and progress of children in a child care program. These assessments are done to describe children's abilities to parents and sponsors and to diagnose children's needs so that future activities may be planned. Techniques for child assessment include: anecdotal records, checklists, rating scales, and structured interviews. Techniques assessing children against age-related norms are called norm-referenced; those tools assessing children's progress toward certain goals are called criterion-referenced.

Maturationist staff use anecdotal records for assessment because they want to capture as large and whole a picture of the children as possible. Observers in behaviorist programs complete assessments by filling out quantitative, precisely written checklists, which are keyed to instructional activities. To evaluate children, cognitive teachers conduct structured interviews in which they can probe children's responses and discover their level of cognitive thinking.

Program evaluation looks at the whole program, judging whether the program is working as planned and whether it is contributing to children's development. The two general kinds of program evaluation are formative and summative. Formative evaluation is collection of data about ongoing operations for the sake of immediate feedback. Summative evaluation, which is often conducted by external observers, measures a program's overall worth over a period of time. Within these general kinds, the distinctive types of evaluation include: management evaluation, cost evaluation, impact evaluation, needs assessment, and program analysis.

References

General

Almy, M., & Genishi, C. (1979). *Ways of studying children: An observation manual for early childhood teachers.* New York: Teachers College Press.

Anderson, S. B., & Ball, S. (Eds.). (1978). *The profession and practice of program evaluation.* San Francisco: Jossey-Bass.

Berk, L. E. (1976). How well do classroom practices reflect teacher goals? *Young children, 32* (1), 64–81.

Borich, G. D. (Ed.). (1974). *Evaluating educational programs and products.* Englewood Cliffs, NJ: Educational Technology Publications.

Borich, G. D. (Ed.). (1977). *The appraisal of teaching.* Reading, MA: Addison-Wesley.

Cahn, M. (1981). Evaluation. *Child Care Information Exchange, 2,* 17–24.

Cartwright, C. A., & Cartwright, G. P. (1984). *Developing observation skills* (2nd ed.). New York: McGraw-Hill.

Cazden, C. B. (1971). Evaluation of learning in preschool education: Early language development. In B. S. Bloom, J. T. Hastings, & G. F. Madaus (Eds.), *Handbook on formative and summative evaluation of student learning.* New York: McGraw-Hill.

Clarke-Stewart, K. A. (1981). Observation and experiment: Complementary strategies for studying day care and social development. In S. Kilmer (Ed.), *Advances in early education and day care, Vol. 2.* Greenwich, CT: JAI Press.

Cohen, D. H., & Stern, V. (1978). *Observing and recording the behavior of young children* (2nd ed.). New York: Teachers College Press.

Dunst, C. J. (Ed.). (1983). *Infant and preschool assessment instruments.* Baltimore: University Park Press.

Educational Products Information Exchange Institute. (1972). *Early childhood education: How to select and evaluate materials* (No. 42). New York: Author.

Evans, E. D. (1974). Measurement practices in early childhood education. In R. W. Colvin & E. M. Zaffiro (Eds.), *Preschool education.* New York: Springer Publishing.

Goodwin, W. L. (1974). Evaluation in early childhood education. In R. W. Colvin & E. M. Zaffiro (Eds.), *Preschool education.* New York: Springer Publishing.

Goodwin, W. L., & Driscoll, L. A. (1980). *Handbook for measurement and evaluation in early childhood education.* San Francisco: Jossey-Bass.

Gronlund, N. E. (1976). *Measurement and evaluation in teaching* (3rd ed.). New York: MacMillan.

Hambleton, R. K., Swaminathan, H., & Cook, L. (1982). *Evaluation methods in early childhood program personnel.* Boston: Allyn and Bacon.

Horowitz, F. D., & Paden, L. Y. (1973). The effectiveness of environmental intervention programs. In B. M. Caldwell & H. N. Ricciuti (Eds.), *Child development and social policy. Review of child development research: Vol. 3.* Chicago: University of Chicago Press.

Irwin, D. M., & Bushnell, M. M. (1980). *Observational strategies in child study.* New York: Holt.

Kamii, C. (1971). Evaluation of learning in preschool education: Socio-emotional perceptual motors, cognitive development. In B. S. Bloom, J. T. Hastings, & G. F. Madaus (Eds.), *Handbook on formative and summative evaluation of student learning.* New York: McGraw-Hill.

Loveland, E. H. (Ed.). (1980). *New directions for program evaluation: Measuring the hard-to-measure.* San Francisco: Jossey-Bass.

Mattick, I., & Perkins, F. J. (1973). *Guidelines in observation and assessment: An approach to evaluating the learning environment of a day care center* (2nd ed.). Washington, DC: Day Care and Child Development Council of America.

Medinnus, G. R. (1976). *Child study and observation guide.* New York: Wiley.

Messick, S., & Barrowes, T. S. (1972). Strategies for research and evaluation in early childhood education. In I. J. Gordon (Ed.), *Early childhood education.* Seventy-first yearbook of the National Society for the Study of Education. Chicago: University of Chicago Press.

Miller, L., & Dyer, J. L. (1975). Four preschool programs: Their dimensions and effects. *Monograph of the Society for Research in Child Development, 40* (5–6, Serial No. 162).

Montes, F., & Risley, R. (1975). Evaluating traditional day care practices: An empirical approach. *Child Care Quality, 4,* 208–215.

Palmer, F. H., Cazden, C., & Glick, J. (1971). Evaluations of day care centers: Summative and formative. In E. J. Grotberg (Ed.), *Day care: Resources for decisions.* Washington, DC: Office of Economic Opportunity.

Popham, W. J. (Ed.). (1974). *Evaluation in education.* Berkeley, CA: McCutchan.

Shelly, M., & Charlesworth. R. (1980). An expanded role for evaluation in improving the quality of educational programs for young children. In S. Kilmer (Ed.), *Advances in early education and day care: Vol. 1.* Greenwich, CT: JAI Press.

Takanishi, R. (1979). Evaluation of early childhood programs: Toward a developmental perspective. In L. G. Katz (Ed.), *Current topics in early childhood education: Vol. II.* Norwood, NJ: Ablex.

Travers, J. R., & Light, R. J. (Eds.). (1982). *Learning from experience: Evaluating early childhood demonstration programs.* Washington, DC: National Academy Press.

Weinberg, R. A., & Moore, S. (Eds.). (1975). *Evaluation of educational programs for young children.* Washington, DC: Child Development Associate Consortium.

Weiss, C. H. (1972). *Evaluation research: Methods of assessing program effectiveness.* Englewood Cliffs, NJ: Prentice-Hall.

Zimiles, H. (1977). A radical and regressive solution to the problem of evaluation. In L. G. Katz (Ed.), *Current topics in early childhood education: Vol. I* (pp. 63–70). Norwood, NJ: Ablex Publishing.

Observation Instruments and Guides

Boehm, A. E., & Weinberg, R. A. (1977). *The classroom observer: A guide for developing observation skills.* New York: Teachers College Press.

Boyer, E. G., Simon, A., & Karafin, G. (1973). *Measures of maturation: An anthology of early childhood observation instruments: Vols. I–III.* Philadelphia: Research for Better Schools.

Buros, O. K. (Ed.). (1974). *Tests in print II.* Highland Park, NJ: Gryphon Press.

Evaluating children's progress: A rating scale for children in day care. (1973). Atlanta: Southeastern Day Care Project.

Garwood, S. G. (1982). (Mis)use of developmental scales in program evaluation. *Topics in early childhood special education, 1* (4), 61–69.

Gordon, I. J., & Jester, R. E. (1973). Techniques of observing teaching in early childhood and outcomes of particular procedures. In R. M. W. Travers (Ed.), *Second handbook of research on teaching.* Chicago: Rand McNally.

A guide for teacher recording in day care agencies. (1965). New York: Child Welfare League of America.

Harms, T., & Clifford, R. M. (1980). *Early childhood environment rating scale.* New York: Teachers College Press.

Head Start Test Collection. (continuously updated). Princeton, NJ: Educational Testing Service.

Hoepfner, R., Stern, C., & Nummedal, S. G. (Eds.). (1971). *CSE-ECRE preschool/kindergarden test evaluations.* Los Angeles: Center for the Study of Evaluation, UCLA.

Johnson, O. G., & Benmarito, J. W. (1973). *Tests and measurements in child development: A handbook.* San Francisco: Jossey-Bass.

Medley, D. M. (1983). Systematic observation. In H. E. Mitzel (Ed.), *Encyclopedia of educational research* (5th ed.). Chicago: Rand McNally.

Stallings, J. A. (1977). *Learning to look: A handbook on classroom observation and teaching models.* Belmont, CA: Wadsworth.

Walker, D. K. (1973). *Socio-emotional measures in preschool and kindergarten children.* San Francisco: Jossey-Bass.

Wodrich, D. L. (1984). *Children's psychological testing: A guide for nonpsychologists.* Baltimore: Paul Brookes Publishing.

Summary Supplement: A Comprehensive Program Plan

In the last five chapters we have presented a systematic approach to thinking about the design of child care programs. In Chapter 2 we constructed a daily care pattern and discussed the eight activity blocks that comprise the basic structure of all programs: arrival, breakfast, morning activity, snack, lunch, rest, afternoon activity, and departure. Every child care program, regardless of clientele, location, sponsor, or purpose, can be reduced to some combination of these eight activity blocks. The three developmental viewpoints are maturationist, behaviorist, and cognitive. Each offers an appropriate foundation for program design when it is conceptually consistent, linking philosophy to theory to practice. We advocate the choice of a single developmental viewpoint as the basis for program design. Local programs need to identify idiosyncratic features of their situation that will impact the program. Programs should also develop a program rationale setting forth the local program's understanding and adaptation of specific developmental principles and local conditions as they blend to form the basis for all subsequent program design and planning.

Chapters 3, 4, 5, and 6 have described the major components of program operation from each of the three developmental viewpoints. With this background one can design a program with the essential, compatible components and an integrity of focus based on a single developmental viewpoint.

A *comprehensive program plan* is the application of these design concepts to the systematic planning of a local program. It is the best means to sustain integrity of developmental viewpoint on a daily basis. The written plan serves three purposes for daily program implementation:

1. *Vision* The program plan records the synthesis of philosophical planning efforts that director and staff have accepted as the basis for the design of the local program. The program plan is the collective, official vision of what the program can and ought to be.
2. *Balance* Through discussion and dialogue general program procedures for staffing, environmental design, materials and equipment, and evaluation are devised. Every local program is a special case requiring compromises and adjustments between theoretical viewpoint and practice. The written plan documents the range and depth of the match between program practice and theory and is a record of acceptable balances.
3. *Standard* The local program plan becomes a standard, or a set of criteria against which intent, quality, and completeness of daily practices can be judged. Evaluation completes the circle in the process of program design, giving summative evaluation information about success as well as formative evaluation information useful for fine-tuning and adjustment. Using the basic framework for program design, described in Chapter 2, local program planners can design, implement, and evaluate child care programs that mold theory and practice to local circumstance and need.

Box S.1 lays out a step-by-step procedure for

Box S.1 Writing a Comprehensive Program Plan

Step One: Construct a Daily Care Pattern

A. Consider the contributing factors for basic care and developmental curriculum opportunities.
B. Adjust the sequence and timing of the daily care pattern to reflect contributing factors.
C. Retain contributing factor lists from Chapter 1 for further use.

Step Two: Identify the Program Designer

A. Designate a person to coordinate, design, and implement the program.
B. Consider the responsibilities of the person in charge of program implementation (probably the director).
C. Consider the personal viewpoints of this person and significant others.
D. Give that person sufficient time, resources, and support to perform the job.

Step Three: Choose a Program Viewpoint

A. Review options.
   1. Survey local situations and biases—parents, staff, funding agency, and operational concerns.
   2. Refer to updated contributing factor lists from Step 1.

B. Assess personal position.
   1. Rate the three developmental viewpoints according to:
      1 compatible, feels comfortable
      2 potentially O.K., not sure
      3 not appealing, actively dislike
      Discard any viewpoints rated 3.
   2. For viewpoints rated 1
      a. Reread that section of Chapter 2.
      b. Obtain and review one or more recommended follow-up references for that viewpoint.
      c. Consider whether you can serve as an information resource and trainer for this viewpoint.
      d. Repeat steps 2a–c for other viewpoints rated 1, or 2 if answer to 2c is not clear-cut.
      e. Select a single perspective.
   3. Generate a statement of program rationale and include:
      Statement of beliefs about the nature and course of development
      Developmental goals and objectives
      Role of the child and explanation for change
   4. Circulate your program rationale. Solicit comment and feedback. Assess the response. If favorable, proceed. If not favorable, review your work. Does the problem lie with your choice of theoretical foundation? Be prepared to resign as program designer or director if you must change strongly held personal views in order to function within the local situation. Work diligently to articulate your views and establish your program leadership in favorable situations.

Step Four: Specify Program Practices

A. Use the statement of program rationale from step 3 for the first section of the program plan.
B. Specify Staffing Component

   Caregiving Behaviors
   1. Write procedures and/or guidelines for routines and transitions.
   2. Identify common caregiving behaviors; list and write guidelines for staff.

   Teacher Role
   3. Identify and list teacher tasks.
   4. Describe general teaching strategies.
   5. Develop examples of teaching situations.

   Interaction Technique and Style
   6. Identify personal qualities desired in staff.
   7. Describe the relationship program expects children to build with staff.

C. Specify Environmental Design

   Setup of Facility
   8. Using an activity and capacity plot, prepare a set of blueprints of the physical setup of the facility (see text for complete description).

   Management of Groups and Individuals
   9. Use the time schedule to prepare a grouping pattern chart for enrolled children.
   10. Prepare a set of guidelines for discipline. Include examples for individual and group.

Cover preventive measures, supervisory procedures, and handling of unacceptable behavior.

Time Schedule for Activity Blocks

11. Prepare a local program version of the basic care pattern. Make this time schedule in two forms: (1) a general activity block version and (2) a specific, detailed version.

D. Specify Materials and Equipment

Selection of Activity Content

12. Select the activities, topics, and/or experiences that will be emphasized in the program.
13. Prepare a master outline of activity content.
14. Write objectives for each major outline point. Objectives should be written in language appropriate for the program's developmental viewpoint.

Sequencing and Pacing of Content

15. Select and use guidelines to sequence objectives.
16. Prepare samples of daily, weekly, monthly, and year-long activity content and objective sequencing.

Selection of Materials and Equipment

17. Describe general criteria for selection of materials and equipment.
18. Prepare a master inventory of current collection of items.
19. Categorize items in the master inventory by objectives prepared in D-14.
20. Identify additional items needed. Prioritize within objectives. Note which can be locally made and which must be purchased.
21. Use these prioritized lists as a guide when purchasing materials and equipment.
22. Inventory and update quarterly.

E. Evaluation

Assessment of Children

23. Work from program objectives to identify types of information needed to assess children's progress.
24. Select or devise procedures and instruments to collect desired child assessment information.
25. Schedule assessment procedures. Assign responsibility and set up necessary records.
26. Plan periodic review and dissemination procedures. These may be staff sessions, parent conferences, consultations, and so on.

Program Evaluation

27. Formative
    a. Review specific sections of the plan periodically. Try to rotate these minireviews so all major program components are reviewed at least twice during the year. Use consultants, in-service sessions, and any other techniques that seem appropriate. Keep notes. Make adjustments in practice or plan as seems necessary at the moment.
    b. Organize a yearly concept review of the theoretical foundations of the program and the details of implementation in the program plan. Revise the plan as needed.
28. Summative
    a. Assess the average daily match between program plan and practice. Identify points of similarity and discrepancy with the plan standard.
    b. Interview parents and staff and any other stakeholders. Summarize comments.
    c. Summarize results of child assessment information. Relate to overall program goals.
    d. Prepare a yearly "state-of-the-program" report. Note areas of strength and points that are weak. Make recommendations for areas of effort for the next year.

devising a comprehensive program plan. It puts into practice all the design elements presented in the previous chapters. You can use this procedure to think, dream, and plan a new program. Or, you can analyze and describe a program that is already operational, which is a good exercise in formative evaluation!

The resources included here supplement the more specific, topical resources in the preceding chapters. You will find excellent general programming resources for each of the developmental viewpoints.

Resources

General Programming

Abbott, M. S., Galina, B. M., Granger, R. C., & Klein, B. L. (1981). *Alternative approaches to educating young children.* Atlanta: Humanics Limited.

Auerbach, S. (Ed.). (1978). *Creative homes and centers: Vol. III.* New York: Human Sciences Press.

Blueprints: Building educational programs for people who care for children. (1980). St. Paul, MN: Toys 'n Things Press.

Cherry, C., Harkness, B., Kuzma, K. (1973). *Nursery school management guide.* Belmont, CA: Lear Siegler.

Click, P. (1981). *Administration of schools for young children* (2nd ed.). Albany, NY: Delmar.

Decker, C. A., & Decker, J. R. (1980). *Planning and administering early childhood programs* (2nd ed.). Columbus, OH: Charles E. Merritt.

Evans, E. B., Shub, B., & Weinstein, M. (1971). *Day care: How to plan, develop and operate a day care center.* Boston: Beacon Press.

Hess, R. D., & Croft, D. J. (1975). *Teachers of young children* (2nd ed.). Boston: Houghton Mifflin.

Schickedanz, J. A., York, M. E., Stewart, I. S., & White, D. A. (1983). *Strategies for teaching young children* (2nd ed.). Englewood Cliffs, NJ: Prentice-Hall.

Spodek, B. (1972). *Teaching in the early years.* Englewood Cliffs, NJ: Prentice-Hall.

Sprung, B. (Ed.). (1978). *Perspectives in non-sexist early childhood education.* New York: Teachers College Press.

Maturationist Programming

Althouse, R. (1981). *The young child: Learning with understanding.* New York: Teachers College Press.

Armington, D. (1968). *A plan for continuing growth.* Newton, MA: Educational Development Center.

Ashton-Warner, S. (1963). *Teacher.* New York: Bantam.

Association for Childhood Education International. (1969). *Nursery school portfolio.* Washington, DC: Association for Childhood Education International.

Bettelheim, B. (1969). Psychoanalysis and education. *School Review, 77,* 73–86.

Biber, B. (1964). Preschool education. In R. Ulick (Ed.), *Education and the idea of mankind.* New York: Harcourt, Brace.

Biber, B. (1969). The challenges ahead for early childhood education. *Young Children, 24* (4), 196–207.

Biber, B. (1970). Goals and methods in a preschool program for disadvantaged children. *Children, 17,* 15–20.

Biber, B., Shapiro, E., & Wickens, D. (1971). *Promoting cognitive growth: A developmental-interaction point of view.* Washington, DC: National Association for the Education of Young Children.

Butler, A. L., Gotts, E. E., & Quisenberry, N. L. (1975). *Early childhood programs: Developmental objectives and their use.* Columbus, OH: Charles E. Merrill.

Caplan, F., & Caplan, T. (1973). *The power of play.* New York: Anchor Press/Doubleday.

Davis, D., Davis, M., Hansen, H., & Hansen, R. (1973). *The playway handbook: Playway method for early childhood education.* Minneapolis: Winston Press.

Dittmann, L. L. (Ed.). (1977). *Curriculum is what happens: Planning is the key* (rev. ed.). Washington, DC: National Association for the Education of Young Children.

Engstrom, G. (Ed.). (1971). *The significance of the young child's motor development.* Washington, DC: National Association for the Education of Young Children.

Featherstone, J. (1971). *Schools where children learn.* New York: Liveright.

Henderson, R. W. (1971). *Mindlessness in and about the open classroom.* Tucson: University of Arizona. (ERIC Document Reproduction Service No. ED 058 955)

Hendrick, J. (1984). *The whole child: Early education for the eighties* (3rd ed.). St. Louis: C. V. Mosby.

Hill, D. M. (1977). *Mud, sand, and water.* Washington, DC: National Association for the Education of Young Children.

Hirsh, E. (Ed.). (1974). *The block book.* Washington, DC: National Association for the Education of Young Children.

Isenberg, J. P., & Jacobs, J. E. (1982). *Playthings as learning tools.* New York: John Wiley.

Leeper, S. H., Dales, R. J., Skipper, D. S., & Witherspoon, R. L. (1974). *Good schools for young children* (3rd ed.). New York: Macmillan.

McDonald, D. T. (1979). *Music in our lives: The early years.* Washington, DC: National Association for the Education of Young Children.

Moore, S. G., & Kilmer, S. (1973). *Contemporary preschool education: A Program for young children.* New York: Wiley.

Pitcher, E. G., & Ames, L. B. (1975). *The guidance nursery school* (rev. ed.). New York: Harper & Row.

Rathbone, C. H. (Ed.). (1971). *Open education: The informal classroom.* New York: Citation Press.

Read, K. (1976). *The nursery school: A human relationships laboratory* (6th ed.). Philadelphia: W. B. Saunders.

Rudolph, M., & Cohen, D. (1964). *Kindergarten: A year of learning.* New York: Appleton-Century-Crofts.

Segal, M., & Adcock, D. (1981). *Just pretending: Ways to help children grow through imaginative play.* Englewood Cliffs, NJ: Prentice-Hall.

Silberman, C. E. (Ed.). (1973). *The open classroom reader.* New York: Random House.

Singer, D. G., & Singer, J. L. (1985). *Make believe: Games and activities to foster imaginative play in young children.* Oakland, NJ: Scott-Foresman.

Stant, M. A. (1972). *The young child: His activities and materials.* Englewood Cliffs, NJ: Prentice-Hall.

Stone, J. G. (1978). *A guide to discipline* (rev. ed.). Washington, DC: National Association for the Education of Young Children.

Taylor, J. (1971). *Organizing the open classroom: A teacher's guide to the integrated day.* New York: Schocken.

Todd, V. E., & Heffernan, H. (1977). *The years before school: Guiding preschool children* (3rd ed.). New York: Macmillan.

Warren, R. M. (1977). *Caring: Supporting children's growth.* Washington, DC: National Association for the Education of Young Children.

Weber, L. (1971). *The English infant school and informal education.* Englewood Cliffs, NJ: Prentice-Hall.

Yawkey, T. D., & Jones, K. C. (1982). *Caring: Activities to teach the young child to care for others.* Englewood Cliffs, NJ: Prentice-Hall.

Behaviorist Programming

Anderson, V., & Bereiter, C. (1972). Extending direct instruction to conceptual skills. In R. K. Parker (Ed.), *The preschool in action: Exploring early childhood programs.* Boston: Allyn & Bacon.

Baer, D. M., & Wolf, M. M. (1966). The reinforcement contingency in preschool and remedial education. In R. D. Hess & R. M. Baer (Eds.), *Early education: Current theory, research, and practice.* Chicago: Aldine.

Becker, W., Engelmann, S., & Thomas, D. R. (1971). *Teaching: A course in applied psychology.* Chicago: Science Research Associates.

Bereiter, C., & Engelmann, S. (1973). Observations on the use of direct instruction with young children. In B. Spodek (Ed.), *Early childhood education.* Englewood Cliffs, NJ: Prentice-Hall.

Bereiter, C. E., & Engelmann, S. (1966). *Teaching disadvantaged children in the preschool.* Englewood Cliffs, NJ: Prentice-Hall.

Bijou, S. W. (1977). Behavior analysis applied to early childhood education. In B. Spodek & H. J. Walberg (Eds.), *Early childhood education.* Berkeley: McCutchan.

Bradfield, R. (Ed.). (1970). *Behavior modification: The human effort.* Palo Alto, CA: Science and Behavior Books.

Bushell, D., Jr. (1973). The behavior analysis classroom. In B. Spodek (Ed.), *Early childhood education.* Englewood Cliffs, NJ: Prentice-Hall.

Cohen, M. A., & Gross, P. J. (1979). *The developmental resource: Behavioral sequences for assessment and program planning: Vols. 1 & 2.* New York: Grune & Stratton.

Engelmann, S. (1969). *Preventing failure in the primary grades.* Chicago: Science Research.

Essa, E. L. (1978). The preschool: Setting for applied behavior analysis research. *Review of educational research, 48* (4), 537–575.

Gewirtz, J. L. (1968). On designing the function environment of the child to facilitate behavioral development. In L. L. Dittmann (Ed.), *Early child care.* New York: Atherton Press.

Gewirtz, J. L. (1971). Stimulation, learning, and motivation principles for day care programs. In E. H. Grotberg (Ed.), *Day care: Resources for decisions* (pp. 173–226). Washington, DC: Office of Economic Opportunity.

Irwin, D. M., & Bushnell, M. M. (1980). *Observational strategies for child study.* New York: Holt, Rinehart & Winston.

Hom, H. L., & Hom, S. L. (1980). Research and the child: The use of modeling, reinforcement/incentives, and punishment. In D. G. Range, J. R. Layton, & D. L. Roubinek (Eds.), *Aspects of early childhood education: Theory to research to practice.* New York: Academic Press.

Homme, L., Csanyi, A. P., Gonzales, M. A., & Rechs, J. R. (1970). *How to use contingency contracting in the classroom* (rev. ed.). Champaign, IL: Research Press.

Kaplan, P., Kohfeldt, T., & Sturla, K. (1974). *It's positively fun! Techniques for managing learning environments.* Denver: Love Publishing.

Madsen, C. M., & Madsen, C. K. (1974). *Teaching/discipline: Toward a positive approach.* Boston: Allyn & Bacon.

Montes, F., & Risley, T. R. (1975). Evaluating traditional day care practices: An empirical approach. *Child Care Quarterly, 4* (5), 208–215.

Moore, O., & Anderson, A. (1969). Some principles for the design of clarifying educational environments. In D. Goslin (Ed.), *Handbook in socialization theory and research.* Skokie, IL: Rand McNally.

Nimnicht, G., McAfee, O., & Meir, J. (1969). *The new nursery school.* Morristown, NJ: General Learning Corporation.

Patterson, G. R., & Gullion, M. E. (1971). *Living with children* (rev. ed.). Champaign, IL: Research Press.

Resnick, L. B. (1967). *Design of an early learning curriculum.* Pittsburgh: University of Pittsburgh, Learning Research and Development Center. (ERIC Document Reproduction Service No ED 018 393)

Resnick, L. (1981). Instructional psychology. In M. R. Rosenzweig & L. W. Porter (Eds.), *Annual review of psychology.* Palo Alto: Annual Reviews.

Sherman, J. A., & Bushell, D. Jr. (1975). Behavior modification as an educational technique. In F. D. Horowitz (Ed.), *Review of child development research: Vol. 4.* Chicago: University of Chicago Press.

Thoreson, C. E. (Ed.). (1973). *Behavior modification in education.* The seventy-second yearbook of the National Society for the Study of Education, Part 1. Chicago: University of Chicago Press.

Cognitive Programming

Athey, I. J., & Rubadeau, D. O. (Eds.). (1970). *Educational implications of Piaget's theory.* Waltham, MA: Xerox College Publishing.

Bereiter, C. (1970). Educational implications of Kohlberg's cognitive-developmental view. *Interchange, 1,* 25–32.

Blank, M. (1972). The treatment of personality variables in a preschool cognitive program. In J. C. Stanley (Ed.), *Preschool programs for the disadvantaged: Five experimental approaches to early childhood education.* Baltimore: Johns Hopkins University Press.

Bruner, J. S. (1966). *Toward a theory of instruction.* Cambridge, MA: Harvard University Press.

Cahoon, O. W. (1974). *A teacher's guide to cognitive tasks for preschool.* Provo, UT: Brigham Young University Press.

Charles, C. M. (1974). *Teacher's petit Piaget.* Belmont, CA: Fearon.

Christenberry, M. A. (1984). *Can Piaget cook?* Atlanta: Humanics.

Duckworth, E. (1972). The having of wonderful ideas. *Harvard Educational Review, 42,* 217–231.

Forman, G. E., & Hill, F. (1980). *Constructive play: Applying Piaget in the preschool.* Monterey, CA: Brooks/Cole.

Hawkins, F. P. (1969). *The logic of action: From a teacher's notebook.* Boulder: Mountain View Center for Environmental Education, University of Colorado.

Hohman, M., Banet, B., & Weikart, D. P. (1979). *Young children in action: A manual for preschool educators.* Ypsilanti, MI: High/Scope Press.

Kagan, J. (1971). Cognitive development and programs for day care. In E. H. Grotberg (Ed.), *Day care: Resources for decisions* (pp. 135–152). Washington, DC: Office of Economic Opportunity.

Kamii, C. K., & DeClark, G. (1985). *Young children reinvent arithmetic: Implications of Piaget's theory.* New York: Teachers College Press.

Kamii, C., & DeVries, R. (1976). *Piaget, children and number.* Washington, DC: National Association for the Education of Young Children.

Lavatelli, C. S. (1970). *Piaget's theory applied to an early childhood curriculum.* Boston: American Science and Engineering.

Parker, R. K. (1974). Theory in educational curricula. In R. W. Colvin & E. M. Zaffiro (Eds.), *Preschool education.* New York: Springer.

Schwebel, M., & Raph, J. (Eds.). (1973). *Piaget in the classroom.* New York: Basic Books.

Weikart, D. P., Rogers, L., Adcock, C., & McClelland, D. (1971). *The cognitively oriented curriculum.* Washington, DC: National Association for the Education of Young Children.

Part III

Understanding Types of Programs

7

Infant Care

Introduction

Infant care is an unsettled and to many an unsettling subject. The image of a close mother-child pair is a cherished, popular cultural norm. Mothers who work and obtain child care for their infants go against the norm. The area of infant care also raises very complex societal and programmatic issues. So far, neither practice nor research findings have alleviated concerns about child care for infants.

The very young children who attend organized, formal infant care programs typically receive meticulously planned and executed caregiving programs. The vast majority of infants with working mothers are *not* in these model or center-based programs and are *not* in licensed family day care homes but are cared for through informal arrangements. Professionals, laypersons, public agencies, and legislators all debate whether infant care should be provided at all, what kind of care should be provided, who should pay for the care, and who should be given priority to receive services.

Demonstration projects in infant care, changes in social consciousness, and greater demand in infant care have contributed to the trend toward increasing provisions for infant care programs. The issue of whether to provide infant care at all is not decided. This chapter is both practical and analytical. We'll begin by defining infant care, describing the settings and purposes of programs. Since full-time workers in the field do not often have time to explore current research, we offer an overview of themes in recent infant developmental research. The section on implementing programs outlines the characteristics of an infant caregiver, ideas for daily activities, concerns of staff-child ratios, and the need for health and safety planning. Finally, we'll identify several controversial issues of infant care.

Characteristics of Infant Care

Infant care programs are similar to other forms of child care occurring in center and home settings. Yet the age of the children involved makes infant care a special kind of child care. The developmental needs of infants are perceived as requiring substantially different and perhaps more careful program practices. Child care, by definition, is substitute care for part of the day. The value of a strong infant-mother bond is celebrated in song and supported by research data. Concern for the effects of disruptions and substitutions (however handled) of this infant-mother bond underpins all programming practices in infant care programs.

Age of Children Served

The term *infant care* is used to refer to care provided for children between the ages of birth and three years. More familiar labels for children during this period are infants and toddlers: *Infant* generally refers to children from birth to age one, and *toddler* describes children age one to three. Children at the lower end of the age range, birth to six months, are not as frequently seen in group care programs as children at the upper range of two to three years.

Children from birth to six months are often cared for by their biological mothers for a number of reasons: maternity leaves that provide the mother with time after the birth of the child; pediatricians' recommendations concerning when to return to work; feeding practices that support weaning from breast to bottle around six months; and to an extent the personal desires of mother to remain with the child during the early months when schedules and rhythms are gradually firming up. In some locations regulations prohibit providing service for children below the age of six months. "It is for this youngest group that day care opens up new possibilities of early stimulation. It is for this youngest group that there is concern about the possible negative effects of separation from the mother or exposure to infection." (White, Day, Freeman, Hantman, & Messenger, 1973, p. 202) However, very young infants are found in some programs.

Older infants and young toddlers (children six months to a year and a half) participate on a regular basis in a number of different kinds of infant care programs. Children in this age range are increasingly independent, mobile, talkative, and competent in handling their world. Concern seems to be less intense that daily, temporary disruption of the infant-mother bond for children in this age range will have critical consequences for later development. However, older infant and young toddler care programs are still subject to stringent regulation or prohibitive statutes designed to carefully control and monitor services provided.

Toddlers are probably the most numerous participants in infant care programs. Three years of age has long been the accepted age for entering nursery school or regular child care. Many areas allow children to enter such programs in the latter half of their second year, effectively lowering the age of entrance to around two years, nine months. Children in this age range are generally the least controversial group for service. In the public's mind toddlers are not that different from three-year-olds; to professionals, while the differences between toddler and preschooler are great, the general developmental needs are equally critical.

The Issue of Separation

Concern regarding the appropriateness of child care for children from birth to age three is not evenly distributed across the age range. Programs for young infants are more likely to draw criticism and face constraints than programs serving three-year-olds. When someone asks, "Is it okay for babies to be in child care?" they are asking about separation, not safety. Separation is a constant factor in child care experiences for children. Each child is separated from family and home in order to come to the program and then separated from caregivers, friends, and program when returning home. Learning to cope with repeated temporary separations is an integral part of child care demands on the child.

When considering separation, we are haunted by images of deprivation—the listless, pathetic look of institutionalized children that suggests lack of interest in and connectedness to objects and people in their environment. This kind of deprivation results from extreme separation and unattachment to the world. Without some special relationship young children are stunted and developmentally withered. All the factors that promote attachment—physical closeness, time spent together, simultaneous activity, joint participation, sensitivity to one's needs, "reading" behavior cues—are part of child care. A well-planned child care experience encourages children and caregivers to become attached and provides a developmentally sound basis for substitute care. A later section of this chapter, "Human Relationships," will examine separation and attachment.

Settings

The Home. The unquestionably appropriate setting for infant care is the infant's home. Although homes vary considerably in psychological and physical characteristics relevant to child rearing, the stereotypical home with infant-mother pair has become the standard against which formally organized settings for infant care programs are judged. The home setting and all the supposed advantages of daily, continuous infant-mother interaction provides an abstract standard to use in assessing infant care settings and the patterns of interactions and physical equipment for normal infant development. Many parents make arrangements for in-home care for their infants and toddlers. Called housekeepers, babysitters, governesses, nannies, or au pair girls, these are private agreements between families and the employee. We do not cover details of this situation in this book. Recently, a very small number of training programs for nannies or in-home caregivers have been started. (Wheelock College, Boston, MA has one we recommend you look at if you are interested in pursuing this further.) Perhaps this is the beginning of a new trend in child care service and training that will merit more extensive coverage in the future.

The Family Day Care Home. The home of a caretaker of similar educational and cultural background, economic circumstances, and geographical proximity to the infant's parents is presumed by many to provide the closest approximation of "in-home" care for the infant. Many areas will allow only family day care homes to care for very young infants, older infants, and toddlers. Infants placed in family day care homes are essentially in a homelike family grouping with children of different ages, although some may place restrictions on the ages that may be mixed in a single family day care home.

The Infant Center. Infants may receive child care in a center-based setting either as the youngest members of a large, multiage center or as the only age group served by a specialized center. In either case, there are likely to be several infants of roughly the same age in the center at any time. Staffing concerns mount as caretakers may need to handle several children whose developmental needs are similar.

Physically, a center setting differs markedly from a typical home. There is special equipment, open space, and facilities for sanitation. They do not suggest homelike qualities of coziness and warmth. Even spacious, attractive centers remind people of institutions. Adults are simply not used to seeing a group of infants crawling around together.

In summary, center settings suffer most when contrasted with the ideal home setting. The advantages of center settings are not necessarily captured by describing the center in terms of what homelike qualities are *not* present and what institutional qualities *are* present. Center settings for infant care raise the most vocal critical concern, but also appear to offer the greatest hope for delivery of adequate care for infants in child care programs.

Groups of Infants and Single Infants

We mentioned the differences in age mixes typically found in home and center care settings for infants. Infants in their natural home setting may be part of a mixed-age group of siblings in the same family. At best, in the family day care situation, the caretaker has a single infant in a particular developmental period. Other children are usually older and not in the same developmental category as the infant or toddler in the setting. This closely approximates the ideal of the single infant-caretaker unit in the natural home setting.

Center-based care for infants poses additional questions concerning the effectiveness of handling young infants and toddlers in groups. By design, children in centers are in groups. Caretaker ratios hold down the size of any one

Many feel that center settings are too institutional for young children. One must be careful, however, not to confuse functional equipment with caregiver warmth, which is much more critical for young children. (Courtesy of U.S. Department of Health and Human Services, Washington, DC.)

group, but the infants are in groups with other infants of similar age. In addition, the range of ages in specialized infant care programs does not approximate the same spacing of siblings found in homes. A home may have a single six-month-old and a two-year-old. Appropriately staffed, a center may be operating with six six-month-old babies and ten two-year-olds, which is certainly not a formal family sibling group.

The caregiving patterns necessary to deal with groups of infants and toddlers are, then, not directly related to the type of caregiving that occurs naturally in homes. Questions arise concerning the health and safety needs of groups of infants and toddlers and the kinds of caregiving that can simultaneously manage the group and handle very intense individual needs for basic care and interaction. Patterns of management and caregiving for infants as members of groups have not been formulated in our society. Experts are still asking whether the developmental needs of infants are substantially altered by the presence of the group and whether the group facilitates or hinders meeting the developmental needs of individual infants and toddlers.

A country's form of social organization is related to the rearing of children in groups. Socialized and collectively organized cultures, such as the collectives in China or the Kibbutzim in Israel, value the emphasis such group-rearing puts on the needs of the group and the relationship of individual needs to the demands of the group. A capitalistic, democratic society does not stress the common good to the exclusion of the individual need. Early childhood, in particular, is seen as a period in which individualism must be stressed and reinforced. Those who try to answer questions about group care of young children solely on the basis of psychological research on developmental impact are ignoring the crux of the issue—it is essentially a societal question. Infant care addresses a very real critical period in societal philosophy. At what point is the individual's identity strong enough to withstand the influence of the group? Is infancy too early? Are toddlers too young to assert self-identity in the face of group living arrangements for part of the day? Society views groups of infants very differently from groups of preschoolers. Those who want to provide child care for infants need to consider these attitudes.

Purposes of Infant Care

Why are infants and toddlers enrolled in child care? Increasingly, the answer is because their mothers have gone to work. Statistics are usually reported for mothers with children under six entering the work force. Over the last few years, the totals have steadily risen. Closer inspection of these statistics indicates that while mothers with children between ages three and six have gone to work in record numbers, mothers with younger children, ages birth to three, are also contributing to the overall increase. Demand for care may make the debate over provision of infant care irrelevant.

The 1960s and 1970s saw a tremendous resurgence of interest in early childhood education. These early, formative years were seen as essential building blocks for later years of achievement and skill development. One slogan of the movement could have been "the earlier the better." Using a combination of infant and parent education techniques, planners created model programs to offset or prevent early negative biases in children's development. They subsequently generated a wealth of practical materials, operational protocols, and research data. Directed at infants, toddlers, and their parents, these programs were not child care service programs, but were educational programs intended to stimulate development in measurable ways. The resultant documents and reports are good resource material for curriculum design in infant child care programs today.

Emerging in the early 1970s were somewhat broader programs aimed at infants thought to be "at risk" developmentally because of family circumstances. These programs are clearly child care services, each a mixture of customized design and special research programs. Often referred to in discussions of infant care, all are high quality, professionally supervised, demonstration projects. Research findings and practices tested in these programs form the basis for much of what is considered to be "good practice" in infant child care. Descriptions of several of these programs are in Box 7.1.

Impact of Child Care on Infants

No compelling negative evidence exists regarding the effects of group care on infants. Group care appears to be satisfactory in settings of high quality. These findings occur despite the fact that much of the research on infant care has been looking for harmful effects:

> The preponderance of available research revealed few differences between infants and toddlers attending group day care and peers who stayed at home with their mothers . . . the value of the research to date is this clear consensus that a priori day care is not harmful to young children. (Kilmer, 1979, p. 103)

> It appears from the data that children from low-income families can be cared for in group care during the day beginning in early infancy without adversely affecting their health, their mothers' attitudes toward them, or their attachment to their mothers. Further, it also appears that high quality day care provides substantial intellectual benefits that are detectable as early as the second year of life. (Ramey, 1981, p. 75)

Still, we cannot assume that infant care has been given a clean bill of health.

> To even say that the jury is still out on day care would be in our view both premature and naively optimistic. The fact of the matter is, quite frankly, that the majority of evidence has yet to be presented, much less subpoenaed. (Belsky & Steinberg, 1978, p. 946)

Box 7.1 Model Infant and Parent Programs

Title Home Start
Sponsor Administration for Children, Youth and Families
Dates 1972–75
Description A three-year demonstration program that provided Head Start-type comprehensive services to young children (three- to five-year-olds) and their families in their homes. Offered education, health, nutrition and social services. Showed parents how to teach their children using as materials everyday objects and routines of family life.
Materials Roggman, L., DeBolt, C., Davis, J., Lemon, J., Glance, P., & Stokes, J. (1976). *Home start curriculum guide.* Washington, DC: Office of Child Development. (ERIC Document Reproduction Service No. ED 188 737)
References Goodrich, N., Nauta, M., & Rubin, A. (1974). *Natural home start evaluation interim report V: Program analysis.* Washington, DC: Office of Child Development. (ERIC Document Reproduction Service No. ED 134 319)

Title Florida Parent Education Projects
Sponsor Ira J. Gordon
Dates 1966–72
Description Home-centered family services for cognitive, language, and personality development of mother and child, based upon the use of paraprofessional educators, themselves members of the population served.
Materials Gordon, I. J. (1970); (1977). *Baby learning through baby play; Baby to parent, parent to baby.* New York: St. Martin's Press.
References Gordon, I. J. (Ed.). (1969). *Reaching the child through parent education: The Florida approach.* Gainesville, FL: University of Florida, Institute for Development of Human Resources.

Title The Family Development Research Program
Sponsor Alice S. Honig and J. Ronald Lally
Dates 1971–76
Description A family enrichment program that provided developmental day care for the children (six to thirty-six months) and a home visitation program with the families. All families were low income and 85% were single-parent families. The home visitation program provided positive family social and learning experiences for the children. The children experienced interactions with a variety of adults in a 1 : 4 adult-child ratio in the open-education settings of the Syracuse University Children's Center program. Multiage, family-style groupings facilitated child-child interactions.
Materials Honig, A. S. (1972). *The family development research program: With emphasis on the children's center curriculum.* Syracuse, NY: Syracuse University. ERIC Document Reproduction Service No. ED 135 484)
References Honig, A. S., & Lally, J. R. (1972). *Infant caregiving: A design for training.* New York: Media Projects, Inc.

Just because these desirable consequences *can* occur for children in group day care does not mean they *will* occur. (Ramey, 1981, p. 75)

It would be wrong to conclude that day care, any more than home care, is without effects, and it would be misleading to assume that it carries no risks (even though these have been greatly exaggerated in the past). (Rutter, 1982, pp. 22–23)

Developmental Foundations

Infants and toddlers grow up so quickly! The pace of development and the obvious changes that occur in physical and mental abilities during the first three years of life are profound and dramatic. Babies are endearing and lovable. Anyone regularly caring for an infant or toddler

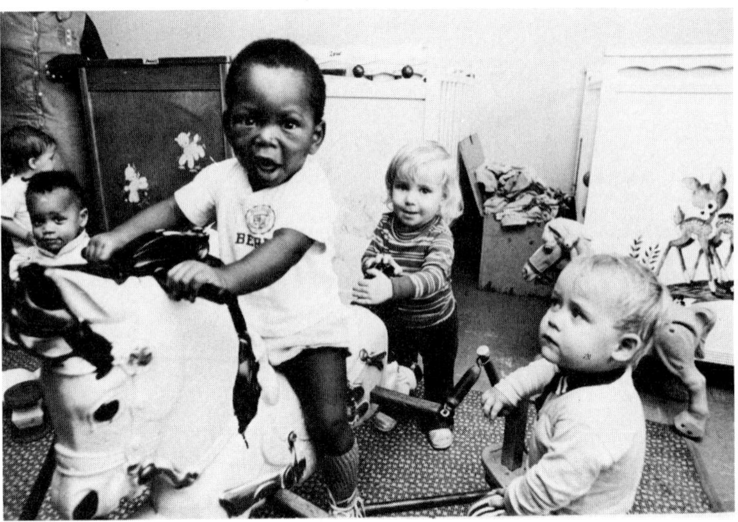

Toddlers love to try out new ways to move. (Courtesy of U.S. Department of Agriculture, Washington, DC.)

easily gets caught up and captivated by the sweep of developmental gains. In common questions such as "When do babies smile?" "Can two-year-olds handle a cup?" "Do twelve-month-olds have nightmares?", we are asking for information on the developmental time line to help us understand a child's behavior. Developmental theory provides that framework; it describes current events and helps predict the course of later development. It is an essential foundation for infant-toddler child care programs.

Theories are constructed from careful observation and accumulating evidence of research. Theory and research are intertwined, each fueling and refining the other. Nowhere is this relationship more dynamic than in the area of infant development. The more we know about the beginnings of development, the better we can predict or influence later development. These research findings frequently have direct and meaningful application in infant-toddler child care.

No longer are infants perceived as dull blobs or sleepy nothings. Our changed conception of the importance of infancy recognizes that the infant is a complex organism who can do lots of things. The potential of the human infant has attracted the attention and captured the imagination of medical, psychological, and educational professionals. Those working in infant-toddler child care programs need to understand the direction of current research efforts as well as existing developmental theories.

Themes of Research in Infancy

The typical caregiver in an infant-toddler program probably has neither the time nor the resources to systematically track down, read, and evaluate research reports. Single studies may attract widespread media attention, but one study is *not* complete evidence of anything. Periodic summaries and critical reviews of research findings are good resources. Some are technically oriented (for example, Lipsett, 1981, 1982; Osofsky, 1979; Stone, Smith & Murphy, 1973); others relate research more directly to caregiving and programmed practices (for example, Evans & Ilfeld, 1982; Lewis & Rosenblum, 1974; Weissbourd & Mussick, 1981). What follows is a brief review of major themes of current research.

Capacity of Infants. Research has demonstrated that infants are capable and well-equipped organisms. They can see, seeming to prefer faces and able to discriminate patterns very early; hear, responding especially to higher pitched sounds such as female voices; and feel, reacting differentially to levels of pain, sensation, and temperature. Neonates (early period after birth) in particular have a much wider range of perceptual and response capabilities than ever realized before.

Physiological maturation seems to set the stage for critical and sensitive periods. Many animals have *critical* periods—biological peaks of developmental preparedness when certain behaviors or events must occur. Death or permanently impaired growth results if critical periods are missed. Humans have *sensitive* or *optimal* periods, when appropriate conditions are present for certain skills or qualitative organizations to occur. If sensitive periods are missed or not maximized, problems may occur. Opinions vary on whether makeup is possible; later change is definitely difficult.

We know human infants are remarkably resilient. They can get back on track. Also, no single "right" prescription can be written for human infant development. Research has documented that there are many ways to achieve acceptable developmental outcomes.

Roots of Intelligence. The human infant responds initially to everything with "all he's got." This rudimentary physical response pattern gradually differentiates as infants gain control and skill with their body. Knowing, perceiving, and doing are intimately connected. Developmental theorists describe these early months and years with the terms *sensory* and *motor*. Sensorimotor experiences are the child's first ways of connecting with the world, and they form the roots of intellectual development.

The quality and detail of early sensorimotor behaviors provide clues about the infant's learning style and abilities. The individual organization and timing of infants' and toddlers' behaviors should show some kind of progressive, positive change. All of the first two to three years of life may be one long optimal period for sensorimotoric stimulation of intelligence. Questions about the role of stimulation and education for infants are motivated by the desire to take full advantage of growth opportunities, particularly if the effects have the potential to be long-lasting.

Human Relationships. Infants need a close, continuing relationship with a special person. In our culture that special person is usually mother. Thus, much of the research in this area is about the mother-child bond, or lack of it. The concept of maternal deprivation is related to attachment and separation. We have come to believe that infants' needs can be met by "mothering" figures other than the biological mother. Fathers, aunts, grandmothers, friends, and caregivers can be "special" people for the infant if positive, warm feelings and physical closeness characterize the relationship over time. Infants can develop more than one simultaneous and significant attachment.

In the psychological literature *maternal deprivation* is defined as the lack of bonding with a central figure. This may occur because a central figure is not available or amenable to bonding or because the infant is somehow incapable of bonding. The terms *attachment* and *separation* are used to describe two major behavior clusters related to maternal deprivation. Attachment describes the bonding behaviors and feelings; separation describes the reactions and feelings related to both short- and long-term absences of the central figure. The classic work of John Bowlby (1968, 1969, 1973) has been a seminal foundation for contemporary researchers and program practitioners.

Researchers who have examined the nature of the bond that exists between infants and their special people have concluded that the "feel" of the relationship is critically important. Based on responsiveness and reciprocity of action and communication, there develops a "bi-directionality" of effects—that is, each member of the pair affects and alters the behavior of the other. These findings along with Erikson's theoretical conceptions of trust have lent credibility to the idea that it is *quality*, not quantity, of time spent together that counts. When parents and infants are emotionally invested in one another, they may not need to spend long hours together to reap developmental rewards. Substitute caregivers who are responsive can also provide quality time for infants and toddlers.

Potentially so much is at stake with infants that continued research and evaluation in this area is necessary.

Infants at Risk. For infants considered to be at risk the presumed chance of developmental delay or damage is high. Infants are always vulnerable to risks, although contributing causal conditions vary in type and severity depending on the infant's current development state. Prenatally, fetuses are at risk from a number of genetic and environmental factors. Drugs, alcohol, smoking, and maternal diet are known to affect the unborn child. Disease, complicating delivery events, inadequate medical care, and lack of early screening and treatment for progressive genetic problems affect neonates' chances of satisfactory survival. After earliest infancy, accidents account for most child deaths and injury. Since the 1960s, however, our definition of "at risk" has also come to encompass social and environmental factors that limit a child's horizons and restrict opportunity. This broadened definition focused research attention and intervention efforts on a large, new category of children. Social and economic risk means that we must consider the context of children's lives. One result has been efforts to reach young children and their family units.

For infants with disabilities, the prevailing research trends have been toward early identification and assessment strategies. Accurate and early diagnosis allows prompt corrective or compensatory treatment.

Developmental Mileposts

From birth to maturity, differentiation and individuality characterize development. Mothers of several children routinely comment on how even as newborns their children showed differences in need for sleep and reactions to noise and to cuddling. Over time these differences magnify with one child a sound sleeper with regular naps, and another a "night owl" who never seems to sleep much. These early simple differences probably anticipate the considerably more complex differences in personality and ability that characterize siblings. Differentiation starts with something simple and results in something complex. Developing children become increasingly different from one another. Newborns are genetically different from one another, but children grow up in different environments and develop at different rates. The more behaviors they have, the more opportunities they have to show differences.

Charts of behavioral characteristics are useful guides for caregivers of infants and toddlers (see Table 7.1). Behaviors are organized by category and sequenced. Age ranges give an approximate indication of when most children can be expected to exhibit similar behaviors. These charts represent observations of children's development over time.

Infant development depends on interactions with adults. The responses of the infant and the adult serve to stimulate each other. The reciprocal nature of the interaction is described by Provence (1982, p. 49):

> Playful behavior, social play, and play with toys characterize the infant who is developing well. It is known that a young child who does not or cannot play is a child in trouble. . . . Playful interaction with adults is initiated by well cared for infants beginning at around four months when spontaneous social smiling and vocalization are actively used to engage the adult. If adults respond, this social play becomes progressively varied and complex. Mutual imitation is an important factor in its development. Throughout the

first year at least, much of the baby's play goes on in relation to the care of his body. . . . Adults are important as arrangers of an environment that encourages play; they also provide the protection and social atmosphere in which the child is secure enough and stimulated enough to play. They are comforters, organizers and sources of renewed energy. They are also play partners, and this partnership ranges widely from, for example, a game of peek-a-boo to helping the toddler make sand pies, work a puzzle, manage a rocking horse, feed a baby doll, negotiate with another toddler, etc. Infant day care providers need to appreciate the value of their personal involvement as facilitators of play and to be aware that planning a program of playtimes for infants and toddlers is more fluid and informal than is true for older children.

Basic Care Pattern

The eight blocks of the daily care pattern can be used to illustrate some typical individual variations of programming for infants and toddlers (see Figure 7.1). For Yetreta, an infant of three months, a daily schedule of alternating naps and feeding, changing, and alert periods represents almost a total merger of basic care and curriculum opportunities. John, at fifteen months, has a schedule in which some periods of the day are devoted exclusively to play activity. Basic care periods still occupy a large portion of the day and are secondary opportunities for developmental enhancement. The pattern for three-year-old Carol is the familiar preschool pattern characterized by two long activity blocks and relatively contained basic care periods.

Implementing Programs

Current practices in infant care are a reflection of research findings, developmental norms, social mores, and traditional procedures. In quality programs the individual needs of infants and toddlers are the basic determinants of structure. Programming is highly personalized. The guiding philosophy of many programs is to provide the essentials for optimal development, relying on the caregiver-child relationship for guidance on specific details. Programs are, therefore, heavily dependent on the empathy and character of each caregiver-child unit. Within the overall goals of the program, caregivers can adapt routines and activities. Flexibility, spontaneity, and a sense of humor are essential for survival.

The program components described in this section are those for which practices in infant-toddler child care are generally different from preschool and school-age care. Through commentary and example we illustrate the particular features of operation that differentiate infant-toddler care. Where possible, we use examples from programs that are *not* model or demonstration programs. This shows that local talent and resources can produce quality child care service for infants and toddlers.

Caregivers

Who are these important people who tend infants and toddlers? The Infant/Toddler Day Care Study and the Supply Study, substudies of the National Day Care Study (NDCS), reported some interesting facts on caregivers.

The Infant/Toddler Day Care Study was a small, naturalistic substudy designed to describe child care arrangements for children under three years of age. While having less formal education, infant-toddler staff had slightly more experience (4.5 vs. 4.1 years) and worked longer hours (33 vs. 29.9 per week) than staff for older children. Fewer than half of the infant-toddler staff contacted in the study reported having had specific training for work with infants and toddlers.

Caregivers of infants and toddlers must possess the same personal qualities desired for staff in all child care programs: concern for children and familiarity with child development, organization and initiative, patience, and stamina. Of

Table 7.1 Developmental Behavior

BIRTH TO SIX MONTHS	
Thinking	Baby discriminates mother from others, is more responsive to her Acts curious, explores through looking, grasping, mouthing Recognizes adults, bottle, discriminates between strangers and familiar persons Shows he or she is learning by anticipating situations, responding to unfamiliarity, and reacting to disappearance of things Uses materials in play such as crumpling and waving paper Looks a long time at objects he or she is inspecting
Language	Baby coos expressively, vocalizes spontaneously Vocalizes over a sustained period of time to someone who is imitating sounds Babbles in word-sounds of two syllables
Body Expression and Control	Baby develops own rhythm in feeding, eliminating, sleeping and being awake—a rhythm that can be approximately predicted Quiets self through rocking, sucking, or touching Adjusts posture in anticipation of being fed or held (in crib, on lap, at shoulder) Head balances Turns to see or hear better Pulls self to sitting position, sits alone momentarily Coordinates eye and hand in reaching. Baby reaches persistently, touches, manipulates
Body Expression and Control (*continued*)	Retains objects in hands, manipulates objects, transfers from hand to hand Engages in social exchange and self-expression through facial action, gestures, and play
Social Play and Responsiveness	Baby imitates movements Gazes at faces and reaches toward them, reacts to disappearance of a face, tracks face movements Responds to sounds Smiles to be friendly Opens mouth in imitation of adult Likes to be tickled, jostled, frolicked with Makes social contact with others by smiling or vocalizing Quiets when someone approaches, smiles Takes part in a mutual exchange between adult and child through smiling, play, voice, and bodily involvement
Self-awareness	Baby smiles at own reflection in the mirror Looks at and plays with hands and toes Feels things about self through such actions as banging
Emotions	Baby shows excitement through waving arms, kicking, moving whole body, face lighting up Shows pleasure in anticipation of something, such as bottle Cries in different ways to indicate cold, wetness, hunger, and so on Makes noises to voice pleasure, displeasure, satisfactions Laughs
SIX TO NINE MONTHS	
Thinking	Baby shows persistence in doing things Becomes aware of missing objects Makes connections between objects—pulls string to secure ring on the other end, uncovers a hidden toy Increases ability to zero in on sights or sounds he's interested in Has prolonged attention span Shifts attention appropriately, resists distraction
Language	Baby babbles to people Says "da-da" or equivalent Notices familiar words and turns toward person or thing speaker is referring to Shows understanding of some commonly used words
Body Expression and Control	Baby sits alone with good coordination Manipulates objects with interest, understands the use of objects—rings a bell on purpose

(*continued*)

Table 7.1 (*continued*)

	SIX TO NINE MONTHS		
Body Expression and Control (*continued*)	Practices motor skills, crawls, and stands up by holding on to furniture Uses fingers in pincer-type grasp of small objects Increases fine-motor coordination of eye, hand, and mouth	Self-awareness	Baby listens and notices own name Makes a playful response to own image in mirror Begins to assert self
Social Play and Responsiveness	Baby cooperates in games Takes the initiative in establishing social exchanges with adults Understands and adapts to social signals Shows ability to learn by demonstration	Emotions	Baby expresses some fear toward strangers in new situations Pushes away something not wanted Shows pleasure when someone responds to self-assertion Shows pleasure in getting someone to react
	NINE TO EIGHTEEN MONTHS		
Thinking	Baby unwraps an object, takes lids from boxes Recognizes shapes in a puzzle board Names familiar objects Becomes increasingly curious about surroundings, sets off on own to explore further than ever before Becomes more purposeful and persistent in accomplishing a task	Social Play and Responsiveness	Baby plays pat-a-cake, peek-a-boo Responds to verbal request Imitates actions Stops own actions on command from an adult Uses gestures and words to make wants known Focuses on mother as the only person permitted to meet needs
Language	Baby jabbers expressively Imitates words Says two words together	Self-awareness	Baby becomes aware of ability to say "no" and of the consequences of this Shows shoes or other clothing Asserts self by "getting into everything", "getting into mischief" Wants to decide for self
Body Expression and Control	Baby stands alone, sits down, walks with help Is gradually gaining control of bodily functioning Throws ball Becomes more aware of own body, identifies body parts Stands on one foot with help Walks up and down stairs with help Needs adult as a stable base for operations during growing mobility and curiosity	Emotions	Baby shows preference for one toy over another Expresses many emotions and recognizes feelings in other people Gives affection—returns a kiss or hug Expresses fear of strangers Shows anxiety at separation from mother, gradually masters this
	EIGHTEEN TO TWENTY-FOUR MONTHS		
Thinking	Child says the names of familiar objects in pictures Explores cabinets and drawers Begins to play pretend games	Body Expression and Control	Child has increasingly steady hand coordination—can build tower of many blocks Climbs into adult chair Runs with good coordination Climbs stairs, using rail Uses body actively in mastering and exploring surroundings—an active age
Language	Child uses two-word sentences Has vocabulary of 20 to 50 words Begins to use *me, I,* and *you* Follows verbal instructions Listens to simple stories		

(*continued*)

Table 7.1 (*continued*)

Eighteen to Twenty-four Months			
Social Play and Responsiveness	Child scribbles with crayon in imitation of adults' strokes on paper Likes parents' possessions and play that mimics parents' behavior and activities Follows simple directions Controls others, orders them around Tests, fights, resists adults when they oppose or force him to do something Child is able to differentiate more and more between people	Emotions	Has intense feeling of self-importance—protests, wants to make own choices Child desires to be independent, feed self, put on articles of own clothing Shows intense positive or negative reactions Likes to please others, is affectionate Shows some aggressive tendencies—slaps, bites, hits—which must be dealt with Shows greater desire to engage in problem-solving and more persistence in doing so Develops triumphant delight and pride in his own actions Becomes frustrated easily
Self-awareness	Child recognizes body parts on a doll Identifies parts of own body Takes a more self-sufficient attitude, challenges parents' desires, wants to "do it myself"		
Twenty-four to Thirty-six Months			
Thinking	Child can name many objects Begins to grasp the meaning of numbers Child's memory span is longer Child's ability to reason, solve problems, make comparisons develops Child grasps the concepts of color, form and space Begins to respect and obey rules Shows strong interest in investigating the functions and details of household objects	Social Play and Responsiveness	Child tests his limits in situations involving other people Says "no" but submits anyway Shows trust and love Enjoys wider range of relationships and experiences, enjoys meeting many people other than parents Likes to try out adult activities, especially around the house, runs errands, does small household chores
Language	Child uses language as a way of communicating his thoughts, representing his ideas, and developing social relationships Child enjoys using language, gains satisfaction from expressing himself and being understood Understands and uses abstract words such as "up", "down", "now", "later"	Self-awareness	Child becomes aware of himself as a separate person, can contrast himself with another Expresses preferences strongly Expresses confidence in own activities Expresses pride in achievement Values his own property
Body Expression and Control	Child can jump and hop on one foot Child walks up and down stairs, alternates his feet at each stair Begins to notice the differences between safe and unsafe activities Expands his large muscle interests and activities Tries hard to dress and undress himself	Emotions	Child strives for mastery over objects Child can tolerate more frustration, more willing to accept a substitute for what he can't have Shows strong desire for independence in his actions Gradually channels his aggressive tendencies into more constructive activities Uses language to express his wishes and his feelings toward others Shows a developing sense of humor at surprises, unusual actions, etc.

Source: Adapted from *Day care 2: Serving infants* (pp. 36–39) by D. S. Huntington, S. Provence, and R. K. Parker, 1971, Washington, DC: U.S. Department of Health, Education and Welfare.

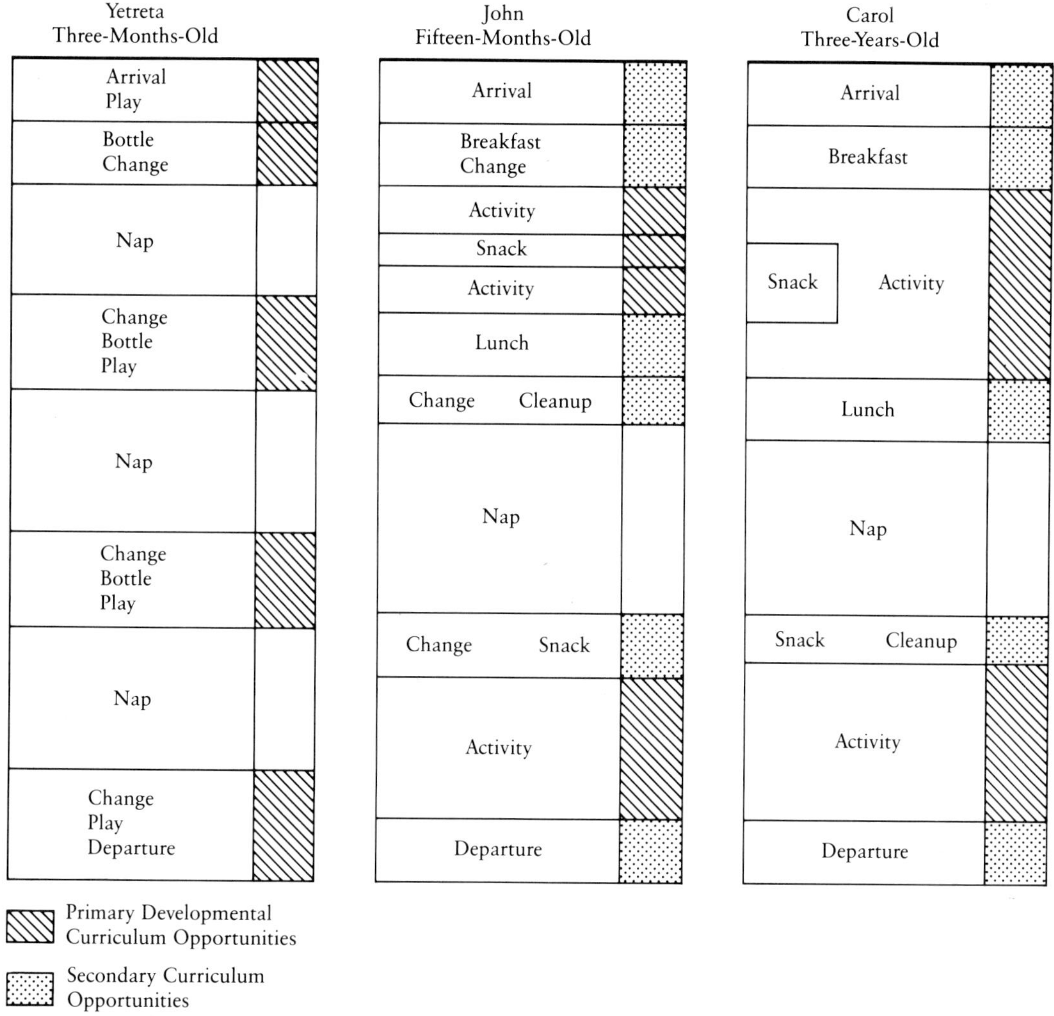

Figure 7.1 Adaptations of the daily care pattern for infant care.

critical importance for good infant caregivers is the ability to establish close, personal bonds with the children in their care. The examples of desirable caregiver qualities described in Box 7.2 illustrate the very strong emphasis that is placed on feelings and emotions.

The same study also indicated that among caregiver behaviors talking, touching, and social interaction with children were predominant (see Table 7.2). This is more evidence about the nature of the personal relationship between caregiver and infant that is the basis for daily care experiences.

Daily Activities and Curriculum

Activities for infants and toddlers are organized by the sequence and reciprocity that develop during physical care routines. A great deal of

Box 7.2 Characteristics of Good Caregivers

Obviously, no one person will have all the qualities described here. Initially, however, a caregiver should already have some of these characteristics; others may be acquired through training and experience. In general, the following qualities are important for a good caregiver:

1. Should be patient and warm toward children. This warmth is the basic ingredient in the caregiver-child relationship. Only with patience can the child be helped to develop, and the caregiver survive the strains of this type of work.
2. Should like children, be able to give of [himself or] herself to them, and receive satisfaction from what they have to offer. Must be able to appreciate the baby as an individual, since this is vital to his [or her] growing self-acceptance. A caregiver also needs to have a sense of humor.
3. Should understand that children need more than simple physical care. Should have some knowledge of the practical care of children and be willing and able to learn from other people.
4. Must be able to adjust to various situations, understand feelings, and help children to handle fear, sadness and anger, as well as to experience love, joy and satisfaction.
5. Should be in good health. Since children possess abundant energy, the caregiver must be energetic and imaginative in order to teach and discipline them.
6. Must be aware of the importance of controlling undesirable behavior, but must not be excessively punitive or given to outbursts of anger.
7. Needs to show initiative and resourcefulness in working with children and be able to adapt the program to meet their individual needs and preferences.
8. Must be acquainted with, accept and appreciate the children's cultures, customs and languages if they are different from [his or] her own. Helping the child develop a sense of pride in his [or her] own uniqueness is vital.
9. Must respect the child and parents, regardless of their backgrounds or particular circumstances, thus helping the child learn to respect himself [or herself]. The caregiver's own self-respect will aid in imparting this quality to others.
10. Should be able to work with other adults and get along with the other staff members in order to provide a harmonious atmosphere at the center.
11. Should have a positive interest in learning, understand the importance and variety of learning needs in a young child, and be responsive to the child's attempts at learning in all spheres.

Source: Adapted from *Day care 2: Serving infants* (pp. 28–29) by D. S. Huntington, S. Provence, and R. K. Parker, 1971, Washington, DC: U.S. Department of Health, Education and Welfare.

the caregiving day for infants and toddlers is devoted to body care and basic care activities. Eating, sleeping, and cleaning up form continuous cycles of activity. For the most part these are activities requiring the caregiver's full attention. As children grow older and sleep less, time becomes available for play and exploration. After breakfast a six- to ten-month-old may be alert and playful for an hour or so before taking a morning nap. A two- to three-year-old will typically take only an afternoon nap, leaving the full morning and late afternoon for activity. From early infancy on, sleep patterns vary enormously, but the pattern is for longer and longer wakeful periods as children develop.

Caring for young children is physically demanding work. Bending, fetching, following, picking up, even chasing are part of a normal day's workout. Much of the work is repetitive janitorial duty: washing hands and faces, changing diapers, and wiping up spills, spits, and burps. One active child, one fussy child, or

Table 7.2 Observed and Rated Behavior of Caregivers and Children in Infant and Toddler Classrooms

Caregiver Behavior	Infant Groups		Toddler Groups	
	Mean Percentage[a]	*Standard Deviation*	*Mean Percentage*[a]	*Standard Deviation*
Management Activity	4.0	3.1	7.2	6.0
Social Interaction	52.0	12.8	52.9	15.6
Cognitive-Language Stimulation[b]	8.5	6.1	21.5	15.2
Administrative Tasks	18.4	7.6	18.0	10.2
Observes Children	13.7	7.3	14.9	9.0
Touches Children	40.8	16.2	30.2	13.2
Talks with Children	46.8	22.1	50.5	23.4
Talks with Adults	13.6	9.1	8.8	7.9

[a] This figure represents the average, across all caregivers observed, of the frequency with which behavior was observed.
[b] Constructed from codes indicating both formal and informal instruction.
Source: From "The Infant/Toddler Day Care Study," in *Children at the Center: Vol. 1. Final Report of the National Day Care Study* (p. 267) by R. Ruopp, J. Travers, F. Glantz, and C. Coelen, 1979, Cambridge, MA: Abt Associates. Used with permission.

one alert child can fully occupy a caregiver. Getting dressed to go outside and undressed when back inside can easily take longer than the time spent outside. Personalities and temperaments come in all combinations. Some babies balk, some are slow to warm up, some charge ahead fearlessly, some frazzle easily, some are loud, others are quiet. Life with infants and toddlers is never dull, never quite predictable, and never uninteresting (see Table 7.3 for recommended matches between infant characteristics and caregiver actions).

Whether in home or center setting, a great deal of the caregiver's interaction time with infants occurs during changing and diapering. In the following example both Jason and his caregiver give each other lots of cues for behavior and stimulation during this time.

Jason may

- kick vigorously when diaper area is exposed (accompanied by gurgling sounds)
- lie very still trying to maintain eye contact with caregiver as she talks to him while changing diaper
- resist slightly or passively help arms get into sleeves of clothes
- swipe at caregiver's face or clothes as she leans over him

Caregiver may

- hold Jason firmly on changing table
- sing song to him about what is happening, keeping up a running patter of words
- react with changes in her voice or facial expression to his reactions of cold, dislike, or confinement

Marsha, a toddler, is one of four children in a small group that is the responsibility of one caregiver. Marsha's mobility and stamina enable her to engage in many activities and bring her in proximity with other children and other caregivers. Eating is a big part of Marsha's day. Along with her group members she participates in feeding herself and is learning to handle utensils. For her foods are not only things to eat but are also raw materials to explore.

Eating is a time when a child gets food. Eating can be a time when a child learns how to sit and get along with others. Eating can be a time when an older infant learns language. Eating can be a time when a child learns about textures. Eating can be a time when an older infant learns manners. Eating can be a time when a child practices hand and eye skills. Eating can be a time when a child expresses competence and independence. Eating IS a

Table 7.3 Children's Needs and Characteristics with Related Implications for Caregiver Behaviors and Attitudes

	Child	Teacher
Social-emotional	Needs to feel sense of belonging	Establishes a close relationship that is caring and nurturing
		Is alert to child's needs for people and social experiences
		Includes child in group activities, either as spectator or as actual participant
	Likes to be with or near other children (sociocentric)	Provides opportunities to watch or join other children
	Is self-centered (egocentric)	Does not insist on group involvement, sharing behaviors, etc., that are beyond child's level of functioning
	Likes to be independent	Offers opportunities for child to do things for and by self; provides chances for child to assume responsibilities
		Provides materials and experiences that require initiative or problem-solving by child
	Needs adult guidance and support	Is accepting and appreciative of child's efforts
	Needs affection and praise	Gives child unlimited affection and appropriate praise; helps child learn socially acceptable ways of showing interest or affection
	Has a good sense of humor	Plays with child; offers appropriate discrepancies in actions and words; laughs with child
	Is easily stimulated	Recognizes the fine line between enough and too much
	Is easily frustrated	Recognizes that a young child will persist only when successful, and may be able to handle only one or two failures with a task before giving up
		Provides challenges that match child's level of functioning
	Needs to experience success	Plans cumulative program of new experiences based on previous ones, so as to provide an appropriate match for the child's current level of functioning
	May have "unreasonable" fears of strangers or changes in environment or routine or activities	Understands that fearful children usually regress in their behavior; is soothing and supportive; shows love with body contact and quieting language
		Introduces changes slowly, one step at a time
	Is dependent upon all adults, but very dependent upon significant adults for social-emotional development	Is a "significant" adult by forming a close, nurturing, consistent relationship
Physical-behavioral	Is very active	Provides opportunities and space for free and vigorous movement
	Has developmental control of large muscles; beginning control of fine muscles	Provides large muscle activities and equipment; gradually adds such activities as self-feeding, drawing, painting
	Tires easily	Adapts schedule to individual child's physiological needs
	Is highly susceptible to communicable diseases	Is alert to any change in child's usual behavior or appearance; is able to recognize early symptoms of child diseases; instills and enforces habits of cleanliness
		Expects irregular attendance at the center

(*continued*)

Table 7.3 (*continued*)

	Child	Teacher
Physical-behavioral—cont'd	Has a small tummy	Provides meals on schedule, but snacks should always be available
	Is establishing handedness and eyedness	Provides activities and materials that require use of either or both hands
	Is far-sighted	Does not force near-vision activities; should let the child determine closeness
	Is progressing from nonverbal cry to verbal communication	Listens, responds, imitates; initiates "conversations"
	Is very dependent upon adults for satisfying physical needs	Responds to needs with appropriate actions immediately or as soon as possible
Cognitive	Is intensely curious and eager to learn; learns by doing	Provides a wide variety of materials and experiences in an interesting environment; provides opportunities to explore, manipulate, and discover
		Eliminates safety hazards in the environment
		Allows time and space for individual explorations with only the necessary restrictions for the sake of safety
		Is alert for new signs of interest
		Knows progression of mental development and provides opportunities that match and stretch the child's behavior and thinking
	Has a very short attention span for other-initiated tasks	Allows time and freedom for self-initiated tasks that tend to encourage greater persistence
	Understands through sensorimotor experiences	Provides time and opportunity to experience many kinds of things and activities
	Enjoys "playful" experiences with language and activities	Smiles, laughs, enjoys, and adopts "playful" attitude toward routines and interactions
	Is dependent upon all adults, but very dependent upon significant adults for learning	Is a "significant" adult by forming a close, nurturing, consistent relationship; reinforces and encourages child's behaviors in all areas of functioning

Source: From *Group care and education of infants and toddlers* (pp. 41–42) by M. G. Weiser, 1982, St. Louis: C.V. Mosby.

> time, and you have to decide what it is and what you want to happen. (Tronick & Greenfield, 1973, p. 43)

Play is the most significant activity for young children. It is through play that children come to know their world by trying out and testing ideas and skills. In infant and toddler programs no clear distinction exists between routines and activities. Everything and anything are experiences and the play mode allows young children to incorporate these experiences. For young children, play involves people, objects, and actions or ideas. Of these ingredients people are the most important—relating and connecting to people attracts the child. Objects are of interest, but more so when someone shares the exploration. Caregivers can set up play opportunities and through comment, suggestion, and demonstration extend the quality and depth of the infant's activity. Box 7.3 has two examples.

Box 7.3 Activities for Infant Care

A Talking and Doing Activity: Peek-a-Boo

Why

Learn language.
Learn to be attentive.

What You Need

Scarf

Talk About What You Do

(Use your own language. This is an example.)
"See this thing I am holding? It is a scarf. Sometimes Mommy wears this on her head."
"I'm going to hide behind this scarf. See. I'm going to peep around to see if I can find you."
Look around scarf and say, "Peek-a-Boo." Look on the other side and say, "Peek-a-Boo. I see you."

Things To Do Another Time

Play other hide-and-seek games.

Teach Through Play

Be excited.
Laugh a lot.

Source: From *Education of children aged one to three: A curriculum manual* (p. 99) edited by P. H. Furfey, 1972, Washington, DC: Catholic University, used with permission.

Watch Where I Go: The Concept of Direction

Follow The Leader with Trucks or Dolls

You select one truck (or doll) and your child selects another. Take the two on a trip around the room, talking about where you are as you move about. First you be the leader, and then when your child catches on, let him or her have a try.

Source: P. 73, from *Learning through play*. Copyright © 1972, by J. Marzollo and J. Lloyd. Reprinted by permission of Harper & Row Publishers, Inc.

A ready supply of ideas, a dose of caregiver creativity, and sensitive judgment about timing constitute the curriculum for infant and toddler child care. Curriculum is embedded in the rituals and routines of caregiving. Formal written guidelines, lessons plans, objectives, and procedures are nothing more than props. Caregivers use these props to help organize their actions and to increase their sensitivity to potentials for stimulation. Curriculum plans and corresponding child development training help boost caregivers' resources and confidence. Stimulating development presumes an orderly sequence of growth and skill achievement. A curriculum identifies mileposts of development. Caregivers' daily interactions with children should encourage progress through practice and accumulated experiences. In summary, curriculums in infant-toddler programs are for caregivers. They are a set of examples and a decision process that can be a valuable resource tool. The judgment, wisdom, and sensitivity of the caregiver to the immediate situation produces the real plan of action. Examples of published curriculum guides are given in the Resource section entitled "Implementing Programs" at the end of the chapter.

Staff-Child Ratios and Group Composition

Ratio, the number of caregivers to children, continues to be of great concern in infant-toddler child care. Low ratios are clearly indicated. Children and caregivers need assured and unstressed access to each other if the critical qualities of bonding are to develop. State standards on number of caregivers to infants and toddlers prevail. However, in the course of the revision of the Federal Interagency Day Care Requirements, which do not apply now to any child care programs, strong opinions were expressed for and against different ratio figures.

For children birth to two years, a ratio of one to three was suggested. This strict ratio conformed to recommendations of the Child Fire Life Safety Code. Child development experts felt that the one-to-three ratio was an acceptable context for the intensive physical and social contact required by children under two. A slightly higher one-to-four ratio was proposed for children two years old.

State regulations in 1975 generally permitted much higher staff-child ratios than professionals recommended. Lowering state standards to match the proposed Federal Interagency Day Care Requirements (FIDCR) meant child care costs would increase as more staff salary money would be needed. Many feel that one contributing factor to the demise of the FIDCR revisions was the controversy over staffing standards for infants and toddlers with the prospects of cost increases.

Group size is the total number of children in a group. The assumption is that it is a group that stays together. Group size combined with staff-child ratio is group composition. The Infant/Toddler Substudy of the NDCS reported that group composition is related to the behavior of caregivers and the quality experiences of infants and children.

> Caregivers spend less time "managing" children and infants and toddlers cry less (show less distress), in groups where there are fewer children and higher staffing ratios. In infant groups, high ratios are associated with lower levels of child apathy and potential danger. (Abt, 1979, p. 253)

Recognition of group composition as a component of quality care conditions was promoted by the NDCS. A group of six two-year-olds with two caregivers is a vastly different social environment than three two-year-olds with one caregiver. Research and opinion support the conclusion that group composition is an important quality indicator for infant and toddler care, perhaps more so than for preschoolers. Group size figures in the FIDCR revisions were a group size of six for birth to two-year-olds, and a group size of twelve for two-year-olds.

The concept of group composition as a "regulatable" quality index is somewhat new. In the past many states have specified only ratio figures, not group composition.

The "Special Person"

The developmental literature points strongly to the need to have *one* person (mother, aunt, father, and so on) or a small number of special people with whom the infant can build a close reciprocal relationship. Low ratios and small groups are ways of meeting the child's need for a special person. Implicit in much of this discussion of daily activities and caregiver responsibilities has been the equation of *one* caregiver with the *same* caregiver. Compliance with a ratio requirement of one to four does not, however, automatically mean the same caregiver throughout the day. We must pay attention to *continuity* of caregiver assignment, continuous assessment of *caregiver burden,* and an appreciation of *contact hours.*

Continuity The same caregiver is available to and responsible for the infant every day. Stability and predictability in the infant-caregiver relationship builds positive feelings and is thought to be conducive to overall adjustment. In practical terms this means that caregivers, infants, *and* parents must feel comfortable with each other. When accepting employment in a center, caregivers must try to make a long-term commitment, perhaps arranging vacations and leave times to minimize program disruption. Infant and toddler caregivers tend to work longer shifts than staff for older children.

Caregiver Burden The job requires stamina. Some children demand more and drain more from their caregivers. Caregivers respond according to their strengths and skills. Balancing the "burden" of children on caregivers necessitates a blend of wisdom and intuition, and continual monitoring and support from the director. Within the parameters of staff-child ratios and group size there is room for careful, personal "matches" and "pairings" of children and caregivers. This process cannot be controlled perfectly. Openings occur, children change, and caregivers leave. All have good and bad days. Some tensions and burdens are probably inevitable.

Contact Hours Defined as the number of hours a caregiver is "on-duty" in actual contact with children, contact hours may be a better estimate of adult-child interaction than ratio. Calculated by dividing the total number of staff hours by the total number of child hours (adjusted for absenteeism), this estimate was formulated in the NDCS to reflect the availability of staff to children. For infant and toddler programs contact-hour figures can give a perspective on the effects of long staff days and the ameliorating effects of uneven child attendance because of staggered schedules or absences.

By definition, the only caregiver present in family day care homes is the mother (called provider or caregiver). Group size is regulated around this constant in the ratio of caregiver to children. For example, an appropriate ratio might be one to six or seven—that is, one caregiver for six or seven children.

Restrictions are typically placed on the number of children present of different ages in an attempt to moderate the caregiver burden and ensure reasonable contact hours for younger children. For example, the Health, Education and Welfare Day Care Rules (HEWDCR) Final Rules on group composition are as follows:

> (a) In a day care home in which one caregiver cares for children of all ages, including children under two years of age, the group size at any given time shall not exceed five. No more than two of these children may be under two years of age. The caregiver's own children younger than six and not yet in full day school shall count towards the group size requirement.
>
> (b) In a day care home in which one caregiver cares for children who are all under two years of age, the group size at any given time shall not exceed three. There may be no other children in the home besides the caregiver's own children over the age of six years. (Rules and Regulations, *Federal Register, 45* (55), March 19, 1980, p. 17884.)

In centers, similar provisions are made for mixed-age groups. In order to protect the youngest children in a group, ratios and group sizes are conservatively regulated in mixed-age groups.

Health and Safety

While many diseases of childhood (polio, mumps, and measles) are now controlled through immunization programs, today's young children still get colds, fever, flu, chicken-pox, and other infections. One way we try to protect infants and toddlers is to keep them healthy. Regulations and program practices for health and sanitation are designed to limit the spread of disease in a child care program. For caregivers and parents infections seem to run in never-ending cycles. Decisions about absence or exclusion from care and isolation and management of sick children within a program are difficult. One often expressed concern about caring for young children in group-settings is the fear that they will be exposed to and contract more illnesses. We have little information that confirms or disputes this concern. For infant and toddler programs, however, some guidelines for diapering and feeding help caregiving staff reduce problems arising from these contact sources. The real desire to shield very young children from unnecessary illnesses imparts more urgency to the otherwise routine health practices.

Diapering. The potential for contamination and spread of infection is high unless diapers are handled sanitarily, changing surfaces and equipment are kept clean, and staff wash their hands *every* time diapers are handled. Even for a small group of young children the logistics of perhaps thirty diaper changes a day are challenging. Good staff habits, practical facilities, and constant supervision are needed.

Contact. Infections are spread through contact and droplets. When young children play, contact occurs. Fingers and mouths explore objects and each other. Small spaces and limited toys increase contacts. With larger spaces and generous supplies of toys, opportunities to spread infections can be decreased. Infants and toddlers do not share well anyway. The solitary and parallel play situations characteristic of this age are healthy. Even very young children can be encouraged to use tissues and cover their mouths when coughing. Vigilant caregivers can minimize the spread of infection.

Different children of different ages in different parts of the country have different infections. In a stable environment of the same caregivers and the same peers young children will be healthier. New people bring new germs. Thus, there are health reasons as well as developmental reasons for promoting continuity of caregiving.

Isolation. Does removing sick children from the company of others reduce the spread of infection? Not really. By the time children show symptoms of illness they have already had the chance to infect others. (Contagious diseases such as chicken-pox are an exception.) Working families may find that staying home from jobs to care for mildly sick children is a hardship. Parents may be tempted to disguise or ignore children's symptoms. Invoking isolation means deciding who is too sick to stay and who can stay; this is not easy to do. Sick children need care, but often not much more than the ordinary. Programs need to establish workable, realistic policies for the management of sick children. State and local codes may set the parameters of such policy.

Safety. Toddlers and infants are curious and busy. They are totally dependent upon adults for safety and protection from danger. Three factors contribute to sound safety practices in child care programs:

1. Constant and alert supervision
2. Child-proofed environment
3. Carefully chosen toys and equipment

Supervision for infants and toddlers is best characterized as anticipatory. As children play

Table 7.4 Infant Hazards and Preventative Measures

Age	Characteristics	Accident Hazards	Measures for Prevention
Birth–4 months	Eats, sleeps, cries Rolls off flat surfaces. Wriggles	Bath-Scalding	Check bath water with elbow. Keep one hand on baby.
		Falls	Never turn back on baby who is on table or bed.
		Toys	Select toys that are too large to swallow, too tough to break with no sharp points or edge.
		Sharp objects	Keep pins and other sharp objects out of baby's reach.
		Smothering	Filmy plastics, harnesses, zippered bags and pillows can smother or strangle. A firm mattress and loose covering for baby are safest. Babies of this age need *complete* protection.
4–12 months	Grasps and moves more. Puts objects in his mouth	Play areas	Keep baby in a safe place near attendant. The floor, full-sized bed, and yard are unsafe without supervision.
		Bath	Check temperature of bath water with elbow. Keep baby out of reach of faucets. Don't leave him alone in bath for *any* reason.
		Toys	Large beads on strong cord and unbreakable, rounded toys of smooth wood or plastic are safe.
		Small Objects	Keep buttons, beads, and other small objects from baby's reach. Children of this age still need full-time protection.
		Falls	Don't turn your back on baby when he or she is on an elevated surface.
		Burns	Place guards around registers and floor furnaces. Keep hot liquids, hot foods, and electric cords on irons, toasters, and coffee pots out of baby's reach. Use sturdy and round-edged furniture. Avoid hot steam vaporizers.
1–2 years	Investigates, climbs, opens doors and drawers; takes things apart; likes to play	Gates, windows, doors	Keep doors leading to stairways, driveways, and storage areas securely fastened. Put gates on stairways and porches. Keep screens locked or nailed.
		Play areas	Fence the play yard. Provide sturdy toys with no small removable parts and of unbreakable material. Electric cords to coffee pots, toasters, irons, and radios should be kept out of reach.
		Water	*Never* leave child alone in tub, wading pool, or around open or frozen water.
		Poisons	Store all medicines and poisons in locked cabinet. Store cosmetics and household products, especially caustics, out of reach of child. Store kerosene and gasoline in metal cans and out of reach of children.
		Burns	Provide guards for wall heaters, registers, and floor furnaces. Never leave children alone in the house. Close supervision is needed to protect child from accidents.
2–3 years	Fascinated by fire. Moves about constantly. Tries to do things alone. Imitates. Runs and is lightning fast. Is impatient with restraint	Traffic	Keep child away from street and driveway with strong fence and firm discipline.
		Water	Even shallow wading pools are unsafe unless carefully supervised.
		Toys	Large sturdy toys without sharp edges or small removable parts are safest.
		Burns	Keep matches and cigarette lighters out of reach of children. Teach children the danger of open flames. Never leave children alone in the house.

(*continued*)

Table 7.4 (*continued*)

Age	Characteristics	Accident Hazards	Measures for Prevention
		Dangerous objects	Lock up medicine and household and garden poisons. Store dangerous tools, firearms, and garden equipment in a safe place out of reach of children. Teach safe ways of handling appropriate tools and kitchen equipment.
		Playmates	Accidents are more frequent when playmates are older—the two-year-old may be easily hurt by bats, hard balls, bicycles, and rough play.

Source: From *Day care 6: Health services* (pp. 37–38) by A. F. North, 1971, Washington, DC: Department of Health, Education and Welfare.

with toys and move around, caregivers develop the habit of "guessing ahead," trying to anticipate which of many things the child may do next. Each age group has its share of probable accidents and dangers (see Table 7.4).

State and local regulations contain many safety provisions, covering items such as gates for every stairwell, covered electric outlets, protective coverings on hot water pipes and radiators, medicines stored in locked cabinet, and lead-free paint. Keep in mind that no degree of regulatory rigor or stringent code enforcement makes an environment totally safe for young children.

Special mention needs to be made about automobile safety. Highway accidents are *the* leading cause of death for young children. Infants and toddlers are not safe riding in cars unless they are in approved and correctly used crash-tested child restraints. Young children have a high center of gravity—they are top-heavy. In crashes and sudden stops they tend to go "head first." A child riding loose in a car is a missile all too likely to be hurt in sudden stops and crashes *even* at low speeds.

Points of Controversy

Family Policy

Care services for infants and toddlers are a reflection of family policy in this country. Ambivalent support of care services in the face of rising numbers of mothers entering the work force is policymaking by default. It neither supports families nor attempts to protect infants and toddlers who are placed outside their families for care. The economic necessities or incentives of working apparently outweigh personal beliefs or cultural norms in favor of full-time parental care. This is a reality, but it may not be an informed choice. Can we educate and inform parents about the choices and trade-offs involved in infant and toddler care? Does support of care services automatically mean we are discouraging home care of young children? Can we work toward a family policy that has the "best interests of children" as its highest priority—whatever the chosen circumstances of care for the age of the children?

Supplying Infant and Toddler Care

Infants and toddlers are the minority age group in center-based care. Many more are cared for in licensed family day care homes or through private arrangements. State regulations for infant care in centers are generally considered to range from cautious and conservative to outright restrictive. Costs of quality care are high because staff-child ratios need to be low. Staff salaries, specialized equipment, and facility management contribute to higher per child care costs. Who should pay? Family day care home care is cheaper. Is this care better or just as good? Should public resources be channeled into upgrading and extending day care homes to reach more children, or should a few children be subsidized in high quality center care? Can private enterprise help? What market incentives and licensing conditions would facilitate private proprietary involvement?

Standards for Infant and Toddler Care

Regulatory standards are intended to ensure a minimum level of service. Licensing is a protective and preventive function. Young children are highly susceptible to environmental impact on development. Extra age-differentiated standards are clearly indicated for infant and toddler care. Can regulations be used as a tool for ensuring quality care? Are there enough observable, concrete indicators of quality care on which monitoring and enforcement procedures can focus? The implicit assumption of regulations is the middle-class home as the model setting for care. Does this unduly restrict definitions or allowable practices of care?

Impact of Care

Are we gathering evidence that will allow conclusions to be reached about the efficacy and impact of care alternatives? A number of researchers and analysts think we don't even ask the proper questions when we try to look at the impact of early child care. There is more to competence then cognitive functioning or intelligence. Do we have the patience, vision, resources, and will to do long-term assessments and surveys? Can we hope to do objective analyses, or will some overlay of emotion and caution always circumscribe impact studies?

Summary

Infant care is defined as programs for children aged from birth to three years. Because the infant-mother bond is viewed as an important developmental factor, there is still a great deal of debate as to whether infant care programs ought to be provided at all.

One of the chief issues in infant care is that of separation, but well-planned programs allow children to learn to form attachments with caregivers and cope with temporary separations from families. The three common settings are the infant's home, a family day care home, and an infant center. In mixed-age groups an infant's environment approximates the ideal of a natural home, but we are still questioning the developmental effects of caring for groups of infants together in an infant center.

Research in infant development is examining the infant's capacity to respond and discriminate, and the optimal periods when these capacities are at their peak. The infant's sensorimotor experiences are children's first ways of connecting with the world around them, and they form the roots of intelligence. Infants need an intimate, continuing relationship with a special person or persons. Infants may be put at risk of developmental delay or damage due to genetic, environmental, or social factors.

Much of an infant caregiver's time is spent in talking and touching and in social interaction with the children. Curriculum is embedded in such daily routines as eating and diapering. Staff-child ratios are of concern in infant care. For children from birth to two years, a ratio of one to three is recommended; two-year-olds may be cared for in a ratio of one to four. Since infants need a relationship with a "special person," caregivers must be alert to providing continuity in personnel, sharing the caregiver burden, and monitoring each caregiver's contact hours. A few simple guidelines for diapering and feeding can help to reduce potential health problems arising from periods of social contact.

Among the issues concerning infant care are the education of parents about the best choice for child care and the possible sources of financing quality infant care.

Resources

Overview

American Academy of Pediatrics, Committee on Infant and Preschool Child. (1971). *Standards for day care centers for infants and children under three years of age.* Evanston, IL: American Academy of Pediatrics.

Cataldo, C. (1982). *Infant and toddler programs: A guide to very early childhood education.* Reading, MA: Addison-Wesley.

Cohen, M. D. (Ed.). (1976). *Understanding and nurturing infant development.* Washington, DC: Association for Childhood Education International.

Denenberg, V. H. (Ed.). (1970). *Education of the infant and young child.* NY: Academic Press.

Elardo, R., & Pagan, B. (Ed.). (1976). *Perspectives on infant day care.* Little Rock, AK: Southern Association on Children Under Six (SACUS).

Haith, M. M. (1972). *Day care and intervention programs for infants.* Atlanta: Avatar Press.

Infancy in the eighties: Social policy and the earliest years of life. (1983). Washington, DC: National Center for Clinical Infant Programs.

Keister, M. E. (1970). *"The good life" for infants and toddlers.* Washington, DC: National Association for the Education of Young Children.

Kilmer, S. (1979). Infant-toddler group day care: A review of research. In L. Katz (Ed.), *Current topics in early education: Vol. 2* (pp. 69–115). Norwood, NJ: Ablex.

Provence, S., Naylor, A., & Patterson, J. (1977). *The challenge of day care.* New Haven: Yale University Press.

Ruopp, R., Travers, J., Glantz, F., Coelen, C. (1979). The infant/toddler day care study. In *Children at the center: Vol. 1. Final report of the national day care study.* Cambridge, MA: Abt Associates.

Silverstein, L. (1981). A critical review of current research on infant day care. In S. B. Kamerman & A. J. Kahn (Eds.), *Child care, family benefits, and working parents: A study in comparative policy.* New York: Columbia University Press.

Weissbourd, B., & Musick, J. S. (Eds.). (1981). *Infants: Their social environments.* Washington, DC: NAEYC.

White, S. H., Day, M. C., Freeman, P. K., Hantman, S. A., & Messenger, K. P. (1973). *Review of evaluation data for federally sponsored projects for children: Vol. II. Federal programs for children: Review and recommendations.* Washington, DC: Department of Health, Education and Welfare.

Witmer, H. (Ed.). (1967). *On rearing infants and young children in institutions.* Washington, DC: U.S. Department of Health, Education and Welfare, Children's Bureau.

Developmental Foundations

Ainsworth, M. D. S. (1973). The development of infant-mother attachment. In B. M. Caldwell & H. Ricciuti (Eds.), *Review of child development research: Vol. 3* (pp. 1–94). Chicago: IL: University of Chicago Press.

Bowlby, J. (1965). *Child care and the growth of love* (2nd ed.). Baltimore: Penguin.

Bowlby, J. (1969, 1973). *Attachment and loss: Vol. 1. Attachment. Vol. II. Separation.* New York: Basic Books.

Brazelton, T. B. (1969). *Infants and mothers.* New York: Dell.

Brazelton, T. B. (1974). *Todders and parents.* New York: Dell.

Dittmann, L. L. (Ed.). (1984). *The infants we care for* (rev. ed.). Washington, DC: NAEYC.

Evans, J., & Ilfeld, E. (1982). *Good beginnings.* Ypsilanti, MI: High/Scope Press.

Fraiberg, S. H. (1959). *The magic years.* New York: Scribner's.

Frank, L. K. (1966). *On the importance of infancy.* New York: Random House.

Goldhaber, D. (1979). Does the changing view of early experience imply a changing view of early development. In L. Katz (Ed.), *Current topics in early education: Vol. 2* (pp. 117–140). Norwood, NJ: Ablex.

International Children's Center. (1979). *Infant stimulation: A review for educators and primary care personnel.* (ERIC Document Reproduction Service No. ED 188 359)

Kagan, J. (1981). *The second year of life: The emergence of self-awareness.* Cambridge, MA: Harvard University Press.

Kagan, J. et al. (1978). *Infancy: Its place in human development.* Cambridge, MA: Harvard University Press.

Lewis, M., & Rosenblum, L. (Eds.). (1974). *The effect of the infant on its caregiver.* New York: Wiley.

Lipsitt, L. (Ed.). (1981, 1982). *Advances in infancy research: Vol. 1 and 2.* Norwood, NJ: Ablex.

McCall, R. B. (1979). *Infants.* Cambridge, MA: Harvard University Press.

Osofsky, J. D. (Ed.) (1979). *Handbook of infant development.* New York: Wiley.

Parkes, C. M., & Stevenson-Hinde, J. (Eds.). (1982). *The place of attachment in human behavior.* New York: Basic Books.

Provence, S. (1982). Infant day care: Relationships between theory and practice. In E. F. Zigler & E. W. Gordon (Eds.), *Day care: Scientific and social policy issues* (pp. 33–55). Boston: Auburn House.

Segal, M., & Adcock, D. (1979). *From birth to one year/from one to two years.* Rolling Hills Estates, CA: Winch and Associates.

Smart, M. S., & Smart, R. C. (1978). *Infants: Development and relationships* (2nd ed.). New York: Macmillan.

Stone, L. J., Smith, H. T., & Murphy, L. B. (Eds.). (1973). *The competent infant.* New York: Basic Books.

Werner, E. E. (1984). Resilient children. *Young Children, 40* (1), 68–72.

Implementing Programs

Anselmo, S., & Peterson, J. D. (1976). *A manual for caregivers of infants and toddlers.* Iowa City, IA: University of Iowa, Early Childhood Education Center. (ERIC Document Reproduction Service No. ED 152 408)

Appalachian Regional Commission. (1970). *Programs for infants and children.* Washington, DC: Appalachian Regional Commission.

Bailey, R. A., & Burton, E. C. (1982). *The dynamic self: Activities to enhance infant development.* St. Louis: C. V. Mosby.

Bond, L. A., & Joffe, J. M. (Eds.). (1982). *Facilitating infant and early child development.* Hanover, NH: New England Press.

Caldwell, B., & Stedman, D. (Eds.). (1977). *Infant education: A guide for helping handicapped children in the first three years.* New York: Walker.

Castle, K. (1983). *The infant and toddler handbook: Invitations for optimum development.* Atlanta: Humanics Ltd.

Cohen, M. (Ed.). (1977). *Developing programs for infants and toddlers.* Washington, DC: Association for Childhood Education International.

Eheart, B. K., & Leavitt, R. L. (1985). Supporting toddler play. *Young Children, 40* (3), 18–22.

Evans, E. B., & Saia, G. E. (1972). *Day care for infants.* Boston: Beacon Press.

Fowler, W. (1980a). *Curriculum and assessment guides for infant and child care.* Boston: Allyn and Bacon.

Fowler, W. (1980b). *Infant and child care: A guide to education in group settings.* Boston: Allyn and Bacon.

Furfey, P. H. (Ed.). (1972). *Education of children aged one to three: A curriculum manual.* Washington, DC: Catholic University.

Gonzalez-Mena, J., & Eyer, D. (1980). *Infancy and caregiving.* Palo Alto, CA: Mayfield.

Gordon, I. J. (1970). *Baby learning through baby play.* New York: St. Martins Press.

Gordon, I. J. (1970, 1975). *The infant experience.* Columbus, OH: Charles E. Merrill.

Herbert-Jackson, E., O'Brien, M., Porterfield, J., & Risley, T. R. (1977). *The infant center: A complete guide to organizing and managing infant day care.* Baltimore: University Park Press.

Hirshen, S., & Ouye, J. (1973). *The infant care center: A case study in design.* Washington, DC: Day Care and Child Development Council of America.

Honig, A. S., & Lally, J. R. (1981). *Infant caregiving: A design for training.* Syracuse, NY: Syracuse University Press.

Hunt, J. M. (1981). Toward a pedagogy for infancy and early childhood. In S. Kilmer (Ed.), *Advances in early education and day care: Vol. 2.* Greenwich, CT: JAI Press.

Huntington, D. S., Provence, S., & Parker, R. K. (Eds.). (1971). *Day care 2: Serving infants.* Washington, DC: U.S. Department of Health, Education and Welfare.

Infant care (rev. ed.) (1980). Washington, DC: U.S. Department of Health and Human Services.

Jones, E. (Ed.). (1979). *Supporting the growth of infants, toddlers and parents.* Pasadena, CA: Pacific Oaks.

Lally, J. R., & Gordon, I. J. (1977). *Learning games for infants and toddlers.* Syracuse, NY: New Readers Press. (ERIC Document Reproduction Service No. ED 149 860)

Marzollo, J., & Lloyd, J. (1972). *Learning through play.* New York: Harper & Row.

Maxim, G. (1980). *The very young: Guiding children from infancy through the early years.* Belmont, CA: Wadsworth.

Maxim, G. (1981). *The sourcebook: Activities to enrich programs for infants and young children.* Belmont, CA: Wadsworth.

Moss, H. A., Hess, R., & Surft, C. (Eds.). (1982). *Early intervention programs for infants.* New York: Haworth.

Neugebauer, R., & Lurie, R. (Eds.). (1980). *Caring for infants and toddlers: What works, what doesn't.* Belmont, MA: Child Care Information Exchange.

Neugebauer, R., & Lurie, R. (Eds.). (1982). *Caring for infants and toddlers: What works, what doesn't: Vol. II.* Redmond, WA: Child Care Information Exchange.

O'Brien, M., Porterfield, J., Herbert-Jackson, E., & Risley, T. (1979). *The toddler center: A practical guide to day care for one- and two-year-olds.* Baltimore, MD: University Park Press. (ERIC Document Reproduction Service No. ED 175 571)

Provence, S. (1975). *Guide for the care of infants in groups.* New York: Child Welfare League of America.

Robertson, A., & Overstad, B. (1979). *Infant-toddler growth and development: A guide for training child care workers.* St. Paul, MN: Toys 'n Things Press.

Segal, M. (1984). *Birth to one year: Month by month descriptions of baby's development with suggestions for games and activities.* New York: Mailman Family Press.

Tronick, E., & Greenfield, P. M. (1973). *Infant curriculum.* New York: Open Family, Media Projects, Inc.

Tyler, B., & Dittmann, L. (1980). Meeting the toddler more than halfway: The behavior of toddlers and their caregivers. *Young Children, 35* (2), 39–45.

Weiser, M. G. (1982). *Group care and education of infants and toddlers.* St. Louis: C. V. Mosby.

Willis, A., & Ricciuti, H. (1975). *A good beginning for babies: Guidelines for group care.* Washington, DC: NAEYC.

Women's Action Alliance. (1983). *Beginning equal: A manual about nonsexist childrearing for infants and toddlers.* New York: Women's Action Alliance.

Issues

Belsky, J., & Steinberg, L. D. (1978). The effects of day care: A critical review. *Child Development, 49,* 929–949.

Bloom, K. (Ed.). (1981). *Prospective issues in infancy research.* Hillsdale, NJ: Lawrence Erlbaum Associates.

Clarke-Stewart, A. (1977). *Child care in the family: A review of research and some propositions for polity.* New York: Academic Press.

Fein, G. G. (1976). *Infant day care and the family: Regulatory strategies to ensure parent participation.* Report prepared for the Office of the Assistant Secretary of Planning and Evaluation, DHEW.

Fraiberg, S. (1977). *Every child's birthright: In defense of mothering.* New York: Basic Books.

Frye, D. (1982). The problem of infant day care. In E. F. Zigler & E. W. Gordon (Eds.), *Day care: Scientific and social policy issues* (pp. 223–242). Boston: Auburn House.

Honig, A. S. (1972). *Infant development: Problems in intervention.* Washington, DC: Day Care and Child Development Council of America.

NAEYC public policy report. (1981). Advocacy strategies: The care of infants and toddlers. *Young Children, 36* (2), 51–56.

Ramey, C. T. (1981). Consequences of infant day care. In B. Weissbourd & J. S. Musick (Eds.), *Infants: Their social environments* (pp. 65–76). Washington, DC: NAEYC.

Rutter, M. (1982). Social-emotional consequences of day care for preschool children. In E. F. Zigler & E. W. Gordon (Eds.), *Day care: Scientific and social policy issues* (pp. 3–71). Boston: Auburn House.

Scott, M., & Grimmett, S. (Eds.). (1977). *Current issues in child development.* Washington, DC: NAEYC.

Seitz, V. (1982). A Methodological Comment on "The Problem of Infant Day Care". In E. F. Zigler & E. W. Gordon (Eds.), *Day care: Scientific and social policy issues* (pp. 223–242). Boston: Auburn House.

Newsletters

Zero to three
National Center for Clinical Infant Programs
733 15th St. N.W. Suite 912
Washington, DC 20005

Caring for infants and toddlers: What works, what doesn't.
Resources for Child Care Management
P.O. Box 669
Summit, NJ 07901

8

School-Age Care

Introduction

During the hours of school attendance, school personnel have responsibility for the supervision and safety of children. Supervision of children's activities for the hours before and after school, and during holidays, summer vacations, and times of illness is presumed to be the responsibility of parents. However, we know from our study of statistics about families and economic indicators that few parents have continual, personal supervision of their children outside of school hours. Care for school-age children when school is not in session is an issue of increasing concern in the United States.

Where are the children? Who is watching? The answers to these questions are as varied as the families involved. Children's interests, labor force status of mother, family composition, income, race, and availability of care alternatives tell us that there is a dizzying array of care solutions for school-age children. Some are formal programs, some are informal arrangements, and many are "no care" or self-care by a child (often called latchkey children). Few school-age children are found in center-based care.

This chapter tells you what is happening in the field of school-age care, helps you understand why and how programs operate, and then gives you the tools and resources to go forward yourself. We begin with a summary and analysis of current school-age care alternatives. A discussion of developmental concepts and processes related to school-age children contributes a theoretical perspective and builds on the three points of view (maturationist, behaviorist, and cognitive) used in previous chapters. Summary charts of developmental characteristics of school-age children are also given since they are necessary for program implementation.

Because school-age children spend increasing amounts of time outside the family circle, we need to discuss some of the social influences on development, including chemical substance abuse, sex-role stereotyping, and maternal employment.

Our school-age program design framework considers children and parents to be almost equal co-consumers of care. The role of the professional is more reactive than directive in determining the initial focus of care programs in any given locality. However, the model clearly supports considerable professional input for the implementation and administration of different kinds of programs. The basic care and curriculum components of the daily care pattern are adapted to the particular demands of school-age care. Among the programs we consider are center-based, school-based, family day care, focused activity, and parental or self-supervision situations. Finally, we explore several controversial issues in this area, such as latchkey children and the role of the schools.

Characteristics of School-Age Programs

Informal or parent care is the modal form of care for school-age children. Formally organized programs for school-age care do exist, but not many are available and participation rates among potential users are low. Those programs that do exist are now receiving considerable attention as more people become aware of the need for school-age child care. The characteristics of current programs are of interest because they help us understand the range of alternatives and identify program dimensions that are related to demand, participation, and children's developmental growth.

School-age care includes care that substitutes for parental care of the child during those periods when school is not in session. The child care may be formal or informal; it may involve adult supervision or self-supervision by the child. School-age children are aged six to fourteen years. Children older than fourteen (or sixteen in some states) are presumed to be able to care for themselves for short periods of time.

A Profile of Current Programs

Drawing on published case studies, critical analyses of programs, surveys of current practices, and extensive personal experience, we have constructed the following profile of current programs. First, most programs are organized to provide after-school care. A few settings allow for easier management of before-school care. A very few programs temporarily expand hours to cover vacations. Some programs operate for summers only. Almost no night care or weekend care is available. Care for sick children is very rare.

Children ages six to nine years are most frequently enrolled in center settings either as an "add-on" program to a preschool center or less frequently as a school-age special purpose program. Younger children are more likely to receive before-school care as well as after-school care. Older children are more frequently found in after-school programs based in community facilities. Children ages ten years and up are least likely to be found in organized programs.

Center settings are more frequently found for younger children. School-based settings can be found for all ages. Family day care homes in children's neighborhoods appear to be the most frequent mode of care other than parent or informal care. Very few programs operate in community facilities such as a "Y" or recreation center. The more formal the program, the more likely it is to provide basic supervision and a fixed choice of activities. Some settings and sponsors offer single-purpose activities. Very few programs offer changing combinations of settings and activities.

School-age programs are not usually the hub of a constellation of comprehensive services. Those that provide a service array are receiving federal or other public funds and are accountable to federal and state regulations. These programs are most likely to provide snacks, meals, and transportation. Little comparable data exist on costs to parents and costs of operation. The diversity of programs means that costs are either not available separately or are reported in ways that are not comparable. It is expensive to operate a program with so much "down time." Facilities and staff are hard to hold on to for just a few hours a day. Overall, few public funds are used to purchase school-age care. Some costs are absorbed by sponsors; most are paid from parent fees. Sponsorship for school-age programs is rarely vested in one source. Community groups, parents, school, and corporations have been involved in partnerships to provide care. Programs using public funds must meet established licensing and regulation requirements in areas such as staffing, programs, and services. Many school-age programs are not "good matches" with requirements because scope, facility, or sponsorship are not easily categorized according to licensing specifications.

Staffing is a function of applicable regulations. In many localities staffing regulations for school-age programs are not very different than those for younger children. Because school-age children are older and likely to be in care for very different periods of time, many professionals question the appropriateness of simply extending regulations designed for younger children in different care situations. Should certified school teachers be used as staff in school-age programs? This is an unresolved issue because such teachers are perceived to have training and skills that are not necessarily required for caregiving staff. Also, pay can be an issue if the child care staff is to be paid on the same scale as the classroom teacher.

Many child care arrangements can be categorized as informal or parent supervised. These may in fact be a sequence or collection of related child participation activities (such as sports or lessons) that are coordinated or monitored by the parent. Thus, what is reported as parent care may actually be an individually tailored child care program. The nature of informal arrangements and parent supervision needs to be explored since no available information systematically describes self-care situations.

Goals for Programs

When we consider all types of formal programs and care arrangements for school-age children, we can identify four major program goals: supervision, recreation, diversion, and stimulation. Many care experiences incorporate all four goals into program formats; others have services keyed to one goal or another.

1. *Supervision* Supervision includes basic care and physical monitoring of children's activities and whereabouts. This is the "shelter and protection" component of child care. Supervision ranges from passive to active. Passive supervision is nothing more than providing a place for the children to go, a time to be there, and a time to leave. What happens in between is left up to the children. Most parental or self-care supervisions are presumed to be such passive supervision. In contrast, active supervision situations place adults in face-to-face contact with children and require that some program staff be responsible for children at all times during care.

   Basic care encompasses the provision of food (snacks and meals) and comfort (emotional and physical). Supervision should be a fundamental building block of all care experiences for school-age children, but often it is not. Many care situations are short on comfort and questionable in terms of adequate supervision.
2. *Recreation* Many programs operate under the assumption that after many hours in school children need a change of pace. Play, both mental and physical, is refreshing for the body and mind. Recreation activities can foster considerable skill development and serve as the basis for many personal growth opportunities. They can also be reduced to supervised play or organized chaos if children are continually allowed to go their own way with equipment or activities.
3. *Diversion* Child care experiences in this category are those involving a strong element of attention. These activities elicit or demand considerable involvement from children. Recreation activities may or may not be diversionary. Diversionary activities include craft projects, trips, jobs and chores, theater or play groups, and other activities that capitalize on children's interests and keep them busy.
4. *Stimulation* This category is for all the experiences that are educational. The common theme is providing experiences from which children can learn. Stimulation activities may be recreational and command attention, but they are also developmental and teach children new ways of behaving and interacting. They do not always provide basic care or supervision, especially if stimulation activities are scheduled once a week or less and children are left to their own devices at times when formal lessons or practices are not scheduled.

Developmental Foundations

The ages from six to fourteen correspond to elementary through junior high school. This period is one of increasing mental competence and

Sports programs exemplify a recreational focus. Exercise and amusement are the objectives for activities and games. (Courtesy of U.S. Department of Health and Human Services, Washington, DC.)

diverse socializing experiences. The developmental needs and characteristics of school-age children are a logical source when designing school-age care programs. Major psychological changes occur during this period; development is also heavily influenced by factors in children's general social and emotional environments. Obviously, too, the developmental status and needs of children do not remain the same throughout this age range. Children at different points of the age range are sufficiently different to require separate planning for their care experiences. Typically, children at six years are learning to read while children around fourteen years are entering a period of intense search for self-identity.

Patterns of Development

For young children (infants and preschoolers) developmental progress means many changes in physical characteristics, increases in mental complexity and competence, acquisition of language skills, and new ways of participating in familiar social groups.

For school-age children, no single developmental viewpoint appears to be adequate by itself as a means of providing a comprehensive basis for child care programming. In general, physical development slows down during the six- to fourteen-year-old period. Baby teeth are replaced by larger, permanent teeth; muscles and bones grow in mass and strength; coordination improves and stamina increases. During the entirety of this school-age period, however, no qualitative change in physical structures occurs that is comparable to the peak of walking for the toddler or the onset of puberty for the adolescent. Language mastery is achieved, and language becomes a tool that is refined and used in mental tasks such as reading. Increasing language skill for the school-age child is a function of both instructional opportunities and cultural situations. The school-age child emerges from the relatively sheltered cocoon of family life and begins to grow some social wings. Gradually,

Interest and participation in social group play peak during the six- to ten-year-old period. (Courtesy of U.S. Department of Health and Human Services, Washington, DC.)

throughout the six- to fourteen-year-old period, the child increases and consolidates all developmental gains in the context of an enlarging social group, which expands to include the gang, the team, and the class.

Within the school-age period it is possible to identify three rather homogeneous age groupings that correspond to this gradually increasing involvement of the child with others. The social status of the child within each of these age groups suggests goals for child care experiences that are compatible with the social context of the child's development. These age groupings are a function of the interaction of development and social opportunity, and can be discussed independent of particular developmental perspectives. If you observe school-age children at work and at play, you will find children's activities clustered around these age groupings. The groupings are approximate; individual children will vary in exhibiting the behavior patterns for each grouping.

1. *Family and Friends—Ages Six to Nine or Ten* This period corresponds to schooling from first grade through third. Frequently kindergartners, aged five, will become part of this group if school entrance and play opportunities are similarly timed. At the beginning of this period familiar playmates are sought and children have a loose, easily defined circle of friends. By age nine or ten the "gang" is an important part of a child's life. Rules can be rigid, play very much sex segregated, and exclusion from the group painful. It is the social structure that is important, with much less emphasis on the content of the play. Activities are fanciful, complex, and varied; what is most important, however, is *who* plays and *how* everything operates.

   Few school-age children participate in center-based day care, but those who do are most likely to be ages five to nine or ten. The grouping patterns of center activities plus the program's ability to fill in for hours outside school are conducive conditions. Children of six to ten need adult supervision for comfort, security, and stimulation. Thus, this age group is a prime target for prevailing forms of school-age care programs.
2. *Consolidation—Ages Eleven to Twelve* This period marks a comfortable phase for the late elementary school-age child. School and extracurricular achievements begin to give children some distinctive characteristics. Specific friends within the group are selected. Most children have a sense of security and the skills to handle basics of daily living such as packing their lunch, bathing and washing their hair, doing errands, making store purchases, bus riding, and telephoning.

   Single-purpose activities, lessons, and hobbies all appeal to children in this age group. Some children intensively pursue activities in a chosen field and develop real expertise playing musical instruments, dancing, or playing sports. Some children require specialized staff to pursue their interests, others merely need space and time for stamps, model building, and reading. The individual child's need for adult supervision will be partly a function of the child's growing independence and the parents' confidence in relaxing supervision. Few children in this age range are found in formal, organized day care programs. Rather, children's after-school experiences may vary daily depending on the child's interests, activity opportunities, and the flexibility allowed by the parent for self-supervision.

3. *Preadolescence—Ages Thirteen to Fourteen* The junior high school child is just on the threshold of adolescence. The preadolescent years are characterized by new physical energies, the sporadic beginnings of real physical sexual changes, and some unpredictability in behavior and personality. Where harmony and industry once prevailed, strains occur in the child's relationships with family, peers, and friends. Some children continue to pursue favored activities and interests, but a qualitative change in the child's participation behavior occurs. Children begin to be conscious of themselves as unique people. Their quest for self-identity, which is the hallmark of adolescence, has its beginnings about age thirteen to fourteen. Children begin to examine themselves in the context of the familiar activities of childhood. The activities and relationships that once seemed so fulfilling are no longer sufficient. Many of the same activities and programs that appeal to children ages eleven to twelve will continue to attract preadolescents. But changes in social behavior, emotional needs, and physical concerns will require sensitive adult handling. Children may turn away from their parents to other adults or peers for information and support in understanding their changing bodies and feelings. Children and parents eventually confront the issue of independence and may struggle mightily to reach a satisfactory balance of self-supervision and parent control. Very few children in this age range receive child care through homes or centers. Except for unusual situations, the demand for child care services for these children is nonexistent. Perhaps by default, parents and program planners accept the fact that children this age determine their own activities.

Developmental Theories

The social context in which school-age children's development occurs, which we just described, forms a backdrop for examining the specifics of developmental change. Each of the three theoretical perspectives must recognize the influence of social behavior within the three age groupings. Our discussion here is limited to those ages and corresponding theoretical assumptions and developmental periods that are particularly useful for planners of school-age care programs.

The Maturationist Viewpoint. Over the years Gesell and his colleagues compiled extensive word portraits of children's typical behavior at each age (Gesell, Ilg, & Ames, 1977). School-age child care planners are, of course, most interested in those descriptions for ages six to fourteen years. Table 8.1 presents several normative capsule descriptions for ages six to twelve years. You are encouraged to obtain the complete developmental chart if you are working with school-age children. Many feel that in the upper ages these normative descriptions are too superficial to be of much help to program planners. At these ages unique personal and social factors impact so much on the genetic patterns of development that the normative approach appears to be too simplistic to capture all important behavior patterns.

Erikson extends and shapes a view of development drawn from Freud's work (Erikson, 1968). For Erikson, development follows a genetically programmed plan that unfolds within a social context. At each of eight stages in life, a person must resolve a major psychosocial crisis for development to proceed. Early crises are due to the child's conflicts between instinct and reality, while later crises relate to nuances and decisions in social situations.

Erikson's Stage IV, roughly from the sixth

Table 8.1 Samples of Normative Data on School-Age Children

School Grade	Characteristic	
One	*Physical*	*Social*
	Growth is varied between boys and girls. Girls are about a year more mature than boys. Height is about two-thirds of adult height. The body is about two-fifths of adult size.	Still admires parents most. Mother is not center of attention. Father gets better obedience. Child is demanding, hesitant, and companionable with parent. Interest is lost in family membership.
Three	*Emotional*	*Physical*
	Feelings become more sensitive, emotions more concealed. Child may cry easily and is sensitive to criticism.	Large muscles are still developing. Strength and improvement of motor skills and body controls are rapidly improving. Arm and leg muscles are not strongly developed, resulting in a look of spindly weakness.
Five	*Emotional*	*Social*
	Happiness and contentment are prevalent. Simple occasions are pleasurable. Bursts of happiness and demonstrative affection are frequent.	Relations with peers: Peers are dominating influence; their approval is sought. Group cooperative spirit is combined with competitive spirit. More organized games and sports with rules are played. Boys develop teamwork and team loyalty.
Seven	*Physical*	*Social*
	General development: Sleep is again less heavy. Health is good, but may not be consistent. Fatigue may come easily.	Group loyalties are well developed. The spirit of the game has meaning. There may be membership in a club. Small groups are preferred.

Source: "Chart of development" by F. Lanning and R. Robbins. Reprinted from *Instructor,* August–September 1966. © 1966 by Instructor Publications, Inc. Used by permission.

year to puberty, is of interest to planners of school-age programs. Prior stages bring children through crises of trust versus mistrust, autonomy versus shame and doubt, and initiative versus guilt. In these earlier stages the children's social sphere expands from mother to the basic family as the children achieve some self-control and purposeful direction. In Stage IV the dominant psychosocial crisis revolves around industry versus inferiority. Children achieve method and competence as they focus on work that requires skillful activity. Their social sphere broadens beyond the family to include school and neighborhood. This is a period of cooperation, competition, and factual mastery. Learning takes precedence over maturation and children come to identify themselves in terms of their achievements. Inferiority feelings occur when children think themselves unable to master the basic skills expected of them by society. As children gain confidence and develop industrious behaviors, they think positively about adult autonomy. Erikson's approach to development has much intuitive appeal for those who work with school-age children since he provides a coherent, realistic explanation of the dynamics of development that appear to dominate this period.

The Behaviorist Viewpoint. The behaviorist assumes that all behavior is learned, and development occurs as gradual, incremental changes in behavior. The older the child, the broader the learning base of experiences and the more likely that generalization and transfer will occur. Skills such as tying transfer from shoelaces to hats, sashes, and ropes in many uses. Self-help behaviors that start as simple tasks such as pouring juice, crossing the street, and combing one's hair become complex, general skills such as making breakfast, running an errand, and independent bathing and dressing. Model programs derived from behaviorist theories rely on purposeful teacher behavior, sequential content arrangement, and systematic reinforcement to effect learning. Curricula protocols from these projects can serve as models for school-age day care program staff who need to teach specific skills. However, few school-age programs are likely to be organized on the assumption that adults in charge will specify activities, arrange events, and control reinforcement, leaving the child in a passive, responding situation. While learning does take place in school-age programs, it is usually not the primary goal of program activities.

The Cognitive Viewpoint. The work of Piaget (Flavell, 1963; Inhelder & Piaget, 1958) and Kohlberg (1969) has important implications for planners of school-age child care programs. Piagetian theory uses a series of universal, qualitative stages to describe the invariant sequence of development. Stage III—concrete operations, ages seven to eleven—represents a period when logic and objectivity characterize the child's thought patterns. Children can typically classify objects, order or seriate objects, and transform or reverse actions. All these mental operations are handled in relation to actual events and objects—thus the stage name of concrete operations. Formal operations—Stage IV, ages eleven to fifteen—describes the child as moving toward abstract thinking and rationalization, no longer tied to the physical reality of objects and events. Many observers consider Piaget's theory to be lopsided because of its emphasis on mental functions. The complicated vocabulary and complex mental processes Piaget describes leave many practitioners feeling that the theory is not easily applied to daily program needs. For the school-age day care program planner, a general understanding of the mechanisms and stage achievements related to Piaget's theory will prove helpful in working with children since children think in ways that are different from adults. Adults working with children must respect that and be able to respond accordingly.

Kohlberg formulated an interactional view of development based on the idea that a child's cognitive structures result from the interaction of mental and social conditions. Applying his theory to moral socialization, Kohlberg describes six stages of morality organized into three levels. In Stages I through IV, the child is essentially egocentric. The Stage V child sees the possibility for changing morality by mutual consent in some situations. The Stage VI child exhibits a moral conscience that guides action toward the goal of general community. Kohlberg maintains that the growth of morality occurs during the first through sixth grades. However, not all and perhaps not many people ever reach Stages V and VI. Many feel that Kohlberg's point of view cannot accommodate all situations or individual needs and incentives that may affect specific moral judgments. This theoretical position is helpful to school-age day care program planners, however, because it highlights the existence of different levels of moral response and provides some guidelines against which questions about morality can be evaluated.

Social Influences on Development

The school-age child is especially vulnerable to social influences. Much of the "fuel" for development comes from the people and social environment around the child. General aspects of society and culture shape development, both positively and negatively. How school-age chil-

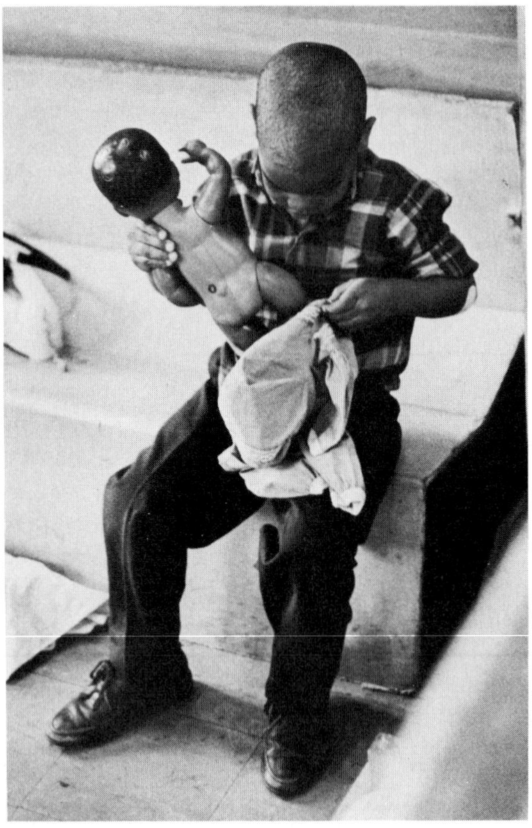

We are more conscious today of providing children with role models and play opportunities that are not sex-specific. (Courtesy of U.S. Department of Health and Human Services, Washington, DC.)

dren come in contact with and deal with these forces influences personal growth.

Chemical Substance Abuse

No responsible adult working with school-age children should remain ignorant of the signs of chemical substance abuse. Drugs, alcohol, and tobacco are more accessible, and use is more prevalent than most of us like to think. Patterns of use change. Strong peer pressure to experiment, personal needs to reduce inner tensions, or generalized rebellion at authority may provoke children to try chemical substances.

Many schools and child care programs routinely discuss chemical substance abuse and provide information on drawbacks of use. Many give strong emotional support for resisting dependency. Some formal curriculum programs for abuse prevention stress decision-making skills and build self-esteem. Child care programs can help children and parents contact community services or professionals capable of providing therapy for chemical substance abuse problems.

Sex-Role Stereotyping

The visible indicators of the women's liberation movement are such sights as girls in Little League uniforms and boys in home economic classes. Children of both sexes may grow up equally fond of dolls and with reasonable access to a wide range of athletic activities. Yet the arguments rage over whether this equality is "ethically" right or whether innate, biological differences between the sexes really prevail and matter. Some families rigidly equalize activities for children of both sexes, some rigidly segregate chores and promote feminism and masculinity. Most families fall in between.

Programs for school-age children do reflect the general loosening of sex-role stereotyping to the degree that staff, parents, and children have adopted new attitudes. Occasionally tension arises as children, staff, or parents perceive program activities to be inconsistent with their attitudes toward sex-appropriate activities. Local conditions and people will determine whether a program's position is activist, status quo, or passive.

Maternal Employment

Developmental psychologists have increasingly concentrated research efforts on the effects of maternal employment on school-age children's development. Clarke-Stewart (1977) concluded from a review of studies on maternal employment that mothers' satisfaction with work status is associated with positive benefits for children. However, the picture is not completely encouraging. According to Clarke-Stewart, "supervision of the child while the mother is working is also relevant—particularly to the child's intellectual development. Unsupervised children (who are almost inevitably from low-income families) tend to experience much greater cognitive impoverishment than those who are supervised." (1977, p. 48)

Hoffman (1979) reported that the developmental needs of school-age children fit well with the situation of a working mother. Independence skills, social adjustment, and academic achievement are positively related to maternal employment. For daughters especially, maternal employment appears to enhance competence and socialization. Findings for sons differ by social class. For lower-class sons there may be strain in the father-son relationship, but there is little indication of adverse effects on socialization or cognitive ability. However, for middle-class sons, maternal employment has been frequently associated with diminished academic performance. Further research is necessary to determine the conditions and circumstances associated with these differences between boys and girls.

Children's Interests

Developmental needs are not the sole determinant of program content or quality. Children ages six to fourteen years are capable of expressing vigorous and effective opinions regarding their extended care experiences. They are "co-consumers" of child care programs. The melding of children's interests and their perceived developmental needs probably accounts for the very wide range of activities found in programs. The following list describes five common areas of interests (Military Child Care Project, 1982):

School-age children want to choose and do real work This might include caring for animals, shopping for groceries, painting equipment or furniture, caring for younger children, or building a clubhouse.

School-age children want to practice and show off their skills Children like to be the best at what they do. They will practice and learn the skills needed to excel in anything from sports to reading, riding a bike, or painting.

School-age children like clubs Children love to have activities organized as clubs with rules, meeting places, and emblems. Centers can recognize and serve this need.

School-age children want to learn leisure activities School-age children like to learn hobbies, individual sports, and creative ways to use their leisure time. Centers can fill the gap that schools may ignore.

School-age children want to learn about the community Make other parts of the community as much a part of the child care environment as possible. This can include field trips and recreation like bowling or swimming. It is also a great benefit to the children if they can safely walk to and from these various activities.

We can make two critical points regarding children's developmental characteristics and the demand and need for school-age care. First, there is a dynamic interaction between children's interests and choice or participation in extended care programs. Second, the child's increasing maturity influences participation. At some point parent and child agree on a reduction of adult supervision.

Framework for Program Design

For school-age children, there are many paths to quality programs. Rather than stress the differences among programs, and rather than overwhelm the program planner with masses of detail about program operations in different locales, we advocate starting with the basics and finding similarities. All programs must provide basic care, which is important even for school-

Time	Activity Unit	Basic Care	Care Decisions
3:00 P.M.	Arrival	Accountability	Who checks child in? What are program responses to "no-shows"? Is transportation included in the program? How are sick children or emergencies handled?
	Snack	Nutrition	Who decides kind of food and portion size? Who pays for food? Are food service standards applicable?
	Program Activities	Protective Environment	Are facilities, equipment, and activities safe and appropriate for children? What kind of on-going staff supervision is provided? Is the program insulated from intrusions and disruptions?
6:00 P.M.	Departure	Accountability	What are checkout procedures? Is transportation provided? Are children's belongings accounted for each day?

Figure 8.1 Basic care for school-age care.

age children. All programs have periods during which children and staff pursue curricular activities. Certain features such as staff, equipment, and facilities are common in all programs. Finally, all programs operate with a set of goals, implicit or explicit, that shape daily and long-term activities. The components of school-age care programs, therefore, form a basic framework for program design that applies to centers, homes, recreational facilities, or any other setting. When we analyze quality programs, we find consistency in the experiences that children have and an explicit logic about the relationships of program parts. Planning and operating school-age care programs can and should be a deliberate effort.

The planning model illustrated in this chapter applies to all sponsorship and setting conditions and all program goal and activity variations. Current programs can use the model to identify and analyze components and their relationships.

Basic Care

Basic care is an obligation of programs. Basic care can be overemphasized, of course, sometimes to the point where nothing else happens in programs. However, because it is necessary, our program design model begins with basic care elements.

Since after-school care is the major focus of most programs, let's use that time period (3 P.M. to 6 P.M.) for illustration of the model (see Figure 8.1). Actual program hours will vary somewhat. Four activity units occur during that period: arrival, snack, program activities, and departure. These four activity units correspond to basic care services of accountability, nutrition, protective environment, and accountability again. For each basic care component, programs must make decisions about the type and amount of attention the program will expend on monitoring basic care.

Figure 8.2 provides examples of basic care services provided by a parent-child supervision situation and a recreation program. In both instances, accountability procedures are present, food is available, and activities occur in protected environments. In which situation would you want your child? How do such factors as age of child, geographic location of program, or transportation affect your assessment of the adequacy of these basic care situations? At what points or under what conditions can programs and/or parents take "reasonable risks" and

Time	Activity Unit	Parent/Self Supervision Basic Services
3:00 P.M.	Arrival	Child (7-year-old) walks home with sixth grader. Uses own key to enter house, locks door behind, calls mother at work to check in.
	Snack	Helps self to fruit, crackers, and yogurt as mother said. Finds old Halloween candy to eat.
	Program Activities	Watches TV, eats more, calls friend on phone, sets table, plays with dog, reads comic books, does some homework. Calls mother twice.
6:30 P.M.	Departure	Mother and father arrive home.

Time	Activity Unit	Recreation Program Basic Services
3:00 P.M.	Arrival	Activity leaders take attendance. Look for children who were in school but are not at program. No calls to parents made.
	Snack	Children bring food from home or use vending machines. No special snack time.
	Program Activities	Each activity has specially trained instructors who run planned skill development activities. Supervision is continuous. Hall monitors roam corridors and watch doors.
5:00 P.M.	Departure	Children leave as they return swim towels and collect gear. Most take city bus home.

Figure 8.2 Examples of basic care.

limit some features of basic care? These are highly personal questions that no model can answer, but studying basic care tells you that programs and parents need to address these questions.

Developmental Program Opportunities

Developmental planning, unlike basic care, implies that programs are sensitive to children's needs and use some acceptable standards for selecting and organizing activities. In the school-age program model, one unit—program activities—offers the greatest opportunity for developmental emphasis. Many factors influence the decisions about program focus and curricular goals. A particular program chooses a particular line of developmental activities because of local factors. For example, in some localities programs could not operate at all without public school involvement. That involvement may be dictatorial or cooperative with respect to program goals. In other locations, need may be greatest for care facilities for older elementary children. Suburbia can be a wasteland for twelve- to fourteen-year-olds after school. Other communities with well-developed recreation and parks staffs may choose to capitalize on that resource and plan after-school programs with a recreation focus. By identifying decision factors that enter into local program decisions, you can assess the adequacy of program resources and work toward a "good fit" with those resources.

Implementing Programs

The best way to understand school-age child care programs is to observe several programs in operation and talk to staff, directors, parents, and children; then gather up documents, notes, and other materials for further study. This sounds good but is not practical for most of us. The next best method is to look at program descriptions and try to piece them together. This section does just that, giving you practical details on program operation. These descriptions are composites of several program types and include useful examples of practice. Resources for further reading are at the end of the chapter.

To put everything in perspective, remember that we identified three developmental curricular modes: recreation, diversion, and stimulation. These labels refer to the activity focus and goals of a program. The programs described in this section are examples of those activity modes. Some programs have a single focus; others are mixtures.

Center-Based School-Age Programs

The center-based program for school-aged children is typically both an extension of and an adaptation of prevailing forms of center-based care for preschool children. This model appeals to many because it is a relatively known quantity.

The two major types of center-based programs are add-on programs that build school-age care around an ongoing preschool program, and group programs that serve *only* school-age children. Both have the potential to provide quality care. The operational characteristics of add-on and group programs are similar. Important differences will be highlighted in the following descriptions and examples.

Hours of Operation. Center-based programs for school-age children are organized to provide care on a daily basis around the hours of school attendance. Some programs are responsive to care needs for full days when school is not in session. A few programs may operate only for periods of the year such as winter holidays or spring vacations, or summers only.

Before-school hours range from 6:30 A.M. to 9 A.M. Add-on programs are often set up to receive children of early shift workers and provide breakfast, but some programs do not accept school-age children before school because of transportation difficulties. Group programs may not be able to enroll enough children before school to warrant operating for this short time period. Lack of breakfast facilities and transportation may also preclude group program operation before school. After-school hours are considered to be the major time period for school-age programs. Hours range from 3 P.M. to 6:30 P.M. Add-on and group center programs often operate only during this time period. Some add-on programs may serve only kindergartners for this after-school period. Figure 8.3 shows a daily schedule for an add-on program.

Ages of Children. Many state regulations assume that children up to ages fourteen or sixteen years will be served by child care centers. In practice, most center programs find that ages nine or ten are about the upper limits for add-on programs. Group programs and those add-on programs that can handle a school-age group in addition to preschoolers typically enroll children ages five to about twelve years. In centers dependent on public funding, subsidized care is allocated to younger children in greater proportion than to older school-age children, lowering the average age of children served in these centers. Both add-on and group centers provide the closely supervised activity and familiar setting thought to be developmentally advantageous for children in the early school years.

Settings and Facilities. Churches, community halls, store fronts, and other facilities become the base of operation for school-age programs. Licensing and zoning regulations affect the locations and buildings that can be used for center care. Add-on programs benefit from the cost effectiveness of facilities that are in continuous use. Any efforts expended on facility upgrading to meet standards can be amortized over all the children and programs using the facilities. Group programs and vacation-only programs may face unrealistic costs in improving facilities to meet standards. Standards for centers typically cover children ages three to fourteen or sixteen and are written in the most restrictive sense. That is, the center facility is considered safe for the youngest, most vulnerable user; to many it is then overly protective of the oldest users or, more importantly, it becomes too expensive to establish a center facility for the short period needed for group care for school-age children.

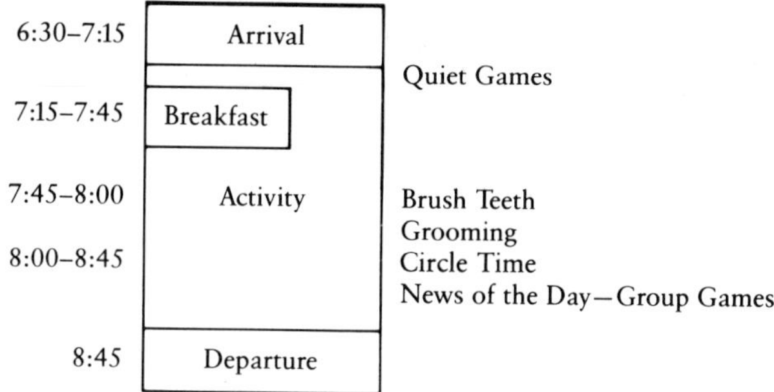

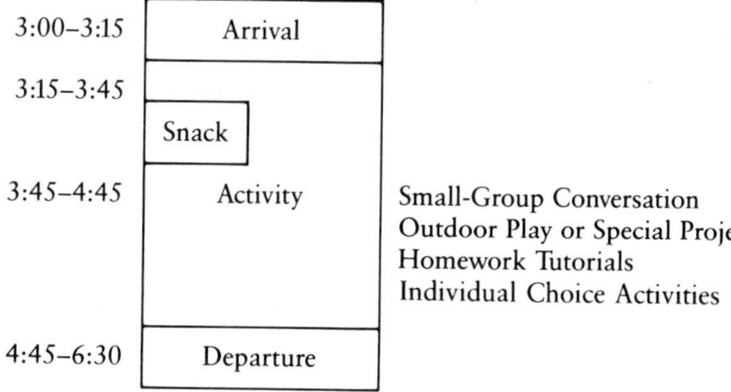

Figure 8.3 Daily schedule for an add-on school-age program.

Program Activities. School-age children in add-on programs draw upon the equipment and staff resources of the entire program. Activities are keyed to children's interests and energy levels. They may include the following activities or games (*School Age NOTES*, November/December, 1983; used with permission):

Activities

- Growing plants
- Cooking
- Gardening
- Race-car Making
- Health Awareness—teach real skills such as how to use and read thermometer, first-aid, and CPR (Cardio Pulmonary Resuscitation)
- Publish newspaper
- Learn another communication method: Sign language, Braille, and Morse Code
- Field trips
  - X-Ray Dept.—local hospital
  - Computer Office
  - TV and/or radio station or newspaper office
  - Local campus (high school and/or college)
  - A *real* dairy where cows are milked

Games with Rules

- Dodge Ball
- Kick Ball
- Hockey Pockey
- Playing Cards: Concentration, War, Go Fish, I Doubt It, Slap Jack, Crazy Eights, Rummy, Hearts, Twenty-one, Solitaire
- Board Games: Monopoly, Boggle, Scrabble, Life, Clue, Checkers, Chinese Checkers, Jackstraws, Chess, Tic-Tac-Toe, and Bingo
- Treasure Hunt
- Scavenger Hunt
- Marbles
- Jump Rope
- Soccer
- Badminton
- Volleyball
- Jacks

An add-on program may choose to devote considerable after-school time to tutorial work and homework. Another add-on program may consider after-school time to be children's personal time and hold periodic group planning meetings at which children help select and plan special projects and activities. Some programs follow a more formal curriculum plan, using seasonal themes, recreation skill development, or community events for which staff can provide special guidance.

Services. Child care centers, particularly publicly funded centers, are the hub of a network of social and health services available for eligible children. Center-based programs are likely to be able to provide such service or referral for school-age children. However, this is true primarily of add-on center programs that coexist with preschool programs. Proprietary centers are not likely to provide service or referral for social or health care because costs would have to be borne directly by the program.

Costs and Fees. Costs for school-age center-based programs are difficult to determine. Comparative costs are misleading because cost units are very different from program to program. In general, center programs must carry specialized staff costs because the short hours of service and long downtime of facility use increase unit costs. Transportation needs, specialized equipment, and activity fees all add to overall cost. Box 8.1 shows a sample budget.

Sponsorship. Add-on programs are generally under the auspices of a public agency or contractor providing services for public assistance recipients. Group center-based programs may be operated by parent cooperatives, church groups, or community organizations. Eligibility for enrollment is determined by sponsorship.

Staffing. Staffing is of special concern in center-based programs. For the add-on programs, attention must be paid to the length of a staff member's day. An eight-hour day that includes morning and early afternoon with preschoolers or toddlers and then late afternoon with school-age children is too tiring and demanding. Not all staff can or want to work with both age groups. Equally, however, few staff people want to work just two and a half hours a day in the late afternoon either. School-age programs may need staff members with specialized talents and staff who have some specific knowledge of developmental needs for school-age children. Staff turnover is a problem. Careful staff selection, frequent positive supervision, and livable wages are necessary conditions to attract and keep staff.

Parent Participation. Sponsorship conditions and preschool center care experience affect parent participation. Those parents who are "old timers" to center-based care will continue to be involved with parent meetings, parent advisory committees, fund raisers, and other events. Add-on programs draw parents into the mainstream of the center's parent activities. Group programs with heavy parent investment in sponsorship through agencies or cooperative groups can expect involvement in policy and financial matters.

School-Based Programs

School-based programs enjoy some degree of affiliation or support from local school officials. Programs sponsored fully by school officials are one major form of care. Programs that use school facilities but are sponsored by parent groups or other agencies seem to be increasing in number. Basing the child care program at school appeals to many as a cost-efficient and convenient solution to some of the financial and transportation hassles faced by center-based care programs. The program sponsorship—community or school—influences the program. Program descriptions and examples given in the following sections highlight the similarities and differences of programs that can be attributed to sponsorship.

Hours of Operation. School-based programs provide care primarily during after-school hours: 3 to 5:30 P.M. A few programs provide

Box 8.1 Two Center-Based Program Budgets

The following examples are for ongoing programs not including start-up (initial furnishings and supplies), major purchases (for example, computer), or major repairs (building).

Low Overhead Program

A church program or school-based care with all income from parent fees.

Typically there might be no rent (or minimum charge) and no transportation expenses (or very little).

Description: 25 children
2 staff 1 : 12 ratio
$20 per week fee

Operates before-and-after school and full days when school is out except for summer. Budget based on forty weeks, split shift, program operated five hours plus one hour for planning, preparation, and cleanup.

$ 8,400	Teacher/Director $7/hr for 6-hr day
5,400	Caregiver $4.50/hr for 6-hr day
2,500	FICA, unemployment, substitutes, full-day help, teacher liability insurance
1,250	Food @ 25¢ per child per snack (sack lunches on full days)
1,500	Supplies and equipment
250	Gasoline (van loaned when needed)
700	Phone, program insurance, and so on
0	Rent
$20,000	

81% of budget is personnel costs.

High Overhead Program

A nonprofit program with a sliding fee scale, receiving funding from donations, government subsidies, and parent fees.

Typically might have high rent, transportation, and food costs and strives for an extra good adult child ratio.

Description: 48 children
5 staff 1 : 10 ratio
$32.03 per child per week

This program might typically have a preschool component with it and have summer care for school-agers. For comparison purposes we will base budget on a similar forty-week before-and-after school program.

$ 4,800	Director $10/hr based on 30% of time
7,200	Head Teacher $6/hr for 6-hr day
5,700	Caregiver $4.75/hr for 6-hr day
5,700	Caregiver $4.75/hr for 6-hr day
5,400	Caregiver $4.50/hr for 6-hr day
4,500	Aide $3.75/hr for 6-hr day
1,800	Cook $4.50/hr base on 25% time
4,000	FICA, unemployment, substitutes, and so on
7,200	Food @ 75¢ per child per day breakfast served and on full days lunch
4,000	Van transportation
5,200	Rent and utilities
2,000	Phone, insurance, computer rental, and so on
4,000	Supplies and equipment
$61,500	

Source: From "Director's Corner" by R. Scofield, 1983, *School Age NOTES, 4,* pp. 10–12; used with permission.

before-school supervision for an hour or two. Very few provide breakfast or planned activities before school. Most do not operate on days when school is not in session or for summer vacation.

Ages of Children. Children ages six to twelve or first through sixth grade, the common enrollment group for elementary schools, are served. Grade groups are not rigidly preserved for after-school activities, and children may be clus-

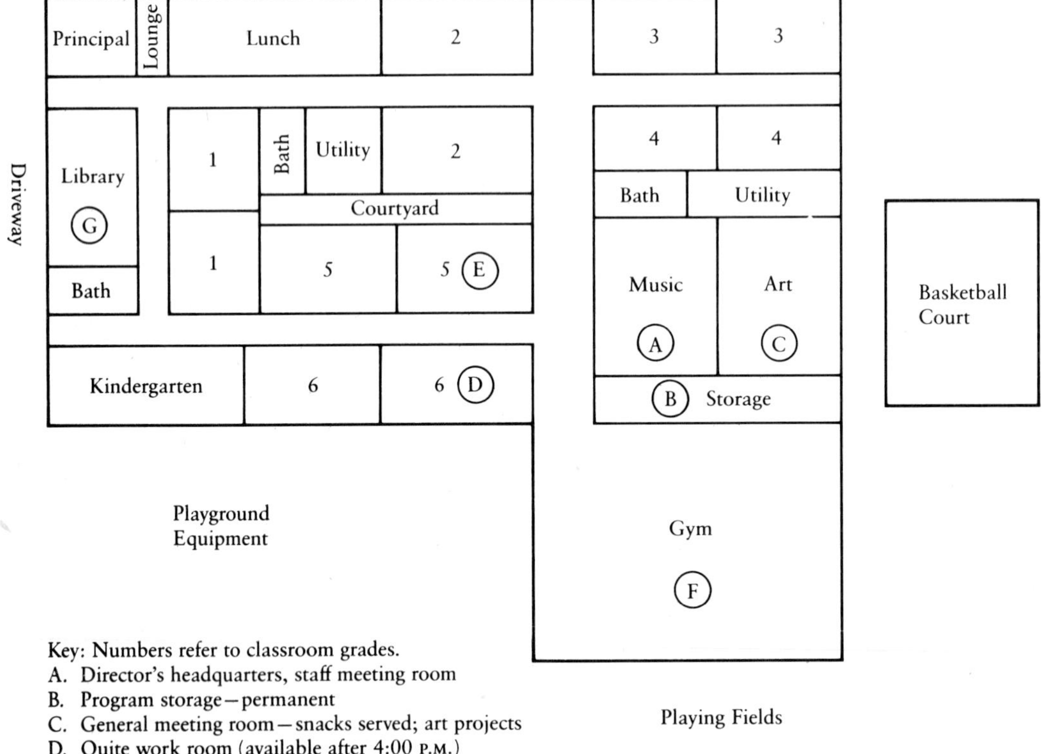

Key: Numbers refer to classroom grades.
A. Director's headquarters, staff meeting room
B. Program storage—permanent
C. General meeting room—snacks served; art projects
D. Quite work room (available after 4:00 P.M.)
E. Special project room (available after 4:00 P.M.)
F. Multipurpose program room—often several groups use different areas of room.
G. Library (available when program assigns staff member to supervise)

Figure 8.4 Floor plan of school used for after-school activities.

tered in family age groups or grouped by interests. As space permits, children are usually enrolled on a first-come, first-served basis.

Setting and Facilities. School facilities present both a problem and a resource for programs. On the plus side, school buildings have plenty of space, special equipment, and playgrounds and playing fields. Problems can arise, however, when these resources are reluctantly shared or withheld. A lack of goodwill toward mutual use of facilities can undermine the program. Many programs find that time, close daily contact, and visible program effects usually help smooth out the situation.

Figure 8.4 shows one school-based program's physical use of a school facility. This program enjoys excellent athletic and project facilities. The director has no permanent office, and the program is a long distance from the principal's office and driveway. Telephone messages and departures occasionally require special handling or disruption of the program activities.

Program Activities. One criticism of school-based programs is that children have already spent many hours at school. Programs counter this argument by pointing to the change of pace and variety of activities offered to children after school. Relaxation, athletics, art, music, and science are typical activities. Staff expertise and children's interests shape the program. The school can become a base for children's participation in community activities if such activities are nearby or if transportation is available.

Staffing. School-based programs are the most likely to have college-trained and well-paid staffs. Proximity to the public school staff accounts for the high salaries for the program staff. School-sponsored programs may require day care staff to meet teacher certification standards or child care staff may be part of the teachers' collective bargaining unit. Community-sponsored programs may have close enough affiliation to the local school to be affected by school salaries and education requirements, but this is less likely. Also, school-based programs tend to have high visibility within the community and are under social pressure to deliver quality care services; programs tend to hire and pay staff accordingly. Almost no specialized training exists for school-age day care professionals in this country.

Parent Participation. One common lament of school-based programs is the lack of parent involvement. School programs may have great difficulty extracting anything but fees from parents. Community programs often benefit from parent involvement in advisory activities but do not get much parent participation or staff-parent contact. One explanation is, of course, that parents are busy working and that school-age children are fairly reliable "reporters" about their experience whereas preschoolers are not. Most school-based programs owe their existence and continued access to school facilities to parents because parents are a political power—they vote. School officials across the country are responding to parents' expressions of the need for school-age care.

Family Day Care Programs

In the minds of many, family day care most closely replicates what children would do if parents were at home. Family day care homes usually serve a mixture of children, ranging in age from infancy to junior high. Care in such homes is a varied proposition, however. Quality depends almost entirely on the caregiver, or family day care mother. Private caregivers usually do not have the support services that a caregiver affiliated with a network is likely to have.

Hours of Operation. Children may spend time before school in a family day care home. Breakfast with the caregiver's family and school departure with the caregiver's children can be conveniently arranged. After school, children return to the home and spend time under the caregiver's supervision until parents pick them up. Snacks, and perhaps dinner, are provided. The presence of the other children during dinner preparation and the meal hour is disliked in some families. This is seen as a time for the home family to be together privately. Late departures or unreliable pickups can cause strained relations.

Program Activities. Family day care homes do not routinely provide formal activities for children. Private homes may offer "babysitting" and "find your own fun." Many private caregivers conscientiously interact with children and attempt to involve them in ongoing home activities. Children may bring projects or caregivers may provide raw materials for children to use. Affiliates are likely to routinely provide activity ideas, supplies, and perhaps some supervision.

Caregiver. The caregiver, usually a mother, is the sole staff person in the home. The caregiver's judgment, talent, and energy determine the atmosphere and quality of the home. Many feel isolated from adults even though they view themselves as providing an important service.

Private caregivers mention difficulties in dealing with parents, handling finances, or managing children if day care home and family standards of behavior differ. For some caregivers, school-age children are a joy; their lessened physical dependence and supervision requirements make them easy to handle and keep busy. For these reasons, caregivers may be tempted to accept many children for after-school care, thus diluting their ability to interact individually with children.

Availability. Parents find day care homes through neighborhood contacts, newspaper ads, or referral groups. Family day care homes are not always operating legally. Parents may not care, relying on their own judgment or desperation of need for services. Affiliate homes that are sponsored by agencies receiving public funds will enroll children who are screened and referred by the sponsoring agency. State and local standards for homes may be limiting the availability of "legal" homes. It is easier, quicker, and cheaper to simply take a few children for after-school care for a few hours a day than to go through a lengthy inspection and licensing process that may require costly improvements in the home. Because of funding sources, affiliate homes are usually required to be licensed or registered.

Focused Activity Programs

The school-age years are prime time for learning how to do things. Lessons and practices can occupy children's time and interests. Children may pursue one thing singlemindedly or may dabble in many subjects. These lessons and practices are most likely to occur during after-school hours, becoming by virtue of frequency, a form of child care for school-age children. Children may be taking private lessons that are paid for and arranged by parents with highly trained and specialized instructors. Recreation agencies may offer after-school programs that feature team sports, sports skill development, or practice time.

Focused activity programs are child care because they provide stimulating experiences for children after school. Of course, many children and parents choose the activities because of personal pleasure or gain, not just because they fill time when children may need something to do or someone to watch them. Focused activity programs do not "cover" all the hours of every day that children may need care. They do not account for children and accept responsibility for their arrival, departure, or subsequent activity involvement. The sequencing of experiences and overall mix of activities for purposes of fostering development is up to children and their parents. When logistics can be managed, other forms of school-age child care may use focused activity lessons and practices as a desirable complement to their programs. Older elementary children, in particular, value the opportunities to pursue interests or skill development on an individual basis.

Parental or Self-Supervision

Children, especially school-age children, do stay home alone before and after school and for vacation periods. Some have responsibility for younger siblings. Some come home alone every day; others do so only when no other activities are scheduled. Some do chores, play outside, or visit friends; others watch TV, eat, or make mischief. There do not seem to be any developmentally sound reasons for children ages six to twelve having to rely on themselves day after day or for long periods of time. There are, however, financial or lack-of-alternative reasons. For children ages twelve to fourteen, self-care is not so bothersome. Some can handle it, and some cannot. All need to grow into self-responsibility and are beginning to show signs of such maturity.

Like everything else, there are degrees of difference in the self-supervision that school-age children experience. The following comments are illustrative:

> I called home every half hour the first few months. Sometimes they didn't answer the phone, and I went nuts. When I got home I inspected the house with a fine-tooth comb. We had problems—the older one didn't like having to watch the younger one; but I said, "Look, if I don't work, we don't eat and you don't get designer jeans!" That hit home. (Mother of two girls ages seven and thirteen)

> A half sick kid is the pits. Can't go to school and can't go anywhere else. Yeah, I turn the TV on, go to work, call, come home for lunch, come home early. And I try not to feel guilty. (Mother of twelve-year-old boy)

Some communities and volunteer groups are creating support systems for children who are home alone after school. The project described in Box 8.2 was designed to help children feel physically and psychologically safe if they were home alone after school.

Points of Controversy

The Need for Care

More school-age children than ever before have working mothers; unfortunately, however, there has been no corresponding change in usage or perceived supply of child care alternatives for this group of children. Parents are the most common source of care for school-age children. Some children also receive care through informal, neighborhood arrangements, schools, or with relatives. Parents generally appear to be satisfied with present care arrangements. But is the status quo really satisfactory? Will future events spur an increased demand for more or different child care options for school-age children? Box 8.3 has more information.

Named for the house key dangling from a neck chain or tied to a shoelace, latchkey children leave and/or return to homes without adult supervision. The most recent statistics on daytime care of children aged seven to thirteen years show that in-home care by parent, other relative, or child caring for self constitutes the most common form of care arrangement. Organized child care centers supply virtually no care for children seven to thirteen years. Bane, Lein, O'Donnell, Stueve, and Wells (1980) concluded that "for six to thirteen-year-olds, the public school is the major caretaker, supplemented by parents and other arrangements." (p. 52)

These parents, however, are supposed to be working. Jones (1980) questioned similar 1975 Department of Labor conclusions saying that parents were probably afraid to admit that they left children alone at home. She pointed out that most mothers of school-age children hold full-time jobs and are working all day, not just when their children are in school. A recent reader survey conducted by *Family Circle Magazine* (Whitbread, 1979) found that nearly 30 percent of the children aged six to thirteen were left home alone.

Many more school-age children than we think may be home alone. If so, we need to decide if this is a national emergency for which remedies should be sought.

The Role of the Public School

It is difficult to phrase a question to capture the essence of this controversy without biasing the answer. For example: Should the public schools be involved in child care for school-age children? This question implies a yes or no answer. It implies that the lines of battle are drawn, and the fight will be waged, and the outcome will be decisive. That is not the case.

Another question: What contributions can public schools make to child care services for school-aged children? This question is open-ended and implies positive but perhaps passive relationships in the schools. It raises the ques-

Box 8.2 An After-School Support System

Kids!

You're alone at home after school and you can't reach your Mom or Dad . . .
Maybe you're lonely or scared.
Maybe you feel like talking to a friend.
Maybe you hear a strange noise or you think your pet might be sick.

When you need somebody,
Call PhoneFriend
at the Kids' After-School Help-Line .
234-3355
any school day between 2:30 and 5:30 p.m.

PLEASE PLACE THE ATTACHED STICKER ON OR NEAR YOUR TELEPHONE SO YOUR CHILDREN CAN FIND IT EASILY.

ESIGNED AS A PUBLIC SERVICE BY BARASH ADVERTISING.

Parents

In cooperation with the Women's Resource Center, the State College Branch of the American Association of University Women has instituted PhoneFriend as a public service.

PhoneFriend is *not* meant to replace usual emergency numbers (such as fire and police) or your established family emergency procedures. It acts as a supplement to emergency services.

Trained volunteers will answer PhoneFriend from 2:30 to 5:30 p.m. each school day, beginning on Sept. 8, 1982.

State College Police & Fire: 234-0234. **Bellefonte Police: 355-5441**

Source: Phone Friend, P.O. Box 735, State College, PA 16804. A project of the American Association of University Women—State College Branch; used with permission.

Box 8.3 U.S. Senate Caucus on Children

June 9, 1983—Forum on Latchkey Children
Excerpts from Testimony

"No massive infusion of public funds is needed, nor large-scale construction of new facilities. Rather, what is needed is to make the most of some ideas and facilities we already have," said Edward Zigler, director of the Bush Center in Child Development and Social Policy at Yale University.

The most logical place for before- and after-school programs to take place is in the public schools, Zigler and other witnesses told the caucus.

More Than 5 Million

A conservative estimate on the number of latchkey children is 5 million, Thomas J. Long, coordinator of the counseling program at the Catholic University of America, told the forum. "There is the strong possibility that when the actual number of all children who routinely care for themselves during nonschool hours while their parents work is known, it will be in excess of 15 million," he said.

Children who are unsupervised during these hours run the risk of sustaining both physical and emotional injury, the witnesses agreed.

Long, who has been studying latchkey children since 1979, has found that children who care for themselves express more feelings of fear, loneliness, and boredom than children who constantly have adults caring for them.

More Harm Than Good

Zigler also disputed the notion that leaving a child alone or caring for younger children builds independence and responsibility. "Although an eight-year-old might be developing a sense of responsibility by watching a younger brother in the back-yard while the parent is in the house, the same child might be overwhelmed by the day-to-day responsibility of meeting all his brother's needs or making crucial decisions in times of danger and crisis."

Children taking care of younger siblings is not an isolated happening, the witnesses said. "We know of children as young as eighteen months who are routinely left home unattended or attended by a sibling only slightly older than they," Catholic University's Long said.

Congressional Action

In the fall of 1984 Congress passed legislation authorizing support for school-age child care services and for school-age care information and referral services. The measure was a compromise worked out after action on the initial School Facilities Child Care Act passed the House (HR-4193) but stalled in the Senate (S-1531). The authorizing legislation passed as a block grant attached to the Head Start Reauthorization Bill. The 99th Congress is expected to begin work on the appropriation measure in 1985. Until the appropriation measure passes, there will be no funds available to implement this legislation.

---

tion of whether schools can afford to contribute anything.

Still another question: Does school-age care need the public schools to survive? This is closer to the heart of the issue. One institution may need the other.

Albert Shanker, President of the American Federation of Teachers (AFT) drew fire when he presumed prime sponsorship by the schools for any national child care efforts in testimony before Congress in 1974. The AFT position, expanded in 1976, represents to many an attempt to buttress the public schools by giving them a new mission to fill the void created by declining school populations. The traditions of child care are philosophically and programmatically very different from those of public education. Child care professionals seem to want to preserve their tradition and tend to see linkage with the public schools as an invitation to merger and a loss of identity. Parents may be the bridge between the public schools and child care. They

Table 8.2 Advantages and Disadvantages of Using School Facility for After-School Care

	Facilities	Needs of Children	Needs of Parents	Needs of Staff	Needs of Community	Needs of Programs
Schools						
Advantages:	Extends function of schools; enhances image; builds parent support. May increase enrollment or help with desegregation efforts.	Familiar and suitable space; oriented for school-agers; availability of additional spaces—gym, lunchroom, playground, etc. Convenient—no long bus rides—and allows maximum time to be spent in program; in child's own neighborhood; may give continuity to child's day.	No transportation costs or worries; consider school a "safe" place; deal with one environment/institution; program easily accessible for pick-up; affordable.	Allows communication between school teachers and SACC[a] staff.	Draws people to public schools and to the community. Good use of taxpayers' dollars.	No transportation costs; may have flexible locations to meet changing needs; custodian, facilities, equipment, utilities are already on premises; building set up for SACC; has potential for lowest cost to program; well located with access to other city resources.
Disadvantages:	Another program to worry about; fears regarding liability, accountability, and costs.	Same environment all day; institutional restrictions and limitations; possible negative associations with school accrue to program.	May have negative feelings about school.	School personnel may not welcome staff; may lack access to cooking and food preparation facilities; staff may need to "take down" the program daily.	Use may be questioned by private sector or taxpayers.	Space is often shared or has common usage; SACC program may be moved if school activities are seen as taking precedence; storage space may be limited; program may be unable to alter or change space; may be unavailable during summers, vacations (or costs may increase dramatically).

Source: From *School-Age Child Care: An Action Manual* (pp. 72–73) by M. Seligson, R. K. Baden, A. Genser, and J. A. Levine (School-Age Child Care Project), 1982, Boston: Auburn House Publishing Company; reprinted by permission.

[a] School Age Child Care Project.

have the political power to get cooperation from local schools. The provision of child care services for school-age children requires some rethinking of the partnership of family and society, or parent and school, that has prevailed for so long (see Table 8.2).

School-age children will be the beneficiaries of any cooperative efforts and involvement of the schools. Many who speak to this issue do not single out school-age children; they include much younger children and all forms of child care. Where the issue is narrowed at the community level to school-age children in school facilities for child care, cooperation seems desirable whether the schools or community assume program responsibility.

James Levine, while with the School-Age Child Care Project at Wellesley College, wrote extensively on the relationships and issues connected with child care and the public schools. He believes that diversity and flexibility are likely to be the norm:

> The arrangements worked out will no doubt vary from community to community, based on the capability, power and influence of schools, other agencies and parents. That is, in the short term, the matter of prime sponsorship will be played out at the local level, and in terms of community politics, not national politics. (Levine, 1979, p. 21)

Advocates for school-age care must provide leadership that promotes a variety of program options while strengthening stability of programs. Vesting sponsorship responsibilities in any one group will give that group significant influence over the character of school-age care services.

The Federal Role in School-Age Care

Society provides for school-age children through the provision of public schooling, which is a function of state and local governments. Matters other than education that affect the development of the child have historically been the right and responsibility of the family. Child care, with its comprehensive developmental focus, appears to some as a threat to family sovereignty.

In the past, federally sponsored child care was targeted at children thought to be "at risk." Over the years the definition of "risk" has expanded to include sociocultural as well as physical factors, and the emphasis of federally sponsored child care has shifted to protection for the child and prevention of deterioration of development. Today most federal funds support child care for preschool children of low-income families in center settings. Efforts of federal agencies to monitor and improve the quality of federally supported child care have contributed to raising standards in the field and increasing the general professionalism of all involved in service delivery. However, school-age children are not now generally served by federally funded programs. Many school-age children who are potentially users of care do not qualify for federal programs. Child care for school-age children offers an opportunity for a level of federal leadership and involvement that could affect care options for all children, regardless of family status or developmental risks.

Issues Ahead for School-Age Care

Target Population Should we continue to work for child care for all school-age children age six to fourteen years? Or should we focus on a narrower age span? Should special efforts be made to provide care for school age handicapped, migrant, and native American children? Will conditions of federal funding limit care options for low income children and families?

Purposes of Care Can child care make a sustained, positive contribution to school-age children's development? What are reasonable programs and delivery mechanisms for school-age care?

Regulation In what ways and for what purposes does school-age care need to be monitored?

Should the regulatory bureaucracy and licensing mission for school-age care be different from existing federal and state procedures?

Political Action for Alternatives How can the presumed concerns of working parents be translated into political power and local action to provide care options? What are the parameters of need, demand, and preference for care alternatives? How do parents and children choose care?

Summary

School-age care includes any overseeing of children when parents are absent and school is not in session. It may be formal or informal, and it may involve adult supervision or self-supervision by the child.

Most school-age programs are for after-school care. Family day care homes are the most common form, other than parent or self-supervision. Among all types of programs, the four program goals are supervision, recreation, diversion, and stimulation.

Within the six- to fourteen-year-old age range there are three general age groups: (1) ages six to nine or ten; (2) ages eleven or twelve; and (3) ages thirteen to fourteen. Each of the three developmental viewpoints can contribute to planning a school-age program. The maturationist viewpoint describes normative behavior for each age in brief capsule portraits and describes the psycho-social context of development as a basis for program planning. The behaviorist viewpoint prescribes a specific program of purposeful teacher behavior, sequential content arrangement, and systematic reinforcement. The cognitive viewpoint enables caregivers to appreciate children's own way of thinking and to recognize their different levels of moral response. Social influences to which the school-age child is vulnerable include chemical substance abuse, sex-role stereotyping, and maternal employment.

All school-aged child programs must satisfy the basic care needs of accountability, nutrition, and a protective environment. Developmental program opportunities will depend on local resources and children's interests. Center-based programs may be an add-on to a preschool program or a program only for school-age children. They generally operate after school for children aged six to nine or ten. School-based programs take advantage of the cost efficiency and convenience of existing facilities. Problems can arise if resources are reluctantly shared or withheld.

Family day care most closely replicates the child's natural home, but the quality of care depends entirely on the caregiver. Focused activity programs include team sports, sports skill development, or private lessons. Many children must be alone for parts of the day due to parents' employment and the inability to find or afford alternative care.

School-age children are perhaps the most underrepresented group in child care programs. Finding alternatives to the latch-key child remains a challenge for parents and program planners.

Resources

General

Diffendal, E. (1972). *Day care for school age children.* Washington, DC: Day Care and Child Development Council of America.

Rodes, T. W., & Moore, J. C. (1975). *National child care consumer study.* Washington, DC: UNCO.

Ruopp, R., Travers, J., Glantz, F., & Coelen, C. (1979). *Children at the center: Summary findings and their implications. Final report of the national day care study: Vol. I.* Cambridge, MA: Abt Associates.

School-age day care study: Executive summary. (1983). Washington, DC: Office of Program Development, Dept. of Health and Human Services.

School Age Day Care Task Force. (1972). *Report.* Washington, DC: DHEW, Office of Child Development.

Seligson, M., Genser, A., Gannett, E., & Gray, W. (1983). *School-age child care: A policy report.* Wellesley, MA: School Age Child Care Project, Wellesley College.

Westat. (1971). *Day care survey—1970.* Rockville, MD: Westat Research.

Developmental Foundations

(The following references are specific to school-age children. See the Resources in Chapter 2 for general resources on each developmental perspective.)

Cohen, D. H. (1972). *The learning child.* New York: Vintage Books.

Collins, W. A. (Ed.). (1984). *Development during middle childhood: The years from six to twelve.* Washington, DC: National Academy Press.

Erikson, E. H. (1968). *Identity: Youth and crisis.* New York: Norton.

Flavell, J. H. (1963). *The developmental psychology of Jean Piaget.* Princeton, NJ: Van Nostrand.

Gesell, A., Ilg, F. L., & Ames, L. B. (1977). *The child from five to ten* (rev. ed.). New York: Harper & Row.

Inhelder, B., & Piaget, J. (1958). *The growth of logical thinking from childhood to adolescence.* New York: Basic Books.

Kohlberg, L. (1969). Stage and sequence: The cognitive-developmental approach to socialization. In D. A. Goslin (Ed.), *Handbook of socialization theory and research.* Chicago: Rand McNally.

McCandless, B. R., & Evans, E. D. (1973). *Children and youth: Psychosocial development.* Hinsdale, IL: Dryden Press.

Worell, J. (Ed.). (1982). *Psychological development in the elementary years.* New York: Academic Press.

Implementing Programs

An after-school program. (1977). In E. Galinsky & W. H. Hooks (Eds.), *The new extended family.* Boston: Houghton Mifflin.

Baden, R. K., Genser, A., Levine, J. A., & Seligson, M. (1982). *School-age child care: An action manual.* Boston: Auburn House.

Bender, J., Flatter, C. H., & Schuyler-Haas Elden, B. (1984). *Half a childhood: Time for school-age child care.* Nashville, TN: School Age NOTES.

Blau, R., Brady, E. H., Bucher, I., Hiteshew, B., Zavitkovsky, A., & Zavitkovsky, D. (1977). *Activities for school-age child care.* Washington, DC: National Association for the Education of Young Children.

Cohen, A. J. (1984). *School-age child care: A legal manual for public school administrators.* Wellesley, MA: School Age Child Care Project, Wellesley College.

Cohen, D. J., Parker, R. K., Host, M., & Richards, C. (Eds.). (1972). *Day care 4: Serving school age children.* Washington, DC: U.S. Government Printing Office.

Collins, A. H., & Watson, E. L. (1977). *Family day care.* Boston: Beacon Press.

Editorial—Leaving schoolage children alone . . . A topic behind closed doors. (1983). *BANANAS Newsletter, 8* (5), 4–5.

Genser, A., & Baden, C. (Eds.). (1980). *School-age child care: Programs and issues.* Urbana, IL: ERIC Clearinghouse on Elementary and Early Childhood Education.

Hoffman, G. (1972). *School-age child care: A primer for building comprehensive child care services.* Washington, DC: DHEW.

Lanning, F., & Robbins, R. (1966). Chart of development. *Instructor,* August–September, 130–132.

Levine, J. A. (1978). *Day care and the public schools: Profiles of five communities.* Newton, MA: Education Development Center.

Medrich, E., & Roizen, J. A. (1983). *The serious business of growing up: A study of children's lives outside school.* Berkeley, CA: University of California Press.

Military Child Care Project. (1982). *Caring for school-age children* (Staff Development Series). Washington, DC: U.S. Government Printing Office.

Military Child Care Project. (1982). *Creating environments for school-age child care* (Child Environment Series). Washington, DC: U.S. Government Printing Office.

Nall, S. W., & Switzer, S. E. (1984). *Extended day programs in independent schools.* Boston: National Association of Independent Schools.

Neugebauer, R. (1979). School age day care: Getting it off the ground. *Child Care Information Exchange, November,* 9–15.

Neugebauer, R. (1980). School age day care: Designing an effective structure. *Child Care Information Exchange, April,* 27–32.

Neugebauer, R. (1980). School age day care: Developing a responsive curriculum. *Child Care Information Exchange, January,* 17–20.

Neugebauer, R. (1980). School age day care: Selecting and motivating staff. *Child Care Information Exchange, November,* 27–31.

Prescott, E., & Milich, C. (1974). *School's out! Group day care for the school-age child.* Pasadena, CA: Pacific Oaks College.

Prescott, E., & Milich, C. (1975). *School's out! Family day care for the school-age child.* Pasadena, CA: Pacific Oaks College.

School age children (excerpts from *Texas Child Care Quarterly*). (n.d.). Austin, TX: Corporate Child Development Fund for Texas.

Stickney, F. (1981). *Latchkey cares for kids.* Moraga, CA: Fred Stickney Publisher.

Strommer, E. A., McKinney, J. P., & Fitzgerald, H. E. (1983). *Developmental psychology: The school-age child* (rev. ed.). Homewood, IL: Dorsey Press.

Survival training for latchkey kids. (1980). *Newsweek,* October 6, 100.

Issues

AFT Task Force on Educational Issues. (1976). *Putting early childhood and day care services into the public schools.* Washington, DC: American Federation of Teachers.

Appropriateness of the federal interagency day care requirements. (1978). Washington, DC: DHEW, Office of the Assistant Secretary for Planning and Evaluation.

Bane, M. J., Lein, L., O'Donnell, L., Stueve, C. A., & Wells, B. (1980). Child care arrangements of working parents. *Special Labor Force Reports* (233), 50–56.

Bergstrom, T. M., & Dreher, D. L. (1977). *The evaluation of existing interagency day care requirements: Day care for the school-age child.* Washington, DC: DHEW, Office of the Assistant Secretary for Planning and Evaluation.

Clarke-Stewart, A. (1977). *Child care in the family.* New York: Academic Press.

Community solutions for child care. (1979). Washington, DC: National Manpower Institute.

Garbarino, J. (1980). Latchkey children: Getting the short end of the stick. *Vital Issues, 30,* unpaged.

Hayes, C. D., & Kamerman, S. B. (Eds.). (1983). *Children of working parents: Experiences and outcomes.* Washington, DC: National Academy Press.

HEW day care requirements final rules (HEWDCR). (1980). *Federal Register, 45* (55), 17855–17870.

Hill, C. R. (1977). *The child care market: A review of evidence and implications for federal policy.* Washington, DC: DHEW, Office of Assistant Secretary for Planning and Evaluation.

Hoffman, L. W. (1979). Maternal employment: 1979. *American Psychologist, 34* (10), 859–865.

Jones, L. W. (1980). Who knows? Who cares? *Journal of the Institute for Socio-economic Studies, 5* (9), 55–62.

Levine, J. A. (1978). *Day care and the public schools.* Newton, MA: Education Development Center.

Levine, J. A. (1979). Day care and the public schools: Current models and future directions. *Urban and Social Change Review, 12* (1), 17–21.

Long, T. J., & Long, L. (1981). *Latchkey children: The child's view of self care.* (ERIC Document Reproduction Service No. ED 211 229)

Rubin, V., & Medrich, E. A. (1979). Child care, recreation, and the fiscal crisis. *Urban and Social Change Review, 12,* 22–28.

Scofield, R. (1983). Director's corner. *School Age NOTES,* IV (1), 10–12.

Smith, R. E. (1979). *Women in the labor force in 1990.* Washington, DC: Urban Institute.

U.S. Bureau of the Census. (1976). *Current Population Reports,* Series P-20, No. 298. Daytime Care of Children: October 1974 and February 1975. Washington, DC: U.S. Government Printing Office.

U.S. Senate, Committee on Finance. (1977). *Child care: Data and materials.* Washington, DC: U.S. Government Printing Office.

Whitbread, J. (1979). Who's taking care of the children? *Family Circle,* February 2, 88–103.

Woods, M. B. (1972). The unsupervised child of the working mother. *Developmental Psychology,* 6, 14–25.

Organizations

School-Age Child Care Project (SACC)
Wellesley College Center for Research on Women
Wellesley, MA 02181
The project is a valuable source for technical assistance and information on school-age care programs. Contact them directly for details.

School-Age NOTES
P.O. Box 120674
Nashville, TN 37212
A newsletter for school-age child care workers and administrators published bimonthly. Edited by Rich Scofield.

9

Family Day Care

Introduction

By all estimates, family day care is the most widely used form of child care in this country. Demand for family day care is expected to increase as mothers continue to enter and to stay in the labor force. The result is that many children will spend significant periods of their daily life in family day care homes. The prevalence of family day care arrangements and the sheer numbers of children involved command the attention of child care leaders and advocates. Yet, for the most part, family day care is outside the mainstream of organized child care. Arrangements are usually informal personal agreements between parents and caregivers that do not involve agencies, inspectors, or contracts. Also, there appears to be no grassroot parental concern to change the low profile of family day care. Can we assume, therefore, that the major participants in family day care—parents, children, and caregivers—find the current situation satisfactory? Perhaps, but questions abound.

What is family day care? Is it care by relatives? Full-day care? Care in a home? Playing and watching TV?

Who are the caregivers? What kind of qualifications and experience do they have? How well do they do the job?

Is family day care good for children? Are children safe in homes? Are daily activities stimulating? Are there disadvantages?

Why is family day care so popular? Are costs, convenience, and flexibility major factors? Do parents prefer family day care?

Should family day care be organized? If so, how? Will regulation and closer monitoring improve care? Does family day care need to be more professional?

Serious and systematic efforts to understand the conditions and status of family day care are relatively new. The most ambitious of the efforts has been the federally financed National Day Care Home Study (NDCHS) conducted from 1976 to 1980. The material in Box 9.1 describes the study and some of its findings.

Through circumstance and serendipity family day care's time in the sun has come. Increasingly, child care administrators and program specialists can expect to work with family day care—licensing homes, training caregivers, and organizing and managing networks of homes. More caregivers are choosing to formally structure their homes either as independent businesses or as part of the home day care systems that we'll describe later in this chapter. Child care organizers are looking at family day care homes as a cost-effective means of delivering child care services with fewer public dollars.

Family day care homes differ in many ways from center-based programs. The home setting is special and creates a distinctly different set of administrative and programming conditions. This chapter begins with an overview of the characteristics of family day care homes, including the general types of homes, the chil-

Box 9.1 The National Day Care Home Study (NDCHS)

Description

> Initiated in 1976, the National Day Care Home Study was a four-year study of urban family care in three major American cities—Los Angeles, Philadelphia, and San Antonio. The principal goal of this research was to understand the many dimensions of family day care as it operates in different geographic, cultural, and structural settings for children of different ages. It is the first large scale study of family day care in this country and the first to study all of the major participants—children and their parents, caregivers, programs administrators, agency officials and advocates in the day care community. It is thus the first study to approach family day care from an ecological point of view as a comprehensive and complex phenomenon interwoven throughout the fabric of American life. (Fosburg, 1981, p. x)

Comment

The NDCHS has generated a wealth of detailed and comprehensive information about family care. The study, however, is not statistically representative of all family day care across the country; while extremely useful, the findings are not universally applicable. Procedural decisions and sampling trade-offs in the research design limit the generalizability of the findings in specific ways. The NDCHS has achieved a reasonable balance between research rigor and the pragmatics of the situation, but users of the data should understand limitations on interpretation such as the following:

1. This is an urban study. No rural or suburban homes are included in the sample.
2. Sampling procedures were used to ensure adequate representation of black and Hispanic caregivers in order to capture the richness and diversity of family day care. White caregivers are underrepresented in the sample in proportion to their numbers as caregivers.
3. Only full-time care for at least twenty hours a week for pay is included. The study does not include incidental, part-time care for less than twenty hours or care where no money changed hands.
4. Because of sampling constraints, the income of parents in the NDCHS is lower than the national average. Middle and upper income levels and job status are underrepresented in the sample.

In general, the NDCHS sample and research design was developed to provide federal policymakers with usable data on which to base policy decisions and determine programming support for subsidized family day care. The NDCHS estimates that only 3 percent of all children currently in family day care are in sponsored homes that might receive some form of subsidy. Findings of the NDCHS are considered to be reasonably representative of urban sponsored and independent regulated homes, but caution must be exercised in extending interpretation of the study's findings to all other types of family day care.

Unregulated Homes

- Homes tended to be less stable, discontinuing provision of care services over time.

dren, activities, caregivers, and parents. The second half of the chapter on implementing family day care home programs is written from the perspective of a program administrator, or someone who works with several family day care homes. We expect few readers of this book will themselves become caregivers in family day care homes, but many will find themselves working in some professional capacity with family day care homes. Accordingly, sections on administration, recruiting and training caregivers, and planning for children emphasize the tasks and decisions likely to be encountered by family day care program directors and supervisors. The focus is on family day care systems rather than individual day care homes. (Appendix A, "Setting Up a Family Day Care Home," outlines the steps and procedures necessary to

- Relative care was especially common among unregulated caregivers.
- Enrollment tended to be smaller than in regulated homes at two out of three sites.
- The majority of homes, regardless of regulatory status, were in compliance with age and group size requirements.
- Caregivers in unregulated homes had the lowest levels of interaction with one- to five-year-olds.

Characteristics of Children

- The younger the child at the start of family day care experience, the longer the child remained in care.
- Children cared for by relatives entered care at younger ages and remained in care longer.
- Toddlers (ages nineteen to thirty-six months) were the largest age group in care, particularly in sponsored homes.
- School-age children were the largest age group in care in unregulated homes.
- As group size in the home increased, there was more caregiver-group interaction and less individual caregiver-child interaction.
- Presence of infants in a home tended to elicit special behavior from caregivers—comforting, affection, attending to physical needs.

Family Day Care Home Activities

- Caregivers in all settings spent the majority of the day in direct interaction, supervision, or preparation of children's activities.
- Caregivers in sponsored homes spent more time teaching children.
- Caregivers with training tended to display more structured behaviors.
- Homes with own children or relatives' children tended to be less formal and structured.

Caregiver Characteristics

Group 1 Young white mothers in late twenties and thirties caring for own children as well as others; unregulated homes; small numbers of children in care.

Group 2 Hispanic and black women in their forties and fifties caring for relative (usually grandchild); unregulated homes; small numbers of children in care.

Group 3 Women in their thirties to fifties caring for children of friends, neighbors, and others in community; large proportion of sponsored or regulated homes; larger numbers of children in care; most caregivers with some training.

Parent Characteristics

- Parents of children in sponsored care had lower incomes than parents of children in regulated or unregulated care.
- Parents used care in order to work and chose family day care for financial reasons, special attention for child, or unavailability of center care.
- Most found their care arrangements through personal sources.
- Parents wanted caregivers to be reliable and to provide opportunities for children to acquire cognitive and linguistic skills.
- Parents cited social growth and a chance to play with other children as a benefit of family day care.

open a single family day care home operated as a private, independent business.)

Characteristics of Family Day Care

Family day care is a complex, diverse collection of child care arrangements. Definitions of family day care are based on the common denominators of care arrangements and emphasize the aspects of family day care that can be regulated. The incredible variations in terms of participants and circumstances of individual family care arrangements tend to be masked by general definitions. Nevertheless, definitions are helpful and provide a standard for judging specific care arrangements.

Family day care is nonresidential care pro-

The family day care home is generally within the same neighborhood as the child's home. Transportation is easy and quick. Here several children leave for school after an hour or so of early morning care and, perhaps, breakfast. (Courtesy of U.S. Department of Health and Human Services, Washington, DC.)

vided in a private home other than the child's own, for six or fewer children including the caregiver's own, and for any part of a twenty-four-hour day. The most distinguishing characteristic of family day care is the extent to which arrangements are *informal agreements between parent and caregiver.* Estimates of the proportion of unregulated, informal arrangements for family day care are uniformly over 90 percent of all family day care in the United States.

Background

Home-based child care (now called family day care) is a legacy from an earlier era in this country when neighborhoods were stable and extended families were accessible and willing to share with parents the burdens of child care. These arrangements were informal and based largely on personal relationships or recommendations. Usually such setups did not involve established institutions or attract the attention of licensing agencies. Care might be provided without charge, bartered, or provided for small amounts of cash. By all accounts this "naturally" occurring child care system functioned quite well, though it was not systematically studied. Many participants in this informal child care network would not have called it child care and did not see themselves as anything but babysitters.

Times have changed. Close extended families in stable neighborhoods are not as common now. Grandmothers and aunts, as well as mothers with young children, are likely to be in the work force. In every neighborhood there are still some people who will care for young children of working mothers, but subtle changes have come about in these informal child care arrangements. More parents seem to be looking for child care, and many expect more than just babysitting. Likewise, caregivers recognize that they provide a service and are beginning to act in a more businesslike manner.

Types of Homes

Family day care homes are not all alike. Let's take a look at what they have in common and how they differ.

Home as a Setting for Care. *Home* is an emotion-laden word. It brings to mind images of safety, security, warmth, affection, care, and parents. If one believes young children belong at home with a parent, and this parent (mother or father) joins the work force, then the next best thing for the young child is to be at home, even if the parent is not. Forthright reasoning such as this may not consciously be part of parents' decision-making in choosing child care arrangements, but it is appealing logic as an ex-

Box 9.2 What Does a Family Day Care Home Offer?

A "home away from home" quality family day care home offers all the nurturing, love, attention, and family living experiences children would have in their own home. Informal in nature, daily activities in a good day care home are carefully planned to give each individual child the type of care and experiences he or she needs to grow emotionally, socially, physically, and intellectually. These activities give each child the opportunity to:

- Participate in usual household routines.
- Live with both younger and older children.
- Do the same things and use the same community resources as others one's age in the neighborhood.
- Be oneself—to feel angry, shy, or happy—to eat chosen foods and to rest and play as necessary.
- Feel comfortable and confident in the safety and security of a home.
- Have basic needs fulfilled, helping the child to grow socially, emotionally, physically, and intellectually.

Source: Adapted from *Day care no. 9: Family day care* (p. 9) edited by C. Seefeldt and L. L. Dittmann, 1973, Washington, DC: U.S. Department of Health, Education and Welfare, Office of Child Development.

planation for the seemingly overwhelming use of family day care (see Box 9.2). Do not underestimate the strength of sentiment and value placed on *home* as an appropriate setting for child care.

Home-based care offers the advantage of a familiar environment for children. Going from one's own home to another for care is thought to be a manageable separation experience for parent and child. For both families involved, only modest adaptations in family life are required. In rural areas home care may be the only reasonable alternative since driving to centralized programs may be prohibitively time consuming and expensive. To an extent, neighbors can act as natural monitors of the care arrangements as a part of the normal daily exchanges among homes in the neighborhood.

Physically, home settings for care are considered appropriate and safe environments for children. If the caregivers have their own children at home, other parents assume that this parent will take the necessary precautions for all children. No expensive addition or renovation of the home seems necessary to most caregivers and parents, although regulatory and licensing inspectors may disagree. State and local standards for family day care homes are designed to be protective and preventive, relying more on physical barriers than caregivers' judgment and alertness. As we have noted before, the overwhelming majority of homes are unlicensed. A part of the controversy over the conditions and purposes of regulation of family day care homes centers on physical factors of the home environment. Zoning is almost never an issue for individual family day care homes unless large numbers of children are cared for or other persons hired to help the primary caregiver. Parking and traffic management are usually not a problem unless users provoke neighbors.

Studies show that most homes have sufficient indoor and outdoor play space. Urban homes are more likely to use parks and other public areas for outdoor play. Both cost of equipment and the caregiver's skill in selection and use determine how much equipment is available in the home. Found materials, interesting junk, and a creative caregiver can mean many happy and busy hours of activity for children. When children become involved in helping with household routines such as cleaning, cooking, and grocery shopping, common household items and furniture are adequate equipment. Obviously, most homes have the equipment resources for many developmentally sound activities if—and it is sometimes a big *if*—the caregiver knows how to pull it all together.

Purchased equipment and materials increase play opportunities for children and can reduce the planning load on the caregiver. Toy-lending programs have developed in many parts of the country to help cut costs of equipment through central purchasing, rotated sharing, and periodic maintenance. These lending programs usually involve training services and aid caregivers in selecting developmentally appropriate equipment for the children in their homes. Unfortunately, most are directed at that small percentage of homes that are in systems or under sponsorship, which are described in the following section.

Status of Family Day Care Homes. The legal and operational status of an individual family day care home is a function of two factors: compliance with applicable regulations and codes, and relationship with a sponsor or system. Family day care homes, therefore, may be categorized as regulated or unregulated, and regulated homes may be independent or part of a system. Systems include sponsored homes, limited affiliates, and provider networks (see Figure 9.1). *Sponsored homes* belong to a system in which all administration and management are handled by a local agency. *Limited affiliates,* or umbrella sponsors, join homes together in order to qualify for the U.S. Department of Agriculture (USDA) Child Care Food Program. Caregivers combine into *provider networks* so that they can exchange information and support one another. At present, no data (including the NDCHS) indicate that quality levels of care are higher in one category of home than another. Nationwide, there is considerable flux in regulatory standards, with many states moving toward less restrictive requirements. Incentives for caregivers to "go public" and affiliate with a sponsor or network are increasing.

The evolution of private family day care arrangements into more public systems is a relatively recent development in the child care field. Systems have been formed in response to a number of different needs expressed by agencies, caregivers, and parents. Agencies have started new homes and incorporated existing homes into family day care organizations to increase the supply (number of slots) of child care in local communities. Eligibility for cash reimbursement and donated commodities, such as the USDA program, has also required that homes have an umbrella sponsor (nonprofit organization) responsible for program administration and financial matters. Caregivers who have recognized the need for business information on home operation and the value of contact and sharing with other day care mothers have formed or joined provider networks that offer such services to their members. Caregivers are also becoming more professionalized and selling themselves as more than babysitters. Equally, parents have difficulty finding homes and evaluating the adequacy of the caregiving situations and have returned to referral services and clearinghouses for help in handling family day care needs.

Specific patterns of regulatory compliance and affiliation depend upon the local climate and the availability of sponsors. Private individuals seem unwilling to bother with complex regulatory procedures when it is relatively easy to operate without them. There are few penalties and no localities have sufficient resources to make enforcement of standards meaningful. The legal status of homes varies within systems and from one system to another. Compliance with existing regulations is a necessity for some, but not all, types of family day care systems.

Unregulated Homes. The majority of family day care homes are unregulated. No one knows whether ignorance of laws, refusal to comply, or evasion from fear of inspection accounts for it. They are essentially unconnected in any formal way to the child care community. Child care in these homes is a free market private enterprise that draws the attention of the public

Independent Homes

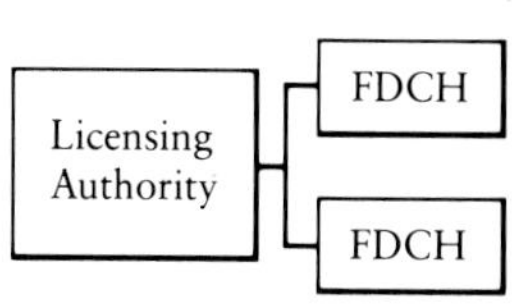

Homes operate as independent businesses. Contact with licensing authority is for inspection and regulatory compliance.

Provider Networks

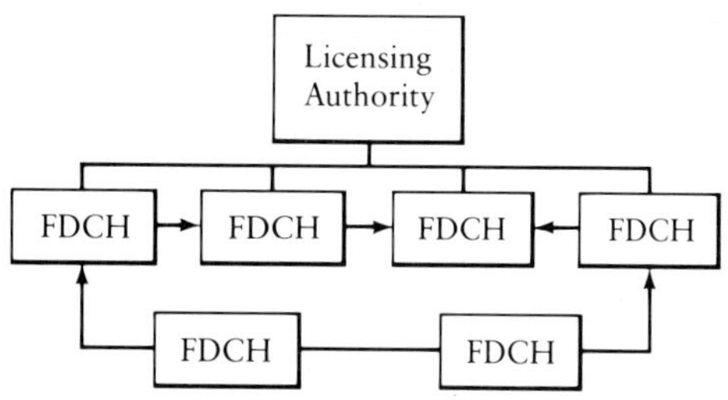

Caregivers form self-sustaining network for informal exchange and support. The network may include unlicensed homes. Homes have direct, independent contact with licensing authority for inspection and regulatory compliance.

Sponsored Homes

SATELLITE HOMES

FDCH
FDCH
FDCH
FDCH

Licensing Authority — Local Agency — Center

FDCH FDCH FDCH FDCH

SYSTEM HOMES

Local agency assumes total administrative control of homes and organizes services as a satellite of existing centers or a system of homes with a system director. Homes are licensed either through authority delegated to this local agency or directly by licensing authority with liaison help from the local agency.

Limited Affiliates

Licensing Authority — Local Agency

FDCH FDCH FDCH

Local agency provides an organizational structure for licensed, independent homes to qualify for the USDA Child Care Food Program (CCFP). Homes may continue to be licensed directly by licensing authority or local agency may become involved.

Figure 9.1 Patterns of family day care home (FDCH) organizations.

only if the welfare of children is involved. The following remarks describe typical cases:

> I knew I needed a license. But this arrangement was going to last for six weeks, afternoons only. David napped most of that time once he got used to being in my house. Then he got up and had a snack together with my two year old. Now really, is that worth the attention of a licensing person? I have known his family for four years, and they know what kind of child care I give. (An urban caregiver, 1981)

> At first Emily just came to play with Sarah. We live so far out on this farm that she doesn't have any one but me to play with. About the time Emily's mother wanted to go to school more, I got Brian. He came after school. Just walked up the lane off the bus. It was good money for me. Then I saw the ad in the paper about getting more kids from the state, so I called them up. What a mess. They said I was OK. But my cellar door needed covering and something was wrong with the toilet—the one in the woodshed we only use in the summer. My husband doesn't like the idea of someone telling him how to fix up his house. So I don't have any kids any more. (A rural caregiver, 1980)

> Jerry has been with Mrs. Walker for three years now. When we first started she told us a few little rules about paying on time and picking up promptly. Now and then we have to discuss some naughty stuff he does. Sometimes she has lots of children in the afternoon, like at holidays when everyone is busy and needs child care at the same time. But, she is real strict about her fulltimers. Only one tiny one at a time, and she gets them out of diapers and on the potty as soon as she can. Her daughter helps some. Once a parent asked her if she was inspected. She was kind of insulted and told them they could look around all they wanted. (A parent, 1981)

Anecdotal accounts and common understandings of family day care lead one to believe that some of the family day care provided in an unregulated home involves relatives' children. Whether or not money changes hands in these situations, the general presumption by those involved is that relatives' homes do not need to be approved by the state. Neither the family nor the state is particularly eager to spend resources legalizing this care situation. The exception comes in terms of numbers of children and whether children other than relatives are being cared for. Children of caregivers and relatives' children count in figuring a home's total enrollment. The point at which the interest of the state should prevail over the privacy of the family is not clear. Care by relatives may keep the pool of unregulated family day care homes high, regardless of the regulatory or advocacy efforts of the child care profession.

Two other gray areas of unregulated family day care are *in-home care* and *play groups*. Both types of care have the potential to become variations of unregulated family day care. In-home care may become a piggyback arrangement if two or more families choose to share the cost of the one caregiver. One family may hire a caregiver and set him or her up in their home. In order to share costs or provide playmates for their child, they may advertise for other children to join the care arrangement. For those extra children the home is a family day care home and may be subject to regulation. The in-home family does incur some legal liabilities similar to those incurred by a family day care mother in her own home.

Once-a-week rotations and exchanges among mothers can become scheduled obligations—every Monday at Mary's or this week at Claudia's. Depending upon local statutes, play groups may become eligible for family day care regulation. Much in-home care piggybacking and play group scheduling can be traced to mothers' needs for part-time child care or odd hour and sporadic work obligations. Experience suggests this is how many women cope with irregular or low level child care needs. If we discount these marginal family day care arrangements, we may lose sight of what family day care is all about and why unregulated family day care is such a large part of child care in this country.

Regulated Homes. Legal family day care homes comply with prevailing local and state standards. Regulated homes are visible within the child care community and accountable for care. States and local governments have statutory authority to regulate family day care. Federal child care dollars can be used to purchase or provide care only in homes and centers that are in legal compliance with prevailing statutes. Public funding conditions have played a major role in family day care regulation by focusing caregiver, agency, and public attention on the specific regulation standards. Regulated family day care homes are important beyond their numbers because of this attention. Public funds, especially the USDA Child Care Food program monies, have been the carrot that has enticed many homes and agencies to fulfill compliance requirements, provoking many to criticize prevailing standards and procedures. Regulation of family day care homes serves two purposes: (1) to protect taxpayer dollars, ensuring accountability and value for money spent; and (2) to protect the interest and welfare of all children.

Family day care regulation involves three fundamental components: (1) specification of standards including a description of the liable population; (2) inspection and verification procedures; and (3) enforcement and revocation procedures. State agencies are responsible for family day care regulations. In some instances, responsibility for verifying compliance with regulations may be delegated to agencies running family day care systems. At this time no federal regulations apply to family day care.

Licensing is formal permission to operate. Homes that are licensed according to state regulation frequently must meet local codes (fire, sanitation, health, zoning) in order to meet all the provisions of the state standards.

Registration is another form of legal permission to operate. Registration standards may differ from licensing standards. Self-inspection by the caregiver and parent monitoring may substitute for state inspection except for a small number of spot checks. Regulation may be voluntary or mandatory.

Certification is used when care is purchased with public dollars. Certification standards can be identical to licensing standards in a state. The purpose of certification is to account for service value in the expenditure of public funds.

Regulated homes are of two types: independent and sponsored. Independent homes are private businesses operated by an individual caregiver. Any connection or contact they have with the general child care community is solely through the initiative and interest of the caregiver. Sponsored homes allow organizational networks or sponsoring agencies to assume responsibility for administrative and financial management tasks. Some common organizational patterns are described in the section on family day care systems later in this chapter. In all these organizational patterns, the caregiver may be a direct employee or may be providing services under contract to the organization. Because of closer monitoring, sponsored homes comply more strictly with regulations.

The best estimates of home status, numbers of homes, and numbers of children involved are projections from data in the NDCHS (see Figure 9.2). It is clear from these projections that the vast majority of children in family day care are in homes outside legal and child care professional surveillance. Children in these homes are, potentially, too vulnerable for comfort. Regulated homes are a miniscule percentage of family day care. Yet, regulated homes, regulations, and organizations and networks command almost all the attention. We believe that some level of information, training, support, and regulatory oversight is appropriate to ensure the well-being of all the children involved. Consequently, this chapter focuses on the administration and supervision of legal family day care homes.

Children Served

Children of all ages can be cared for in family day care homes. The mix of ages typically present in family day care settings promotes positive and stimulating social experiences for the children. Siblings often attend together. Since only a small number of children are present in the home, the caregiver is accessible and able to respond to children individually. Mildly ill children can often be cared for in the home setting. For descriptive purposes children are often identified as *resident* or *nonresident*

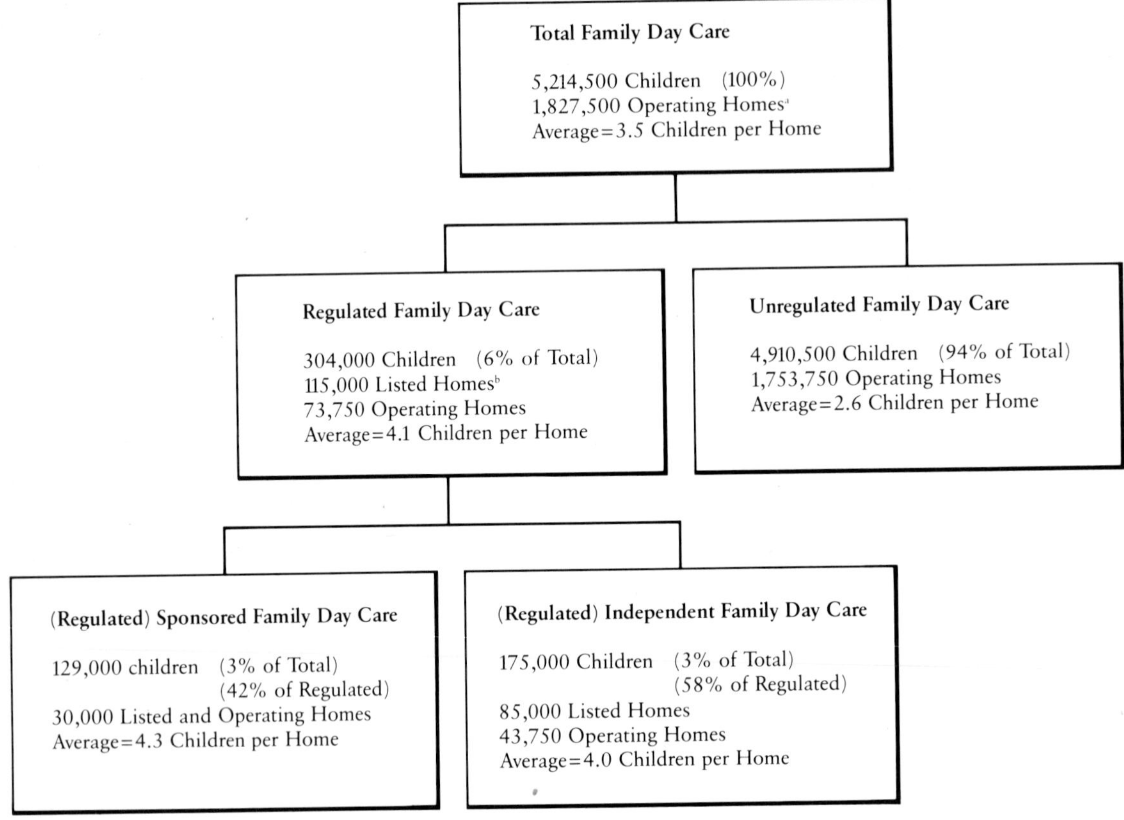

Figure 9.2 Types of family day care. (From *Family day care in the United States: Summary of findings: Vol. 1. Final report of the National Day Care Home study* (p. 7) by S. Fosburg, 1981, Washington, DC: U.S. Department of Health and Human Services.)

and *related* or *unrelated* to the caregiver. The following four groups are the typical categories of children in family day care.

Infants and Toddlers The flexibility and mobility afforded by the family day care setting is thought to be particularly responsive to the needs of infants and toddlers. Individual schedules fit the biological rhythms of each child. The caregiver-child ratio is especially well adapted to infant care. Toddlers will find the experiences offered in home and neighborhood good matches for their developing skills. Regimentation and structure can be minimized in the home environment.

Finding care for infants is difficult for parents. Very few group or center-based programs are set up to handle infants, and parents have few options other than family day care. In many states, regulations restrict the number of infants that a home can care for at one time or limit the number of children of all ages allowed in the home if infants are present. The rationale is that infants place a greater burden on caregivers and that group size limits based on age mixes will balance the caregiving load.

Regulated homes have "slots" for more children if infants are not present. Caregivers may not want to accept infants because they may be more expensive to care for, they require more special supplies (diapers, formulas, and changes of clothing), fees and reimbursements are not generally higher for infants despite their higher costs.

Children ages eighteen to thirty-six months are the most common age group found in family day care homes. Over the years family day care homes have tended to care for toddlers while preschool-age groups have increased in center-based care situations. Children of this age are "just outside" the three-year-old age limits for many formally organized programs, and parents use family day care arrangements to fill the gap until children are eligible for other care.

Preschoolers Most public subsidy dollars for child care go to buy care for preschoolers in centers. The small number of subsidized slots in family day care homes are also occupied, for the most part, by preschoolers. Depending on family circumstances, children aged three to five years can attend Head Start, kindergarten, or a wide range of local nursery school programs. This reduces the number of hours of care still needed to cover a working parent's schedule. Transportation logistics need to be worked out, but family day care homes offer an attractive and flexible option to cover the hours other than formal programs. This use of family day care is part-time, and many of the children are in unregulated homes.

School-age Children Family day care has distinct advantages for school-age children. They can remain in their own neighborhoods, attend the local school, use neighborhood resources freely, and function as they would in their own homes. Many caregivers become involved in helping children with their homework and take an interest in children's school activities. Except for vacations and holidays, school-age children are part-timers in family day care settings. Their greater maturity and skills make them more independent and place fewer demands on the caregiver. Accordingly, state regulations frequently allow greater numbers of school-age children in a home care setting. Older school-age children residing in the home may not be counted in determining the total number of slots a home has available for care. Not many school-age children can be found in sponsored, regulated homes where standards are most strictly enforced. Again, we expect that unregulated homes are handling much of the demand for school-age family day care.

According to the NDCHS, several points emerge concerning the characteristics of children served in family day care homes:

1. Ages of children served are a rough guide to caregiver burden. Amount of care required and type of care are a function of the age-related developmental needs of children.
2. The number of children served becomes a trigger for a regulatory liability. Residency in home and relationship to caregiver affect how total numbers are computed. This varies from state to state. Sponsored homes are likely to be monitored most strictly.
3. Age mix of children or group composition is a way of balancing caregiver burden. But regulatory restrictions build in economic disincentives to care for infants and school-age children, shifting demand for care for these children to unregulated homes.

Program Activities

What do children do all day in family day care homes? Children in fulltime care in a family day care home can spend up to ten hours a day in care depending on the work hours and transportation time of parents. To a large extent the activities that are offered depend on the type of home and the caregivers' motivation, training, and experience. The following comments of family day care mothers provide a typical cross-section:

> Mostly my day care children play. We go outside every morning and once in awhile I plan something special like pasting or treasure hunts outside. (Licensed home)

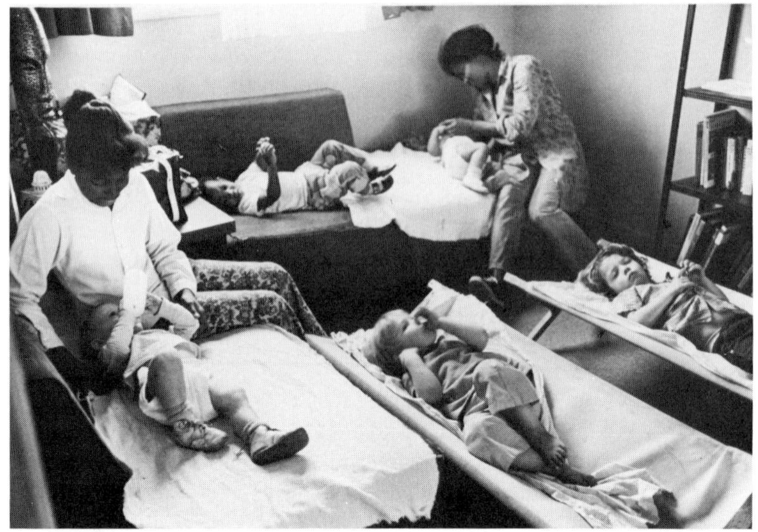

Typical daily activities in a family day care home are a blend of basic care and learning opportunities. (Courtesy of U.S. Departments of Health and Human Services, and Housing and Urban Development, Washington, DC.)

See my daily schedule; it's over by the telephone. I like to plan activities. It makes things more interesting for all of us. My worker [agency program aide] usually brings me books and art supplies and helps me think about how to plan lots of different kinds of activities. (Sponsored home)

I don't do anything special. It is just me and the kids. A few extra don't matter much. (Unregulated home)

I'm always trying something new. We went on the bus last week and then spent several days reliving the trip. We even made up a song about what we saw. (Unregulated home)

Caregiver Characteristics

Called *caregiver, provider,* or *family day care mother,* she is the central figure around whom the entire care experience revolves. (Despite increased flexibility in gender roles and the emergence of house husbands, caregivers in family day care are still usually women.) She is director and staff rolled into one. Her attitudes, practices, personal qualities, and resources are related to everything that happens in the home. And she is on her own. Everyday, all day she is responsible, in charge, and on call. Older children, husbands, relatives, or neighbors may occasionally help and workers from sponsoring groups or state agencies may visit now and then, but the primary family day care unit is one caregiver with several children.

Women become caregivers for a variety of reasons:

- They like to work with children and derive satisfaction and pleasure from being with them.
- They want extra income but don't want to leave their own children and don't want to work outside the home.
- They want companions for their own children and something to do while their own children are young.
- Their own children are getting older and they want to have some little ones around.
- They provide care as a favor for a relative or friend.
- They feel confident of skills in caregiving, but are less sure of other marketable skills.

Caregivers come from all races, classes, and ethnic backgrounds. Whites seem to be the most frequent users and providers of family day care. There is a tendency for caregivers to be older and less educated than users. Also, caregivers are more likely to be part of an intact family than users.

Few caregivers report any special training in caring for children. The basic premise behind training is that child care involves knowledge skills and attitudes that are not necessarily intuitive. According to the NDCHS:

> The effects of training are strong and positive. This is perhaps the most encouraging of the study findings, for it means that an investment in caregiver training can influence the ways in which caregivers interact with children. Thus, the quality of the family day care environment can be enhanced by this means. (Fosburg, 1981, p. 90)

At present, training opportunities for caregivers are tied to home status. Caregivers in sponsored regulated homes participate in a variety of direct and indirect training experiences. There may be workshops, courses, home visits, newsletters, and other means of sharing. Independent regulated homes and unregulated caregivers are simply not reached by the majority of current training programs. Many in this group are not interested or willing to participate in training. They consider child care to be a natural ability and feel that training programs are an invitation to regulatory attention.

Being a family day care mother is hard work. The hours are long, the pay is poor, and job status is low. Caregivers report feeling isolated and lacking in companionship and support from other adults. Caring for small children is physically exhausting. After a full day of child care, the day care mother must also tend to the needs of her own family and home. Financial matters, record-keeping and legal matters must be managed in a businesslike fashion, and many caregivers are naive or uncertain about these matters. Caregivers and parents must deal directly with one another. There is often no one available to help with difficulties, counsel, or find solutions to problems.

Caregivers who are part of networks may find that their sponsors can help. But even for these caregivers, low pay, daily job isolation, and double workloads are problems. When things get intolerable, caregivers quit. Family day care has no career ladder and does not offer meaningful respites such as paid holidays to help caregivers recoup and refresh.

Parent Preferences

It would be easy to assume that family day care is the preferred type of care arrangement for children of all ages. Yet studies consistently conclude that the desire to work rather than the availability of child care is what propels mothers into the work force. Is family day care the care option of choice? Or, for most parents, is it the only available option? Eligibility criteria and space limitations result in a very low percentage of young children cared for in public or private center programs, but parents often mention two common themes:

1. When my child is old enough (or there is room), I will put him or her in a day care center.
2. I think children learn more in group programs. I want my child to be exposed more to learning activities.

There seems to be a tendency for older children to move into more formally organized programs. For older children, parents express desire for emphasis on cognitive development and language experiences. For younger children in family day care, safety and supervision are of utmost concern. Many parents believe that only formal programs can provide learning opportunities for children because of their structure and professional staff. As a result, many parents make no demands on the family day caregiver to provide more than basic care. In a 1974 study of 116 family day care arrangements, Emlen and Perry looked at the sources of tension and satisfaction in the parent-caregiver relationship. Their findings are typical of most studies. The mother's satisfaction depended on the adjustment of the child. The caregiver's satisfaction depended on the relationship to the mother. She tended to be happy with the child unless the mother's discipline or other behavior was of concern. For both parent and caregiver the concern of the other woman for the child was extremely important. Mutual satisfaction characterized most relationships. However, there was evidence of parent satisfaction at the expense of caregiver dissatisfaction. The caregiver accommodated, at some cost in role strain and emotional drain, to the inconsistencies in the parents' schedule.

The following excerpt is an example of advice to parents when choosing family day care.

> Because family day care is given in a person's home, it can take on a more intimate quality than care given in a center. A parent, in fact, is choosing more than just the provider herself—you will also be accepting the home atmosphere, other family members, neighborhood environment, etc. So, the first criteria in selecting family day care is an acceptance of the provider and her family as people you would feel comfortable having your child be around and learn from. If that acceptance and basic trust doesn't seem to exist when you visit and chat with a potential provider, then the physical facility, the program, the rates, don't really matter. You must *like* the person caring for your child or you will never be satisfied with the child care. That doesn't mean the provider has to have identical values and parenting style to your own—differences can be complementary. But, your feelings about children and the provider's must be compatible for trust to exist. If you find several providers whom you are comfortable with, then other factors such as group size, physical setting, discipline, etc. come into play in making your final selection.
>
> Family day care is a private business; each provider sets the tone she wants for her program. You cannot make over a provider's life style or attitudes to suit what you want in child care. If you don't like what is going on in a family day care home and the provider (after discussion) is clear that she is not going to change her approach, don't leave your child in care. Having a child care provider you like and trust means that you can work or go to school or take time for yourself without having to feel guilty or worried about your child. (*BANANAS handout: Choosing family day care*, 1981, Oakland, CA: BANANAS, Child Care Information & Referral and Parent Support; used with permission)

Costs

Expenses for family day care are direct and indirect. Direct expenses include food, insurances, consumable supplies, equipment, and toys. Getting started can require home repairs or remodeling to meet regulations and may involve advertising and printing costs. Affiliated and sponsored homes may have some of these expenses absorbed by the umbrella organization. Indirect costs include increased frequency of home maintenance, automobile expenses related to care, and convenience purchases and services desired because of loss of caregiver's free time. Many caregiving expenses qualify for tax deductions for the provider.

Fees for family day care are low and tend to reflect prevailing estimates of the value of the service. Fees do not reflect expenses; in fact the relationship between fees and expenses is not often considered. Care for profit is usually suspect or irrelevant as a motive for entering into a family day care arrangement. Private care fees are set in accordance with current community rates; the local competition determines the allowable range of fees. Private, unregulated caregivers would need to offer some extraordinary services to justify fees that are out of line with most local fees.

For government-purchased care, individual providers or sponsoring groups are paid a set fee, or reimbursement rate, for each child in care. Reimbursement is calculated according to formulas that can take account of several things; for example, they may consider average expenses of care across several regions, predetermined caps on allowable expenses for particular budget items, and absolute limits on dollars available for care purchased. Reimbursement rates are flat and do not vary in relation to known differences in caregiver burden (number and ages of children) or qualifications (training, years of experience, home resources). Neither fees nor reimbursement rates result in minimum wages for caregivers.

The following summary describes both sides of the cost issue (dollar values are those at the time of the study):

> From the parents' perspective, family day care may appear a costly endeavor. An average of 60 cents per hour must be paid for the care of each child. Since many children are in care for 40–50 hours a week, this expense could easily exceed $30 per week. From the provider's perspective, however, family day care is not a lucrative profession. The average weekly wage for providing care is $50.27 to $62.09 after payments are made for food, supplies, and insurance. As a result, many caregivers' earnings are significantly below the poverty level. They work long hours, frequently have no provisions for sick time or for vacations, and often are not even aware of tax advantages for which they are eligible. (Fosburg, 1981, p. 103)

Administration and Management

Family Day Care Systems

Increasingly, the trend is for individual family day care homes to become part of a system. The status of a home within a system can range from limited affiliate, to full sponsorship, to a loose network relationship. Within a system the group responsible for legal, contractual, and administrative obligations is often a local human services *agency*. The remainder of this chapter, which describes the implementation of day cares, applies to family day care homes within a system.

With very few exceptions, the family day care homes in systems are licensed and regulated. Systems vary on three characteristics:

1. *Sponsored Homes* Systems may intervene or assist in the licensing process or may be delegated full responsibility by authorities to license homes directly.
2. *Limited Affiliates* Systems may have full administrative and programmatic control over the homes or may serve merely as a convenient conduit for administrative paperwork.
3. *Provider Networks* Caregivers within a system may have minimal contact with one another or may be the dominant influence over system policy and activities.

Government agencies find family day care systems to be a convenient administrative unit. It is more efficient to negotiate and monitor public subsidies for child care with one system than it is to negotiate and monitor each individual home in the system. One system contract may cover a hundred homes with 350 children in subsidized slots. The USDA Child Care Food Program (CCFP) requirement that participating homes be sponsored by an umbrella organization has given considerable impetus to the current move toward formation of family day care systems and the licensing of family day care homes.

System Functions. The division of responsibility between system and provider depends on the purpose of the system. The core responsibilities of a provider are to provide an adequate care environment, exercise appropriate caregiving skills, and perform necessary record-keeping tasks. A full sponsorship system will provide these support services:

- Recruit caregivers.
- Screen children.
- Maintain enrollment levels of home.
- Inspect or aid in licensing of home.
- Monitor regulatory compliance.
- Train caregivers.
- Provide technical assistance.
- Serve as a vehicle for parent involvement.
- Collect fees, keep financial records, and pay caregivers.
- Assist with insurance.
- Distribute supplies.
- Loan equipment.
- Provide a communication network among providers.

Central Staff. A fully developed, large family day care system will have several central office staff people; some will work directly with providers and homes, while others will concentrate on contracts, external relations, and overall system management.

Program Director Oversees the internal management of the homes in the system; liaison and chief program officer for dealings with other components of the sponsoring agency and in handling external contacts for public relations and contracts.

Home Visitor Responsible for site monitoring, caregiver communication, and supervision of programs; serves as liaison between individual homes or caregiver and agency.

Trainer Provides group or individual training on specific topics related to children, program planning, or home management.

Social Worker Recruits and screens children; does eligibility determination for subsidies; in conjunction with home visitor, places children; handles referrals for special needs; serves as liaison between this and other services.

In small systems these job responsibilities may be combined into one position. Or the family day care unit may share the services of a social worker or trainer with other programs administered by an agency.

Files and Records. One indicator of the scope and importance of the administrative work of the family day care system is the documentation that the system creates and maintains. This "paper trail" is concrete evidence of the activities and management burden that a system can assume in running a group of family day care homes. An agency's files and records might include contracts, home inspection reports, purchase orders, USDA meal counts, payroll and benefit records, education and health records, menu plans, newsletters, and enrollment and attendance records.

Legal Concerns

This section highlights those legal concerns and issues that are particularly relevant for family day care. Chapter 13 gives a comprehensive analysis of the legal terms and situations that commonly arise in child care.

Regulatory compliance and licensing are the most obvious legal concerns for family day care homes. Licensing status affects the contractual relationship between agency and home and between home and parent. When a family day care home operates outside of the registration, certification, or licensing statutes that apply, it is illegal. No state or local jurisdiction appears to be aggressively searching out and punishing "illegal" family day care homes. In fact, there is considerable disagreement over the substance and procedures of family day care regulations among providers, professionals, advocates, parents, and even the lay public. However, noncompliance *is* illegal and carries some risk for provider, agency, and parent. The extent of the risk usually becomes apparent only when accidents or problems occur. Compliance does not prevent problems, but it does provide a firm legal context for operation.

Discussions of regulation of family day care homes tend to focus on state and/or federal regulations. There is often a provision in the state standards that homes must comply with all applicable codes. Local fire, building, and zoning codes can apply to family day care homes. Separate local inspections can be required to meet fire and building codes. Copies of these inspections are then submitted with the state licensing application. Local zoning codes may affect the operation of a family day care home if the code restricts parking and traffic in residential areas or limits the use of private homes for business purposes. Zoning codes are highly variable in interpretation and variances are often allowed. Neighbors' concerns and community property values contribute to zoning situations. In some localities the number of children present in the home is the "trigger" for applying local codes. For example, a home with twelve or more children (often called a group family day care home) might be subject to local fire codes and building safety inspection, while state regulations would apply to all homes caring for two or more unrelated children. Agencies and individuals interested in setting up family day care homes should check with local authorities about applicability of local codes.

Contractual Obligations. Contracts are legally binding agreements, oral or written, that spell out the terms and conditions between two or more parties. A contract is the legal basis of judging disputes over service or products delivered. Detailed written contracts are preferred in all situations. Caregivers and parents in family day care most frequently enter a caregiving situation with only vague oral contracts. Problems with fee payment, hours of pickup, termination of service, responsibilities for food and diapers and other needs can all be eliminated through use of clearly written contracts signed by both parent and caregiver.

Caregivers who provide family day care as a part of a system of affiliated or sponsored homes usually do so on a contract basis. They contract to provide their services as caregivers. The provider's agency contract sets forth the circumstances and conditions of care and details the services and assistance that the agency will provide. Providers under contract are *not* subject to minimum wage laws. Contracts alleviate legal problems with unemployment benefits, FICA, and similar matters. (Only when providers work as direct employees of an agency are they definitely eligible for benefits and covered by minimum wage laws.) Another important aspect of agency-provider relationships is an "exclusive use" contract or contract provision. In this situation the provider agrees to care only for children placed by the system; it allows the agency to have greater control over the home caregiving situation. See Box 9.3 for a sample contract between a caregiver and an agency.

Family day care systems receive public money for subsidized care through a "purchase-of-service" contract. This contract states the conditions and requirements of care, the reimbursement rate for care, and usually the number of children (or slots) to be funded. For example, agency ABC may have a purchase-of-service contract for thirty family day care slots; the slots may be dispersed over 40 homes or may be clustered in six or seven homes. How agency ABC structures its program to deliver services depends on the local situation and funding conditions as well as the availability of homes.

Box 9.3 Agreement Between the Caregiver and the CDC

AGREEMENT BETWEEN THE CAREGIVER AND THE CDC

Made this day______(DATE) between the Child Development Council, hereinafter known as the Council, and____________________(CG NAME), hereinafter known as the Caregiver.

The Caregiver, in consideration of certain fees and/or other remunerations, agrees to provide care at________________________(ADDRESS) for children enrolled by the Council with said Caregiver.

In consideration of which the Council agrees to pay the Caregiver a fee of $___ per day for each full-time child (over 5 hours per day) and a fee of $___ per day for each part-time child (under 5 hours per day). Care is not to be provided but payment will be made for the following holidays: New Year's Day, Memorial Day, Independence Day, Labor Day, Thanksgiving Day and the day after, Christmas Eve Day and Christmas Day, plus two additional days to be announced.

REIMBURSEMENT to the Caregiver is made on a semi-monthly basis. The pay periods end the 15th day and the last day of each month. Evidence of the children's attendance (i.e., a completed DCH/GDCH Attendance Sheet) must be provided to the Council within 2 working days after the last day of each month. If it is not received within that time, payment will be postponed until the following pay period and only if proof of attendance is provided.

The Council agrees to reimburse the Caregiver for attendance at TRAINING SESSIONS as follows: (A) During care hours--Caregiver receives regular wage plus pay for substitute based on attendance and is reimbursed for mileage. (B) During noncare hours--$15.00 if entire session is attended, plus reimbursement for mileage.

The Caregiver understands and agrees that the Caregiver is not an employee of the Council but an INDEPENDENT CONTRACTOR. Therefore, Council does not cover the Caregiver with Workmen's Compensation or unemployment compensation and that there will be no taxes or social security deducted from her pay. The Caregiver is soley responsible for these obligations.

The Caregiver agrees to comply with all State and Federal REGULATIONS governing Family Day Care and all Day Care Homes Program Policies and Procedures now in effect or hereafter enacted or adopted (see attached). The Caregiver understands that if she is found to be out of compliance with these regulations, this Agreement will be terminated immediately.

The Caregiver understands that she enters this agreement under a PROBATIONARY PERIOD of three months, during which time it will be determined by the Field Supervisor, Program Director and Caregiver whether the Agreement shall be continued beyond the probation period.

The Council cannot GUARANTEE to place a set number of children in the Caregiver's program, but the Caregiver will agree to accept at least three Council children.

The Caregiver agrees to work closely with a FIELD SUPERVISOR on the development and management of her program. The Caregiver understands that her Field Supervisor will visit her program at least two times per month and that one of these visits will be unannounced.

The Caregiver shall provide (at her own expense) LIABILITY insurance coverage on her home or rented space to protect both the Caregiver and the Council from losses resulting from accidents or injuries arising out of this Agreement. Additional liabiltiy coverage will be provided by the Council when the Caregiver provides the Council with the square footage of primary care area in her home and her liability insurance policy numbers.

The Caregiver represents to the Council and covenants and agrees with the Council that there are not now nor will there be during the time this agreement is in effect and while children are in the Caregiver's care no persons present including herself in the family day care home who have been convicted of a CRIME involving child abuse or neglect, moral corruptness or physical violence; is awaiting trial on charges listed above; evidences drug addiction, alcoholism or child abuse.

This Agreement may be TERMINATED verbally by either party subject to two weeks notice.

____________________	____________________
Caregiver's Signature	DCH Director Signature
________	________
Date	Date

Child Development Council

Daycare Specialists 111 Sowers Street State College, PA 16801

814-238-5480

Source: Child Development Council of Centre County, 111 Sowers St., State College, PA 16801; used with permission.

Insurance. By most accounts family day care homes, whether operated independently or through systems, are not adequately insured. Insurance is protection; it reduces risk. In return for protection, a premium is paid. This premium is an expense for a day care home. Family day care homes should have three types of insurance:

1. *Medical/accident* to cover costs of injuries
2. *Liability* to cover costs of damages
3. *Automobile* to cover transportation needs

Caregivers may have existing homeowner or automobile policies to which a rider or endorsement can be attached (for an extra fee) to cover the insurance needs of the operation of the day care home. Separate, individual policies can be purchased to cover the home, or insurance may be obtained under a group policy sponsored by a family day care system or professional association. Insurance, like contracts, tends to be ignored in the informal atmosphere of family day care until the need is acute. One way to lessen insurance costs is to ask parents to pay a portion of the insurance costs as part of the fee for care, making it clear to them that the insurance protection benefits them in covering medical costs in the case of accident or injury. Parents are sometimes asked to sign waivers, or a waiver of liability statement, which is a prior informed consent release from responsibility in the case of accidents. Still, there are situations in which caregivers or programs can be held responsible even when parents have signed the waiver. Waivers are not equivalent to insurance.

Other Legal Matters. Family day caregivers can find themselves confronted directly with some situations that seem to demand patience, wisdom, and the presence of a lawyer. The best defense is anticipation and preparation of a contingency plan. Circumstances, support services, and laws will vary from place to place, but all caregivers need to be prepared for:

Sick children This includes conditions of care or refusal of care for an ill child as well as provisions for medical care in an emergency and life-threatening situation.

Custody disputes Abiding by the conditions of a child custody agreement can be difficult if parents are feuding or uncooperative with each other. This can involve problems in releasing the child to one parent or the other and accepting directions for care from one or the other.

Child abuse Caregivers may suspect child abuse and they need to know the local procedures for reporting suspected abuse as well as the responsibilities incurred by such reports.

Money

Family day care is thought to be cheaper to provide than center-based day care. On the surface the figures appear to support this since caregiver wages, parent fees, operating costs, and reimbursement rates are all lower for family day care. Most of the dollar totals and cost estimates for family day care are for care provided in homes that are administered by a sponsor or affiliate system. Such sponsored, regulated homes are a very small fraction of the homes providing care, so these dollar totals do not reflect the cost and fees of the vast majority of family day care provided through informal, private arrangements.

Patterns of funding for homes in family day care systems reflect the subsidy requirements for system organizations. The fifteen systems surveyed in the NDCHS reported 72 percent of total income from government reimbursement including USDA-CCFP, 5 percent from parent fees, and 23 percent from other contributions, including 13 percent in-kind donations (Grasso & Fosburg, 1980, p. 76).

Caregivers' wages are the major cost of care. In the NDCHS sample of family day care systems, the average wage for family day care providers was $5,800 per year. In stark contrast, the NDCHS found the average wage for all caregivers in the sample (sponsored, regulated, and unregulated) was only $2,600 per year.

Box 9.4 Family Day Care Income Taxes

The following is intended as a guide for general information purposes. If you have specific questions about your family day care income taxes, contact a tax specialist or the IRS.

There are two kinds of deductions: *direct*—which can be totally claimed and *indirect*—which can be claimed only on a percentage basis. One of the easiest ways to keep your family day care records is to open a checking account just for your business. Deposit all parent fees into the day care account and pay all your *direct* day care bills including your "salary" from this account. Pay your *indirect* expenses from your family checking account and "bill" your day care account either monthly or quarterly for its percentage share of the indirect costs. If you choose to have just one checking account for both your family and day care business, you must be sure to indicate which deposits are parent fees and you still must separate your expenses into direct and indirect expenses. Regardless of the method used, save receipts (not check stubs). If you are ever audited, these will be necessary. Save your tax returns for five years (even if you stop doing child care); tax audits are often two or three years after you file. You must be licensed in order to claim these deductions.

Direct Expenses

Expenses *just for* your day care business use. (This list is not all-inclusive; other items may be deductible.)

Toys or equipment
Supplies
Groceries
Legal fees and tax preparation
Advertising
License costs
Maintenance
Education
Dues, subscriptions
Gifts
Field trips and entertainment
Insurance
Parking fees, bridge tolls, etc.
Telephone
Assistants' salaries and substitutes' salaries

Indirect Expenses

Expenses for items used both by your family and your child care children. You can only claim a percentage of these expenses as child care costs. The formula for figuring out what portion you can claim is given with each item.

- *Groceries and Household Supplies* (such as toilet paper, laundry soap, etc.) Often it is easier to purchase these items all at one time since they are used by both your family and your child care children—then apply a percentage formula to figure out your child care costs. *Sample Formula:* If there are 3 in your family and you serve your family 3 meals a day and you care for 6 children serving them 2 meals a day plus 2 snacks (count 2 snacks as one meal), you are serving a total of

Family day care is inexpensive, therefore, because providers' wages are low—below minimum wage *and* poverty guidelines. Since centers must pay minimum wage, center care costs are automatically higher.

Family day care subsidies are calculated on unique cost data across the country. Service functions are not comparable and no uniform counting units have been developed. As a result reimbursement rates vary widely. In 1977 the NDCHS found a range of \$.59 to \$1.53 per child hour in reimbursement rates.

In day care homes that operate independently, either regulated or not, caregiver income is presumed to be solely from parent fees. Occasional community contributions or in-kind donations may supplement the cash income. Since weekly fees are lower in independent homes than in systems homes, independent caregivers earn less than system caregivers. Caregivers do

153 meals for the week (63 meals to your family and 90 to your child care children). The child care portion of your food and household bill for the week would be 90/153 or 59%. Be sure to subtract any liquor, pet food, cigarettes, etc. before applying the percentage. Save all the receipts and your math in figuring the percentage of each receipt. *If you participate in the Federal Food Program,* and your actual food costs are higher than your reimbursement, you can claim the difference as a deduction. Of course, you will need to be able to demonstrate this with records.

- *Mileage* IRS allows 20½ cents a mile [up to 15,000 miles and 11 cents a mile after that] for child care-related business such as pickup of children, field trips, child care shopping, meetings, classes, etc. Keep a notebook in your car and jot down mileage for each child care-related trip.

The following indirect expenses must be computed using the IRS business percentage formula given below:

General maintenance
Insurance
Rent or taxes and interest
Utilities
Telephone
Depreciation of large appliance
Depreciation of house

Determining Business Percentage of Home (use on federal and state Schedule C)

1. Find total area of home.
2. Find area of individual rooms for business.
3. Determine the number of hours each room is used for business during the week; include cleanup time.
4. Find the percentage of time each room is used for business during the week (number of hours per week used for business divided by 168—168 is total number of hours/week.)
5. Multiply area of each room by the above percentage and total the results.
6. Divide the above total by the total area of home for percentage of home used for business.

Any room used specifically for child care and never for personal family use is 100% deductible.

Source: From *BANANAS handout: Family day care income taxes* (rev.) by N. Ott, 1981, Oakland, CA: BANANAS, Child Care Information & Referral and Parent Support; used with permission.

not get rich providing family day care. Few even earn enough money to support themselves and their families.

Tax Concerns

Caregivers are often in a good position to deduct a portion of their household expenses because they use their home to operate their business. Unfortunately many caregivers do not know how to properly document and claim their expenses. Box 9.4 has more information.

Caregivers

A good caregiver is the key to a quality day care home. In a home setting the importance and duties of the caregiver extend beyond those of staff with comparable roles in a center pro-

It's no accident that caregivers in family day care homes are usually called day care *mothers*. (Courtesy of U.S. Department of Health and Human Services, Washington, DC.)

gram. The home caregiver is director, teacher, aide, cook, janitor, and driver all rolled into one. No easy substitutes or opportunities for daily breaks are available. Aside from naps, the caregiver is "on duty" every minute the children are in her care. The job demands stamina, commitment, devotion, and resourcefulness to a degree unlike any other child care job except perhaps mothering.

It is no accident that these caregivers are sometimes called day care *mothers*. Recognizing the element of mothering that is part of the caregiver's role helps clarify two important attitudes that influence large-scale implementation of family day care sponsor and affiliate organizations. First is the idea that anyone who is a mother—who has had life experiences caring for children—can be a good family day care mother. Second is the notion that mothering comes naturally. If these ideas were universally true, homes would not need to be inspected and licensed, caregivers would not need to be credentialed and supervised, and training and support services for caregivers would be eliminated. However, experience contradicts this simplistic equation of mothering and caregiving. The job of a caregiver in family day care does encompass many aspects of mothering and such experiences are a helpful qualification, *but* caregivers in family day care are providing a service in a demand and supply situation. However loosely organized the care arrangement may be, caregivers are in the *business* of mothering. We like to think of a caregiver in family day care as a professional mother, someone who is providing a service for which standards, accountability, and conditions of operation are quite appropriate. Selection, retention, training, and evaluation of caregivers are the most time-consuming tasks and the largest expense items for family day care organizations.

Qualifications

Family day caregivers must meet applicable regulatory qualifications for education, experience, and training. State qualifications might cover such areas as age, criminal record, and histories of mental illness or drug and alcohol addiction. Sponsoring agencies may have additional criteria and characteristics that they think are desirable for caregivers to possess.

Recruitment

The need for agencies to recruit caregivers is continuous. For a number of reasons, children leave care placements and caregivers discontinue providing care. Keeping a reasonable balance between actual and projected demands for care and available caregivers is a constant juggling task. Many care arrangements are quite stable, but others are short term. Turnover is high even in well-managed systems.

Waiting lists of children and approved caregivers can be used to control the flow of changes. Homes may be kept deliberately under-enrolled so that the system has some flexibility to respond immediately to needed changes. Child enrollment may be limited to specific calendar periods with little opportunity for switches between periods. Systems may set quotas on the number of children to be served or the number of children of different ages to be served.

Recruitment of caregivers is a lengthy process. Time lapse between initial contact with the caregiver and final approval of the contract and employment papers and licensing or certification of the home may take a month or more, particularly if more than one agency must inspect and approve the home. Not all potential caregivers will emerge as licensed caregivers. Dropouts occur as caregivers become better informed about the demands of the caregiving job, homes fail to meet standards, and the central office staff assess caregivers strengths and weaknesses.

Recruitment procedures should be systematic. Forms and procedures need to be readily available and easy to follow. The example given here highlights the general purposes and desired outcomes of a recruitment process that is suitable for a moderately large system.

Step 1: Finding Each Other A large part of the task of identifying potential caregivers is public relations (see Box 9.5). Publicity and a high visibility profile within the community increase the appeal of caregiver jobs as well as position the agency as an effective provider of needed community services.

The goals of recruitment advertising are to make the public aware of the need for caregivers and to entice people to consider the job. Agencies will find that asking applicants how they "heard about the job" or coding replies differently for each type of ad will quickly tell them which techniques were most effective in reaching large numbers of people. Ads may be in newspaper classifieds, posted on bulletin boards, circulated in co-op newsletters, broadcast on local radio stations or TV programs, or distributed door to door as flyers.

Step 2: Getting Acquainted If all goes well, many prospective caregivers will contact the agency in response to recruitment advertising. Once prospective caregivers and the agency are in contact with one another, more detailed exchange of information can begin. Exchanging a few pieces of critical information early is a means of screening serious contenders from the larger pool of respondents. The agency can send respondents an information package with a brief description of the job, a summary of regulatory procedures, copy of agency newsletter, a checklist for the remainder of the formal recruitment procedure, and an application.

Next comes a follow-up phone call to solicit minimum information about the prospective caregiver so the agency can decide about proceeding further. This second phone call may be placed after an application is submitted or may be used to encourage or discourage an application.

Step 3: Serious Consideration After receiving the application and the written report of the telephone interview, a staff member from the central office will visit the home and interview the prospective caregiver. The visit will last two to three hours and will include a close inspection of the home facility. Agencies need to know if licensing or certification of the

Box 9.5 "Love for a Living" Recruitment Campaign

THINK OF IT AS A LICENSE TO LOVE
Poster—10 × 12½ Contents: At first glance, it may look like just another official document. But if you like kids, you might come to regard it as a license to love . . .

This promotional campaign was specifically designed to:

- Attract qualified people to become licensed family day care providers
- Establish the image of child care as a respected community profession
- Inform the public that training and education is available in the child caregiving profession
- Increase the amount of child care available to working and student parents, especially those with infants

The series, valued at over $15,000, was designed by a leading Minneapolis advertising agency, and has been successful in the St. Paul/Minneapolis metropolitan area. The "Love for a Living" Series includes five posters, one brochure, and two radio spots.

Source: From Toys 'N Things Press, a division of Resources for Child Caring, Inc., St. Paul, MN 55103; used with permission.

home will be possible, and they need to assess the qualities of the applicant for caregiving. A written report of this interview visit should be made using a standard format designed by the agency. A small committee at the agency should review these interview visit reports and decide how to proceed. More than one person should participate in the decision. If the decision is positive, the agency is committing staff time to certify (or to aid in the licensing application) the home as well as accepting the person as a caregiver for the agency. Negative decisions can result from perceived personal inadequacies or the expectation of great difficulties with licensing the home. Either way, the applicant should be notified of the decision and a written record should be kept of the proceedings.

Step 4: Formalizing the Relationship The agency should prepare copies of all contracts and agreements and forward them to the caregiver to sign. Licensing, certification, and inspection procedures should begin immediately. A second home interview visit is often needed to finalize facility compliance. The second visit is the beginning of caregiver preservice training and orientation. Caregivers begin working with program supervisors to prepare items such as daily schedules and meal plans. Inspection delays, central office paperwork, and other problems can hinder completion of the process at this point. Program supervisors may feel that preservice training should begin anyway in order to continue positive momentum and strengthen the new relationship with the caregiver.

Training

In a sense every contact between agency and caregiver is an opportunity for training—an opening for the exchange of information or discussion of problems and recognition of available support services. Often this incidental training can have a significant impact on the caregiver's behavior because information is given when it is needed. Specific training for caregivers in child care appears to be associated with desirable caregiver behaviors and better care experiences for children.

Orientation Training. As caregivers enter formal relationships with the sponsor or affiliate agency, orientation training begins in earnest. This covers the mechanics of running a family day care home—setting up the home and becoming familiar with the record-keeping and procedural requirements of the agency. A combination of individual sessions and group meetings may be used for initial orientation. New caregivers can be given sample forms and asked to work through forms and procedures in self-instructional practice exercises. Extensive orientation programs can even include observation visits to other day care homes. Caregivers should receive reference notebooks and resource lists and be guided in setting up a filing system and a work space in their home.

The agency may periodically schedule orientation "updates" to keep everyone current and accurate. New caregivers may be assigned to experienced caregivers in a variation of the buddy system, or small contact circles of caregivers may be formed to help disseminate information. Agencies need to recognize that once the big push of orientation training is over, caregivers still need information about administrative procedures. This need is rarely enough to warrant a full-scale training meeting, but there will be errors and difficulties that can undermine efficient operation unless some attention is given to maintaining accurate procedures.

Competency Training. The topic emphasized the most in training programs is child development. Other topics such as selection of materials, planning activities, discipline, and planning meals are usually integrated into sessions as examples of how to apply basic child development information. Agencies and family day care staff will probably need to tailor the content of training programs to meet the individual needs of caregivers. Commercial materials and numerous model training programs are also available and can serve as the basis for local programs, concentrating local staff efforts on the logistics of delivery of the training program rather than the planning.

The conditions under which caregiver training must be accomplished are simultaneously limiting and challenging. For instance, grouping caregivers for training purposes is difficult because caregivers work apart from one another. Finding time for training may not be easy since family day care homes may have children in care for ten to eleven hours a day. Caregivers may also have to be convinced that training is really needed. Finally, motivation may be a problem because higher pay and moving up a career ladder do not result from training.

As agencies and caregivers across the country have struggled to find ways to arrange training opportunities, they have found some very resourceful strategies including credit course work at local schools, workshops, field trips, home visits, newsletters, TV programs, self-instruction courses, group meetings, telephone conferences, monthly meetings at centers, paraprofessionals as consultants, "master" day care mothers, liaisons with center program staff, and interagency coordination of home visitors.

From an agency perspective training programs can be risky. Staff resources are diverted from daily program management to implement training programs. Only fairly mature, smoothly managed systems can tolerate this segmenting of staff resources. Lower caregiver attrition rates are cited as one positive benefit of training, and, to the extent this is true for a local system, training efforts are rewarding. Systems may have to weigh the relative benefits of upgrading current care services against expansion of care to serve more families. Resources are always limited and these trade-offs are necessary.

Independent caregivers have virtually no incentives other than personal reasons for pursuing training. If training increases professionalism, costs of care may go up. Parents as consumers, and the government as a purchaser of care, definitely have limits on how much they are willing and able to pay for care. Training in caregiving increases costs and quality of care.

Monitoring Caregivers

Although phone and mail contacts are used for routine communication, the circumstances of family day care make a home visit virtually the only reliable method of monitoring caregiver behavior and children's activities.

Purpose of Home Visits. The more distant, authoritarian, and forbidding the home visitor, the less likely the home will function normally during the visitor's stay. Infrequent visitors and visits for purposes such as inspection and regulatory compliance will be surrounded with formality and anxiety. Local agency staff may need to perform some of these formal functions and must accept certain levels of artificiality in response.

Home visits for purposes of program monitoring and caregiver's support need to be conducted under very different circumstances. Familiar visitors who come periodically, who are genuinely interested in the caregiver's work, and who make a practice of always leaving something of value (such as an idea, a suggestion, a good feeling, or useful materials) have the potential to serve as effective liaisons between agency and caregiver. Short and frequent visits, each with a clearly defined objective, are most likely to contribute to a positive relationship between caregiver and agency. Many organizations assign one staff member the responsibility for a group of homes. All home visits and agency contacts with that home are channeled through that staff member. Other agencies may assign staff to specific functions for all homes. One staff member may handle licensing, another training, another operational management, and so on. Each approach has advantages. Caregivers may prefer the familiarity of a single staff member or may appreciate the chance to interact with several individuals with varying areas of expertise. Agency budgets and staffing patterns will dictate which approach is used.

Home Visit Protocol. Opinions differ about whether home visits should be scheduled or whether caregivers should be surprised and always alert and ready. Travel time and visitor flexibility should be considered. It can be hard to predict the exact hour of arrival or know in advance precisely how long a visit is necessary to accomplish objectives. Further, while most homes can be expected to follow routine schedules, special events or spontaneous changes do happen and can conflict with planned visit schedules. Common sense dictates that home visiting be scheduled flexibly.

Home visits will proceed best if caregivers are prepared to use the time efficiently. This means caregivers need to know the purpose of the visit in advance and be able to schedule their own activities accordingly. Home visitors can be assured that over a period of time caregivers will relax, and visitors will come to understand how much of what they observe at each time is reflective of typical daily activities. Good days and bad days average out. Consistent patterns of caregiving emerge in the context of receptivity and trust. The success of monitoring through home visits results from equal measures of the sensitivity of the visitor to the caregiver's personal situation and the skill of the visitor in responding to particular caregiver needs in meeting visit objectives.

Record-keeping and Evaluation. Written records are maintained of every home visit. Home visitors should keep logs of visit that include the purpose, time, activities during the visit, and follow-up plans. Every home visit should be entered in a cumulative visit record in each caregiver's file. All pertinent reports should be completed and entered in both the visitor's and the caregiver's logs and then filed. Phone contacts and messages should be treated similarly. Agencies will want records to document program compliance with legal and funding requirements. Forms for this purpose are often supplied by the licensing authority or the funder. If these forms are not suitable for direct use with caregivers, agencies may design other forms to collect the information and then transfer it to the standard report forms. Information collection, recording, and dissemination are major tasks for family day care agency staff. Examples of forms and reports include cumulative attendance records, cumulative meal counts, meal planning reviews, fee records, referral reports, inspection checklists, field trip permissions, travel expense reports, caregiver evaluations, home activity reviews, parent contact information, training records, and child eligibility determination.

In Chapter 6 we discussed the purposes and techniques of evaluation from two perspectives: child assessment and program evaluation. Much of that information applies to family day care. Child assessment procedures, observation instruments, and interpretation of findings are a joint responsibility of home visitor and caregiver. Agency program evaluation for family day care rests mainly in the review and updating of compliance documents for legal and funding authorities. This produces summary descriptive statistics such as the number of children served, the costs, and caregiver working hours to quantify the characteristics of the program.

Formative evaluation is built into every contact between home and agency. Decisions about quality and effectiveness, suggestions for change, and directions for caregiver behaviors and home activities to meet overall program goals underlie every action of agency staff. Clear and mutually accepted goals and objectives for home programs guide these activities. Consider that agency staff are managing perhaps thirty to sixty separate day care homes, each one a small-scale version of a care program. Some similarities are present, but each home program is distinct, and agency staff must deal with program quality and formative evaluation at that level.

Planning for Children

Children are the most vulnerable participants in family day care—they are the least able to manipulate services and the most sensitive to variations in quality. Parents, caregivers, agency staff, and regulatory authorities all have some stake in the service delivery and some corresponding responsibility for the welfare of the children. Coordinating the interests of these various stakeholders and overseeing the daily experiences of children in a family day care home is the task of agency staff. Agency staff need to recognize the double role they have in family day care. At times they act as agents and interpreters of public policy, and at times they are responsive to the personal needs of individuals. Public and personal needs can differ and conflicts may arise. Planning for children in family day care programs is a task of compromise—a search for the middle ground that will enable the agency to provide quality services consistent with local circumstances and in conformance with public standards.

Three agency staff activities influence directly the experiences of children in family day care and give the agency opportunities to influence the quality of care. Through child enrollment and parent activities, agencies define the scope of care requirements and build critical parent support. Children's activity schedules and related caregiver training and resources determine the nature of the child's care experience. Finally, the level and accessibility of support services from other agencies and community sources enrich the basic care experience.

Enrollment

Children come to be cared for in family day care homes either through voluntary enrollment by their parents or through referral and subsidy by public service programs. Age of the child and parental need for care further affect the likelihood of enrollment in a family day care home. Enrollment requires matching the child and parent pair with a caregiver and home. Factors of personality, compatibility, existing home group composition, and convenience of the home location must be taken into account in placing children in specific homes.

If the system depends primarily on *voluntary enrollment,* parents need to be made aware of the availability of the service. Advertisements, announcements of openings, and information brochures can be used to spread the message. A widespread information outreach like this is most appropriate where few or no restrictions are placed on enrollment. Waiting lists can be maintained to equalize access to available spaces in homes.

At the opposite end of enrollment procedures is the situation where all children in care are subsidized by public funds. Enrollment is allowed only for children whose family circumstances place them in categorical eligibility groups. Service levels are determined to comply with current reimbursement rates for family day care. Parents make contact with the family day care system through referral from other social service agencies. The family day care program must maintain a high profile and good working relationship with these agencies. The capacity (number of slots available) is predetermined under contract provisions with the funding agency. In this situation widespread recruitment of children from the local community does not make sense. Many persons reached by general announcements will not be eligible for services. Agencies may wish to do needs assessment to find out how many eligible children are in the community; then they can compare need for service with capacity of the present day care homes. Some heavily subsidized programs may have a few spaces available for private full-fee paying parents. These can usually be filled without resorting to extensive publicity campaigns. Public funding conditions tend to limit the mix of income levels and socioeconomic backgrounds of children in the day care program. This has direct implications for the kinds of recruitment activities and enrollment procedures that a local agency needs to establish for family day care homes.

Eligibility Determination. This is a formal, legal procedure for assessing the status of children and families to determine eligibility for publicly funded services. Family descriptors such as income level, income source, parents' work or training status, and physical disabilities of the child or parent are used to assess the status of the child and the family. If a child and family qualify for category placement, they have "categorical eligibility" for service. These category profiles are established using federal guidelines along with state data compiled by set formulas to determine cut-off levels or caps for local conditions. Programs receiving public funds must enroll or reserve service slots for children who are categorically eligible for subsidized care.

Application Procedures. Application procedures serve two purposes: acquainting parents with the care service and completing required forms and information materials. Several items will be needed:

Application A formal request for care services, it includes personal data on parents and basic summary of contact information.

Information form A more extensive questionnaire about needs for care, family situation, expectations. May be filled in together with agency staff. Used in making decisions about which home to place a child in.

Developmental history Parental report of progress and attainment of developmental milestones. Gives comprehensive picture of child's activities and accomplishments. Used in making decisions about placement.

Health appraisal Physician's report of child's health status. Helpful in diagnosing and screening for developmental problems. Can help in pinpointing areas of concern or identifying possible problems.

Emergency cards Notarized cards listing parent contact information and health insurance information.

Emergency consent Permission of parents for caregivers or the agency to act in their behalf if children need immediate medical attention. Form may be accepted by local hospital or physician in advance.

General consent forms Blanket permission for field trips, routine car transportation, photographing, and other similar items. Special events permission slips will still be obtained from parents.

Eligibility determination Form varies with local programs.

Contract for care Statement of conditions and costs of care.

When the application procedure is completed, the agency will reach a decision regarding enrollment of the child. If space is not available and parents wish to be placed on a waiting list, only certain parts of the application procedure may be completed. Forms such as health appraisal and emergency cards may be done only upon actual enrollment in the home.

Home Placement. In agency situations a staff member in the cental office usually makes a preliminary placement decision based on a review of the application papers and a review of existing vacancies in homes. This placement will take into account location and transportation time as well as items such as length of care day and any special requests of the parent. When the caregiver accepts the child, the parent is contacted and arrangements are made for an orientation visit.

The agency staff member participates with the parent, the child, and the caregiver in a brief orientation meeting at the caregiver's home. Unless serious problems arise, the placement is finalized and plans are made to initiate care. The caregiver receives copies of all consent forms before the first day of care. Depending on the circumstances, shorter days may be used to gradually introduce the child into the home situation. Essentially, the caregiver takes over and interacts directly with the parent in managing the placement after the orientation meeting. The agency staff person checks back periodically to monitor progress. Some agencies use a formal child placement period and review events in a conference before finalizing the placement. The goal of home placement is to find a stable and satisfactory match that will stand the test of time and child growth.

Parent Responsibilities. Parents' responsibilities are to meet the conditions of their contract for care regarding fees, length of care, time of arrival and pickup. Every care situation becomes to a certain extent a mutually comfortable relationship between parent and caregiver. The purpose of contracts and statements of responsibility is to ensure that no one's rights are unduly trespassed as minor daily variations in the care arrangement occur.

Family day care parents rarely associate with one another. At individual homes parents may cross paths at arrival or pickup times, but meetings are fleeting and conversation among parents is brief. Most attention is directed to the caregiver and the child. Systemwide newsletters are helpful to keep parents abreast of events and relevant information. Family day care parents usually do not have a sense of community and shared purpose and need. Organizing family day care parents under these circumstances is difficult. Chapter 14 presents a wealth of background information and suggestions for involving parents of children in child care.

Children's Activities

"I'm more than just a babysitter" has become almost a rallying cry for caregivers in family day care as they seek to define the valuable service they provide and upgrade their image. We tend to associate babysitting with simple custodial acts and watchful supervision interspersed with play activities. That is what family day care looks like to the casual observer. With an untrained caregiver that is, in fact, all it may be. Figure 9.3 illustrates sample daily schedules for children in family day care aged infant through school age. A large portion of children's time and activities revolve around basic care. Large blocks of time are available for supervised play. Children's activities in family day care homes are a mix of the necessary basic care and predictable curricular opportunities time blocks that are common to all other child care programs. How these activity blocks are meshed by the single caregiver in a home setting with a small, multiage group of children distinguishes family care from all other forms of child care.

Basic Care. As in center programs, the basic requirement for quality child care is adequate provision for children's bodily needs and assurance of safe, protective care. In center programs basic care services benefit from presence of several staff. The caregiver in a family day care home is the sole adult available. More younger, dependent children—toddlers and infants—are likely to be present. Care routines are more individualized in response to particular children's preferences and rhythms. Often in a family day care home more time is spent on basic care by the caregiver. As Figure 9.3 shows, in a home with infants and toddlers, the odds are high that someone will always be eating, sleeping, or toileting. When planning children's activities, caregivers must recognize that curricular opportunities can be woven into custodial care routines for individual children, and some children will need custodial care while others are involved in curricular activities.

Basic care dominates family day care home activity programs. Program planning must begin with basic care routines and work toward maximizing caregiver-child interactions at those times. Caregivers can do this by embedding curricular opportunities in routines and by extending custodial routines to include related activities. The possibilities are limited only by the caregiver's resourcefulness and sensitivity to individual children's interests and developmental levels.

Agency staff who supervise and train caregivers in family day care can use the daily care pattern and the concept of embedded and extended custodial care routines as a basis for building activity plans. A firm grasp of the logistics of basic care services underlies the smooth management of daily activities so that caregivers will feel and act like "professionals"—not just babysitters.

Theoretical Point of View. In Chapter 2 we presented extensive and strong arguments for the adoption of a single theoretical point of view on children's development as a basis for the design of child care programs. For family day care program planning, we recommend a modification of the program design process that takes into account the unique circumstances of family day care.

Maturationist Approach. Family day care home programs should be unabashedly based on maturation principles of development and derived practices. Popular wisdom on childhood development as well as the physical features of the home lend themselves to easy implementation of a program using the maturationist "folk curriculum"—cooking, dress-up, carpentry, water play, crafts, and so forth. Well-devel-

The times given are only approximate and will depend on the situation.

		Infants	Toddlers	Preschoolers	School-Age
Arrival					
Breakfast	7 A.M.	All children and their families are greeted warmly as they arrive. Many of the children will require some nourishment now, depending on their needs.			
		Babies may be changed, fed, and allowed to rest.	Some children may want to 'cat nap' or be rocked or cuddled for a while. Quiet toys—beads to string, puzzles, dolls, books—can be available.		After eating, the children can read, finish homework, watch TV, or play a quiet game until time for school.
Activity	9 A.M.	When the baby wakes, and feeding is completed, a game of peak-a-boo, or other play is enjoyed. Put the baby's seat or playpen near the activity of the children so he can watch.	Special Activities Art activities—painting, drawing, modelling, or other activity—cooking, playing with water or sand, making puppets, might be prepared for the children for in or outdoor play.		
Snack			A light snack is enjoyed midway through the morning.		
		Babies will probably require a full morning nap.	Many toddlers will require a full nap.	Preschoolers may need a quiet time to stretch out and rest.	
	11 A.M.	Some time for outdoor play—a walk around the block, to the store or playground—can be planned. Following this period of active play, the children prepare for lunch by washing, helping with the food preparation, or reading stories.			
Lunch	Noon	Babies may be fed earlier, and may be ready for an afternoon nap.	Toddlers can learn to feed themselves.	Preschoolers can set the table, help to prepare the meal and help clean up.	Lunch is ready for the children.
Rest			After lunch help the children brush teeth and prepare for nap. Toddlers will probably require a full nap.	Preschoolers can brush their own teeth and prepare for rest. Many will nap, others will rest by playing quietly.	
	1 P.M.	The children are allowed to sleep as long as they wish. Usually a refreshing drink or snack is welcome after napping.			
Activity	3 P.M.	Floor play—with baby placed on a blanket or in a playpen—can be planned.	Active in and/or outdoor play follows nap. Some special activity, a game, story, or walk can be arranged.		A snack is ready for the children or they can fix their own. The children decide what to do with their time—building, sewing, painting, doing homework, going to clubs, listening to records, playing with friends.
Snack					
Departure	5 P.M.	Preparing the children for going home helps them to make a smooth transition from your home to theirs. This is a good time for story reading, to gather together the things that each child will take home, or perhaps for a light snack to tide the children over until their parents prepare dinner.			

Figure 9.3 A suggested day. (Adapted from *Day care 9: Family day care* (p. 51) edited by C. Seefeldt and L. L. Dittmann, 1973, Washington, DC: U.S. Dept. of Health, Education and Welfare.)

oped, normative descriptions of children's developmental patterns by ages and stages can be used as the basis for planning and selection of activities. Maturationist principles are acceptable to all. Caregivers can become quickly comfortable and competent in using these developmental principles.

Behaviorist Approach. In general, behaviorist principles will be most helpful to caregivers in family day care in specific situations rather than as a basis for overall program design. Task analysis for behaviors such as toileting, shoelace tying, and throwing a ball can show caregivers how to help children acquire these skills.

Techniques of behavior modification can help caregivers manage troublesome behaviors. Children with certain physical or mental disabilities may progress faster with clear-cut behavioral expectations and reward conditions. Without considerable training, caregivers probably cannot independently set up and use behaviorist strategies. However, problem situations and children's special needs may permit judicious use of behaviorist techniques. In such situations, caregivers should expect close supervision and help from agency staff or related support services.

Cognitive Approach. Understanding cognitive (Piagetian) principles of development and designing program activities demand study and training. While some slightly different supplies and materials are desirable for this perspective, the major difference from the maturationist approach is the caregiver's cognitive role as questioner and his or her ongoing efforts to challenge children to mentally extend themselves. Caregivers in family day care homes can become quite effective and run home programs with a strong cognitive foundation. Many may have inclinations in this direction and naturally interact with children this way. Given the greater complexity of the perspective and the necessity for staff and caregiver time for training, however, we do not feel that the cognitive perspective is the best place to start with family day care home programs. Individual caregivers may eventually be motivated to seek out cognitive training. Agency staff will find that cognitive principles give them a perspective on children's development that increases their personal resources for program counseling.

Support Services

Support services are the psychological, medical, dental, social work, health, and nutrition service programs that operate in communities to meet basic and special needs of the local population. Child care has traditionally been viewed as a means to deliver a host of social services to children and their families. Enrollment in a child care program was seen as the first contact—a point of entry to meet various family needs. The term *comprehensive child care* refers to the array of support services that can be added to or clustered around the child care service itself. Support services remain an integral part of child care for two reasons. Children who meet categorical or criterion requirements for eligibility for child care often qualify on the same basis for other services such as primary medical care. Unless these services come as part of a comprehensive service package constituted by the child care program, these children would simply not get them. A second reason is a straightforward result of opportunity. Identification, assessment, and diagnosis of need for services can be accomplished efficiently as children are observed daily in child care settings. Child care gives access and opportunity to deliver support services to needy children.

Children in family day care homes are routinely observed by caregivers and professionals other than parents. Based upon these daily observations, periodic developmental assessments, and special diagnostic tests, children who have particular developmental difficulties can be identified. In addition, if because of family status, children are entitled to receive basic health benefits, participation in these programs can be encouraged. Caregivers and sponsoring agencies work together to identify service needs and eligibility or opportunity situations for children in care.

Caregivers and/or agencies use referral to connect children and families with support service providers. Referrals can be automatic if screening tests indicate needs for glasses, hearing screenings, or other services, or can be on a case-by-case basis for problems requiring further testing or special therapy. Agencies may have standing referral agreements with other service agencies or may make arrangements on an individual basis. The extent to which caregivers are trained to spot needs for referrals and to which agencies are geared up to process and monitor referrals varies considerably.

Caregivers in family day care are more likely to become involved in follow-up of social services than their counterparts in centers. They are very aware of and may need to schedule the home's daily schedule around children's absences for other services. They can be intimately affected by the therapeutic benefits or lack thereof of the support service. Because of the close relationship with a child, the caregiver may need or want help in dealing with the child's problems or understanding about how to adapt activities to the child's needs. On occasion, caregivers may take children to receive support services or checkups.

Without the help of an agency to oversee identification of need and referral, individual caregivers can become overwhelmed with the logistics of support service coordination. Yet, simultaneously, the closer and more personal context of the home care situation can motivate caregivers to look to support services for help with individual children and their families.

Points of Controversy

Legitimacy

Family day care has an image problem in relation to the more widely recognized center-based programs and other formally structured early childhood programs. Phrases such as "part of the underground economy" have come to describe the vast majority of private and unregulated child care arrangements that characterize family day care. The location of care (the home), the sex and work status of the caregiver (female, housewife), and the low wages are all negative contributions to family day care's image. The informal and personal nature of the arrangements further the impression that family day care is not legitimate work. Finally, family day care homes tend to be isolated from the mainstream of child care activity. They are not connected with more visible center-based programs. They are rarely licensed by authorities, and they are known only to a small circle of people in the immediate neighborhood of the home. It is understandable that under these conditions the general public, and even caregivers and parents, underestimate the value of family day care services.

While initially it may appear that legitimizing family day care is a good idea, there are trade-offs. Obviously much about the current state of affairs is acceptable for parents and caregivers; each has difficulties at times, but arrangements are fluid and flexible. Formalizing the system by introducing checkpoints and service requirements could destroy desirable aspects of current arrangements. Nevertheless, the controversy over legitimizing family day care is really focused on the extent and ways of legitimizing efforts rather than on whether family care should be recognized and formally acknowledged by the child care community.

Demand

Changing social and economic factors have increased the demand for child care services of all types. Diminished public subsidy of care appears to be shifting the burden of supplying care to the private sector. Parents of all income levels use family day care; most children in child care are in some kind of family day care arrangement. These factors have brought recognition and a form of legitimacy to family day care. By choice or default through lack of other options, family day care will continue to be the most frequently used form of child care in this country for at least the next decade.

Regulation

Closely related to the controversy over legitimizing family day care services is the question of regulation. Compliance with regulatory standards confers a very formal kind of legitimacy on day care homes—the legal right to provide care services. Every family day care home is a small business, organized to provide care for young children. Governments have a statutory obligation to monitor such activities to ensure adequate protection for citizens.

The regulatory controversy surrounding family day care stems from several attitudes and opinions:

- It's ridiculous to have so many liable but unregulated homes. The current system is not working well for anybody.
- There is no strong consensus on the value and need for family day care home regulation.
- There is no convincing case for benefits and incentives that could ensue from licensing.
- Regulation would be a reliable point of contact with the many independent family day care homes that exist, helping to pull family day care into the mainstream of day care support services.

The mood today in society in general is definitely one of deregulation—moving away from restrictive regulations to more permissive guidelines for operation. What form regulation for family day care homes should take as well as the substance of the standards themselves continues to be a topic for debate.

Family day care is not an ordinary business. Many caregivers are ignorant of the fact that they should meet regulatory standards and be licensed. The number of children present in the home is the most common "trigger" for licensing liability. It is a complex process; some estimate there are up to twenty different tasks required to achieve licensing. Those caring for relatives' children may feel it is an unnecessary intrusion into private family affairs. There is no incentive to meet standards and more importantly no sanctions for not complying. As consumers of care, parents may also be ignorant of the need for a home to be licensed. Or they may discount it since they see no value in a formal license. They may prefer instead to trust their own judgment in selecting a good place for their child.

Licensing personnel do not now have the resources to inspect the hundreds of existing unlicensed homes. Forcing more homes into the current bureaucratic system is not the answer, especially since many regulatory standards are thought to be overly strict and perhaps misdirected.

Quality

What constitutes quality in a family day care home? There are as many definitions of quality as there are caregivers, parents, children, and interested observers. The generally accepted program goals of protecting children from harm and enhancing their development can be reached by varying combinations of activities and circumstances. It would seem that indices and measures of quality programming could best be left to the discretion and judgment of participants in each care arrangement.

Concern for the welfare of children, however, is pervasive—so much so that no one (advocates, laypersons, or professionals) is really willing to let quality programs just happen. Although imperfect, regulation is seen as a means to ensure quality care programs for children, and few people are willing to omit some kind of program oversight, even though the move toward permissive guidelines is widely supported. How can quality result from regulations? If we are not really sure what quality is, how can we presume to write standards that will compel its presence? Emerging from current thinking on the subject is the idea that some program factors are more closely linked with quality care experiences than others. Finding quantifiable (and hence regulatable) indices of these factors could selectively direct licensing procedures to critical care variables. Both the National Day Care Study and the National Day Care Home Study pinpointed *group composition* and *caregiver training* as factors with great potential for impact on quality of care. If and how these findings can be translated into meaningful practices for family care is a point of controversy and challenge in the immediate future.

Summary

Family day care is nonresidential care provided in a private home other than the child's own, for six or fewer children, and for any part of a twenty-four-hour day.

Family day care homes may be categorized as regulated or unregulated. Approximately 90 percent of all family day care homes in the United States are characterized as unregulated, informal arrangements. Regulated homes are either independent or part of a system. Systems include sponsored homes, limited affiliates, and provider networks.

Children of all ages attend family day care homes, which often congenially mix infants and toddlers, preschoolers, and school-age children. Caregivers in family day care, who are usually women, come from all races, classes, and ethnic backgrounds. They work long hours, earn low wages, and are accorded a relatively low status. Fees tend to reflect prevailing estimates of the value of the service, rather than the caregiver's actual experience.

Individual family day care homes have increasingly opted to become part of a system. In sponsored homes all administration and management are handled by a local agency. Limited affiliates come together in order to qualify for the USDA Child Care Food Program. Provider networks offer a way for day care homes to exchange information and support one another. Systems can recruit and train caregivers, enroll children, inspect homes and aid in licensing, collect fees, distribute supplies, and loan equipment.

The two areas of legal concern for day care homes are regulatory compliance and licensing. To reduce the potential for problems with fee payment and hours of pickup, caregivers may sign a contract with parents. Caregivers whose day care is part of a system may also contract with that system to provide their services.

It is often mistakenly thought that anyone who has had experience as a mother can be a good caregiver in a family day care home, and that mothering comes naturally. In fact, the caregiver job encompasses many aspects of mothering, but a caregiver is really in the business of mothering and, as such, the work requires training.

Because even well-managed day care homes experience a high turnover, family day care home systems must have a systematic recruitment procedure for caregivers. Agency staff must overcome the problems of isolation and lack of motivation to provide training for caregivers. Family day care homes can be effectively monitored only by well-planned, sensitive home visits.

Family day care home systems can lend individual homes help in enrollment, activities, and support services. Enrollment involves following a complete, formal application procedure and determining eligibility for publicly funded services. Caregivers can maintain basic care and offer educational experiences by embedding curricular opportunities in routines and by extending custodial routines to include related activities. Because caregivers are in close contact with the children, they may be best suited to identify and refer children for support services.

The future challenge for planners is to find ways to lend some degree of legitimacy to family day care homes and to regulate appropriately while retaining the already attractive qualities of this form of child care.

Resources

General Overview

Alston, F. K. (1983). *Caring for other people's children: A complete guide to family day care.* Baltimore: University Park Press.

BANANAS, Inc. (1981). *Choosing family day care.* Oakland, CA: BANANAS, Inc.

Collins, A. H., & Watson, E. L. (1977). *Family day care.* Boston: Beacon Press.

Davison, J. L., & Ellis, W. W. (1980). *Family day care in the United States: Parent component: Vol. 4. Final report of the national day care home study.* Washington, DC: U.S. Department of Health and Human Services.

Day care survey—1970. (1971). (Summary report and basic analysis). Rockville, MD: Westat. (ERIC Document Reproduction Service No. ED 051 880)

Emlen, A. C., Donoghue, B. A., & LaForge, R. (1971). *Child care by Keth: A study of the family day care relationship of working mothers and neighborhood caregivers.* Portland, OR: Oregon State University. (ERIC Document Reproduction Service No. ED 060 955)

Emlen, A. C., & Perry, J. D., Jr. (1974). Child-care arrangements. In L. W. Hoffman & F. I. Nye (Eds.), *Working mothers.* San Francisco: Jossey-Bass.

Fosburg, S. (1981). *Family day care in the United States: Summary of findings: Vol. 1. Final report of the national day care home study.* Washington, DC: U.S. Department of Health and Human Services.

Fosburg, S. (1982). Family day care: The role of the surrogate mother. In L. M. Laosa & I. Sigel (Eds.), *Families and learning environments for children.* New York: Plenum.

Murphy, K. (1984). *A house full of kids.* Boston: Beacon Press.

Sale, J. S. (1973). Family day care—A valuable alternative. *Young Children, 28,* 209–215.

Singer, J. D., Fosburg, S., Goodson, B. D., & Smith, J. M. (1980). *Family day care in the United States: Research report: Vol. 2. Final report of the national day care home study.* Washington, DC: U.S. Department of Health and Human Services.

Statewide assessment of family day care. (1977). *Final Report:* Vol. 1. Albany, NY: Welfare Research.

Travis, N. E., & Perreault, J. (Eds.). (1982). *Building bridges: Report of a family day care conference, April 1981.* Atlanta: Save the Children/Child Care Support Center.

Urich, H. (1972). *A study of family day care systems in Massachusetts.* Cambridge, MA: Child Care Resource Center.

Regulations

Adams, D. (1982). Family day care regulations: State policies in transition. *Day Care Journal, 1* (1), 8–13.

The appropriateness of the federal interagency day care requirements: Report of findings and recommendations. (1978). Washington, DC: U.S. Department of Health, Education and Welfare, Office of the Assistant Secretary for Planning and Evaluation.

Class, N. E. (1972). The public regulation of family day care: An innovative proposal. In *Family day care west: A working conference.* Pasadena, CA: Pacific Oaks College. (ERIC Document Reproduction Service No. ED 070 511)

Comparative licensing study: Profiles of state day care requirements. Washington, DC: Lawrence Johnson and Associates, 1982. In Appendix F, *Model Child Care Standards Act—Guidance to states to prevent child abuse in day care facilities.* Washington, DC: U.S. Department of Health and Human Services, 1985.

Galambas, E. C. (1971). *Problems in licensing family day care homes.* Atlanta: Southern Regional Education Board. (ERIC Document Reproduction Service No. ED 058 959)

Morgan, G. (1980). Can quality family day care be achieved through regulation? In S. Kilmer (Ed.), *Advances in early education and day care* (pp. 77–102). Greenwich, CT: JAI Press.

Morgan, G. (1974). *Alternatives in regulation of family day care homes in children.* Washington, DC: Day Care and Child Development Council of America.

Wattenberg, E. (1980). Family day care: Out of the shadows and into the spotlight. *Marriage and Family Review, 3* (3/4), 35–62.

Organizations

Collins, A. H., & Watson, E. L. (1969). *The day care neighbor service: A handbook for the organization and operations of a new approach to family day care.* Portland, OR: Tri-County Community Council. (ERIC Document Reproduction Service No. ED 049 810)

Grasso, J., & Fosburg, S. (1980). *Family day care systems:* Vol. 5. *National day care home study.* Washington, DC: U.S. Department of Health and Human Services.

Open the door . . . See the people. A descriptive report of the second year of the community family day care project. (1972). Pasadena, CA: Pacific Oaks College. (ERIC Document Reproduction Service No. ED 071 737)

Organizing tools for family day care systems. (n.d.). Washington, DC: Day Care and Child Developmental Council of America.

Sales, J. S. (1974). A self-help organization of family day care mothers as a means of quality control. Paper presented at the fifty-first annual meeting of the American Orthopsychiatric Association, San Francisco, CA. (ERIC Document Reproduction Service No. ED 094 306)

San Diego County Family Day Care Association. (1983). *Quality family day care: The choice is yours.* San Diego: Committed to Kids Press.

Seefeldt, C., & Dittmann, L. L. (Eds.). (1973). *Day care 9: Family day care.* Washington, DC: U.S. Department of health, Education and Welfare, Office of Child Development.

Training for Child Care Project. (1977). *Family day care associations in the South.* Atlanta: Southern Regional Education Board.

Training for Child Care Project. (1978). *Establishing a family day care agency.* Atlanta: Southern Regional Education Board.

Playgroups and In-Home Care

Broad, L. P., & Butterworth, N. T. (1974). *The playgroup handbook.* New York: St. Martin's Press.

Magg, P. B., & Ornstein, M. R. (1981). *Come with us to playgroup: A handbook for parents and teachers of young children.* Englewood Cliffs, NJ: Prentice-Hall.

Playgroups: Do it ourselves child care. (1975). San Francisco: Childcare Switchboard/Single Parent Reserve Center.

Playgroups: How to grow your own. (1974). Cambridge, MA: Child Care Resource Center.

Ruderman, F. A. (1968). *Child care and working mothers.* New York: Child Welfare League of America.

Business

Child care resources federal income tax and audit guide. (1982). Mound, MN: Quality Child Care Press.

Getting it all together: Recordkeeping for family day care. (1981). Mound, MN: Quality Child Care Press Division, Day Care Fair, Inc.

Ott, N. (1981). *BANANAS handout. Family day care income taxes* (rev.). Oakland, CA: BANANAS Child Care Information & Referral and Parent Support.

Treadwell, L. W. (1980). *The family day care provider's legal handbook.* Oakland, CA: BANANAS, Child Care Project.

Daily Activities—Guides for Providers

Child Development Training Program. (1971). *Handbook for home care of children.* Detroit: Wayne State University.

Seefeldt, C., & Dittmann, L. L. (Eds.). (1973). *Day care 9: Family day care.* Washington, DC: U.S. Department of Health, Education and Welfare, Office of Child Development.

Squibb, B. (1980). *Family day care: How to provide it in your home.* Harvard, MA: Harvard Common Press.

West, K. (Ed.). (1980). *Family day-to-day care* (rev. ed.). Mound, MN: Quality Child Care.

Training and Support for Caregivers

Colbert, J. C., & Enos, M. M. (1976). *Educational services for home day caregivers: Final report.* Chicago: Roosevelt University. (ERIC Document Reproduction Service No. ED 134 341)

Crawley, M., & Whiren, A. (1982). The process of planning a family day care conference. *Day Care Journal, 1* (1), 55–57.

Developing training support systems for home day care. (1973). Denver: Colorado Department of Education. (ERIC Document Reproduction Service No. ED 087 558)

Wattenberg, E. (1974). *The family day care consultant: An invention of a strategic catalyst to upgrade the quality of family day care homes.* (ERIC Document Reproduction Service No. ED 088 583)

Issues

Burton, J. (1973). Family day care. In P. Roby (Ed.), *Child care—Who cares?* New York: Basic Books.

Emlen, A. C. (1972). Family day care research: A summary and critical review. In *Family day care west: A working conference.* Pasadena, CA: Pacific Oaks College. (ERIC Document Reproduction Service No. ED 070 511)

Prescott, E. (1972). *Group and family day care: A comparative assessment.* Washington, DC: Children's Bureau. (ERIC Document Reproduction Service No. ED 060 945)

Sparks, G. B. (1972). Problems and alternatives related to provisions of family day care. In *Family day care west: A working conference.* Pasadena, CA: Pacific Oaks College. (ERIC Document Reproduction Service No. ED 070 511)

Associations

Technical assistance, publications, newsletter:
Family Day Care Advocacy Project
Children's Foundation
1420 New York Ave. N.W. Suite 800
Washington, DC 20005

Information, forms, and administrative materials:
TOYS 'N THINGS Press
Resources for Child Caring, Inc.
906 North Dale St.
St. Paul, MN 55103

Part IV

Making Programs Work

10

Program Management

Introduction

Child care programs depend to an extraordinary degree on the competence and performance of one person—the program director. Any discussion of the preparation, responsibilities, and role of the child care director is shaped by two realities: the national child care field and the nature of individual programs. Nationally, the field is changing at a rapid rate through redefinition and standardization. Child care is complicated by federal law, regulation, and funding; by state licensing, regulation, and standards that differ markedly from one state to another; and by hundreds—perhaps thousands—of local community codes, ordinances, requirements, and regulations. Such legal complexities influence the management responsibilities of the director.

As regards the nature of individual programs, directors function in a variety of administrative structures. In a complex administrative hierarchy, the director is responsible to one or more of the following: a board of directors, an executive director, a program supervisor, or a general administrator. In addition, the director often works with a social service worker, a parent involvement coordinator, and a program specialist. In a less complex organization or in a self-contained center, the director is responsible for program management and for many of the duties and responsibilities that come under the jurisdiction of special personnel in the more complex systems.

This chapter examines the administrative and leadership role of the child care program director. We'll begin by defining what we mean by *administration* and *management,* and describing three common structures of organization. Overall, the director's role is to assume responsibility for a variety of tasks, interpret the program's philosophy and carry out policy decisions. The responsibilities that we'll discuss include managing the children's program, maintaining the facility, record-keeping, and public relations. Because the director's job is more than accomplishing tasks, we'll look at styles of action, or what constitutes leadership, and the necessary qualifications for the position.

Administration and Management

Administration and management are very similar. Both refer to systematic and deliberate processes that are used to achieve an organization's goal. In child care, the goal of the organization is to deliver a service—child care—to children and their families. We define *administration* as the tasks, activities, and jobs necessary to do the work of delivering the service. We define *management* as the leadership and supervision necessary to accomplish these administrative tasks and deliver the service. In practice, administration and management are inseparable and you will often see the terms used interchangeably.

Undermanagement is the single biggest problem confronting most child care organizations. It leads to management by crisis, or directors attending to whatever tasks are most compelling at the moment. Priorities cannot be set and routines cannot be followed because all efforts must focus on the immediate task. Without long-range planning directors find themselves endlessly repeating the same tasks and responding to, rather than preventing, problems. It is difficult to disengage from the immediate needs of children, staff, and program and concentrate instead on the concepts of administration and management. Nevertheless, formal and deliberate management is the best tool a director has for delivering quality child care services to children and families.

Organizational Patterns

Programs with a large staff usually formalize the job specifications and work relationships, but even the smallest and most informally run center has an implicit organizational structure. One of the most important tools for management, therefore, is a picture of the organization. An organizational chart for a child care program can usually be easily drawn. The chart provides the director with a blueprint of the relationships between people and positions and clarifies authority lines. It also identifies the management level of the director. With these basic pieces in place, the director can identify communication lines, work contacts, and discrepancies between what is written on the chart and actual daily practice.

There are three patterns of child care program management: family, ray, and line management. Each has distinct advantages and promotes particular types of management roles for the director. Often as a program grows in size and as the director gains management skill, the organization evolves from one pattern to another.

Family Organization

All programs probably have some characteristics of the family style of organization (see Figure 10.1). This pattern tends to encourage group commitment and can elicit impressive cooperation among staff members. Such "esprit de corps" is very helpful. Small centers where staff have frequent contact with each other and with all children are likely to be family organizations. Programs in which directors are director-teachers often have this organizational pattern because the director must move in and out of a management role. Contacts outside the organization are handled by the staff as the need arises. Administrative tasks are moderate and can be handled through informal means and group consensus. This director is one person among equals.

Stresses occur in this organizational pattern for two reasons. If outside demands increase, the time required for response can place demands on the group. It becomes more efficient for the director to become the "point" person and separate from the group to meet the demands. These external demands may be funding problems, public relations needs, or regulatory and inspection difficulties. Internal stresses may arise because of staff incompatibility or increases in child enrollment, requiring changes in job assignments. Family organizations are flexible, and on a temporary basis, can respond to such stresses; if there are sustained pressures, however, a change in the organizational pattern is needed.

Ray Organization

In this pattern the director is clearly differentiated from the staff and acts as the spokesperson for the center (see Figure 10.2). Many family organizations evolve to the ray pattern. It allows the director close contact with the staff but

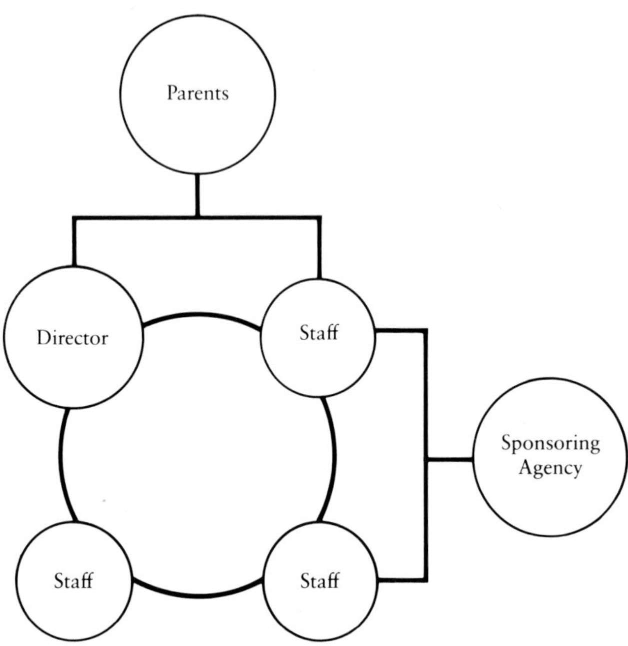

Figure 10.1 Family organization.

also provides sufficient detachment for the exercise of authority and better response to groups outside the organization.

The director has immediate contact and control over all staff. Directors assume the entire burden of administration, delegating few tasks. With this kind of immediate involvement, the director can respond quickly to situations and is usually informed about events in the program. Stresses occur if too many demands are made on the director. If the director has to spend much effort on tasks such as proposal writing or parent meetings, he or she may have little time left for daily management and staff supervision; no one is in a position to substitute. Similarly, if daily program activities and staff concerns dominate the director's time, no one can assume the work with outside groups. One solution is to have an assistant director who performs parts of the director's tasks.

Line Management Organization

The traditional business pattern of organization is characterized by delegation of authority and midlevel management. This pattern is necessary with a large staff. It requires clearly defined responsibilities for each level of management. Line management offers directors the potential to maximize planning efforts. Once fundamental decisions are made, other staff members can implement them. With functioning midlevel managers a director is free from the details and routine decisions of the daily program.

Figure 10.3 illustrates a simple line management organization for a child care center. There can be many variations, but all would reflect the notion of delegation of authority. Figure 10.4 presents a line management organization for a large, complex center.

Line management organizations need directors who are managers. Stresses occur when the director does not delegate authority or tasks and does not function fully as the leader and decision maker. Management must be deliberate and goal directed. Supervision is essential and performance evaluations are necessary to keep all levels of the organization functioning smoothly. To do the job the director must use the authority and communication lines of the organization.

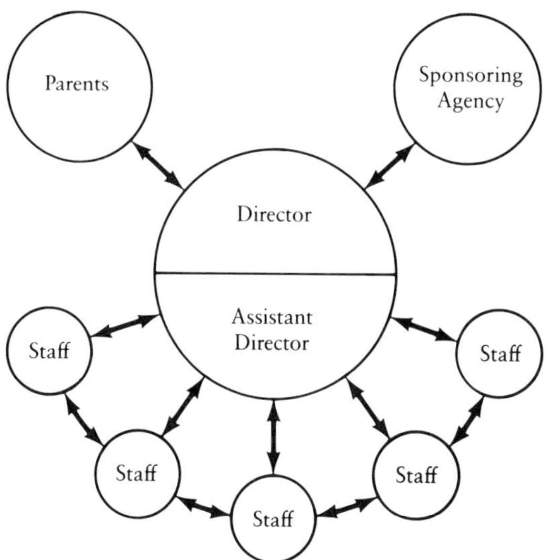

Figure 10.2 Ray organization.

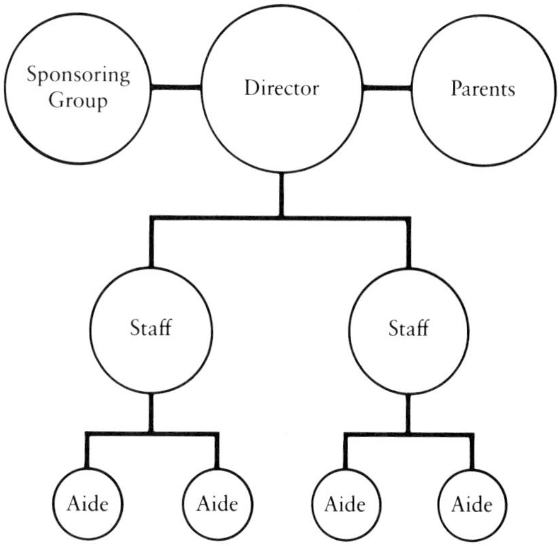

Sponsoring Group
Director
Parents
Staff
Staff
Aide
Aide
Aide
Aide

Figure 10.3
Line management organization—simple.

Role of the Director

In general, the director manages the daily operation of a child care program. The director is the ultimate authority who ensures that the program (1) contributes to the individual growth and development of children; (2) complies with applicable federal, state, and local standards and regulations; and (3) reflects the philosophy and goals of quality child care.

The director's job is, on the one hand, a challenging opportunity for professional contribution and personal development. Among other things the director is a problem solver, decision maker, instructor, evaluator, personnel manager, recruiter, public relations expert, fund raiser, and child advocate. In all fairness, however, enthusiasm for the positive and creative aspects of management should not obscure the mundane and frustrating elements. After all, the director is also often a fee collector, bookkeeper, file clerk, secretary, cook, telephone-answering service, janitor, and general maintenance specialist. At times the job is unpleasant, especially when handling suspected cases of child abuse, settling staff disputes, and being frustrated in finding solutions for the many problems experienced by children and their families.

The director influences the emotional climate of the program, the quality of the program, the organization of the physical setting, the tempo of the daily operation, and the personal relationships of everyone. The program reflects the capabilities and the limitations of the director—no other single individual is as important or exerts as much power.

Administrative Tasks

Directors have six major administrative tasks. The specific duties and functions vary according to the needs of individual programs, but all directors' jobs are composites of duties from each of these areas:

1. Management of the children's program
2. Coordination of program support functions
3. Maintenance of the physical facility
4. Record-keeping for legal and fiscal purposes

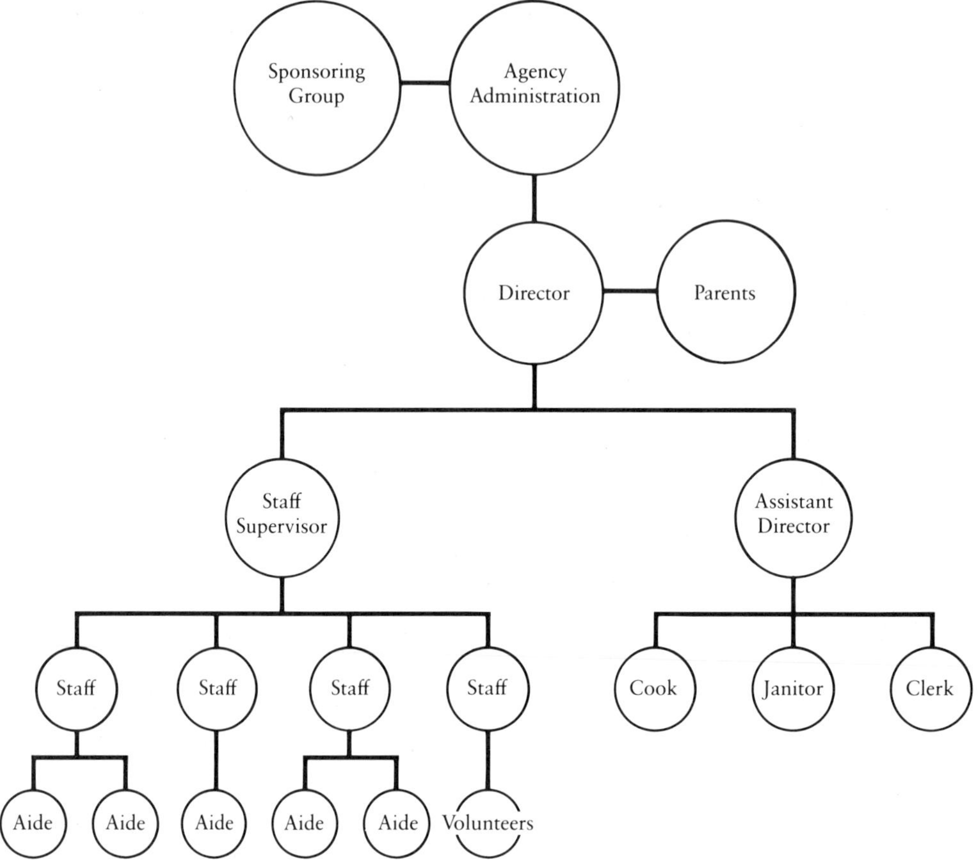

Figure 10.4 Line management organization—complex.

5. Staff management
6. Public relations

Figure 10.5 illustrates the daily time commitment in each of these areas for a director of a moderate-size center. Percentages were derived from averages based on a week's observation of a director's daily activities. Numerous studies have produced similar time distributions.

Every administrative task is composed of three processes: (1) preparation, (2) implementation, and (3) evaluation. Since directors perform many administrative tasks each day, they are always in the midst of several different cycles of task administration. It is easy to lose track of direction in this kind of situation, and it is also easy to start thinking that the overall task of management is impossible. It is not. Administration is a skill. Directors can learn "how to" administer and can improve their techniques.

Systematic approaches are required to organize all elements of operation. Directors must first organize their own time and duties. They must be in control of their own productivity if they are to achieve any kind of efficiency and control over the ongoing operation of the program.

Directors also need two types of information: *professional information,* which is best

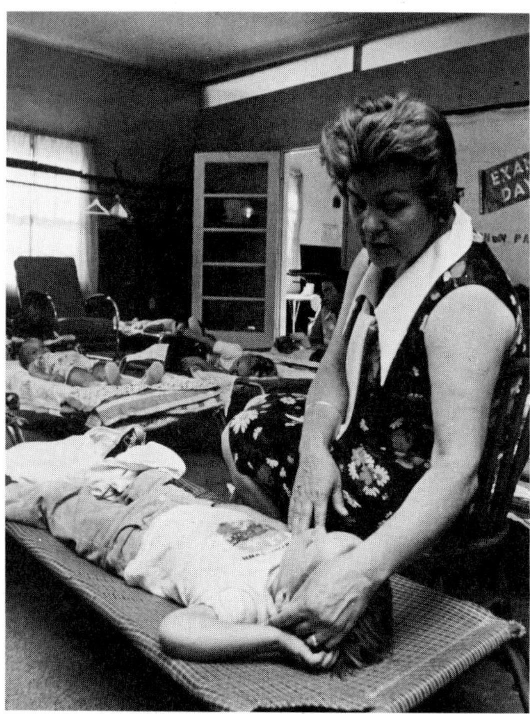

The director of a program for children of migrant farm workers comforts a child napping during midday. Most directors, whatever their formal administrative roles, value opportunities to interact with the children in the program. (Courtesy of U.S. Department of Agriculture, Washington, DC.)

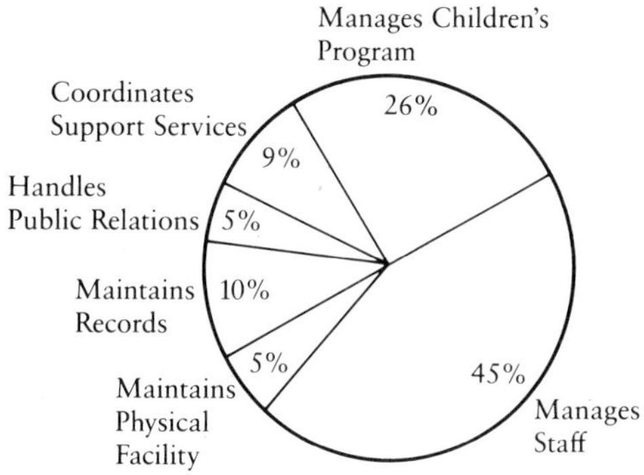

Figure 10.5 Daily percentage time estimate by responsibility areas for the director.

obtained by professional training and through reading, discussion, and course work; and *operational information,* which is continuous, practical information about the ongoing program.

The following sections describe the six specific administrative tasks of the director and the informational requirements of those tasks.

Management of the Children's Program. What happens for children everyday in the program is the most important outcome of the director's administrative efforts. The most visible aspect of child care is the children's program—the activities and events that are part of the lives of children. For sound management, as well as for the sake of morale, the children's program occupies much of the director's time. The following lists show typical administrative activities and information needs for this task.

Activities

- creates program philosophy and organization
- coordinates writing of program plan
- oversees setup of physical environment for program
- updates professional library and resources for center staff related to program
- monitors execution of program philosophy
- approves and arranges program activities (field trips, cooking projects, etc.)
- helps to select and plan program activities

Operational Information

- reads professional literature on program activities
- receives input from staff on effectiveness of planned activities
- initiates staff planning sessions for unit activities

Professional Information

- knowledge of current trends and practice
- knowledge of child development
- special expertise in program area
- skill in designing program and curriculum

Of all staff members, the director is in a unique position to contribute to program management as a result of his or her breadth of duties. The director's complete understanding of program philosophy and operation and sensitivity for the needs of the children, parents, and community enables him or her to determine the most useful program emphasis and program improvement and the most appropriate methods for program development.

Coordination of Program Support Functions. Program support includes those activities that are directly related to the children's program as well as activities that are a part of a comprehensive network of social services available to eligible families. Directors manage parent involvement and education, attend board and committee meetings, and coordinate referrals and services with community agencies. Many programs are not legally required or do not have a tradition of coordinating these social services for eligible families. If a director or a board sees the program as the pivot in an array of comprehensive services, considerable importance will be attached to referral activities. The following lists present administrative activities in this area.

Activities

- organizes and leads parent meetings
- arranges babysitting for parent meetings
- writes and produces parent newsletter
- works on parent manual
- organizes parents for work, fund raising, etc.
- initiates and participates in parent conferences
- helps families with unexpected crises and temporary problems
- distributes information on social services
- sets up appointments, provides transportation, and encourages follow-up for social and medical services
- attends board and sponsoring group meetings
- functions as program's liaison with other groups or program's representative in internal management structure of sponsoring group

Operational Information

- informed by parents about family problems
- collects and disseminates information from authorities pertinent to parents
- informed by staff of severe and continuing problems with individual children and families
- knows who to call or where to go for various services
- can identify needs of program and resources
- can lobby or present program's viewpoint with peers and decision-makers

Professional Information

- familiar with community mores and culture
- interpersonal skills to organize and coordinate parent groups
- knowledge of function and limitations of various types of professional services
- skill in identifying and facilitating situations that require professional specialists
- knowledge of a variety of evaluation techniques and uses of information
- effective oral and written communication skills

It is a mistake to assume that everyone in a sponsoring agency favors child care. Directors must be able to represent their program within the internal organizational structure of a sponsoring group. "Defending turf" is a cliché appropriate to describe many directors' activities when they operate within a larger human service organization or sponsoring group.

Maintenance of the Physical Facility. The director is responsible for the management of a safe and attractive physical environment. In addition to complying with regulatory standards, the director supervises ongoing maintenance and establishes procedures for evaluating the environment. Both regulatory standards and government jurisdiction vary depending upon the location, the state department licensing authority, and the funding or sponsorship arrangement. Therefore, the director must be aware of national standards, state laws, and local codes that apply to the program. In general, the facility and grounds used by the children must meet the requirements of the appropriate safety and sanitation authorities. Minimum requirements include: (1) adequate indoor and outdoor space; (2) nonhazardous and clean floors and walls; (3) adequate ventilation and heating; (4) safe and comfortable nap arrangements; and (5) isolation of sick children. Specific regulations about the environment involve detailed examination of sewage disposal systems, water supplies, pest and rodent control, food temperature storage, the ratio of toilet and washbowl units to number of children enrolled, disposal of single service diapers, and the number of foot-candle units for adequate lighting. For many directors there is a continuing need to work with authorities who often are stringent and critical monitors.

Activities

- monitors custodial work
- supervises requisition and inventory of supplies
- maintains staff lounge and work area with mailboxes and bulletin boards
- plans and sets up procedures for handling routines

Operational Information

- informed from staff about supply and maintenance problems
- current regulations applicable to facility

Professional Information

- skill in delegating responsibility

A monthly safety inspection tour by the director and staff provides a systematic examination of the physical setting as a means for identifying hazardous conditions. Typical safety checklists identify:

- *Fire hazards* Blocked stairways and exits; unmarked exits; nonfunctioning fire extinguishers; accumulated debris; faulty heating, wiring, lighting, and cooking equipment.
- *Insufficient lighting* Dark or insufficient illumination in hallways, stairwells, entrances, and rooms.
- *Hazardous materials and equipment* Sharp edges, broken parts, chipped paint, missing or small pieces of equipment; dangerous toys; dirty materials.
- *Improper storage of materials* Unprotected poisonous substances; accumulated trash or combustible materials, cluttered rooms, exits, and passageways; improper food storage.
- *Unsatisfactory floor conditions* Slippery, cold, or drafty; improper floor covering; accumulation of dirt.
- *Dangerous playground conditions* Broken glass; faulty equipment; unprotected from traffic; hard surface playing areas.
- *Walls* Damp, unclean, peeling or lead-based paint.
- *Windows* Unscreened, not able to be locked, drafty.

The physical environment does not have to be antiseptic, but an uncluttered and clean setting is necessary. The director must supervise the janitorial and food preparation staff in much the same manner as he or she supervises the caregiving staff.

Three areas of particular concern are food preparation, toileting facilities, and nap facilities. Directors must understand the sanitation aspects of food handling and the education and supervision of the meal preparation staff. Toilet facilities require daily cleaning with antiseptics, and the mats, cots, and blankets used for nap time should be marked with the child's name. They should be scrubbed and disinfected regularly.

The director is also involved creatively in designing a setting that is attractively arranged, pleasing to the eye, and comfortable for children and adults. Children who spend the greatest portion of their day at the center and adults who work within that environment are directly influenced by the physical atmosphere and deserve pleasant surroundings. Even programs with a limited budget can provide attractive facilities through effort and ingenuity. The director can stimulate staff interests in an attractive environment by encouraging pride in the arrangement of activity areas, by helping to create colorful and interesting displays, and by creating homelike touches with plants, pillows, and rugs. Children need little encouragement to contribute to the beauty of the center. They can collect and arrange materials from nature, display their artwork, create sculptures, and exhibit favorite collections. The director should try to arrange a quiet area with a few comfortable chairs, a small table, and coffee and tea as a setting for staff relaxation and for parent conferences and meetings. An entry way can double as a communications center for parents. Display of children's art, individual mailboxes, and a bulletin board filled with articles of interest can stimulate parent curiosity about the program and communicate interest in parents as well as in children.

Record-Keeping for Legal and Fiscal Purposes. The most tedious duty of directors is often thought to be record-keeping. With the advent of computers and government concern for accountability in human service programs, the record-keeping demands on administrators have increased. Whether directors keep all records themselves or assign the task to administrative assistants, the orderly and swift collection, storage, and retrieval of information are an integral part of management. Activities and information needs associated with this task are shown in the following list:

Activities

- keeps attendance records, fee records, etc.
- answers correspondence
- reports verbally and in writing
- works on budgets
- develops forms as needed
- enrolls children

Operational Information

- reads current literature and regulations on child care
- informed of all changes involving money and client services

Professional Information

- secretarial skills
- minimal bookkeeping skills
- familiar with agency and state regulations

The management of record-keeping systems includes a number of processes: (1) *identification* of records demanded by governmental departments and sponsors and essential records used in daily operation; (2) *organization* of records into an efficient storage system; (3) *filling out* of records with duplication as required; (4) *filing* of records, including the preparation of file folders and procedures for storage and retrieval; and (5) *updating* records by revising, discarding, and refiling. The director controls the management of record-keeping systems by setting some guidelines:

1. Information collection has a definite *purpose*. Record-keeping does not exist for its own sake. Rather, records are kept for a valid reason. In general, information is needed if it is essential to program operation or if it is required by a government agency or sponsor. Only minimum information should be collected and stored.
2. The record-keeping system should be *efficient*—simple enough to be easily understood, but complex enough to be complete. Filing patterns must be logical so that the system is easily understood by all who use it. Standardized forms and summary sheets consolidate information and reduce repetition.
3. The records should be *confidential*. Record retrieval should be controlled by the director who authorizes access to the information. Highly confidential and personal information should be stored in a locked file cabinet. All individuals who use records should fully understand the confidential nature of the information.

The child care program should have written policies and guidelines outlining the financial responsibility of the director. These fiscal guidelines should define the director's power and control over the expenditure of money, responsibility for financial record-keeping, duties for budget preparation and fund raising, and the financial circumstances requiring board action or approval. Any director with financial responsibility should be bonded. Some of the financial management responsibilities of the director are:

Budget preparation The director may have sole responsibility for preparing the budget or may advise a financial manager or finance committee in budget preparation.

Budget administration The director supervises and controls the expenditure of monies; validates expenditures with receipts, invoices, and financial statements; and maintains records for the purchase of goods and services.

Financial record-keeping Records for fee setting and collection; budget preparation, projection, analysis, and administration; payroll management; purchasing and distributing goods and services; and financial reporting are typical examples of director's responsibilities.

Goods and services purchasing The director supervises the process and purchases goods and services. He or she must know exactly what goods and services are needed, where and how to purchase, which forms to use for purchase and proof of purchase, and how to acquire and use a tax-exemption status.

Fee-setting and collection If the center charges fees, the director is often responsible for setting the fee scale or administering a state or agency fee scale, collecting fees, and recording fee payments.

Staff Management. The quality and vitality of a child care program depend to a large extent upon the competence of the director in selecting, training, and supervising staff. The composition of the staff reflects the program philosophy and goals. Men and women of various ages with diverse educational and personal backgrounds and different ethnic and racial heritages enrich the child care experience for children.

The director supervises a variety of other staff members such as social service assistants, staff supervisors, caregivers, assistant caregivers, aides, practical nurses, secretaries, cooks and cook aides, and housekeepers and janitors. Depending upon the program, the director also supervises volunteers, interns and practicum students, student teachers, and other trainees.

Staff management is the skill of forming positive working relationships with and among the individuals associated with the center. The success of the director in performing his or her duties is directly related to this skill. The director organizes the duties and responsibilities of personnel. This includes developing staff work patterns, preparing individual job descriptions, and assigning staff duties. It also includes the delegation of responsibility to competent personnel for support activities. The following lists describe the activities and information management:

Activities

- plans and chairs staff meetings
- interviews volunteers and new staff
- organizes new staff orientation
- prepares staff manual
- prepares guidelines for substitutes
- maintains smooth communication and relationships
- evaluates staff
- schedules staff working hours

Operational Information

- mediates staff problems and disputes
- informally observes staff working
- receives volunteered information from individual staff regarding their activities

Professional Information

- knowledge and competency in supervision principles
- capable of organizing and executing workshops and skill sessions
- skill in personnel selection and management

Public Relations. Directors increasingly feel the need to be advocates—advocates for their programs within community life and advocates for children and child care as political and economic trends seem to threaten the stability or even the survival of their programs. Many directors have added a new set of tasks related to public relations to their responsibilities:

Activities

- lectures to community and student groups
- prepares brochures describing program
- solicits new children

- maintains positive relationship with other groups using facility
- handles newspaper publicity
- prepares testimony for public hearings
- speaks out on community issues involving children

Operational Information

- informed of all church and agency activities
- seeks out information from staff in activities appropriate for newsletter or newspaper

Professional Information

- public speaking
- writing and editing skills
- organize and coordinate interested individuals and groups

Child Care Philosophy

Program directors should be able to recognize the relationship between child care theory and its practical application, and should be knowledgeable about the impact of early childhood experiences on physical, intellectual, social, and emotional development. The operation of the program will be easier if the personal philosophy of the director coincides with the program philosophy and the philosophy of the staff. However, at times, conflicting views do spark growth and change.

Policy

Policy serves as the overall plan by which program philosophy becomes action. The director uses policy as a decision-making tool to keep the program and its management consistent with the organization's goals and to create a workable system of procedures to manage recurring processes and events. Absence of policy means that decisions must be made for each situation. Policy should meet these five standards:

1. Policy reflects program goals and philosophy. If policy is to serve as the bridge between philosophy and action, then each statement of policy must be consistent with philosophy. For example, if a program goal is parent involvement at the decision-making level, the policy that "75 percent of the members of the board of directors must be parents of children enrolled in the program" reflects that goal. An analysis of the composition of the board would determine if practice is consistent with the policy.
2. Policy is written. Lengthy documents of policy are unnecessary, but adequate written policy statements are essential for management and as an information base for the persons affected by policy. For example, if parents are charged a fee for child care, then written fee scales, fee determination procedures, and fee payment procedures must be provided for parents and administrators. This policy ensures that parents are aware of fees and provides management practices about fee assessment and collection.
3. Policy is a guideline for action. Policy should be consistently administered, but provisions for extenuating circumstances and unusual situations are also desirable. Deviation from accepted policy usually requires approval from the board of directors or another such committee. For example, the board might have the prerogative to extend sick pay or grant a salary advance for an employee in an emergency even if this is not an established procedure.
4. Policy has a purpose. Many programs are burdened with policy that serves little or no purpose in bridging philosophy and action. Policy facilitates a workable management system. For example, policies for the admission of children in the program should satisfy admission requirements, offer a workable admission process for administrators, and facilitate the admission procedure for parents.
5. Policy is regularly evaluated and changed as necessary as the program alters in size or complexity and as established policy becomes obsolete.

Program policies should address issues in the following areas:

Administrative structure Policy determines the size of and the membership criteria for the board of directors, committees, advisory groups, and parent councils. These standards and other information pertinent to these groups are stated in the organization's bylaws and procedural guidelines.

Program and services Policy states the type and emphasis of the child care program (that is, a bilingual preschool center or a recreational after-school program). The hours of operation, specific days when the center is closed, and procedures for alternative child care exemplify policy for program operation. The nature and extent of program services as well as any requirements for service eligibility are outlined for health care, meal provision, social services, and the care of children with special needs. This area of the policy should also delineate program limitations regarding the age and maximum number of children served, the staff-child ratio, and any special conditions for child attendance or parent participation.

Admissions Policy factors pertaining to the admission of children are specified. Common criteria include eligibility requirements; the age of the child; the social, economic and employment status of the parents; pre-enrollment medical examinations and medical history; requirements for the admission of children with special needs; governmental and agency rules for the determination and documentation of family need; and fiscal requirements for the assessment and payment of fees.

Personnel Regardless of their size or complexity, child care programs need a comprehensive written policy concerning the rights, responsibilities, benefits for, and the restrictions upon employees. Personnel policy addresses the recruitment and selection of employees, provisions for training and advancement, exact terms of a probationary period, complete job descriptions, wage rates, and payroll dates; employee benefits and benefit eligibility requirements; descriptions of required staff records; procedures and reasons for employee discipline and dismissal; and staff grievance procedures.

Financial Good management and legal accountability require accurate, well-defined fiscal policy. All programs must demonstrate financial accountability. The primary fiscal policy document is the budget. In addition, financial policy describes the individuals responsible for financial management and fiscal record-keeping and the extent of their duties; those persons permitted to disburse money; the conditions and procedures for spending; the system of bookkeeping, audit, and accountability; the purchase of program insurance; and the bonding of employees involved in the financial process.

Other Most programs discover the need for general policies that do not fit into a specific category. Examples include policies concerning field trips, photographing children at the center, observation of the program by visitors, transportation arrangements, personal belongings at the center, and parental permissions for such possibilities as the treatment of children in emergency situations.

The management responsibility of the director in regard to policy includes *formulating, administering, interpreting,* and *disseminating* policy.

The role of the director in formulating policy varies. Some directors, especially in proprietary (for profit) centers and small programs, are the sole author of policy. Other directors serve as advisors or acting members of policy-making teams. In these cases, the team recognizes the director's closeness to the actual operation and relies on director assistance, guidance, and suggestion in the setting of policy. As a working member of the team, the director exerts great influence over the actual policy decisions.

The director is the primary agent for administering policy. As the connecting link between board members, parents, staff, and children as well as between policy and practice, the director translates policy into the daily program. Administering policy is essentially creating a workable system of procedures for the management of recurring processes and events. The initial step for smooth and efficient center operation is the organization of policy statements into a useful reference system such as a policy manual. The manual need be nothing more than a looseleaf notebook divided into sections for policy in areas such as personnel, admissions, program, and curriculum. The manual is a convenient and versatile master file for policy; new policy can be easily added; references to specific policy are easy; and appropriate sections can be duplicated for parents, staff, and board members.

Directors must also interpret policy through daily associations with parents and staff. They state and review policy, answer questions concerning policy intent or application, refer to appropriate policy for planning, and demonstrate the implications of policy for staff, parents, and program operation. Policy interpretation occurs anytime and is often impromptu. However, planned policy discussions are also a vital part of preservice training for staff and the pre-enrollment interview with parents. Likewise, policy must be reviewed periodically during staff and parent meetings.

Finally, the director ensures that written policy is available to all individuals affected. Policy statements can be posted on a conspicuous bulletin board or duplicated for distribution. Employees should have access to the staff manual, which states personnel policy; program goals, philosophy, and description; detailed job descriptions; policy and procedures for recurring events; and proper procedures for completing time sheets, mileage reimbursements, and similar forms.

Leadership

Program management is not simply the sum of parts of administrative tasks and management decisions. Carrying out these tasks and decisions reflects the style of action, or leadership, of the director. Every director brings a distinctive set of personal qualities to the performance of the job. These personal, stylistic differences among directors contribute to the diversity of programs for children and allow individual approaches to flourish at the local level. Some directors may approach every situation in the same manner—whether it be calm, prepared, frantic, controlled, or flexible. Others may react differently to each situation—now calm, now frantic. Some directors inspire or command considerable cooperation from staff and parents; others prefer to assume control and work alone. Each style of action can be valid and appropriate for an individual director and specific program. Directors may not even be aware of the patterns of action they employ; they may not realize exactly which patterns of action produce which results. They may also not have the information that would enable them to deliberately match a style of action to a particular task at hand.

Leadership Theories

The systematic study of leadership styles and techniques has been of interest to researchers in such disciplines as social psychology, politics, and organizational behavior. Most modern theories of leadership revolve around physical attributes and personality traits, behavior patterns, principles of group dynamics, and social power ideas.

Physical and Personality Traits. Superficially, certain physical and personality traits appear to be common to leaders. We often think of leaders as taller or larger than their followers. Although physique and size can make an individual conspicuous or give the impression of energy or strength, many successful leaders, of course, possess no outstanding physical attributes. Physical attractiveness and appearance can generate notice in some social situations or in certain occupations such as modeling, but these attributes don't seem to matter in other areas. Although leaders are generally more intelligent than their followers, just which intelligent individual is a leader depends on many factors, including the goals of the group.

Some common personality traits of leaders include self-confidence, stability, adjustment, and dominance. However, leaders are not always extroverts. In fact, influential persons may be introverts capable of depth of thought, deliberation, and reflection.

Leadership Behaviors. The study of leadership behaviors examines the actions of leaders. This approach attempts to define the specific behaviors of leaders that place them in their unique positions. Four clusters of leadership behavior appear to be dominant. In the order of their importance they are

1. *Consideration for individuals* Leaders show consideration for others through the warmth of their interpersonal relationships; the mutual trust between leader, associates, and followers; the readiness of leaders to explain their actions and decisions; a willingness to listen to the ideas and opinions of others; and the ability to delegate meaningful roles to subordinates.
2. *Initiation of structure* Leaders provide structure by organizing processes and procedures, developing systems of operation, maintaining standards of performance, following operational procedures and policies, making roles clear and understandable, and assigning individuals to tasks.
3. *Orientation to productivity* Leaders stress productivity by accentuating task completion and scheduling deadlines for goals or task completion, and by encouraging subordinates to goal achievement.
4. *Sensitivity orientation* Leaders are sensitive to others by their attention to feelings, beliefs, and emotions; understanding the shortcomings and failures of others; ability to change their own inappropriate decisions and actions; acceptance of blame for their own errors; and demanding no scapegoat for mistakes.

Child care programs must have organizational structure and goal-oriented leadership to deliver services to children and their families, but they are also working atmospheres that must meet the sensitive human needs of staff members. Both the program and the atmosphere will clearly reflect the emotional well-being of the staff as well as the personal and professional relationships of the director and the staff. Because of this, the director must be considerate of and sensitive to individuals in addition to fulfilling administrative responsibilities.

Principles of Group Dynamics. Although all leaders do not have the same personalities or physiques, all leaders do have followers. One social-psychological theory regards leadership as the *natural property of groups.* The theory is that leaders emerge as the group functions. All groups strive to function as a unit and accomplish tasks. Individuals comprising the group must interact as a unit if the group is to reach its goal; thus, the group members are interdependent upon each other. Basically, two types of leaders emerge as the group functions: one leader is task oriented and moves the group toward its goal (accomplishing its task), and the other is a social-emotional leader who maintains the group's cohesiveness (functioning as a unit). The task leader organizes, structures, assigns duties, summarizes, and precipitates action. The result of this action is often tension and conflict that threatens the unity of the group. To ease pressure and ensure group cohesion, the social-emotional leader reassures, praises, encourages, listens, and explains. The director must be skillful in both roles and, depending upon the circumstances, emerge as one or the other type of leader.

Social Power Theory. Social power theory views leadership as the exercise of either institutionalized or informal influence over other individuals. Leadership based on social power can be of four types: primitive, legitimate, referent, and expert. The exercise of *primitive* social power depends upon the leader's ability to control the reward and punishment resources. The leader's constant surveillance of subordinates is also primitive social power. *Legitimate* social power is based on broad general norms that define appropriate behavior and attitude. The traditional and internalized values of others provide a set of prescriptions for acceptable personal relationships and for standards of conduct. Obedience to authority and acceptance of role in the established social structure are examples of legitimate social power. *Referent* social power occurs whenever others identify with the leader. Subordinates wish to be similar to the leader, to imitate the leader's actions in an attempt to achieve leadership likeness. Thus the actions and behavior of the leader constitute a goal to be obtained by others. In their desire to identify with the leader individuals follow the leader's standards, meet his or her demands, and fulfill the requests of the leader. *Expert* social power relies on either the actual or the perceived superior knowledge and ability of the leader. The extent of this power varies according to the amount of knowledge attributed to the leader, the actual degree of expertise the leader exhibits, and the relationship of the leader's knowledge to the goals of others.

Leadership Style

The way in which an individual exercises authority and influence is leadership style. Styles of leadership are often categorized as authoritarian, democratic, or laissez-faire approaches. Classifying leadership into three basic approaches is simplistic, but helpful distinctions between leadership styles and trends in leadership can be recognized by such categorization. Wise administrators do not limit themselves to one leadership style. Instead they choose an approach based upon the unique elements of each particular situation, individual circumstances, and specific individuals.

An *authoritarian* leader relies on psychological distance for a secure concentration of power. By remaining aloof from subordinates, the leader is able to dictate policy and procedure, and to dispense praise and criticism without challenge. Group members have no personal stake in the success or failure of the venture; that responsibility is the sole possession of the leader. Authoritarian leadership is often considered offensive or a negative style of leadership. However, authoritarian leadership is both effective and appropriate in many situations. For instance, the center director relies upon this approach in times of crisis, in emergency situations demanding immediate action, and in circumstances that require privileged information. In such situations, the director is obligated to make a decision, act upon that decision, and accept the consequences of that action.

A *democratic* approach permits the leader to function as a member of the group. He or she offers suggestions, recommendations, and choices for group consideration, but the decisions are made by the group. Because the leader and the group mutually determine solutions and actions, the responsibility for success and for failure is their joint concern. Individuals consider the collective goals and decisions of the group as their own. Many directors favor this approach to management. When democratic leadership is successful, each individual respects the contributions of others, knows his or her own opinion is valued, and feels a personal responsibility for the operation of the center.

The *laissez-faire* leader is passive, permitting other individuals or the group to make decisions and maintaining a position of noninterference. Usually the leader offers suggestions, opinions, and recommendations only if pressured to do so by the group. The responsibility for decision making and its consequences is easily ignored or refused by both the leader and by the group.

Applying Leadership Techniques

The relationship between leadership theory and director behavior is not always obvious. This section provides guidelines for extracting and applying appropriate leadership principles as part of a personal style of management.

Leadership Is An Art. People in leadership positions recognize that success requires fundamental skills and creative vision, all with a sen-

A rare opportunity to get together—a group of child care program directors meet to exchange ideas and share resources. Even here, though, children and staff are just a phone call away. (Courtesy of U.S. Department of Housing and Urban Development, Washington, DC.)

sitivity to the "people climate" of the organization. Theories can guide, but ultimately it is the personal style responding to the situation at hand that produces leadership. This charismatic aspect of leadership has led many to believe that leadership is an internal ability or that certain individuals are predisposed to leadership. This is not necessarily true. Center directors can maximize their personal leadership talents through clear statements and understandings of personal philosophy and acceptable practices of child care. Directors who work from stable personal positions, who have a strong and persistent commitment to a point of view on child care, and who have consistent guidelines for the selection and support of particular practices attract followers. The art of child care leadership evolves from sharing this program vision.

Leadership Skills Are Acquired and Improved. The director has a responsibility to develop and improve leadership skills. This process includes self-analysis and evaluation of leadership techniques. By examining the duties and responsibilities of the position, a director can identify specific skills and abilities that are essential for effective management. This provides the basis for the director's evaluation of his or her leadership strengths and weaknesses in relationship to job responsibilities. Thus, a plan of action for improvement can be developed to take full advantage of personal and professional assets and to secure assistance with leadership deficiencies.

As directors manage on a daily basis, they must be aware of leadership strategies in relationship to situations, individuals, and decisions. This awareness uncovers patterns of personal style and techniques, areas of personal deficiency, and successful leadership methods and behaviors. The director can consciously increase successful strategies and become aware of ineffective techniques, thus perfecting management and leadership skills. Books, manuals, and pamphlets provide information in a variety of areas including problem-solving, reflective listening, and leadership theory. Local high schools, universities and colleges, and other agencies offer continuing education programs that are usually inexpensive and geared to working adults.

One often overlooked resource is the local association of child care directors or early childhood educators. Association with such groups provides opportunities for the exchange of ideas and the exploration of new developments in child care and education. In addition, it draws together the local leaders of child care services.

Leaders' Effectiveness Varies. Of course, directors have limitations, both in knowledge of and skill in management. Directors will make mistakes of judgment and action. Although admitting mistakes truthfully is important, the real value of an error is the ability to analyze and learn from the experience. Directors often create an atmosphere of acceptance for and assistance with their own errors by treating the mistakes of others in a positive and understanding fashion.

Most directors are more effective leaders in one area than in others. To compensate, they may seek assistance from others. Leadership is not so much great knowledge in all areas as it is an ability and a desire to obtain needed information and to use the knowledge and abilities of others. With this in mind, directors can strengthen contacts with community services and agencies and with individuals. They can share leadership responsibility with staff, parents, and board members and delegate meaningful roles. Finally, effective directors realize that in some situations their leadership is minimal. In those instances, their best role is that of follower.

Leaders Are Goal-Directed. Directors set both long-term and short-term objectives for their own performance and the performance of staff. They determine program goals for children and their parents. They also interpret the purpose and philosophy of the center to staff, parents, board members, and the community. The quality of the program and its daily operation is largely determined by the director's orientation to these goals.

Program personnel should understand their function, how to accomplish their duties and responsibilities, and why meeting goals and standards is important. Directors rely on a number of techniques to educate staff about goals and task achievement:

- Compile written job descriptions for each member of the staff to be explained during preservice training, reviewed after observation and evaluation of staff members, and revised as the program develops.
- Examine and evaluate program purpose and goals as a regular part of in-service training and staff meetings.
- Discuss the total operational structure of the program and each individual's role in that structure to achieve efficiency; ensure that all directions are explicit and that standards for task accomplishment are understood.
- Provide for regular, periodic observation and evaluation of staff.
- Set goals for their own performance and evaluate their accomplishments and shortcomings.

Leaders Show Consideration for Others. Perhaps the vital element in leadership behavior is the personal and professional interest that the director shows in others. This consideration is extended in various ways: instituting formal and informal communication channels; encouraging initiative and self-direction in others; rewarding individual creative efforts; praising and acknowledging the accomplishments of others; acting as a resource person for staff and parents; listening to the ideas and perceptions of others; and creating an atmosphere of mutual sharing among individuals. Techniques vary. Informal conversations with individual staff members may be held during the day. Even something as simple as relieving a harried aide for a coffee break may be appropriate. Other examples are celebrating an employee's birthday, holding monthly social gatherings for staff and parents, greeting parents in the evening, and maintaining an open door office policy.

Social Power Exists in Organized Systems. Many directors are uncomfortable in admitting that social power exists in the program or in exercising an influence over others. The competent exercise of authority depends upon the director's intelligent understanding of social power and its judicious application.

The director exercises social power in programs that offer merit pay, provide staff benefits for noteworthy job performance, and withhold advantages as disciplinary action. As a staff supervisor and evaluator, the director plays a major role in the distribution of rewards and sanctions—both material and psychological. The director who sets program standards determines the competencies required of employees to achieve good ratings.

The director often draws upon social power for control in emergency situations. In case of fire, accident, or sickness, the director requires staff obedience to authority. He or she expects prompt execution of orders and instructions and a conformity with established emergency procedures.

A director inspires others to achieve their potential by using social power. Techniques such as trust in subordinates, an eagerness to perfect skills and knowledge, and an open-minded fair treatment of co-workers can be used by the director to stimulate the admiration and imitation of staff members. When the director displays expertise in child care and management principles and sets high standards for her own job performance she is using expert social power. Communicating positive expectations for co-workers and adhering to established policy and procedures are other appropriate procedures.

Communication and Management

Given the complex relationship among boards, committees, staff, children, parents, and community, the child care program depends upon accurate communication. Precise communication implies not only the exchange of information but also the transmission of meaning; that is, the listener interprets the message in the same manner that the speaker intended. The director is the major program spokesperson to individuals and groups outside of the program and the central communication link within the program.

Generally, five communication systems operate within a program. Each has its own membership, and each is useful to the director.

1. The *external communication system* exists between personnel and outside groups such as community agencies, vendors, governmental bodies and representatives, professional contacts and associates, parents, and the public media. The director uses this external system to inform others about the program through open houses, fairs, and social events; displays and posters in community businesses and agencies; newspaper articles; listing in community service directories; and speaking engagements. Contact with parents includes conferences, worknights, newsletters, bulletin boards, and parent meetings. Communication with governmental bodies involves written and oral reports, proposals, meetings, and telephone contact. The director communicates professional concerns through participation with early childhood and child care associations on local, state, and national levels and by meeting with other directors.
2. The *formal communication system* follows the levels of authority within the organizational structure of the program. These communication pathways link boards, committees, and personnel. The director relays information between these groups and also presents written and oral reports, recommendations, and program data to them. In addition, the director actively participates in meetings with boards, committees, and staff.
3. The *work relationships communication system* flourishes as co-workers accomplish their daily jobs within the organization. The director passes along information, directives, decisions, and comments to staff as the daily work of the program proceeds. In turn, the staff shares remarks, comments, and information with each other and the director.
4. The *informal communication system* operates between employees who are friends or who have similar interests other than child care or the life of the program. This communication system is simi-

Communication with staff members is a vital and ongoing part of a director's job. Often directors must deal with staff concerns as they arise, make suggestions, and give criticism on an impromptu basis. (Courtesy of U.S. Department of Agriculture, Washington, DC.)

lar to the work relationships system except that its membership is more selective and the topics of communication extend beyond program interests. Because the communication is more personal than professional, the director gains insight into individual members of the staff and better understands the personal side of employees.

5. The *grapevine communication system* passes accurate and inaccurate information throughout the entire organization at a rapid rate. Usually the grapevine is viewed as a negative communication system for it is often fed by rumor and innuendo and it is usually difficult to control. However, the director gains valuable information concerning the emotional climate of the program and the attitude of staff through attention to grapevine information.

It is tempting but foolish to assume that a knowledge of communication systems and an expertise in their use guarantees accurate communication. Even under the best conditions, communication often has a life of its own that defies control. Therefore, the director should be aware of the types of communication barriers operating within the program. Communication is interpersonal, so whatever interferes with the relationship between individuals is a potential barrier to their communication. The most common barriers to communication within the center are:

Distance Communication interference through distance can be physical (the director who never mingles with staff), theoretical (staff members who view child care from opposing perspectives), and psychological (an employee who is personally threatened by program evaluation).

Distortion Individual perceptions color and often distort the intent and meaning of events, actions, comments, and information.

Need and prejudice All individuals possess personal needs and ingrained prejudices. These internalized factors, often unrecognized by the individual, threaten interpersonal communication.

Structural organization The levels of authority and the structural organization of the program can frustrate the flow of formal communication.

Vague job descriptions All employees must know what is expected of them; how the job is to be performed; when routines, activities, and events occur; and why their job is to be accomplished in a particular manner.

Problems with written information Communication with external agencies and along internal formal channels is frequently in written form. Typical problems with written communication include incomplete or ambiguous information, misuse of words, and obtuse writing style. Words, both written and spoken, are highly susceptible to personal interpretation.

Personal incompatibilities Communication is highly interpersonal and thus is adversely affected by individual dislikes and animosities. It is difficult for individuals to ignore or overcome their negative reactions to the message if they personally object to the communicator.

The personal and professional relationships of the individuals associated with the program directly influence the quality of center communication. Close attention to the work relationship, informal, and grapevine communication systems reveals personal preferences for communication outside the formal communication system. The director should study which persons communicate to each other and the reasons for that communication. Communication in group situations is facilitated if the director as the group leader is conscious of which individuals communicate, and how often and how much they communicate.

Communication within the program is effective if the director establishes a cooperative group climate that encourages the equal participation of all members and promotes the feeling that each individual's ideas and views are of value. To function effectively, the director must adopt a two-way, open communication procedure, develop a cooperative climate, and facilitate interaction among individuals.

Qualifications

The responsibilities of organizing child care services and providing leadership in program settings pose difficult questions for the preparation, training, and credentialing of center directors. Program management requires administrative, fiscal, personnel, and public relations skills as well as knowledge and training in curriculum planning and child development. The scope of the job requirements means that few directors find their previous training and experience adequate for the job. Most directors learn on the job by trial and error, by getting advice from colleagues, and by pursuing needed skill development on their own.

Legal Qualifications

State regulations lack uniform requirements for the education and training of directors. They also reflect a wide variety of acceptable educational experiences for the position. Often state requirements vary according to whether the child care program is publicly funded or an independent, proprietary program. Sometimes the regulations vary according to the size of the program, the number of children enrolled, or the number of centers overseen by the director or administrator. In general, state regulations about director's qualifications concern age, education and training, and experience.

Age Age minimums range from eighteen to twenty-two years. A few states specify no age minimum for center directors.

Education and training Some states do not specify any particular formal education and training requirements for directors. Most states have regulations that require directors to have some combination of formal education and child care work experience. In the majority of states a person can qualify to become a child care director with a high school diploma (or equivalent) and some child care-related experience. A number of states require course work in child development for those who want to be directors.

Experience Child care, teaching, and administrative experience are most commonly specified in regulatory qualifications for directors. Such on-the-job experience can be used in lieu of formal degrees for director candidates in many states.

Pragmatic Qualifications

Local programs always have the prerogative to go beyond the state regulations and seek candidates who possess strong education credentials and considerable experience in administration. Thus, while state regulations give a picture of minimal qualifications for directors, in practice, hiring committees often use more stringent criteria.

It takes a very special person to be a good center director. While directors report little difficulty recruiting and hiring teaching and support staff, boards of directors seem to have a hard time finding day care directors. Salaries for directors gener-

> ally range from $8,400 for a center with an average daily attendance of twenty-five children to $10,450 for a center serving seventy-five children. And most boards want people with early childhood education degrees or a great deal of experience in the field of child care (Ruopp, O'Farrell, Warner, Rowe, & Freedman, 1973, pp. 25–26)

What qualifications are important for potential directors? Realistically, what do boards look for, and what do candidates present when the task of selecting a director is at hand?

Personal Attributes. Personality factors that enable a director to function successfully are subjective and not easily translated into explicit criteria that are useful for evaluation of job candidates. Yet, as boards and hiring committees and potential directors participate in the process, many of the questions related to a particular candidate's qualifications will revolve around personal characteristics. For example, the ability to learn from mistakes, openness to new ideas, sensitivity to others, a sense of perspective, and the future director's physical and mental stamina may be questioned. Personal interviews and references are typical approaches used to assess directors' qualifications.

Openness to Challenge. The successful director is enthusiastically open to new ideas and possibilities and willing to learn and use new techniques and materials. A director inspires the creativity, individualism, and experimentation of others if he or she is excited about change and is not bound by familiar methods and procedures. The director must constantly strive for a balance between consistency and change.

Sensitivity. The perceptive director exhibits a sensitivity to others' personalities. By respecting the individuality and unique personality of each staff member and parent, the director implies acceptance of each person as he or she is and the expectation that individuals will give their best. Through supporting and accepting each individual's rights, needs, and abilities, the director provides leadership.

Perspective. A balance between seriousness and humor is essential to the emotional well-being of the director and the climate of the program. This sense of perspective is a balancing influence and enables the director to separate the trivial from the important. A well-developed sense of the ridiculous often saves the director from an inflated sense of importance and an exaggerated view of the position. In the daily life of the center, humor reduces tension. It can save the day when nothing goes right.

Stamina. The daily job of managing a child care program is a demanding one and requires physical and mental strength and energy. Even a well-organized and efficient operation suffers if a director is chronically absent or in poor health. Vitality and stamina are required to meet the volume and pressure of the many responsibilities and duties of the position.

Formal Education and Training

Valid transcripts and certificates should be obtained to document education and training for all directors. It is particularly important for boards and hiring committees to be able to document satisfaction of those requirements set by regulations. As hiring committees screen candidates for the director position, attention should be paid to matching the specific local job duties with the candidate's educational record and experiences. A program with pressing financial problems does not need a director who has no experience with budgets. A program with a strong parent involvement component can probably train an inexperienced director on the job provided that individual is receptive to gaining more skill in working with parents. Supervisory experience and proven in-service training capabilities are essential for directors who will oversee large or relatively untrained staffs. Directors can expect to grow and acquire information on the job, but there is no advantage to ignoring individuals' strengths and predictable areas of job demands. Hiring or becoming a director is a gamble; the odds of success for the program and the person can be greatly enhanced through judicious selection procedures and rigorous matching of qualifications with job demands.

Is It For You?

Many individuals working with young children find themselves attracted to the idea of directing a child care program. As their education and/or experience in the field increase, many feel that assuming a directorship is a logical next step in their career. The self-assessment inventory in Appendix C is to help you compare your current levels of education and experience with job requirements and qualifications needed for directing a child care program.

Issues

Issues related to management revolve around the personal and professional status of the director. Directors average about three years on the job. What causes this high turnover? Are there any ways that program management can or should be changed?

Director Burnout

Burnout seems to be the catchy disease of the 1980s for professionals who work in social service positions. The phenomenon occurs when job stresses build, when feelings of powerlessness or hopelessness prevail, or when relaxation and vacations seem impossible to achieve. Psychologists suggest that professionals who work in people-intense service situations are the most likely candidates for burnout. Simply put, the job consumes them, wears them out, leaves them with few resources to cope with their personal life outside the job. Perhaps it is inevitable that over a period of time, despite the best management strategies and conservation of personal resources, a director will say, "Enough is enough." Directors cite worry over funding, the unending needs of families in crisis and children with difficulties, and staff with personal problems as high contributors to burnout in their situations. Directing a center is often lonely work. Peers or other directors are busy and far away. Support is hard to find. Low pay and long hours are not sufficient compensation for the effort.

Credentials for Directors

Child care leaders and early childhood educators are debating the issue of accreditation for directors. Decisions about adequate training and standardized requirements are complicated. Some of the confusion happens because we don't agree about the purpose of child care in the United States. The care and education of young children was and, to an extent, still is divided between two schools of thought—social welfare and education. Recent interest of educators concerning child care is partly due to an increasing emphasis on the merits of early education for all children and the decreasing need for trained teachers in the public schools. Social welfare advocates argue that directors must possess a background in that discipline; educators stress the need for accreditation in education-based fields. Consequently, little progress is made in combining pertinent aspects of both disciplines with a consideration for the administrative and business management of child care services.

Many child care services existed before national and state standards were written. Thus, many field-based child care professionals resist increasingly stringent standards that may endanger their positions. Other professionals realize that national standards are not the solution. Federal standards are too narrow in scope because they apply only to programs utilizing federal monies. States, too, often have different standards for publicly funded and privately funded programs.

Even if credential standards for directors could be agreed upon and the financial means for implementation secured, specific opportunities for training in child care administration are limited. In most cases the prospective director must augment a social welfare or education major with other disciplines such as home economics, business administration, psychology, and sociology. We hope uniform minimum standards for professional credentials will be instituted as state and local governmental supervision and control of private and public child care increase. Nevertheless, government regulation does not guarantee quality or the means to implement training and educational programs.

Another issue involving director qualification is the acceptance of experience in lieu of academic credentials. Proponents of job and life experience as a desirable alternative to academic training for child care directors argue that formal education has little relationship to the real world of administration, that the experiences of working in a center and progressing along its career ladder better equip individuals for director positions, and that the operation of a center can be accomplished without an academic degree. Still, serious questions involve setting standards for experience-based credentials. It is not easy to specify standards for the quality and type of previous experiences, individual job performances, and the relevancy of these experiences to the position of director.

Director Authority

Another critical problem area is the degree of power and responsibility delegated or assumed by the director. Some directors are virtually powerless to manage the center environment or to effect change. Although the committee structure guarantees a voice for parents and community leaders, controlling through committees has negative aspects. In some cases, the director is unable to conduct any management without permission from the board or parent council. At times these committees refuse to delegate any of their responsibility for decision making to the individuals that they have hired. This lack of trust in the ability and expertise of administrators destroys director authority and places an unnecessary strain on human relations within the organization. On the other hand, too many committees delegate all their power and authority to the administrator. This forces the director to make decisions that, by right, belong to the committee. This absence of a power base undermines effective management because the director has no support in times of crisis or when he or she makes an unpopular decision. At its best, the committee structure is frustrating in its slowness. Balanced committee action and director responsibility work well only in the presence of mutual trust and clear guidelines for shared power and decision making.

Summary

The operation of a child care program depends to an extraordinary degree on the competence and performance of the program director.

The three patterns of management organization in child care programs are family, ray, and line management organization.

Program directors are responsible for six administrative tasks: management of the children's program, coordination of program support functions, maintenance of the physical facility, record-keeping, staff management, and public relations. Managing the children's program, which is the most visible of the tasks, occupies much of the director's time. Directors must have a firm grasp of the program's philosophy so they can recognize the relationship between theory and practice. Directors also must take charge in formulating, administering, interpreting, and disseminating policy.

The way in which different directors carry out their tasks reflects their style of action, or leadership. Various types of leadership have been explained by theories regarding physical and personality traits, leadership behaviors, the principles of group dynamics, and social power. Leadership styles may be categorized as authoritarian, democratic, and laissez-faire. Good child care program directors are not necessarily born with leadership talent; they need to acquire and constantly improve leadership skills. Directors must learn to set goals and to be considerate of others in the program.

Successful child care programs rely on accurate communication among staff, committees, children, parents, and the community. The director's role is to facilitate effective communication and to interpret messages. The five communication systems operating within a program are the external, formal, work relationships, informal, and grapevine communications systems. Among the barriers to good communication are distance, distortion, need and prejudice, vague job descriptions, and personal incompatibilities.

The legal qualifications to be a program director, usually required by the state, specify the age, education and training, and experience necessary. Beyond these state regulations, programs evaluate such qualifications as personal attributes, openness to challenge, sensitivity, sense of perspective, and stamina.

Issues of concern regarding program directors include recognition and prevention of burnout, the establishment of credentials, and appropriate levels of directorial authority.

Resources

Role of the Program Director

A Former Director. (1980). You gotta laugh. *Child Care Information Exchange, 11,* 1–5.

Axelrod, P. G., & Trager, N. (1972). Directing a day care center. *Children Today,* November–December, 29–32.

Hammond, M. (1981). Women as directors—Reactions to the role. *Child Care Information Exchange, 22,* 5–9.

Kyle, J. E. (1980). The extrospective early childhood administrator. *Child Care Information Exchange,* April, 33–37.

Levine, J. (1974). Letters to a day care director. *Day Care and Early Education,* January, 5–10.

Rogolsky, M. (1979). Psychologist views the role of the day care director. *Child Care Information Exchange, 9,* 1–5.

Travis, N. E., & Perrault, J. (1981). *The effective day care director.* Atlanta, GA: Save the Children Care Support Center.

Yablans-Magid, R. (1981). The process of administering early childhood programs. In M. Kaplan-Sanoll & R. Yablans-Magid (Eds.), *Exploring early childhood: Readings in theory and practice* (pp. 341–348). New York: Macmillan.

Administrative Tasks

Auerbach, S. (Ed.). (1976). *Child care: A comprehensive guide: Model programs and their components:* Vol. 11. New York: Human Sciences Press.

Butler, A. L. (1974). *Early childhood education: Planning and administering programs.* New York: Van Nostrand.

Cherry, C. (1973). *Nursery school management guide.* Belmont, CA: Lear Siegler/Fearon.

Hewes, D. W. (Ed.). (1979). *Administration: Making programs work for children and families.* Washington, DC: National Association for the Education of Young Children.

Hewes, D., & Hartman, B. (1979). *Early childhood education: A workbook for administrators.* San Francisco: R and E Research Associates.

Hitchcock, S. (Ed.). (1983). *The effective nonprofit executive handbook.* San Francisco: Public Management Institute.

Host, M. S., & Heller, P. B. (1971). *Day care 7: Administration.* Washington, DC: U.S. Department of Health, Education and Welfare, Office of Child Development.

Jorde, P. (1982). *The administrator's start-up kit.* Alama, CA: Small Wonder Enterprises.

Ruopp, R., O'Farrell, B., Warner, D., Rowe, M., & Freedman, R. (1973). *A day care guide for administrators, teachers, and parents.* Cambridge, MA: MIT Press.

Save the Children. (1981). *Recruiting and enrolling children.* Atlanta, GA: Child Care Support Center.

Schon, B. (1981). Director's survival kit: Marketing. *Child Care Information Exchange, 19,* 17–24.

Sciarra, D. J., & Dorsey, A. G. (1979). *Developing and administering a child care center.* Boston: Houghton Mifflin.

Stine, S. (Ed.). (1983). *Administration: A bedside guide.* Pasadena, CA: Pacific Oaks College.

Starting a day care center. (n.d.). St. Louis, MO: Child Day Care Association of St. Louis.

Wilson, G. B. (1981). *Humanics limited system for record keeping*. Atlanta, GA: Humanics Limited.

Time Management

Bliss, E. C. (1976). *Getting things done: The ABC's of time management*. New York: Scribner's.

Lakein, A. (1973). *How to get control of your time and your life*. New York: New American Libarary.

Save the Children. (1980). *Time management for day care directors*. Atlanta, GA: Child Care Support Center.

Winston, S. (1978). *Getting organized*. New York: Warner Books.

Leadership

Hewes, D. W. (1981). Leadership in child care: What contingency theory can show us. *Child Care Information Exchange, 17,* 11–14.

Kidder, L. H., & Stewart, M. V. (1975). *The psychology of intergroup relations: Conflict and consciousness*. New York: McGraw-Hill.

Neugebauer, R. (1982). Director's survival kit: Making decisions. *Child Care Information Exchange, 23,* 17–24.

Schon, D. A. (1983). *The reflective practitioner: How professionals think in action*. New York: Basic Books.

Sentz, B. C., & Wofford, J. (1979). *Leadership and learning: Personal change in a professional setting*. New York: McGraw-Hill.

Tannenbaum, R., & Schmidt, W. H. (1981). How to choose a leadership pattern. In M. Kaplan-Sanoll & R. Yablans-Magid (Eds.), *Exploring early childhood: Readings in theory and practice* (pp. 350–361). New York: Macmillan.

Wofford, J. (1979). "Know-thyself": The key to comparing your leadership style. *Child Care Information Exchange,* November, 19–25.

Qualifications

Almy, M. (1975). *The early childhood educator at work*. New York: McGraw-Hill.

Day Care and Child Development Council of America. (1969). *Gould Foundation conference on training of day care administrators (Edited transcript)*. February 14, New York City. (ERIC Document Reproduction Service No. ED 031 806)

Lawrence Johnson and Associates. (1978). *Comparative licensing survey: Appendix A. Profiles of state day care licensing requirements* (Vol. 6). Washington, DC: Lawrence Johnson Associates.

Seaver, J. W., Cartwright, C. A., Ward, C. B., & Heasley, C. A. (1979). *Careers with young children: Making your decision*. Washington, DC: National Association for the Education of Young Children.

Additional Information Sources

Exchange
P.O. Box 2890
Redmond, WA 98073
Bimonthly magazine for program directors

Resources for Child Care Management (RCCM)
P.O. Box 669
Summit, NJ 07901
Training, conferences, publications, information

Training seminars and courses for program administrators

Bank Street College of Education
New York, New York

NOVA University
Fort Lauderdale, FL

Pacific Oaks
Pasadena, CA

Wheelock College
Boston, MA

11

Personnel Management

Introduction

Program staff are the most important resource that a director has for implementing the child care program. Although some of the effort required to manage a child care staff entails nothing more than administrative detail and recordkeeping, much of the management involves the interpersonal dynamics of staff. People must be hired and, unfortunately, sometimes fired. Supervision, performance evaluation, in-service training, and general staff meetings require time and energy.

This chapter presents a comprehensive view of staff management for a child care program. First, to establish exactly what we mean by personnel, we define the variety of positions within a staff. We describe efficient methods for selecting staff and sound procedures for interacting with staff once they are hired. Following that, a section explores the basic issues of child-caregiver ratios, group sizes, and staff scheduling. The last half of the chapter looks at supervision, in-service, and training as opportunities for improving the quality of care in a particular program.

Staff Positions

Child care staff include a wide spectrum of ages, educational experiences, and ethnic backgrounds. People with degrees in education, social welfare, child development, and other fields may hold the same positions as high school graduates. A career in child care is possible if one loves children, is willing to learn on the job, and accepts low pay and job status as the "givens" of employment.

The vast majority of child care workers are women. Turnover is high. In spite of some notable exceptions, years of service average three to four years. Nevertheless, the pool of potential new caregivers always remains high. Many workers regard positions in this field as accessible, entry-level jobs. In addition, child care benefits when workers from such diminishing fields as education and social work turn to child care jobs as alternatives.

One of the long-standing symbols of the difference between child care and other early childhood education programs has been the terminology used to label staff positions. *Teacher* was reserved for degree-trained professionals who worked in programs with goals for young children in cognitive and social-emotional development. *Caregiver* was used to identify child care workers, implying less than full professional training. The incorporation of the word *care* in the term was a signal that children's custodial care came first in the program's priorities. Such distinctions are no longer appropriate or useful. Providing basic physical care for children is not seen as a lowly act to perform, nor is competent teaching considered to be solely the province of the professionally certi-

Caring is the essence of working with children. (Courtesy of U.S. Department of Health and Human Services, Washington, DC.)

fied. The terms are used interchangeably and child care staff are proud to wear either label.

Program needs, budget, and applicable regulations determine the number of staff positions needed in a given child care program. Job titles as well as job responsibilities vary greatly from program to program. Staff members may wear two hats: cook and bus driver, teacher and assistant director, for example. Important staff, such as medical and social service workers, may not be on the program's payroll but may have continuing, substantial input into daily program operations. This section divides the descriptions of typical staff positions in child care into three categories: program staff, support staff, and service staff.

Program Staff

The largest group of employees are *program staff*. They are generally responsible for daily implementation of the program. These staff members are the primary caregivers who interact with children. Staff in this category are covered by regulations about experience, education, and training.

The teacher is responsible for planning and conducting a daily program for a group of children. Teachers are team leaders and usually must coordinate the activities of a number of lower-level staff members. Large programs may have several teachers. One teacher, designated an assistant director, may assume some management duties.

Aides in some programs may be called assistant teachers, helpers, or small-group leaders. It typically takes many aides to run a program. Their duties and responsibilities vary according to program needs and their ability to maintain comfortable working relationships with staff in higher authority positions. The cost of losing an aide is high because often a program invests time and money in training this person.

Support Staff

Centers that serve hot, prepared meals have full-time cooks. They may be assisted by meal aides and dietitians. The kitchen is the cook's domain, and all things having to do with food selection, preparation, and serving are the cook's responsibility. Cooks, however, can also extend their influence beyond the kitchen doors by their sensitivity to staff and children's food favorites, willingness to share recipes, and receptivity to little cooking helpers.

Since children in a program are usually busy with lots of activities, all staff must perform maintenance functions continuously. Heavy and thorough cleaning, though, falls to the custodian, janitor, or cleanup crew. Security and safety checks may also be part of the job. In addition, all too frequently, the custodian is the only male staff employee. Many programs choose to exploit this situation by enlarging the scope of job responsibilities to increase contact with the children.

Depending on program size and budget, other staff, such as accountants, secretaries, or bus drivers, may be hired to perform specialized functions. Central office or sponsoring agencies may rotate such staff to several programs. These specialized staff free regular staff to concentrate fully on children's activities and reduce the need for program staff to perform clerical or administrative tasks.

Service Staff

Child care programs may be eligible to use the services of state or local medical, social, and psychological workers. These services may be provided to the program or on a case-by-case basis to individual children. Any child care program may enroll children whose family situation gives them eligibility or entitlement status for service. Service workers dealing with young children will frequently seek to work cooperatively with child care program staff to increase the impact of their services. Applicable codes regarding confidentiality, privacy, and access to records must be observed by all personnel involved in service coordination efforts.

Substitutes

For irregular and unplanned staff absences every child care program needs a plan for short-term substitutes. Vacations and staff leaves create the need for longer-term substitutes. Directors must seek to minimize the impact of staff absence on the children's program and activities, maintain legally required staff-child ratios and group sizes, and meet the extra salary costs incurred by the program to pay substitute salaries.

Programs should maintain a list of available substitutes. Each person on this list should complete an application or information form, sign a statement of understanding regarding pay level and conditions of payment, and file a list of available hours. If substitutes are volunteering time, that should be recorded and clearly understood.

Special Staff

Child care programs often have access to other programs that can provide staff members. In return for these special staff, the child care program may be asked to provide documentation and some supervision for the assigned person.

Student Teachers and Interns. Increasingly, university early childhood programs are seeking to include child care programs as one of the several sites used for field training for beginning professionals. A field placement gives a student the opportunity to become acquainted with the demands of staff roles in child care programs. Students may be placed as aides with child care programs for a few hours a week or may complete a full-time student teaching practicum. College supervisors seek to maintain a liaison among college, student, and program and typically assume considerable responsibility for evaluation and record-keeping.

Internships for more advanced students give students practical experience as directors, social workers, or parent trainers. Internships may be for short-term specific job tasks or may be used as full-scale trials in a job position.

Foster Grandparents. The Foster Grandparents project provides meaningful work for retired persons or the elderly while offering child care programs a rich resource for volunteer staff. Mature, reliable, and often highly dedi-

Using volunteers effectively takes skill and patience, but the rewards can be great for both child and volunteer. (Courtesy of U.S. Department of Health and Human Services, Washington, DC.)

cated Foster Grandparents make good role models for children and supply an extra set of hands for staff in many activities.

Volunteers

Volunteers perform services on a regular basis without pay. Many programs find that volunteers are both a blessing and curse. Volunteers can help programs save money on staff salaries, relieve staff for needed breaks, and provide special skills at timely moments in the program. Managing a volunteer program or even the occasional volunteer, however, necessitates planning and effort. Effective use of volunteers requires that a formal volunteer program be established and that volunteers be selected and supervised as carefully as regular staff. Many programs fail to plan or they underestimate the managerial demands of volunteers. Good volunteers cost time and planning; programs must be willing to pay that price.

Planning for a volunteer program begins with a survey of jobs that volunteers could perform in the program. The survey should pay special attention to time of day and number of hours desirable for volunteer help. It should also note whether there is a need for the same individual over a period of time or whether a series of different volunteers could perform the job as well. If a program is planning to use volunteers on a regular basis to meet mandated staff-child ratios, the director will have to carefully plan scheduling and duties.

For many programs parents are the primary source of volunteers. An organized volunteer program is often used as an adjunct to the parent involvement program. Individuals associated with the program's sponsoring agency or connected with the immediate program staff and facility are another ready supply of potential volunteers.

Other sources include:

Schools High schools, colleges, school health programs and school nurses, vocational or technical schools, and business schools.
Businesses Businessperson's groups, medical services, hospital dietitians, labor organizations, clinics, and the state health department.
Community organizations Church groups, retired persons, off-duty military personnel, police, firefighters, youth organizations, and service groups such as Lions, Rotary, or Kiwanis.

Recruitment of volunteers can be done successfully through informal methods. Personal phone calls, notices posted on bulletin boards, and word-of-mouth are all effective means in small communities. Public recruitment through newspaper ads and lectures to groups of potential volunteers may help to reach persons outside the informal network of the child care program and may be the best way to reach groups likely to have special skills or little prior knowledge of child care programs. Points to emphasize when recruiting are:

- Volunteers are serving the public interest.
- Volunteers are supplementing tax dollars by helping to improve problems that may be costly in the future.
- Volunteers may work with expectations of career opportunities or part-time work.
- Volunteers will benefit from being close to children, meeting the public, or filling an empty day.
- Volunteers will learn ways of teaching preschoolers.

Ask potential volunteers to fill out a simple application or information form and talk personally to each volunteer. You may want references and credentials if volunteers are going to function in responsible staff positions. Ask for health records and TB tests if such are required for staff. Assess each volunteer candidate's skills and availability and assign volunteers to jobs within the center accordingly. Accept the fact that some willing volunteers may not fit into the needs and time slots of the program. Programs should select volunteers carefully. They will have responsibility for children's welfare.

Setup and post a weekly volunteer schedule. Assign each volunteer to a specific job within instructions to report to or work with a specific staff member. Be sure the staff member is aware of and capable of overseeing the volunteer. Have volunteers sign in and sign out.

The minimum training a volunteer should receive is a personal tour and opportunity for discussion with program staff. Some programs provide volunteers with copies of the program manual or a volunteer manual. Training should emphasize orientation and program procedures. Expect volunteers to learn on-the-job by example of the supervisory staff member. Since volunteers come and go, training procedures should be short, easy to repeat individually, and applicable to all volunteer jobs in the program.

Expect volunteers to function reliably and competently. Monitor their performance. At no time should the performance of volunteers interfere with the quality of children's care or take staff attention away from their duties with the children. If this occurs, either remove the volunteer or consider changing the level of performance and responsibility expected from the volunteer.

Records need to be kept. Often persons use volunteer work as a way of trying out a career field. Be prepared to write references for volunteers based on documented hours served and duties performed. Note that the resources section of this chapter includes several helpful publications about volunteers. Information about working with volunteers is available from The National Center for Citizen Involvement, P.O. Box 4179, Boulder, CO 80306.

Staff Selection

Staff turnover, program growth, or program change result in the periodic need for new staff throughout the year. Every program should, therefore, establish a general set of procedures to guide the selection process.

Directors are responsible for staff selection for most child care programs. Sponsoring agencies and parent committees may be involved in interviewing or contract processing, but the program director generally assumes administrative management of the selection process. The two goals of the hiring process are to use efficient and legal screening and selection procedures, and to select staff who will be competent and compatible with existing program staff and policies.

Employee selection is a high priority area for all businesses. Child care directors can profit by basing their own selection procedures on the successful experiences of other businesses. Directors should be sure they understand laws about personnel matters, especially laws about hiring and fair treatment of employees.

Recruitment

Job Description. Staff selection begins with the preparation of a detailed job description. This portrait includes a description of actual duties, responsibilities, and authority and a list of qualifications, skills, and abilities that are required or desired. The description might also include a profile of the program and an explanation of how the job fits in the total program. The position description along with program public relations brochures, policy manuals, and similar materials forms a more elaborate information package to distribute to serious job candidates.

Advertising. The job may be advertised in local job classified ads or professional publications. The purpose of recruitment is to notify a wide pool of potential applicants of the position vacancy. The more qualified people who can be encouraged to apply for the job, the greater the likelihood of finding a satisfactory candidate. A balance must be struck so that candidates are provided with enough information to realistically assess themselves in relation to the job, but good candidates are not discouraged from applying if there are minor inconsistencies between the position and personal characteristics.

Job Application. Candidates should be asked to complete a job application. The job application provides information about the candidate's education, health status, previous work experiences, and references. Depending on the position description, additional details such as car ownership, special skills, and hobbies may be requested. It is helpful to ask why the applicant is seeking the position. Candidates whose credentials are unsuitable for the job can be removed from further consideration based upon an initial screening of job applications. Candidates may be asked to submit transcripts, copies of publications, or certificates to support information given on the job application.

Interviews

The personal interview is an important tool in the selection of child care staff. Directors find that personality factors weigh heavily in selecting staff compatible with program goals. Comparing information concerning the position and the candidate's job application assists the director in formulating questions. If a committee is to conduct the interview, time ought to be set aside to review the applicant's materials beforehand so all committee members approach the candidate with the benefit of that knowledge.

When several candidates are being interviewed for the same job, interview questions should be somewhat standardized. This gives the interviewers a basis for comparing responses.

Job-interviewing techniques vary, but an informal approach usually elicits more information than a rigorous questioning. A comfortable arrangement of chairs, a conversational approach, and a mutual discussion of the applicant's qualifications in relationship to the position create a pleasant experience and draw out the necessary information. During the interview the director asks thoughtfully formulated questions. Open-ended questions, such as "What would you do if . . . ," reveal the applicant's child care philosophy, attitudes, and feelings. Other questions about the applicant clarify and enlarge upon the information on the job application. Be aware that the law prohibits questions that can be construed as discriminating if the employer cannot show such information is essential for the job. The interview should be conducted in private and without interruptions, and sufficient time should be given for an unhurried and complete discussion. At the end of the interview the director may briefly describe the program and conduct a short tour of facilities. During the tour the director observes the applicant's reaction to the program, staff, and children and introduces applicant and staff members to each other.

A written record should be made of the interview. As soon as possible after the interview, the director should record highlights of the candidate's responses and relevant judgments of the interviewer(s). Committee comments should be solicited immediately.

Documentation of Credentials

Before the final hiring decision is made, the director must document the candidate's education and experiences. The standard procedure is to ask for certified copies of transcripts and to contact references by phone or letter. No one minds a legitimate request for such information, but programs should exercise good judgment in collecting such information and should do so only for serious candidates. No employee should be hired before certificates and references are checked. There is no excuse for laziness or sloppiness in such a critical personnel matter. These documents form the basis of the successful job candidate's personnel file and may be needed to verify compliance with staff training and qualification regulations. Where needed, medical forms should be submitted or hiring should be contingent upon acceptable exams.

Screening

Screening takes place at several points:

1. As responses to the job advertisement are received, the contact person encourages seemingly qualified, interested candidates to submit formal applications. Obviously unqualified applicants should be discouraged at this time. Don't waste their time or yours.
2. The director and/or a committee screen completed job applications and select top candidates for further consideration. If the selection process will be prolonged and if certain applicants will not be considered further under any circumstances, they should be notified at this point.
3. A few top candidates are selected for interviews. A second group of candidates may be identified at this time and their names set aside for follow-up if the top candidate group does not pan out.
4. Top candidates are interviewed and a dialogue established to exchange information about candidate and job. Be sure candidates learn enough about the program and the job that, should you decide to offer the job, they will want it.
5. Be aware that most states are in the process of establishing mandatory screening procedures for child care workers. Checks of FBI and criminal records may be required in some form as a preventive measure against child abuse by caregivers in programs.

Final Selection

Following the personal interviews, the director considers all information—the preliminary data concerning the position, the job application forms, the personal interview, and all staff reactions. If unable to reach a decision, the director can schedule further personal interviews with top applicants or readvertise in the hope of attracting additional candidates. When a choice has been made, the director should immediately notify in writing those candidates not selected to fill the position. A letter should also be sent to the chosen individual, offering the position and listing information such as the title of the position, salary, hours, starting date of employment, and the duration of the job if it is for a limited time.

Probationary Work Periods

The purpose of a probationary work period is to allow the new employee and the child care program a chance to "try each other out" under actual conditions. The glamour of the recruitment process wears off quickly under the stresses and strains of daily tasks. Both employee and child care program should have a chance to test each other.

Probationary periods are for set periods of time—perhaps two weeks to six months—depending on the scope and complexity of the employee's job responsibilities. Pay during the probationary period may be slightly less than that of a full-fledged employee. This reflects the fact that a new employee is not functioning at full levels at first and provides a reward as employees move to full-pay status when the probationary period is over.

If a probationary period is used, the conditions of the probationary period should be clearly stated and communicated in writing to the new employee. Of particular importance are the provisions for moving from probationary to full status. One common method is to state that at the end of the agreed-upon probationary period either employee or child care program can choose to terminate the employment arrangement for any reason. Should the employee move to full status, he or she will enjoy the rights and protections accorded to all employees of the program. Probationary work periods are worth the managerial effort required for setup and monitoring. Together with the preservice orientation sessions for new staff described in a later section of this chapter, probationary work periods give program directors a strong position for handling staff management in a child care program.

Personnel Procedures

Contracts

A signed contract is a written record of the offer and acceptance of employment. Contracts can be very simple or filled with "legalese." They protect both the employee and the child care organization. Together with job descriptions and personnel policies, contracts establish the legal circumstances governing the employee-program relationship.

Personnel Policies

Written personnel policies are an important contribution to smooth staff management. Employees have the right to know the conditions of their employment and the program's expectations for their behavior and performance. Box 11.1 includes suggested topics to be included in a set of personnel policies and procedures for a day care center.

Personnel Records

A personnel file should be started for each new employee. This file serves as a central repository for all information that the program acquires or produces about the employee. Personnel records are confidential, and access to these files needs to be tightly controlled. Personnel records include:

- Initial employment application and any supportive documentation submitted by the employee
- References
- Copies of transcripts, certificates, and documentation of training experiences
- Health records, reports of physical examinations, special tests, and other relevant medical data
- Correspondence related to the employee
- Employment record and termination date
- Records of promotions, salary changes
- Performance evaluation reports, including disciplinary actions
- Reports of conferences with the employee
- Information the employee wishes to have included (these may be employee responses to evaluation, explanations of health data, or responses to complaints or disciplinary actions)
- Record of requests for references

Personnel files should be periodically updated and purged of inappropriate material. When an employee leaves the program, be sure that the file is complete and accurate at that point. If an exit interview is conducted, a report should be placed in the file.

Salaries and Employee Benefits

Staff salaries are the single largest item in a program budget. Salary levels are a growing fiscal issue in child care. Chapter 12 includes detailed examples of child care salaries and a discussion of the issues related to staff wages and working conditions.

Employee benefits refer to support for employees in addition to salary income. Sometimes called "fringe benefits," these benefits represent a significant financial commitment for the program. Some benefits translate directly to dollars; for example, employers often provide health and life insurance plans to which they make contributions. Other benefits are in the form of released time for sick leave, jury duty, or pursuit of educational programs. Ultimately, these benefits "cost" the program because substitutes must be hired to cover while the regular employee uses the released time.

Some benefits are mandated by law, and others are provided at the discretion of the employer. Voluntary benefits are usually not as generous in child care and other human service agencies as they are in business and industry. Some estimates are that compensation in addition to salary (that is, benefits) may add as much as an additional 30 to 40 percent to an individual's income.

Mandated benefits refer to Social Security, unemployment insurance, and Workman's Compensation. Social Security payments involve a fifty-fifty split in the employee-employer contribution. The employer deducts the employee's share from each paycheck and then pays the total tax (both shares) to the Internal Revenue Service on a quarterly basis. Unemployment insurance payments and policies depend on both state and federal requirements. Eligibility and benefit levels vary from state to state, but the federal government sets baseline standards under which state systems must operate. Workman's Compensation insurance protects the employer from liability for injuries to employees while they are engaged in organization activities.

Voluntary benefits typically include health and life insurance plans, disability insurance, retirement plans and tax-deferred annuity plans, and provisions for leaves or released time with or without compensation. For example, vacations, holidays, and sick leave are often time-off with pay. Other leaves may include general personal leaves, maternity and paternity leaves, educational leaves, and bereavement time-off. Provision of training programs and meals for employees are also services that may be provided at no cost to the employee as part of the total benefits package.

The Child Care Employee Project (CCEP) is an organization for child care workers dedicated to collecting information and doing advocacy work for better working conditions for staff. You can contact CCEP by writing: P.O. Box 5603, Berkeley, CA 94705. Their newsletter, "Child Care Employee News," is available on a subscription basis.

Grievance Procedures

Grievance procedures are appeal systems that allow employees to ask for reconsideration of an issue or review of employment situations if they feel they have been treated unfairly. The procedures vary depending on whether the employees are members of a union. Typically, the grievance procedure begins with the employee first discussing the concern with an immediate supervisor. If the employee does not feel that adequate attention has been given to the concern, he or she can then submit the grievance to the next higher level of supervision and so on until the program director or chief administrator for the program is reached and makes the final decision. At each step written decisions should be presented to the employee and deadlines for making the decisions should be specified (for example, a decision must be rendered within

Box 11.1 Suggested Contents of Personnel Policies

I. Statement of Employer Philosophy Toward Employees

II. Process for Establishment and Amendment of Personnel Policies
   - A. Description of how a board of directors or its personnel committee will work with staff in the development of personnel policies.
   - B. Statement of how often the policies will be reviewed.

III. Employment and Employee Status
   - A. A definition of the types of employee status. Permanent and probationary employees are the most common. It may be desirable to define or discuss temporary employee status (e.g., a substitute teacher) and the terms of promotion and transfer.
   - B. A statement that the program is an equal opportunity employer.
   - C. A description of the process by which a vacancy is filled.
   - D. A description of the process for resigning, and the required period of notice.
   - E. The policy regarding retirement.

IV. Basic Employment Description and Expectation

   This includes the length of the workday and workweek; policy for documenting time; statement about when salaries are paid; recommendations or requirements concerning type of clothes to wear; areas in the building in which smoking is permitted or prohibited; whether staff are expected to eat lunch with the children (required in the day care licensing standards in some states) or are permitted a separate lunch period; if desirable, a statement prohibiting employees from eating or drinking foods which the children do not have (e.g., eating candy or coke in the classroom); a statement of health tests (TB, physical, VD, etc.) which may be required for employment in day care; information about parking, or areas of the building which can be used for breaks or planning work; and policies on use of the telephone and personal calls.

V. Salary Plan and Description of Fringe Benefits
   - A. Included in the salary plan should be a statement of the employer's philosophy on salaries, how base salaries are established and are reviewed, and under what conditions salary increases will be made available.
   - B. Included in the fringe benefit discussion should be a description of required fringe benefits (usually workman's compensation, unemployment insurance and social security) and a description of optional fringe benefits (e.g., medical insurance, life insurance, retirement plan). Information about the pros and cons of choosing various optional fringe benefits should be available and could be included in the Personnel Policies and Procedures document.

VI. Attendance and Leave
   - A. Definition of expectations regarding regular attendance, procedure for notifying if employee will be late, policy when an employee is absent without authorization.
   - B. Definition of vacation and sick leave—how it is accumulated, whether unused leave may be carried over at the end of a year, how soon to apply in advance for vacation leave, whether sick leave must

be documented by a doctor's statement, definition of other family members whose illness would justify the use of sick leave.

C. Definition of leave for special purposes, such as jury duty, voting, serving as an election officer, and attending a funeral. Some programs have a policy to cover when the program is closed due to bad weather.

D. Definition of educational leave where applicable.

E. Definition of maternity leave.

VII. Disciplinary Actions and Appeal Procedure

A. This should include a description of the process by which discipline will be administered. It could include the steps of probation, suspension, and dismissal, although often it only includes a dismissal process.

B. The actions of an employee which could cause a dismissal should be stated. Some of the most common reasons are: The employee uses physical force in disciplining child, the employee has falsified employment information, consistent failure to carry out assigned duties, failure to comply with the program's licensure regulations and, in some programs, the violation of confidential information—such as discussing a child's behavior with someone other than staff or a child's parents.

C. A description of how an individual employee may appeal a disciplinary action or other decision related to employment.

D. A description of how general grievances of employees can be brought to the attention of an upper level of supervision or the board.

VIII. Employee Evaluation

A process of periodic evaluation of employee performance is common in most day care programs. Discussion should include purposes of the evaluation, its frequency, whether the evaluation will or will not be used in making decisions about promotion or salary increases, and usually a statement that the employee is required to sign the evaluation.

IX. Miscellaneous Topics

Other possible subjects that some day care programs have found necessary to include are:

A. Policies related to nepotism—that is, whether relatives of current employees or board members can be hired or be the supervisor of a relative.

B. Policies of what kinds of political activities an employee can engage in; this only applies to centers which are subject to certain federal laws (Chapter 15, Title V of the United States Code—formerly known as the Hatch Act—and/or Sections 606 (6) and 213 of the Economic Opportunity Act).

C. Special meetings or workshops which employees are expected to attend.

D. Policies of whether an employee's child can be enrolled in the program or not.

E. Statement related to employees' travel and conditions under which they will be reimbursed for expenses.

Source: From *Day care personnel management* (pp. 59–60), 1979, Atlanta, GA: Southern Regional Education Board.

five working days). Grievance procedures should be included in the personnel policies.

Termination

A director who is responsible for hiring staff must also have the power to dismiss unsatisfactory employees. This authority should be stated in written program policy and clearly understood by staff. In addition, administrators need a well-conceived disciplinary policy outlining the circumstances, process, and procedure for employee discipline and dismissal. Seasoned directors maintain comprehensive written records of employee misconduct such as tardiness, absenteeism, incompetence, or lack of cooperation. Regardless of the strained relationship between an unsatisfactory employee and the director, the director must ensure that the employee has access to all documentation and a fair hearing and that the termination process is followed carefully.

Staff Deployment

How many staff members should a program employ? What hours should each staff member work? How many children of what ages should be in which staff member's groups? These are fundamental questions a director must answer.

You might think that figuring the number is a straightforward calculation. It is not. The questions seem simple, but there are complex regulations and program factors to consider. Staff-child ratios, group size, and staff training have all been the subjects of heated debate, and until recently the target of regulatory reform. No satisfactory resolution of the issues has been reached, and efforts for regulatory reform have been suspended. When the national, political, and budgetary climates change, the issues will be raised once more and reform pressures will mount again.

Recent Political Background

Child care, especially center-based programs for preschool children, has long been subject to comprehensive regulation by government authorities to ensure that public monies are being spent properly. Private, proprietary, and non-center-based programs have not been the objects of public scrutiny and concern as often. Staff characteristics, in particular, have been the focus of regulation for two reasons: (1) intuitively to the professionals and laypersons who drew up regulations, staff seemed to make a difference in quality of care; and (2) staff can be counted and qualifications documented, thus making regulation feasible. For a number of years at the national, state, and local levels child care programs coped with diverse, unevenly enforced, sometimes contradictory specifications for staff-child ratios, group size, and staff qualifications.

Title XX child care funding gathered momentum as advocates learned to compete at the state level for a share of the social service pie. In general, child care had high visibility as the rise in working mothers meant more demand for child care at all economic levels. Child care became a priority area for the Administration for Children, Youth and Families (ACYF) in the U.S. Department of Health, Education and Welfare (HEW). ACYF funded a four-year National Day Care Study (NDCS) to look at quality and cost in center-based care for children ages three, four, and five, and to an extent for children in infant and toddler care.

Meanwhile Title XX focused attention on the amended FIDCR. Efforts were started to revise the FIDCR again in response to continuing concerns about proposed staffing standards. Data from the NDCS were available to help shape the recommendations for new federal standards, which became known as HEWDCR. The NDCS found that:

- *Group size* was consistently related to measures of quality; smaller groups were associated with better

Table 11.1 Three Policies of Group Size and Caregiver-Child Ratio

	Maximum Group Size		Maximum Caregiver-Child Ratio	
	Attendance[a] *Basis*	*Enrollment Basis*	*Attendance Basis*	*Enrollment Basis*
Policy A	14	16	1:7	1:8
Policy B	16	18	1:8	1:9
Policy C	18	20	1:9	1:10

Note. An evaluation of the three options indicates the following:

- Policy A would have the most positive impact on the quality of day care provided with public funds.
- Given the importance of group size for quality, all three options would provide higher quality than current FIDCR requirements for four- and five-year-olds. Policy A would provide higher quality than FIDCR requirements for three-year-olds as well.
- All three options would reduce the cost of care relative to current regulations in the range of an estimated minimum of 6 percent for Policy A to a maximum of 16 percent for Policy C. This would allow a potential increase of up to 19 percent in the number of children served at current expenditure levels.
- Between 75 and 90 percent of centers currently providing publicly funded care would be in compliance with all three policy options, without any changes in current operations.
- Depending on the option chosen, between 30 and 60 percent of the centers in the United States not currently serving publicly funded children would immediately be eligible to provide care.

[a] Differences between attendance-based and enrollment-based regulatory levels assume the 12 percent child absence rate prevailing nationally, and also assume that absent staff will be replaced by substitutes.

Source: Final Report of the National Day Care Study, Children at the Center: Executive Summary (p. 5) by Abt Associates, 1979, Washington, DC: ACYF-OHDS, Department of Health, Education and Welfare.

care; variations in group size affected cost only slightly.

- *Staff-child ratio* within the 1:5 to 1:10 range showed a slight relationship to measures of staff and child behavior; ratio was found to be the strongest determinant of program cost.

The NDCS research team came up with three policy options (See Table 11.1) based on the data. It is helpful to review these recommendations since this is the best data base available for evaluating ratios and group sizes. The options are various ways of relating group size and caregiver-child ratio. None of these options was adopted by the federal government.

After considerable public debate and comment, the HEWDCR were published in final form in the *Federal Register*. Title XX funds had been used to provide staff training and a series of $200 million Title XX grants had been earmarked to help states come into compliance with the revised HEWDCR. Congress, however, voted to postpone the effective dates indefinitely. The Department of Health and Human Services (HHS) has now announced that federal child care regulations no longer will apply to Title XX funds now provided through Social Services Block Grant (SSBG) to states. One source of pressure on Congress was parents, who did not want to see child care costs go up and the number of children served go down as an expected result of the new regulations.

Thus, despite all the time, preparation, comment, and money expended, regulatory revision never occurred. Why? Partly because of concern that staff-child ratios and group sizes would adversely affect cost and availability. These events coincided with a general federal move away from regulation. The issues of staff-child ratio and group size were not resolved and will need to be addressed again.

Ratios and Grouping Patterns

Directors must manage staff in order to meet applicable state and local legal requirements for the number and ages of children in the program. Many directors feel that regulatory requirements set only minimum levels and these directors routinely exceed the levels in order to deliver services consistent with their program plan. Staff working hours and enrollment peaks can force directors into a balancing act as they consider minimum and optimal levels on a daily or hourly basis.

Compromises need to be made because there is often not enough money available for staff salaries. This section defines terms and discusses concepts for determining operational staff-child ratios and grouping patterns.

Definitions. Staff-child or caregiver-child ratios seem to be the typical unit used when describing a program. Parents often ask, "How many staff do you have?" or teachers say, "I have ten children to watch in the morning." Ratios are a convenient way to express the responsibility of a staff member and the corresponding access a child has to staff attention. A *ratio* is the number of staff divided by number of children. For example, four staff divided by twenty-four children is a ratio of 1 : 6.

Ratios can be calculated on a center basis or a classroom group basis. Regulations will tell you which method to use. Centerwide ratios give programs more flexibility. By pooling all ages of children, only one leftover or underratio group is possible. Group ratios open the possibility of considerably more unfilled groups since each group ratio calculated can result in undersized groups to be staffed. However, group ratios may reflect more adequately the specific activity needs of center program. Center ratios may be useful for routine activities such as nap, meals, or outdoor play. However, ratios vary according to how *staff* is defined, time of day, and ages of children.

The most honest ratio would count only the number of staff actually working directly with children. Directors, cooks, janitors, bus drivers, and others who do not usually oversee daily child activities would be excluded from this count. Even staff who do work directly with children are not all equal in training and competence. One head teacher and three aides is a qualitatively different staff than four head teachers. Volunteers and student teachers further complicate the determination of ratios.

Regulations and inspectors' interpretations will limit staff counts. Often volunteers cannot be counted and directors can be counted only if over half of their time is spent teaching. But there is frequently considerable latitude in designating which staff members count for ratio determination. It is here that directors must make judgments based on program needs and cost factors. If legal ratios can be met by counting staff who are only marginally involved in program activities, many directors count and report those ratios. Minimum ratios may need to be exceeded if program activities are to proceed as desired.

Child care programs use two methods to report the number of children in the program:

1. *Number enrolled* The total number of children whose enrollment requirements have been met and whose fees are current. For example, fifty children enrolled divided by five staff = 10 : 1 ratio.
2. *Average Daily Attendance* (ADA) The average number of enrolled children who are present at the program, which is typically a lower figure than number enrolled. For example, fifty children enrolled or forty-two attendance average divided by five staff = 8 : 1 ratio.

Basing ratios on enrollment figures can result in higher staff-child ratios than are actually needed to operate the program. Larger centers may routinely have absence rates that are equal to one staff position. When money is tight, carrying an extra staff member can be a big budget item. Some programs in this situation count the director (or other support staff) as a teaching staff member but actually only use the director as a teacher on days when attendance nears enrollment figures. This depends on regulatory constraints and judgments concerning program needs.

Ages of Children. Minimum ratios are set according to the ages of children. Generally, the younger the children, the more staff, and the lower the ratio required.

The example presented earlier of the three policy alternatives from the NDCS (Table 11.1) illustrates ratios by age ranges. The purpose of these age ranges is to establish some correspondence between children's developmental levels and the need for adult attention. Specific age ranges vary from state to state, and often from one program type to another (center, home, school-aged).

Time of Day. Enrollment and attendance fluctuate throughout the day. Peak hours for children need to correspond to the highest staff levels. Ratios required to meet regulations and implement the program can vary throughout the day. Before 8:30 A.M. and after 4:00 P.M. only five or six children may be present. A mixed-age group ratio could require only one staff member present. Yet, between 8:30 A.M. and 4:00 P.M., the presence of forty children and varying groupings will require perhaps six staff.

Child care programs that have children in more than one age group must meet staff-child ratios for each age range separately or ratios for mixed-age groups. Mixed-age groupings, if they match program goals, are one way to spread staff numbers across more children. Mixed-age ratios are figured on the average age of the group and are set forth in regulations. Once again, the program director must balance staff costs against regulations to determine grouping patterns and staff numbers.

Ratios and Costs

Staff-child ratios are a critical issue for child care programs. Ratios are the keys to quality and to costs. Staff salaries are a program's biggest cost. The more staff, the higher the budget. Yet good staff, well-trained and satisfactorily paid, are capital investments in quality.

Developmentally appropriate age ratios and well-composed groupings of children advance child care from a mere protective service to a service that enhances children's experiences. Existing minimum ratios are protective, conservative, and often arbitrary. The challenge for directors is to identify ratios that maximize program quality and control costs.

Staff Scheduling

The basic plan for coordinating staff is the work schedule. The work schedule determines the daily work periods of all staff including volunteers, students, and paid employees. When devising the staff work schedule, the director considers hours of center operation, regulatory staff-child ratios, ages of the children, arrival and departure time of the children, daily routines and activities of the program, and availability of volunteers and substitutes.

The process for determining a workable staff schedule is two-fold. First, the director constructs a graph, recording the enrollment numbers of children by age of child as they vary throughout the day. Using this information and the staff-child ratios for the youngest children enrolled, the director estimates how many staff need to be present for each half-hour period. This results in a maximum estimate since staff-child ratios will be higher for older children and mixed-age groups. Starting with a maximum staff estimate allows leeway in matching actual staff working hours with regulatory requirements. This step helps to ensure that actual staff levels will be legal. Box 11.2 shows a step-by-step approach to determining staffing for a program.

The second step of the process is to schedule work shifts. Here the director considers:

- The program activity needs: What levels of staff are needed at various times of the day? When must

Box 11.2 Child-Staff Ratio Plan for Maximum Staff Estimates

1. Construct a chart showing each half-hour period the center is in operation.
2. Write in the number of three-, four-, and five-year-olds enrolled for each half-hour period.

9:00–9:30			9:30–10:00		
3 Yrs.	4 Yrs.	5 Yrs.	3 Yrs.	4 Yrs.	5 Yrs.

   (Use other age levels if appropriate.) Work from enrollment figures at this point even if regulations allow staff ratios to be calculated on average daily attendance figures.
3. Use the number of three-year-olds (or youngest age group) to determine the number of adults needed each half-hour segment. Use the current regulatory ratio for your program.
4. Figure the overstaff number. This overstaff figure represents the number of *additional children* that would be covered to "fill-up" the three-year-old staff-child ratios.
5. Write in the number of four- and five-year-olds enrolled for each half-hour period. (Use other age levels if consistent with regulatory ranges.)
6. Subtract the three-year-old overstaff number from the four- and five-year-child enrollments for each half-hour, thus "filling up" the three-year-old staff-child ratios. The remaining four- and five-year-old figures are what the four- to five-year staff-ratio is calculated upon.
7. For each half-hour segment, calculate the total staff needed to serve the adjusted enrollment using the current regulatory ratio for your program.
8. There may be an overstaff or understaff figure at this point. Clearly indicate how many and what age children are involved. Note that this is likely to occur when child enrollment totals are just above or just below totals needed to "fill" a group for one staff-child ratio. If regulations permit use of average daily attendance figures to calculate ratios, use these lower figures to adjust maximum staff estimates downward at this point.

aides and head teachers be present; when are cooks needed; and so on?

- Employee stamina: A staggered work schedule is necessary to cover a long day. No single employee, the director included, can or should be expected to work directly with children more than six hours at most (see Box 11.3). However, few employees want to work short or split shifts.
- Overlap in staff work schedules means that the smooth routine of the day is not broken by abrupt staff changes, and staff members can pass information easily to one another. Some built-in overstaffing can allow for this.
- The working hours of male and female staff are scheduled so that both men and women are present in the center during the entire day. Similar attention should be paid to the presence of ethnic and minority staff members where appropriate.
- Most of the day does not depend on volunteer aid to meet staff-child ratios. Instead such individuals are used to supplement the staff during mealtimes, naptimes, special activities, and excursions. Volunteers can be very dependable. However, realistically, no director should consistently allow legal compliance with staff ratios to rely on staff who are not contractually bound to the program.

Supervision

Supervision of staff, whether it is formal or informal, is an integral part of all child care programs. Frequent observation of program activity, staff functioning, and child growth allows directors to monitor program operations. One distinguishing feature of child care programs is the team of adults that is involved in daily activities and caregiving for young children. Informal supervision of the team is needed to ensure that all adults are reasonably consistent with and aware of what others are doing. Formal supervision is often neglected, especially if everything seems to be going smoothly. Or, formal supervision may be a periodic, required ef-

Box 11.3 Contact Hours*

Contact hours are the total number and sequence of hours a child care staff member is directly interacting with children. Contact hours equal the caregiving time.

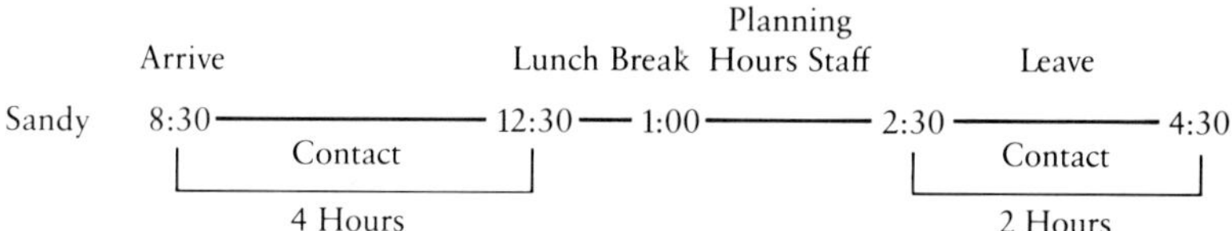

Six hours is considered plenty of caregiving time by seasoned child care staff members. Time for personal needs and planning is essential. Remember, wages are low and few employees should be expected to use nonworking time for preparation purposes.

* The concept of *contact hours* first appears in child care literature as part of the research procedures of the National Day Care Study.

fort to evaluate staff performance. As such, staff supervision becomes linked with feelings of anxiety and the desire to "do it right" while the supervision is occurring. The result is that everyone is glad when the supervision is over and things return to normal. Neither of these approaches to supervision capitalizes on the potential benefits of systematic, ongoing supervision, and neither encourages the professional growth that ultimately creates the type of working atmosphere for staff most beneficial for children's experiences.

What Is Supervision?

Supervision is an essential management tool for monitoring the quality and activities of program staff. It is a three-part process.

1. Establishing objectives and conditions for supervision.
2. Collecting information, usually through observation of the staff member on-the-job. Records and planning papers related to the job may be reviewed.
3. Making evaluative judgments about the staff member with selected information obtained through supervision.

Often both teacher and supervisor get so caught up in attending to the child-teacher interaction that they neglect to systematically exploit the fact that they are adults working together to solve problems and enhance children's development. The adult-adult interaction in the process is almost always allowed to simply happen; it is rarely seen as the relationship critical to supervision.

Staff *attitudes* toward supervision are crucial. Attitudes toward oneself as a teacher in need of change and toward another adult (supervisor) as a resource for change do not spring forth fully developed when a person begins employment in a child care program. Staff need to be guided in acquiring the skills and attitudes needed for supervision.

The child care supervisor must be skilled in negotiating personal relations and handling feelings. The following expectations form a workable series of competencies for a positive adult-adult supervision interaction:

Stage 1 The staff member must become used to being observed. Many are used to having a product observed while they are not present. In child care, however, it is the ongoing process of caregiving that is to be evaluated while it is occurring.

Stage 2 Staff members have to recognize the need and be able to talk about their own behavior with the children. Many staff members cannot easily describe what actions they have taken with children. They forget what they said or did in a situation. Even more important, they may be unable to express reasons for their actions or relate their behaviors to overall program goals.

Stage 3 Staff should learn to pose their own questions about their actions as teachers. They cannot become complacent, expecting a supervisor to take responsibility for isolating aspects of their performance. The effective staff member continually raises questions about actions as a teacher. Unless this personal criticism is operating, hopes for improvement on the job are limited.

Stage 4 Staff must be able to use the feedback they receive from a supervisor. They must be able to take constructive criticism and integrate this feedback into future performance.

Supervisors cannot expect to start functioning with a staff member at stage four. Each staff member will progress through these supervision stages at an individual pace.

Purposes of Supervision

Directors can use supervision not only to monitor program quality but also to motivate staff members. Close attention to the details of a staff member's performance, coupled with analysis, praise, and a positive personal rapport, enhance this motivation. Systematic observation and one-to-one conferences with staff members increase the director's understanding of the staff person's contribution to the program and provide a legitimate means to reward desirable performance. Staff will be more receptive to supervision when the outcome is recognition of good performance and mutual effort toward increasing job satisfaction.

Supervision allows a director to collect a broad base of information about the ongoing operation of the program. How well daily events match or combine to support the program's goals and philosophy is best determined by grouping data. Judgments about the program and the depth to which philosophy is implemented can be made only if supervision is systematically related to job descriptions, program goals, and observation findings. Through supervisory observations and related staff conferences, directors may generate ideas for useful in-service or training experiences for staff members.

Supervising at Different Staff Levels

Child care staff reflect a wide variety of educational and experiential backgrounds. In addition, staff have varying degrees of responsibility for program implementation. Supervision should reflect the role of positions in the overall program structure.

Supervision of Aides. Aides work with a more experienced teacher. Supervision for aides must consider the duties and the limits of responsibility given to aides. Many aides lack formal training in early childhood specialties, but bring a great deal of personal experience and positive feelings to their jobs. An aide may be an excellent caregiver but lack the skills of analysis and technical knowledge to describe the rationale behind daily actions. Supervisors can help aides articulate the reasons why they do what they do and provide assistance and resources to support their effectiveness in the program.

Supervision of Teachers with Early Childhood Training. Supervisors can help trained professionals realize their potential as a model for other personnel in the program. Generally, the supervision, which is very specific, extends the teacher's skills in implementing a particular model program, diagnosing special needs of children, and adapting to leadership within the staff team.

Supervision of Teachers with Related Training. Many teachers do not have specific or extensive education in early childhood development and techniques. The supervisor needs to extend prior training and help these teachers transfer familiar principles and techniques to the early childhood level. Demonstration, explanation, and analysis of teaching strategies suitable for the child care setting can greatly help during the initial period of adaptation for those professionals.

The Director As Supervisor

Directors are responsible for staff supervision. This is a logical outcome of a director's role in the hiring and firing of staff and of the director's responsibility for overall management of the program. Occasionally, supervision responsibility for some employees can be delegated; for example, an assistant director may supervise support personnel such as a cook or janitor, or a head teacher may assume supervision responsibility for aides or volunteers. Supervision is usually performed by a person outside the particular child-caregiver relationship in which the staff member works. An aide should not be supervised by an assistant teacher or teacher if that teacher's own job performance directly interacts with the aide's. Distance lessens personal involvement and increases the likelihood of objectivity. Also, if problems are observed, an outside supervisor can work with all staff involved. For directors who must assume teaching responsibilities and function part-time as director-teachers, achieving the necessary distance for effective supervision can be very difficult. Few programs have the financial resources or large enough staffs to justify a full-time supervisory position.

Directors insert supervision into their schedule by:

- planning short, unannounced spot checks for frequent observation of program and staff;
- varying working hours to gain an overall picture of the total day;
- observing daily routines for meals, naps, and transitions from one activity to another in order to check center processes and procedures;
- choosing different days and hours to observe individual staff members for comprehensive supervision; and
- scheduling large time blocks for critical observation of individual employees and program activities for further evaluation and planning.

Problems in Supervision

Two problems stand out as obstacles for directors involved with supervision: knowing how to supervise and finding the time to do it. Neither problem is easily remedied.

Knowing How to Supervise. Specific training in supervision principles and techniques is offered in advanced graduate courses. Master's degree candidates or supervisory certificate candidates (who typically already have a master's degree) enroll in these courses. Child care directors need only have a high school diploma, associate degree, or bachelor's degree with early childhood course work to be hired to manage a child care program in all states. Few directors will have had supervisory training at colleges and universities.

Directors learn to supervise by trial and error, by taking the initiative to attend child care administrative workshops offered on the topic or by making an extra effort to locate and read resources. Many directors trade ideas with each other when opportunities permit. If a director does not have some personal talent for supervision, along with access to some resources or support services for supervision skill development, staff supervision will not be effectively used as a center management tool.

Finding Time to Supervise. Supervision is time consuming. Procedures and forms need to be planned, observations made often, conferences held with staff, and reports written and filed. In the press of daily demands and when weighed against higher priority tasks, supervision can appear to take too much time and to promise benefits too far in the future.

Supervision Record-Keeping

Supervision procedures and outcomes must be documented. Supervision requires paperwork and filing.

Procedures and Forms. The personnel handbook should contain a listing of the major steps in the sequence of supervision for each type of employee, a copy of all observation forms and rating scales to be used, and a statement of the purpose of supervision and the use of supervision data. If there is no supervision section in the personnel handbook, the director should prepare this set of papers and distribute them to each employee well in advance of any actual supervision. Whenever changes or additions are made in supervision procedures, staff should receive written notice. Supervision is too important, and the resulting information too often used in a legal context, for the forms and procedures to be a surprise to employees. If employee contracts require supervision information for salary increase or continuation decisions, the forms and procedures for these purposes must be clearly labelled.

Supervision Schedules. The staff work schedule is a helpful tool for planning and organizing supervisory activities. The schedule helps the director identify potential trouble times, staff transition periods, and peaks for child enrollment and program activity. After observing a particular staff member, the director can place the date in the appropriate time slot for that employee. At a glance the director can see who has been observed and the date and time of observation.

Once a month the director should review the staff work schedule on which overall supervision dates are recorded. With month-by-month planning, the director should be assured of maintaining a balanced supervision schedule and be able to plan to meet any deadlines for supervision information required for contract reasons.

Organizing A Supervisory Program

Planning a supervision program begins with two questions. How a director answers these two questions determines the overall goals for supervision and the supervision strategies that will be compatible with achievement of the stated goals.

1. What is the reason for supervision in the program?
   - to monitor staff job performance
   - to identify areas for staff development
   - to ensure program integrity
   - to meet staff contract provisions
2. What information should be obtained through supervision?
   - observation data describing staff job performance
   - assessments of staff strengths and weaknesses useful for planning in-service and training experiences
   - assessment of activity selection and implementation in relation to the curriculum plan and philosophy of the program
   - summary ratings of staff performance

Meeting all these goals requires a number of interrelated supervision strategies: information sharing, observations, and conferences. Individual directors may choose a variety of techniques from each of these categories depending upon their personal supervision skills and the complexity of the programs they administer.

Supervision is a cyclical process with each phase leading into the next. Observations are followed by conferences, which in turn often lead to information sessions, which are designed to provide ideas and resources that will enhance staff performance.

Information Resources

The entry point into a supervision cycle should be information resources about the goals of supervision, observation instruments, and the conference process. Supervision is not "snoopervision," and staff have a right to know what the process and procedures will be. The following resources may be helpful in this respect:

Role Playing An active technique to teach and provide staff with practice in the skills of managing children's behavior and handling activity interactions effectively.

Questioning Demonstration of various levels of questioning to aid staff in developing children's thinking skills and to encourage flexible adult responses to situations.

Log A daily diary, either free form or organized around specific questions, in which staff record daily happenings and insights concerning children's behaviors and curriculum activities.

Materials Display An area for access to materials that could enhance skills. Allows staff to use resources at their own pace and initiative.

Weekly Meeting A forum for informal, but guided discussion and sharing of staff activities and concerns. Staff can use peers as resources.

Films Effective media to show classrooms, developmental levels, and teaching strategies as models.

Texts Organized study courses or guided reading with supervisor follow-up provides a common reference point for understanding children's behavior and curriculum planning.

Observation Techniques

Observation is by far the most widely used supervision strategy. Supervisors position themselves near an ongoing activity and record details of the staff member's performance. Supervisory observation is nonparticipatory, requiring the supervisor to blend into the background and observe activities as they naturally occur. Supervisors may record events during an observation or may do so immediately afterwards, depending on how distracting the recording would be to children or staff. Supervisors move with the flow of activity, but do not become involved or seek unnecessary eye-contact with children or staff member. The more frequently supervisors observe, the more staff and children become used to a supervisor's presence. Supervisors should actively intervene in ongoing activities *only* when the well-being of children or staff members is threatened.

The purpose of *observation instruments* is to systematize the recording of observation data and to help supervisors focus on pre-selected areas of staff performance. Instruments can be as simple as a set of questions that the supervisor responds to after observing. Or, instruments may be elegant coding schemes to capture both verbal, non-verbal teacher-child interactions. Supervisors may need special training to use these effectively. Observation instruments can be "home-grown"—developed by staff and director to meet the needs of the local program, or may be selected from a number of published instruments designed to be appropriate in a variety of early childhood settings.

Several variations on direct supervisor observation are useful for collecting information involving staff in the supervisory process and for documenting situations.

Self-evaluation provides an opportunity for staff to look closely at their behavior and growth. Staff can be asked to use whatever procedures and instruments the supervisor uses.

Tape recordings can be used to analyze the

effectiveness of the staff member's voice and types of questions the staff member is using when dealing with children in a variety of situations. They also provide documentation of questions and vocabulary of children. Videotape recordings allow staff to see themselves in a teaching role. They are excellent for picking up nonverbal communication and the total context affecting children's behaviors.

Conferences

Conferences should follow soon after the supervisory observations. If possible, give the staff member written feedback (a copy of the completed observation instrument, for example) at the conclusion of the observation. Supervisor and staff member then begin the conference on an equal footing. Keep conferences short (twenty to thirty minutes).

Whenever a staff member is formally observed, the director should conclude the observation with a written notice of a conference date. Using the staff work schedule, the director can select a conference time that is reasonable and make any necessary arrangements for substitutes or volunteers. Conferences should follow observations very closely in time.

At the conference the director should complete all forms and give the employee a copy. If any conference notes are to become part of the supervisor's record, the director must make duplicate copies for the employee. All records and forms should be placed immediately in the employee file and be considered confidential information.

In-Service and Training

For a center or program director, in-service and training experiences are fundamental management tools. Through these experiences the director meshes the skills and abilities of individual staff members with the activities and goals of the child care program. Often the terms *in-service* and *training* are used interchangeably, or combined as *in-service training*. We feel, however, that the terms should be distinguished since the goals, costs, and time frame are frequently different.

Generally, in-service experiences are characterized by:

- Meetings, workshops, and related activities that focus on the immediate tasks of staff as they implement the child care program
- Participation of entire staff or program area staff units
- On-site or nearby location
- Short duration
- Experiences emphasizing single topic in self-contained sessions
- Planning by program or sponsoring agency personnel or resource personnel from local community

Generally, training experiences are characterized by:

- Conferences, courses, seminars, and related activities selected to extend the skills and general knowledge base of individual staff members
- Higher costs since travel to institutions or conferences may be involved or substitutes hired to replace staff in training
- Longer durations, including several sessions and follow-up work
- Academic credit or formal certification of work completed, allowing the staff member to document participation

Role of In-Service and Training

In the broadest sense in-service and training experiences represent a continuous quest for quality. Trying to do better, seeking new ideas, refreshing interest, and fine-tuning current practices contribute to the dynamics of an active program. No matter how small the program or low the budget, no director can ignore in-service and training.

Staff Development. Staff come to programs with a wide variety of educational backgrounds and experience levels. Most staff benefit from specific information regarding the history and purpose of child care as differentiated from other types of early education programs. Staff also need immediate help in establishing themselves as part of a team of caregivers. The development of a person's "self-image" as a child care worker is the first goal of in-service experiences. As staff members acquire skills and years of service, continual clarification of this "self-image" is essential.

Program Support. In-service and training also fulfill a program support function. All child care programs develop their own routines and practices. Staff need to know the mechanics of local program implementation. In-service sessions on field trips, greeting and good-bye routines, meal procedures, and so forth help new and experienced staff work consistently and harmoniously together.

Children need activities. Programs need equipment. Sessions about the design of activities help staff to provide a consistent learning environment for children. Sessions that fire up the creative juices provide many ideas for activities; sessions that distribute the chores and budget dollars help to unite staff efforts. Many directors can easily handle program support sessions and schedule them on a frequent basis.

Staff who have participated in extensive training experiences outside the center may be able to plan program in-service for the entire staff.

Administrative Climate. Staff that know their job, know how the program operates, and feel part of a mutually supportive team of caregivers foster a positive administrative climate for the director. Delegation of tasks is easier, burdens and limitations can be shared, and difficulties can be faced together.

Staff work sessions can be social occasions as well as helpful periods for the program. Here staff members are making multiple sets of games to extend children's play opportunities. (Courtesy of U.S. Department of Housing and Urban Development, Washington, DC.)

Director's Responsibilities

The director is responsible for all aspects of planning, implementation, and assessment of the in-service and training experiences of the program staff. Decisions to use external training resources and to allocate in-service budget funds also reside with the director.

Designing Preservice Orientations. All new personnel need preservice training. A well-planned preservice experience provides incoming staff with information concerning the center and eases new employees into established center routine. Directors should take the time to draw up a checklist for these orientations. Box 11.4 presents some general guidelines. Note that employees must verify receipt of several personnel items. Indicate to employees that they are ex-

Box 11.4 Guidelines for a Preservice Orientation

Program

- Introduce program—brief history, auspices, structure
- Describe service and clientele
- Describe program structure (Provide employee with copy of descriptive materials on program)
  - Assumptions concerning children and their care
  - Program objectives
  - Program context
  - Support services
  - Parent role
- Tour center
- Observe program
- Meet with staff

Personnel

- Present written job description (A)
- Present copy of contract with hours, wages, and other terms of employment (B)
- Present copy of program personnel policies (C)
- Obtain signed statement that employee has received A, B, and C above
- Provide opportunity for employee to talk to appropriate person about benefits, payroll procedures, and so on
- Set up personnel folder for employee

Program Policy

- Review record-filing system
- Review confidentiality provisions for records
- Provide copy of daily schedule and discuss routines
- Review emergency procedures
- Review procedures for excursions and visitors

pected to become familiar with those policies and procedures. Some directors may wish to add items to cover specific jobs; for example, the cook will need a thorough review of financial procedures for food purchasing and an introduction to storage of meal preparation equipment. It is not necessary to schedule the center's preservice orientation on one day. Allowing several days will give the new employee an opportunity to observe more, meet staff in small groups, and have time to reflect on areas to question.

Assessing In-Service and Training Needs. The child care director can collect information about in-service and training needs by asking the staff as a group what kinds of in-service or training experiences they would like to have, and by reviewing staff performance and personnel records and identifying areas where individual staff could profit from further training experiences. A conference with individual staff members may be a useful adjunct to this procedure.

The simplest staff survey is an open-ended question: "What do you want to know more about?" or "What would you like for in-service this year?" Staff then write down topics, and the director tallies and ranks the topics. With just a little more effort a director can get additional, more detailed input from staff. For example, the director might use a series of questions such as the following:

- Would you like to have more information on the developmental aspects of the particular age you are working with?
- Do you need more information on particular content areas: science, math, language development?
- Would you like to see comparisons of educational approaches in different programs?
- Do you feel the need to have help in developing self-control in the child's behavior?
- Could you use tips on classroom management and organization?

- Do you need help in involving parents and developing parent rapport?
- Would you like to develop better observation skills?
- Do you feel the need for more information about first aid or on observing possible health problems?
- Would you like to find ways to increase staff morale or improve professionalism among the staff?
- Do you need to make free play more constructive or creative?
- Could we define tools to evaluate children's progress more effectively?

For individuals, privately compare job descriptions and staff performance ratings for each staff member. Look at details and content of child care-related educational training. Prepare a list of course work or content areas for further study. Meet with the staff member and finalize the list. Where possible, encourage the staff member to seek training on his own. Discuss use of early work release, training monies, or other support the program could offer. For each staff member try to finalize a list that identifies high priority training areas, areas of interest, and training required for advancement.

The director must look at the final list of topics from the staff survey and a similar list of training and in-service topics generated from the individual staff review and compile a master list of in-service and training topics. Since the director also has to make some decisions about funds and available resources, he or she should be prepared to present at a staff meeting three categories of in-service topics:

Rejected List of topics rejected and reasons why (repetition, not available, too expensive, inappropriate).

Priority List of topics for which resources are most favorable. The director will use this list to develop a yearly plan for in-service (see following section).

Possible List of courses, workshops, and conferences that individuals may attend with partial or full support from program. This list would include sessions provided through sponsoring agencies as part of their regulatory responsibility.

Tracking Participation. Attendance should be taken at all staff meetings and in-service sessions and recorded on a master sheet. When the director meets with the employee for periodic job performance evaluation, attendance figures should be transferred to the employee's file. The personal training plan should be revised as needed. Employees should submit copies of transcripts of all work taken outside the center, brief reports of all trips or meetings financed by the program or attended on their own time, and copies of all certificates awarded for work or participation in child care related trainings sessions. Documentation of in-service and training experiences gives the director an accurate picture of the extent and direction of individual staff development and provides a basis for discussing career development and progress toward desired educational levels.

Yearly Plans

The yearly plan for in-service training starts with a calendar marked with holidays, special events, and other staff program commitments. Next, the director looks at the list of in-service topics and makes a preliminary sorting of topics by format and likelihood of assembling resources or leaders for the sessions. Topics such as first aid, child abuse, or crisis counseling are probably best handled by specialized professionals from the community. The director can begin immediately to contact these professionals and schedule sessions as far in advance as possible. Where possible, substitutes or volunteers can be arranged for to cover the program while staff participate in these sessions. By being early in making a request and being very flexible about dates, directors stand the best chance of receiving the donated services or outreach efforts of these professionals. Directors may negotiate to pay material costs and provide meals and transportation, but they should try to minimize fees for consultant's time when possible. Chapter 15 discusses sources and strategies for finding such people. Certainly, if specific topics or the time of a particular professional is judged to be especially valuable for the staff, the director can allocate the in-service and training monies necessary and contract for their services. For some of these special topic in-service sessions the director may choose to invite parents or the general community to the session as well as staff. This larger audience can be an attraction for session leaders as it increases their outreach efforts.

Reviewing the remaining topics on the proposed in-service list, directors will find that some can be handled through "in-house" or director-initiated efforts. Four or five topics that are appropriate for intensive, two- to three-hour sessions should be selected. Directors can then schedule those sessions, blocking out appropriate times on the yearly calendar. Planning files for those sessions can be set up, and the intermediate deadlines for preparing materials for the session can be noted on a personal calendar.

Staff Meetings

In addition to in-service sessions the director plans and conducts regularly scheduled staff meetings. Because a child care center combines intense activity and team effort, frequent meetings are essential for staff communication and coordination. Staff meetings work best on a weekly basis, but scheduling meetings so frequently is difficult due to the long day the center is in operation, the staggered work schedule of employees, and the personal commitments of staff in the evenings and on the weekends. Often judicious use of volunteers during children's nap time can free staff for short meetings.

Staff meetings should be short, focused, and crisply conducted. The agenda for every meeting should include:

1. Center Business
   - Announcements about program procedures and activities (that is, new forms, fees, or enrollment procedures)
   - Descriptions of events affecting the program (that is, inspection reports or sponsoring agency meetings)
   - Discussion of staff activities
   - Polling of staff when appropriate to decide consensus for problem resolution
2. Information Sharing
   - Presentation of new resources and equipment
   - Distribution of articles or bibliographies of interest to staff
   - Reports from staff who have attended meetings or training sessions
3. Social Time
   - Special snacks and drink for staff (Staff may wish to rotate responsibility for this.)
   - Informal sharing of personal events and activities
4. Definite End
   - Nap and or snack bell for children is one signal

Staff Credentials

Regulations specify minimum educational or training levels required of staff in child care programs. Many staff exceed minimum requirements. Regulations frequently require some combination of an earned degree or course work and practical experience with young children.

Credentials or certificates are used by public education departments to categorize and verify the preparation and training levels of teachers. By graduating from an approved training program or by submitting records for review, individuals can obtain a teaching certificate. The teaching credential represents a "professionalization" of preparation and standardizes skill descriptions.

Many states have special certificate requirements for persons who want to teach young children. A teacher may be certified for Nursery–Third Grade (N-3), Kindergarten–Sixth

Grade (K-6), or Nursery-Kindergarten (N-K). These credentials almost always apply to persons wishing to teach in public or private schools. Child care staff may earn these credentials, but usually no credential is needed according to child care regulations.

It is tempting to support certification for child care staff along the lines of established public and private certificate requirements for teachers of young children. To do this, however, ignores three important realities of child care:

1. Many child care staff who are effective workers do not have (and may not want) the four-year college degree that a certification program requires.
2. Studies such as the National Day Care Study and the general weight of opinion indicate that workers trained in child development and tasks specific to the child care program perform as well as workers with broader, less specific training.
3. Money is very tight for child care programs. To raise staff qualification requirements in a manner that would increase costs to workers for preparation would inevitably "bust the budget" for staff salaries. Wages need to be higher now for all workers, not just for a highly trained, credentialed few.

The Child Development Associate (CDA) National Credentialing Program is an innovative and promising approach to recognizing and standardizing child care staff qualifications. The program operates under the auspices of the U.S. Department of Health and Human Services. Some are working to have the CDA incorporated into state licensing standards. Initially, the CDA was developed to assess competencies for caregivers who worked in centers with preschoolers, but recently ways have been developed to extend the CDA to home visitors, family day care providers, and caregivers who work with infants or with handicapped children. The CDA Credential is explained thoroughly in an application book available from the Child Development Associate National Credentialing Program, 1341 G Street, NW, Washington, DC 20005.

Issues

As might be expected with such a critical program component as staff, concerns are many and varied. Some are legitimate, universal concerns common to child care programs across the country. Others arise from particular mixes of local conditions. Whatever the issue, discussion of options must recognize three perspectives:

1. *Staff Perspective* For each staff member a job in the child care program is, at the minimum, a source of money to live on. For many staff members the job is also professionally meaningful, allowing them to work in an area and do tasks they enjoy.
2. *Parent Perspective* Parents entrust their children to staff members. Staff are the personal faces of child care. Whatever the program philosophy or parental reasons for using child care, there exists between parent and staff an expectation that the child will be taken care of, loved, and protected from harm by staff.
3. *Director's Perspective* Representing the program, the director must view staff as a precious resource that must be efficiently used to maximize the return on the dollar cost of staff salaries. Directors cannot be oblivious to personalities, but staff decisions need to be considered first from a management perspective.

Staff, parent, and director perspectives are not always compatible. Even when all three agree in principle, issues remain if lack of money, opportunities, or materials forces compromises.

Money: Staff Wages and Parent Fees

At the root of many disputes over staffing practices is the absence of enough money to meet all program expenses at desired levels. Staff want minimum wages as well as yearly merit and/or cost-of-living raises. Parents want affordable child care that does not eat up their after-tax income. Funding services set caps on funds available or do not raise support in line with increasing costs. There is no easy solution to resolving the issue of budget crunches; every solution will require staff, parent or program to make trade-offs each would deem undesirable.

Working Conditions: Burnout and Unions

Staff in child care programs generally function like a family. The strong interpersonal skills possessed by most child care workers as well as the atmosphere created by busy, happy, loving children contribute to the "family feeling." "We're all in this together" is a common expression of this comaraderie. Yet problems occur. Caring for children amidst limited resources and meager financial rewards often results in high turnover and burnout. Child care is a people-intense activity. Sociologists tell us that without special attention, workers in such activities often lose their motivation and get "used up" as they try to compensate personally for the many deficiencies of material and money. Often it is the best of the staff that burns out. Turnover deprives programs and children of experienced staff.

Frequently, staff are expected to make sacrifices to keep a program running on a low budget. These sacrifices may create daily working conditions that are uncomfortable or illegal. Benefits may be cut or may be nonexistent. Prolonged sacrifices, abuse of workers' rights, or simply unattractive working conditions are conducive conditions for union activity. Child care workers hope to ensure themselves that their voice is heard and needed at budget planning time through union organizations.

Training: Career Ladders and Certification

NAEYC has recently adopted a position statement dealing with job titles and career ladders, along with salaries and benefits. It offers a useful standard and yardstick of comparability to those concerned with this issue.

Increasingly, research findings point to staff-child interactions as the key to quality child care. Staff with training in child development, early childhood education, and supervised field experiences with young children appear to be the best qualified. Specific training rather than formal degrees seems to be appropriate for child care workers. In the future child care workers can expect some kind of pressure to acquire such training. Debate continues over whether formal certification for child care workers is needed or is desirable. Training experiences and relevant degree-granting programs are in short supply. Who pays for the training? If trained workers are more desirable, will they cost more in salary demands? Can we afford trained child care staffs? Can we afford *not* to have them?

Very few people spend a lifetime in child care. One reason they leave is lack of adequate job challenge. After three years as head teacher, or five years as director, what next? Some degree of challenge can be obtained by moving to another program or perhaps increasing job responsibilities in the current one. But, in reality, the career ladder in child care is a short one. To go from teacher to director *is* a major change and requires that a person have managerial and financial skills in addition to child care expertise. To go beyond program director, though, removes a person almost totally from direct child care and requires advanced degrees. Careers in child care are built primarily around the personal rewards and intrinsic challenges a person can maintain on the job. Low pay and low status for child care workers mitigate strongly against longevity in the job.

Recruitment: Males and Minorities

Program directors and parents often mention that children should be exposed to good role models and experience care from a number of concerned adults. Many programs make special efforts to hire men as staff members. Parents may influence programs to recruit staff who are compatible and sympathetic to their culture and language.

Summary

All child care programs rely on a staff of skilled workers to perform a variety of tasks. Program staff, who are responsible for the daily implementation of the program, include teachers and aides. Support staff, such as cooks, custodians, and secretaries, do essential jobs that would otherwise take teachers away from the children. Other occasional staff include substitutes, student interns, Foster Grandparents, and volunteers.

The selection of staff should follow an orderly, planned sequence: recruitment, interviews, documentation of credentials, screening, and final selection. As part of the record-keeping duties associated with personnel management, the director must create and file contracts, write and disseminate a comprehensive personnel policy, and maintain detailed records for each employee. It is the director's responsibility to inform all staff members of salary scales, benefits, and grievance procedures.

To satisfy legal requirements and meet program needs, staff have to be deployed effectively throughout the day. The director can calculate the most efficacious staff-child ratios based on enrollment figures or average daily attendance.

Supervision involves the regular observation of program activity, staff functioning, and child growth in order to monitor the program's quality. Staff attitudes toward supervision are crucial, and the director can help staff members accept and learn to use the supervision. The supervisor generally unobtrusively observes a staff member's activity and records details of the interchanges with children. Later a conference between supervisor and staff member allows time for discussion and evaluation.

In-service experiences are educational meetings or workshops for the entire staff in the center itself. Training sessions are typically selected for individual members for particular skill-building and often take place away from the center. Both in-service and training offer the benefits of staff development, program support, and a positive administrative climate. Directors are responsible for organizing orientations for new employees, assessing the need for in-service and training, and tracking the staff's participation in such programs.

An important issue for child care staff today is certification, or credential programs. Credentialing may raise the quality of child care, but it may also increase the cost to parents as wages go up. One promising approach is the Child Development Associate (CDA) program.

Resources

General

Almy, M. (1982). Interdisciplinary preparation for leaders in early education and child development. In S. Kilmer (Ed.), *Advances in early education and day care: Vol. 2.* Greenwich, CT: JAI Press.

Butler, A. L. (1974). *Early childhood education: Planning and administering programs* (Chap. 3). New York: Van Nostrand.

Cherry, C., Harkness, B., & Kuzma, K. (1973). *Nursery school management guide* (Chap. 10). Belmont, CA: Lear Siegler/Fearon.

Click, P. (1981). *Administration of schools for young children* (2nd ed.) (Sec. 3). Albany, NY: Delmar Publishing.

Combs, A. W., Avila, D. L., & Purkey, W. W. (1971). *Helping relationships: Basic concepts for the helping professions.* Boston: Allyn and Bacon.

Decker, C. A., & Decker, J. R. (1980). *Planning and administering early childhood programs* (2nd ed.) (Chaps. 6 & 7). Columbus, OH: Charles E. Merrill, 1980.

Evans, E. B., Shub, B., & Weinstein, M. (1971). *Day care: How to plan and operate a day care center* (Chaps. 7 & 8). Boston: Beacon Press.

Katz, L. G. (1970). Teaching in preschools: Roles and goals. *Children, 17* (2), 42–48.

Peters, D. L., & Fears, L. M. (1974). Program personnel. In R. W. Colvin & E. M. Zaffiro (Eds.), *Preschool education.* New York: Springer.

Provence, S., Naylor, A., & Patterson, J. (1977). *The challenge of day care* (Chap. 9). New Haven, CT: Yale University Press.

Sciarra, D. J., & Dorsey, A. G. (1979). *Developing and administering a child care center* (Chaps. 9 & 11). Boston: Houghton Mifflin.

Spodek, B. (Ed.). (1974). *Teacher education.* Washington, DC: National Association for the Education of Young Children.

Stevens, J. H., & King, E. W. (1976). *Administering early childhood education programs* (Chap. 7). Boston: Little, Brown.

Staff Positions

Boressaff, T. (1983). *Children, the early childhood classroom & you: A guide for students and volunteer assistants.* New York: Early Childhood Council of New York City.

Bouverat, R. W., Skeen, B. S., & York, M. E. (1983). *A survey of state certification requirements of young children.* Washington, DC: National Association for the Education of Young Children.

Brophy, J. E., Good, T. L., & Nedler, S. E. (1975). *Teaching in the preschool.* New York: Harper & Row.

Fogarino, S., & Reynolds, A. (1974). *Careers in child care.* Washington, DC: Day Care and Child Development Council of America.

Hart, B. (1982). So that teachers can teach: Assigning roles and responsibilities. *Topics in Early Childhood Special Education, 2* (1), 1–8.

Hess, R. D., Price, G. C., Dickson, W. P., & Conroy, M. (1981). Difference roles in mothers and teachers: Contrasting styles of child care. In S. Kilmer (Ed.), *Advances in early education and day care: Vol. 1.* Greenwich, CT: JAI Press.

Host, M. S., & Heller, P. B. (1971). *Day care 7: Administration.* Washington, DC: U.S. Department of Health, Education and Welfare, Office of Child Development.

NAEYC Position statement on nomenclature, salaries, benefits, and the status of the early childhood profession (1984). *Young Children, 40* (1), 52–55.

Rose, I. D., & White, M. E. (1974). *Child care and development occupations: Competency based teaching modules.* Washington, DC: U.S. Government Printing Office.

Schindler-Rainman, E., & Lippitt, R. (1977). *The volunteer: Community creative use of human resources.* La Jolla, CA: University Associates.

Seaver, J. W., Cartwright, C. A., Ward, C. B., & Heasley, C. A. (1979). *Careers with young children: Making your decision.* Washington, DC: National Association for the Education of Young Children.

Spodek, B. (1972). Staff requirements in early childhood education. In I. J. Gordon (Ed.), *Early childhood education: The seventy-first yearbook of the National Society for the Study of Education: Part II* (pp. 339–365). Chicago: University of Chicago Press.

Todd, V. E., & Hunter, G. H. (1973). *The aide in early childhood education.* New York: Macmillan.

Staff Selection and Termination

Buese, R. (1984). Staff selection: Using group employment interviews. *Exchange,* October, 29–31.

Cannon, N. (1979). Rights of child care workers: A prototype code of rights. *Child Care Information Exchange, 10,* 6–8.

Child Care Staff Education Project. (1982). How to develop an effective grievance procedure. *Child Care Information Exchange, 23,* 37–39.

Day care personnel management. (1979). Atlanta, GA: Southern Regional Education Board.

Neugebauer, R. (1982). Selection interviews: Avoiding the pitfalls. *Child Care Information Exchange, 23,* 1–6.

Recruitment and selection of staff: A guide for managers of preschool and child care programs. (1985). Washington, DC: U.S. Department of Health and Human Services.

Staff Deployment

Blake, M. E. (Ed.). (1972). *Day care aides: A guide for inservice training* (2nd ed.). New York: National Federation of Settlements and Neighborhood Centers.

Cohen, M. D. (Ed.). (1971). *Helps for day care workers 1: A lap to sit on . . . and much more.* Washington, DC: Association for Childhood Educational International.

McFadden, D. N. (Ed.). (1972). *Early childhood development programs and services: Planning for action.* Washington, DC: National Association for the Education of Young Children.

Morgan, G. G. (1973). *Regulation of early childhood programs* (rev. ed.). Washington, DC: Day Care and Child Development Council of America.

Prosser, W. R. (n.d.). *Day care in the seventies: Some thoughts.* Washington, DC: Office of Planning Research and Evaluation, Office of Economic Opportunity.

Ruopp, R. R., & Travers, J. (1982). Janus faces day care: Perspectives on quality and cost. In E. F. Zigler & E. W. Gordon (Eds.), *Day care: Scientific and social policy issues* (pp. 72–101). Boston: Auburn House.

Supervision

Goldman, R. M., & Anglin, L. (1979). Evaluating your caregivers: Four observation systems. *Day Care and Early Education,* Fall, 40.

Litman, F. (1971). Supervision and involvement of paraprofessionals in early childhood education. In R. M. Anderson & G. H. Shane (Eds.), *As the twig is bent* (pp. 368–377). Boston: Houghton Mifflin.

Madle, R. A. (1982). Behaviorally based staff performance management. *Topics in Early Childhood Special Education, 2* (1), 73–83.

Marks, J. R., Stoops, E., & King-Stoops, J. (1978). *Handbook of educational supervision* (2nd ed.). Boston: Allyn and Bacon.

Seaver, J. W., & Cartwright, C. A. (1983). A tri-level model for internship and supervision. *Revista Cayey, 15* (38), 46–55.

In-Service and Training

Adler, J. (1981). *Fundamentals of group child care: A textbook and instructional guide for child care workers.* Cambridge, MA: Ballinger.

Diamondstone, J. (1980). *Designing, leading, and evaluating workshops for teachers and parents: A manual for trainers and leadership personnel in early childhood education.* Ypsilanti, MI: High/Scope Press.

Donaldson, L., & Scannell, E. (1978). *Human resource development: The new trainer's guide.* Reading, MA: Addison-Wesley.

Early childhood teacher education guidelines. (1982). Washington, DC: NAEYC.

Farrell, G. (n.d.). *Guidelines for the development of the XX training plan criteria.* Washington, DC: U.S. Department of Health, Education and Welfare, Administration for Public Services.

Greenberg, P. (1975). *Day care do-it-yourself staff growth program.* Washington, DC: The Growth Program.

Greenman, J., & Fuqua, R. (Eds.). (1984). *Making day care better: Training, evaluation, and the process of change.* New York: Teachers' College Press.

Haupt, D. (1972). Personnel and Personnel Training. In D. M. McFadden (Ed.), *Early childhood development programs and services: Planning for action* (pp. 111–116). Washington, DC: NAEYC/Battelle Monograph Series no. 2.

Honig, A. S., & Fears, L. M. (1974). Practicum. In R. W. Colvin & E. M. Zaffiro (Eds.), *Preschool education* (pp. 171–198). New York: Springer Publishing.

Jones, L., Hardy, S. B., & Rhodes, D. H. (1981). *The child development associate program: A guide to program administration.* Washington, DC: U.S. Department of Health and Human Services, Office of Human Development Services.

Kasindorf, M. E. (1980). *Competencies: A self guide to competencies in early childhood education.* Atlanta, GA: Humanics Limited.

Moore, S. (1972). The training of day care and nursery school personnel. In D. M. McFadden (Ed.), *Early childhood development programs and services: Planning for action* (pp. 117–126). Washington, DC: NAEYC/Battelle Monograph Series no. 2.

Rothenberg, D. (Comp.). (1979). *Directory of education programs for adults who work with children.* Washington, DC: National Association for the Education of Young Children/ERIC-EECE.

Schwertfeger, J. (1972). Issues in cooperative training, the university and the center. In D. M. McFadden (Ed.), *Early childhood development programs and services: Planning for action* (pp. 101–110). Washington, DC: NAEYC/Battelle Monograph Series no. 2.

Seaver, J. W., & Cartwright, C. A. (1976). *Early childhood student teaching.* University Park, PA: Pennsylvania State University, College of Education. (ERIC Document Reproduction Service No. ED 130 759)

Shaw, S. (1982). Facilitating professional development of early childhood personnel. *Day Care Journal, 1,* 43–48.

Warnat, W. I. (1980). Early childhood education programs: How responsive is higher education to training needs? *Journal of Teacher Education, 31* (4), 21–26.

Staff Meetings

Hoge, C. S. (1975). *Better meetings: A handbook for trainers of policy councils and other decision-making groups.* Atlanta, GA: Humanics Ltd.

Managing meetings. (1982). *Child Care Information Exchange, 26,* 17–24.

Schindler-Rainman, E., & Lippitt, R. (1975). *Taking your meetings out of the doldrums.* San Diego, CA: University Associates.

Smith, C. A. (1975). *Better meetings.* Atlanta, GA: Humanics Ltd.

Successful meetings. (1980). San Francisco, CA: Public Management Institute.

This, L. E. (1972). *The small meeting planner.* Houston, TX: Gulf Publishing.

Issues

Ade, W. (1982). Professionalization and its implications for the field of early childhood education. *Young Children, 37* (3), 25–32.

Cogan, M. L. (1975). Current issues in the education of teachers. In K. Ryan (Ed.), *Teacher education: Seventy-fourth yearbook of the National Society for the Study of Education* (pp. 204–229). Chicago: University of Chicago Press.

Gold, D., & Reis, M. (1979). *Male teachers in the early school years: Do they make a difference? A review of the literature.* (ERIC Document Reproduction Service No. ED 171 387)

Jorde, P. (1982). *Avoiding burnout: Strategies for managing time, space, and people in early childhood.* Alamo, CA: Acropolis.

Peters, D. L., & Kostelnick, M. J. (1981). Current research in day care personnel preparation. In S. Kilmer (Ed.), *Advances in early education and day care: Vol. 2.* Greenwich, CT: JAI Press.

Whitebrook, M. et al. (1981). Who's minding the child care workers? A look at staff burn-out. *Children Today, 10* (1), 2–6.

12

Budgets and Funding

Introduction

Child care services are directly affected by money. Total dollars available to a program and the source of those dollars define the services that the program can provide. Managing child care money is an exercise in accounting guided by policy. Whether it's petty cash disbursements for Halloween pumpkins, equipment orders for tricycles, proposal applications for new programs, or pay raises for staff—every financial transaction is an example of program policy in action.

Directors must manage funds according to established priorities and policies. They must have basic accounting skills, understand budgeting, and be able to use money to achieve program goals through effective financial management techniques. Directors frequently cite stress and worry about money as one of the primary factors contributing to burnout and job dissatisfaction (see Figure 12.1). Securing program funds is never an easy effort, and few directors are well prepared initially for the tasks of financial management. Directors who understand the processes, however, have a powerful tool and, ultimately, control the shape and quality of the child care program.

This chapter covers all the dollar issues of child care. We begin with a broad look at money's influence on a program and the way program staff decide money questions. Then we get down to the nuts and bolts: types of budgets and procedures for designing a budget; accounting methods; and standard financial management techniques. Costs and fees, the most obvious elements of money management, can be handled in a variety of ways. Apart from parent fees, income may come from public and private sources through reimbursements, funding proposals, and fund raisers. Finally, we examine child care programs financed by employers or chain organizations.

Money and Program Policy

Money is a yardstick of worth: High price tags have become synonymous with great worth. This notion influences the child care system directly in terms of how much money is available to programs, and more subtly in terms of the value we place on child care services. In spirit and rhetoric we acknowledge the importance of child care, yet with pocketbook and votes we do not support high child care costs. Those who work in programs know that good child care costs money. What mothers and families have been doing for generations—tending and rearing children—costs dearly when purchased on the open market. Also, as more mothers enter and remain in the work force, there is increased need for *paid* child care. Demand and changed social circumstances have moved child care away from the old practices of free or bartered care. Public attitudes, however, do not seem to have changed to reflect this difference. Parents who say they cannot afford to spend large percentages of their wages on child care still want high quality care. Staff who are not paid salaries commensurate with their training, experience, and work responsibilities are still expected to provide quality care. Many programs continually push against capacity limits in the name of economy of scale and size efficiency. Cutting corners, keeping costs down, and making do are coping strategies familiar to child care administrators.

Figure 12.1 Raising money for child care has never been easy. (Children's Defense Fund, Washington, DC; used with permission.)

How Money Shapes A Program

Contrary to popular opinion the answer to every director's dream is not an unlimited amount of money. Directors still need to allocate funds, make selective purchase decisions, and justify expenditures in terms of program goals. The total number of dollars available to a program is an insufficient indicator of program quality or service levels. Many programs rely heavily on volunteer time, donated materials, and other "in-kind" contributions. Certain kinds of child care require more dollars to run—infant care more than school-age care, care in urban areas more than in rural locales, care that meets federal standards more than privately purchased or most proprietary care.

Three factors—source of funds, stability of funds, and established spending patterns—influence the impact of total dollar amount on program operation.

Source of Funds. Child care dollars always seem to come with strings attached. Government funds require programs to meet specified standards and may give priority or restrict service to certain client groups. Matching dollars may be required, forcing programs to secure local support. Funds may be restricted to food purchases, program supplies, or special consultant salaries. These restrictions make good sense in light of the funder's priorities, but they can curtail a program's fiscal flexibility. When parent fees are high, parents may have stronger feelings about their participation in policy decisions or their right to have their service expectations met. Whatever the source of funds, the door is opened for some outside participation in program policy decisions and, perhaps, daily operation.

Stability of Funds. Reliable funding levels give programs the luxury of time for preparation, planning, and anticipation of events. The stability of income sources for a program determines the "crisis" threshold and the amount of staff time that must be diverted from daily operation to survival. Special funds for start-up costs, periodic capital equipment outlays, and one-time expenses such as a bus purchase or bathroom renovation are generally easily incorporated into program routines. Seed-money for special ideas, demonstration projects, and supplementary program services are often less easily accommodated over the long term since these additional funds help set up new services but also generate high expectations for future services. If the funds run out, many programs scramble to keep things going and struggle to adjust expectations to less ambitious activities that are more in keeping with the program's long-range capabilities.

Nonprofit child care programs may operate so close to the edge financially that minor fluctuations in what are basically reliable funding sources cause major problems. Fee collection may be delayed because the program was slow to reach capacity enrollment. Reimbursement payments may be late, causing cash on hand to be insufficient to meet a payroll; or the program may be unable to afford the interest on a short-term loan. Sometimes fiscal crises are unavoidable. Good fiscal management techniques call for identifying potential crises, calculating the odds, and then taking steps to "buffer" crises when they do occur.

Established Spending Patterns. One of the trickiest budget situations to manage arises when program expenditures seem to be set in concrete, either through legal obligation (for example, mortgage payments, employee salaries and benefits, or other contractural agreements) or force of habit (for example, deciding to buy new puzzles every year or never to pay more than twenty dollars a day for consultant's travel). Certainly, legal obligations must be met, but some programs lock up such a large percentage of their total budget that the director may feel that all that's left is petty cash. Changing prior spending patterns takes persuasion and assertiveness. Each budget expenditure should be justified in a manner that is consistent with current program goals. It is the only way to ensure that each year's budget fits the program, the personnel, and the circumstances of that year.

Who Controls Money Decisions

In an owner-operated program, one person is likely to be in complete charge of all financial decisions. However, for most programs, control over money is spread over several administrative positions. What is significant then is the extent of each individual's control and his or her relationship (either through authority or influence) with the program director. Directors must have real control over most money decisions directly related to daily program operations and must be able to exercise credible influence over other financial matters that indirectly affect their programs. The goal for program financial management within the organization is to establish useful fiscal checks and balances to protect the organization's interest but allow the director fiscal responsibility on matters that affect daily program operation.

Accountants. *Accounting* is the system and procedures for keeping track of fiscal activity. Accountants are professionally trained to set up, maintain, and audit program fiscal records. They can be hired as consultants or as employees in a large organization. An accountant can help a program gather fiscal information, set up recording procedures, and organize the information. Accountants cannot be expected to decide such things as whether raising fees will change the client mix of the program. But they can tell a program, for example, that on the basis of current accounts more income is necessary to meet expenses and that raising fees is one of several financial options. Accountants, especially those familiar with social service agencies, can provide valuable assistance in relating financial data to program decisions.

Bookkeepers. The actual process and work of accounting is called *bookkeeping*. A central office staff bookkeeper may keep account ledgers and bank account records for most financial matters. Competent bookkeeping allows a program director to assess the current state of accounts, observe cash-flow patterns, and spot developing fiscal problems before crisis occurs.

Many of the typical check and balance techniques used to monitor fiscal expenditures involve bookkeeping procedures. For example, two-signature check accounts operate under the assumption that if two people approve the expenditure it must be okay. (Actually, in practice this is often a spurious monitoring procedure, because the second person assumes the first person must have checked and both may resent the hassle of obtaining two signatures.) Positive attitudes and convenient procedures are necessary for monitoring to be effective. It is worth the time and effort to determine which procedures are most appropriate for child care programs.

Since bookkeeping records are basically information, they must be understandable and accessible to those who need the information. Miscommunication and personality differences between bookkeeper and director can inhibit the flow and exchange of information. Directors may not be able to "read" account ledgers and may have little motivation to quiz the bookkeeper about meaning and interpretation of numbers. Directors who keep their own books may find that the time needed for daily entries is hard to squeeze out of an already busy workday.

All of this points to bookkeepers and bookkeeping procedures as a primary trouble spot in financial management procedures for programs. This is where the director's fiscal decisions mesh with the existing formal accounting procedures of the organization. The measure of true financial control is how well the director negotiates this juncture.

Board of Directors. Ultimately the board of directors or a similar advisory group sets the overall fiscal policy for the program. Decisions about where to pursue external funds, how much to ask for, and what purposes and programs to support are the province of the board. Boards may be involved in labor contract negotiations that set staff salaries and benefits. They have responsibility for approving major capital projects, overseeing building programs, and approving facility rental agreements and renovation plans. Boards may also hire accountants, tax lawyers, and auditors. Chapter 15 includes an extended discussion of the role and responsibilities of a board of directors, including the board's fiscal activities.

Money Management

> If child care centers were generously funded, the consequences of ineffective money management would not be so severe. Most centers, however, are seriously underfunded and are barely able to pay their bills from month to month. The waste of a few dollars here, or the loss of some expected income there, can cause a center to delay or even cancel a payday. If income and expenses are not carefully planned and controlled, a center can go out of business in a remarkably short period of time. (Neugebauer, 1979, p. 31)

Money management begins with a budget. A *budget* is an itemized statement of income and expenditures. It summarizes financial data and formats the data to allow efficient comparison and analyses of information. Budgets translate program services into dollars. Every item in the budget represents a decision about the program. A carefully developed and administered budget requires intimate knowledge of the daily operational requirements of the child care program. Whoever controls the budget process controls the program.

The budget process is more than a meeting or two at which votes are taken on budget adoption. It is a series of working sessions that thrash out priorities and document needs. Without active participation in these working sessions, directors will find their control over program expenditures limited.

Once adopted, a budget serves as a reference point and a guide for financial activity. Careful analyses of budget account activity throughout the year help directors monitor the program's fiscal status. Adjustments can be made in income and expenditure levels before major crises develop. Effective money management affects the daily operation of the program and builds confidence among staff. Everyone can focus on the care and activities of children knowing that bills are paid, wages assured, and supplies available to support their efforts.

Budgets and Accounting

Budgets set financial goals for an organization and reflect internal management decisions regarding type and priority of services. Accounting systems and bookkeeping procedures provide the tools to record financial activities and to track the organization's fiscal progress. Only when total dollars are viewed in relation to program goals can we begin to assess how much money is needed to operate the program. Even then the task is not straightforward.

This section provides a brief introduction to the terms, principles, and procedures involved in budget making and bookkeeping. It is designed to increase your familiarity with financial aspects of program management. Those who need to set up or maintain budgets and books and who want additional guidance will find several excellent books and guides listed in the resources section.

Types of Budgets

Budgets are prepared on an annual basis and cover a twelve-month period called a *fiscal year* (FY). A program's fiscal year may be a calendar year, January 1 through December 31, or it may be chosen to coincide with the fiscal year used by funding agencies.

The *annual operating budget* is, in reality, often a composite of all the various budgets a program needs to prepare to meet funding and reporting requirements. Child care programs may prepare different versions of annual operating budgets to match fiscal years and budget categories used by different funding sources. This common problem somewhat complicates the budget planning process. While each budget version includes the same financial data, they differ in their time periods, rationales, and uses. Some common examples are:

Subsidized-Deficit Budgets Community organizations such as United Way, the county commissioners, church charities, and service organizations may require documentation for subsidies. The budget estimates costs and projects income to identify the amount of deficit. This type of budget is used to secure operating fund support.

Service Contract Budgets Local, state, or federal units contract with the program to provide child care services. This budget specifies the costs, kind, and amount of service the program will provide as an agent for the funding body. Conditions of service and payment are given. Contracts are monitored for service delivery and fiscal compliance. A service contract budget is not necessarily a complete fiscal picture of the child care program. It emphasizes those services and costs associated with the contract. An agency or sponsor may have other child care services that are not fiscally related to the contract. Service contracts are the basis of public funding. This is a balanced budget in which costs should be fully covered by payments.

Grant Budgets Demonstration projects and special programs funded by external groups require budgets. Grants are almost never awarded to cover recurring operating expenses. Grant budgets are prepared on an annual basis for the duration of the grant. They tend to be more flexible than other types of budgets. Grants provide sufficient money to carry out proposed projects. Programs need to be fiscally accountable for the awards, but problems with insufficient funds are rare. Grant budgets are set to expend the total amount of the grant award before the end of the grant period.

Start-Up Budget Starting a child care program from scratch is costly. Initial capital and cash outlays are high and income is delayed and unpredictable. A start-up budget includes items that are one-time costs necessary to open the program. Obtaining funds for initial capital outlays is difficult, if not impossible, for many programs. It is also a guesstimate of regular annual operation costs and income. Until a program has been in operation for awhile it has no financial track record. Start-up budgets

Table 12.1 Tracking Income Sources

INCOME SOURCE	1980 INCOME	1981 INCOME	1982 INCOME	1983 INCOME	1984 INCOME
Gifts	$15,200	$15,195	$250	$295	$250

require serious, careful attention and involve budget and accounting analysis techniques specifically geared to the questions and conditions of start-up. If you are thinking of starting a program, we urge you to review the books *Managing the Day Care Dollars* (Morgan) and *Day Care Financial Management* (Travis & Perreault) for detailed analyses of budget considerations for program start-up.

The annual operating budget that most directors work with and that guides the fiscal management of a child care program is a self-supporting budget, or a budget that meets or exceeds expenses. This budget may project a year-end balance between income and expenditures or a profit depending on the fiscal goals of the program. Throughout the year, interim financial reports are related to this budget.

Developing a Budget

There are two parts to a budget: income and expenditures. Budget preparation involves the identification and documentation of all contributing factors to program income and expenses. Program directors, accounting staff, administrators, and committees such as the finance committee of the board of directors share in the task. The first step is to create a comprehensive, centralized data bank about income and expenditures.

Estimating Income. The cash resources available to a program for its operating budget constitute income. For budgeting purposes each source of income is identified separately. Actual dollar totals (if known) and conservative projections are used to establish an estimate of total cash income. The following list of sources illustrates the range of possibilities:

Fees
Transportation charges
USDA Food Program (if applicable)
Other government sources (excluding USDA)
Gifts and donations (grants, memorials, bequests, legacies, pledges, and endowments)
Investment income (dividends, interest, bank accounts, distribution or earnings, and revenue from rental or leasing of property)
Loans
Sale or exchange of property
Fund raising

When developing a budget, programs may use a simple historical tracking approach to estimate income for the coming year. In the example shown in Table 12.1, the program received large demonstration grants in 1980 and 1981. In subsequent years gifts consisted of irregular contributions from local organizations and individuals. In the absence of any expected large grants or progressive giving campaign the budget projection for FY 1984 is realistically set at $250. Similar budget projections can be calculated for each of the income sources using past performance levels plus knowledge of current or qualifying conditions.

Utilization Rate. Parent fees represent a big source of income for programs. Programs can be financed entirely by parent fees. Maximum fee income is determined by multiplying the capacity of the program by the fee charged per child per month. For example:

25 (child capacity)
× $150 (monthly per child fee)
× 12 (months)
= $45,000 (maximum fee income)

Actual fee income never equals maximum fee income. Centers frequently are underenrolled (part-time children, delays in enrollment), fees are not paid (bad debts), or fee policies are based on actual attendance, not enrollment, thus reducing the fee income from individual children because of illness, vacations, and holidays. Reimbursement from government-funding sources may be based on actual attendance, not enrollment. Morgan (1982) presents a detailed discussion of the problems and considerations for fees based on attendance versus enrollment. Dividing actual fee income by maximum fee income results in a figure that represents the utilization rate (expressed as a percentage) for the program. For example:

$$\frac{\text{actual} \quad \$42{,}578}{\text{maximum} \quad \$45{,}000} = 94.6\% \text{ utilization rate}$$

When estimating fee income for budgeting purposes, directors use the utilization rate to adjust the budget projections. For example, a director anticipating an increase in fees from $150 to $165 per month may project income from fees by computing the new maximum fee income and multiplying that by the utilization rate for the previous year.

new maximum fee
= 25 (child capacity)
× $165 (new monthly fee per child)
× 12 = $49,500

projected income from fees
= $49,500 (maximum fee)
× 94.6% (previous year's utilization rate)
= $46,827

In-Kind Donations. Payment in kind, or *in-kind donations,* are a special and valued source of income for child care programs. Donated supplies and services can make it possible for an underfunded program to provide a reasonable quality level of service. The following are common examples:

Supplies and materials
- Food for snacks, parties, or picnics
- Equipment and toys
- Art supplies
- Space for program

Services
- Clerical services (typing, bookkeeping)
- Utility repairs (plumbing, electricity)
- Repair and maintenance

Trips and entertainment
- Field trips and tours with guides
- Fee waivers for admission
- Visiting theater groups or performers

Time
- Professional consulting
- Unpaid staff overtime
- Parent time for fund raising
- Volunteers
- Committee work or meetings

To qualify as an in-kind donation, supplies and services must be useful to the program. They should be distinguished clearly from cash income but assigned a cash value equal to the cost of purchase. Some auditors believe that in-kind donations have to meet a test of control and direct administration by the program. This precludes programs from counting, as in-kind donations, services (such as medical screenings) routinely provided by other agencies.

Accurate estimates of the cash value of in-kind donations allow programs to calculate realistic costs for services provided. For many programs, in-kind donations are substantial parts of their budgets. Facility space may be donated. Transportation costs may be assumed by another group. Volunteers may be needed to maintain acceptable staff-child ratios. Ignoring the value of these in-kind services makes the program look as if service is cheaper than full costs would indicate. The term *fully costed* refers to a program budget based on cash and in-kind donations as income sources balanced against expenditures. Fully costed programs can be meaningfully compared as to level of service delivery and cost per service unit. Ignoring or disguising in-kind donations only deludes

Consultant services are an extremely valuable in-kind contribution. A university teacher leads a staff training session on child development. (Courtesy of U.S. Department of Health and Human Services, Washington, DC.)

parents and the public into thinking that child care is not expensive.

In-kind donations play a particularly important role for programs in which funders or sponsors require matching funds. Funders often want some assurance that local communities support programs. Additionally, some funders feel that in order to have a true stake, programs must commit some of their own resources to the effort. Local programs may be required to provide 5, 10, or 25 percent of the total funding amount. Conditions vary, but in most instances documented in-kind donations will be accepted as match. In view of the cash-strapped state of most child care programs, the importance of in-kind donations for match requirements cannot be overemphasized.

Loans. Delays in contract payments, reimbursements, and fee payments sometimes create cash shortages for a program. New programs may find that income from fees and other sources increases more slowly than planned. A short-term loan may be sought. Loans cost money for interest, but may be a reasonable solution instead of shutting down the program. Loans are also used for capital expenditures such as equipment and building renovation. Loans that work toward asset and equity accumulation are not as risky for individual program survival as loans that are substitutes for operating income.

Estimating Expenditures. The other side of the budget is expenditures (expenses or costs). Programs have two major kinds of costs: annual and capitalized. *Annual costs* are the actual costs, or cash outlays, for the yearly operation of the program. *Capitalized costs* appear in a budget as *depreciation,* or the cost of an asset distributed over its estimated useful life. The rate of allowable depreciation varies by type of asset and is established by tax authorities. Buildings last longer than buses, refrigerators longer than typewriters. Depreciation costs are considered as yearly expenses. The following list shows typical expenses incurred in operating a child care program:

Personnel
- Administrative
- Teaching and child care
- Social services
- Nutrition and food

- Health
- Occupancy

Nonmandated fringe benefits
- Life insurance
- Health benefits
- Retirement plans

Payroll taxes and other personnel costs
- Payroll taxes
- FICA
- Other (unemployment compensation)

Special fees and contract service payments
- Professional fees (medical, dental, legal, and accounting)
- Maintenance contract
- Food catering
- Transportation contract

Supplies
- Teaching and child care
- Food and food service
- Office
- Health
- Vehicle
- Building, grounds maintenance, and housekeeping

Occupancy
- Rental of space
- Depreciation
- Real estate taxes
- Building insurance
- Utilities

Furniture and equipment
- Rental and purchase payments
- Repairs
- Depreciation

Conferences and meetings
- Parent meetings
- Staff training

Other
- Licenses, permits, and fees
- Advertising, printing, and duplicating
- Telephone
- Postage
- Field trips
- Miscellaneous
- Bank charges, loan payments, and interest
- Professional memberships
- Transportation insurance
- Contingency fund payments

Expenses have a way of depressing budget planners and fostering premature cost-cutting and allocation decisions. The first step in building the expense side of the budget is to prepare a straightforward list of expenses. This list should be based on previous expenses and anticipated expenses of newly formulated program plans. You should budget initially as if expense were no obstacle to program plans for the coming year. Ask program personnel for "wish lists" in priority order. Prepare cost estimates for special projects or events.

When expense estimates are complete, the process of budget preparation can begin. Beyond fixed, legally required expenses and necessary expenses, there is considerable maneuvering room on the expense side of the budget. The heart of policy-making in the budget process lies with the trade-offs and compromises that lead to expense allocations across categories and expected disbursements within each category. Staff training may be eliminated in favor of higher allocations for materials and supplies. Repairs may be postponed in order to add salary money for a needed program aide. Snacks may be eliminated and parents asked to donate food. Field trips may be reduced. Maintenance responsibilities may be shifted to staff to eliminate the need for contracted service. The possibilities are endless; only those working in the program can decide what is acceptable and tolerable.

Budget Documents

Budgets and accompanying reports and documents can take any number of forms. The format and collection of forms should meet the information needs of the program and be compatible with the forms and guidelines of funders. Budget forms may be statements, explanations, reports, or analyses.

Budget Statements. A budget statement is a formal proposal of spending for the program for a given fiscal year. It represents the "best" estimates of projected income and expenditures. In a *line-item budget statement* each major income and expenditure category is listed on a separate line. When selecting line-items for a budget, a program can aggregate categories and use those that best cover its fiscal situation.

If the budget statement reflects only the fiscal status of a single program, it is called a *program budget statement.* Large organizations often generate an overall organization budget and then isolate separate budgets for each program under their auspices. In this situation a program budget is a prorated share of the overall budget.

A *functional budget statement* organizes expenditures by service category rather than line-item budget categories. Functions are uniform categories of service that are common to all child care programs. The eight commonly used function categories are teaching and child care, social services, food services, health services, administration, occupancy, staff development, and transportation. Expenses can be allocated proportionately to each function. For example, supplies are required for each function. Instead of summarizing and reporting a total supply cost, a functional budget assigns the portion of the total cost of supplies to each function area. The cost reported for each function area includes the individual costs of every contributing factor. Functional budgets are a reorganization of the expenditures appearing in a line-item budget. Some changes may be required in existing bookkeeping systems so that the cost data needed for functional allocation are easier to assign to functions.

Uniform cost categories permit comparison of cost data from one program to another. Different programs can be accurately compared using the common denominators of functional service categories. Functional budgeting analysis makes it possible to begin to address the question of worth or the market value of a given child care program. Some government contracts base child care payments according to service contracts on functional analysis cost data. Functional budgets also help identify relative costs of services within a program and pinpoint those that seem out of line.

Budget Explanations. Accompanying the budget statement is a more explicit explanation of the budget items. A *budget backup* sheet lists in detail the contributing factors for each income and expenditure item. It may be as detailed as a list of all the bookkeeping accounts for each budget item. A *budget justification* statement is an often lengthy narrative explanation of the budget. It explains unusual budget items, describes methods of computing budget dollar amounts, and discusses considerations weighed in developing the budget. Those who review budgets look to the narrative as implicit evidence that the budget was thoughtfully prepared.

Budget Reports. The organization's bylaws and funders' reporting requirements dictate the type and frequency of budget reports. All budget reports are essentially balance sheets giving the total income and expenditure activity for a particular time period and the current balances. *Monthly reports* take the form of a treasurer's reports at meetings, internal organization summaries, and routine monthly account reconciliation. Staying in close touch with fiscal activities enables an organization to spot potential problems and make adjustments immediately. *Quarterly reports* are balance sheets summarizing fiscal activity for three months. The quarterly report is frequently used to report to funders, sponsors, and government agencies. It may be widely distributed. The quarterly report gives a historical perspective on the organization's activity. It is less useful as an internal management tool because of this, but it is more appropriate to monitor progress toward overall annual fiscal spending targets.

The *annual report* is a comprehensive summary of the past year's fiscal activity. It is often a public document used by the program to report to creditors, funders, sponsors, and the organizational board. Annual reports may be prepared and/or audited by external accountants. The annual report is *not* a budget. It replaces the budget, which was a proposal for spending,

Table 12.2 Conducting a Monthly Cash-Flow Analysis

	JAN.	FEB.	MARCH	APRIL	MAY	JUNE	JULY	AUG.	SEPT.	OCT.	NOV.	DEC.
Cash Taken In	3902	3780	4055	3760								
Expenditures	3856	3560	3515	4062								
Cash Flow	46	220	540	−302								
Cumulative Cash Flow	46	266	706	404								

with a record of actual income and expenditures.

Budget Analyses. Reading a budget requires knowledge and calculation. Familiarity with budget terms, an understanding of the budgeting process, and concentration on the budget figures lead to a solid working knowledge of the budget.

After monthly or quarterly balances are figured, *deviation analysis* is used to compare actual account totals with budgeted account totals. The difference between totals is expressed as a percent. Deviation analysis is a simple calculation that gives information on the rate of fiscal progress toward budget targets. It can be used with line-item or functional budgets, and it can be applied to income and expenditure balances representing any time period within the budget year.

Over the year a budget may project a sufficient amount of money from income to cover expenses. Maybe more income than actually needed comes in and you end the year in the black. Having enough money at the end of the year is not, however, always the point. A program needs cash in its accounts when its bills, payrolls, and loans are due. *Cash-flow analysis* helps to monitor the timing and amount of money flowing into the program. Cash-lag or cash-flow problems are what a program has when cash-on-hand is insufficient to meet current expenses. Programs have to find ways of building reserves (savings, loan sources) to cover cash-flow problems.

A cash-flow analysis tracks the amount of cash coming into a program and relates it to actual cash expenditures. Some portion of a program's cash expenditures is known. These are *fixed expenses* for essential salaries, supplies, and services that remain fairly stable from month to month. An average of these fixed expenses can be calculated. Other expenses such as heat, gas, field trips, fees, and substitute salaries vary from month to month. These are *variable cash disbursements.* Monthly cash flow is computed by subtracting cash expenditures from cash taken in. By adding cash flows from month-to-month the director can track cumulative cash flow. Cumulative cash flow represents the increase or decrease in the cash resources of the program from the beginning of the year. Table 12.2 illustrates a cash flow analysis.

Since cash taken in and expenditures both vary from month to month, negative cash flows are to be expected in some months such as shown for April in Table 12.2. This may have resulted from extra substitute salaries to cover staff on vacation. However, if negative cash flows continue for long the program's resources will be depleted. A cumulative cash flow that is negative is a warning signal that demands attention and immediate action. The solutions may be painful or costly, but nothing is gained by postponing action.

Accounting

As we said earlier, accounting is the system and procedures an organization uses to keep track of its fiscal activity. The five basic concepts of accounting are as follows:

Assets Things you own. (Examples: Cash in bank, petty cash fund, or fees receivable)
Liabilities Things you owe. (Examples: payroll deductions, employer's share of FICA, or accounts payable)
Equity Difference between what you own and what you owe (net worth or capital).
Income Amount of money coming in during a given period for which no assets have to be sold or liabilities incurred. (Examples: fees or government allotments)
Expenses Amount paid out for any given period of time for which an asset is not increased or a liability reduced. (Examples: personnel, occupancy, utilities, or office supplies)

A Chart of Accounts, a set of journals, and a General Ledger are the basic components of a Standardized Accounting System (SAS). Organizations may choose to use more books beyond this basic set. Every financial transaction of the organization, all income and expenses, and any changes affecting assets, liabilities, or equity will be recorded in the system.

Chart of Accounts. The books in the accounting system are set up using a Chart of Accounts, which is a master list of all the names and code numbers of the asset, liability, income, expense, and equity accounts used by the organization. The four- or five-digit code assigned to each account is a detailed classification tag for that account. Table 12.3 shows a sample list of accounts applicable to a child care program. Accounts are of two types. *Real accounts* are assets, liability, and equity accounts carried over from one fiscal year to the next. *Nominal accounts* are income and expense accounts that are closed out at the end of a fiscal period and started anew in the next fiscal period. The accounts used in the bookkeeping process can be clustered into groups for a particular line-item in a budget. The financial transactions that contribute to a single line-item in a budget are recorded in separate accounts. Any budget analysis must aggregate those accounts and match them to budget items.

The Books. An SAS uses a basic set of books of entry journals and ledgers to keep the records of an organization's financial transactions:

Cash Receipts Journal A book of original entries used to record all monies received by program.
Cash Disbursements Journal A book of original entries in which cash outlays are recorded.
Payroll Journal A book of original entries used to record details of a payroll period.
Petty Cash Control Book A book of original entries used to record petty cash transactions.
General Journal A book of original entries in which noncash transactions are recorded.
General Ledger The book of record in which all an organization's accounts may be found. Information from journals is posted to the ledger in summary form. Account balances are cumulative, reflecting all transactions to that account to date.

(Additional specialized books may be needed by some organizations.)

Entries. Entries are made twice in the books to cross-reference, reduce error, and ensure a track record of each transaction. Each entry is recorded once in the appropriate journal and then again in the General Ledger. This system of balance and check entries is known as *double-entry bookkeeping.* Transactions are *debits* entered on the *left* side of an account if they represent an increase in asset or expense accounts and a decrease in liability and equity accounts. Transactions are *credits* entered on the *right* side of an account if they represent a decrease in asset accounts and an increase in liability, equity, or income accounts. To conform with accepted practices, organizations should use an accrual accounting procedure, recording all transactions when they occur even if the money has not been received or disbursed. The cumulative account balances in the General Ledger then reflect the current financial status of the organization.

Table 12.3 Excerpt from a Chart of Accounts

ASSET, LIABILITY, AND EQUITY ACCOUNTS: 1000–3010			
Current Assets	*1000–1051*	*Current Liabilities*	*2000*
Cash in Bank		Accounts Payable	2010
Unrestricted	1000	Notes Payable	2011
Restricted	1011	Mortgage Payable	2012
Petty Cash Fund	1012	Interest Payable	2020
Accounts Receivable		Payroll Control	2022
Fees and Direct Payments	1020	Accrued Regular Salaries	2030
Accounts Receivable		Accrued Substitute Salaries	2031
Other Revenue	1021	Accrued Other Salaries	2032
Accounts Receivable		Employee Benefits	2033
Governmental Sources	1022	Federal Tax Payable	2040
Accounts/Pledges Receivable		State Tax Payable	2041
Contributions	1023	City Tax Payable	2042
A/R-USDA	1024	FICA Payable	2043
Accounts/Pledges Receivable		Unemployment Tax	2044
Notes Receivable	1025	Workmen's Compensation	2045
Marketable Securities		Disability	2046
Unrestricted	1030	Other Taxes	2047
Restricted	1031		
Unexpired Insurance	1040	*Other Liabilities*	*2050*
Prepaid Interest	1050	Unearned Fee Income	2060
Prepaid Rent	1051		
Other	1060	*Equity*	*3000*
		Fund Equity	3010
Fixed Assets	*1090–1190*		
Land	1090		
Building and Building Improvements	1100		
Accumulated Depreciation Building and Building Improvements	1109		
Furniture & Equipment	1110		
Accumulated Depreciation Furniture & Equipment	1119		
Leasehold Improvements	1120		
Accumulated Amortization Leasehold Improvements	1129		
Vehicles	1130		
Accumulated Depreciation Vehicles	1139		
Other	1140		

Source: From *Effective Management in Human Services Programs: Vol. 2. Guide to Bookkeeping and Financial Reporting,* by E. Youngquist and G. Farrell, 1980, pp. 32–33, Washington, DC: Office of Policy Development/HDS, U.S. Department of Health and Human Services.

Financial Management Procedures

Management is the application of accounting information to daily program operation. Directors will find it useful to become familiar with some of the specialized terms of a few common activities.

Payroll. Staff payrolls are the largest expense for most child care operations. A missed payroll affects morale and is a clear signal that management is not conscientious. Pay periods should be stated and employees paid on time. Employees should know the kinds and amounts of deductions made from their salaries. Appropriate written authorization is needed for many deductions. Accurate time sheets are needed. Overtime, sick leave, and vacation days should be monitored and totals should be current. Tax statements are required. Written notification for change in pay status or termination prevent misunderstandings.

Petty Cash. Small amounts of cash can be made available for purchase of incidental or inexpensive items. The Petty Cash Control Book is used to record the date, item, and receipt number of each transaction. Petty cash money is debited to the Cash Disbursements Journal and enters the General Ledger through that journal. Petty cash gives flexibility for minor expenses, but does require controlled bookkeeping. Some organizations prefer not to deal with petty cash and write checks directly for expenses or reimburse people upon presentation of receipts.

Checkbooks. Prenumbered, approved signature (often two required) checking accounts are preferred. Every check is accounted for in the check register and posted by number and amount to an account in the system. A running account balance is maintained. Safeguarding the checkbook from theft or misuse is just as important for organization accounts as with personal checking accounts.

Purchasing. Managing purchasing requires business skill and knowledge of the program. The goal is to purchase good quality supplies at the best prices. A *purchase order* is an order or request for supplies on the organization's letterhead, usually signed by an authorized agent of the organization. An *invoice* is a bill for what was ordered. A *packing slip* is a list of items included in a shipment. Organizations may qualify for quantity discounts on purchases, and some vendors (suppliers) allow charge accounts. Bills may be discounted if paid within five to ten days. Organizations that qualify for tax-exempt status will not have to pay sales tax, and over a year's time this savings can be considerable. Vendors may require copies of the tax-exempt ruling.

Audits. An audit is a third party's procedural review of the accounting records and methods of an organization to establish the financial health of the organization. Certified Public Accountants (CPAs) performing audits will attest to the accuracy of account totals. Funders can require audits as a way of ensuring that money was properly spent. Audit exceptions occur when balances or procedures are in error. Several audit exceptions can result in a contract cancellation. Organizations under audit exceptions may be forced to repay, with interest, any funds considered misspent.

Costs and Fees

The solid fiscal framework that budgets and accounting systems provide for child care programs gives little indication of the concern, controversy, and lack of consensus that surround the actual figures reported. Costs, fees, and reimbursement rates vary widely; they are affected by local situations and distant policymakers. Cost means different things to different people, and each viewpoint raises questions. Are costs calculated in terms of dollars needed to pay the bills, or the cost to parents for care? Is there a cost for children—developmentally or psychologically—of different types of care? Can we put a dollar figure on minimum, acceptable, or superior quality levels of care? What does child care cost society in terms of family stability, work force participation, government subsidy or reimbursement? Who should pay?

Actual dollar figures are available for child care program costs and fees, but rarely are the figures comparable across surveys because units of service and calculation procedures differ. Despite these problems, it is instructive to study the various approaches to costs and fees. Without a firm understanding of the components and calculation procedures for cost compari-

Table 12.4 Sample Salary Schedule*

	Step 1 (0–12)	Step 2 (13–24)	Step 3 (25–36)	Step 4 (37–48)	Step 5 (49–60)	Step 6 (61–)
Group Supervisor						
Level 1	$8,650	$9,027	$9,231	$9,435	$9,639	$9,843
Level 2	8,000	8,364	8,568	8,772	8,976	
Level 3	7,750	8,109	8,313	8,517		
Assistant Group Supervisor						
Level 1	6,533	6,783	6,987	7,191	7,395	7,599
Level 2	6,533	6,579	6,783	6,987	7,191	7,395
Aide	6,533	6,370	6,574			
Food Service Worker						
Level 1	8,000	8,364	8,568	8,772	8,976	9,180
Level 2	7,200	7,548	7,752	7,956	8,160	
Level 3	6,700	7,038	7,242			

* 1982–1983 figures are given. Annual salary increases of about 3–4 percent could be calculated to determine current salaries.
Source: Child Development Council of Centre County, 111 Sowers St., State College, PA, 16801; used with permission.

sons, directors lose a valuable perspective on the stability of their program's fiscal status and the effectiveness of their fiscal management.

Costs

The costs of service are frequently compared when programs are compared with one another, with Head Start, and with public schools. Directors and other program administrators must also be prepared to explain and to defend program costs. Costs vary according to differences in data calculation, pricing discrepancies, and program quality differences. A standard cost unit is, therefore, essential. The first step is to work from common assumptions of the costs to be included.

Since start-up costs are high one-time outlays, they do not represent a true picture of program operation. For most purposes, recurrent operating expenses are preferred as cost figures. Costs are reported by functions. As we noted earlier, functional budgets allocate individual program expenses to a commonly accepted set of eight functions and permit meaningful comparison among service units.

Adjustments must be made in cost data to account for regional price differences and inflation. Department of Labor price indexes are useful for this purpose. The National Day Care Study estimated that prices vary around the country by as much as 100 percent (Ruopp, Travers, Glantz, & Coelen, 1979). Even within states, urban and rural prices may vary significantly.

Salaries. Child care is labor-intensive. Staff salaries account for the biggest portion of expenses (often 55 to 65 percent of the budget). The implications for cost comparison are twofold. First, high staff-child ratios mean high salary expenses. Staff-child ratio is likely to vary most among different types of programs. Regulations establish minimum staffing levels for most types of programs. Infant programs should be compared with infant programs, preschool programs with each other, school-age with school-age, and so forth. Within each of these programs, differences in staff-child ratios and salary costs can be assumed to reflect different quality levels of service. Second, staff salary rates vary around the country, reflecting the employment market in the geographical area where the program is located. For cost comparison purposes, personnel costs must be adjusted for these variations.

Often salary figures do not reflect the education and commitment that staff bring to their

Good staff deserve good salaries. Putting a dollar figure on caring is one of the most difficult decisions that programs must make in budgeting. (Courtesy of U.S. Department of Agriculture, Washington, DC.)

jobs. Low staff salaries are a hidden private "subsidy" helping to keep overall costs down and disguising the true value of the care being provided. Since staff salaries are such a large percentage of a program's budget, there is an obvious direct correlation between staff salaries and parent fees—higher salaries translate to higher fees. Many parents are unwilling and/or unable to pay fees based on reasonable staff wages. Table 12.4 gives salary figures for child care staff.

Salary and related benefits are emerging as one of the most important issues for child care in the future. Efforts range from grass roots, single-center staff demands for specific benefits to broader-based efforts to change job classification titles and definitions of child care work as an occupation. One organization currently very active in this area is the Child Care Employee Project (CCEP), P.O. Box 5603, Berkeley, CA 94705. CCEP is mounting a national effort toward improving working conditions, especially salary and benefits, for child care staff. A newsletter, *Child Care Employee News,* reports on project activities and related news around the country.

Unions are another method of organizing workers and pressing with a unified voice for adequate wages and working conditions. Among the many union locals is District 65, UAW in Massachusetts. (Day Care and Human Services Local; District 65, UAW; 636 Beacon Street; Boston, MA 02215) Some child care and human service workers in Massachusetts belong to this union. District 65 is organizing workers, spotlighting issues of working conditions, and doing state-level political advocacy. Their newsletter *BADWU News* is published bimonthly and is bilingual. Unions in other cities, notably New York, have become effective advocates for child care workers, helping to educate the public and preserve programs and jobs in the face of budget crunches.

Growing demand for care, the clear connection of staff to quality care, and economic realities of high prices and inflation are joining to make raises plus changes in staff salaries inevitable.

Standard Cost Units. Cost is generally reported on a *per child* basis. The general formula is:

$$\text{per child cost} = \frac{\text{costs}}{\text{number of children} \times \text{amount of time}}$$

Depending on the figures used, cost is reported as *per child hour, per child day,* or *per child year*. Let's look at how the figures are obtained for each component of the formula.

Costs Fully costed programs include all income sources—cash and in-kind donations. In-kind donations can drastically reduce the cash expenses incurred by the program yet support a high level of service. If current program services could not be maintained without in-kind donations, that program should be fully costed on the basis of *all* income. Programs may be costed without in-kind donations but should be clearly identified as such. *Total* program costs or *function* costs can be used as the numerator in the formula.

Number of Children Implicitly, this means number of full-time children or full-time equivalents (FTE). Part-time children are added together to produce FTEs. There is, however, no really good way to create FTEs with part-time children. Programs must decide to use hours in care, days enrolled, or some other method will be used. In some respects part-time children generate as many costs as full-time for paperwork, parent meetings, and so forth. On the other hand, costs may be lower for meals, and space and equipment use is distributed over more children. Individual programs must use the method that best captures the actual program costs.

Enrollment and average daily attendance (ADA) are used to report number of FTE children. *Enrollment* is simply the number of children registered for the program generally adjusted to FTEs. Do not confuse enrollment with *capacity,* the number of children the facility is licensed for. Because of part-time children and the variable hours children are in care, capacity is almost never reached. Attendance fluctuates as illness, travel difficulties, and family situations arise. Enrollment numbers represent the availability of service. When the enrollment number is used in the formula denominator, costs are lower than they would be with the ADA because they are spread over all possible children.

Costs reported in terms of ADA are higher. They represent the actual use of service. The ADA is obtained by averaging the number of children present (adjusted for FTE) each day for a month. Accurate attendance records are required for this. Reimbursements are usually based on ADA. Be alert in examining cost data. Know what you are looking at and ask whether it's appropriate for the comparison situation.

Amount of time The standard definition of time is a 10-hour day, 250-day year (52 weeks plus 10 holidays). FTEs are figured on this time unit. The 10-hour figure is used for cost *per child hour,* the 250-day figure for cost *per child day.* Cost per child hour is the preferred reporting figure. An expanded cost formula (cost per child) is as follows:

$$= \frac{\begin{array}{c}\text{Costs:}\\ \text{Program or function}\\ \textit{or}\\ \text{Expenses with in-kind donation}\\ \text{or without in-kind donation}\end{array}}{\begin{array}{c}\text{Children:}\\ \text{Enrollment number}\\ \textit{or}\\ \text{Average daily attendance number}\\ \times \text{ Time: Hour } \textit{or} \text{ day } \textit{or} \text{ year}\end{array}}$$

Cost Data. There are no definitive figures on what it costs to actually run a child care program. Some estimates were generated in the late 1960s and early 1970s through surveys sponsored by the federal government. Specific cost figures are obsolete. Based on prior surveys and allowing for inflation and changes in accounting procedures, we estimate that the costs of operating a program can be allocated as shown in Table 12.5.

Of course the actual costs will differ depending on the size and type of program. As an example of what typical costs might look like, Table 12.6 shows the costs by category for operating a small, private center in 1981.

Fees

Fees are the charges for service. They represent the direct, cash costs of child care for parents, but they are not the only costs parents incur when fee levels are discussed. To fully cost child care for parents, we need to include all the expenses parents incur or are responsible for related to using the program: transportation costs; extra clothing costs; supplies such as diapers, toothpaste, blankets, meals or snacks brought from home; and other similar items.

Fees are income for a child care program. Programs can and do operate with fees as the sole source of income. In other programs, fees supplement income received from external funders and government reimbursement. The circumstances, conditions, and amount of fees charged vary. Differential fees are established according to one or more of these factors:

Enrollment Children are enrolled for specified time periods. Parents are expected to pay the fees for the enrollment periods whether or not children attend. When the program is officially closed (Christmas, July 4), fees are not charged. Otherwise, full-time children are typically given a two-week vacation credit on fees. Some programs treat summer as a separate enrollment period and temporarily suspend fees for those not enrolled until they return in the fall.

- Part-time children may be charged higher fees than full-time children.
- Siblings may be given discounts on fees.
- Reduced fees may be charged if parents are employees of the program sponsor or meet other priority criteria for enrollment.

Age of Child Infants may be charged higher rates than school-aged children, reflecting the higher costs of staffing and supplies. For example, a Texas study done in 1977 showed the average fee *per day* for infants under one year of age in centers was $5.15; for five-year-olds the average daily fee was $4.54.

Family Income Fees may be prorated based on determination of the family's ability to pay.

Table 12.5 Costs of Operating a Program

Category	Percentage Cost	Explanation
Personnel	68	Actual salaries, fringe benefits, and tax requirements. Fringe benefits may include health insurance, sick leave, and vacation: estimate 15% of salary. Substitute costs based on vacation days for staff when replacement is needed plus sick days.
Occupancy	12	Mortgage payments or rent, utilities, maintenance, repair, and insurance.
Equipment	2	Educational materials, kitchen utensils, housekeeping, and office equipment.
Supplies	2	Expendable items that need replacing: crayons, paint, paper, stationery, billing forms, postage, soap, paper towels, etc.
Food	14	One meal and two nutritious snacks per child per day.
Other	2	Advertising, licensing fees, insurance, journal subscriptions, professional memberships, and audit.
Total	100	

Establishing fee levels is a combination of financial management and policy determination. Sound financial management dictates that fees be based on costs. *Break-even analysis* is the technique used to calculate how much to charge parents in order to pay the bills. *Sliding fee scales* are used to reduce fees for some parents, usually for policy reasons to provide care to low-income families. The final measure of fees is cash-in-hand. Fee collection procedures that are fair, but rigorous, are needed to ensure the expected fee income.

Break-even Analysis. Break-even is the point at which program costs are balanced by program income. A break-even analysis looks at the impact of different enrollment numbers and

Table 12.6 Costs for a Small Private Program (serving 45 children in 1981)

PERSONNEL	% OF TIME	ANNUAL SALARY ($)	TOTAL ($)
Director/Head Teacher	100	14,000	14,000
Sec/Bookkeeper	50	8,000	4,000
Teachers (2)	100	12,000	24,000
Aides (1)	100	8,000	8,000
(2)	50	7,000	7,000
(3,4)	30	volunteers	—
Cook/Maintenance	100	7,000	7,000
			64,000
Fringe Benefits @ 15%			9,600
Substitutes @ $3.20/hr. × 8 wks			1,050
			$74,650
OCCUPANCY			
Rent @ $800/month × 12 months			
(2,000 square feet @ $4.80 sq. ft.)			$ 9,600
Heat			2,300
Electricity			1,700
Telephone			500
			$14,100
EQUIPMENT			
Educational			$ 800
Kitchen			500
Housekeeping			200
Office			300
			$1,800
SUPPLIES			
Educational			$1,200
Housekeeping			500
Office			500
			$2,200
FOOD (1 MEAL AND 2 SNACKS)			
($1.60 × 40 × 240 days)			$15,400
OTHER EXPENSES			
Advertising			$ 400
Licensing fees			50
Insurance (liability @ $10/child/year)			450
Subscription/membership			50
Audit			900
			$ 1,850
		Total Expenses	$110,000

Adapted from: *How to start a day care center*. Prepared by the Day Care Council of America for the U.S. Dept. of Health and Human Services, Contract #HDS-90-PD-100010. Washington, DC: 1981, pp. 26–27.

fee charges. A break-even chart (Figure 12.2) gives a graphic picture of the data. Costs are computed and shown as three separate lines on the graph. *Fixed* costs are those costs the program has regardless of number of children enrolled. *Variable* costs are tied to enrollment (supplies, food, and so on) and rise as enrollment rises. *Semivariable* costs rise irregularly when certain enrollment thresholds are reached. Examples might be the need for another staff member when group size reaches a certain point, another van for transportation, or more space or toilets at higher enrollment figures. The costs of new program services (adding infants, extending hours) can be calculated as semivariable costs to see what impact such a change would have on costs and whether fees would need to be raised. Figure 12.2 shows the three cost lines as cumulative totals. The staircase rise of the sum line reflects the irregular rise of semivariable costs at certain enrollment levels. There are no set guidelines for determining whether costs are fixed, variable, or semivariable. Common sense, good judgment, and a working knowledge of the program must guide those who collect the cost data and prepare a break-even chart.

The income line is calculated by multiplying fee income (usually total dollars per year) by number of children. Other income can be added to this total or the break-even analysis can be based on fee income alone. Different income lines are needed for different fee levels and may be put on separate charts. Figure 12.2 shows one income line. It intersects the sum cost line at three points—break-even points. Based on the number of children enrolled and the total income needed at each break-even point, fees that will result in financial stability can be established. If lower fees are chosen, the amount of additional income required to break even is known. Obviously, a break-even chart also shows profit and loss positions for a program.

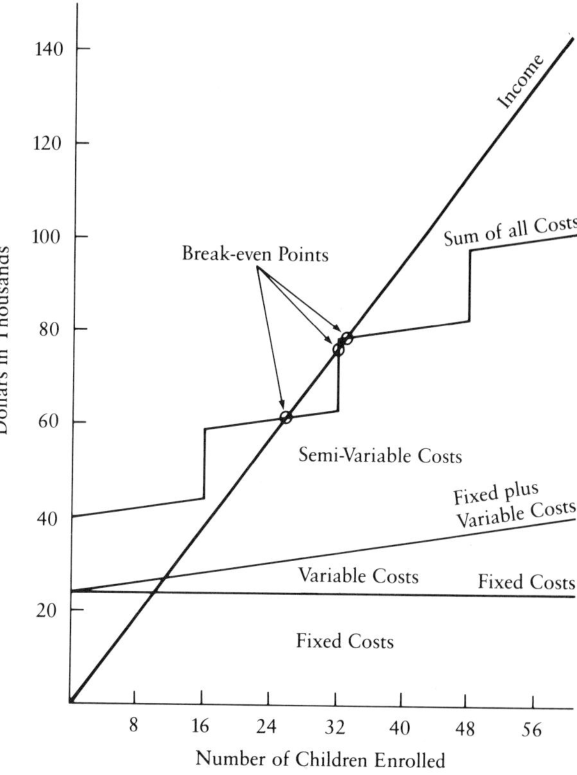

Figure 12.2 Break-even chart. (From *Managing the day care dollars* by G. Morgan, 1982, p. 58, Cambridge, MA: Steam Press; used with permission.)

Sliding Fee Scales. Sliding fee scales are based on an estimate of a family's ability to pay for child care. Family income is most often used to determine eligibility for low fees. Fee scales can be set up so that some families pay more than the actual cost of care to subsidize families who can afford only lower fees. More frequently, fee scales are set with the actual cost of care as the maximum fee. The difference between lower fees and actual costs is made up by subsidy, reimbursement, and/or in-kind donation.

Fee Collection. Fee delinquencies can undermine the financial stability of a program. Programs that operate on tight budgets and try to keep fees as low as possible cannot afford the bad debts of nonpayment of fees. This is true despite the unpleasant idea of refusing care for a child at the door or turning a deaf ear to a pleading parent who is hundreds of dollars behind in payment.

Child Care Information Exchange (January 1980) compiled a list of suggestions for fee collection procedures. Most aim to prevent problems. We have adapted some of their suggestions to produce the following list:

1. Develop and publicize fee policies.
   - Design fee schedules.
   - Set late-payment penalties.
   - Establish procedures for deferments or adjustments if any.
   - Consider a credit card system.
2. Collect fees promptly.
   - Begin in advance to allow time for pursuing late payments.
   - Don't let debts accumulate.
3. Establish safeguards.
   - Collect an enrollment deposit.
   - Enforce late-payment penalties.
   - Minimize bounced check losses.
4. Institute pursuit strategies.
   - Negotiate payment plans.
   - Require signing of a promissory note.
   - Sue in small claims court.
   - Stop providing care.

Public and Private Financial Support

Reimbursements

The fiscal link between child care programs (service providers) and public agencies (purchasers of service) is *reimbursement*. Programs receiving public funds are designated as FFP (federal financial participation) programs to indicate the source of some income and their ability to meet whatever federal standards for care are in force. Reimbursements are intended to cover the costs incurred by a program provider in delivering child care services. Reimbursement payments are income that should balance costs for the programs involved. However, the process is not straightforward, as the following quote indicates:

> The establishment and maintenance of reasonable reimbursement rates for providers of child care services is one of the thorniest and most capricious issues in management. Unlike the exclusively private sector where providers may charge what the market will bear, providers of services to publicly-supported clients may be reimbursed only for actual expenses incurred, *not to exceed limits imposed by state or local agencies* [emphasis added]. Further, expenses must be incurred to support the additional applicable child care standards in order to be eligible for reimbursement. (Entis, 1980, p. 5)

Once a reimbursement rate is established, the total number of dollars a program receives is calculated on the number of children or *slots* to be subsidized. The term *slot* is tossed around by directors and funders alike, and it is easy to lose sight of the fact that slots are real children. But funders don't subsidize vague services or specific individual children. Reimbursement is made for service for one eligible child or one slot. Slot is the unit of service a child care program contracts to provide under a purchase-of-service contract with an outside funder.

A sliding fee scale in combination with a reasonable reimbursement rate should produce income that offsets costs for the unit of service delivered. But, unfortunately, this is not always the case. Reimbursement rates may be set artificially in order to stretch scarce public dollars. Certain service costs may be disallowed and not included in cost calculations. As a matter of policy decision, programs may choose not to make up the reimbursement income shortfall by raising fees. Other sources of income must be found. And, so begins the fund-raising scramble.

A major step forward in the area of public funding and reimbursement rates has been the application of cost analysis techniques to child care and other human services programs. Cost analysis collects, organizes, and analyzes cost information into a uniform system of data. Funding agencies can use cost analysis to establish rates that realistically reimburse service providers for their costs. A four-volume series titled *Analyzing Costs in Human Services Pro-*

grams describes the principles of cost analysis, presents worksheets and instructions for necessary data collection, and discusses the use of cost analysis data and rate setting. Developed by the Human Services Management Transfer Project (funded by DHEW-ADS/ACYF), this series is a valuable reference for program administrators who confront reimbursement rate and cost calculation difficulties. Each volume is listed by author in the reference section.

Costs, fees, and reimbursement rate discussions open a Pandora's box of issues all swirling around the question Who Should Pay? The government's presence in the child care market as a purchaser of care with public funds has complicated costs. Federal standards intended to ensure quality of care levels are thought by many to raise the costs of care unnecessarily high. Conditions of funding have tended to segregate children by family income level in FFP programs. Throughout this chapter we have talked about costs and fees in relation to center-based programs. If parents can be considered to vote for child care preferences with their pocketbooks, then the vast majority opts for unregulated, non-FFP, family day care.

Funding

The process of obtaining or maintaining funding requires a seemingly endless series of tasks. Programs relying on somewhat predictable sources of public funds must meet numerous report, monitoring, and inspection requirements as conditions of funding. Programs that piece together support funding from changing combinations of public and private sources increase the tasks of managing fund solicitation, documentation, and administration. For any program that counts quality of service to children as its highest priority, the time drain of extensive fund-raising activities can be frustrating. Often survival, however, is at stake, and programs have no choice but to give fund-raising activities the highest priority. Self-sufficiency for programs requires individual programs to handle fund raising as a perennial activity. Money for child care programs comes from both public and private sources.

Public Funds. By far the largest source of federal support for child care has been through Title XX of the Social Security Act (P.L. 93-647). Title XX has now been superseded by the Social Services Block Grant (SSBG), allocated to states based on population. Congress continues to keep tight rein on total federal expenditures under this program. Under Title XX child care services enjoyed some favor. Funds were designated (earmarked) to help states upgrade child care services to comply with the Federal Interagency Day Care Requirements (FIDCR), which were being revised. Designated training monies also helped child care directly. However, Congress has suspended work on implementation of any federal child care standards. The Department of Health and Human Services has dismantled agency units devoted to child care.

Under the current SSBG, states have broad discretion in determining both the mix of social services to be delivered and the eligibility requirements for recipients. Child care is one of the social services that states can choose to fund, and in a way, child care "competes" with other social service programs within the state for a portion of the state's SSBG dollars. A 1984 General Accounting Office study of thirteen states revealed that since 1981 child care's share of SSBG dollars has generally dropped. Recent congressional concern regarding the potential of child care staff involvement in child abuse has resulted in a supplemental $25 million to the SSBG to be used to train child care providers in child development and to prevent child abuse. States must have a procedure for screening and conducting criminal history checks of child care workers in place. Failure to meet specific provisions of the law by 1986 will result in drastic funding cutbacks.

Child care advocates consider SSBG funding vital to maintaining reasonable capacity in publicly supported programs. Major decisions regarding allocation of funds and service delivery will continue to be made separately by each state. Despite recent events, few expect that the federal government will move to exert control over state expenditures on child care through the SSBG.

Programs that depend upon public funding will find the government publications described here helpful in locating and monitoring fund sources. All are available from the Superintendent of Documents, Government Printing Office, Washington, DC 20204.

- *Catalog of Federal Domestic Assistance Programs* Considered *the* basic source on federal funding. The catalog is published in June with a supplement available in November. Users of the catalog will find the publication *How to Use the Revised Catalog of Federal Domestic Assistance* by Timothy Saasta very helpful. (Grantsmanship Center, 1031 South Grand Avenue, Los Angeles, CA 90015)
- *Commercial Business Daily* Published daily, CBD has current information on upcoming contract awards, notices of awards, and much other government business.
- *Federal Register* Published daily Monday through Friday, the *Register* has information on new and proposed regulations, program changes, deadlines, and fund availability.
- *The Code of Federal Regulations* Published quarterly with monthly supplements, the *Code* is a compilation of all current federal regulations.

The Budget Process. Legislation creates a program. Regulations define the conditions of service and funding. But, unless Congress, state, or local governments appropriate money for the program, it will not exist as its advocates, sponsors, and users may think it was intended to. The federal budgeting process directly influences the level and quality of child care programs at the local level. The budget process is complicated and the work of politicians in Washington can seem remote and unrelated to programs in Arkansas, North Dakota, or Michigan. The budget process can be understood, however, and Congress is always attentive to voters' priorities. Using resources such as the following, child care advocates can be directly influential in federal, state and local budget processes.

- *Children and the Federal Budget: How to Influence the Budget Process* Available from Children's Defense Fund, 1520 New Hampshire Avenue, N.W., Washington, DC 20036.
- *The Citizen and the Budget Process: Opening Up the System* (Pub. no. 482)—State and local budgets. *The Budget Process from the Bureaucrat's Side of the Desk.* (Pub. no. 483)—State and local budgets, Washington, DC: League of Women Voters, 1974.
- *A Children's Defense Fund Budget: An Analysis of the President's Budget and Children* Washington, DC: Children's Defense Fund, (updated and revised every year).

Private Funds. Through foundation and other charitable organizations, private wealth is made available for the public good. Many people are discovering that private foundations are potential sources of money for child care projects. Applications to foundations have skyrocketed in the last few years. Foundation support for child-related programs has increased significantly as a result of more applicants in child-program areas and an apparent growing recognition by foundations of the importance of such efforts.

The trustees or board of directors of a foundation administer an award program that is funded by the earnings of an endowment. Foundations may have been established by a single donor (individual or corporation), or the endowment may have been built up through numerous gifts and bequests. Each foundation has a particular set of objectives for its awards program.

Tapping foundation funds is hard work. Potential applicants need to locate foundations, identify their major fields of interest, and try to match their needs with the foundation's priorities. Checking recent award lists is an excellent way to assess compatibility. The following are some of the best services for locating, identifying, and assessing foundation sources:

- The Foundation Center
  888 Seventh Avenue
  New York, New York 10019
- The Grantsmanship Center
  1031 South Grand Avenue
  Los Angeles, CA 90015
- Taft Corporation
  1000 Vermont Avenue, N.W.
  Washington, DC 20005
- Public Management Institute
  333 Hayes Street
  San Francisco, CA 94102
- Human Resources Network
  2010 Chancellor Street
  Philadelphia, PA 19103
- National Rural Center
  1828 L Street, N.W.
  Washington, DC 20036

  Publications directed at needs of rural areas and funders active in rural areas.

- Public Service Materials Center
  355 Lexington Avenue
  New York, New York 10017

A review of the directories, publications, and services of any of the preceding groups will quickly impress a grant-seeker with the number and diversity of foundations. Among the resources uncovered will be listings for corporate giving. Large businesses frequently maintain philanthropy programs. If you operate where large, national or international businesses are located, pay particular attention to listings and information on corporate giving. Be on the watch for state foundation directories, also.

Proposal Writing

The basic mechanism for solicitation of funds from government agencies, foundations, and corporations is the proposal. A cover letter, application form, and supporting documents may accompany the proposal. The proposal is essentially an extended essay describing the activity, project, programs, or service your organization hopes the funder will support. The information and evidence presented in the proposal are the basis on which a yes or no funding decision will be made. It is hard to overestimate the important role a proposal plays in the funding process.

While no one can guarantee funding, applicants can certainly increase the odds and avoid costly errors by heeding the following suggestions:

1. Think through your proposed project. Be very clear about your goals and your organization's capabilities. Write down as many details about your project as possible.
2. Locate several potential sources of funds. Check current award lists, analyze mission statements, and funding agendas. Identify several "matches."
3. Visit, call, and write each of these funders. Discuss your project ideas. Ask if your project appears to fit the funder's objectives. Get clarification of the funder's priorities.
4. Assess the situation on the basis of all this information. Go ahead and write the proposal if you are certain there are no major obstacles or automatic disqualifiers lurking ahead.

Proposals must conform to specifications and formats stated by the funder. These specifications are intended to organize the applicant's project information in ways that are compatible with the funder's goals. Similar formats permit easier comparison across competing proposals. Programs submitting proposals to federal agencies or other units for public funds must conform precisely to proposal specifications and deadlines. Rigorous adherence to proposal and review procedures helps ensure that public funds are fairly and legally awarded. Private foundations and corporations often have no precise requirements on proposal format. The general proposal format has the following sequence:

1. *Summary* Summarizes the request.
2. *Introduction* Describes the agency's qualifications or credibility.
3. *Problem Statement or Needs Assessment* Documents the needs to be met or problems to be solved by the proposed funding.
4. *Objectives* Establishes the benefits of the funding in measurable terms.
5. *Methods* Describes the activities to be employed to achieve the desired results.
6. *Evaluation* Presents a plan for determining the degree to which objectives are met and methods are followed.
7. *Future or Other Necessary Funding* Describes a plan for continuation beyond grant period and/or the availability of other resources necessary to implement the grant.
8. *Budget* Clearly delineates costs to be met by the funding source and those to be provided by the applicant or other parties.

(From Kirwitz, N.J. "Program Planning and Proposal Writing" (expanded version), p. 33, *Grantsmanship Center Reprint Series*, May/June, 1979.)

Fund Raisers

Local talent, time, energy and resources are the ingredients of fund raisers. Sooner or later, every child care program will turn to grassroots fund raising for money. Locally raised money may be considered a necessary income source for the program to keep fees low, provide scholarships, or serve as match money for a federal grant. Also, fund raisers can be fun. Everyone pulls together, sharing the labor of the event. Fund raisers, with their attendant publicity, focus the community's attention on the child care program and are good public relations opportunities for many programs.

Fund raisers can also give people headaches. The old reliables end up doing all the work. Nobody volunteers to help. Or, everyone pitches in, and the cash doesn't flow—the "take is low." Morale suffers and the treasury is not enhanced. Roger Neugebauer describes a "fruitless fund raiser":

> A center pours considerable time and energy into a fund raising project which generates only limited funds. For example, a local nursery school sponsors a fair every year. This past year, the school netted $725. after expenses. To earn this amount, parents and staff donated over $100. in cash and 500 hours in labor. If, instead, each parent had donated only $7., the Center would have raised as much money with no effort. (Neugebauer, 1979, p. 32)

Neugebauer suggests doing a cash-benefit analysis before mounting any fund raiser.

> First, estimate the maximum amount of money the project could yield, after expenses. Then estimate the number of staff and volunteer hours required to carry out the project. Finally, divide the dollars by the hours. If the result is less than $10. per hour, the project is probably not worth the effort. From $10. to $25. per hour, it is of marginal value. Above $25. per hour, it is clearly worthwhile. Really successful fund raisers have been known to yield over $100. per hour. (1979, p. 32)

Fund raisers tend to divide into two categories: special events and small fund raisers. *Special events* are large, often annually repeated, efforts that involve many members of the organization and are expected to produce a lot of money. Repeating events capitalize on name recognition in the community and organization "know-how" in running the event. Special events can also be one-time only happenings that build on current events or circumstances—a circus coming to town, the center's tenth birthday, or a local team reaching a playoff in a sports' league. All these may be excellent opportunities for raffles, refreshments, fairs, and so forth. Programs with well-selected, well-oiled special events may be able to raise large amounts of cash with only a few special events each year.

What *small fund raisers* have in common is that no one expects oodles of money to result and organizing efforts are smooth and easy. Typical small fund raisers are movies, bake sales, or a booth at a fair. Chosen wisely, a series of small fund raisers can be managed by different individuals or small groups so no one gets overburdened. Total profit from all small fund raisers may be a good sum.

One of the most profitable local fund raisers is direct solicitation. Individuals, businesses, and groups can be asked to donate money to the program. Prospective donors can be approached by members of the board, friends of the program, or program staff. A thoughtful, well-organized presentation by the solicitor will educate the prospective donor and hopefully stimulate a donation. For more information contact Standards of Charitable Solicitation, Council of Better Business Bureaus, 1150 17th Street, N.W., Washington, DC 20036.

Financial Sponsorship Alternatives

The majority of child care arrangements are sought by parents or provided through subsidy in order for parents to work. Employers, as well as parents, have become increasingly aware of the importance of child care for work force participation. Some astute businesspeople have recognized the profit potential of child care as a service business for working parents. With fewer public subsidy dollars available for child care, private sector services are increasing in number and importance. Programmatically, these services can and do compare favorably with existing publicly supported programs. Characteristics and quality of care are not generally at issue. The patterns of sponsorship and financial resources available in the private sector create a different operating context for child care programs, reflected in facility location, parental involvement, fees, staffing, levels, or overall program management.

Employer-Supported Child Care

Employers become involved in child care for a number of reasons—from enlightened self-interest to the desire to make a contribution to society. Employer involvement in child care ranges from the substantial financial commitment of on-site centers to flexible sick leave policies that permit employees to care for ill children. The large number of women with young children in the work force has led employers to recognize and deal with the parental responsibilities of their employees. Adequate child care is thought to be related to employee morale, work force turnover, tardiness, and absenteeism. Some employers see employer-subsidized child care as a useful recruiting tool or as an incentive for employees to remain with the company. The federal government also encourages employer-supported child care through tax incentives. Businesses are permitted deductions and depreciation allowances for certain expenses related to the provision of child care. The following list indicates some employer assistance options that have been developed to help employees with child care.

Direct Services

- Work-site day care centers
- Summer recreation program
- After-school care
- Family day care homes

Financial Assistance

- Subsidized fees at local centers
- Slots purchased in local programs
- Corporate contributions to local programs

Information and Referral

- Child care location services, exchanges, and clearinghouses
- Counseling programs
- "Getting it all together" seminars and workshops

Work Schedules

- Flex-time
- Part-time
- Job sharing

Box 12.1 An Example of Corporate Child Care

The Zale Child Care Center is located about 50 feet from the main building of the Corporation in Dallas, Texas. The center has a capacity of up to 85 children ranging from infants to five-year-olds. Parents pay a monthly fee to cover operating expenses. (Courtesy of Zale Corporation Photography Department.)

Dr. Michael Romaine, Vice President, Community Relations at Zale Corporation described Zale's child care program as follows:

A carefully planned, well-run, on site child care center offers many advantages to the working parent—and to the company. Morning routines are simplified with parent and child headed in the same direction. The child remains nearby and parents are available immediately in the case of illness or injury. Absenteeism declines.

But convenience is only part of the story. Corpo-

Benefit Plans

- Flexible leave policies
- Choice of benefit packages

On-site or work-based child care centers are one of the oldest and most visible forms of employer support. These programs represent a clear financial commitment by the employer. Support is provided for capital outlays, facility construction and/or renovation, start-up costs, and some portion of ongoing operating costs. Parents are often intensely involved in initiating and planning programs. Very little on-site care existed prior to World War II, but during the war years, large numbers of married women entered the industrial work force as men left their jobs for military service. Government- and industry-sponsored child care centers were established to support the war effort and allow women to work. An outstanding example of this wartime effort is the Kaiser Centers at the Kaiser Shipyards in Portland, Oregon. At their peak the Kaiser Centers served 680 children, while operating three shifts, twenty-four hours a day, seven days a week. By all accounts the rate child care programs are a symbol of caring. In an age when we are all being urged more and more to take responsibility for individual needs, corporate child care is an important innovation. It's an indication that big business has a heart as well as a balance sheet.

Zale's Child Care Center was carefully designed to provide a warm, supportive atmosphere for children and to ensure that they have the personal attention and stimulation needed at each point in their development. Zale's Center is a family-oriented center which strives for a real sense of teamwork between parents and staff to provide the best possible care for the children.

Physically the child care facility near our corporate headquarters in Dallas, Texas, occupies a 5,000 square foot building. Maximum occupancy is 85 children with no more than 24 infants under the age of 18 months allowed. The staff consists of an experienced child care center director, a lead teacher with child development credentials and 10 years of classroom experience, plus a staff of attendants which meets State Licensing Standards . . .

Corporate child care was an idea whose time had come at Zale Corporation. Our company has experienced numerous benefits from the program. Although it is financially subsidized by about $2,500 per month, the benefits far outweigh the costs. In-house child care humanizes our company. It shows our awareness of children and youth and instills the same awareness in our employees. Corporate child care also helps attract women employees as well as bring them back after childbirth. Our center boasts a long waiting list for infants, including the names of some Zale employees who have not even conceived.

In addition to helping us keep trained employees, having the child nearby improves a parent's attitude on the job. Parents have extra time with their child when commuting to and from work and are encouraged to visit during lunch or a break. Other advantages to the parent and child include:

- Parental participation in policy formation
- Ease of reaching child in emergencies
- Child able to visit parental work site
- Parent and child can share holiday themes
- Parent can be present for important development milestones
- Mothers of infants can feed

Source: Courtesy of Dr. Michael Romaine, Vice President, Community Relations, Zale Corporation, Irving, Texas: used with permission.

Kaiser Centers were well staffed and provided excellent child care as well as a host of complementary services, including care for mildly ill children and take-home meals for purchase. After the war the Kaiser Centers and most other industry facilities were closed.

Currently a number of sponsored child care programs are in operation around the country. Many are work-site centers supported by industry and unions. Hospitals and educational institutions are becoming involved in child care supporting centers for employees and students. As employers try to match resources with employee needs for child care, several have turned to variations of the work-site center, including day care homes. An example is in Box 12.1.

Not everyone advocates employer involvement in child care. There is concern that employees may feel trapped in jobs because the cost and convenience of employer-supported child care services cannot be duplicated elsewhere. This is of particular concern in fields where women may tolerate low pay, overtime, and undesirable working conditions because of the company's benevolence in child care areas.

From an employer's perspective, investments

Box 12.2 How to Go about Developing Employer-Supported Child Care

Although each workplace has different needs, administrative structures, and planning techniques, some steps are generally helpful.

1. *Get outside consultation* There is no need to reinvent the wheel! Call us or your local child care information and referral for names of groups in your area who can help you get advice on how to approach the subject and what particular information you will need.
2. *Form a working committee* Be sure to begin with representatives from the widest range of employees at the workplace, including management, clerical, administration, maintenance, etc.
3. *Do a needs assessment* Gather statistics on how many employees need child care, how much they can afford to pay, and what they see as a workable/ideal situation for their children and themselves. Collect information on ages of children, geographical locations of homes, modes of transportation, etc. Consultants can help develop a needs assessment to suit the individual situation as well as help analyze the results.
4. *Make a time plan and try to stay with it* The development of your ideal employer-sponsored child care probably won't take place immediately. Plan the benefits in stages and try to insure some continuity by incorporating child care in the future plans of the company and work force negotiations.
5. *Research the physical availability of child care in your area* This will prevent duplication of existing services. It will also show the met and un-met needs, the open market costs for services, and models of child care delivery. In California there is a network of Child Care Information and Referral agencies to help you find these statistics. Call us for the Information and Referral in your area.
6. *Enlist professional organizations or unions when appropriate* The role of organized labor groups in employer-supported child care is entirely dependent upon the situation of each company or consortia of companies. However, a clear picture of the present and future employment scene in the community should be analyzed when developing child care plans.
7. *Utilize in-house media* Bulletin boards, newsletters, etc. should all include articles on child care as an issue—both for the company and the community.
8. *Don't be afraid to start small* One or two parents with a lot of perseverance can begin to work wonders!

Source: BANANAS HANDOUT: A Look at Employer-Supported Child Care, Oakland, CA: BANANAS, Child Care Information & Referral and Parent Support; used with permission.

in child care are not clearly cost-beneficial. Few employer-sponsored programs break even; most rely on heavy subsidies from employers. Businesses have not taken advantage of tax incentives for child care in any great numbers, either. For most employers, provision of child care reaps rewards in intangible areas such as employee morale and attitude.

Employer-supported child care is an area of increasing interest and action in child care. Work by Dana Friedman, Kathryn Senn Perry, and Sandy Burud has been instrumental in establishing a factual foundation and instigating a dialogue about need, services, and options. The Reagan administration has promoted employer-supported child care through high-level briefings with industry leaders and well-publicized meetings of all interested parties. We predict employer-supported child care will continue to develop as a major vehicle for the delivery of quality child care services to children and families. The resource section at the end of the chapter lists several pivotal references for those who wish to pursue the topic further. Box 12.2 describes a plan for developing employer-supported child care.

Proprietary Child Care

Actions by the federal government indicate a shift away from subsidized nonprofit programs to dependence on the marketplace to meet the child care needs of all but a small number of low-income families. Proprietary, or for-profit, centers are likely to increase in number in order to meet parental demand for child care.

Caring for children on a profit-making basis has long been viewed with suspicion and outright disgust by many in the field. Joseph Featherstone's 1968 article "Kentucky Fried Children" did little to allay concerns. In 1971, Alice Lake surveyed profit centers and asked the obvious question: "What comes first—the child or the dollar?" Despite these concerns, independent, profit-making child care centers continued to exist—many as "mom and pop" businesses and others as part of national chains, regional businesses, or franchises.

Today proprietary child care centers fill a real need for parents who do not qualify in subsidized programs, who cannot afford in-home care, and who want a group experience other than a family day care home for their children. Descriptive information from nationwide surveys, especially Alice Lake's 1980 survey, indicates that quality levels of profit centers compare favorably to nonprofit centers.

> Ten years have passed, . . . I have surveyed the day care business again. My conclusion is that in large measure I and all the other critics were wrong. Like most day care in the United States, corporate care has matured. It is not per se the best or the worst, but represents one part of a smorgasbord of choices: public and private, profit and non-profit. (Lake, 1980, p. 31)

The Child Care Market

How large is the domestic child care industry? Is it attractive to investors? Montgomery Securities of San Francisco estimates the size of the child care industry in the United States to be about $7–8 billion annually. They describe the industry as one that is highly fragmented, suggesting good potential for growth through chain operators:

> It is our belief that long-term success in the child care business requires that centers be managed by local individuals who possess the flexibility to design and administer programs tailored to the needs and desires of the local community. Lacking this local reputation and high degree of operating autonomy, we believe centers will too easily develop a sterile, institutionalized image and will not be successful in winning the trust and confidence of the parents in the community. The most successful chain operator will, we believe, be the one who achieves the most effective balance between these often conflicting goals of centralization and local control. (Montgomery Securities, 1981, p. 3)

The three largest chains, in order of size, are Kinder-Care, LaPetite Academy, and Children's World, Inc. These chains have multistate operations and operate from one hundred to one thousand centers. National Child Care Centers, Palo Alto Pre-schools, and Gerber Children's Centers are smaller, more regional chains operating around thirty to fifty centers. In addition, a number of local chains with three to ten centers have appeared across the country. Mary Moppets' Day Care is the largest franchise operation. Descriptive information is given in Box 12.3.

In 1976–1977, the National Day Care Study (Ruopp, Travers, Glantz, & Coelen, 1979) looked at the legal status and sponsorship of full-day programs for young children; part-day nursery and Head Start programs were excluded from the survey. Proprietary centers accounted for 40 percent of all programs (35 percent independent, 6 percent affiliated with chains or groups). Approximately 60 percent of the programs were nonprofit (19 percent independent, 16 percent church sponsored, and the remaining 25 percent sponsored by various community and government groups). Independent, proprietary centers provide most of the child care capacity of private programs. These programs are frequently operated as small busi-

Box 12.3 The Burgeoning Growth of Child-Care Chains

No manifesto issued by the Women's Movement for the past decade has been complete without a call for government-funded day care, to enable women to work even if they have young children. But except for some centers designed primarily for welfare families and the working poor, the government has paid no attention.

Nevertheless, because entrepreneurs saw the promise of a burgeoning market in an area that the politicians largely chose to ignore, day care for the children of middle-class families has turned into a flourishing business. Today 10 major chains operate about 1,000 child-care centers (the sanitized new name for day-care centers), collecting $100 million annually from the mostly middle-class families whose children attend them.

Although the chains account for only 5% of the country's 19,000 licensed child-care centers—and all licensed centers account for only $2.3 billion of the estimated $7.5 billion spent annually on child care—they are by far the fastest growing segment of the market. Steady increases in the number of working mothers almost ensure even greater future prosperity.

Always there. To working mothers who formerly depended on sometimes unreliable babysitters or sometimes indisposed relatives—and who shunned the custodially oriented government centers—the chain-run centers sound better than Mary Poppins. The typical center boasts college-trained instructors, meals planned by nutritionists, and activities that develop physical, mental, and social skills. And they are always there. "We never go on vacation or call in sick or get another job. Parents know they can count on us," says JoAnn Blasky, director of a center run by Children's World Inc. in Arvada, Colo., a suburb of Denver.

Children's World, which runs 80 child-care centers, is the third largest chain after Kinder-Care Learning Centers Inc., of Montgomery, Ala., with 478 centers, and La Petite Academy, of Kansas City, Mo., a division of CenCor Inc., with 165 centers. Kinder-Care expects to have 520 centers by next summer and 2,000 by 1987. La Petite Academy plans more than 200 centers by next year. Children's World, with headquarters in Evergreen, Colo., projects 90 centers by next year, with 15 more in each following year. All three say that a waiting list forms as soon as they announce building plans.

The typical chain-run center that inspires such enthusiasm resembles a classic nursery school. Divided into groups by age, the children do simple crafts, play, learn their ABCs, eat lunch and snacks and sometimes breakfast, take naps, and go outdoors for fresh air and games. There is free time, group time for stories and discussion (including morale-building talk about "what Mommy does at work"), and field trips to museums and zoos. School-age children are bused to the centers for after-school activities, usually sports, and the centers also run vacation programs.

The average center stays open 12 hours a day to accommodate a variety of parental working hours, although the average child spends only nine hours there. For the parents' convenience, most centers are located on the "morning side" of main highways—the side a driver uses getting from suburban

---

nesses and are closely tied to the personalities of owners and communities. Independent programs are not particularly high-profit businesses. Owners find that sometimes costs exceed the local market's willingness to pay higher fees. Licensing and regulation requirements can be a cause of concern and require continual monitoring for operators.

The National Association for Child Care Management (NACCM), 1800 M St. N.W., Washington, DC 20036, is a nonprofit organization for owners of proprietary centers. NACCM publishes a newsletter and offers a number of services to member businesses. They are conducting membership surveys and raising the profile of the organization among child care providers.

One notable difference between proprietary centers and nonprofit centers stands out. Care in profit centers costs less. Lower staff-child rahome to city office—and have large glass entrances, so that a watching mother can see her child safely inside.

The usual weekly rate is $35; the handful of centers that accept children under the age of two charge $60 for the babies. The federal government subsidizes some of this outlay with a tax credit of up to $800 a year for a family that pays child-care fees for two children as a working expense.

Basically, notes Perry Mendel, president of Kinder-Care, "the working mother has developed a guilt complex, and she is not happy about leaving her child in a substandard facility. When you provide a good facility, the guilt goes away."

The chains do everything possible to forstall the guilt. Many of their centers were specially designed for children, many boast student-to-teacher ratios of 10 to 1 or better, and center directors uniformly stress that their young graduates have fewer adjustment problems when they enter grade school than do children brought up at home. "I don't worry about my son," says Janet L. Jones, an executive secretary with Merrill Lynch, Pierce, Fenner & Smith Inc. in Denver. Three-year-old Michael Jones spends his weekdays at the Arvada Children's World center and says he likes it fine.

Residential. Running this kind of operation is feasible only under the sophisticated auspices of a chain, chain executives insist. Corporate staffs can oversee teacher training, meal planning, and educational activities while providing both financial backing and quality control, they say. "Most mom-and-pop centers don't have the managerial ability and can't conceive of replicating services, whereas the chains come to the business with that idea," says Robert S. Benson, president of Children's World. The average facility, with an enrollment of 100 to 110 children, costs $150,000 to $200,000 to build and equip and nets from $20,000 to $25,000 a year.

Most centers are situated in fast-growing, middle-class suburbs, because the chains have found that mothers prefer to leave their children near home rather than near work. Some chains have experimented with company-sponsored child-care centers: Living & Learning Centers Inc., of Waltham, Mass., runs four centers on the grounds of New England insurance companies, and Kinder-Care recently opened a center on the grounds of Ralston Purina Co. in St. Louis. But the consensus is that the future of child care lies in residential neighborhoods.

Demand for child-care centers should easily outstrip supply during the 1980s, but demographers project that increases in the number of working mothers will slow during the 1990s. Executives of the child-care chains seem unworried. By then, they say, they will have a second-generation market consisting in part of a presold clientele. Says Sherri, a 5-year-old at Children's World in Arvada: "It's boring staying at home alone. I'd rather be here than anywhere else."

tios and lower salaries may be the reason. Or, for centers that are part of large chains, economies of scale may contribute to lower cost. Cost comparisons may be inappropriate because comprehensive, publicly subsidized care is not equivalent to the basic, no-frills service of many proprietary centers. Public dollars buy a lot of child care service, but, for the average children, that may be more service than they need and more care than their parents want to pay for. Proprietary centers fill a need and serve a clientele different from publicly supported centers.

Issues

Who Should Pay for Child Care?

The most straightforward and narrowest response to this question is that parents should pay child care costs. Children are a parents' responsibility. But communities and society as a whole have a vested interest in the well-being of future citizens. Working parents make desirable economic contributions that cannot be dismissed as unnecessary. Children are a shared responsibility of all people. For those who see child care as a support system for working families, it follows that cost containment or subsidies such as the child care tax-credit, SSBG and other federal program funds, and special tax breaks are reasonable strategies. Related issues concern the fairness and universality of such financial help. Does society have the responsibility to help low-income parents and parents with special needs to the exclusion of all parents?

How Can Salaries Be Higher?

Salaries are low, reflecting both the low status of child care as an occupation and the scarcity of funds from all sources to cover child care costs. Higher salaries are necessary to attract *and* keep good staff, who are the dominant factor in quality of care. Raising parent fees will price most parents out of the child care market. Public funds are not the answer since government budgets must absorb real dollar costs and the inflationary erosion of purchasing power. Not until child care is a valued and higher prestige occupation will salaries be uniformly commensurate with staff responsibilities and training. Raising salaries is a symbolic gesture, a single step in changing a complex set of attitudes and traditional practices. Whether raising salaries is the appropriate first step toward necessary change remains to be seen.

Are Public Funding Conditions Limiting Child Care?

Regulations and service requirements for child care provided through public fund auspices are known to raise costs over care provided in informal settings and proprietary programs. Most children are *not* cared for in publicly funded programs, which calls into question the necessity of such requirements. While we want to protect children, enrich their lives, and monitor expenditure of public dollars, we cannot ignore the fact that the majority of parents consistently arrange care outside the monitored child care system. Congress has chosen not to enforce federal child care requirements, leaving states to determine care conditions. Costs are such a critical issue in child care service that parent behavior in seeking tolerable cost alternatives must be considered when monitoring procedures are designed.

What Are the Most Cost-Effective Forms of Child Care?

Center-based programs for preschool children receive most of the attention in discussions of child care. Until recently it was assumed that center programs were appropriate for all children. Grass roots practice is showing us otherwise. Family day care is the preferred mode of care for infants. School-age children are least often found in center programs. If costs are to be controlled child care cannot afford to promote a single, acceptable form of care. Cheaper, more flexible care alternatives for many children are functioning and need to be legitimatized and capitalized upon.

Summary

The services that a child care program can provide are defined by the source and stability of the funding and the program's spending patterns. To manage the program's money directors should have basic accounting skills, understand budgeting, and have the competence to initiate funding proposals or fund-raising activities. Directors share the money management and financial decision-making tasks with accountants, bookkeepers, and a board of directors.

Money management begins with a budget, which is an itemized statement of income and expenditures. An annual operating budget is really a composite of a subsidized-deficit budget, a service contract budget, a grant budget, and a start-up budget. Directors develop a budget by estimating a program's income and expenditures. The utilization rate, which is necessary for calculating income, is found by dividing the actual fee income by maximum fee income. In-kind donations, which are donated supplies or services in lieu of money, should be included in the computation of income.

The three types of budget statements are line-item, which lists each income and expenditure category on a separate line; program, which indicates the fiscal status of just a single program; and functional, which organizes expenditures by service category.

A Standardized Accounting System consists of a Chart of Accounts, a set of journals, and a General Ledger. The journals record cash receipts, cash disbursements, payroll, petty cash, and noncash transactions. Directors must learn proper management procedures for payroll, petty cash, checkbook usage, purchasing, and auditing.

Staff salaries account for the largest amount of a program's costs. The general formula for computing per child costs is to divide costs by the number of children times the amount of time the program operates.

Fees are the direct, cash costs of child care for parents. Break-even analysis calculates the amount to charge in order to pay bills. Sliding fee analysis allows low-income families to pay a reduced fee.

Reimbursements are the public funds intended to cover the balance between a program's costs and its income. To qualify for funding a program may submit formal proposals to government agencies or private institutions for public or private funds.

In addition to nonprofit child care centers, there are employer-supported centers, proprietary centers, and child care chains. Debate continues over the wisdom of involving employers in child care and over the quality of care in proprietary centers. However, the great demand for child care coupled with a general governmental posture favoring marketplace initiative and private sponsorship undoubtably means increasing growth in nonpublic forms of child care service.

Resources

General

Bruce-Biggs, B. (1977). Child care: The fiscal time bomb. *Public Interest, 49,* 87–102.

Levitan, S. A., & Alderman, K. C. (1975). *Child care and ABC's too.* Baltimore, MD: Johns Hopkins University Press.

Model child care standards act: Guidance to states to prevent child abuse in day care facilities. (1985). Washington, DC: U.S. Department of Health and Human Services.

Neugebauer, R. (1979). Managing your money: Avoiding the pitfalls. *Day Care and Early Education,* Fall, 31–34.

Rivlin, A. (1978). *Child care and preschool: Options for federal support.* Washington, DC: Congressional Budget Office.

Rowe, M. P., & Husby, R. D. (1973). Economics of child care: Costs, needs, and issues. In P. Roby (Ed.), *Child care—Who cares?* (pp. 98–122). New York: Basic Books.

Ruopp, R. R., & Travers, J. (1982). Janus faces day care: Perspectives on quality and cost. In E. F. Zigler & E. W. Gordon (Eds.), *Day care: Scientific and social policy issues* (pp. 72–101). Boston: Auburn House.

Ruopp, R., Travers, J., Glantz, F., & Coelen, C. (1979). *Children at the center. Final report of the national day care study: Vol. 1.* Cambridge, MA: Abt Associates.

States use several strategies to cope with funding reductions under social service block grant. (1984). Washington, DC: General Accounting Office.

Summary report of the assessment of current state practices in Title XX funded day care programs. (1981). Report to Congress, October. Washington, DC: U.S. Department of Health and Human Services, Administration for Children, Youth, and Families, Day Care Division. (ERIC Document Reproduction Service No. ED 211 217)

Budgets and Accounting Procedures

American Institute of Certified Public Accountants. (1974). *Audits of voluntary health and welfare organizations.* New York: American Institute of Certified Public Accountants.

Atkinson, J. (1973). *Day care costs. Day care accounting.* Boston: Office of Children, Massachusetts State 4-C Committee.

Beyers, B. B. (1974). *A planning and budget management system for day care.* Washington, DC: Educational Projects. (ERIC Document Reproduction Service No. ED 095 622)

Doyle, D. M. (1977). *Efficient accounting and recordkeeping.* New York: Wiley.

Fox, J. C. (1979). Minimum wage laws and child care: A legal view. *Child Care Information Exchange, 9,* 9–10.

Gilman, K. (1982). *Computers for nonprofits.* San Francisco: Public Management Institute.

Gilman, K. *Computer resource guide for nonprofits.* San Francisco: Public Management Institute.

Gordon, T. P. (1984). When you think you need an audit—points to consider. *Exchange,* October, 22–24.

Gross, M., & Warshauer, W. (1979). *Financial and accounting guide for nonprofit organizations* (3rd ed.). New York: Wiley.

Money management tools—Cash flow analysis. (1981). *Child Care Information Exchange, 19,* 7–10.

Morgan, G. G. (1982). *Managing the day care dollars.* Cambridge, MA: Steam Press.

Travis, N., & Perreault, J. (1981). *Day care financial management: Considerations in starting a for-profit or not-for-profit program.* Atlanta: Child Care Support Center.

United Way of America. (1974). *Accounting and financial reporting: A guide for United Ways and not-for-profit human service organizations.* Alexandria, VA: United Way of America.

United Way of America. (1974). *Budgeting—A guide for United Ways and not-for-profit human service organizations.* Alexandria, VA: United Way of America.

Youngquist, E., & Farrell, G. (1980). *Effective fiscal management in human services programs: Vol. 1. Dollars and sense: An accounting overview for the social service manager and non-accountant.* Washington, DC: U.S. Department of Health and Human Services, Office of Policy Development/Human Development Services.

Youngquist, E., & Farrell, G. (1980). *Effective fiscal management in human services programs: Vol. 2. Guide to bookkeeping and financial reporting.* Washington, DC: U.S. Department of Health and Human Services, Office of Policy Development/HDS.

Costs and Fees

Abt Associates. (1972). *Cost and quality issues for operators.* Washington, DC: Office of Economic Opportunity. (Reprinted by Day Care and Child Development Council of America).

AVCO Corporation. (1973). *A demonstration care review system: Final report. Cost of day care* (Contract HEW SRS 71-48). Washington, DC: AVCO International Division.

Day Care Council of America. (1981). *How to start a day care center.* Washington, DC: Author.

Elliott, P., & Forman, J. (1980). *Analyzing costs in human services program: Vol. 2. Procedures manual.* Washington, DC: U.S. Department of Health and Human Services, Office of Policy Development.

Entis, E. (1980). *Analyzing costs in human services programs: Vol. 4. Rate setting guide.* Washington, DC: U.S. Department of Health and Human Services, Office of Policy Development/HDS.

Forman, J., Elliott, P., & Riesett, R. (1980). *Analyzing costs in human services programs: Vol. 3. Trainer's manual.* Washington, DC: U.S. Department of Health and Human Services, Office of Policy Development/HDS.

Forman, J., Elliott, P., & Riesett, R. (1981). *Analyzing costs in human services programs: Vol. 1. Reader's guide.* Washington, DC: U.S. Department of Health and Human Services, Office of Policy Development/HDS.

Massachusetts Early Education Project. (1972). The costs of child care: Money and other resources. Chapter 8 of *Child care in Massachusetts, the public responsibility.* Reprinted by Day Care and Child Development Council of America, Washington, DC.

Money management tools—Breakeven analysis. (1979). *Child Care Information Exchange, 8,* 27–33.

Money management tools—Fee collection procedures. (1980). *Child Care Information Exchange, 11,* 6–8.

Neugebauer, R. (1984). Implementing a sliding fee scale system in your center. *Child Care Information Exchange,* June, 28–32.

Prosser, W. R. (1977). Day care in the seventies—Some thoughts. In *Child care data and materials.* Washington, DC: U.S. Government Printing Office.

REAP Associates. (1975). *A study of day care costs: Their impact on day care center quality.* Washington, DC: Resources for Evaluation, Analyses and Planning. (ERIC Document Reproduction Service No. ED 121 423)

Seaver, J. W. (n.d.). *The effect of inflation on the Title XX program: A policy paper.* Washington, DC: U.S. Department of Health and Human Services, Office of Policy Department HDS.

Standards and costs for day care. (1968). Washington, DC: Day Care and Child Development Council of America, Children's Bureau, U.S. Department of Health, Education and Welfare.

Winget, W. G. (1982). The dilemma of affordable child care. In E. F. Zigler & E. W. Gordon (Eds.), *Day care: Scientific and social policy issues* (pp. 351–377). Boston: Auburn House.

Fund-Raising Guides

Allen, H. (1981). *The bread game: The realities of foundation fund raising* (4th rev. ed.). San Francisco: Regional Young Adult Project.

Ardman, P. & H. (1980). *The woman's day book of fund raising.* New York: St. Martin's Press.

Child Care Information Exchange. (n.d.). *Fund raising.* (reprint no. 10). Redmond, WA: Child Care Information Exchange.

Dodge, A. B., & Tracy, D. F. (Eds.). (1978). *How to raise money for kids (public and private).* Washington, DC: Coalition for Children and Youth.

Drotning, P. T. (1979). *Putting the fun in fund raising: 500 ways to raise money for charity.* Chicago: Contemporary Books.

Finn, M. (1982). *Fund raising for early childhood programs: Getting started and getting results.* Washington, DC: National Association for the Education of Young Children.

Flanagan, J. (1982). *Grass roots fund raising book: How to raise money in your community.* Chicago: Contemporary Books.

Gurin, M. G. (1981). *What volunteers should know for successful fund raising.* New York: Stein and Day.

Hillman, H., & Abarbanel, K. (1975). *The art of winning foundation grants.* New York: Vanguard.

Kiritz, N. J. (1979). *Program planning and proposal writing* (expanded version). *Grantsmanship Center Reprint Series.*

Lesko, M. (1984). *Getting yours: The complete guide to government money* (rev. ed.). New York: Penguin Books.

Pendleton, N. (1981). *Fund raising: A guide for non-profit organizations.* Englewood Cliffs, NJ: Prentice-Hall.

Successful small fund raisers. (1979). Day Care Administration Bulletin no. 1. Atlanta: Training for Child Care Project/Southern Regional Education Board.

Warner, I. R. (1975). *The art of fund raising.* New York: Harper and Row.

Employer-Supported Child Care

Anderson, K. (1983). *Corporate initiatives for working parents in New York City: A ten-industry review.* New York: Center for Public Advocacy Research.

Avrin, C., & Sassen, G. (1974). *Corporations and child care: Profit making day care; workplace day care; and a look at alternatives.* Cambridge, MA: Women's Research Action Project.

Baden, C., & Friedman, D. E. (Eds.). (1981). *New management initiatives for working parents.* Reports from an April 1981 Conference. Boston: Wheelock College, Office of Continuing Education.

Bureau of National Affairs. (1984). *Employers and child care: Development of a new employee benefit.* Washington, DC: Author.

Burud, S., Aschbacher, P., & McCroskey, J. (1984). *Employer-supported child care: Investing in human resources.* Boston: Auburn House.

Copeland, T. (Ed.). (n.d.). *Parents in the workplace: A management resource for employers.* St. Paul, MN: Toys 'n Things.

A corporate reader: Work and family life in the 1980s. (1983). Washington, DC: Children's Defense Fund.

Corporations and the family in the 1980s. (1982). Philadelphia: Human Resources Network.

Douglas, J. I. (Ed.). (1976). *Dollars and sense: Employer-supported child care. A study on child care needs, and the realities of employer-support.* (ERIC Document Reproduction Service No. ED 129 417)

Friedman, D. E. (1981). *On the fringe of benefits: Working parents and the corporation.* New York: Center for Public Resources.

Friedman, D. E. (1983). *Encouraging employer support to working parents.* New York: Carnegie Corporation.

Friedman, D. E. (1983). *Government initiatives to encourage employer-supported child care: The state and local perspective.* New York: Center for Public Advocacy Research.

Haiman, P., & Sud, G. (Eds.). (1980). *Employer supported child care: An idea whose time has come. A conference on child care as an employee benefit (costs and benefits, successful programs, company options, current issues).* (ERIC Document Reproduction Service No. ED 201 400)

Magid, R. Y. (1983). *Child care initiatives for working parents: Why employers get involved.* New York: American Management Associations.

Manuel, D. (1982). The tycoon and the toddler. *Graduate Woman,* Winter 17–18 & 36.

Murray, K. A. (1981). *Legal aspects of child care as an employee benefit.* (rev. ed.) San Francisco: Bay Area Child Care Law Project.

Perry, K. S. (1980). *Child care centers sponsored by employers and labor unions in the United States.* Washington, DC: U.S. Department of Labor, Office of the Secretary Women's Bureau. (ERIC Document Reproduction Service No. ED 200 331)

Perry, K. S., & Moore, G. T. (1981). *Employers and child care: Establishing services through the workplace.* (Pamphlet 23) Washington, DC: Department of Labor, Women's Bureau. (ERIC Document Reproduction Service No. ED 198 950)

Pettygrove, W. (1981). *Employer sponsored child care: Four issue papers.* (ERIC Document Reproduction Service No. ED 207 688)

Tax incentives for employer-sponsored day care programs. (1982). Chicago: Commerce Clearing House, Inc.

The child care handbook—Needs, programs, and possibilities. (1982). Washington, DC: Children's Defense Fund.

Proprietary Day Care

Child care in the 80's—Status report on for-profit child care. (1981). *Child Care Information Exchange, 17,* 19–26.

Cook, A., & Mack, H. (1974). Business in education—The discovery center hustle. In V. Breitbart (Ed.), *The Day Care Book* (pp. 43–51). New York: Knopf.

Featherstone, J. (1970). The day care problem: Kentucky fried children. *The New Republic,* September 12.

Frost, T. S. (1976). *Where have all the woolly moths gone? A small business survival manual.* West Nyack, NY: Parker Publishing.

Kagan, S. L., & Glennon, T. (1982). Considering proprietary child care. In E. F. Zigler & E. W. Gordon (Eds.), *Day care: Scientific and social policy* (pp. 402–412). Boston: Auburn House.

Lake, A. (1974). The day care business: Which comes first—The child or the dollar? In V. Breitbart (Ed.), *The day care book* (pp. 37–41). New York: Knopf.

Lake, A. (1980). The day care business. *Working Mother,* November, 143–146, 150–158.

Lake, A. (1980). The day care business. *Working Mother,* September, 31–34, 37, 144–146.

Montgomery Securities Institutional Research (San Francisco, CA). (1981). April 22, p. 3.

Small children as a small business: A primer for potential investors in day care center. (1971). New York: Child Welfare League of America.

13

Regulations and Legal Concerns

Introduction

Directors and program staff cannot ignore the regulatory and legal aspects of child care. Licensing officials, fire inspectors, health officers, and building and sanitation inspectors may periodically tour the facility and observe the program in operation. Unless the program complies with the standards and codes represented by these inspectors, it is in legal jeopardy. The Internal Revenue Service (IRS) is very interested in the flow of money in and out of program coffers. Legal assistance is needed to incorporate, to file for tax-exempt status as a nonprofit organization, and to meet business tax obligations. Insurance is necessary to provide risk protection and liability coverage. Even the simplest daily events raise legal questions:

Children walk to a neighborhood market: *Do you have field trip permission?*
Staff member uses private car to take children to school in the afternoon since it is raining heavily and it is a long walk: *Does the program's automobile insurance cover this?*
The new refrigerator won't fit through an inside door, so it is left in the hall: *Should you use it anyway?*
You buy decorations and favors for a Valentine's Day party: *Do you pay sales tax?*

The first section of this chapter covers licensing, regulations, and codes. Here we discuss some of the principles and ideas that lie behind the regulations, the legal authority that supports them, common terms, and the actual content of some regulations. Readers will find it useful to obtain a copy of their state standards and refer to it alongside the text. (Appendix D gives addresses of state licensing units.) The second part of the chapter introduces basic legal concerns of interest to child care administrators. Topics include form of organization, taxes, insurance, and contracts.

Regulation and Licensing

Licensing is formal, legal permission for a program to operate and deliver services. Licensing is intended to "guarantee" an acceptable level of safety and security for those involved in the program. Most people would agree that some form of licensing is necessary for child care, yet there is little agreement in concept, practice, or evaluation as to exactly what and how licensing should function. Whatever one personally believes about licensing, children, parents, and staff deserve the best child care programs possible, and it is unreasonable to suggest or plan for these programs to operate outside the law. Many child care staff, therefore, see a two-fold responsibility in this area: to help programs meet current laws while working to restructure those same laws.

Regulations *are* changing. States and municipalities are responding to the concerns of the child care community and reexamining and rewriting regulations. Several states have achieved model standards and are working on implementation procedures. Still others are just beginning to work seriously at licensing and regulations. Family day care, infant care, and care for handicapped children are coming to be seen as "special care" situations requiring different regulations.

The tensions and frustrations evident in current licensing practices have their roots in historical assumptions that are incompatible with the reality of child care today. Let's look at some of this historical background here.

Basis of Regulation

By the 1940s, nearly all states had licensing standards for foster child care. The stimulus of several White House Conferences on Children and the leadership of the newly formed federal Children's Bureau put public attention on the needs of dependent children in twenty-four-hour care in institutions and foster homes. Agencies with placement responsibilities were covered to some extent by the standards. While these foster child care standards differed greatly in content and scope, all were clearly intended to be protective. The advent of World War II brought a huge influx of women into the industrial work force. Child care centers became necessary to sustain the productivity of these workers. Expediency prevailed. "The result was the 'jamming' of the child day care safeguarding provisions into the existing 24-hour care licensing statute, regardless of the operational fit." (Class, 1980, p. 5) Child care licensing has not yet been disentangled from this early association.

Protection or Prevention? Historically licensing for child care has had a protective function. The state uses its powers to ensure that all children are equally protected in circumstances of potential risk. In the case of foster care or institutional care regulatory protection seems warranted. These situations are not normal conditions for a child—they are outside the focus of family relationships. Is child care an equivalently atypical condition? Is child care outside the family, or a substitute for parental responsibility?

By definition, child care is less than twenty-four-hour care. Child care is a family choice and a supplement to parent-child relationships. The popular position today is to describe child care as an important support for families—a service that enhances the quality of family life and enables mothers to work and families to enjoy economic security. Given this context, it is obvious that a change in regulatory purpose is called for. While society and the state are concerned with the welfare of the child, parents are neither replaced nor unresponsive in a child care situation. Child care licensing should be permissive, permitting a program to operate subject to specified conditions; and in child care, those regulations must be designed to prevent serious mishap or harm.

The question of protective versus preventive purpose of regulation hits directly at who is responsible for children and how that responsibility is put in effect. Overly rigorous regulations may protect children but place so many limits on programs that few children are served. Lax regulations are not the answer. What we need is a balance of preventive regulation and informed parental consumers.

Target Clientele or Consumers? In the past public services were targeted to children and families in need. For reasons related to health, education, economics, or poor judgment, these families required assistance from others. Until the late 1960s, child care's clientele was characterized as "in need."

Today child care draws a clientele from all socioeconomic levels. Regulations and procedures, however, still have a very strong protective bias, even for programs that operate for profit or totally independent of publicly funded services. Child care is no longer just a program provided for needy clients. It is a business operating in the marketplace to meet the demand for child care of a large number of parents and children. Regulations frequently place undue emphasis on the protection of public service clients and accountability for public funds. Many feel that current regulatory practices actually inhibit free-market child care.

Whose Administrative Responsibility? In most states child care licensing is the responsibility of departments of health, human services, social services, or welfare. At the local level, fire, sanitation, labor, and industry agencies join in. The department and agency titles may vary from locale to locale. The point is that child care is *not* considered an educational service. It does not enjoy public education's universality of acceptance and access or its stability of legislative and financial support. Child care is still tied to the question of need implied in public welfare, which helps explain what appears to be an undue emphasis in the regulations on physical variables and administrative characteristics. Overall, many child care regulations have little to say about what children do in a program. Specificity is reserved for observable and documentable items such as square feet of space per child, building temperatures, playground surfaces, health forms and tests, number and nutritional values of meals.

Legal Basis

Licensing is a state activity, and the legal authority for licensing comes from the power of the state to intervene where there is reason to believe individuals need to be protected from identifiable risks. Licensing assumes someone or something to be licensed—for child care these are providers (staff) and facilities. Regulations, or standards, set forth the necessary conditions for licensure in the form of detailed statements of the characteristics and/or conditions that must be present in the program.

State and local governments have responsibility for public safety and health. Child care programs must meet health, sanitation, safety, fire, and building codes, and a host of related permits and inspections. State licensing regulations may back up local codes by stating that copies of applicable inspections and permits are necessary for state licensing. Or, state licensing regulations may impose more stringent or, unfortunately, conflicting requirements in these areas.

Zoning is the one strictly local requirement that child care programs may confront. Zoning is a question of determination of land use and rests on the police power of local government to control use.

Terminology and Procedures

Licensing is a distinct activity with particular terms and procedures. These words have come to have common meaning through general use. Although the definitions are not always precise, a familiarity with the language will help in understanding the process and relationships.

Permission Formal allowance to operate a program. Permission can take many forms.

1. *Licensing* Basic regulatory procedure for program operation. It is the most common and widely used legal permission. Regular licenses are usually for one to two years and are given following application and inspection. Provisional licenses are temporary permits, often used for new programs trying to come up to standards.
2. *Registration* A recently developed procedure aimed especially at family day care homes. It is based on voluntary adherence to state standards. Registration expects caregiver and parent to share with the state responsibility for ensuring that children are cared for under acceptable conditions. Critics feel that registration is illegal and can give consumers a false expectation of state approval. For the most part, family day care homes are unlicensed. To extend existing licensing procedures to all family day care homes would clearly overwhelm any state licensing staff. Registration is a possible solution.

Box 13.1 NAEYC's Center Accreditation Project: National Academy of Early Childhood Programs

The goals of the National Association for the Education of Young Children (NAEYC) Center Accreditation Project are two-fold: (1) to improve the quality of care and education provided for all young children; and (2) to recognize high quality programs for young children.

The NAEYC will work with programs that voluntarily express interest in accreditation in order to achieve care and education of the highest quality.

The following philosophical concepts underlie the project:

- The personnel in early childhood centers should have an interal commitment to improve program quality.
- A partnership based on mutual trust and respect between NAEYC and program personnel will facilitate and stimulate program improvement.
- Active involvement in the evaluation process by all individuals concerned—parents, staff, administrators—is essential for optimal program development.
- Recognition of and respect for individuality and diversity are essential to optimal program development.
- The program must be considered as an integrated whole in order to assess and improve program quality.

Source: "NAEYC's Center Accreditation Project: Goals and Philosophy," 1983, *Young Children, 38,* pp. 33–36. For further information, see NAEYC, *Accreditation criteria and procedures of the National Academy of Early Childhood Programs.* Washington, DC: NAEYC, 1984.

3. *Certification* A process that signifies approval of a program to provide care subsidized by public funds (generally federal). In states with high-level licensing standards, certification and licensing may be simultaneous. The concept of certification allows a public funder to hold subsidized programs to program service levels deemed most appropriate for taxpayer money. In jurisdictions with minimal standards, certification is leverage for upgrading program quality. The idea of certification is, however, under attack for two reasons:
   a. It promotes a double standard for programs—one for publicly funded and another for private (nonprofit or proprietary) programs. Programs that mix public-private funds can be forced to meet higher public standards for *all* clients.
   b. Higher standards almost always mean higher costs. No one is convinced that the resulting differences (if any) in program quality are worth the extra cost.

   In practice, pinpointing certification standards may take some patience and perseverance. Certification standards may be one or more of the following:
   a. the identical regulations for all child care licensing
   b. a completely different set of regulations just for publicly funded programs
   c. a set of administrative guidelines with no onsite inspection provisions
   d. accounting and audit requirements that must be met by programs receiving public funds

   Certification is closely related to rate setting, the formula by which the government pays for child care services. The government determines what level of care is to be offered (as stated in regulations) and then sets a rate at which providers will be reimbursed for that care. According to many providers, rates do not always cover the actual costs of care. This puts the providers in the position of subsidizing the government!

Statements of Worth Formal recognition of quality levels or skill achievement. These are often voluntarily sought and prominently and proudly displayed.

1. *Credential* Education and qualification standards obtained by staff and professional person-

Box 13.2 Comments on Inspections

"We had a pre-licensing visit. It was okay. I was real nervous but the child care inspector was methodical and quick. We got our license. But, you know, it was *two years* before we had a real inspection with the kids here and the program running. I had no idea what to expect in terms of how things would be looked at. We were told our storeroom was messy and that our storage procedures for cots weren't the best. Basically she said most of the centers she visits weren't like ours. She was amazed at how verbal the children were. She didn't come out and say it exactly, but we're doing okay and the time is best spent other places where the licensing regulations are barely being met."

Campus Center Director

"I've been here three years. My licensing inspector regularly visits. Usually it's pretty routine. We've gotten most of the big things straightened out by now. It seems like sometimes they pay closer attention to some things than others. Like maybe it's records check time and they go over everything with a fine tooth comb, and then maybe it's safety alert—doors, outlets, play yard. But we've hit them all by now. I didn't used to be so calm."

Small Town Center Director

"I freeze everytime I see the fire inspector come in. We never pass the first time. I follow him around like a puppy dog. There's always paper on the floor and he doesn't like that. I don't think he likes child care. We have great fire drills, though. Those kids are trained to MOVE. And he checks everything. Always comes at Christmas to double check on the paper stuff."

Rural Center Director

nel. The CDA (Child Development Associate) credential discussed in Chapter 11 is an example.

2. *Accreditation* Notification that program meets standards for model or exemplary programs; an example is in Box 13.1.

Guidelines Actions that have indirect force of law but directly shape program practices.

1. *Administrative procedures* Policies and provisions of an agency that direct actions and help staff perform their duties. These are usually interpretations of regulations and codes.
2. *Funding conditions* Funders can impose definite structure on the operation of a program. Programs trying to meet the requirements of different funders simultaneously can be heavily burdened. The following are examples of funding conditions that "regulate" a program:
   a. Restrictions on capital expenditures causing programs to rent or scramble for equipment
   b. Qualification requirements for staff paid with funder's money
   c. Mandated organization and use of advisory groups, and limiting discretionary use of funds

Monitoring The procedures and activities through which agencies and groups oversee programs. It is "the systematic, periodic surveillance of providers and subordinate levels of management to assess the compliance of their actual ongoing activities and procedures with the applicable regulations." (Pacific Consultants, 1976, p. 114)

1. *Inspections* An on-site visit and interview to document and match program characteristics with regulations, codes, and ordinances. Inspectors often use a checklist or other observation form to record site data. These inspection sheets are available to providers and can help clarify broad regulatory statements (see Box 13.2).

2. *Compliance* Judgment indicating a program meets a regulation or standard.
3. *Consultation* or *supervision* Help provided by licensing personnel in assessing compliance with regulations.
4. *Technical assistance* Specific, planned help intended to transfer information and skills to the child care program.
5. *Enforcement* Activities intended to promote compliance. A *citation,* which is a detailed note of items needing upgrading, results in reinspection *Probation,* or conditional approval for specific time, means reinspection is necessary. *Suspension* is temporary removal of permission. It is correctable and crisis oriented. *Revocation* is formal, public removal of permission.
6. *Waiver* Formal permission that certain standards do not apply or programs will not be held accountable for them.

Regulatory Content

Closely related to the process of licensing is the actual content of applicable regulations. What is regulated and the extent to which certain details are specified varies considerably among the states. On specificity and scope, the regulations range from lax or nonexistent to excessive, laborious detail. This section presents an overview of child care licensing regulations. The *Comparative Licensing Study* (Lawrence Johnson, 1978–1980, 1982) started a comprehensive review and summary of state regulations. The profile categories developed for that study represent the best description of regulatory topics available. The seven major parts of the profile are:

1. State licensing of child day care facilities
2. Administrative and licensing enforcement procedures
3. Staff-child ratios and eligibility
4. Staff qualifications and requirements
5. Operational and program requirements
6. Facility requirements
7. Other state requirements—compliance with other laws, ordinances, and regulations

In the following sections we'll use these seven categories to discuss the research findings, expert opinion, and consensus of practical experience related to the topic area. We also offer examples of actual regulations and summary charts to illustrate actual regulatory practice. The examples are deliberately chosen to represent a range of practice. Within categories only a few selected regulations are cited. No value judgment is implied about the examples used. They are for illustration purposes only.

State Licensing of Child Day Care Facilities. The intent of regulations in this category is to assign responsibility for child care licensing to governmental agencies within the state. Definitions of service and specific exclusions are an important part of these regulations. Without such specific assignment, control of licensing is muddled and no single group is able to coordinate procedures. For example, one study found the following situation in New York:

> The State Department of Social Services (DSS) is responsible for the development and enforcement of all day care licensing standards for centers and homes except for centers in New York City which are the sole responsibility of the New York City Health Department. The actual licensure of centers outside New York City is the responsibility of a special DSS Day Care Licensing Section which deploys state reps who work out of regional offices. Centers in New York City are licensed by the City Health Department. The DSS Day Care Licensing Section also licenses homes operating under state POS contract, outside New York City. Homes in New York City are licensed by the Agency for Child Development, an arm of the State DSS. Homes not located in New York City nor operating elsewhere under contract are sanctioned by licensing examiners operating out of their individual county social service offices. (Pacific Consultants, 1976, p. 15)

Federal Interagency Day Care Requirements (FIDCR) were promulgated in 1968 to establish a set of standards for federally subsidized child care and to provide a guide for states in upgrading the quality levels of licensing regulations. The FIDCR, however, proved difficult to monitor and enforce. A 1972 revision was shelved when related welfare reform legislation failed. In 1975, a slightly modified version of the FIDCR was accepted as funding requirements for child care services provided under Title XX of the Social Security Act. Fiscal penalties were to be applied for noncompliance. Everyone suddenly became quite concerned over the match between FIDCR and state regulations.

In general, states moved to incorporate or attach FIDCR to existing state standards. The federal Department of Health, Education and Welfare embarked on a review of the appropriateness of the 1968 FIDCR, which ultimately resulted in a revision of the regulations (known as the HEWDCR of 1980). To provide data for their decision the agency carried out numerous studies, panels, hearings, surveys, and analyses of state standards, child care monitoring, and management. Anticipating the proposed FIDCR revision, states began to upgrade licensing standards.

The pace was feverish and the debate vigorous. Through the FIDCR revision and related data collection efforts, there was strong federal presence in the child care community. Certain changes in the FIDCR (known now as the HEWDCR)—staff-child ratio, group size, and staff training standards—were particularly controversial. Raising standards would increase costs. Money was tight and getting tighter. Dissatisfaction with regulations in general was growing. The final rules of the HEWDCR were supposed to take effect in September 1980. Implementation was delayed, then postponed. In 1981, with a new president and different priorities, the HEWDCR were permanently set aside. The Budget Reconciliation Act of 1981 amended Title XX to require that child care provided with federal funds meet applicable state and local standards. In late 1981, the Day Care Division of the Administration for Children, Youth and Families was dismantled. Now the federal role in child care is diminished. With no federal standards or federal child care bureaucracy, states have the major role today in shaping child care through state licensing standards.

Administrative and Licensing Enforcement Procedures. We tend to think of licensing from the perspective of state regulations, procedures, and inspections. In reality, licensing is also tied to a number of local safety permits and inspections that must be obtained prior to state licensure. The steps required to obtain a license vary from state to state and also according to the type of program. While no general statement will apply to every situation, the following steps are typical of a large number of states and may give some idea of the time and effort needed to obtain a license (Cohen, 1974, p. 52):

1. Locate your licensing office. Find out about the licensing requirements and other requirements that have to be met.
2. Get an informal appraisal to learn if your building can meet building safety and fire codes.
3. Submit floor and building plans to city hall for zoning approval. Is the location zoned to permit child care? If not, a public hearing may be needed to obtain a special permit.
4. Submit floor and building plans to the city hall building inspector and sometimes to the fire department as well. The inspector will visit the facility and may issue a building permit if it is new or remodeled. If the building meets both state and local fire and safety codes, the inspector will issue a building safety certificate.
5. Contact the local health department to learn if the building meets state and local sanitation requirements. When these requirements are met, you can apply for a license.
6. Contact the licensing office once more. A staff member will visit your facility to check requirements and make recommendations. If all requirements are met, you will receive a license.
7. Expect the licensing staff to visit regularly to make sure that standards are being maintained. You may want to ask for advice during these visits.

To frustrated participants the licensing "game" may seem like a special form of bureaucratic roulette. Delays and inconsistencies are numerous and will be the norm for some time to come. Many state agencies have worked diligently to streamline licensing procedures and negotiate compromises where state and local safety codes conflict, but licensing staff are government employees who are vulnerable to cutbacks and reductions too. Heavy licensing workloads are one explanation for delays.

Several states have been working on establishing licensing and monitoring procedures for effective, efficient regulation of child care programs (Ferrar, Gleason, Smith, 1980; Pacific Consultants, 1976). In an effort to disseminate exemplary procedures the Children's Services Monitoring Transfer Consortium was established. Member states are California, Michigan, Pennsylvania, Texas, West Virginia, and the City of New York. A number of monitoring tools and techniques have been developed for transfer, including a Generic Checklist for Day Care Monitoring (1985). Each state retains separate, state specific procedures. Pennsylvania uses the Child Development Program Evaluation (CDPE), an assessment tool designed to measure compliance with applicable regulations, to determine program training and technical assistance needs, and to measure the impact of such assistance on the program. The CDPE is part of a comprehensive management system that is capable of interfacing with individual programs while simultaneously aggregating information across programs at the state level as a basis for policy decisions and regulatory revision. The work of Richard Fiene and several colleagues has been instrumental in conceptualizing the Pennsylvania CDPE system.

Regulatory content and planning of licensing procedures originate with an advisory group. This group consists of interested persons, experts, politicians, and consumers. They have the opportunity to directly mold the character of state regulations. Those who have concerns with regulations should look to these groups for action.

A continuing issue in licensing is what to do about noncompliance. Few state agencies are in a position to aggressively look for violations such as programs operating in ignorance or defiance of the law. Staff energies are consumed by processing and inspecting the applications of those who do request licensing. The vast number of unlicensed family day care homes is silent testimony to the extent of the problem. Enforcement tools have not been very powerful. Closing a center or prohibiting opening of a program are the most common options. A few states levy financial penalties.

Without effective enforcement procedures child care licensing runs the risk of being selectively focused and unevenly practiced. The movement toward self-accreditation through registration and affadavits transfers this responsibility to provider and/or parent consumer.

Staff-Child Ratios and Eligibility. Staff-child ratio is a characteristic of child care programs that is highly susceptible to regulation. Undeniably, staff-child ratios are connected to supervision and, hence, the safety of children. Prior to the National Day Care Study (NDCS) and the FIDCR revision, state staff-child ratios varied according to local sentiment. No data or cogent analyses favored one ratio figure over another. Common sense and good judgment determined the regulations. The NDCS jolted people's thinking. The most important findings of the study related not just to staff-child ratio, which was found to be related to cost of care, but to a new variable called group size. Together, group size and child-staff ratio are labelled group composition. "Across all study sites, smaller groups are consistently associated with better care, more socially active children and higher gains on two developmental tests." (Abt, 1979, Executive Summary, p. 2) The final rules of the HEWDCR were written to implement a ratio and group size figures based on the NDCS findings and the overall findings of FIDCR revision proceedings.

With federal funds at that time used to achieve compliance with these regulations, the ratios had the potential to dramatically change the costs and characteristics of publicly subsidized programs throughout the country. The changes were not a surprise, however. Helped by Title XX funds earmarked for child care, states had been upgrading and moving toward eventual compliance for some time. Today HEWDCR is not in force, but the recommendations are not just history. Despite the exceptions, waivers, stalls, and complaints along the way, states did begin to adopt the concept of group composition—regulating both staff-child ratio *and* group size by age of child.

Staff Qualifications and Requirements. Staff qualifications are another important regulatory link to quality care conditions for children. Qualifications can be documented for monitoring procedures. Once again the findings of the NDCS slightly altered the prevailing wisdom. Years of experience and formal education were found to be less strongly associated with measures of quality care than simple child-related training. Workers who had child development training specifically related to the ages and characteristics of the children they served were consistently associated with quality care practices.

The emphasis in practice and state regulation today is on in-service training delivered as needed and tailored to the special needs of each staff member. The fine line between licensing supervision and program technical assistance is blurring. Increasingly, licensing workers are seen as the most obvious contacts between state and program for training arrangements. Texas has developed a licensing and technical assistance program that integrates the functions of licensing with follow-up training needs.

Operational and Program Requirements. For all the hours children spend in child care and the countless specialists who have worked with staffs to plan programs to facilitate children's development, existing state regulations on programming are very shallow. They do little more than recognize the need for a planned activity program and provide an umbrella covering all possible local variations of theme and content. An excerpt from the 1980 HEWDCR is a fair representation of the level of specificity of regulations in this area:

> Day Care Center. A day care center shall establish a planned program of developmentally appropriate activities which promotes the intellectual, social, emotional, and physical development of the children it serves. The planned program shall be in writing and shall be made available to parents. The plan shall contain a description of activities children engage in and how those activities meet their developmental needs, including the special needs of children in the center who are multilingual or handicapped. (HEW day care regulations, 1980, p. 17882)

Why is this so? Program practices are difficult to define and even harder to pinpoint for measurement and observation purposes. Local determination of programming is highly desirable. Parents can influence, children's individual needs can be responded to, and staff can function at their levels of competence and interest. Programs are built to capitalize on local equipment and resources.

Can more be done? Isn't there a growing body of tested practice and theory that could be more effectively integrated into child care curriculum activities? The beginning chapters of this book indicate that they could. But whether program regulations should be more stringent is not so easily answered. Quality programming practices for children are the by-products of staff training and group composition. For the time being regulatory practice appears to favor relying on indirect approaches to ensuring good program practices. This has the distinct advantage of preserving local prerogatives and promoting multiple care options.

Facility Requirements. These regulations cover space and factors related to the condition of that space. Programs may be required to have so many square feet of space per child or service function. Specific requirements may be

Box 13.3 Excerpts from Pennsylvania's Physical Facility Regulations

122. All floors, walls, ceilings, and other surfaces shall be kept clean and in good repair.
123. All stairs used by the children shall have right-hand descending handrails and be illuminated by artificial or natural light. Landings or gates shall be provided beyond each exterior and interior door which opens into a stairway.
124. Where glass is used in traffic areas, a visual strip or other visual identification shall be provided so that the glass is noticeable.
125. A means of ventilation shall be provided in the child care areas. If windows are present, they shall be operable except in air conditioned or mechanically ventilated buildings. All operable windows and doors used for ventilation shall be securely screened.
126. All windows above ground level in areas used by children under school age shall be constructed, adapted or adjusted to limit the exit opening to less than six inches (15 centimeters) to prevent children from falling.
127. Hot water pipes and other sources of heat accessible to children exceeding 110° F (43° C) shall be equipped with protective guards or insulated to prevent children from coming into direct contact with them.

Source: From *Regulations for Child Day Care Centers* (p. 18) by Pennsylvania Department of Public Welfare, 1978, Harrisburg, PA: Department of Public Welfare.

given for lighting, ventilation, heating, and air conditioning. Regulations may prohibit specific materials such as lead paint and prescribe other materials and equipment such as exit signs, push bars on doors, outward opening windows, safety glass, and so on. Cleanliness and soundness of the facility is of concern as evidenced in Box 13.3.

Other State Requirements. State codes often contain provisions that require child care programs to meet local codes in the areas of fire, health, sanitation, and building inspection.

Satisfactory certificates of inspection are required as a condition for program licensing in most states. In some situations physical facility standards are incorporated or subsumed in the ordinances of the fire, sanitation and health, and building codes.

Zoning is solely a local requirement, and coordination of standards is a major problem. Zoning is the regulation of land use and buildings. Size of buildings, yards, location and type of fences, and parking are covered by zoning. Zoning is often a serious problem for child care programs. Because of playground noise and parking traffic, programs may be zoned out of residential areas. There is little evidence that programs create these problems; however, programs may be zoned out of commercial areas because this environment is deemed unsuitable for children. Child care programs should be treated as community facilities, comparable to elementary schools for zoning purposes. Until some resolution is reached, zoning will continue to be a potential obstacle for child care program licensing. Facilities may be restricted to a few areas, conditional or special permits may be required, and zoning ordinance standards may greatly exceed licensing regulations for such things as lot size and outdoor play area.

The regulatory situation in these areas is characterized by a jumble of stringent and lax standards, overlapping and often uncooperative jurisdictional questions, and confusion about the whole purpose of public safety inspections. Inspections also can cause substantial licensing delays. In 1973, an Office of Child Development Study reported these delays in licensing attributable to code inspections: fire inspection (65 days), sanitary inspection (35 days), health inspection (35 days), and zoning (50 days).

Safety officials may not understand child care. Many may not approve of it. Codes and attitudes may have many obstacles preventing the setup of child care programs. Similarly, child care people do not seem to fully appreciate the purpose of safety codes. Inspectors are trained to look for and eliminate potential hazards to safety. Mistakes mean injury and death for innocent people. In this context it is quite understandable that inspectors stick to the letter of the law.

Progress is being made as safety groups and child care people communicate and share information. Safety codes and state licensing standards can be reviewed for compatibility. Communication and a transfer of ideas are occurring between licensing workers and code inspectors. Family day care homes continue to be a problem. Codes designed for public use facilities seem excessive when applied to private residences, especially since the caregiver's own children will be in the home whether it passes inspection or not.

Facilities are important. However plain, sparse, old, or weathered, facilities and equipment must meet regulatory standards in order for programs to operate legally. (Courtesy of U.S. Department of Health and Human Services, Washington, DC.)

Legal Concerns

Child care is a business. The fact that small children and family values are involved does not excuse child care programs from good business practices. Like shoe repair shops or dry cleaners, child care programs must establish a legal identity. Whether public or private, profit or not-for-profit, day care home or center, sole proprietor or large corporation, programs have legal obligations regarding the organizational structure of the service, tax and reporting requirements, and insurance needs. It is risky and foolish to operate a child care program relying on goodwill and circumstance. The laws apply to all who engage in business. Box 13.4 provides further information.

Legal statutes and child care regulations vary from state to state. You should seek assistance on legal matters from local lawyers. Remember that many lawyers are specialists. Look for a lawyer who is trained to handle your program's particular needs. Large firms and local bar associations do offer *pro bono* (for the public good) assistance. Perhaps your program qualifies. Competent legal advice is always cheaper than defending suits and paying court costs or penalties.

Several excellent references on legal concerns are listed in the "Legal Issues" section of the Resources at the end of this chapter. For more information contact: Child Care Law Center,

Box 13.4 Why Child Care Needs Lawyers Now

Like all other complex social issues, child care has a legal dimension. Yet because child care issues are given little or no attention by public interest lawyers and are not sufficiently fee-generating to attract the private bar, there is a tremendous unmet need for legal advocacy and services to child care. The needed services cover the full range from routine services to child care providers and nonprofit institutions to representation before legislative and administrative bodies, negotiations before governmental agencies and, where appropriate, impact litigation. The constituency includes child care providers, child care advocacy organizations and, perhaps most importantly, the parents and children who desperately need additional child care programs.

Legal Services

Many of the legal problems of child care programs are those typical of a small, highly regulated business. Unfortunately, almost all child care programs operate on a very tight budget and cannot hire lawyers. As a result, they often make serious mistakes which legal service would have prevented and which, once they become a problem, cannot be solved without a lawyer.

Typical child care program legal problems include (1) licensing of centers and family day care homes; (2) contracts, both with parents and with people providing products or services to the program; (3) zoning and relationships with neighbors and with the community in general; (4) child abuse, the child care worker's obligation to report suspected abused and the child care worker's role when a child in her care has reportedly been abused; (5) family law, when a provider is asked to refuse to allow a child to leave the center with one of his/her parents or when a child care worker is asked to testify in a custody dispute; (6) taxes, including the tax consequence of owning a family day care home, of incorporating a child care center or of hiring an employee. Furthermore, parents and advocates require legal assistance in negotiating for the maintenance of existing programs and in the creation of new ones.

Source: From Treadwell, Lujuana Wolfe. *Why Child Care Needs Lawyers Now.* San Francisco: Bay Area Child Care Project, 1980, p. 1.

625 Market Street, Suite 815, San Francisco, CA 94105.

Legal areas, such as those in the following sections, are central to the operation of child care programs. Decisions and requirements in these areas directly affect the activities of the program. All staff should be familiar with these issues and be alert for instances of application in daily events.

Form of Organization

Child care programs may be organized as sole proprietorships, partnerships, or corporations.

Sole Proprietorships. As a sole proprietor the owner (who is usually also the operator) has full personal liability for the financial consequences of all aspects of the center's operation. This includes liability for debts, breaches of contract, and taxes. The liability is called "full" because it is not limited in amount.

Sole proprietorships also have complete decision-making authority. They can sell, even give away, the program to anyone at anytime. They may also decide at anytime to end the program and go out of business. The program has no tax obligation because the income is regarded as the owner's personal income. Finally, only one document, the True Name Certificate, is required to legally open a sole proprietorship. (Kotin, Crabtree, & Aikman, 1981, pp. 13–14)

Partnerships. In a general partnership each partner has full personal liability for program obligations. Each partner is co-equal in decision-making, and the decisions of one general partner are binding on all general partners. All partners must consent to the transfer or selling of a partnership. There is no partnership tax obligation; there is only an individual tax obligation. An informational form must be filed with the IRS. The partnership ceases to exist automatically upon the death or incapacitation of any partner. Only a True Name Certificate is required to establish the partnership.

In a limited partnership, each partner's fiscal liability is limited according to the extent of his or her capital contribution. Limited partners are investors not decision-makers concerned with daily management details. In addition to a True Name Certificate, a Limited Partnership Certificate must be filed to legally establish the partnership. Both limited and general partnerships are strongly advised to prepare a Partnership Agreement, which covers the details and contingencies of the partnership. (Kotin, Crabtree, & Aikman, 1981, pp. 15–16, 23)

Incorporations. A corporation is created by several people. It has a legal existence of its own. With limited exceptions, people involved in the corporation have no personal liability for corporate actions and consequences. Corporations must have an organization and are governed by a board of directors. Documents required in order to incorporate include articles of incorporation, bylaws, financial statements, and minutes of annual meetings and director's meetings.

Several state licensing laws require incorporation as a condition for licensing. In effect this uses incorporation requirements as a regulatory tool. Funders may choose to deal only with not-for-profit groups, which is a legal status available only to incorporated programs.

Profit-making corporations pay taxes and distribute any profits to shareholders as dividends. Not-for-profit, or more commonly nonprofit, corporations can and do make money. This excess money must be used to support the purposes of the organization—more equipment, higher staff salaries, or expansion.

Tax Status. Tax-exempt status is available to not-for-profit programs that meet certain tests of purpose and fiscal expenditures. It is desirable because the organization thereby doesn't have to pay certain federal and state taxes, thus saving money on purchases. Also, donors can deduct their donations to the organization on their personal income tax, which is an incentive for giving money or supporting fund-raising activities.

Programs must file for tax-exempt status. Child care programs usually file with the IRS under Section 501 (c) (3) of the tax code. Separate forms must be filed for tax-exempt status from state and for local taxes. Tax-exempt status is not automatic. Forms and documents must be filed regularly.

Insurance. Insurance is protection from risk. Liability is responsibility for risk. How much and what kind of insurance a program carries depends on how likely an event is to occur and the amount of money required if the event does occur. The probability of events and the cost consequences must be balanced against the cost of insurance coverage.

Liability insurance Protects against the consequences of accidents occurring on program premises.

Automobile insurance Provides liability and personal property protection for program-owned vehicles. Coverage should extend to any vehicles permitted to transport children for program purposes.

Fidelity bonds Protect the program from financial losses caused by employee misconduct.

Health Insurance Provides fringe benefit health protection for employees.

Coverage options and insurance fees vary greatly. Shop around. Check with professional organizations about special plans or group policies that are usually cheaper. Nonexistent or

Ceiling of Quality

	Accreditation	Standards of quality for model programs
	Credentialing	Standards spelling out qualifications to be required of staff
Rate Setting	Fiscal Regulation	Funding standards
	Inspection and Approval	Administrative standards for publicly operated programs
Fire and Safety Sanitation Regulations	Day Care Licensing	Basic preventive requirements or standards

Floor of Quality

Operating a day care program without a license is a crime.	Child Abuse and Neglect	Below an acceptable standard the state punishes as crimes behavior deemed abusive or neglectful.

Figure 13.1 Regulating levels of quality. (From "Federal Day Care Standards in Context" by G. G. Morgan, August, 1977, DHEW, Washington, DC.)

inadequate insurance is one of the most common mistakes of child care programs of all types.

Contracts. A contract is a legal obligation. The three essential legal components of a contract are:

1. Offer Proposal of product and price (statement of care conditions and cost for child at child care center)
2. Acceptance Indication of acceptance of product plus price terms (parent signs agreement)
3. Consideration Value or price of exchange (hour of care = $2.50)

When these three elements are present, a contract is legally enforceable. An oral agreement can be a contract. No documentation is required, and no money has to change hands. Contracts are a particular problem for family day care, because the nature of the care seems to encourage casual agreements that neither parent nor provider is concerned about until misunderstandings over hours of care or responsibility for food and diapering supplies arise. Legal assistance may be required to draw up contracts.

The Future

Child care, particularly family day care (which has been operating mainly outside legal frameworks) is in great demand. The federal government, however, is out of the position of regulating child care since the HEWDCR were never implemented. The dominant force shaping child care in the 1980s is the regulatory standards of individual states. State licensing standards are the mechanism for achieving a minimum quality of protection and developmental support for children. Figure 13.1 illustrates the regulatory levels leading toward a quality program.

As child care programs try to cope effectively with reduced public funding and meet increasing market demand for services, questions of legal and business procedures will become increasingly important. Regulations, legal status, and sound fiscal procedures are the foundation of child care's future.

Summary

All child care programs must comply with state and local standards and codes and must meet the legal obligations concerning ownership, taxes, and insurance.

Licensing is the formal, legal permission for a program to operate and deliver services. Today's regulatory standards were originally designed to be protective, to serve a clientele "in need," and to be administered by welfare services.

Permission, which is the formal allowance to operate a program, may take the form of licensing, registration, or certification. Statements of worth, such as a credential, are formal recognitions of quality levels or skills. Guidelines are actions that have indirect force of law; an example is a funding condition. Agencies oversee programs through monitoring, which takes the form of inspections, consultation, and enforcement.

Since the early 1980s and the suspension of federal standards, states have played a major role in setting licensing standards. Licensing procedures are typically lengthy and plagued with delays. One element of child care that is particularly susceptible to regulation is the staff-child ratio. Regulations may also cover staff qualifications. Regulations are not easily written to help upgrade program content. Facility inspections are often the most trying part of the regulatory process for child care programs.

Child care programs should operate in a legal, businesslike fashion, which means learning and following certain legal obligations. The three types of program organization are sole proprietorship, partnership, and incorporation. Tax-exempt status allows some programs to avoid paying certain federal and state taxes. Insurance, in areas such as liability and auto, is a necessity for child care centers. Directors should arrange for contracts to be drawn up for any agreement before misunderstandings arise.

Resources

Regulations and Licensing

American Academy of Pediatrics. (1971). *Standards for day care centers for infants and children under three years of age.* Evanston, IL: American Academy of Pediatrics.

Class, N. E. (1968). Licensing for child care: A preventive welfare service. *Children,* September-October, 188–192.

Class, N. (1980). Some reflections on the development of child day care facility licensing. In S. Kilmer (Ed.), *Advances in early education and day care: Vol. 1* (pp. 3–18). Greenwich, CT: JAI Press.

CWLA Standards for day care service. (1984). New York: Child Welfare League of America.

Ferrar, H. M., Gleason, D. J., & Smith, B. (1980). *A state-of-the-art report on state monitoring of child care facilities.* Washington, DC: Social Services Research Institute. (Prepared for U.S. Department of Health, Education and Welfare, Office of Human Development Services)

Guides for day care licensing. (1973). Washington, DC: USDHEW, Office of Child Development. (DHEW Pub. No. (OCD) 73-1053)

Lounsbury, J. W., Lounsbury, K. R., & Brown, T. P. (1976). The uniformity of application of day care licensing standards. *Child Care Quarterly, 5,* 248–261.

Model child care standards act: Guidance to states to prevent child abuse in day care facilities. (1985). Washington, DC: U.S. Department of Health and Human Services.

Morgan, G. G. (1974). *Alternatives for regulation of family day care homes for children.* Washington, DC: Day Care and Child Development Council of America.

Morgan, G. G. (1973). *Regulation of early childhood programs* (rev. ed.). Washington, DC: Day Care and Child Development Council of America.

NAEYC. (1984). *Accreditation criteria and procedures of the National Academy of Early Childhood Programs.* Washington, DC: NAEYC.

Policy issues in day care: Summaries of 21 papers. (1971). Washington, DC: Center for Systems and Program Development. (USDHEW Contract No. 100-77-0017)

State Practices

Adams, D. (1982). Family day care regulations: State policies in transition. *Day Care Journal, 1* (1), 8–13.

Allen, S. V. (1973). Early childhood programs in the states. In P. Roby (Ed.), *Child care—Who cares?* (pp. 191–227). New York: Basic Books.

Children's Services Monitoring Transfer Consortium. (1985). *Generic checklist for day care monitoring.* Washington, DC: Office of Policy Development, Office of Human Development Services, Department of Health and Human Services.

Cohen, D. J. (1974). *Day care 3: Servicing preschool children* (Chap. 5). Washington, DC: USDHEW.

Collins, R. C. (1973). Child care and the states: The comparative licensing study. *Young Children, 38,* 3–11.

Early Childhood Project. (1975). *Day care licensing policies and practices: A state survey.* Denver: Education Commission of the States.

Fiene, R., Douglas, E., & Kroh, K. (1979). *Child development program evaluation: Center licensing revision—Manual.* Harrisburg, PA: Department of Public Welfare.

Fiene, R., & Woods, L. (1984). Theory of compliance indicator checklist statistical model instrument based program monitoring information system. Paper presented at Pennsylvania System Workshop, Medicine Hat College, Medicine Hat, Alberta, Canada, August 15–16.

Lawrence Johnson & Associates. (1978–1980, 1982). *Comparative licensing study: Profiles of state day care licensing requirements.* Washington, DC: Lawrence Johnson.

Pacific Consultants. (1976). *Child day care management study.* Washington, DC: Pacific Consultants.

FIDCR-HEWDCR

Appropriateness of the federal interagency day care requirements: Report of findings and recommendations. (1978). Washington, DC: USDHEW, Office of the Assistant Secretary for Planning and Evaluation.

Federal interagency day care requirements 1968. (1969). *Code of Federal Regulations,* Title 45, Subtitle A, Part 71. (34 F.R. 1390, January 29)

HEW day care regulations (proposed rules). (1979). *Federal Register,* June 15, *44* (117), 34754–34781.

HEW day care regulations (final rules). (1980). *Federal Register,* March 19, *45* (55), 17870–17885.

Morgan, G. G. (1977). Regulating levels of quality. In *Federal day care standards in context.* Washington, DC: Department of Health, Education and Welfare. (ERIC Document Reproduction Service No. ED 156 343)

Gleason, D. J. (n.d.). *Assessment of factors affecting implementation of the HEW day care requirements: Final report.* Washington, DC: Social Services Research Institute. (Prepared for DHEW, Administration for Public Services)

Nelson, J. R., Jr. (1982). The politics of federal day care regulation. In E. F. Zigler & E. W. Gordon (Eds.), *Day care: Scientific and social policy issues* (pp. 267–306). Boston, MA: Auburn House.

Southwest Federal Regional Child Development Task Force. (1977). *A public review in federal region VI of the federal interagency day care requirements* (Combined 1968, 1972 and Title XX FIDCR). Dallas, TX: Southwest Federal Regional Child Development Task Force.

Federal Role

ACYF down plays day care. (1982). *Report on Preschool Education, 14* (1), 1–3.

Grotberg, E. H. (1980). The roles of the federal government in regulation and maintenance of quality in child care. In S. Kilmer (Ed.), *Advances in early education and day care: Vol. 1* (pp. 19–45). Greenwich, CT: JAI Press.

Orton, R. E., & Langham, B. (1980). What is government's role in quality day care? In S. Kilmer (Ed.), *Advances in early education and day care: Vol. 1* (pp. 47–62). Greenwich, CT: JAI Press.

Malone, M. (1982). *Child day care: The federal role.* Washington, DC: Congressional Research Service. (Issue Brief No. IB81027)

Steiner, G. Y. (1976). *The children's cause.* Washington, DC: Brookings Institution.

Summary report of the assessment of current state practices in Title XX funded day care programs. (1982). Report to Congress, October 1981. Washington, DC: U.S. Department of Health, Education and Welfare, Day Care Division.

Twiname, J. D., Moore, W. A., & Mott, P. E. (1975). *Using Title XX to serve children and youth.* New York: Child Welfare League of America.

Zeitlin, J. H., & Campbell, N. D. (1982). *Strategies to address the impact of the Economic Recovery Tax Act of 1981 and the Omnibus Budget Reconciliation Act of 1981 on the availability of child care for low income families.* Washington, DC: National Women's Law Center.

Zigler, E. F., Kagan, S. L., & Klugman, E. (983). *Children, families, and government.* New York: Cambridge University Press.

Legal Issues

Allen, K. E., & Goetz, E. M. (1983). *Special environmental, policy, and legal implications.* Rockville, MD: Aspen Systems.

Frank, M. (Ed.). (1984). *Child care: Emerging legal issues.* New York: Haworth Press.

Kotin, L., Crabtree, R. F., & Aikman, W. F. (1981). *Legal handbook for day care centers.* Washington, DC: Lawrence Johnson Associates.

Ladd, J. C., & Murray, K. A. (1981). *How to find and use a lawyer.* San Francisco: Bay Area Child Care Law Project.

Melton, G. B. (Ed.). (1983). *Legal reforms affecting child and youth services.* New York: Haworth.

Rose, C. M. (1978). *Some emergency issues of legal liability of children's agencies.* New York: Child Welfare League of America.

Training for Child Care Project. (1979). *Legal and program issues related to child custody and late parents* (Day Care Administration Bulletin No. 3). Atlanta: Southern Regional Education Board.

Treadwell, L. W. (1980). *The family day care provider's legal handbook.* Oakland, CA: BANANAS Child Care Project.

Treadwell, L. W. (1980). *Why child care needs lawyers now.* San Francisco: Bay Area Child Care Law Project.

Treadwell, L. W. (1981). *Child care contracts: Information for parents.* San Francisco: Bay Area Child Care Law Project.

Zoning for day care. (1972). Child Care Bulletin No. 8. Washington, DC: Day Care and Child Development Council of America.

Insurance

Murray, K. A., & Stevenson, C. (1981). *Insuring your program: Liability insurance.* San Francisco: Bay Area Child Care Law Project.

Murray, K. A., & Stevenson, C. (1981). *Insuring your program: Property and vehicle insurance.* San Francisco: Bay Area Child Care Law Project.

Tax

Delmon, D. J., & Staley, C. C. Jr. (1980). Money management tools: Tips for tax planning. *Child Care Information Exchange, 12,* 29–33.

How to apply for and retain exempt status for your organization. IRS Publication 557.

Murray, K. A. (1982). 501 (c) (3) Tax-exempt status: And how to get it. *Child Care Information Exchange, 26,* 27–32.

Neugebauer, R. (1979). Non-profit tax-exempt status: Is it right for you? *Child Care Information Exchange, 9,* 27–30.

Tax guide for small business. IRS Publication 334.

Troyer, T. A., Slocombe, W. B., & Boisture, R. A. (n.d.). *The new tax law: A guide for child welfare organizations.* New York: Child Welfare League of America.

Part V

Working with Parents and Community

14

Parent Roles in Child Care

Introduction

Since parents choose child care programs, they are the consumers of child care. This chapter explores the part parents play in selecting and participating in programs for their children. The first step is to look at who these parents are. Next we'll look at how parents go about picking a program and what decisions they need to make. Once parents have joined a program, they will take part, to some degree, in the program's activities. We'll define this involvement first in general terms, explaining several involvement models. Then we'll discuss parental participation in five specific areas: communication, support, information sharing, daily activities, and policymaking. Finally, we'll give some attention to establishing healthy, productive parent-staff relationships.

Working Parents

As we come into the 1980s, fertility rates are down and families are smaller in size. More mothers are working, and these mothers are starting or continuing to work when their children are very young (see Figure 14.1). The proportion of women who are in the labor force has grown from one-third in 1950 to more than half today. Dramatic increases have occurred for mothers with children younger than age six.

Dual-income families have the financial means to provide children with higher standards of living; that income helps parents meet the costs of child-rearing. Smaller families mean that women spend fewer years engaged in child care. Higher educational achievements raise women's salaries, making labor force participation more rewarding. Education also affects commitment to work; professional women are more likely to continue careers after the birth of children.

Single-parent families headed by women are most likely to have incomes below the poverty level (42 out of 100 for women; 15 out of 100 for men). Sixty-five percent of single-parent women are employed, compared to 50 percent of the women in two-parent families. Half of all black families with children, one-fourth of all Hispanic, and one-seventh of all white families are maintained by one parent—usually the mother. In March 1980, almost 1 out of 4 children lived in a single-parent family. More than any other group, single-parent families influence child care.

Parent Options for Care

Parents do not have unlimited child care options. Choices of child care arrangements depend on many factors and are part of a complex cost-benefit decision for each family.

Basic Factors

Availability A parent's search for care is constrained by whatever the local child care market offers: center-based or home-based, licensed or unregulated, quality program or TV babysitting, and immediate opening or long waiting list.

Child Characteristics Parents want care that they think is appropriate for the age of their children and whatever special needs those children have. Infants and school-age children require different care, handicapped or developmentally delayed children may require special staff or facilities, religious or cultural values may exclude some care options.

Family Finances Parents look for care they can afford. Family income level can determine eligibility for publicly assisted care. Parents may then be required to use only programs that have met certain standards; parents with higher incomes may not have access to those programs.

Personal Factors

Reliability Parents generally want their child care arrangement to be dependable. They want to get to work and want children to feel comfortable about care arrangements. Most place a high value on lack of stress and freedom from having to find last-minute substitute care.

Protection Parents want children to be safe and physically well taken care of while they are away from them.

Continuity As children get older, parents value care arrangements where discipline, attitudes, and affection are close to family ideals.

Activity Parents express a desire for their children to be busy and happy. For some, this means they seek out programs with formal curriculum plans; for others, age-appropriate materials and supervision are sufficient.

Convenience Care needs to be convenient. Transportation to the care site and workplace must be compatible. Hours of work and care must be compatible so that schedules do not get too tight.

Costs Costs of care must be consistent with parents' perceptions of the efforts involved and benefits received. This is a highly personal calculation; it does not reflect any socioeconomic class differences. Tax credits for child care are described in Box 14.1.

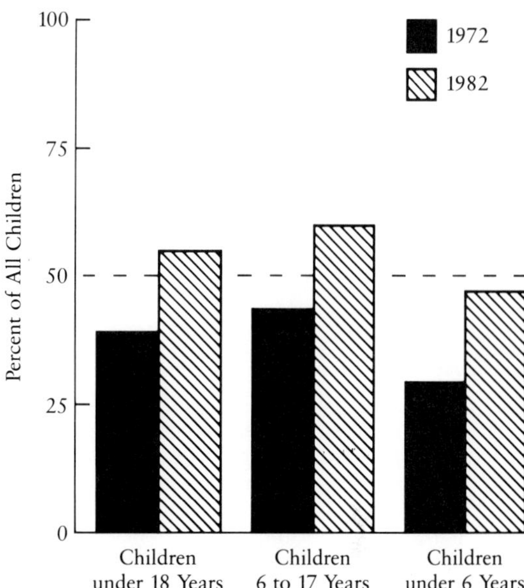

Figure 14.1 Children with mothers in the labor force as a proportion of all children by age of children, 1972 and 1982. (From *Women at Work: A Chartbook* (Bulletin 2168) by U.S. Department of Labor, Bureau of Labor Statistics, August 1983, Washington, DC: U.S. Government Printing Office.)

Patterns of Care

The most striking finding that emerges repeatedly from studies of child care arrangements chosen by working parents is that parents, themselves, still provide most of the child care.

How do parents manage to work and still provide care for children? Juggling work hours so that mother and father "split shifts" of child care is one way. Using paid care for a few hours to cover for parent work schedules, or perhaps leaving children home alone (supervised by siblings, telephone calls or written notes from par-

Box 14.1 Child Care Tax Credit

You may be eligible to receive a federal income tax credit equaling from 20% to 30% of your child care expenses. This credit will be deducted directly from the federal income taxes you owe—you do not have to itemize deductions to take advantage of it.

Who is eligible?

To qualify for the tax credit:

1. You must be employed either part time or full time or in active search for employment.
2. You must live with one or more children under the age of 15 for whom you are entitled to a personal exemption.
3. You (and your spouse if you are married) must have paid over half the cost of keeping up your home.

Must both spouses in a married couple be employed?

Yes. In a two-parent household, both parents must be *gainfully* employed, and they must file a joint return. However, if one spouse is employed and the other spouse is a full-time student for five months a year, both are considered to be gainfully employed.

What expenses can be claimed?

All child care expenses which are necessary to enable you to work can be considered, with the following exceptions:

1. Expenses are limited to $2,400 if you have one child under 15, and to $4,800 if you have two or more children under 15. **Note:** If you have two or more children under 15 with only **one** of them incurring child care expenses, you may still claim expenses up to the higher $4,800 limit.
2. Transportation costs for children between home and a care location are **not** considered eligible child care expenses.
3. Expenses claimed may not exceed the annual earned income of a single parent or the annual earned income of the spouse with the lowest income in a married couple.

Do payments made to day care centers, nursery schools, family day care providers, or babysitters qualify?

Yes. Payments for all these forms of care qualify as long as the care is needed to allow you to work. If you use a day care center or a family day care home, it must comply with state and local licensing regulations.

Do payments made to relatives qualify?

You **cannot** claim payments to your relatives unless:

1. These relatives are providing the child care as employees of another organization, or as self-employed persons in their own home, or as your employees for whom you are withholding Social Security taxes.

ents at work) are other ways. School enrollment is rising for three- to five-year-olds, which means that the hours parents need to provide care at home are fewer. For example, in 1980, according to the Bureau of Census, 53 percent of the three- to five-year-olds were attending nursery schools or kindergartens. This represents an increase from 38 percent in 1970.

Where do children go when parents choose out-of-home care? Consider these answers:

An organized day care center supplies care for children 3 to 13 years old rather infrequently. Approximately 2 percent of children 3 to 6 years old and virtually no older children (7 to 13 years old) are cared for in this way. If the mother holds a job, then about 4 percent of the younger and 1 percent of the older children are usually cared for in a day care center. (U.S. Bureau of the Census, P-20, (298), pp. 2–3)

In terms of both the number of families using care

2. These relatives are not your dependents for the tax year.

If child care fees are partially subsidized, do they still qualify?

You can claim any portion of the fees that you pay yourself. Any portion of the fee paid by another party, whether it be the center itself through a scholarship or the government through a subsidy, cannot be claimed by you as an expense.

How much can I save?

You can deduct from 20% to 30% of your eligible child care costs directly from your federal taxes. The exact percentage you can deduct is based on your family's adjusted gross income. For example, if your adjusted gross income is $15,000 and your child care expenses totalled $1,200, you would be allowed to reduce your tax payment by $324 (27% of $1,200).

Can I claim the credit for previous years?

If you were eligible for the child care tax credit any time in the past three years, but did not claim it on your tax returns, you may still file an amended return for those years.

Does this credit apply to state taxes also?

No. It applies only to federal income taxes. However, 30 states now have a child care credit provision for state income taxes. Check with tax officials in your state for details.

Must I wait until I file my tax return to have the amount of my tax savings refunded?

No. You can spread the credit over the year by having less tax withheld from every paycheck. If your federal income taxes will be reduced by this credit, you can lower the amount of federal income tax withheld from your paycheck by taking additional withholding allowances. To benefit in this way you must file a new W-4 tax withholding form with your employer, taking additional withholding allowances. For details, ask the IRS to send you Publication 505, **Tax Withholding and Estimated Tax.**

How do I claim this credit?

Starting with tax year 1983, you can claim this credit by filing your federal tax return on either Form 1040 (the long form) or 1040A (the short form). Complete and attach Form 2441, **Credit for Dependent Care Expenses,** to your return.

You must retain receipts for your child care fees with the name of the provider, the dates of services, and the name(s) of the child(ren) for whom care was provided. For details, call the IRS's toll-free number (1-800-424-1040) and ask for a free copy of Form 2441 and Publication 503, **Child and Disabled Dependent Care.**

From *Child Care Information Exchange,* 1984, p. 22. Reprinted with permission from *Child Care Information Exchange* (a bi-monthly management magazine for directors), PO Box 2890, Redmond, WA 98073.

and the number of children served, family day care constitutes the most widely used form of day care in the United States. . . . More than half of the full-time children in family day care homes are under six years of age; the greatest proportion of these children are under age three; and approximately 30 percent are aged three to five. Family day care also represents the most prevalent mode of care for the five million school children between 6 and 13 whose parents work. (*Family Day Care in U.S.,* Vol. 1, pp. 2–3)

Decisions for Parents Choosing Child Care

How a particular child comes to be enrolled in a particular program is frequently the result of chance, desperation, and circumstance. Like the proverbial chicken-and-egg question, finding child care arrangements or meeting time demands of a job can be a logistical riddle. Some parents diligently visit and observe many child care programs, trying to locate a situation that pleases them and their child. Because of financial constraints or lack of variety in local programs, other parents may have little choice about child care placement and little incentive to understand program goals and operations. Child care staff cannot and should not assume that all placements at their center are the result of informed choice. Neither should staff assume that child placement represents parental satisfaction with the program. Certainly placement represents a trust, but it is primarily an opportunity to *begin* a cooperative relationship between parent and staff.

For parents, choosing child care involves three basic decisions:

1. To work or not?
2. What kind of child care?
3. How to make it all work?

For each decision, parents will ask and answer for themselves many related questions. They will consider factors such as family transportation, job salaries, relatives' support, and others.

To Work or Not?

Many have no real choice but to work; family survival and personal dignity may be at stake. For others, working when children are young is a personal or career decision. Whatever reason a parent uses to decide to enter the work force, some emotional baggage is inevitable. Feelings can range from guilt to euphoria; rewards may be financial or emotional. Deciding whether, when, and how to enter the work force are the first decisions toward choosing child care.

Child care staff will find that this is not a simple decision for parents. A child's developmental crisis, stress at work, family attitudes, or just vague parental misgivings often makes a parent reconsider the decision to work. Staff can help parents by letting them know that they are not alone. Supportive comments, flexible hours, and parental discussion groups are ways in which staff can respond to parents' needs to explore personal answers to the question about whether or not to work. Check the Resources section for helpful publications.

What Kind of Child Care?

Parents appreciate advice and information. It is a confusing task to choose child care because for most parents the options are not familiar and the criteria for quality care are not obvious. Helping parents learn the vocabulary of child care is a first step. The next step is understanding the organization structure, program goals, and pros and cons of different child care options.

Many programs give introductory booklets to parents. These are helpful and necessary, but parents also need general guidelines that help them see child care options in perspective. Several excellent parent guides are available, but do not appear to be widely known (see Resources). An example from one of these guides is in Box 14.2.

Child care information and referral (I & R) services are an effective and expanding mechanism for meeting parents' information needs. A child care information and referral service gives parents the names of potential providers of child care; provides information about child care; provides information about child care programs and often other services as well; and helps parents to evaluate child care programs. The referral process involves an assessment of parental needs and an attempt to match those needs with available and acceptable choices. It is estimated that there are over 6,000 organizations in the United States providing some child care information and referral services. IBM has recently initiated a child care referral service for company employees. Both Congress and federal agencies have expressed interest in I & R services. *The National Directory of Child Care Information and Referral Agencies* is available from California Child Care Resource and Re-

Box 14.2 Sample Page from *A Parent's Guide to Day Care*

A Day Care Checklist for Parents

This checklist is designed to help you decide what things about a day care arrangement are most important to you and your family. It can also help you make sure your child's arrangement offers the things you believe are important.

Read through the checklist and circle those items you want the arrangement to provide. Then, when you talk to a possible caregiver or visit a home or center, decide whether the arrangement offers those things. Just check "yes" or "no." Use the checked-off list to help you make a decision.

Remember, this checklist tries to be as complete as possible. Not everything will apply to your family's situation. Look at the headlines in the lefthand column to see what you should read and what you can skip.

Does your child's caregiver . . .

	Yes	No
Appear to be warm and friendly?	□	□
Seem calm and gentle?	□	□
Seem to have a sense of humor?	□	□
Seem to be someone with whom you can develop a relaxed, sharing relationship?	□	□
Seem to be someone your child will enjoy being with?	□	□
Seem to feel good about herself and her job?	□	□
Have child-rearing attitudes and methods that are similar to your own?	□	□
Treat each child as a special person?	□	□
Understand what children can and want to do at different stages of growth?	□	□
Have the right materials and equipment on hand to help them learn and grow mentally and physically?	□	□
Patiently help children solve their problems?	□	□
Provide activities that encourage children to think things through?	□	□

Source: From *A Parent's Guide to Day Care,* 1980, Washington, DC: U.S. Department of Health and Human Services, Office of Human Development Services, Pub. No. (OHDS) 80-30254.

ferral Network, 320 Judah St., Suite 2, San Francisco, CA 94122.

How To Make It All Work?

Every parent and child ultimately find ways of dealing with the daily logistics of child care. Organization and planning are necessary; flexibility and humor are essential. Child care staff will find that some parent-child pairs seem able to analyze their situations and change behavior patterns rather easily as the need arises. Other parents seem overwhelmed or easily sidetracked. Frequently, parents will find it reassuring just to read about how others "put it all together." In this way they realize that they're not alone in solving child care problems. Parents will find publications listed in the Resources helpful.

Parent Involvement

Parents are a child's first teachers.
The family shapes the man (or woman!).
Children walk in the footsteps of their parents.

Such common sayings recognize the significant role that parents have in the development of their children. Despite this popular wisdom, however, parents have not always been welcomed as full partners in their children's programs. A little more than a decade ago it was necessary to marshall research evidence and expert opinion to ensure that parents became an integral part of Head Start.

Child care programs today share this legacy of attitudes toward parent involvement. Nevertheless, special program characteristics and unique political issues have recently shaped parent involvement in child care so that it differs from earlier programs. Child care programs sponsor many activities, events, and programs for parents. There are two major trends in these parent programs: (1) a focus on the role of the family in children's lives, including both practical elements and the more illusive elements of societal expectations for family sovereignty, and (2) the gradual shift from parent education to parent involvement.

Historical and Current Influences of the Family

American society assumes that the family has the right and exercises the responsibility to make the best decisions regarding the welfare of its children. Both the immediate social community and the law are unusually reluctant to intervene in family decisions. The ideal American family is pictured as two parents (a breadwinner and homemaker), two-plus children, and a comfortable life-style. This is not, of course, reality. Most families do not fit this stereotype, but it is critically important to recognize that this is the "family standard" that often underlies people's thinking.

Many social service programs are designed to provide for families that do not meet this ideal because of circumstances, loss, or disability. Social Security dependent's benefits aid children whose parents have died. AFDC benefits typically go to unemployed single mothers. Food Stamps, Fuel Assistance, and Medicaid are other examples of benefits provided to eligible families. Head Start, School Lunch and Breakfast, and Early and Periodic Screening, Diagnosis and Treatment (EPSDT) Health Services are examples of services targeted directly at children from eligible families. An array of programs and benefits at both the state and federal level support children and families in need. As families come to rely on these programs for survival and well-being, they relinquish some control over their daily activities. Not every doctor or health facility is available to these families. They do not have any or much choice in which child care facility their children can attend. Food Stamps limit which items families can purchase. Thus, despite widely voiced support for the role, rights, and responsibilities of the family, many of the parents that child care staff will work with have little expectation or experience in exercising these responsibilities.

Families are alive and well in America, but there have been sweeping changes in the work habits of American women and there are growing numbers of single-parent families. Divorces and remarriages are creating dizzying combinations of blended families of "his, hers, and ours" children. We need to change our definition of family to include these diverse groupings of parents and children. The family that child care staff works with must include the "caring unit" of which the child is a part, however spread out it may be. For instance, child care staff may find themselves dealing with complicated communication situations arising from a child's extended family.

Working parents, whether part of one- or two-parent families, have special kinds of pressure on their relationships with their children. There is simply less time for at-home tasks, less time for face-to-face interaction with their children, and less time for family social activities. Much has been written about the advantages of quality time between parents and children. Child care practices can be designed to maximize the quality of time that parents and children have together. Every fund-raising, social, or informative activity for parents sponsored by child care programs should be evaluated in terms of its impact on parent, child, or family time.

Models of Parent Involvement

Prior to the 1960s activities for parents were labeled "educational." Professionals expected to teach parents about child-rearing. These educational activities were intended to increase a parent's competence. Professionals drew upon a relatively stable pool of information. Parents were assumed to be uninformed passive learners. Films, discussion groups, pamphlets, or books were used. The underlying assumption was that parents needed information on child-rearing.

The social changes and civil rights advances of the 1960s eclipsed this narrow view of purposes of parent programs. Parents and children were encouraged to participate in a wide variety of programs aimed at improving the child's chances of educational success. Parents were challenged, stimulated, and sometimes paid to change their parenting behavior.

Since the late 1960s the rapid pace of technological change in our society has meant that parents are expected to prepare their children for a world they have never known. Traditional information is no longer a reliable guide for parenting behavior. Different cultural values lead to more diversity in goals and attitudes for child-rearing. The result of these changes has been the end of traditional parent education and the rise of parent involvement.

Parent involvement is not just a simple change in program labels. Parent involvement legitimizes the right of parents to participate in decisions affecting programs for themselves and their children. Parent involvement means there is no longer a firm line between professional and parent. However valued this new cooperation and shared effort are, in practice they can be difficult. Child care staff may find it difficult to relinquish program decisions to parents who are not well versed in child development. Parents may be suspicious of staff members who do not appear to be familiar with cultural values or community activities.

Hess, Black, Costello, Knowles, & Largay (1971) and Gordon (1970) described four types of parent involvement. These models help practitioners identify the major assumptions for parent programs.

1. *Deficit Model* This model is based on the idea that the young child has missed out on experiences commonly associated with middle-class child-rearing. The child is considered deprived. This phenomenon increases with age, making it a growing disadvantage or a cumulative deficit. Programs for parents and children are remedial when this model is used.
2. *Schools as Failure Model* In this model problems are viewed as arising in the school system, not the family. The school cannot deal adequately with the child's resources. Teacher retraining, curriculum change, and improved communication between school and community are recommended when the schools-as-failure model is used.
3. *Cultural Difference Model* In this model some children are seen as having learning experiences that differ from those of the mainstream school and middle class. Programs need to accommodate this cultural pluralism and maintain the strengths of the child's home culture.
4. *Social Structural Model* Parent's endeavors are related to factors such as their status in the social structure and the demands and expectations of society. Such programs are concerned with community issues and policies and very little with individual children and families.

As child care programs attract clientele from all economic classes, two additional types of parent involvement are becoming prominent. The *Community Support Model* assumes that parents' energies can effectively be directed toward fund raising and local public relations. This model assumes competent parenting, thus eliminating the need to provide parent training. The *Family Cooperative Model* assumes that the child care program is an integral part of the family's life-style. Parent activities are seen as extensions of typical family activities.

Parent involvement is a diverse effort, often requiring compromise and complicated organizational authority lines. It is not always completely successful. Individual programs can expend great effort to involve parents and find that no one is interested. Programs may find that as their parent population changes, parent activities must change also. Other programs may be overwhelmed with parent help. A very few parents may usurp program affairs because of time and leadership talent. Parent involvement is at once a pot of gold and a Pandora's box for child care program. It is a fact of life for child care programs and needs to be managed with wisdom and discretion.

Supportive Evidence

Most staff members find that parent activities come about because of the good ideas and energies of specific staff members with a knack for dealing with parents. As parents and staff leave the program, new activities emerge as new groups of staff and parents see different needs and have new ideas for parent involvement. Why, therefore, should anyone in child care ever need any scholarly findings related to parent involvement? The reason is that sometimes objective evidence is needed. For example, consider the following situations:

- A parent giving testimony for hearings on the state child care allocation.
- Community groups wanting to know whether their contributions make a difference to the families using child care programs.
- The staff member feeling that somehow parents and staff are not really working together but isn't sure why.

For these and many related situations, answers and solutions require more than "seat of the pants" responses. These are the times when it is necessary to gather the evidence and rely on the experts. A large pool of research evidence, program evaluation data, and program materials were produced during the 1970s in support of parents' involvement in programs for young children. Research studies exist about mother-child interactions and mothers' and fathers' roles. Also, research studies have dealt with the effects on development of the child when a mother works. (See Resources for specific titles.)

The evaluation literature on parent involvement ranges from anecdotal case studies to full-scale comparative evaluations. Some parent programs have operated as demonstration projects intended to spark similar programs elsewhere. These notable parent programs may no longer operate exactly as originally designed. Nevertheless, you should be familiar with the descriptions and results of the milestone parent involvement projects such as Head Start, Home Start and related home-based programs, Education for Parenting programs, and school-based programs including Follow Through and Parent-Child centers (see Resources).

Regulatory Requirements

State and local statutes frequently mandate parent involvement. Regulations and interpretations vary from locale to locale. When you visit programs, ask about parent participation regulations and how the program complies.

Board Membership. Child care programs may be required to meet quotas for parent board members. Programs may operate under two boards—one at the program level and one at the agency level if the program is part of a community service agency. Requirements may be designed to give parents a voting majority in the program board and a representative seat on the agency board. Local customs or constitutions may increase the number of parent board members.

On paper, having parents as board members would seem to ensure parent input at the highest levels of policy and financial decision making. Parents can make contributions to program goals as they help exercise responsibility over such things as hiring directors, setting program priorities regarding modes of child care, and pursuing funding from a variety of sources. Board positions, however, are sometimes the most difficult for parents with little time or leadership incentive.

Advisory Committees. Parent Advisory or Policy Advisory Committees (PACs) are standing committees that work with the director and staff of a program. Regulations may require a minimum number of PAC meetings a year. PACs are close to the daily operation of the program and are likely to work with the program director in generating tasks and priorities for meetings. Directors may use the PAC group as a "think tank" for initiating program activities and as a sounding board for resolving program-parent issues. PACs are generally removed from financial decisions on program operation and operate with fewer formal responsibilities than a board of directors.

Committees. Parents volunteer and are volunteered for an unending round of committees for bake sales, Week of the Young Child celebrations, and picnics. None of these specific committees is called for in regulations, but programs often are required to document parents' support, and these are genuine attempts to involve parents in program-related activities. Committee assignments are less time consuming than board or PAC work and can easily include the variety of skills and interest levels of parents.

Communication. Many regulations state that communication must be maintained between program and parent. Here local customs are important. Newsletters, monthly informational meetings, family events, and parent work groups are all examples of activities intended to open communication. Program directors may keep a log of parent participation, meeting attendance, and samples of meeting agendas and handouts to document compliance with the communication regulation.

Conferences. Periodic assessments of children's activities may be used as a basis for parent-staff conferences. Such assessments are usually based on some method that produces comparative observations over a period of time. Conferences for working parents may need to be scheduled in the early morning or evening. At times, the logistical hassles and apparent inconveniences can appear to outweigh whatever benefits may occur from shared discussions about children. Where required, periodic conferences are intended to ensure that staff and parents do occasionally have the time to exchange meaningful information.

Visitation and Observation. Regulations can state the obvious—that parents are welcome to visit and observe the children any time. In organized centers such an open-door policy seems natural. In day care homes it is more understandable that such a provision needs to be stated. Informing parents that their right to access is guaranteed without question can be a basic building block in the trust established between parent and program.

Managing Parent Roles

For the practical aspects of parent involvement, we want to know:

- What do parents do?
- Does parent involvement occur everyday?
- How do programs manage parent involvement?
- How do small or large home or center, infant or school-age programs find parent involvement activities appropriate for their specific programs and parent populations?

The answers to these and related questions are necessarily different for every child care program. While regulations and good practices

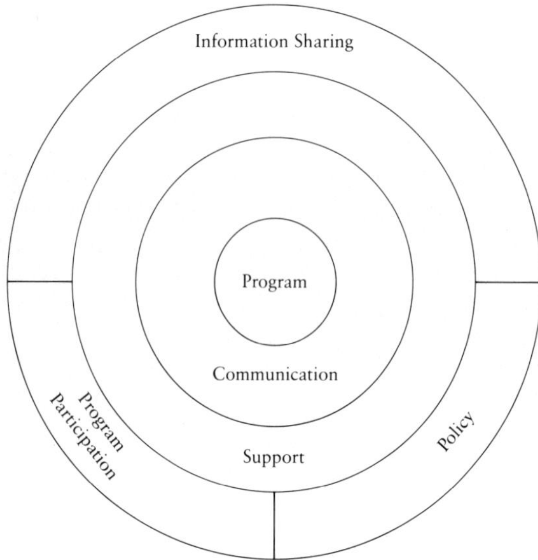

Figure 14.2 Realistic view of parent roles in child care.

Independent Family Day Care Home

Parent involvement revolves totally around daily drop-off and pick-up contacts.
Provider will strive to provide both formal and informal communication.

Center-based Infant Program

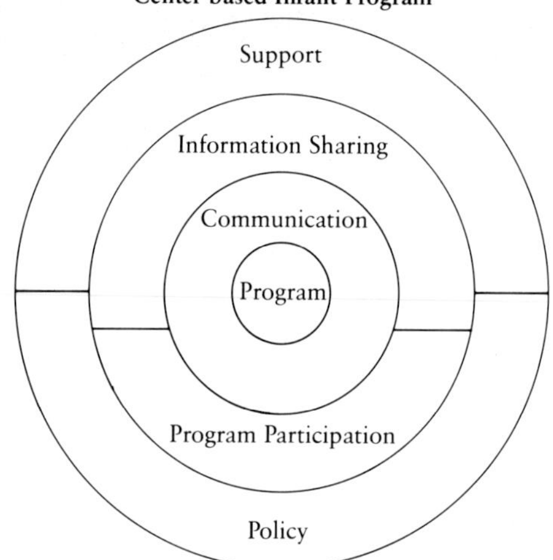

Daily exchange between parents and staff is critical. Child development classes and open access to the program are likely to be stressed. High costs and regulations about parent decision-making may require support and policy roles.

Figure 14.3 Examples of parent roles in child care.

guide all programs, the constraints of time, energy, and talent determine the particular mix of parent involvement for any one program.

In practice, three assumptions guide the selection and management of parent involvement roles.

1. All parents are involved in all programs. Regardless of type of child care program or the characteristics of parents, every program finds some role for parents. The most common parent role is as recipients of information from the program. These contacts may be informal drop-off chats or regular newsletters, but every program builds parent involvement from this base of communication with all parents.
2. Parents have specific needs that define parent roles in the program. Information needs of parents guide the planning of educational sessions or training programs. Families with strong cultural traditions encourage the use of parents in classroom roles and as activity resources.
3. Programs have specific needs that define parent roles. The most obvious example is money, since parents become involved in fund raising to keep the program open. Regulations and general public relations needs of programs require that parents serve in responsible, visible roles related to program affairs.

Five general categories of parent involvement cover the range of parent roles that exist in child care programs:

1. participation through communication
2. supportive participation
3. participation requiring information sharing
4. daily program participation
5. parents as policymakers

It is tempting to rank-order these categories in terms of significance of parent involvement in program affairs. While it is true that when parents make policy decisions they may have lasting influence on the program, this influence tends to be exaggerated. In fact, very few parents function in policymaking roles. More importantly, program practices bend more to the forces of day-to-day contacts with all parents than to the monthly decisions of a few. Many small programs cannot manage elaborate formal programs for parents. Nor do these programs always have extensive committee structures with which to formalize parental decision-making. Yet parents play legitimate and influential roles in these programs.

Recognizing the reality of current practices requires a different perspective on the relationship between parent roles and program influence (see Figure 14.2). The model shown in Figure 14.2 presents a typical situation for a medium-size preschool child care center. The very size of the rings indicates both the smaller numbers of parents involved and the less frequent occurrence of some parent roles. Using this graphic model, child care staff can analyze the parent and program needs of their particular situations in order to identify the appropriate balance of parent roles. Several examples are shown in Figure 14.3.

Participation Through Communication

Communication with parents is the basic parent involvement activity for all types of child care programs. Parents should know what is happening in the program and why. Parents also need frequent, specific information about their own child and his or her activities in the program. Many communication activities are informal and involve no preparation or documentation. Others are formally scheduled or depend on written transactions. Staff-initiated communication activities can be least demanding as a role for parents. The following lists offer examples of important and frequently used communication activities.

Periodic

- Newsletters
- Special announcements
- Bulletin boards

Spontaneous

- Daily conversations
- Telephone calls
- Personal notes
- Activity reports

Scheduled

- Conferences and reports
- Program orientations and parent handbooks
- Home visits

Special

- Crisis contacts

Parents differ in how much they value communication. Staff should be sensitive and prepared to vary their approach. Powell (1977) studied relationships between parents and caregivers with special emphasis on how they communicated. He found three types of interaction styles. The *independent parents* kept their social distance from the child care center and did not see the child care program as a source of information. They relied on newsletters and bulletin boards rather than people in the program for communication. The *dependent parents* had one-way communication patterns—from center

Box 14.3 Sample Weekly Newsletter

Dear Parents and Friends,

Cheers! This is Dr. Lennard's diagnosis on the children and events during the past two weeks. Health and Safety are the continuing themes along with Thanksgiving.

Emergency center

The trip this week was exciting! We met firefighters Lucia, Alexandra and Norman. They showed us how to stop, kneel, and roll if our clothes are caught on fire. Also, crawl and stay down low if the room is smokey. We sat in the firetrucks, honked the horns, and saw a firewoman climb down the pole. Tuesday we will go to the Museum of Natural History.

Calling all nurses, please report to your stations immediately!

We were fortunate to have two nursing students, Dornette and Janis, teach two lessons about our bodies. They discussed body parts, their functions, and the names and shapes of some of the organs. The culminating exercise was the question asked to the children, "which part of your body do you like and why?" Here are some responses . . .

1. Daniel—"mouth to make faces with it."
2. Tad—"head because it is round."
3. Lucas—"toes because you can stand on them."
4. Abbey—"belly-button is my favorite word."
5. Jason—"hands to hold people."

to parent. These parents tended to develop a relationship with one staff member. The third group, *interdependent parents,* believed in sharing information and values back and forth between parents and staff. These parents believed in two-way communication and practiced it.

Periodic Communication Activities

Newsletters, special announcements, and bulletin boards are communication activities that many programs rely on to disseminate information to all parents. Over the course of the year parents begin to expect such communication and it becomes familiar. Program staff should handle most of the responsibility for initiating these activities. Do not overlook the fact that working parents find these activities very compatible with their busy schedules.

Newsletters. Newsletters can be short, one-page summaries of program activity or have many pages with feature story formats. They

Interns/residents corner

Sharon, 3rd year intern, has created "Guess the Object" from the Clue game for Team I. Chris and Andrea, 2nd year interns, discussed Health and Safety procedures with the children. Kadee, a junior intern, had the children decorate apples and watch them shrink and shrivel. A terrific science and art project.

Gastrology department

Special snacks made this week were popcorn with cheese, grilled cheese, fruit salad, scrambled eggs, and deviled eggs.

Pulse rate

Movement and drama activities have been vigorous these past weeks. The children loved the exercises, yoga, dancing to the tempo, and marching to the beat of instruments. Kadee had the children become trees and connect their bodies to one another. In our acting department, *Caps For Sale* was improvised.

Patients schedules

The children have been busy working with playdoh, pasting, cutting, and drawing. Painting with vibrant colors has decorated our Center magnificently. Cutting out feathers for our turkey was also a success. Magnets have been an attraction for the children. They have had to decide which objects were attracted or repelled. Counting objects, people, and actions have been on-going activities. The Dr.'s office and hospital area have been extremely popular the past two weeks.

Optometrists

Heidi, Joanne, and a majority of the University students have contact lenses. We showed the children the difference between the hard and soft lenses. Heidi demonstrated putting them in and taking them out. The children were fascinated how small the glass was and how it fit into one's eye.

Optometry division—looking ahead

We will be closing on Wednesday, November 23, at 3:30 p.m. Thank you for your cooperation. Please let us know if your child will be here on Wednesday. Sign up in the office.

A parent meeting on Feb. 23 has been scheduled. Discussions on varied child/parent situations will take place. The film *Mr. Rogers Talks to Parents* will be shown and followed with a discussion led by our staff psychologist, Dr. Weisbrod.

Cardiac unit

Our hearts were touched by (1) Michael Barker's father fixing the cot hooks, (2) Nancy Stadter, Gregory's mom, for baking the oatmeal cookies, and (3) Tad's mom for picking up the rug squares. We all appreciate it!

Off Duty,
Dr. Lennard and Staff

Source: American University Child Development Center, Washington, DC; used with permission.

may be weekly handouts or quarterly editions. The focus is generally on the child care program with specific attention paid to the children's activities. Written in conversational style, the newsletter may briefly summarize a week or month of curriculum activities, highlight children's responses, and remind families of coming events. This type of newsletter assumes a fairly homogeneous parent population and parent familiarity with the program. Thus, the newsletter transmits news, not background information (see Box 14.3). The short newsletter is most effective in combination with strong spontaneous conversation and adept, sensitive scheduling of educational meetings for specific parent needs.

A feature story newsletter requires more effort, is more expensive, and can be more informative to a wider range of readers. Large centers, networks of day care homes, franchises, or parent activist groups may find that a formal newsletter pays public relations dividends worth the extra effort expended. A feature story newsletter allows more detailed cov-

Few males are present in child care programs. Here a father is spending the morning helping his young son adjust to attending an all-day program. (College of Human Development, Department of Individual and Family Studies, The Pennsylvania State University; used with permission.)

erage of the background and planning activities of the child care program.

Special Announcements. One-page flyers and bright-colored handouts are part of child care operations. These special announcement techniques can be used to get attention and jog people's memories. Simplicity and timing are important. Use headlines, eye-catching graphics, and anything that captures your reader's eye. Then state your case or announce your event concisely. Use a telephone number, contact person, or lengthy brochure as a follow-up for those who want more information. Your initial message should be short, simple, and to the point.

Bulletin Boards. Bulletin boards can be used to encourage parents to stop and look, but they are not fully reliable in reaching all parents. One easy way to increase the visibility of bulletin board notices is to position the bulletin board near the log book or parent's mail boxes.

- Be sure the bulletin board is large enough to hold everything and still allow room for special display.
- Segment the bulletin board into areas such as

  For your information Local events, special articles, brochures, book reviews of general interest.
  Program news Upcoming events and meetings involving center staff and parents.
  Parents' exchange Personal notices, requests for babysitters, clothing exchanges.

- Assign a staff member responsibility for updating and arranging the bulletin board. Keep it fresh and interesting, not stale and cluttered.
- Periodically review the impact of your program bulletin board message center.
- See if people look at new notices; from time to time ask parents if they have any reaction to articles that have been posted. If such feedback is not positive, change something. Don't waste staff effort and display space on something that is not working to reach parents.

Spontaneous Communication Activities

Examples of spontaneous communication activities are daily conversation, telephone calls, notes, and quick reports. Staff are likely to do these activities as need or opportunity arises. Staff can also be sensitized to the value of such parent contact and can be encouraged to increase the frequency of these contacts. Most programs consider these contacts informal and not something for which staff needs prior authorization. Documentation of phone or written contacts is good practice, and programs should set up easy procedures for recording dates and content of contacts.

Daily Conversations. This is probably the single most important type of parent involvement. Drop-off and pick-up times are transition periods when staff, parents, and children can help each other immensely. Every child care operation should have a formal plan for handling drop-off and pick-up. Simply signing in and signing out is not effective management practice. Just because we expect this to be an informal time does not mean that very little attention should be paid to procedures.

Pointers for handling drop-off and pick-up times include the following:

- Assign a staff member responsibility for covering this time or assign responsibility for certain children to different staff members.
- Start with greetings—welcome the child, send off the parent. Use words to clearly indicate that these are transition times.
- Pick up on parent comments, ask questions as follow-up, keep the conversation going.
- Observe the parent-child interaction—learn to recognize typical and unusual interactions for each parent-child pair.
- At drop-off, concentrate on the child and strive to ease the child into the program.
- At pick-up, concentrate on the parent. Aim to help parent and child interact smoothly and alert the parent to highlights of the child's day that can be a starting point for them as they come together again.
- If possible, stagger children's arrival and departure times, or assign more than one staff member; don't let numbers produce transition chaos.
- If seemingly important information is picked up, communicate it immediately to other staff.
- If the staff member repeatedly picks up clues of problems at drop-off or pick-up time, more formal contacts may be indicated.
- Above all, keep these chats short and informal; let the frequency of contact help to establish the relationship rather than striving for intense contact.

Telephone Calls. The first time a parent gets called during the day or evening, the response is likely to be "What's wrong?" We tend to limit telephone calls, trying not to impose on parents during work hours or interrupt family privacy. The two basic rules for telephone calls are:

1. Know your parents. Some parents cannot receive calls at work; others are uncomfortable on the phone. Some parents prefer the convenience and willingly indicate time when telephone calls are welcome.
2. Have a good reason for calling. State your reason immediately; then you can limit yourself to the business at hand and complete the call quickly if necessary.

What kinds of business can you conduct by telephone? First, it's not all business. Despite our admonition to be businesslike, remember that telephone calls can be social and can contribute to comfortable relationships between staff and parents. Some reasons to use telephone calls are:

- Parents need to know or be asked immediately about an event, and personal contact is thought to be best (a marriage, death, a great accomplishment, a critical information need, or a referral).
- Solicitation of opinions or ideas: A telephone survey of parents may be better than meeting. This can help to set an agenda for a meeting or guide staff in programming decisions. You lose discussion among parents, but there are often situations where that is not really necessary.
- A specific request such as obtaining a field trip volunteer or asking parents to save egg cartons or other home items.
- Clarification of situations—family status information, tuition reminders, medical or dental updates.
- A specific child situation. This can be similar to a conference in which information sharing between the home and program is the primary purpose. Generally it is related to specific needs. For example, a child is not willing to nap—what suggestions does the parent have? Is the child lacking any special props at the center (blanket, pacifier)?

Child care centers and homes should keep telephone logs, including date, time, name of caller, topic, and person contacted. Since this log needs to be accessible and available for recording for all staff, no personal or confidential information should be entered. If telephone calls produce critical information, separate notes should be made and entered into the child's folder.

Personal Notes. Stock up on small note pads, pads with a message logo at the top (from the center to you), or fold-up postcards with bright designs. Be prepared to write short notes. It may seem that written personal notes are not necessary if staff regularly see parents. Yet, sometimes writing has more impact than conversation, and more privacy than in the hubbub of drop-off and pick-up. Times to write personal notes include:

- Communicating times and dates of conferences, referrals, evaluations that are important for one parent rather than the entire group. The note ensures privacy and provides a written record for the parent.
- Thanking parents for particular contributions or efforts for the program or for the child. Perhaps a child has clean clothes or a bigger lunch now, and everyone is happier as a result. Perhaps a parent has spent a Saturday repairing windows or painting cubbies and deserves special thanks.
- Informing parents of certain events discretely—perhaps Sara was especially uncomfortable today being called names or was unduly upset by a filmstrip about dinosaurs charging around the jungle. If you want to be sure the parent knows this and is told privately, write a personal note.
- Refreshing the memory. Parents may need reminding to pay bills, provide extra clothing, or meet work commitments. Use a personal note to achieve this.

Activity Reports. These should not be confused with more formal reporting procedures. Activity reports are index-card sized activity summaries written with staff and child collaboration. Four- and five-year-olds relish producing these short stories and save them at home. Staff often find that activity cards are a helpful tool in opening up conversation with parents. Directors find that activity cards are a prop to remind staff to interact with parents.

In infant centers parents may receive an activity card report everyday listing naptimes, mealtimes, and elimination information.

Scheduled Communication Activities

Certain parent involvement activities are formal events, occurring because of requirements or program priorities. Conferences and reports, program orientations, and home visits are examples of formally scheduled activities. We include parent handbooks as part of program orientations. These activities require planning, preparation of forms, gathering and recording of information, and careful management of the documents.

Conferences and Reports. Center-based programs generally offer to schedule conferences at parents' requests at any time. Day care home providers are not as likely to feel the need to schedule formal parent conferences.

A conference is a personal meeting between parents and program staff. Reports accompany the conference. Reports are evaluations of children's progress and vary in complexity. They range from anecdotal observations to professionally administered developmental tests. Parents may receive copies of a report prior to a conference or staff may convey report information to a parent during the conference. With all these variations in mind, let's follow a typical procedure for a parent conference.

Let's assume the policy requires the program staff to schedule an annual child progress evaluation conference. With agreement from the staff and the parent advisory committee, the director selects an age-graded developmental checklist for the child progress evaluation. For each age, the checklist gives typical skills and asks the recorder to estimate the degree to which the child can perform the behavior.

To complete the checklists, the director determines which staff have primary contact with each child. That staff member is assigned as the conference person and evaluation recorder for that child. The director holds several short training and information sessions related to the developmental checklists. Staff are encouraged to keep anecdotal records on children to sharpen their observation skills. With some input from other staff, the conference staff person assigned to each child completes the checklist for each child and prepares a short summary to send home to parents. For example:

> Dear Parents,
>
> We have spent several months observing your child's activities at our center. We would like to share our observations with you and discuss the many ways we can work together in helping your child grow and learn.
>
> Please read our observations and share them with others who care for your child. Return the conference sign-up sheet and we'll schedule a conference at our mutual convenience.

Separate statements about developmental areas are included with the letter. For example:

> Jennifer is usually quite cheerful and outgoing. Her fine motor skills have improved considerably and she seems to enjoy her new skills. She spends most of her time playing with other children and is quite active.

At conference time the staff person has available a detailed checklist for the child and several anecdotal notes. The parent has a summary sheet; the staff member has already tackled the job of translating the information into language that is meaningful to the parent.

Holding the Conference

- Confirm the date, time, and place in writing. Send a reminder note or telephone the day before the conference.
- Review materials as close in time to the conference as possible.
- Arrange to meet in a private place; let others know that you are not to be interrupted.
- Be on time yourself; arrange for coats, care of younger siblings, and parking if necessary.
- Plan some ice-breakers; for example, coffee and cookies or a quick tour of a new play area.

Conference Procedures

- Tell the parent something about yourself and the center.
- Be positive about the child—begin with the positive points.
- Ask the parent if he or she has any questions—respond directly to any questions.
- Discuss the categories of the parent report. Elaborate where you can and encourage the parent to ask questions and to provide comments about the child's behavior at home.
- Consider whether you are talking too much or overwhelming the parent.
- Have some stock questions ready in case the conversation lags—for example, "What is a favorite activity at home?" or "Are you concerned about any behavior?"
- Listen and then listen some more. It is generally intimidating for a parent if you take the main role in the conversation. Besides you can't listen if you're doing all the talking.
- Close the conference on time or early if everything goes smoothly; be ready with phrases such as "The last thing we need to discuss is ______" or "I'm glad we had this chance to talk."

Back-up Procedures

- If the parent does not show up, reschedule immediately; take the initiative.
- If the conversation is combative or tense, try other topics, offer to reschedule with director or other staff present, go immediately to director for advice or help, or conclude the conference.
- If the parent is uncommunicative or if you feel the language or cultural barriers are too great, change the pace (take a tour or go together to meet other staff), ask another staff member to join you, or reschedule when another staff member can be present.

Follow-up Procedures

- Write a brief summary of the conference.
- File all documents together in the child's folder.
- Decide if any conference information should be shared with the rest of the staff; discuss with the director how to do this.
- Initiate any referrals and be sure to follow through on any commitments made to parents during the conference.

Program Orientations and Parent Handbooks. Parents should know the "facts of life" about the particular program in which their child is enrolled. The wise director or provider does not assume that a new parent knows or remembers everything. Once enrollment is official, take the time to orient and inform parents.

Program orientation is a guided tour. It is appropriate and helpful in the smallest home or the largest center. Ask the parent(s) to come at a convenient time just for this tour. If children are to have extra clothes, they should be ready and brought for this tour.

The tour might include the following activities:

1. *Inspect facilities and equipment* Visit all areas, have floorplans with you, and go outside and point out nearby buildings and places.
2. *Meet all staff* Provide a list of names and job titles for the parent. Include relevant agency personnel even if not at the site.
3. *Meet the children* Provide a list of names for the parent.
4. *Walk the parent through a typical day* Have a copy of your schedule available; then go to each place and discuss activity highlights.
5. *Locate all parent-child personal places* Cubby, mailbox, and sign-in logs.
6. *Review program finances and organizational structure.*
7. *Introduce parent to other parents, if possible.*

Floorplans, staff and child lists, schedule, and organizational structure may all be in the parent handbook.

Parent handbooks are vital tools for parent communication. Used alone or in connection with an orientation tour, parent handbooks can be an essential repository of program information. Minimum contents for a parent handbook include:

- *Program data* Location, sponsor, and phone numbers
- *Staff data* Names and selected personal information
- *Child list* Names and addresses
- *Personal sheet* Fees, record of emergency numbers, and medical information
- *Daily schedule* Indication of child's enrollment hours
- Checklist of enrollment procedures and items to provide

Tear-out or return sheets are also helpful:

- Field trip permission slip
- Photographic permission slip
- Testing permission slip
- Emergency and medical information
- Statement of understanding of fees and hours

Home Visits. The visit of a caregiver to a child's home is a big occasion. Young children may not know how to react to seeing their caregiver in the setting of their home. Home visits are scheduled by programs and providers for a number of reasons:

1. *Introductory social visit* Programs may use home visits as a way to introduce the child to his or her new teacher. These visits give parents an opportunity to ask questions and discuss program activities informally. Teachers find it helpful to see the child in his or her home and observe the kind of play opportunities available for the child. This type of visit can be the first step in an open communication link between program and home.
2. *Periodic home visits* These visits may replace formally scheduled parent conferences. In rural areas where children are transported to the center, it may make more sense for the caregiver to travel to the parents for conferences.

3. *Special purpose visits* The program may use home visits as part of a traveling resource project. Teachers may bring toys, books, or equipment to loan to parents. Visits may focus on topics such as funding, making toys, or language development. They can be personalized education sessions for parents. Programs may occasionally schedule special-purpose visits, or these may be part of a supplemental formal training program for parents.

Special Communication Activities

Crisis Contacts. Parents and children attending a child care program can find themselves in a situation that suddenly affects their ability to function normally. As part of the extended care family, the staff often must decide if and how to help. Some examples of these situations are a parent losing a job, fire destroying all household possessions, an injury to a child, a serious illness or death in the family, older siblings with problems, or a relative involved in a criminal activity.

Suggestions for handling these situations are:

- Have one person contact the family to assess the situation and offer immediate, child-related support and aid. This is compassionate first aid.
- Determine any privacy problems or family conditions that would establish a framework for longer-term help.
- If appropriate, involve the program staff and the larger parent group in support activities that are genuinely helpful and use the program support capacity effectively.
- Refer the case to other professionals as appropriate; remain supportive over the long term, but keep a reasonable perspective on the capacity of the child care program to sustain long-term aid for highly specialized difficulties.

Supportive Participation

Nurturing a common sense of purpose and shared commitment among parents is an important goal and a frequently overlooked outcome of parent involvement. Supportive participation activities are for fostering goodwill and friendship among parents. Such events may be purely social or may revolve around program support activities that bring parents together for short-term work efforts. Supportive participation activities are generally sporadically scheduled. Some occur spontaneously or in response to a perceived need of the parent group.

Good times and shared fun are important. From time to time every child care program can sponsor social events. Social events bring people together and promote a sense of community. They also help group members meet one another. Parties, family events, and morning coffees are examples of social activities that can promote parents' commitments to the program. Carefully selected social activities can also contribute to the child care families' time together, providing both parents and children with enjoyable activities. Some activities are "social-plus" activities. They require parents and staff to work together for short periods to produce some tangible results. Equipment work days, small fund raisers, and other charitable endeavors are common examples of constructive activities. Success must be measured in terms of both the product and the secondary social support opportunities for parents.

Information Sharing and Education

Do all parents need help? It seems inevitable that at some point all programs want to offer to parents activities that are called educational. These educational activities may result from parent requests for information. Or, the program staff may feel that parents could benefit from training in areas such as child development. Some people think that educational activities tend to set people off in separate categories—parents versus program staff, the uninformed versus the informed, the layperson versus the expert, or the student versus the teacher. These separations tend to exaggerate differences between parents and staff and between home and program. On the other hand, the educational activity may serve to bring parents and staff closer by reducing the information gap and skill differences between the groups. The result of educational activities could be closer agreement between parents and program staff on matters of child development. To achieve this result, information sharing and educational activities must be organized around guidelines:

1. *Content planning* Include a reasonable range of information and skill levels. Assume that different levels of expertise exist among parents, and incorporate those varying levels in the activity. Without this range of information you cannot expect growth to occur as parents and staff reach toward compatible information levels.
2. *Format devices* Parents' learning skills will vary, sometimes from nonreaders to Ph.Ds. Discussions, panels, lectures, films, printed materials, public meetings, and private sessions—all have a role in educational activities. Present content using a format that is a "good fit" for the intended parent audience. Modify available materials or seek out others to achieve this good fit.
3. *Parent attitude* Think about attitudes and reactions to proposed educational activities. Try to identify possible areas of difficulty ahead of time. Alert program staff and help the staff prepare to deal with positive and negative outcomes of the program through in-service training or individual counseling. Identify concrete ways that staff can build on the educational activity content in working cooperatively with parents.

The following list shows several types of information sharing and educational activities that could be used in child care programs:

Dissemination

- Pamphlets and materials
- Resource libraries
- Resource staff

Organized Activities

- Focused meetings
- Educational programs
- Committees

Large-scale Efforts

- Toy-lending libraries
- Home visits and home tutors
- Model programs

Dissemination

Modest in scope and easy to organize and operate, dissemination activities are useful for all types of child care programs. Common examples are pamphlets, a resource library, and a resource staff. Each can be started on a small scale and added to as staff and money resources permit. Occasional mention of the resources in newsletters or at other meetings will serve to maintain visibility and promote use by parents.

Pamphlets and Materials. Free stuff! Or perhaps a few pennies apiece. Child care programs can quickly tap into a large supply of pamphlets and materials that are produced as public information efforts by companies and organizations. Possible sources are local dairy councils, food companies, insurance companies, toy manufacturers, and, of course, the U.S. government. Much information available through these sources is highly relevant and closely related to the topics that parents frequently ask questions about.

Spend a little time setting up a system for pamphlets and brochures. For example:

1. Solicit: Watch the ads in professional magazines, ask around in your local community, ask other programs, or write to Toys 'n Things Training Resource Center, 906 North Dale Street, St. Paul, Minnesota 55103 for their "Potpourri of Child Care and Development Pamphlets." They reviewed over 400 brochures and for a fee will pro-

vide you with a list of the 100 best and single copies of 25 of them. This is a good start for building a pamphlet collection.
2. Review brochures and decide which are worth having in quantities. Set up an index file and make a card for each, listing ordering information and price. Record each request for copies on this card.
3. Display brochures and leave out extra copies or instruct people how to ask for copies.
4. Store brochures in one place. When supplies get low, pull the appropriate order card and note on your calendar when to reorder.
5. Ask a parent, volunteer, or staff member to handle the system.
6. Newsletters for parents may be helpful (see Appendix F).

Resource Libraries. A single shelf of books with a pad for sign-out can work as a resource library. Often multiple copies of the same book are a better investment than many titles. However, as money and donations permit, expand the library. Call parents' attention to new books and refer parents to books when they ask questions. The resource library could be the focus of a parent-staff lounge if space permits.

Resource Staff. One person may be designated as an information resource person. Frequently, programs will have one staff member who just seems to "know about things." Formalize the position and give that person some time to read, locate resources, and set up procedures for dissemination. Encourage informal use of this person's capabilities. Refer parents who may want information to this person.

Organized Activities

For many, meetings and lectures and panel discussions *are* the real educational activities for parents. The combination of extensive planning, formal setting, and parents' commitments to participate are thought to be the necessary ingredients for education to occur. And, for many parents, these organized educational activities are their primary, formal contact with the program.

Focused Meetings. General large group meetings are probably the most frequent parent educational activity planned by child care programs. A speaker, film, panel, or discussion may be scheduled to coincide with the business meeting or to precede or follow a social event. If there is enough interest, it may stand alone as a topical meeting. Some programs are adept at drawing on local experts and resources, others are hard-pressed to find presenters. All programs find it necessary to advertise these events and find they must work to "get parents out."

Educational Programs. These are different from focused meetings because they usually involve a series of related meetings. Parents may be asked to register and pay small fees for the program. The child care program may combine staff training and parent education and run the educational program for both groups.

Committees. Parents are always serving on committees for child care programs. Standing committees that concern themselves with curriculum, finance, or personnel are frequently overlooked as targets for educational activities. Careful agenda planning, distribution of brochures, introductory remarks, or the availability of resource consultants are techniques that allow committee members to learn and work at the same time. Programs have much to gain by treating committee assignments for parents as learning opportunities.

Large-Scale Efforts

Some educational activities require considerable resource commitment.

Toy-Lending Libraries. Toy lending is much like book lending. A centrally located collection of toys (cataloged and maintained by a staff) is available to members for short-term loan. Toys circulate throughout the membership, providing each member access to toys that might not be available otherwise. Members with special toy needs can share the costs of those needs with others in similar circumstances. Family day care homes can change the mix of toys available to children and share the costs and use of large outdoor equipment or special equipment for handicapped children. Center programs can share costs and use for expensive large equipment and rotate a large supply of instructional materials through their programs. Toy-lending libraries may deal directly with parents as part of home-based parent education programs or as extensions of community library services. Parents and children check out new toys each week and may receive printed suggestions for games or demonstrations by the toy librarian.

Toy-lending libraries caused quite a stir among early childhood professionals in the 1960s. Many people recognized the creative and efficient potential of toy libraries as resource pools for child care programs and as appealing educational programs for parents. Several excellent practical guides are listed in the Resources section.

Home Visits and Home Tutors. Child care programs may use home visits as a regularly scheduled supplement to the children's experiences in the program. Staff are specifically trained and equipped to use the home visit as a teaching and learning session for parents and children. Parents may be instructed during these visits in a number of child development areas and may be given assignments to tutor or play special games with their children.

Home-based programs require extensive curriculum planning and staff training. Case histories, program descriptions, and packaged curriculum materials are available from a number of successful programs (check the Resources section).

Model Programs. Planned Variation Programs in Follow Through and Head Start spawned a few well-developed model programs for parent education. Since that time, other federal funds have been used to initiate other quality programs for parent education. Child care programs will find that these models are useful guides in developing their own parent education programs. Many model programs have curriculum packages that can be purchased for local use. Several listings of relevant programs are given in the Resources section.

Daily Program Participation

Parents can make special contributions by working in a child care program. Center and home programs benefit from parents' intimate involvement in daily activities. Parents learn through experience and gain understanding of the program by being a participating observer. Staff and parents working side by side can lead to good rapport and easier personal relationships. Sometimes frictions and misunderstandings do occur. Frequently this is more because of the responsibilities of the work than because a parent is doing the work. However, smoothly integrating parents into a program does require thought and preparation.

Parents can work as paid employees of the program or they can contribute their time. Parents who work in a program on a regular basis should pay attention to how they and their child cope. Children may have difficulty separating from a parent and pursuing activities with other staff members. Parents should not play favorites. The parent-child relationship is different from the staff-child relationship. Recognizing such differences and dealing with them in ways that the child can accept is necessary.

Protecting confidentiality of information is essential when parents work in programs. As regular staff members, parents can expect to have access to and need for some personal information on children's families. Clear-cut rules regarding such information need to be communicated to all parents and staff.

Paid Employment

Child care programs may employ parents for a number of reasons. Certain publicly funded programs pay the salaries of workers in training. The child care program may be a selected work site, and a parent may be eligible for such a funded position. Parents may be trained professionals who have good qualifications for the program jobs. Or, they may seek entry-level employment as program aides because they like taking care of children. Some programs may prefer not to employ parents or may restrict parents of enrolled children to certain jobs such as cook, bus driver, or janitor. Such policies may be illegal and certainly don't suggest harmonious and trusting relationships between staff and parents and the community. After all, child care programs can be parent cooperatives in which parents fill all the jobs and run the whole show quite successfully. Programs with restrictive or discouraging employment policies for parents need to reexamine their practices and work toward more accepting work situations.

Program Support

Parents may help with daily program activities as volunteers, special project leaders, and field trip aids. Such roles bring parents into the program for brief periods of interaction with staff and children. Many of the same conditions and cautions about parents as employees can apply to parents in program support roles. Usually, however, the contact is brief and directed at specific activities.

Child care programs may exert strong pressure on parents to contribute volunteer time. Programs can actually rely on volunteers to meet staff-child ratios or to adequately staff activities. Parents are the most readily available pool of volunteer talent for a child care program. Volunteers, unfortunately, can be just more adults poorly managed and integrated into the program. The Resources section of Chapter 11 has more information.

The talents and skills of parents can also be used in special projects. For example:

- Have a parent who is a plumber come and explain sinks and toilets and give children a chance to use simple tools.
- Have a parent help with a cooking project—grandma's special molasses cookies, tortillas, or stir-fried rice and vegetables.
- Have a stewardess parent wear her uniform, describe her job, and perhaps arrange for the children to tour a plane.

There are many ways of discovering contributions that parents can make. You can ask parents directly or use a general survey form. For example, send a note home asking "What ideas and activities can you share with the children? Let us know. We would like to have you come to our program." As the staff gets to know parents, they may be able to suggest contributions that even parents had not thought of.

Trips away from the program require closer supervision of children, and parents can be helpful in this way, too. Children need to be in small groups on trips so that they can more easily ask questions about new sights and experience. Be considerate of parents' time. Make a realistic time schedule with some slack for dawdling or prolonged activities and then try to stick to that schedule for the field trip. Let parents know if lunches are needed or if special clothing or equipment is required. Give parents sufficient notice about field trips so they can rearrange work schedules if they want to participate. Keep track of which parents come on field trips. Try to encourage all parents to come at some time. Avoid always imposing on the same parents if you can. Express appreciation

Sometimes just being there is the best kind of contact that a parent can have with a program. (Courtesy of U.S. Department of Housing and Urban Development, Washington, DC.)

for their time, and prepare children for trips so that parents are not confronted with difficult behavior.

Parents As Policymakers

Policy statements are the written principles that guide the administration of the day care program. Policies are formulated by program staff, parents, sponsoring agencies, and community representatives. Many consider parent participation in policy decisions to be the ultimate form of parent involvement. PACs are the policy group for individual day care programs. Parents from the program serve with interested others from the community on standing committees and on the PAC itself. The PAC formalizes parent participation and authority in policy formulation.

Parent representation on a child care program board is necessary. If PACs operate effectively, they serve as a source and training experience for parent board members. All board members—parents or not—should be willing to and capable of performing board functions and responsibilities. Chapter 15 discusses board structure and function.

Staff-Parent Relationships

Parent involvement is built around staff-parent relationships. Implicit in any discussion of parent involvement activities is the critical role that child care staff plays as the personal link between parent and program. To many parents, staff members *are* the program. Much of the discussion about parent roles is from the perspective of the parent and the effects of activities on parents. However, staff concerns related to parent involvement deserve special attention as well.

Each staff member in a child care program has a set of duties designated for his or her position. Programs with good personnel practices provide staff members with a detailed list of job duties and responsibilities. In one way or another, staff are told that part of their job is to work with parents.

Staff usually see their primary job duties in relation to children and activities with the children. Activities with parents are secondary. As parent activities occur at night or on weekends and thereby add hours to a staff member's day, it will seem as if parent activities are an extension of a staff member's duties. Extended parent activity requires extra time and effort. Some form of compensation, recognition, or motivation becomes necessary. For example:

- Programs may evolve strong norms of staff-parent participation. Staff derive personal feelings of satisfaction and group identity from working with these obviously committed parents and staff.
- Staff contributions to parent activities may be recognized through service awards, compensatory vacation time, extra pay, or higher evaluation ratings from supervisors.
- A large program staff may rotate the responsibility for parent involvement activities. Over a period of time all staff will do their fair share.

Program directors and leaders need to honestly pay attention to staff feelings and grievances related to the extra time and efforts required for parent involvement. Invoking authority or enforcing participation is not likely to result in good staff-parent relationships. With some probing and questioning, program leaders may find that staff discontent is a reflection of lack of skill or poor attitudes.

Lack of Skill

Working with parents requires the ability to "get along with" other adults. An open and friendly personality, backed up by the status of the staff position, is enough of a basis for most staff to deal comfortably with parents on an informal level. Problems and difficulties come when staff skills do not match those required by different kinds of parent involvement activities. Consider the different communications skills necessary to:

- Moderate a panel discussion.
- Be hostess at a parent coffee.
- Introduce a speaker.
- Give a tour of the facility.

With training and practice, most staff members might be able to do all of these things. Training in skills that are directly related to parent activities can be a priority topic for in-service training or a good reason for staff to attend workshops and conferences. Use staff where they are comfortable and able. Work toward increasing skills and minimizing situations where staff feel vulnerable.

Attitudes

Staff with high motivation and good skills may still find parent involvement activities a hassle. Why? Can attitudes be changed toward more favorable perceptions? One overlooked reason for poor staff attitudes is that the effects and progress that result from parent activities are often very gradual. Parents don't change magically or exhibit visible evidence of benefits or appreciation of parent activities overnight. Staff need help in identifying the slow time factors of parent involvement and help in recognizing small and subtle cues about their impact. People like to know that their time and effort were worthwhile. Poor staff attitudes can result when there is no feedback or too much delay in seeing that the activity has been successful.

More difficult to deal with are those staff attitudes about parents that lead to feelings of superiority. Staff may have trouble seeing parents as educators in a professional sense. Or, staff may have difficulty accepting some parents as competent caretakers of their children. Staff attitudes such as these are communicated to parents in informal ways and can jeopardize the entire parent involvement effort of a program. The remedy in poor attitude situations is individual; some staff members respond to counseling, others to frank discussions, others to peer pressure or actual experience with parents. Intolerant and inflexible staff should be removed from parent contact even if that means leaving the program.

Issues

Five issues are likely to arise in the area of parental roles in child care. How programs respond to these issues shapes their parent involvement efforts. For each issue we present several different viewpoints.

What Is the Appropriate Relationship of Child Care and the Family?

Child care is a service to families that is intended to supplement and complement the caregiving of parents and other relatives. Families can expect a child care program to be responsive to their needs, reflect cultural values, and enhance the quality or ease of family life.

Or, child care is a positive experience for growing children. All children should have the opportunity to participate in child care. All families should have access to child care arrangements that are compatible with their needs. Society should ensure universal access to child care.

Or, child care is a necessary service. For social, economic, or other reasons some families need or should be helped with child care. Child care experiences can probably be designed to support or, at best, not harm children's development. Parents, children, and programs make trade-offs in child care service components as conditions demand.

Or, child care is not a public responsibility. The fundamental position here revolves around responsibility. If families choose child care as a caregiving service, then full financial responsibility for the service is also assumed for the parents.

Or, child care should not exist. Children should be cared for by their families. Often supporters of this position view child care as an undesirable intrusion into family life.

Do Working Parents Have Time for Program Participation?

YES! The child care program is so important to parents, allowing them pursuit of an income, that they make time for participation.

Parents believe participation is beneficial for their children. They are highly motivated to participate in parent activities.

The program makes participation convenient. Activities are appealing and well-scheduled.

The program needs parents' time and resources in order to survive.

The program values parents' cultural contributions and uses them to enrich curriculum activities.

NO! Parents work all day. They are too tired to take on the extra job of child care program supporter.

Parents are away from their children enough. They should be able to spend as much time as possible with their children. Program participation interferes with that time.

Parents don't have enough time to really get involved and learn enough about program practices and policies. No parent involvement is better than uninformed parents trying to do things.

Parents can usually do things only at night or on weekends. The staff wants a break and doesn't always like to participate in program-related activities at those times most convenient for parents.

Who Benefits from Parent Involvement?

Parents. Parents gain greater understanding of their children's activities and find it easier to relate to their children's experiences and the program.

Parents may feel less anxious about working if they have a meaningful role.

Parents may learn skills that make them more competent or comfortable as parents.

Parents may form friendships or support

workers among the adults in the child care program group.

Children. Parent involvement can make programs run more smoothly.

If parents are comfortable and active in the program, children may benefit from closer continuities between home and program.

All children may benefit from the advocacy efforts of parents for quality child care.

Program. Parent involvement can mean more hands and heads to do all the work. Programs may find financing and management easier with extensive parent involvement.

Programs that reflect parents' values and that respond to parents' wishes for "good care" for their children can be exciting, vital places that are their own best public relations.

How are the Effects of Parent Involvement Assessed?

There are at least four ways of looking at this.

1. Benefits of parent involvement activities are best assessed on an informal basis. So many variables are involved that controlled evaluations are not feasible. Case studies, comparative analysis, and self-assessments are methods appropriate for program resources and are likely to capture locally meaningful effects.
2. Hard data of good quality are essential to determine whether efforts at parent involvement are worthwhile. The more program resources are poured into parent involvement activities, the greater the need for data about effects to justify the use of those program resources.
3. Many parent involvement activities, such as parent education and training, aim to change parents' behavior. The measurement of behavior change can be difficult since it is sometimes hard to identify clearly the amount of change that occurs from program participation versus the behavioral change naturally occurring over the same period of time. There are sampling and statistical procedures available, but these do not always lend themselves easily to the dynamics of parent activities in child care programs.
4. Timing of assessment is an important consideration in looking for effects of parent involvement. Some effects may be immediate, some long-term. Effects may be temporary or sustained, or may carry over in the parents' interactions with younger children in the family. Different parent involvement activities can be expected to have different timelines for optimum effects to emerge. Programs may want to limit resources for parent involvement to activities that will show effects in the short term.

Does the Changing Parent Population Have a Negative Effect?

As children grow older, they will spend less time in a program or leave it completely. Parents who are no longer child care consumers can be expected to stop participating in involvement activities. As parent leadership turns over, do parent activities recognize this and continually strive to identify and train new leaders? When parent priorities change, can programs change to meet differing parent expectations and welcome fresh ideas without losing the essentials of program integrity? Since some parents are always new to the program, can staff and involvement activities meet the challenge of repetitive cycles of orientation, motivation, and rapport building with new groups of parents? Although parents value the child care experience, do parents remain child care supporters, advocates, and responsive voters once the immediacy of their need has passed?

Summary

As the consumers of child care, parents have a part to play in any successful program.

In recent years the characteristics of parents choosing child care have changed. More are working parents, many are part of dual-income families, and many are single working mothers. Parents choose a particular program based on availability, appropriateness for their child, their financial situation, and the program's reliability, protection, and continuity. For most parents choosing child care actually involves three decisions: whether or not to work, type of child care, and ways to make it all work.

Parents' role in child care has changed over the years because the family and our expectations for it have changed and because child care programs have shifted from educating parents to involving them. Six general models of parental involvement are the deficit model, the schools as failure model, the cultural difference model, the social structure model, the community support model, and the family cooperative model. Some state and local laws regulate parental participation in aspects such as board and committee memberships and visitation rights.

In most programs parents participate in five broad areas: communication, support, information sharing, daily activities, and policymaking. Communication involvement includes periodic contact such as newsletters, spontaneous contact such as daily conversations, and scheduled contact such as conferences. Support participation may be a party or fund raiser. Parents may come to the program for information sharing in the form of pamphlets or books, meetings, or talks with a resource staff member. Some parents may decide to work at a program on a daily basis for a salary or as a volunteer. The contribution of parents to policymaking can be as a member of a PAC or the program board.

The relationship between staff and parents can suffer because the staff lack a particular communication skill or because the staff have a poor attitude toward parent involvement. Parents and staff are partners in the child care experience.

Resources

Background

Bane, M. J., Lein, L., O'Donnell, L., Stueve, C. A., & Wills, B. (1979). Child-care arrangements of working parents. *Special Labor Force Report 233.* Washington, DC: U.S. Department of Labor, Bureau of Labor Statistics.

Characteristics of American Children and Youth: 1980. (1982). Current Population Reports, Special Studies Series P-23, no. 114. Washington, DC: U.S. Department of Commerce, Bureau of the Census.

Duncan, G., & Hill, C. R. (1975). Modal choice in child care arrangements. In G. Duncan & J. Morgan (Eds.), *Five thousand American families: Patterns of economic progress: Vol. III.* Ann Arbor, MI: Institute for Social Research.

Family day care in the United States: Summary of findings. Vol. I. (1981). DHHS Pub. No. (OHDS) 80-30282. Final Report of the National Day Care Home Study. Washington, DC: Department of Health and Human Services.

Frost, J., & Schneider, H. (1971). *Types of day care and parents' preferences. Final report: Part VII.* Minneapolis, MN: Institute for Interdisciplinary Studies. (ERIC Document Reproduction Service No. ED 068 195)

A growing crisis: Disadvantaged women and their children. (1983). Clearinghouse Publication 78. Washington, DC: U.S. Commission on Civil Rights.

Haskins, R. (1979). Day care and public policy. *Urban and Social Change Review, 12* (1), 3–10.

Hofferth, S. (1979). Day care in the next decade: 1980–1990. *Journal of Marriage and the Family,* August, 649–658.

Kurz, M., Robins, P., & Spiegelman, R. (1975). *A study of the demand for child care by working mothers:* Research Memorandum 27. Stanford, CA: Stanford Research Institute, Center for the Study of Welfare Policy.

Lamb, M. E. (Ed.). (1982). *Nontraditional families: Parenting and child development.* Hillsdale, NJ: Lawrence Erlbaum.

Lein, L. (1979). Parental evaluation of childcare alternatives. *Urban and Social Change Review, 12* (1), 11–16.

Lewis, V. (1975). Is there much demand for federally financed day care centers? In M. A. Larson (Ed.), *Federal policy for preschool services: Assumptions and evidence:* Research Memorandum EPRC 2158-24 (pp. 81–95). Stanford, CA: Stanford Research Institute, Educational Policy Research Center.

Low, S., & Spindler, P. G. (1968). *Child care arrangements of working mothers in the United States.* Washington, DC: Children's Bureau, U.S. Government Printing Office.

Rivlin, A. (1978). *Child care and preschool: Options for federal support.* Washington, DC: Congressional Budget Office.

UNCO, Inc. (1975). *National child care consumer study: 1975.* Washington, DC: U.S. Government Printing Office.

U.S. Bureau of the Census. (1976). *Current population reports,* Series P-20, No. 298, Daytime Care of Children: October 1974 and February 1975. Washington, DC: U.S. Government Printing Office.

Waldman, E., Grossman, A. S., Hayghe, H., & Johnson, B. L. (1979). Working mothers in the 1970's. A Look at the Statistics. *Special Labor Force Report 233* (pp. 39–49). Washington, DC: U.S. Department of Labor, Bureau of Labor Statistics.

Westinghouse Learning Corporation and Westat Research, Inc. (1971). *Day care survey—1970.* Washington, DC: Office of Economic Opportunity.

Women at work: A chartbook. (1983). Bulletin 2168, August. Washington, DC: U.S. Government Printing Office/Department of Labor, Bureau of Statistics.

Choosing Child Care

Auerbach, S. (1981). *Choosing child care.* New York: Dutton.

Auerbach, S., & Freeman, L. (1976). *Choosing child care: A guide for parents.* San Francisco: Parents and Child Care Resources.

Bergstrom, J., with L. Joy. (1981). *Going to work? Choosing care for infants and toddlers? A guide.* Washington, DC: Day Care Council of America.

Breitbart, V. (1974). *The day care book.* New York: Knopf.

Checking out child care. (n.d.). Washington, DC: Day Care and Child Development Council of America.

Endsley, R., & Bradbard, M. (1981). *Quality day care: A handbook of choices for parents and caregivers.* Englewood Cliffs, NJ: Prentice-Hall.

Galinsky, E., & Hooks, W. (1977). *The new extended family: Day care that works.* Boston: Houghton Mifflin.

King County Child Care Coordinating Committee. (1973). *In-home care checklist, family day care home checklist, day care center checklist.* Washington, DC: Day Care & Child Development Council of America.

Lake, A. (1980). The day care business. *Working Mother,* September, pp. 31–37, 144–146; November, pp. 143–158.

A parent's guide to day care. (1980). Washington, DC: U.S. Department of Health and Human Services, Office of Human Development Services. Pub. No. (OHDS) 80-30254.

Powell, D. R., & Eisenstadt, J. W. (1980). *Finding child care: A study of parents' search processes.* Detroit, MI: Merrill-Palmer Institute.

Siegel-Gorelick, B. (1983). *The working parents' guide to child care: How to find the best care for your child.* Boston: Little, Brown.

For Working Parents

Bird, C. (1979). *The two-paycheck marriage.* New York: Pocket Books.

Child care tax credit. (1984). *Exchange,* March, p. 22.

Curtis, J. (1976). *Working mothers.* New York: Doubleday.

Fraiberg, S. (1977). *Every child's birthright: In defense of mothering.* New York: Basic Books.

Greenleaf, B., & Schaffer, L. (1978). *HELP: A handbook for working mothers.* New York: Crowell.

Hersh, S. (1979). *The executive parent.* New York: Sovereign Books/Simon & Schuster.

Hope, K., & Young, H. (1976). *Momma handbook: The source book for single mothers.* New York: New American Library.

Kramer, R. (1982). *In defense of the family: Raising children in America today.* New York: Basic Books.

Kramer, S. (Ed.). (1976). *The balancing act: A career and a baby.* Chicago: Chicago Review Press/Swallow Press.

Kramer, S. (Ed.). (1981). *The balancing act II.* Chicago: Chicago Review Press.

McBride, A. (1973). *The growth and development of mothers.* New York: Harper & Row.

Parent Involvement

Auerbach, A. S. (1968). *Parents learn through discussion: Principles and practices of parent group education.* New York: Wiley.

Berger, E. H. (1981). *Parents as partners in education.* St. Louis: C.V. Mosby.

Brock, H. C. III. (1976). *A practical guide: Parent volunteer programs in early childhood education.* Hamden, CT: Shoestring Press.

Carson, J. (1975). *The role of parents as teachers.* Philadelphia: Temple University, The Recruitment, Leadership, and Training Institute.

Coletta, A. J. (Ed.). (1976). *Working together: A guide to parent involvement.* Atlanta, GA: Humanics Ltd.

Core, M. (1982). Parent communication: Making the most of transition time. *Child Care Information Exchange, 26,* 33–39.

Curry-Rood, L., Rood, L. A., & Carter, S. E. (1981). *Head start parent handbook* (rev. ed.). Mt. Ranier, MD: Gryphon House.

FOOTSTEPS. Available from the National Audio Visual Center in Washington, DC. This includes 30 one-hour episodes that examine everyday situations and problems confronting parents of young children. Discussion guides are available.

Galinsky, E. (1980). How understanding parental growth will help you as a care giver. *Child Care Information Exchange,* September, pp. 25–32.

Goetz, E. (1975). Parent conferences can work. *Day Care and Early Education, 2* (4), 13–15.

Gordon, I. J. (1970). *Parent involvement in compensatory education.* Urbana, IL: University of Illinois Press, ERIC ECE Clearinghouse. (ERIC Document Reproduction Service No. ED 039 954)

Gordon, I. J., & Breivogel, W. F. (Eds.). (1976). *Building effective home/school relationships.* Boston: Allyn and Bacon.

Gotkin, L. G. (1968). The telephone call: The direct line from teacher to family. *Young Children, 24* (2), 70–74.

Harms, T. O., & Cryer, D. (1978). Parent newsletter: A new format. *Young Children, 33* (5), 28–32.

Haskins, R., & Adams, D. (Eds.). (1983). *Parent education and public policy.* (Vol. III of Child and Family Policy Series). Norwood, NJ: Ablex.

Hess, R. D., Beckum, L., Knowles, R. T., & Miller, R. (1971). Parent training programs and community involvement in day care. In E. Grotberg (Ed.), *Day care: Resources for decisions.* Washington, DC: Office of Economic Opportunity.

Hess, R. D., Black, M., Costello, J., Knowles, R. T., & Largay, D. (1971). Parent involvement in early education. In E. Grotberg (Ed.), *Day care: Resources for decisions.* Washington, DC: Office of Economic Opportunity.

Honig, A. S. (1975). *Parent involvement in early childhood education.* Washington, DC: National Association for the Education of Young Children.

Ideas for effective parent conferences. (1979). *Child Care Information Exchange,* November, pp. 26–30.

Joffe, C. E. (1977). *Friendly intruders: Childcare professionals and family life.* Berkeley, CA: University of California Press.

Kessler, F. (1975). How to plan, execute, and evaluate a successful field trip. *Social Studies Journal,* Spring, *4* (2), 17–21.

Klinman, D. G., & Kohl, R. (1984). *Fatherhood USA: The first national guide to programs, services, & resources for & about fathers.* New York: Garland Publishing.

Kuykendall, C. (1976). *Developing leadership in parent/citizen groups.* Columbia, MD: National Committee for Citizens in Education.

Lane, M. B. (1975). *Education for parenting.* Washington, DC: National Association for Young Children.

Levine, J. A. (1982). The prospects and dilemmas of child care information and referral. In E. F. Zigler & E. W. Gordon (Eds.), *Day care: Scientific and social policy issues* (378–401). Boston: Auburn House.

Lillie, D. L. (Ed.). (1972). *Parent programs in child development centers.* Chapel Hill, NC: Technical Assistance Development System.

Lundberg, C. M., & Miller, V. M. (1972). *Parent involvement staff handbook.* Washington, DC: Day Care and Child Development Council of America.

Marion, M. C. (1973). Create a parent space: A place to stop, look and read. *Young Children, 28* (4), 221–224.

Miller, B. L., & Wilmshurst, A. L. (1975). *Parent and volunteers in the classroom: A handbook for teachers.* San Francisco: R & E Research Associates.

Nedler, S., & McAfee, O. D. (1979). *Working with parents.* Belmont, CA: Wadsworth.

Parent involvement in day care: A resource manual for day care providers. (1982). Washington, DC: Creative Associates.

Pickarts, E., & Fargo, J. (1971). *Parent education: Toward parental competence.* New York: Appleton-Century-Crofts.

Powell, D. (1978). The interpersonal relationship between parents and caregivers in the day care settings. *American Journal of Orthopsychiatry, 48,* 680–689.

Rich, D., & Maltox, B. (1976). *101 activities for building more effective school-community involvement.* Washington, DC: Home and School Institute, Trinity College.

Rothenberg, B. A. (1982). *Parentmaking: A practical handbook for teaching parent classes about babies and toddlers.* Menlo Park, CA: Banster Press.

Rutherford, R. B., Jr., & Edgar, E. (1979). *Teachers and parents: A guide to interaction and cooperation.* Boston: Allyn and Bacon.

Stevens, J. (1978). Parent education programs, What determines effectiveness? *Young Children, 33,* 59–65.

Taylor, K. W. (1981). *Parents and children learn together* (3rd ed.). New York: Teachers College Press.

Model Parent Programs

Bache, W., & Nauta, M. J. (1979). *Home start follow-up study: A study of long-term impact of home start on program participants. Executive summary.* Cambridge, MA: Abt Associates. (ERIC Document Reproduction Service No. ED 192 904)

The cognitive curriculum. Program report. (1971). Berkeley, CA: Far West Lab. (ERIC Document Reproduction Service No. ED 125 742)

Collins, R. C. (1980). Home start and its implications for family policy. *Children Today,* March-April, 9 (2), 12–16.

The DARCEE teacher's guide (preschool series) and DARCEE resource unit materials. Description of teacher inservice education materials. Summary information. (1977). Washington, DC: National Education Assoc. (ERIC Document Reproduction Service No. ED 169 005)

Demonstration and research center for early education (DARCEE): Program report. (1971). Berkeley, CA: Far West Lab. (ERIC Document Reproduction Service No. ED 125 740)

George Peabody College for Teachers Demonstration and Research Center for Early Childhood: Final report to the Office of Economic Opportunity. (1970). Nashville,

TN: George Peabody College. (ERIC Document Reproduction Service No. ED 133 064)

Guide for trainers of DARCEE teachers (preschool series). Description of teacher inservice education materials. (1977). Washington, DC: National Education Assoc. (ERIC Document Reproduction Service No. ED 169 006)

Levenstein, P. (1969). *Toy demonstrator's "visit" handbook.* Mineola, NY: Family Service Association of Nassau County. (ERIC Document Reproduction Service No. ED 059 788)

Levenstein, P. (1975). *The mother-child home program.* Freeport, NY: Verbal Interaction Project. (ERIC Document Reproduction Service No. ED 146 306)

Levenstein, P. (1978). *The parent-child network: The verbal interaction component.* Freeport, NY: Verbal Interaction Project. (ERIC Document Reproduction Service No. ED 167 265)

Levenstein, P., Adelman, H., & Kochman, A. (1971). *Verbal interaction project: Manual for the replication of the mother-child home program.* Mineola, NY: Family Service Association of Nassau County. (ERIC Document Reproduction Service No. ED 059 780)

MCHP/VIP: Mother-child home program of the verbal interaction project. (1978). Freeport, NY: Verbal Interaction Project. (ERIC Document Reproduction Service No. ED 167 266)

Nevius, J. R., & Filgo, D. J. (1977). *Home start education: A guideline for content areas.* (ERIC Document Reproduction Service No. ED 147 013)

Quillian, B. F., Jr., & Rogers, K. S. (1972). *Nine model programs for young children: Program summaries for potential implementation. Vol. I.* St. Ann, MO: National Coordination Center for Early Childhood Education. (ERIC Document Reproduction Service No. ED 129 402)

Roggman, L. (1976). *Home start curriculum guide.* Logan, UT: Millville Home Start Training Center. (ERIC Document Reproduction Service No. ED 188 737)

Rosenfield, A. H. (1978). *Mother-child home program, Parent-child program series, Report no. 1.* Mineola, NY: Family Service Assoc. of Nassau County, Inc. (ERIC Document Reproduction Service No. ED 175 184)

Silverman, C. (Ed.). (1979). *The high/scope report. Number four.* Ypsilanti, MI: High/Scope Educational Research Foundation. (ERIC Document Reproduction Service No. ED 176 856)

Weikart, D. P. (1971). Learning through parents: Lessons for teachers. *Childhood Education,* December, *48,* 135–137.

Weikart, D. P. (1972). Open framework: Evolution of a concept in preschool education. *National Elementary Principal,* April, *51,* 59–62.

Research on Parent Topics

Chilman, C. (1973). Programs for disadvantaged parents. In B. M. Caldwell & H. N. Ricciuti (Eds.), *Review of child development research. Vol. 3: Child development and social policy.* Chicago: University of Chicago Press.

Clarke-Stewart, K. A. (1973). Interactions between mothers and their young children: Characteristics and consequences. *Monographs of the Society for Research on Child Development, 38,* Serial no. 153.

Datta, L. (1973). *Parent involvement in early childhood education: A perspective from the United States.* Washington, DC: National Institute of Education. (ERIC Document Reproduction Service No. ED 088 587)

Freeberg, N., & Payne, D. (1967). Parental influence on cognitive development in early childhood: A review. *Child Development, 38,* 65–87.

Harman, D., & Brim, O. G., Jr. (1980). *Learning to be parents: Principles, programs and methods.* New York: Sage Publications.

Hayes, C. D., & Kamerman, S. B. (Eds.). (1983). *Children of working parents: Experiences and outcomes.* Washington, DC: National Academy Press.

Hess, R., & Shipman, V. (1965). Early experiences and the socialization of cognitive modes in children. *Child Development, 36,* 869–886.

Hoffman, L. W. (1979). Maternal employment: 1979. *American Psychologist, 34,* (10), 859–865.

Kamerman, S. B., & Hayes, C. D. (Eds.). (1982). *Families that work: Children in a changing world.* Washington, DC: National Academy Press.

Lazar, J., & Chapman, J. (1972). *A review of the present status and future research needs of programs to develop parenting skills.* Washington, DC: Social Research Group, George Washington University.

Powell, D. R. (1977). The interface between families and child care programs. Detroit, MI: Merrill-Palmer Institute.

Schaefer, E. (1972). Parents as educators: Evidence from cross-sectional, longitudinal and intervention research. *Young Children, 27,* 227–239.

Toy Lending Libraries

McNeles, J. R. (1974). *A practical guide for planning and operating a toy lending library.* Washington, DC: American Institutes for Research. (ERIC Document Reproduction Service No. ED 145 962)

Nimnicht, G. P. (1971). *Librarian manual for the parent/child toy lending library.* Berkeley, CA: Far West Lab for Educational Research and Development. (ERIC Document Reproduction Service No. ED 179 216)

Nimnicht, G. P. (1975). *Using toys and games with children.* San Francisco, CA: Far West Lab for Educational Research and Development. (ERIC Document Reproduction Service No. ED 129 462)

A project to support a utilization program for the parent/child toy lending library: Final report. (1973). San Francisco, CA: Far West Lab for Educational Research and Development. (ERIC Document Reproduction Service No. ED 150 964)

Rosenfield, A. J. (1978). *Cultural enrichment by means of a toy library. Parent-child program series, Report no. 2.* Washington, DC: American Institutes for Research in the Behavioral Sciences. (ERIC Document Reproduction Service No. ED 175 185)

Toys 'n Things, Training and Resources Center, Inc., St. Paul, MN 55103. They have several publications on toy lending library setup and management.

Legal Rights

Cartwright, G. P., Cartwright, C. A., & Ward, M. E. (1984). *Educating special learners* (2nd ed.). Belmont, CA: Wadsworth.

Cross, B., & Cross, R. (1977). *The children's rights movement.* New York: Doubleday.

Family day care as a child protection service. Atlanta, GA: Child Care Support Center/Save the Children, 1979. (ERIC Document Reproduction Service No. ED 183 290)

Goldstein, J., Freud, A., & Solnit, A. J. (1973). *Beyond the best interests of the child.* New York: Free Press.

Justice, B., & Justice, R. (1976). *The abusing family.* New York: Human Sciences Press.

Kempe, R. S., & Kempe, C. (1978). *Child abuse.* Cambridge, MA: Harvard University Press.

Legal and program issues related to child custody and late parents. (1979). Atlanta, GA: Child Care Support Center/Save the Children. (ERIC Document Reproduction Service No. ED 192 912)

Rosenheim, M. K. (1973). The child and the law. In B. M. Caldwell & H. N. Ricciati (Eds.), *Child development and social policy, review of child development research: Vol. 3.* Chicago: University of Chicago Press.

Schimmel, D., & Fischer, L. (1977). *The rights of parents.* Columbia, MD: The National Committee for Citizens in Education.

15

Community and Professional Resources

Introduction

The most effective support networks that a child care program can build are those including both community and professional contacts. Communities offer a veritable "treasure-chest" of manpower, materials, money, services, and support for child care programs. Programs that are sensitive to the social and ethnic personalities of their communities and fulfill their obligation to educate the community about the purposes and practices of child care can reap enormous benefits. Programs, however, must usually take the initiative.

This chapter explores the resources that are available to most programs. We begin with some of the most visible elements of community support: community organizations, churches, and the military. Related to this is the program's own efforts at community outreach. Here we describe a program's board of directors and public relations. Professional resources fall into three categories: consultants, professional organizations, and a program library.

Participation in professional organizations strengthens the child advocacy network, thus affecting child care policy for all programs. This chapter concludes with a look at child advocacy—what it is, how it is practiced, and why it is necessary. For the individual in child care, personal and professional growth inevitably leads to child advocacy.

Community Support

Community Organizations

Child care is a community issue. No segment of a community remains untouched by the societal changes that have occurred as more and more mothers of young children enter and remain in the work force. Local civic, service, special interest, and political groups are increasingly involved in and approachable for support of community child care programs. Several organizations have had national initiatives or passed resolutions related to support and concern for child care. Some of these groups, such as the Lions Clubs and the League of Women Voters, have traditionally been involved in projects related to young children. Others, such as the Junior Chamber of Commerce and the Rotary, with good public education, advocacy, and persuasion among local people are undoubtedly candidates for support and donations.

Church Sponsorship

> The church has a unique opportunity to respond to the need for child care. It can offer communities throughout the United States two very valuable assets for the creation of child care facilities—buildings and people. (Gilbert, n.d.)

In communities throughout this country, church basements and meeting rooms ring with

Box 15.1 When Churches Mind the Children

Under the auspices of the Child Advocacy Office of the National Council of Churches, New York, member parishes were surveyed regarding the existence and description of child care programs sponsored locally. The results of that survey provide a unique data base of church-sponsored child care, even though the survey was limited to National Council of Churches denominations. The numbers in this survey, despite sampling caveats, clearly indicate that churches are major providers or co-providers of child care in this country.

Distribution of Programs by Type Based on Responses to the Initial Survey (8,767 Respondents; 14,589 Programs)

Program Type	Number of Programs Reported	Type as % of All Programs
Infant Programs	903	6%
Toddler Programs	1,935	13%
Preschool Programs	7,272	50%
Disabled Children	326	2%
Before/After School	1,276	9%
Emergency Drop-off	421	3%
Mother's Support Program	1,528	11%
Other	928	6%
Total Programs	14,589	100%

From *When Churches Mind the Children* (p. 24) by E. W. Lindner, M. C. Mattis, and J. R. Rogers, 1983, Ypsilanti, MI: High/Scope Press, 600 N. River Street 48197; used with permission.

In a follow-up in-depth survey of church-housed child care programs in the original sample, centers were classified by three pairs of variables. As shown in the figure, most church-housed centers were church-operated (56%), nonprofit (90%), and full-time preschool programs (79%). Primary contributing factors to this profile were found to be availability of space in churches, convenience of church location within the community, and existence of tax-exempt status for the church.

One myth that the study debunked was that churches use child care programs to further their religious education mission. In fact, most church-housed programs are open to all in the community with little or no direct spiritual connection to the sponsoring church. Why then do parishes come to open their buildings to child care programs? Several reasons are given below. While a sense of churchly mission underlies all these reasons, it is apparent that formal religious education is not a main criterion for church involvement.

Among the conceptions or theologies of mission that inform the decision of a local parish to become involved in the provision of child care are those outlined [here]. Often these concepts work in conjunction with each other or provide only a partial basis for a parish's decision to be involved in child care.

Christian education. A nursery school or child day care program with an explicit religious education component may be part of the mission undertaken by a parish. When this is the motivation, spiritual development will be central to the program.

Pastoral care. Child care may be viewed as part of a larger program of care and nurture of families within the congregation. Again, religious teachings and/or values clarification may be part of the program. Congregations motivated to be involved with child care by concern for either Christian education or pastoral care will often, though not always, serve primarily children and families of their own membership.

Evangelism. Some programs of child care are viewed within a larger context of evangelism or proclamation of the Christian faith to those outside the congregation. Thus child care programs may be seen as a way of expanding the fellowship of the parish and ultimately increasing the membership.

Stewardship. All parishes make decisions regarding the allocation of their financial resources. Some view the physical plant and equipment as a trust that they must use in the larger expression of ministry as they best see it. Under this conception, child care may be viewed as an appropriate use whether by members or non-members.

Community service. Like stewardship conceptions, ideas of ministry related to community service hold

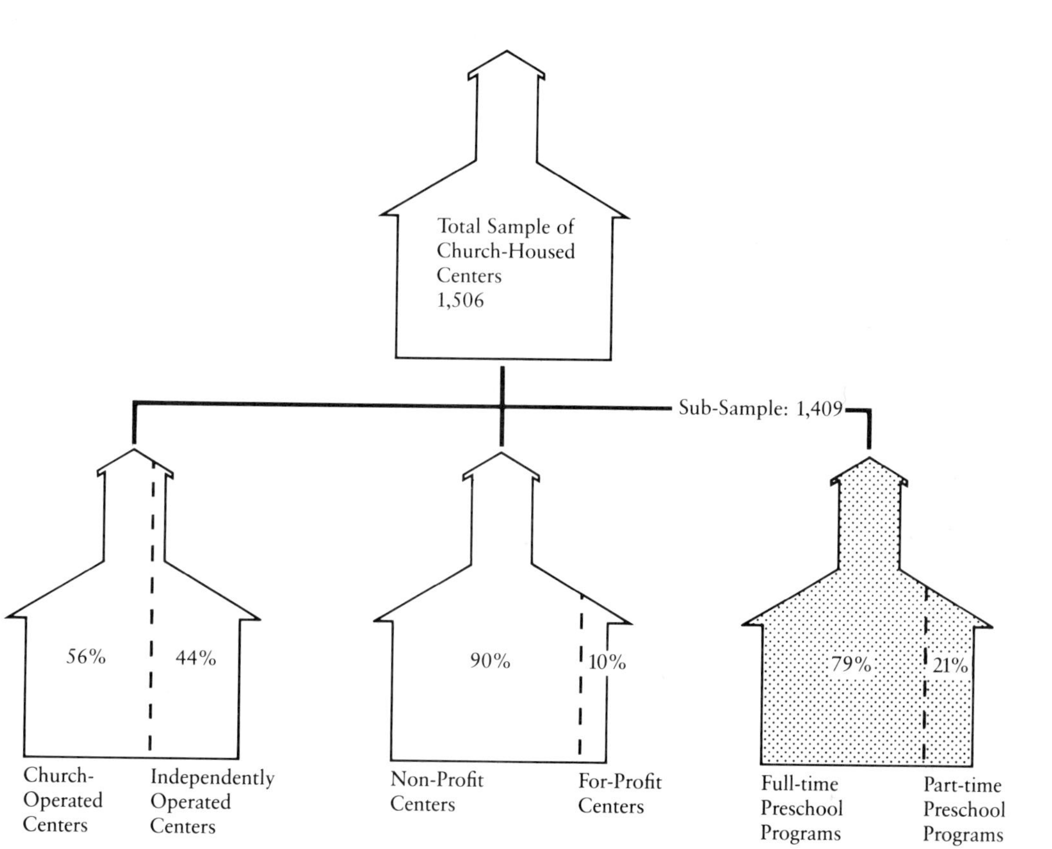

Division of Church-Housed Child Day Care Centers into Contrasting Types.

that the church has some general responsibility to meet the needs of others. Under this conception, programs are likely to be open to persons outside of the membership. It is this view of ministry that often leads churches to respond positively to requests from child care directors to take up residence within the church building. A wide range of programs may be considered within this conception of ministry.

Social justice. Congregations that view themselves as having a significant role to play with regard to the promotion of social justice may introduce child care programs as part of that ministry. Often these programs serve particular populations, such as disabled children, single parents, low-income groups, or racial/ethnic minorities.

Source: When Churches Mind the Children (pp. 20–21) by E. W. Lindner, M. C. Mattis, and J. R. Rogers, 1983, Ypsilanti, MI: High/Scope Press, 600 N. River Street 48197; used with permission.

the laughter and sounds of busy children. The value of the space and utilities donated or subsidized by church groups is simply beyond calculation. Where would many child care programs be without the provision of church-owned space? Box 15.1 describes the extent of church involvement.

Wilkinson in *Church Options for Day Care* (1973) states that concern for the needs of children should guide church involvement in child care. In an excellent analysis and summary of possible modes of sponsorship, she describes how church buildings and administrative energies can be used to establish care programs for children of varying ages and needs. It appears that the vast majority of child care programs connected with churches operate without direct religious curriculum requirements. Even programs that include discussion and observance of religious events enroll children without discrimination or exclusionary priority categories.

Military Day Care

The military services and bases have not been immune to changing patterns of need for child care either. Child care centers are beginning to open on bases around the world, taking their place beside the schools traditionally run for military dependents. The military services are hiring early childhood coordinators, providing and upgrading facilities, and hiring and training staff. Additional information is available from Military Early Childhood Alliance (MECA), c/o Maxine Henry, 1021 North Main Street, Minot, ND 58701. MECA, which is an affiliate group of NAEYC, publishes a newsletter for members. In addition, a series of handbooks for military child care programs is available from the U.S. government.

Community Outreach

To attract the attention of potential sponsors and to create a responsible image in the community, programs must do a certain amount of outreach. The two important elements here are a board of directors and a public relations plan. The board, which provides authoritative counsel, acts as a liaison between the program and the community. Public relations helps to inform the community about the program and maintains a favorable public impression of the program.

Board of Directors

The legal governing group for most child care programs is the board of directors. Board membership is an honor and responsibility for local citizens. The formal organization of a board, its responsibilities, and functions vary according to the legal requirements of the state and the bylaws developed by the local board to govern its activities. A well-connected, hardworking, committed board is one of the most valuable assets a local child care program can have.

Role of the Board. Boards advise and consent. Authority and responsibility for all decisions pertaining to the operation of the program are vested with the board. Tne three primary functions of a board are:

1. to establish, implement, and monitor organizational policies and procedures.
2. to ensure financial support and accountability for the program.
3. to represent and interpret the program to the public.

A sponsoring agency or institution may have a board of directors whose domain includes all programs operating under its auspices. The child care program may be one of many social service, educational, or vocational programs run by the board. In this situation each agency program may elect a specific number of board members, or an advisory committee may be formed by the larger board to more closely monitor each separate program. In situations where the board of directors has as its sole responsibility operating the child care pro-

Box 15.2 Examples of Bylaws

Article V.—Staff

Sec. 1. There shall be an Executive Director and such other members of the staff as the Board of Directors shall deem necessary to carry on the work of the Agency.

Sec. 2. The Executive Director shall employ such staff as are required to carry out the purposes and objectives of the Agency in accordance with policies established by the Board of Directors. The Executive Director shall keep the Board fully informed on all aspects of the Agency program, and shall keep a record of all information of value to the Agency and shall be the medium of communication between all departments of the Agency and between the Agency and the community.

Article VII.—Standing committees

Sec. 1. Committee on Personnel
This committee shall:
a. Recommend to the Executive Committee for employment of an Executive Director.
b. The Executive Director may confer with the Personnel Committee on matters pertaining to personnel and they shall serve as a review board in personnel procedures.
c. Review annually and subject to the approval of the Board, revise personnel practices, job descriptions, and salary scales.

Sec. 2. Committee on House and Grounds
This committee shall:
a. Handle problems in connection with obtaining equipment and maintaining office quarters for the Agency and the day care centers.

Source: Day Care 7: Administration (p. 17) by M. S. Host and P. B. Heller, 1971, Washington, DC: USDHEW, Office of Child Development.

gram(s), lines of authority and influence between program and board are more clear-cut.

Organization of the Board. A charter or articles of incorporation creates the board. Individual liability is limited under incorporation since the corporation becomes legally responsible for all acts. Board members and some employees may be bonded, which is a further protection for them and the corporation in the case of legal problems arising from performance of duties.

The constitution and bylaws state the purpose of the organization, the rules governing selection and role of board members, the duties of officers, and committee structure and responsibility. Boards operate according to recognized and accepted parliamentary procedure. Examples of bylaws are in Box 15.2.

The board of directors usually has an executive committee made up of the officers (president, vice-president, secretary, and treasurer). The number and responsibilities of board committees will depend on the size of the board and the complexity of the programs involved. Committees help distribute workload and help to ensure that adequate research and analysis are possible for issues before the board. Committees on finance, program personnel, buildings and grounds, social services, and health and medical matters are typical.

On a day-to-day basis the board of directors delegates responsibility for program operations to an executive director. The executive director is employed by and responsible to the board and is the major link between board policy and program practice. The executive director's talents, personality, and competence do more to create a public image of the program than anyone else. Among the executive director's many duties are keeping informed about community needs and potential financial resources, recommending fiscal policy, negotiating contracts, re-

Look for board members who are committed to children, child care, and quality services in their local community. One of the biggest challenges is to cultivate and educate prospective board members, encourage commitment, and build advocacy attitudes. (Courtesy of U.S. Department of Housing and Urban Development, Washington, DC.)

viewing administrative structure, and ensuring regulatory compliance regarding employment.

Selection of Board Members. Service on a board is work. Members must have time for study, counsel, and attendance at meetings. Few programs thrive with figurehead boards. When composing a board, local programs should strive for a judicious mixture of prominence, commitment, interest, and involvement from board members. Board members should represent the community—all socioeconomic levels, special interests, professions, and political groups—with particular effort paid to attracting parents of program children to serve on the board. Some desirable groups are:

Prominent Community Members Persons with high standing or wide recognition in the community lend credibility and visibility to the child care program. These persons may be helpful in making contacts, opening doors, and putting the program in touch with other service and support networks within the community. What they perhaps cannot contribute in terms of hours of detail work is balanced by the leverage of their contacts.

Expertise Lawyers, doctors, accountants, child development specialists, and others can serve as resources on the board or as leaders of advisory groups for special projects or task forces.

Service and Business Leaders Reporters, real estate brokers, bankers, and officers of other groups are all in a position to give to the child care program and perhaps use their work skills to extend program impact and educate the community.

Parents Parents provide an essential check and balance and perspective on program operations and quality.

Staff There is debate over whether program employees should formally serve on a board. This issue may be solved by having staff participate on committees, but not be voting members of the board. Labor relations decisions may preclude staff voting membership.

Board Activities and Functions. Meetings are held monthly or quarterly. A typical agenda includes old and new business, committee reports, and reports by the executive director and perhaps other program staff. Occasionally the board may meet in "executive session," closing the meeting to all but voting board members to consider personnel actions or other business of a private nature. Since the board has a responsibility to create a written record of its activities and proceedings, minutes are recorded of all meetings including committees.

Board members may be asked to work on fund raising and public relations within the community. Several publications, which are listed in the Resources section, describe strategies for effectively using board members for solicitation of funds and local publicity.

Host and Heller (1971) recommend providing board members with a handbook. They suggest using a loose-leaf binder that can be easily updated and including material about the following topics:

- Brief history of the organization
- Copy of the bylaws
- Copy of the organization's statement of purpose
- List of board members with addresses, phone numbers, and their board offices or positions
- List of standing committees and the current chairperson of each
- Copy of current personnel practices
- List of facilities used by the program with addresses of each and name of staff member in charge
- List of key staff members, including their titles and locations of their offices
- Board's current annual work schedule
- Calendar of dates of board meetings and of special events of importance to board members
- Organizational chart
- Brief description of each service offered by the day care program
- Sample of children's daily program schedule

Public Relations

Public relations, or PR, is no longer just a catch-all tag for Madison Avenue ad types or high pressure publicity campaigns. Knowledgeable and conscientious handling of public relations is essential for child care programs and other nonprofit organizations that depend on community support and goodwill. A good program image and a strong, positive reputation for child care service within the community are invaluable assets as programs try to market services, attract children, raise funds, and advocate issues. Public relations potential is embedded in every program activity, from field trips to press releases and staff parties. Staff, parents, and children all function as emissaries and representatives of a program.

Information and education are a vital part of public relations. Unless the public understands what child care is and what happens in child care, they are not likely to support local programs. Printed materials need to be available to describe the program. Procedures are necessary to ensure that publicity and media reports favorably represent the program in a timely manner. Persons with particular skills (such as speaking or writing) should be identified and made available for public relations activities.

Media events (TV, radio spots, newspaper articles) tend to receive the most attention when public relations efforts are organized within programs. Obviously, these kinds of events can reach large numbers of people. Equally important, however, are a variety of details, small events, and activities that fewer people may be connected with, but that have contacts that are more intimate, personalized, and ultimately more influential in impact. These activities are also more costly in terms of time demands on the staff.

The Printed Image. Words and pictures can quickly convey an image of a child care program. Printed materials, however, must be able to stand alone. No one from the program will be there to explain or correct impressions. The following printed materials provide an introduction or reference point for persons outside the actual program:

Logo and Name A logo is a combination of graphics and letters with high visual appeal. Logos are designed to capture and convey something of the spirit and uniqueness of the child care program. They are intended to provide a point of quick recognition and stimulate recall of information about the program. As public relations shorthand, they help identify and link all program materials. Get professional help in designing a program logo. Perhaps an art student or graphic studio would be willing to contribute their design expertise. Logos are forever (well almost!). Your program will use the logo a lot and over a long period of time. Be sure the design is appropriate and satisfactory.

Correspondence Identify all program correspondence. Use printed letterhead and envelopes with the program logo. Arrange to have a variety of memo pads printed, have a rubber stamp made. Encourage staff and parents to use printed correspondence materials for activities related to the program, but safeguard these materials from irresponsible or unauthorized use.

Brochure This is the single, most widely used public relations material for child care programs. It introduces the program and its goals, details services, and describes the ongoing activities. The brochure should be comprehensive enough to satisfy most information requests and routine publicity purposes. The excerpt in Box 15.3 may be helpful in this respect.

Supplementary Materials Beyond routine information requests, programs should be prepared to put together in-depth information packages for specific recipients such as: (1) serious, prospective parents; (2) media reporters; (3) important visitors and observers of the program; and (4) board members and program consultants. These prepared materials may include:

- Statement of program's mission and goals
- Detailed program history
- Staff names, along with short biographical details
- Daily program schedules
- Copies of forms and contracts required for enrollment
- Copies of current applicable regulations
- Copies of promotion pamphlets on child care or reprints of similar general information articles
- Descriptive material on sponsoring agency and funding sources where appropriate
- Copies of recent program newsletters
- Copies of press releases and other media coverage

Contacts. Control and plan access to your program. Welcome parents at all times, but give them guidelines for observing and visiting so the experience is informative for them and not disruptive for children or staff. Regulatory inspections can occur unannounced. Be able at a moment's notice to locate all documents and files pertinent to all inspection visits your program may have. Decide in advance how supervisory responsibilities will shift if the director or other designated staff member must give individual attention to visitors. Expect the unexpected and be prepared. Good public relations comes from careful preparation.

Schedule visitors and observers in advance. Let your staff know who to expect and for how long. Consult with staff to be sure children's routines will not be upset or their activities unduly affected. Be concerned first with the ongoing daily needs of the children in the program. The public relations aspects of visitors are secondary. Whatever the visitor's purpose, try to elicit impressions of the program and give counsel in understanding events observed. Escort visitors in and out of the program—avoid allowing people to drift away.

Open house is a festive day when everyone puts their best foot forward. An open house is an excellent chance for neighbors, community people, parents, and relatives to visit the program in comfortable circumstances. Flyers and newspaper ads can announce the open house. Programs can recruit volunteers to act as guides, to provide refreshments, to conduct slide shows, and to stage short group presentations (repeated at scheduled intervals) for visitors.

Many programs find that telephone inquiries, while welcome, are time consuming, repetitive, and not a productive use of staff time. Staff might follow these guidelines for telephone inquiries:

1. Courteously answer caller's questions.
2. Ascertain caller's interests and purpose.
3. Offer to send appropriate information materials.

Box 15.3 How to Develop a Brochure

Convey an Appropriate Image

In designing your center's brochure, you should give utmost attention to the image it conveys about your program. Your choice of paper, language, graphics, lay-out, and printing all shape the appearance of the brochure—and this appearance in turn shapes the reader's initial image of your center. If the brochure is haphazardly put together, this may reflect a careless image. If it is professionally done, it may communicate a sense of competence. If it is too slick, it may suggest a lack of warmth. If it is creatively done, it may convey an impression of creativity.

Before you set out to plan the brochure, therefore, it is useful to decide exactly what image you are trying to convey. Then evaluate every aspect of the completed brochure to be sure this image consistently shows through.

Tell Your Message Clearly

The brochure should tell as much about the center as possible in as few words as possible. At a minimum, give readers the basic information they will need to decide whether or not to seriously consider your center: the center's philosophy or curriculum goals; ages served; hours and months open; location and transportation; staff qualifications; fees and scholarships; and application procedures. To effectively communicate all this information:

- Break the copy into small chunks separated by subheads. Give the reader the option of reading the entire brochure or perusing just the areas that are of primary interest.
- Make the copy personal. Use personal pronouns and everyday language.
- Keep sentences short (not longer than seventeen words, if possible). Alternate short and long sentences.
- Avoid complex sentences and the overuse of adjectives and adverbs.
- Have someone who knows nothing about your program read the copy to see if the message is clear and complete.

Don't Cut Corners on Design

If no one associated with your center has had experience or training in layout and design, you should seriously consider securing outside help in this area. If your budget cannot afford consulting with a professional graphics artist, you may be able to get free advice from your printer or inexpensive assistance from students at a college graphics department. In any case the following design guidelines should be considered:

- Give special attention to the graphics on the cover. The cover sets the tone for the brochure. Keep it simple yet striking, but not gimmicky.
- Use good paper stock. Paper isn't the place to skimp. Even if the brochure isn't an award winner in design, quality paper will make the overall effect pleasing.
- All text should be typeset. There should be no handwritten headlines.
- Don't use photographs unless they are top-rate with high contrast. Line drawings reproduce better and offer more flexibility.
- Don't go to the expense of more than two-color printing. Use the second color sparingly to add emphasis to your main points. When including photos, use black ink on white paper. People are not used to looking at blue people.

Plan Ahead to Cut Costs

While you don't want to save money by seriously compromising the quality of the final product, there are ways to reduce costs. Printers' prices vary considerably so get quotes from a variety of sizes and types of printers. Consult with the printer in advance as to which sizes, folds, paper stocks, color combinations, and types of graphics are least expensive. Print as many brochures at one time as possible. You may come out ahead by printing information that changes from year to year—dates and fees—on a separate insert, so that you can print several years' supply of brochures at one time.

Source: Child Care Information Exchange, 1981, *19*, 21–22. Reprinted with permission from *Child Care Information Exchange* (a bi-monthly management magazine for directors), PO Box 2890, Redmond, WA 98073.

Appealing pictures of young children make ideal public relations information. (College of Human Development, Department of Individual and Family Studies, The Pennsylvania State University; used with permission.)

4. Write a cover memo to be included with the mailed materials, giving the caller specific instructions on what to do next or who to ask to talk to if further contact seems warranted.
5. Record the call, date, name, information sent, or purpose of call; place caller's name on possible follow-up list according to instructions given in memo.

Media Coverage. Local newspapers, radio, and TV stations are constantly on the lookout for feature stories, news events, and items of local interest. With a little initiative and some understanding of the media's news requirements, child care programs can obtain good coverage of events and enhance local public image. Several guidelines on media coverage are given in the Resources section.

Press releases, which can be prepared by the program, provide extensive background information, statements on issues, or announcements of events. Public interest articles, or feature stories, can be written by the child care center and sent to media outlets or be written by a reporter as a result of contacts and education.

TV and radio coverage for local programs can generate considerable interest in child care. Spot announcements, press releases, feature stories, and special event coverage are ways to obtain news attention. Often all that is required is for someone in the local program to cultivate reporter contacts, research and identify likely newsworthy events, and then provide TV and radio with timely announcements. Children are intrinsically appealing local subjects for news.

Professional Resources

Most of those in the child care field have discovered that their work frequently requires additional education and insight. Because the field is dynamic, ideas are continually changing and being refined. New data allow experts to reach new and original conclusions. Since the profession is in a caring, human services area, many staff members may have a strong desire to improve their contribution. The three chief resources for the profession are consultants, professional organizations, and a program library.

Consultants

A *consultant* is a person with special knowledge, experience, and expertise who can work with child care staff to improve the quality of services. Over the course of a year, child care staff members may work with a variety of consultants whose areas of expertise, abilities to work smoothly with individual staff members, and strategies for consultation vary widely. Consultants in child care work with local programs under a number of service agreements ranging from third-party negotiated contracts to *pro bono* service work. Coordinating and meshing the work of child care consultants with the particular needs of a local program is the task of the program director.

Why Use a Consultant? Child care programs undertake relationships with consultants for one of three reasons.

1. *Need* The staff, director, parents, or other concerned individuals may have identified a problem area in the operation of the program. This may take the form of an expressed need for more information, guidance, or suggestions in solving a situation. There may be a feeling of unease or a lingering but noticeable lack of confidence in the group's current ability to deal with a problem. A crisis may occur, making it obvious that outside help is needed. Or, the need may take the form of a generalized desire to improve and extend staff capabilities.
2. *Obligation* Funding circumstances and contracts with community agencies may require that a program accept certain levels of consultation services or have staff participate in programs. While these services may be scheduled at the convenience of the program and staff, there is some risk that the topics covered will not be salient for the local program. However, few programs, even if they are able, are likely to refuse available consultation services. Careful preparation and follow-up by the program director can help to tie these consultation sessions in meaningful ways to staff interests and needs.
3. *Opportunity* Community professionals are often eager to work with social service groups on a *pro bono* basis. Medical and health care professionals consider outreach activities an intrinsic part of their profession and part of their personal contribution to the public welfare. Businesses may offer information services and sessions that, while promoting their products and activities, are also useful training for those participating. Extension agents and university faculty committed to service are often available as consultants. Neophyte consultants, students, and retired people may be looking for opportunities to become involved or get some experience as consultants.

Typical Consultation Services. The consultant-client relationship is mediated most directly by the child care program director. It is up to the director to ensure that the consultant's work is directed toward program needs and performed in a manner consistent with program operations. It is also the director's responsibility to prepare the staff for the consultant.

Typical services are in several categories:

Program-Related Services

- Obtaining licensing, meeting funder requirements, setting up administrative policies and procedures
- Designing curriculum and planning activities
- Using outdoor time creatively and constructively
- Extending the program to age groups not now served

Child-Related Services

- Dealing with difficult child behaviors (biting, screaming, tantrums, and other disturbances)
- Assessing developmental problems—coordinating referrals
- Teaching discipline and self-control
- Recognizing typical developmental landmarks
- Toilet training
- Mainstreaming special needs children

Staff-Related Services

- Helping aides and teachers work together
- Developing good communication and rapport among staff
- Recognizing and reporting child abuse
- Building a staff training program
- Improving parent-staff relationships

Other

- Promoting day care in the community
- Writing funding proposals
- Developing fund-raising events
- Working with community agencies

Selecting Consultants. The cardinal rule for selecting consultants is to choose someone whose education, expertise, and skills fit your needs. Before looking for a consultant, prepare a brief statement of need that includes a description of the problem, the kinds of information you are looking for, and any preferences you may have regarding the strategies for help. Use this statement to introduce your needs to prospective consultants. It can serve as a basis for finalizing an agreement of service when you have located a consultant. Staff may be very interested and helpful in writing this brief, informal description of service desired.

Consultants can be hard to find. Few advertise or consult full-time. Recommendations are a good source. Telephone places where people with the expertise work. Ask board members, staff members, and other child care directors. Keep track of your contacts and file names of people even if you can't use them right now. Expect to use a chain of contacts: Don't hesitate to say, "Ms. S suggested I call you." Be specific about your needs, direct about your program's ability to pay, and convincing in your description of your program and your need for the service.

It would seem that if locating a consultant is hard, all comers should be accepted. Restrain yourself and pledge to do a minimal credential review before hiring anyone. Even when services are free, you do yourself and your staff no favors to commit them to spend time and energy in consulting sessions that are terrible. Ask directly about the prospective consultant's training and experiences that qualify him or her to perform your job. Look beyond degree titles, and ask about specific course work, areas of concentrated study, and themes of research and writing that will give you a clue about the special areas of knowledge the consultant has developed. Past experience tells you two things: how and where consultants have applied their special knowledge, and whether they can adapt their expertise and reach your staff in meaningful ways. Be cautious about hiring consultants who have never been in child care centers, worked directly with young children, or taught adults. Consultants need to be more than professionally competent to work effectively and really be of service to child care programs. Consultants have to exhibit some critical attitudes and interpersonal skills.

Ask for names of others for whom the consultant has worked. Be sure your search process and selection criteria are consistent with the time and dollar outlays you plan for consulting services.

At a minimum, there should be a letter of agreement that formalizes the consultant-client relationship. Do this even for consulting services that are free. It is a simple way to record pertinent information on time of session, date, length, division of responsibilities, and remuneration, so that everyone begins the relationship with the same expectations.

For long-term consulting services the child care organization should use a formal contract signed by both parties. Attachments to the contract may specify the exact duties and content of the consulting services. Rates of pay and maximum amounts, if any, should be specifically stated.

For consultants time is money. Consultants may quote rates on a daily or hourly basis. When you are discussing costs of services and trying to reach an agreement on total amount, be sure that you and the consultant understand how preparation and travel time are to be handled. A typical example would be:

Example: 4 Hours—Workshop session with staff
3 Hours—Preparation time
1 Hour—Travel time
8 Hours—Total
Bill for One Day of Time at $150/Day

Also, discuss negotiable supplementary costs. Are you going to reimburse actual travel expenses (air fare, mileage, meals away from home) in addition to the consultant's daily fee? Who is going to pay for photocopying workshop handouts or purchase copies of texts that consultants may wish to use in the workshop?

These are legitimate expenses and should be discussed for every consulting session. Sometimes consultants provide all materials as part of their daily fee. Other times it makes sense for programs to pay supply costs. Discussions about time and costs are not necessarily adversarial or difficult. Both consultant and client are best served if all understand the details of the consulting arrangement.

Strategies for Consultation. Every consultant has a personal style and preferred way of working with clients. Certain kinds of problems and client needs are best dealt with using particular strategies. These can be specified ahead of time or selection of a strategy can be reserved until the consultant and client have the opportunity to become better acquainted.

Workshops are a catchall term for almost any kind of information exchange session. Topically focused and varying in length from an hour to all-day sessions, workshops are intensive experiences. Participants are exposed to information through lectures and handouts and are asked to become actively involved through small group discussions, role-playing, and simulations of real-life problems. The consultant is responsible for the content, format, and delivery of the workshop. Groups are usually small, with all participants aware of the reasons and objectives for the session. Discussion, suggestions, and examples can all be individualized and adapted to the interests and skill levels of the participants.

A case consultation is a very focused session revolving around a single child, particular problem, or individual need. The consultant will gather information, review materials, and then work directly with the staff. The consultant brings an objective viewpoint to the situation, helps organize and identify relevant information, and suggests several resolutions or activities. The staff learn more about the particular case and come to understand how to generalize their skills to other similar situations. Case consultation may require several sessions to establish rapport and extend developing staff skills.

Professional Organizations

Membership and active participation in professional organizations bring a multitude of benefits for day care directors and staffs. Professional organizations offer the opportunity to join with many concerned, committed people working toward better conditions for young children. Individuals, local programs, and agencies can pool talents and share resources. Professional organizations help strengthen the voice of individual opinion. Whatever their size or scope, professional organizations offer at least three categories of opportunity to members:

1. Association with others of common interest and/or shared commitment
2. Access to information and services through publications
3. Action potential derived from the collective weight of opinions and views on issues

Child care program staff have a wide range of responsibilities and professional interests. Each staff member will find organizations that closely fit his or her particular professional frame of reference. No single organization should be expected to be suitable for all. In addition to professional concerns, staff may be drawn to certain organizations because of ethnic, personal, or religious concerns. Some staff will place high priority on organizations that meet social needs or provide services such as insurance. Others may join organizations that are political and issue-oriented and place little emphasis on daily program service details and requirements. Others look to professional organizations for ideas and a sense of identity as a child care worker. All are legitimate, desirable reasons for child care staff participation in a wide range of professional organizations. Appendix E lists names of professional organizations that currently serve the needs of the early childhood field. Readers are encouraged to write to these organizations to request current membership information, description of services, and statement of purpose.

Every organization has particular goals that direct the activities and services provided to members. Early childhood organizations are likely to emphasize one of five distinctive missions: research, continuing education, political action, public relations, and working conditions. Publications, services, and member activities will be focused on the primary mission of the organization.

Organization Structure. Many national organizations have affiliate groups or branches for local groups. In these local groups members fill all positions; paid staff are not usually used. One of the biggest hurdles for new organizations is to become strong enough financially to use central office staff and conserve the contributions and energies of members for policy and substance work. In the child care field there has been a longtime concern that too much centralization moves the organization too far away from the concerns of the grassroots members. Large national organizations often create or sponsor special interest groups or task forces to meet the special needs of members. Another approach has been to create small, highly specific separate organizations or to form geographically limited organizations to tackle local issues.

Membership. Membership in organizations serving the early childhood and child care field is usually open to anyone who wishes to join. By paying dues, individuals become eligible to receive services, participate in events and elections, and contribute to organizational activities. This self-selection mechanism works to attract interested, active members. The disadvantage is that unless there is some kind of public relations or recruitment efforts, some individuals may not be aware of the existence or benefits of certain organizations. Some organizations limit membership to individuals who hold particular jobs (social worker, psychologist), who have earned degrees in particular fields (educational research, child development), who are recommended (nominated) for membership, or some combination of these things. The purpose of membership requirements is to ensure a comparable level of competence and knowledge among members in order to promote interactions.

Organizations frequently establish different membership categories, such as:

Individual Membership Open to any individual upon payment of dues. Usually includes voting privileges, participation opportunities, subscription to magazines, and member discounts on publications or access to services.

Agency Membership Open to agencies, groups, or organizations. Dues are usually higher than individual memberships. Includes multiple copies of publications, discounts, access to services, and some form of prorated voting and participation opportunities.

Institutional Membership Primarily for libraries and other organizations. Dues may cover only copies of periodicals and publications with no other membership services offered.

Student Membership Reduced rate individual memberships available to bona fide students.

Comprehensive Membership An individual membership that includes additional services and publications. Dues are higher than a straight individual membership but represent a savings on the cost of all benefits offered.

Membership dues along with proceeds from publications and services represent the largest source of income for most organizations. Dues levels are set to cover costs and can range from $10 to more than $100 a year. Public interest and advocacy organizations may not have memberships in the usual sense. They receive funds from grants and foundations to subsidize operating expenses.

Professional organization dues can be considered tax-deductible for income-tax purposes. Individuals should check to see if their circumstances qualify them for such a deduction. Multiple memberships quickly add up and, on the typically low salaries of child care workers, represent a considerable personal investment in professional growth and commitment. Careful consideration of organizational goals and membership benefits will help everyone realize the best return on their money.

Publications. Generally, membership dues pay for a year's subscription to periodicals sponsored by the organization. Periodicals reflect the organization's mission. They may contain research reports, "how-to" articles, samples and descriptions of methods, common interest information, and paid advertisement. Event calendars, announcements, job information, and organizational happenings are also included.

Other publications are separate, irregularly printed materials such as books and pamphlets. These may be single topics of current interest (child abuse, mathematics for children, budgets) or compilations of related writings (research on effects of TV for children). Members can often purchase publications at a discount. Organizations are sometimes responsible for publishing very specific books on topics of vital concern to early childhood people.

A number of very good periodicals are not published or sponsored by early childhood organizations. Published by individuals or companies, these periodicals are aimed at filling gaps in information coverage of existing journals and are targeted at specific reading audiences (directors, school-age careworkers, family child caregivers, child care staff). They are characterized by practical, no-nonsense writing and timely topics. (See Appendix F.)

Conferences and Meetings. A trip to an annual conference can be the highlight of the year, tonic for a "burning-out" staff member, or the genesis of a new perspective and effort on program activities. National organizations host an annual conference about once a year, rotating the site around the country so that travel costs average out over the years for everyone. Child care is a year-round job, however, and not everyone can be released to attend a conference at the same time. Smaller regional meetings may be held on a more frequent basis.

Organizations and their members must expend considerable time and energy planning conferences. They normally solicit membership participation in the form of speeches, presentations, workshops, and demonstrations. Tours, side-trips, and observations in local programs may be planned. At some point a business meeting may be held and votes taken on organizational actions. Members may organize informal special-interest group meetings, caucus amongst themselves, and go about the business of making contacts with others.

Conferences and meetings cost money, including registration, travel, meals, lodging, and expenses. Programs may be able to defray part of the cost for staff or none at all. Under certain circumstances these expenses can be tax-deductible.

Services. Economy of scale and centralized membership files allow organizations to offer services to members that might be more costly or difficult for members to arrange individually. In some instances, members may need these services only occasionally, if at all, meaning that without the ongoing support of an organization it would be difficult to maintain the service.

Insurance Child care workers do not, as a rule, have good benefits. Those working alone do not have access to group rates in insurance plans. Increasingly, one important service of national organizations has become group insurance packages available to members.

Job Advertising and Placement Conventional job banks and classified advertising in organizational periodicals help prospective candidates locate jobs. Employers can reach a large audience of qualified candidates this way. Local affiliates and regional organizations have pioneered in establishing some extremely effective job advertising schemes to help match programs with staff.

Consulting and Technical Assistance Organizations can maintain lists of interested and qualified members available for consultation work. Some organizations put together assistance teams and offer or sell the teams' services to members. Services such as this help meet the special needs of members and make good use of the organization as a clearinghouse. Organizations may or may not guarantee the service depending on how prior screening and listing are done.

Program Library

Resource, reference, and current topical information is essential for child care staff and directors. Since most day-to-day decisions regarding program operation are necessarily spontaneous, it is easy to forget how important information resources can be for long-range planning. Professional information is any print or media resource that program staff might use in the planning, delivery, and evaluation of the entire child care service operation.

Everyone finds favorite sources—books of ideas or inspiration—that we turn to again and again for help. Or, we develop strategies for finding information and turn to these routinely when needed—talking with colleagues, browsing through old journals, or calling a friend for advice. The pace of child care is intense, time for reading and reflection is short, and the need for information is usually immediate. Much of the literature that is useful in child care is not readily available; it includes mimeographed, small press publications, or requires a costly, time-consuming process of mail order (too late to be useful this time!). Staff will continue to have little time, and resources are likely to remain scattered and not widely available. In addition, few programs have budgets to cover large-scale purchases of books and media for staff. How then can a program begin assembling a program library?

- *Anticipate Information Needs* Take a few minutes or perhaps a half hour at a staff meeting to think about the kinds of information the program will need. Once you have generated a list of topics, identify those that are critical. Use your energies and available funds to acquire materials accordingly. Keep your list handy in case extra funds or donations become available.
- *Select Materials Carefully* Make some coolheaded decisions about cost and usefulness. Consider periodical subscriptions. These can offer a potpourri of ideas, subjects, and book reviews.
- *Continually Add to the Collection* Purchase, beg, or borrow, but continually add to the collection. Over time even the smallest collection gets larger.
- *Care For and Protect Materials* Right from the beginning set up a simple check-in and check-out system. Assign someone to monitor the collection at regular intervals to clean up and weed out old material. Store the collection in a safe but conveniently accessible place for staff.

While every program library will ultimately be a unique collection of material, tailored as such by budget as information needs, a few categories of materials will be common to all. The reference lists throughout this text are extensive, and readers undoubtedly will find titles that interest them and appear to meet their program needs. Rather than give specific recommendations, we have chosen to describe a balanced program library by type of material as follows:

Books

In general, buy paperback books and reinforce covers as needed. Avoid books that have little practical, applied information. Do not avoid theory altogether, but be sure the bulk of your book collection is readable, appealing, and potentially useful for *all* the staff.

- One or two general, comprehensive texts on child care and child development (like this one!).
- Single topic books for areas of special interest or need. For example: curriculum or activity books, books on games and outdoor play, and develop-

mental information on age of children in the program.

Film. Rent films, filmstrips, and videotapes. Unless your organization is primarily in the business of training child care staff, not running an actual program, purchase is not recommended. Large centers or agencies with multiple programs may find some media purchases worthwhile, but remember that media can get outdated. Always preview media before purchase and, if possible, before use with staff. (See Appendix G.)

Reports and Handouts. One of the best sources of cheap and timely information is conventions and meetings. Presenters, publishers, and suppliers make available a large number of handouts for attendees. Expect conference attendees to routinely request copies and add them to the center collection. Government reports and other research reports are often available free or at low cost; they should be added to the collection as appropriate.

Pamphlets. Many organizations and companies publish and distribute free or at very low cost information pamphlets. Topics may include nutrition, car seats, day care, and first aid. Most are attractive, easily readable, and contain basic information. Many are good as handouts to parents or directly to children.

Periodicals and Journals. For programs on tight budgets, periodicals and journals offer a lot of information for the money. A judicious mix of items from advocacy, activities, research reports, and popular press magazines can help stimulate staff, meet a variety of information needs, and keep everyone up-to-date.

Advocacy

Children are a permanent minority in our society. Children depend on the commitment and goodwill of adults for the general quality of their life experiences as well as for daily essentials. Individually and collectively, children are vulnerable in our society because they do not participate directly in our political processes. Children cannot vote and they are not direct purchasers in the marketplace. Only through the concern and participation of adults are children's needs and interests represented. Child advocacy is the conscious, deliberate, and public representation of children's viewpoints. Ours is not a child-centered society. We may revere and prize qualities of youth, investing time and money in its preservation, but that is not child advocacy. As Westman states, "Child advocacy really is a state of mind that guides action." (1979, p. 54) Laws, social policies, customs, and individual behaviors come to reflect an awareness and constant sensitivity to children. *Advocacy is thinking of children in everything we do.*

Child advocacy exists in many forms. Specific issues vary widely. Some recent and ongoing efforts include:

- TV ads aimed at children
- Prison conditions for juveniles
- Representation of children's interests in custody disputes
- Adequate nutrition during prenatal and early childhood years
- Basic health care including diagnosis and treatment as well as routine preventive care.

Advocacy work within the field of child care reflects the priorities and special challenges faced in local programs. Efforts range from lobbying work on federal staff child ratios to local zoning variances to permit operation of child care programs (see Box 15.4). Whatever the level of effort or content, advocacy work is an intrinsic part of child care. In the course of operating a program, child care staff and administration almost inevitably come to use the tools of advocacy to maintain, extend, or improve service. Parents in coalition with child care professionals are natural and influential advocates

Box 15.4 Child Advocacy Tools

One advocacy publication entitled *It's Time to Stand Up for Your Children* (Beck, 1979, pp. 34–37. Children's Defense Fund, Washington, D.C.; used with permission.) describes the following advocacy tools:

Organizing Sometimes sheer numbers will create changes that the most persistent individual cannot. Always look for ways to involve others in your child's problem. Identify and call up parents of children with similar problems and try to meet with them. Working with others has advantages other than sheer numbers. It gives you moral support when you're tired or discouraged. And it multiplies the talents you have.

Publicity Call and talk to the reporter in your town who writes about education or the school board. Ask him or her to do a story about your child's problem. You may even want to write a pamphlet or statement to hand out to the press and others who are interested.

Public Education Begin educating the people closest to you. What groups are you already a member of? Churches, civic organizations, clubs? At your next meeting, arrange to talk about your child's problem. See if others have had similar problems. Ask your group to take a specific action to show their support of your position.

Advisory Boards Find out who is on these boards and if they are speaking up for your children's needs. If not, educate them; or try to become a board member yourself.

State Plans and Comments on Regulations In addition to advisory boards, there are two other ways to influence how federal and state funds are spent in your area. One is to comment on state plans, which are required for an increasing number of programs. The second way is to comment on the federal regulations that govern how federal funds are to be spent. These regulations are developed in Washington by the agency responsible for enforcing the laws Congress passes.

Negotiating Use whatever publicity you have gotten as a position of strength from which to negotiate with officials. Have specific things they can and should do. Tell them they will have your support if they make these changes and they will have your whole group and other sympathetic parents and professionals to contend with if they do not.

Grievance Procedures and Complaints Many policies and laws also have built-in systems for parents who disagree with an official decision. Sometimes these systems are called grievance procedures. You may have to file what is known as a complaint, which is simply your statement of what you think is wrong about a particular decision or program affecting your child. Do not be embarrassed to file a complaint or ask for a hearing. That is why they are written into law—for you to use them. They are your legitimate way of letting officials know when they are not responding to your child's needs.

The Courts If you cannot get officials to listen or to budge, and if you have tried everything else, then as a last resort begin a lawsuit. Litigation may not always be necessary, but the courts and judges are there to enforce the laws protecting your children.

Lobbying You are a taxpayer and a citizen. Your elected officials are there to serve you and the best interests of children. You have every right—in fact, the responsibility—to make your problems and preferences known.

for children. Adults involved in child care have the opportunity to be active advocates for children. The child care community has a pivotal leadership role in child advocacy.

Parents and child care professionals advocate for individual children all the time. The parent who directs staff attention toward a child's worries and fears, who alerts staff to a child's food dislikes, and who seeks explanations for children's reports and activities is an advocate. Staff members who provide transportation for children to medical services, who arrange and follow up social service referrals, and who monitor children's health and well-being and counsel parents accordingly are practicing advocacy. Advocacy on a daily basis for individual children in a child care program is expected; perhaps it is even taken for granted and not clearly identified as advocacy. We tend to label activities as advocacy when more than one child is involved, when some organized effort is required, or when the advocacy effort requires dealing with an institution, agency, or government body in a formal manner. We may continue to advocate for one child, but as advocacy activities increase in scope and formality, those involved tend to state their case and seek solutions for *all* children who may have similar situations. Class action advocacy begins often with the needs of one child and a small core of committed adults. As this group gathers information, marshals its resources, selects activities, and targets solutions, others are drawn in, attracted by the energy, momentum, and justice of the effort. General policies are formulated to include many children and their many specific needs. From humble beginnings, advocacy efforts can effect major changes in public policy and law.

Westman (1979) defines advocacy as activities that lead to asking questions that are important to children. He describes six key characteristics of advocacy work that help to delineate the child orientation of advocacy and the context in which it occurs.

1. *System-Bridging* Advocacy efforts aim to bring together the key people in a child's life, taking into account the instructions and daily experiences that are part of his or her world.
2. *Developmental Orientation* Children change and gain in competence and maturity. Advocacy issues cannot be premised on immutable expectations of child dependence. Advocacy is forward looking and flexible, and it facilitates developmental progress for children.
3. *Conflict Resolution* Advocacy involves inevitable and optimal conflicts. Striking balances among the needs and wishes of children, parents, institutions, and society is at the heart of advocacy.
4. *Fact-Finding Techniques* Advocacy is data based. Specific, accurate, detailed knowledge is needed particularly in advocacy situations involving one child. Gross generalization and superficial assumptions do not contribute to effective solutions. Credible generalizations are essential as a basis for establishing public policy in class advocacy situations.
5. *Interdisciplinary Teamwork* Issues in child advocacy work are multidisciplinary. Children's problems rarely fit into neat, narrow categories. Advocates must integrate and coordinate a wealth of knowledge and the perspectives of professionals from several disciplines.
6. *Protection and Promotion of the Legal Rights of Children* Those who have influence and control over the lives of others should be regulated. Advocacy sets a productive tension between advocates and children's rights.

Advocacy Strategies

The four cornerstones of advocacy strategy are knowledge, strength, action, and money. Every advocacy strategy, whether national or local, is a variation on these basic building blocks.

Knowledge Information is a critical component for advocacy. Clearly defined problems, well-supported issues, and documented needs demonstrate you mean business. Facts and figures help establish your credibility, and provide a basis against which progress and change can be evaluated.

Strength Join with others; there is strength in numbers. Vocal individuals *can* cause quite a stir, but many people command sustained attention from the public and politicians. Besides increased influence outside the group, advocates can help support each other through the stress and strain of advocacy work and share the burden of work.

Action Speak out, write often, make yourself known through your actions. Keep your concerns public. Let others know you care and that you are monitoring their actions and commitment. Time and energy are natural resources for advocates.

Money Advocacy costs money—cash for paper, duplicating, ads, and travel. Advocates are usually volunteers willing to commit long hours and personal resources. Even with admirable individual commitments, however, advocacy efforts can stall if financing is not adequate. Dollars for advocacy can return high dividends in terms of volunteer efforts underwritten or leveraged against minimal dollars.

The Children's Defense Fund (CDF) is probably the premier advocacy organization concerned with children in this country. Its statement of purpose describes it as:

> a national, non-profit public charity created to provide long-range and systematic advocacy on behalf of the nation's children. Through research, public education, litigation, technical assistance to state and local groups, community organizing and monitoring federal administrative and legislative policies and programs, CDF seeks to change policies and practices resulting in the neglect and mistreatment of millions of children. Our goal is to place the needs of children and their families higher on the nation's public policy agenda. (Beck, 1979)

Through services, publications, example, and leadership CDF is an unmatched resource for anyone considering or involved in advocacy work for children.

Advocacy Efforts

Child Care Action Campaign (*C-CAC*) Leaders from a range of organizations in the child care field, media, and women's groups established the C-CAC in 1983. It is dedicated to informing the public about child care services and issues. Activities include a strong media campaign, support to local groups working on child care, work with government officials and politicians, and start-up of an information network for national and local agencies. C-CAC is organizing and making accessible a vast amount of information on selected issues of immediate concern to parents and others in the field of child care. A series of topical information sheets are now available. A bi-monthly newsletter provides general information, reviews, and resources. Address is C-CAC, 99 Hudson St., Rm 1233, New York, NY 10013.

Voices for Children Project This is a project of the Center for the Study of Public Policies for Young Children of the High/Scope Educational Research Foundation (600 North River St., Ypsilanti, MI 48197). Advocates have targeted business and civic leaders as key individuals whose actions can effect young children. Through state projects, national associations, and conferences, the Project intends to publicize and disseminate information supporting early childhood education.

CDF Action Council A grass roots lobby sponsored by the Children's Defense Fund. Through the Children's Action Network advocates will receive materials and information, which will support their efforts in working toward a broad spectrum of children's issues in the political arena. Address is: CDF Action Council, 122 C St. N.W., Suite 400, Washington, DC, 20001.

Child Watch Sponsored by the Children's Defense Fund in collaboration with the Association of Junior Leagues, Child Watch is an effort to train people to look out for children in their local communities. Child Watch is a practical, action-oriented program that disseminates the skills and advocacy resources of Children's Defense Fund through local sponsors to communities throughout the country.

Week of the Young Child In April of each year NAEYC celebrates the Week of the Young Child. In communities across the country child advocates plan activities and media campaigns that focus public attention on young children. Over the years the Week of the Young Child has gathered momentum and is now an important event for local NAEYC chapters and members. NAEYC has developed posters, flyers, artwork, decals, buttons, etc. which can be used for promotional activities.

White House Conferences Every decade since 1909, White House Conferences have been scheduled to provide a forum for discussion and analysis of the status of children in our society. Participants assemble, debate issues,

Box 15.5 Lobbying and Lobbyists

Taking its name from the corridors and halls where it supposedly occurs, lobbying is a traditional and heavily practiced activity. Skilled lobbyists use information and persuasion in attempting to influence the voting of legislators and to procure the passage of bills. Lobbyists who work for pay are required by law to register and report certain details of their activities.

What is the difference between lobbying and advocacy? The difference is based on purpose and resources. Lobbyists work to influence or procure passage of legislation. Advocates work to influence the general public, and to educate and inform others regarding the merits of a particular position or attitude they espouse. Thus, a lobbyist would work for influencing votes on increasing Head Start funding. An advocate would publicly support Head Start and disseminate information to convince others of its worth. Many nonprofit child care and early childhood organizations are careful not to overstep the bounds and lose their tax-exempt status. The Office of Management and Budget (OMB) has proposed new restrictions on political advocacy for groups that receive federal funds. Be aware of current, applicable lobbying limits for your organization.

formulate recommendations, and publish reports. Over the years, conferences have focused on varying issues with each conference coming to serve as a review of progress rather than a launching pad for new initiatives. For example:

- *1960* Children and Youth focused on youth, alienation, juvenile problems, and family breakdown.
- *1970* Two conferences—one on Children, one on Youth—to some extent worked at government role in supporting families.

White House Conferences attract a lot of attention and do serve to focus public attention on children and bring advocates together, but little of lasting substance seems to result. No legislative initiatives result, no strong momentum is generated, and coalitions formed during the conferences often do not hold together in the intervening ten years. Critics have called the conferences routine, institutionalized child advocacy that falls disappointingly short of any fruitful outcomes.

Windows on Day Care Written by Mary Dublin Keyserling in 1972, this book is based on a series of community surveys carried out by members of the National Council of Jewish Women. It is an excellent example of advocacy in action, documenting the status of day care and need for changes in service delivery and quality. It continues to be cited as an information source on conditions of care, even today.

Summary

Access to and use of community and professional resources strengthens a program and sustains the people involved. Moving outside the boundaries and circumscribed tasks of daily service delivery gives all a better perspective on the value of work in child care. The social and political progress of all human service programs is characterized by slow gains, inadequate funding, and difficulties in educating the public to understand goals and practices. Child care must compete for resources and support at all levels and in every sphere of activity.

Many community civic and service organizations have become interested in child care and may be available to support a local program. Sponsorship by churches has been crucial for many programs, providing meeting rooms and facilities for child care. Military bases have also begun opening up facilities for child care centers.

A program's outreach to the community has two important mechanisms—a board of directors and public relations. The board's role is to monitor procedures, assist in financial support, and represent the program to the public. Members should be a mix of prominent community members, experts, businesspersons, parents, and staff.

Public relations efforts are necessary to keep the community apprised of the program. Printed materials include a logo, a brochure, and in-depth information packages. Direct person-to-person contacts can be made at open houses or through phone inquiries. Programs can utilize media coverage by preparing press releases or writing feature stories.

To learn more about their field and particular issues, staff may turn to the professional resources of consultants, professional organizations, or a program library. A consultant is a person with special expertise who can help staff to improve their services. Consultants may help by designing curriculum activities, advising on difficult child behaviors, or creating a staff training plan.

Staff members may join a professional organization to meet others in their profession, to obtain information, or to pursue actions. Organizations generally emphasize one of five missions; research, continuing education, political action, public relations, or working conditions. Organizations offer publications, periodic conferences, and services such as insurance and job placement.

A program library should contain comprehensive child care textbooks, films, pamphlets, and relevant magazines.

Child advocacy is the public representation of children's viewpoints. The strategy of advocacy is based on knowledge, strength, action, and money. Ultimately, everyone involved in child care is a potential advocate for children.

Resources

Community Situations

Community needs and resources assessment guidebook. (1976). Boulder, CO: National Center for Voluntary Action.

Friedman, D. E. (Ed.). (1979). *Community solutions for child care.* Washington, DC: Department of Labor, National Manpower Institute.

Grosett, M. D., Simon, A. C., & Stewart, N. B. (1971). *So you're going to run a day care service! A handbook for citizens concerned with day care programs.* New York: Day Care Council of New York.

Church-Sponsored Child Care

Couch, R. A. (1980). *Church weekday early education: Administrative guide.* Nashville, TN: Convention Press.

Gilbert, R. (n.d.). *The children are waiting.* St. Louis, MO: Central Distribution Service.

Halbert, W. H., Jr. (1977). *The ministry of church weekday early education.* Nashville, TN: Convention Press.

Lindner, E. W., Mattis, M. C., & Rogers, J. R. (1983). *When churches mind the children: A study of day care in local parishes.* Ypsilanti, MI: High/Scope Press.

McMurphy, J. R. (1981). *Day care and preschool handbook for churches.* Chappaqua, NY: Christian Herald Books.

Murphy, F., & Puckett, M. (1971). *Church child care/day care curriculum planning guide.* Dallas: Baptist General Convention of Texas.

Stentzel, C. (1983). *In celebration of children: An interfaith religious action kit.* Washington, DC: Children's Defense Fund.

Wilkinson, H. (1973). *Church options for day care.* Philadelphia: Geneva Press.

Board of Directors

The board member of a social agency: Responsibilities and functions. (1957). New York: Child Welfare League of America.

Grach, A. S. (1980). *Board members are child advocates: A plan for action.* New York: Child Welfare League of America.

Guide for board organization in social agencies. (1975). New York: Child Welfare League of America.

Host, M. S., & Heller, P. B. (1971). *Day care 7: Administration.* Washington, DC: U.S. Department of Health, Education and Welfare.

How to be an effective board member. (1980). San Francisco: Public Management Institute.

Revitalize your board of directors. (1980). *Child Care Information Exchange, 13,* 6–9.

Staff members on the board of directors: Centers' experiences. (1979). *Exchange, 9,* 15–16.

Vixman, R. (1967). *Robert's rules of order.* New York: Pyramid.

Public Relations

Brigham, N. (1982). *How to do leaflets, newsletters, and newspapers.* New York: Hastings House.

Burke, C. (1974). *Printing it.* Berkeley, CA: Wingbow Press.

First, J. (1977). *A public relations handbook for early childhood organizations.* Little Rock, AK: Southern Association on Children Under Six.

Gaining access to radio and TV time: A union member's guide to the broadcast media. (1980). Washington, DC: American Federation of State, County, and Municipal Employees.

If you want air time. (1981). Washington, DC: National Association of Broadcasters.

Klein, T., & Danzig, F. (1984). Publicity: *How to make the media work for you.* New York: Scribners.

Ma Bell and child care: Handling telephone inquiries. (1982). *Child Care Information Exchange, 27,* 17–24.

Martinez, B. F., & Weiner, R. (1979). *Guide to public relations for non-profit organizations and public agencies.* Los Angeles: The Grantsmanship Center.

Media kit (n.d.). (Pub. No. 163). Washington, DC: League of Women Voters.

Neugebauer, B. (1982). Publishing your center newsletter: A practical guide to layout and design. *Child Care Information Exchange, 28,* 6–10.

Neugebauer, R. (1982). Tips on publishing a center newsletter. *Child Care Information Exchange, 27,* 26–31.

O'Brien, R. (1977). *Publicity: How to get it.* New York: Harper & Row.

Public information public relations: A do-it-yourself kit. (n.d.). Day Care Administration Bulletin, No. 2. Atlanta: Southern Regional Educational Board. Includes copies of *Public information/Public relations for rural day care programs* by Save the Children Appalachian Program. Schon, B., & Neugebauer, R. (1978). Marketing strategies that work in child care. *Child Care Information Exchange,* (3). Martinez, B. F., & Weiner, R. (1977). *Guide to public relations for non-profit organizations and public agencies.* Reprinted from *The Grantsmanship Center News.*

Schon, B. (1981). Marketing. *Child Care Information Exchange, 19,* 17–24.

Successful public relations techniques. (1980). San Francisco: Public Management Institute.

Professional Resources

Diamondstone, J. (1980). *Designing, leading and evaluating workshops for teachers and parents: A manual for trainers and leadership personnel in early childhood education.* Ypsilanti, MI: High/Scope Press.

Kiester, D. J. (1969). *Consultation in day care.* Chapel Hill, NC: Institute of Government, University of North Carolina.

Scarlett, W. G., Sheaffer, K., & Braun, S. (1980). On using consultants: Suggestions for administrators and teachers. *Child Care Information Exchange, 11,* 26–29.

Wolf, D. On hosting researchers: Guidelines for centers. *Child Care Information Exchange, 11,* 30–33.

Woodburg, M. L. (1982). *A guide to sources of educational information.* Arlington, VA: Information Resources Press.

Advocacy

Beck, R. (1979). *It's time to stand up for your children.* Washington, DC: Children's Defense Fund.

Beck, R. (1973). The White House Conferences on Children: An historical perspective. *Harvard Education Review, 43,* 653–668.

Building a house on the hill for our children: CDF's children's public policy network. (1980). Washington, DC: Children's Defense Fund.

Children's Defense Fund. (1983). *Restrictions on political activities of 501 (c)(3) and other non-profit federally funded organizations.* Washington, DC: Children's Defense Fund.

Franzel, D. (1982). *Advocacy for day care: From sandbox to soapbox.* Washington, DC: Day Care Council of America.

Hass, E. (1975). Getting support for children's programs: Organizing child advocacy. In S. Auerbach (Ed.), *Rationale for child care services: Programs vs politics: Vol. 1.* New York: Human Sciences Press.

Jewett, P. A. (1980). *Kids and politics do mix: The role of the early childhood professional in influencing public policy.* (ERIC Document Reproduction Service No. ED 207 690)

Keyserling, M. D. (1972). *Windows on day care.* New York: National Council of Jewish Women.

Kyle, J. E. (1980). The extrospective early childhood administrator. *Child Care Information Exchange, 13,* 33–37.

Melton, G. B. (1983). *Child advocacy: Psychological issues and interventions.* New York: Plenum.

Rodham, H. (1973). Children under the law. *Harvard Education Review, 43,* 487–514.

Rosenheim, M. K. (1973). The child and the law. In B. M. Caldwell & H. W. Ricciuti (Eds.), *Review of child development research: Vol. 3.* Chicago: University of Chicago Press.

Senn, M. J. E. (1977). *Speaking out for America's children.* New Haven, CT: Yale University Press.

Statement on child advocacy. (1981). New York: Child Welfare League of America.

The child watch manual. (1982). Washington, DC: The Children's Defense Fund.

Westman, J. C. (1979). *Child advocacy.* New York: Free Press.

Young, D., & Nelson, R. (1973). *Public policy for day care of young children.* Lexington, MA: Lexington Books.

Data Sources

America's children and their families: Key facts. (1979). Washington, DC: Children's Defense Fund.

Characteristics of American children and youth: 1980. (1982). Current Population Reports, Special Studies Series P-23, No. 114. Washington, DC: U.S. Department of Commerce, Bureau of the Census.

Congressional yellow book. (1985). Washington, DC: Washington Monitor. (Updated four times a year)

Employed parents and their children: A data book. (1982). Washington, DC: Children's Defense Fund.

Facts for United Way long range planning and where to find them. (1980). Alexandria, VA: United Way.

Federal yellow book. (1985). Washington, DC: Washington Monitor. (Updated six times a year)

Shur, J. L., & Smith, P. V. (1980). *Where do you look? Whom do you ask? How do you know? Information resources for child advocates.* Washington, DC: Children's Defense Fund.

Local Government and Politics

Anatomy of a hearing (1972). (Pub. No. 108) Washington, DC: League of Women Voters.

Derfner, C. (1975). *City hall: An important resource for your organization.* Los Angeles: The Grantsmanship Center.

Gans, S. P., & Horton, G. T. (1975). *Integration of human services: The state and municipal level.* New York: Praeger.

Know your state (1974). (Pub. No. 137) Washington, DC: League of Women Voters.

Know your county (1974). (Pub. No. 180) Washington, DC: League of Women Voters.

Know your community (1974). (Pub. No. 208) Washington, DC: League of Women Voters.

Making an issue of it: The campaign handbook (1976). (Pub. No. 613) Washington, DC: League of Women Voters.

The politics of change. (1972). (Pub. No. 107) Washington, DC: League of Women Voters.

Appendix A

Setting Up a Family Day Care Home

Jan Bogrow

Child Development Center
American University
Washington, DC

Licensing or Registration

	Date Initiated	Date Completed	Comments
A. Procedure to Obtain License or Registration			
1. Contact local child care licensing and zoning offices for copy of regulation forms.			
2. Read thoroughly and create a checklist of tasks.			
3. Recontact licensing (registration) office for verification of possible problems.			
4. When checklist of tasks is completed, contact appropriate inspectors and set up an inspection visit.			
5. Submit forms when all requirements have been met.			
B. Areas of Regulation			
1. Zoning regulations			
a. neighborhood restrictions: commercial vs. residential			
b. outdoor space requirements may differ from child care regulations			
2. Space requirements			
a. square footage per child			
b. lighting			

Licensing or Registration (*continued*)

	Date Initiated	Date Completed	Comments
c. heating/air conditioning/ventilation			
d. plumbing			
3. Building Code Regulations			
a. type of construction			
b. number and pathways of exits			
c. fire doors			
d. electrical			
4. Health requirements			
a. immunization records for children			
b. medical examinations for care-givers and children			
c. first-aid training			
d. sick child care policies			
e. medical administration			
5. Fire regulations			
a. emergency evacuation plan			
b. fire drill schedule			
c. smoke detectors			
d. fire drill procedures			
e. maximum allowable number of children			
f. number of exits			
g. fire doors			
6. Food preparation and nutrition requirements			
a. types of food to be served daily			
b. proper preparation and storage of food			
7. Emergency plans			
a. evacuation plans			
b. medical emergency procedures			
c. substitute caregiver			
8. Group size and adult-child ratio			
9. Caregiver requirements			

Licensing or Registration (*continued*)

	Date Initiated	Date Completed	Comments
10. Program requirements			
a. philosophy, including discipline			
b. daily activities			
c. parent involvement			
d. equipment and supplies			
11. Record-keeping			
a. child registration			
b. health record			
c. emergency care			
d. caregiver/assistant employment record			
e. financial management			

Personal and Community Assessment

	Date Initiated	Date Completed	Comments
A. Personal Assessment			
1. Personal health			
2. Communication skills with parents and licensing officials			
3. Ability to handle emergencies			
4. Decision-making skills			
5. Planning skills			
6. Knowledge of child care and child development			
7. Interest in pursuing further child care/child development ideas and information			
8. Willingness to work long hours for little financial reward			
9. Financial assets to begin a family day care home			
10. Love and respect for children			

Personal and Community Assessment (*continued*)

	Date Initiated	Date Completed	Comments
B. Community Assessment			
1. Number of homes in area in operation			
2. Specific location of existing homes			
3. Ages of children being served			
4. Hours per day and days per week existing homes are operating			
5. Number of unfilled spaces			
6. Number on waiting lists			
C.			
1. Questionnaire for parents' distribution			
a. specific neighborhoods			
b. local child care centers			
c. local elementary schools			
d. local businesses			
e. local churches			
2. Contacting the local child care agency			
3. Surveying the ads for child care needs in the classified section of the local newspaper			
4. Counting the number of family day care homes listed in the Yellow Pages			
5. Census information from the local government planning office			

Communication with Parents

	Date Initiated	Date Completed	Comments
A. Contracts—see Financial and Legal Management			
B. Handbooks			
1. Hours of operation			
2. Fees and payments			
3. Holiday and emergency closings			

Communication with Parents (*continued*)

	Date Initiated	Date Completed	Comments
4. Policies of health, illness, and safety			
5. Educational program including trips			
6. Meals and snacks			
7. Daily requirements (i.e., diapers)			
8. Philosophy			
9. Daily schedule			
10. Parent involvement policy			
11. Special services offered			
12. Additional information particular to setting			
13. Enrollment checklist			
C. Forms			
1. Family and child questionnaire			
2. Emergency care information			
3. Parental consent form			
4. Daily/weekly children's reports			
5. Health records			
D. Verbal Communication on a daily basis			
E. Monthly Newsletter			
F. Family Events (i.e., potluck suppers)			

Financial and Legal Management

	Date Initiated	Date Completed	Comments
A. Budget Preparation			
1. Food and related supplies			
2. Art supplies			
3. Toys, indoors and outdoors			
4. Assistant and substitute salaries			
5. Advertising			

Financial and Legal Management (*continued*)

	Date Initiated	Date Completed	Comments
6. Dues for associations of family day care providers			
7. Transportation (field trips and supply pick up)			
8. Insurance			
9. Office expenses			
10. Postage			
11. Maintenance and cleaning supplies			
12. Repair costs			
13. Telephone			
14. Personal income requirement			
15. Licensing application fee			
B. Setting Fees			
1. Meeting personal income requirement			
2. General fee in the community			
3. Charges based on hours reserved			
4. One fee for all children or sliding scale based on family income			
C. Fee Collection			
1. Require payment in advance			
2. Invoice monthly or weekly			
3. Contracts			
a. payment rate and procedure			
b. hours of child's enrollment			
c. deposit requirement			
d. returned checks			
e. refunds and credits			
f. withdrawal notice			
g. child suspension for unpaid balances			
h. health insurance requirements			

Financial and Legal Management (*continued*)

	Date Initiated	Date Completed	Comments
D. Bookkeeping			
1. Income			
a. daily attendance record			
b. monthly tally of hours			
c. arrival and departure times			
d. yearly tally of individual child's payments			
e. record of fees charged, collected, and balance due			
2. Expenses			
a. a checking account solely for child care related expenditures			
b. keep all receipts from purchases			
c. a book solely for expenditures listing amount spent, item purchased, and date			
d. file of all cancelled checks			
e. indirect expenses of home utilization			
1. rent			
2. utilities			
3. equipment bought for home use and child care use			
4. square footage of space utilized and amount of time the space is used for child care			
E. Internal Revenue Service Information			
1. Record of expenses			
2. State and local taxes			
3. Property tax bill			
4. Record of previously owned child care items			
5. Family day care license			
6. Square footage of total home and that used for child care			

Financial and Legal Management (*continued*)

	Date Initiated	Date Completed	Comments
7. Previous year's tax return			
F. Salary, Social Security, and Taxes			
1. Social Security self-employment tax			
2. State and local taxes			
3. Federal employer identification number			
4. Social security and federal, local, and state taxes for assistant or substitute			
G. Additional Information			

Equipment and Supplies

	Date Initiated	Date Completed	Comments
A. Toys			
1. Puzzles			
2. Dolls			
3. Trucks			
4. Manipulative games			
5. Books			
B. Art			
1. Crayons			
2. Paper			
3. Scissors			
4. Paste			
5. Water colors/tempera paints			
C. Equipment			
1. Table and chairs			
2. Portacribs, cots			
3. Playpens			
4. Shelves			
5. Food preparation equipment			
D. Where to Purchase			
1. Consignment/thrift shops			

Equipment and Supplies (*continued*)

	Date Initiated	Date Completed	Comments
2. Yard sales			
3. Closing schools and day care centers			
4. Parent donations			
E. Additional Information			

Advertising

	Date Initiated	Date Completed	Comments
A. Types of Materials			
1. Brochures			
2. Flyers			
3. Classified ads in local newspaper			
4. Posters			
B. Where?			
1. Shopping centers			
2. Libraries			
3. Laundromats			
4. Restaurants			
5. Children's stores			
6. Supermarkets			
7. Community centers			
8. Schools			
9. Businesses			
10. Universities and colleges			
11. Churches and synagogues			
12. Day care centers			
13. Hospitals			
14. Classified section of newspaper			
15. Feature section of newspaper			
16. Word of mouth			

Advertising (*continued*)

	Date Initiated	Date Completed	Comments
C. Information to Include			
1. Name, address, phone number			
2. Ages of children			
3. Hours of operation			
4. Fees			
5. Opening date			
6. Brief statement about provider and program			
7. Enrollment procedure			

Government Subsidy and Loans

	Date Initiated	Date Completed	Comments
A. Government subsidies are available but limited. Contact the local licensing specialist or local child care association for information.			
B. Loans			
1. Finance companies			
2. Insurance companies			
3. Credit unions			
4. Commercial banks			
5. Savings and loans associations			

Family Day Care Associations

	Date Initiated	Date Completed	Comments
A. Affiliations			
1. County			
2. City/town			
3. Regional			

Family Day Care Associations (*continued*)

	Date Initiated	Date Completed	Comments
4. State			
5. Public school system			
B. Services			
1. Training workshops			
2. Mini-grants for home/program improvement			
3. Toy-lending libraries			
4. Group insurance			
5. Federal child care food program sponsorship			
6. Substitute care network			
7. Equipment purchasing services			
8. Federally funded Title XX subsidy administration			
9. Support services (i.e., social worker, nutritionist)			
10. Providers discussion groups			

Appendix B

Material and Equipment Suppliers

ABC School Supply, Inc.
437 Armour Circle, N.E.
P.O. Box 13086
Atlanta, GA 30324

Ablex Publishing
355 Chestnut Street
Norwood, NJ 07648

Abt Books
55 Wheeler Street
Cambridge, MA 02138

Academic Press
111 Fifth Avenue
New York, NY 10003

Adapt Press, Inc.
1298 West Bailey
Sioux Falls, SD 57104

Addison-Wesley's Teacher Center
2725 Sand Hill Road
Menlo Park, CA 94025

American Guidance Service
Publishers' Building
Circle Pines, MN 55014

Angeles Toys, Inc.
8106 Allport Avenue
Santa Fe Springs, CA 90670

Argus Communications
7440 Natchez Avenue
Niles, IL 60648

Aspen Systems Corporation
1600 Research Blvd.
Rockville, MD 20850

Auburn House
131 Clarendon Street
Boston, MA 02116

B. L. Winch and Associates
45 Hitching Post Drive
Building 23H
Rolling Hills Estates, CA 90274

Barrows Corporation
2205 Langdon Farm Road
Cincinnati, OH 45237

Beckley-Cardy
7423 Diog Drive
Garden Grove, CA 92640

Brigham Young University Press
206 UPB
Provo, UT 84602

C. V. Mosby Company
11830 Westline Industrial Drive
St. Louis, MO 63141

Charles E. Merrill Publishing Co.
1300 Alum Creek Drive
Columbus, OH 43216

Chaselle, Inc.
9645 Gerwig Lane
Columbia, MD 21046

Childcraft Educational Corporation
20 Kilmer Road
Edison, NJ 08818

Children's Learning Center, Inc.
6113 Allisonville Road
Indianapolis, IN 46220

Children's Press
1224 West Van Buren Street
Chicago, IL 60607

Climbing Thing
P.O. Box 1283
Tampa, FL 33601

Community Playthings
Rifton, NY 12471

Constructive Playthings
2008 West 103rd Terrace
Leawood, KS 66206

Continental Press, Inc.
Elizabeth, PA 17022

Creative Curriculum, Inc.
15681 Commerce Lane
Huntington Beach, CA 92649

Creative Playthings
P.O. Box 1100
Princeton, NJ 08540

Cuisenaire Company of America, Inc.
12 Church Street
New Rochelle, NY 10805

Curriculum Associates
6 Henshaw Street
Woburn, MA 01801

David C. Cook Publishing Company
School Products Division
Elgin, IL 60120

D. C. Heath and Company
125 Spring Street
Lexington, MA 02173

Delmar Publishers, Inc.
50 Wolf Road
Albany, NY 12205

Delta Education, Inc.
P.O. Box M
Nashua, NH 03061

Denison
9601 Newton Avenue South
Minneapolis, MN 55431

Didax Educational Resources
6 Doulton Place
Peabody, MA 01960

Early Childhood Bookhouse
822 N.W. 23rd
Portland, OR 97210

EBSCO Curriculum Materials
Box 486
Birmingham, AL 35202

Economy Company
P.O. Box 25308
1901 North Walnut Street
Oklahoma City, OK 73125

EDUCAT Publishers, Inc.
P.O. Box 2891
Clinton, IA 52735

Educational Activities, Inc.
P.O. Box 87
Baldwin, NY 11510

Educational Aids
845 Wisteria Drive
Fremont, CA 94538

Educational Teaching Aids
159 West Kinzie Street
Chicago, IL 60610

Encyclopedia Britannica
425 North Michigan Avenue
Chicago, IL 60611

Fawcett Publications, Inc.
Fawcett Place
Greenwich, CT 06830

Fearon Publishers
6 Davis Drive
Belmont, CA 94002

Follett Publishing Company
1010 West Washington Blvd.
Chicago, IL 60607

Golden Press
Educational Division
150 Parish Drive
Wayne, NJ 07470

Goodyear Publishing Company
P.O. Box 486
Pacific Palisades, CA 90272

Greenwillow Books
Box CM-EDEC
105 Madison Avenue
New York, NY 10016

Growing Child
P.O. Box 620
Lafayette, IN 47902

Grune and Stratton, Inc.
111 Fifth Avenue
New York, NY 10003

Gryphon House, Inc.
P.O. Box 275
Mt. Ranier, MD 20712

Hammett Company
Early Childhood Division
Box 545
Braintree, MA 02184

Harper and Row
10 East 53rd Street
New York, NY 10022

High/Scope Foundation
600 North River Street
Ypsilanti, MI 48197

Holt, Rinehart and Winston
521 Fifth Avenue
New York, NY 10175

Hospital Play Equipment Company
Dr. Victor C. Dye
1122 Judson Avenue
Evanston, IL 60602

Houghton Mifflin
1 Beacon Street
Boston, MA 02108

Humanics Limited
P.O. Box 7447
Atlanta, GA 30309

Human Sciences Press, Inc.
72 Fifth Avenue
New York, NY 10011

Ideal School Supply Company
11000 South Lavergne Avenue
Oaklawn, IL 60453

Instructo/McGraw-Hill
Malvern, PA 19355

Johnson and Johnson
Baby Products Div., Child Dev. Products
Grandview Road
Skillman, NJ 08558

Jossey-Bass, Inc.
433 California Street
San Francisco, CA 94104

Kaplan Corporation
600 Jonestown Road
Winston-Salem, NC 27103

Kendall/Hunt Publishing
2460 Kerper Blvd.
Dubuque, IA 52001

Knowledge Tree Group
360 Park Avenue South
New York, NY 10010

Kurtz Brothers
Clearfield, PA 16830

Lakeshore Curriculum Materials Co.
16463 Phoebe Avenue
LaMirada, CA 90637

Learning Line
P.O. Box 1200
Palo Alto, CA 94302

Lego Systems, Inc.
555 Taylor Road
Enfield, CT 06082

Lexington Books
125 Spring Street
Lexington, MA 02173

Lippincott Co.
East Washington Square
Philadelphia, PA 19105

Little People's Workshop
Box 99608
Louisville, KY 40299

London Bridge
P.O. Box 5964
1205 Greenwood Road
Baltimore, MD 21208

Love Publishing Company
6635 East Villanova Place
Denver, CO 80222

Lyons
530 Riverview Avenue
Elkhart, IN 46514

Macmillan
866 Third Avenue
New York, NY 10022

McGraw-Hill Book Company
1221 Avenue of the Americas
New York, NY 10020

Milton Bradley Company
Springfield, MA 01101

Mother's Manual, Inc.
441 Lexington Avenue
New York, NY 10017

Nancy Renfro Studios
1117 West Ninth Street
Austin, TX 78703

National Dairy Council
6300 North River Road
Rosemont, IL 60018

National Pediatric Support Services
30 Rockrose Way
Irvine, CA 92715

Nienhous Montessori U.S.A., Inc.
320 Pioneer Way
Department 4
Mountain View, CA 94041

NOVO Educational Toy and Equipment Corp.
124 West 24th Street
New York, NY 10011

Open Court Publishing Company
LaSalle, IL 61301

Parenting Press
7750 31st Avenue, N.E.
Seattle, WA 98115

Peacock Publishers
401 West Irving Park Road
Itasca, IL 60143

Pitman Learning, Inc.
6 Davis Drive
Belmont, CA 94002

Playhouse
1406 32nd Avenue
San Francisco, CA 94122

Plenum Publishing Corporation
233 Spring Street
New York, NY 10013

Portage Project Materials
412 East Slifer Street
Portage, WI 53901

Prentice-Hall
General Book Marketing Division
Englewood Cliffs, NJ 07632

Preschool Curriculum Resources
P.O. Box 319
Redding Ridge, CT 06876

Princeton Center for Infancy
306 Alexander Street
Princeton, NJ 08450

Programs for Education, Inc.
Box 85E
Lumberville, PA 18933

Psychological Corp.
757 Third Avenue
New York, NY 10017

Puppet Productions, Inc.
P.O. Box 82008
San Diego, CA 92138

Quality Child Care Press
P.O. Box 176
Mound, MN 55364

R & E Research Associates, Inc.
936 Industrial Avenue
Palo Alto, CA 94303

Random House
201 East 50th Street
New York, NY 10022

Reader's Digest Services, Inc.
Educational Division
Pleasantville, NY 10570

Research Press
Box 317702
Champaign, IL 61820

Rhythm Band, Inc.
P.O. Box 126
Ft. Worth, TX 76101

Rifton
Route 213
Rifton, NY 12471

Salco Toys, Inc.
Route 1
Nerstand, MN 55053

Schocken Books
200 Madison Avenue
New York, NY 10016

Scholastic Book Services
904 Sylvan Avenue
Englewood Cliffs, NJ 07632

Schoolyard Big Toys
Northwest Design Products
3113 South Pine Street
Tacoma, WA 98409

Science Research Associates, Inc.
259 East Erie Street
Chicago, IL 60611

Scott, Foresman & Company
1900 East Lake Avenue
Glenview, IL 60025

Silver Burdett Company
250 James Street
Morristown, NJ 07960

Snow Corporation
P.O. Box 9800
Ft. Worth, TX 76107

Special Learning Corp.
P.O. Box 306
Guilford, CT 06437

Spectrum Educational Supplies, Inc.
P.O. Box 6607
Bridgewater, NJ 08807

Teachers College Press
Teachers College
Columbia University
New York, NY 10027

Teaching Resources Corp.
50 Pond Park Road
Hingham, MA 02043

Toys 'n Things
Training & Resource Center, Inc.
906 North Dale Street
St. Paul, MN 55103

Toys to Grow On
P.O. Box 17
Long Beach, CA 90801

Trend Enterprises
Box 3073
St. Paul, MN 55165

Troubador Press
385 Fremont Street
San Francisco, CA 94105

University Park Press
300 North Charles Street
Baltimore, MD 21201

University Press of America
P.O. Box 19101
Washington, DC 20036

VORT Corp.
P.O. Box 11757A
Palo Alto, CA 94306

Webster-McGraw-Hill
1221 Avenue of the Americas
New York, NY 10020

Western Psychological Services
12031 Wilshire Blvd.
Los Angeles, CA 90025

Western Publishing Co., Inc.
1220 Mound Avenue
Racine, WI 53404

Weston Woods
Weston, CT 06883

Wiley Professional Books—By Mail
P.O. Box 063
Somerset, NJ 08873

Wingbow Press
2940 Seventh Street
Box D
Berkeley, CA 94710

Winston Press
430 Oak Grove
Minneapolis, MN 55403

Wood Etc. Corp.
940 North Beltine #137
P.O. Box 3484E
Irving, TX 75061

Woodland Structures, Inc.
3539 85th Avenue North
Brooklyn, MN 55443

Xerox Educational Publications
1250 Fairwood Avenue
P.O. Box 16629
Columbus, OH 43216

Yale University Press
92A Yale Station
New Haven, CT 06520

Appendix C

So You Want to Be a Program Director: A Self-Assessment Inventory

Program management, administration, and staff leadership combine to make directing a child care program a complex and challenging job. Many individuals working with young children are attracted to the idea of directing a child care program. As their education and/or experience in the field increase, many feel that assuming a center directorship is a logical career step. This self-assessment inventory is organized to help you compare your current education and experience status with the job requirements and qualifications needed for directing a child care program. This systematic assessment procedure will give you an indication of where your strengths lie as a potential child care director. If you are already a center director, the self-assessment inventory can help you chart a personal plan for growth and training based on your current capabilities.

Credentials

A. Education

	Where	Year Graduated	Comments
Grade School			
High School			
GED			
Associate Degree			
Bachelor's Degree			
Master's Degree			
Doctorate			

Indicate in the comments column, course specialization in child development and related fields. Assign a number to each education credential. Use Ed-1, Ed-3, and so on. You will use these in a later section of the self-assessment.

B. Training

Date

Special Courses—List Titles and Credits Earned

Certificates—Describe Course of Study or Purpose of Certificate

In-service—List Title and Duration

Conference Workshops—List Title and Duration

Assign a number to each different training experience. Use Tr-1, Tr-2, Tr-3, and so on. You will use these in a later section of the self-assessment.

C. Experience

Job Title	Duties	Time Period	Reference
1.			
2.			
3.			
4.			
5.			

List most recent experiences first. Include volunteer work if references are available to document your duties and performance. Assign a number to each job listed. Use Job-1, Job-2, Job-3, and so on. You will use these numbers later in the self-assessment.

II. Personal

Answer each set of questions briefly. Ask someone who knows you well to do the same. Talk about any discrepancies in your self-perceptions. Using this information, rate yourself for each question using the following scale:

Key

1. No. Almost never
2. Rarely
3. Maybe
4. Usually
5. Yes

A. Are you healthy? Is your energy level high? Can you sustain hard effort over long periods of time?	1	2	3	4	5
B. What kinds of contact do you enjoy with adults? Can you get along with people in almost all situations?	1	2	3	4	5
C. To what extent are you prepared to sacrifice financial reward and personal or social time for your job?	1	2	3	4	5
D. To what extent are you comfortable with exercising authority and being viewed as an authority figure?	1	2	3	4	5

III. Skills and Abilities

Six skill areas related to center management and leadership are listed. Specific skills often required in each skill area are clustered under the general statement. Complete the following two steps:

1. Read the general statement and specific skill statements. Using the numbers you assigned to your education, training, and experiences in previous sections, note where you have demonstrated those skills. These should be skills that you can ask a reference writer to verify or that you can document in some way.
2. Use the rating scale to evaluate the extent to which your experiences indicate competence in that skill.

Key

1. No experience
2. Little experience
3. Moderate experience
4. Frequent experience
5. Considerable experience

A. Management of Children's Program

1. Know current practices of various program approaches.	1	2	3	4	5
2. Design a program curriculum.	1	2	3	4	5
3. Seek out and understand information on program effectiveness.	1	2	3	4	5
4. Identify and articulate personal philosophy on child care.	1	2	3	4	5
5. Substitute and/or teach, if needed.	1	2	3	4	5

B. Coordination of Program Support Functions

1. Know purposes and goals of professional social service fields.	1	2	3	4	5
2. Identify need for professional specialists.	1	2	3	4	5
3. Maintain relationships with parents.	1	2	3	4	5
4. Organize parent activities.	1	2	3	4	5
5. Handle referrals and follow-ups for social services.	1	2	3	4	5

C. Maintenance of the Physical Facility

1. Know and understand current federal, state, local, and agency regulations.	1	2	3	4	5
2. Set up and maintain flexible routines.	1	2	3	4	5
3. Keep inventories.	1	2	3	4	5
4. Handle on-site inspections.	1	2	3	4	5
5. Monitor facility for compliance with regulations.	1	2	3	4	5

D. Record-keeping for Legal and Fiscal Purposes

1. Set up and maintain files.	1	2	3	4	5
2. Have skill in record-keeping.	1	2	3	4	5
3. Have basic accounting skills.	1	2	3	4	5
4. Know procedures and sources for purchasing.	1	2	3	4	5
5. Handle enrollments and screening.	1	2	3	4	5
6. Collect fees.	1	2	3	4	5
7. Prepare budgets.	1	2	3	4	5
8. Write proposals.	1	2	3	4	5

E. Staff Management

1. Interview and make recommendations to board on prospective personnel.	1	2	3	4	5
2. Organize orientations.	1	2	3	4	5
3. Organize staff meetings.	1	2	3	4	5
4. Maintain smooth personal relationships with staff.	1	2	3	4	5
5. Mediate staff problems.	1	2	3	4	5
6. Evaluate staff.	1	2	3	4	5
7. Specify duties for volunteers.	1	2	3	4	5
8. Organize workshops for in-service training of staff.	1	2	3	4	5

F. Public Relations

1. Speak in public comfortably.	1	2	3	4	5
2. Write and edit effectively.	1	2	3	4	5
3. Have experience with public relations.	1	2	3	4	5
4. Prepare newsletters or brochures.	1	2	3	4	5

Assessment

We're going to ask you to total your ratings for each category and then compute a percentage score for yourself. Use the following form to record your totals and percentages. These percentages will give you a rough guide to how strong a candidate you are for a director's job. Look at those areas where you appear to be well qualified. Look at where you appear to be still inexperienced.

Use these assessments as a basis for planning additional work or training experience. Use them as a basis for presenting your qualifications when competing for a director's job. And, good luck!

Personal	**Possible Total**	**Your Total**	**Compute %**
A. Health and Stamina	5	______	______
B. Relationship with Adults	5	______	______
C. Job Demands	5	______	______
D. Exercising Authority	5	______	______
Skills and Abilities			
A. Management of Children's Program	25	______	______
B. Coordination of Program Support Functions	25	______	______
C. Maintenance of Physical Facility	25	______	______
D. Record-keeping for Legal and Fiscal Purposes	25	______	______
E. Staff Management	25	______	______
F. Public Relations	25	______	______

Appendix D

State Licensing Offices

Office of Program Administration
64 North Union Street
Montgomery, AL 36130

Department of Health & Social Services
Pouch H-05
Juneau, AK 99811

Arizona Department of Health Services
1740 West Adams
Phoenix, AZ 85007

Department of Social and Rehabilitative Services
P.O. Box 1487
Little Rock, AR 72203

Department of Social Services
744 P Street, Mail Station 17-17
Sacramento, CA 95814

Department of Social Services
1575 Sherman Street, Room 420
Denver, CO 80203

State Department of Health
79 Elm Street
Hartford, CT 06115

Department of Health & Social Services
P.O. Box 309
Wilmington, DE 19899

Department of Human Services
1905 E Street, S.E., 5th floor
Washington, DC 20003

Department of Health and Rehabilitation Services
1311 Winewood Boulevard
Tallahassee, FL 32301

Department of Human Resources
618 Ponce de Leon Avenue
Atlanta, GA 30308

Division of Social Services
P.O. Box 2816
Agana, GU 96910

Department of Social Services and Housing
P.O. Box 339
Honolulu, HI 96809

Department of Health and Welfare
Statehouse
Boise, ID 83720

Department of Children and Family Services
1 North Old State Capitol Plaza
Springfield, IL 62706

State Department of Public Welfare
100 North Senate Avenue, Room 701
Indianapolis, IN 46204

Department of Social Services
3619 ½ Douglass Avenue
Des Moines, IA 50310

Division of Health & Environment
Building 740, Forbes AFB
Topeka, KS 66620

Department of Human Resources
Fourth Floor East
275 East Main Street
Frankfort, KY 40601

Department of Health & Human Resources
P.O. Box 3767
Baton Rouge, LA 70821

Department of Human Services
Augusta, ME 04333

Department of Health and Mental Hygiene
201 West Preston Street
Baltimore, MD 21201

Office for Children
120 Boylston Street
Boston, MA 02116

Michigan Department of Social Services
116 West Allegan
P.O. Box 80037
Lansing, MI 48926

Department of Public Welfare
Centennial Office Building, 4th Floor
St. Paul, MN 55155

State Board of Health
P.O. Box 1700
Jackson, MS 39205

State Department of Social Services
Broadway State Office Building
303 W. McCarthy Street
Jefferson City, MO 65103

Montana Department of Social and Rehabilitation Services
P.O. Box 4210
Helena, MT 59601

Department of Public Welfare
P.O. Box 95026
Lincoln, NE 68509

Division of Youth Services
505 East King Street
Carson City, NV 89710

Office of Social Services
Hazen Drive
Concord, NH 03301

New Jersey Department of Human Services
1 South Montgomery Street
Trenton, NJ 08623

Health and Environment Department
725 St. Michael's Drive
P.O. Box 968
Sante Fe, NM 87503

Mr. Jason Edwards
P.O. Box 2348
Room 519, Pera Building
7th and New Mexico
Santa Fe, NM 87501

New York State Department of Social Services
40 North Pearl Street
Albany, NY 12243

Office of Child Day Care Licensing
P.O. Box 10157
1915 Ridge Road
Raleigh, NC 27605

Child and Family Services
Russell Building—Box 7
Highway 83 North
Bismark, ND 58505

Bureau of Licensing and Standards
30 E. Broad Street, 30th Floor
Columbus, OH 43215

Department of Public Welfare
P.O. Box 25352
Oklahoma City, OK 73125

Department of Human Resources
198 Commercial Street, S.E.
Salem, OR 97310

Pennsylvania Department of Public Welfare
Room 423, Health & Welfare Building
Harrisburg, PA 17120

P.O. Box 11398
Fernandez Juncos Station
Santurce, PR 00910

Department of Social & Rehabilitative Services
610 Mount Pleasant Avenue
Providence, RI 02908

South Carolina Department of Social Services
P.O. Box 1520
Columbia, SC 29202

Department of Social Services
Richard F. Kneip Building
Pierre, SD 57501

Tennessee Department of Human Services
111-9 7th Avenue North
Nashville, TN 37203

Texas Department of Human Resources
P.O. Box 2960
Austin, TX 78769

Division of Family Services
P.O. Box 2500
Salt Lake City, UT 84110

Department of Social and Rehabilitative Services
81 River Street
Montpelier, VT 05602

Department of Social Services
P.O. Box 539
Charlotte Amalie
St. Thomas, VI 00801

Department of Welfare
8007 Discovery Drive
Richmond, VA 23229

The Department of Social & Health Services
State Office Building #2
Mail Stop 440
Olympia, WA 98504

Department of Welfare
1900 Washington Street, East
Charleston, WV 25305

Division of Community Services
1 West Wilson Street
Madison, WI 53702

Division of Public Assistance & Social Services
Hathway Building
Cheyenne, WY 82002

Appendix E

Professional Organizations

American Academy of Pediatrics
1801 Hinman Avenue
Evanston, IL 60204

American Alliance for Health, Physical Education, Recreation and Dance (**AAHPERD**)
1900 Association Drive
Reston, VA 22091

American Association for Gifted Children
15 Gramercy Park
New York, NY 10003

American Association for the Advancement of Science (**AAAS**)
1515 Massachusetts Avenue, N.W.
Washington, DC 20005
- *Science 85*

American Association of School Administrators
1801 North Moore Street
Arlington, VA 22209

American Association of University Women (**AAUW**)
2401 Virginia Avenue, N.W.
Washington, DC 20037

American Automobile Association (**AAA**)
Traffic Safety Department
8111 Gatehouse Road
Falls Church, VA 22047

American Educational Research Association (**AERA**)
1230 17th Street, N.W.
Washington, DC 20036
- *Early Education and Child Development SIG* (*Special Interest Group*)
- *Educational Researcher*

American Federation of Teachers (**AFT**)
11 DuPont Circle, N.W.
Washington, DC 20036

American Home Economics Association
2010 Massachusetts Avenue, N.W.
Washington, DC 20036

American Humane Association
Children's Division
P.O. Box 1266
Denver, CO 80201

American Library Association (**ALA**)
50 East Huron Street
Chicago, IL 60611

American Medical Association (**AMA**)
535 North Dearborn Street
Chicago, IL 60610

American Montessori Society
150 Fifth Avenue
New York, NY 10011

American National Red Cross
17th and D Streets, N.W.
Washington, DC 20006

American Occupational Therapy Association
6000 Executive Boulevard
Suite 200
Rockville, MD 20852

American Orthopsychiatric Association, Inc. (**AOA**)
1775 Broadway
New York, NY 10019
- *American Journal of Orthopsychiatry*

American Psychological Association (**APA**)
1200 17th Street, N.W.
Washington, DC 20036

American Society for Public Administration
1225 Connecticut Avenue, N.W.
Washington, DC 20036

American Speech, Language and Hearing Association
10801 Rockville Pike
Rockville, MD 20852

Appalachian Regional Commission (**ARC**)
1666 Connecticut Avenue, N.W.
Washington, DC 20036

Association for Childhood Education International (ACEI)
11141 Georgia Avenue
Suite 200
Wheaton, MD 20902
• *Childhood Education*

Association for Supervision and Curriculum Development (ASCD)
1701 K Street, N.W.
Washington, DC 20006

Association for the Care of Children's Health
3615 Wisconsin Avenue, N.W.
Washington, DC 20016
• *Children's Health Care*

Association of Teacher Educators
1900 Association Drive
Reston, VA 22091

BANANAS, Child Care Information, Referral, and Support Service
6501 Telegraph Avenue
Oakland, CA 94609
(serves counties in CA)
• *Bananas* newsletter

BASICS
P.O. Box 604
Park Forest, IL 60466
• *Learning to Learn*
• *Reading Readiness*
• *Child Care Newsletter*

California Child Care Resource and Referral Network
320 Judah Street
Suite 2
San Francisco, CA 94122
• *CCI&R. Issues*

Center for Community Change
1000 Wisconsin Avenue, N.W.
Washington, DC 20035

Center for Parenting Studies
Wheelock College
200 the Riverway
Boston, MA 02215

Center for Science in the Public Interest
1755 S Street, N.W.
Washington, DC 20009

Child Care Action Campaign (CCAC)
99 Hudson Street
Room 1233
New York, NY 10013

Child Care Information Center
532 Settlers Landing Road
P.O. Box 548
Hampton, VA 23669

Child Care Law Center
625 Market Street
Suite 815
San Francisco, CA 94105

Child Care Resource Center
552 Mass. Avenue
Cambridge, MA 02139

Child Care Support Center
Save the Children Southern States Office
1182 West Peachtree Street, N.W.
Suite 209
Atlanta, GA 30303

Child Study Association of America
9 East 89th Street
New York, NY 10003

Child Welfare League of America (CWLA)
67 Irving Place
New York, NY 10003
• *Child Welfare*

Children's Defense Fund (CDF)
122 C Street, N.W.
Washington, DC 20001
• *CDF Reports*
• *Child Watch Updates*

Children's Foundation
1420 New York Avenue, N.W.
Suite 800
Washington, DC 20005

Community Nutrition Institute
1146 19th Street, N.W.
Washington, DC 20036

Concerned Educators Allied for a Safe Environment (CEASE)
c/o Peggy Schirmer (East of Mississippi)
17 Gerry Street
Cambridge, MA 02138
c/o Terri Fristact (West of Mississippi)
18618 Manzanita Road
Sonoma, CA 95476
• *CEASE News*

Conference Board
Dana Friedman
Work and Family Information Center
845 Third Avenue
New York, NY 10022

Council for Educational Development and Research
1518 K Street, N.W.
#206
Washington, DC 20005

Council for Exceptional Children (CEC)
1920 Association Drive
Reston, VA 22091
• *Exceptional Children*
• *Teaching Exceptional Children*
• *Update*

Council of Better Business Bureaus, Inc.
1515 Wilson Blvd.
Arlington, VA 22209

Council on Interracial Books for Children
Racism/Sexism Resource Center
1841 Broadway
New York, NY 10023

Creative Education Foundation
State University College at Buffalo
218 Chase Hall
1300 Elmwood Avenue
Buffalo, NY 14222

Day Care Council of New York
22 W. 38th Street
New York, NY 10018

Early Childhood Education Council of New York City
66 Leroy Street
New York, NY 10014

Education Commission of the States
1860 Lincoln Avenue
Denver, CO 80295

Education Development Center (EDC)
55 Chapel Street
Newton, MA 02160

Educational Facilities Laboratories
477 Madison Avenue
New York, NY 10022

ERIC Clearinghouse on Elementary and Early Childhood Education (ERIC/EECE)
University of IL, College of Education
805 West Penn Avenue
Urbana, IL 61801
ERIC/EECE Newsletter

Family Resource Coalition
230 North Michigan Avenue
Suite 1625
Chicago, IL 60601
• *FRC Report*

Family Service Association of America
44 East 23rd Street
New York, NY 10010
• *Social Casework*

Food Research and Action Center (FRAC)
1319 F Street, N.W.
Suite 500
Washington, DC 20004

Foundation Center
1001 Connecticut Avenue, N.W.
Washington, DC 20036

Gesell Institute for Human Development
310 Prospect Street
New Haven, CT 06511

Grantsmanship Center
1031 South Grand Avenue
Los Angeles, CA 90013

High/Scope Educational Research Foundation
600 North River Street
Ypsilanti, MI 48197
• *High/Scope ReSource*
• *Keynotes*

Human Resources Network
2011 Chancellor Street
Philadelphia, PA 19103

International Montessori Society
912 Thayer Avenue
Silver Spring, MD 20910
• *Montessori Observer*
• *Montessori News*

International Reading Association
800 Barksdale Road
P.O. Box 8139
Newark, DE 19714

League Against Child Abuse
21 East State Street
Columbus, OH 43215

League of Women Voters of the United States
1730 M Street, N.W.
Washington, DC 20036

Military Early Childhood Alliance (MECA)
c/o Olga Borden
934 Avenida del Sol, N.E.
Albuquerque, NM 87110
• *MECA* newsletter

Multicultural Project
P.O. Box 125
Cambridge, MA 02139

National Association for Child Care Management (NACCM)
1800 M Street, N.W.
Suite 1030N
Washington, DC 20036
• *NACCM News*

National Association for Family Day Care (NAFDC)
c/o Algerine Bridges
P.O. Box 5778
Nashville, TN 37208

National Association for the Education of Young Children (NAEYC)
1834 Connecticut Avenue, N.W.
Washington, DC 20009
• *Young Children*

National Association of Administrators of State and Federal Education Programs
1902 Lundwood Avenue
Ann Arbor, MI 40103

National Association of Counties
1735 New York Avenue, N.W.
Washington, DC 20036

National Association of Early Childhood Specialists in State Department of Education
c/o Ms. Tynette W. Hills
P.O. Box 2019
Trenton, NJ 08625
• *Update*

National Association of Elementary School Principals
1801 North Moore Street
Arlington, VA 22209

National Association of Hospital Affiliated Child Care Programs (NAHACCP)
c/o Rush-Presbyterian St. Luke's Medical Ctr
Lawrence Aronour Day School
630 S. Ashland
Chicago, IL 60607
• *Hospital Day Care Bulletin*

National Association of State Boards of Education
444 North Capital Street, N.W.
Washington, DC 20001

National Black Child Development Institute (NBCDI)
1463 Rhode Island Avenue, N.W.
Washington, DC 20005
• *Black Child Advocate*

National Center for Clinical Infant Programs
733 15th Street, N.W.
Suite 912
Washington, DC 20005
• *Zero to Three*

National Center for Health Education
30 East 29th Street
New York, NY 10016
• *CENTER*

National Center for Neighborhood Enterprise
1367 Connecticut Avenue, N.W.
Washington, DC 20036

National Certificate for Child Care Professionals
5701 Beechnut
Houston, TX 77074

National Coalition for Campus Child Care
c/o Ohio State University Child Care Program
1895 Summit Street
Columbus, OH 43201

National Committee for Citizens in Education
410 Wilde Lake Village Green
Columbia, MD 21044

National Committee for the Prevention of Child Abuse
Suite 510
111 East Wacker Drive
Chicago, IL 60601

National Congress of Parents and Teachers
1201 16th Street, N.W.
Washington, DC 20036

National Council of Churches Child Day Care Project
National Council of Churches in the USA
Child Advocacy Office
475 Riverside Drive
Room 572
New York, NY 10015

National Easter Seal Society for Crippled Children and Adults, Inc.
2023 West Ogden Avenue
Chicago, IL 60612

National Education Association (NEA)
1201 16th Street, N.W.
Washington, DC 20036

National Employer-Supported Child Care Project
P.O. Box 40652
Pasadena, CA 91104

National Family Day Care Providers Network
5730 Market Street
Oakland, CA 94608

National Foundation, The March of Dimes
School Relations and Health Education
Box 2000
White Plains, NY 10602

National Governors Association
444 North Capitol Street, N.W.
Suite 250
Washington, DC 20001

National Head Start Association
P.O. Box 2276
East Bradenton, FL 33508

National Independent Private Schools Association
2355 Lake Street
San Francisco, CA 94121

National Institute of Child Health and Human Development
National Institute of Health
Building 31, Room 2A34
Bethesda, MD 20014

National Institute of Mental Health (NIMH)
5454 Wisconsin Avenue
Chevy Chase, MD 20015

National Kindergarten Association
8 West 40th Street
New York, NY 10018

National Nutrition Education Clearinghouse
Society for Nutrition Education
2140 Shattuck Avenue
Suite 1110
Berkeley, CA 94704

National Organization for Women (NOW)
425 13th Street, N.W.
Suite 1048
Washington, DC 20004
• *National NOW Times*

National Prenatal Association
1311-A Dolly Madison Blvd.
Suite 3A
McLean, VA 22101

National PTA
700 Rush Street
Chicago, IL 60611-2571

National Rural Center
1828 L Street, N.W.
Washington, DC 20036

National Safety Council
444 North Michigan Avenue
Chicago, IL 60611

National School Boards Association
1055 Thomas Jefferson Street, N.W.
Washington, DC 20007

National School Public Relations Association
1801 North Moore Street
Rosslyn, VA 22209

National School Supply and Equipment Association
1500 Wilson Boulevard
Suite 609
Arlington, VA 22209

National Society to Prevent Blindness, Inc.
79 Madison Avenue
New York, NY 10016

National Urban League
425 13th Street, N.W.
Washington, DC 20004

National Youth Work Alliance
1346 Connecticut Avenue, N.W.
Washington, DC 20036

Non-Sexist Child Development Project
Women's Action Alliance, Inc.
370 Lexington Avenue
Room 603
New York, NY 10017
- *Equal Play*

Nutrition Foundation
Office of Education and Public Affairs
888 17th Street, N.W.
Washington, DC 20006

Parent Cooperative Preschools International
P.O. Box 31335
Phoenix, AZ 85046
- *PCPI Journal—A Magazine of Cooperative Learning*

Planned Parenthood Federation of America
810 Seventh Avenue
New York, NY 10019

Professional Association for Childhood Education
352 Harper Lane
Danville, CA 94526

Public Management Institute
358 Brannan Street
San Francisco, CA 94107

Research for Better Schools
1700 Market Street
Philadelphia, PA 19103

Resources for Child Care Management (RCCM)
P.O. Box 669
Summit, NJ 07901
- *Caring for infants and toddlers: What works, what doesn't*

Resources for Child Caring, Inc.
906 North Dale Street
St. Paul, MN 55103

Resources for Infant Education
1550 Murray Circle
Los Angeles, CA 90026

Rural Education Association
300 Education Building
Colorado State University
Ft. Collins, CO 80523

Save the Children
1182 West Peachtree Street, N.W.
Suite 209
Atlanta, GA 30309

School-Age Child Care Project
Wellesley College
Center for Research on Women
Wellesley, MA 02181
- *SACC Newsletter*

Society for Nutrition Education
1736 Franklin Street
Oakland, CA 94612
- *Journal of Nutrition Education*
- *Communication*

Society for Research in Child Development (SRCD)
University of Chicago Press
5801 Ellis Avenue
Chicago, IL 60637
- *Child Development*
- *Child Development Abstracts and Bibliography*
- *Monographs*

Southern Association for Children Under Six (SACUS)
Box 5403 Brady Station
Little Rock, AR 72215
- *Dimensions*

State Higher Education Executive Officers
One American Place
Suite 1530
Baton Rouge, LA 70825

The Sunday School Board of the Southern Baptist Convention
127 Ninth Avenue, North
Nashville, TN 37234

USA Toy Library Association
5940 W. Touhy Avenue
Chicago, IL 60648
- *Child's Play*

U.S. National Committee of OMEP
World Organization for Early Childhood Education
24000 Lahser Road
Southfield, MI 48034

U.S. Small Business Association
P.O. Box 15434
Ft. Worth, TX 76119

United Way of America
801 North Fairfax Street
Alexandria, VA 22314

Volunteer
The National Center for Citizen Involvement
P.O. Box 4179
Boulder, CO 80306
- *Voluntary Action Leadership*
- *Volunteering*
- *Exchange Networks*

Wakefield Washington Associates
1129 20th Street, N.W.
Washington, DC 20036
- *American Family*

Women's Action Alliance, Inc.
370 Lexington Avenue
New York, NY 10017
- *Equal Play*

Women's Equity Action League (WEAL)
805 15th Street, N.W.
Suite 822
Washington, DC 20005
- *WEAL Washington Report*

YWCA—National Board
600 Lexington Avenue
New York, NY 10022

Appendix F

Periodicals*

Baby Bulletin
Piscataway, NJ 08854

Beginnings
P.O. Box 2890
Redmond, WA 98052
• 4 issues
• teachers of young children

Behavior Today
Behavior Today
Box 2993
Boulder, CO 80302

Boardroom Reports
Box 1026
Millburn, NJ 07041
• semimonthly

Building Blocks
314 Liberty Street
Dundee, IL 60118
• 10 issues
• parents and young children

Building Blocks Child Care Edition
P.O. Box 31-0
Dundee, IL 60118
• 10 issues
• child care professionals

CCI&R Issues
(Child Care Information and Referral)
California Child Care Resource and Referral Network
320 Judah Street
Suite 2
San Francisco, CA 94122
• quarterly
• parents and providers

Center for Parent Education Newsletter
55 Chapel Street
Newton, MA 02160
• newsletter (6 issues)
• parent educators

Child Care Employee News
Child Care Staff Education Project
P.O. Box 5603
Berkeley, CA 94705
• quarterly
• child care workers

Child Care Quarterly
Human Sciences Press
72 Fifth Avenue
New York, NY 10011
• quarterly
• day care professionals

Child Care Resources
Quality Child Care, Inc.
P.O. Box 176
Mound, MN 55364
• newsletter (monthly)
• family day care providers

Child Health Alert
P.O. Box 338
Newton Highlands, MA 02161
• monthly newsletter
• children's health issues

Children Today
Superintendent of Documents
U.S. Government Printing Office
Washington, DC 20402
• bimonthly
• federal, state, and local services for children

Children's Advocate
Berkeley Children's Services
1017 University Avenue
Berkeley, CA 94710
• bimonthly
• issues about children

Children's World Staff Newsletter
Children's World, Inc.
P.O. Box 2298
Evergreen, CO 80439
• monthly
• ideas for classroom activities

* *Note:* Periodicals published by professional associations are listed in Appendix E under the respective organization.

Child Welfare Planning Notes
CWLA/Hecht Institute for State Welfare Planning
1346 Connecticut Avenue
Washington, DC 20036
- biweekly
- agencies, planners, and delivery people

Creative Schooling
P.O. Box 621
East New York Station
Brooklyn, NY 11207
- 10 issues a year
- parents of school age children

Day Care and Early Education
Human Sciences Press
72 Fifth Avenue
New York, NY 10011
- quarterly
- day care community

Day Care USA
Day Care Information Service
8701 Georgia Avenue
Suite 800
Silver Spring, MD 20910
- biweekly
- all day care people

Developmental Review
Academic Press
Journal Subscription Fulfillment Dept.
111 Fifth Avenue
New York, NY 10003
- quarterly
- scholarly, multidisciplinary

Early Child Development and Care
Gordon and Breach
Promotions Department
1 Park Avenue
New York, NY 10016
- quarterly
- professionals

Early Years
P.O. Box 7950
Philadelphia, PA 19101
- 10 issues
- teachers of young children

ECE Options
255 North Road #110
Chelmsford, MA 01824
- newsletter (5 issues a year)
- teacher trainers in higher education

Ecumenical Child Care Newsletter
National Council of the Churches of Christ
475 Riverside Drive, Room 572
New York, NY 10115

Equal Play
Women's Action Alliance
370 Lexington Avenue, Room 603
New York, NY 10017

Exceptional Parent
296 Boylston Street
Boston, MA 02116
- monthly

Exchange
P.O. Box 2890
Redmond, WA 98073
- bimonthly
- program directors

Family Journal
Dept. TL
Post Office Box 118
Peterborough, NH 03458
- monthly
- informed parents

Family Learning
5615 W. Cermak Road
Cicero, IL 60650
- 6 issues
- parents interested in education

FDA Consumer
Superintendent of Documents
U.S. Gov't Printing Office
Washington, DC 20402
- 10 issues a year
- information on product safety and regulations

First Teacher
P.O. Box 29
Bridgeport, CT 06602
- newsletter (monthly)
- caregivers, teachers, and family day care providers

First Teacher for Parents
P.O. Box 29
Bridgeport, CT 06602
- newsletter (monthly)
- parents of preschoolers

Food and Nutrition
Superintendent of Documents
U.S. Gov't Printing Office
Washington, DC 20402
- quarterly
- child nutrition information and programs

For Parents
7052 West Lane
Eden Lane, NY 14057
- 6 issues a year
- positive Christian parenting

FUNDAY
1250 Fairwood Avenue
P.O. Box 16658
Columbus, OH 43216
- a Weekly Reader publication for preschoolers
- 24 issues a year

Gifted Children Newsletter
80 New Bridge Road
P.O. Box 7200
Bergenfield, NJ 07621
- 11 issues
- parents of gifted children

Growing Child
22 North Second Street
P.O. Box 620
Lafayette, IN 47902
- monthly
- parents—keyed to age of child

Growing Child Research Review
22 North Second Street
P.O. Box 620
Lafayette, IN 47902
- monthly
- early childhood professionals

Growing Child Store
Growing Parent
22 North Second Street
P.O. Box 620
Lafayette, IN 47902
- monthly
- parents of young children

Highlights for Children
2300 West Fifth Avenue
Columbus, OH 43272

Imprints
Birth and Life Bookstore
P.O. Box 70625
Seattle, WA 98107
- newsletter and catalog on family, parents, child care topics

Instructor
P.O. Box 6099
Duluth, MN 55806-9799
- 10 issues
- teachers of preschool and elementary grades

Kidstuff
1307 South Killian Drive
Lake Park, FL 33403
- 12 issues a year
- early childhood educators

Learning
Subscription Department
P.O. Box 2580
Boulder, CO 80321
- 10 issues
- elementary and early childhood teachers

MicroNotes on Children and Computers
ERIC/EECE
805 W. Pennsylvania Avenue
Urbana, IL 61801
- bimonthly newsletter
- teachers, parents

Mothers' Manual
441 Lexington Avenue
New York, NY 10017
- 12 issues
- parents

New England Journal of Human Services
P.O. Box 9167
Boston, MA 02114
- quarterly
- managers/supervisors of human services

Newsletter of Parenting
2300 West Fifth Avenue
P.O. Box 2505
Columbus, OH 43216
- newsletter (monthly)
- parents

Nurturing News
P.O. Box 1813
Santa Ana, CA 92702
- newsletter (quarterly)
- men who care for children

Nutritioning Parents
Sara Sloan Nutra
P.O. Box 13825
Atlanta, GA 30329
- monthly
- parents

Parent Connection
700 Grove Street
Worcester, MA 01605
- newsletter (6 issues a year)
- parents of infants and preschoolers

Parents
Subscription Department
Bergenfield, NJ 07621
- monthly

Parents' Choice
Box 185
Waban, MA 02168
- newsletter (6 issues a year)
- parents

Pediatrics for Parents
Box 1069
Bangor, ME 04401
- monthly
- medical information for parents and caregivers of young children

Practical Parenting
18318 Minnetonka Blvd.
Deephaven, MN 55391
- newsletter (monthly)
- parents

Preschool Perspectives
P.O. Box 7525
Bend, OR 97708
- monthly
- preschool administrators and teachers

The Report Card
Learning Services
P.O. Box 324
Fallston, MD 21047
- monthly
- about children's education

Report on Preschool Programs
Capitol Publications, Inc.
1300 North 17th Street
Arlington, VA 22209
- biweekly newsletter
- professionals working with young children in all settings

School Ages NOTES
P.O. Box 120674
Nashville, TN 37212
- newsletter (6 issues a year)
- people who work with school age children in day care settings

Single Parent
Parents Without Partners, Inc.
7910 Woodmont Avenue
Washington, DC 20014
- magazine (10 issues a year)
- single parents

Sticks and Stones
Parenting in the Nuclear Age
P.O. Box 3479
Berkeley, CA 94703
- quarterly newsletter

Supervisory Management
Box 319
Saranac Lake, NY 12983
- monthly

Teaching Research
Infant and Child Center
Special Education Department
Monmouth, OR 97361
- series of newsletters
- early childhood professionals

Texas Child Care Quarterly
Texas Department of Human Resources
P.O. Box 2960
Austin, TX 78769
- newsletter (quarterly)
- caregivers of infants through adolescents

Topics in Early Childhood Special Education
Aspen Systems Corporation
1600 Research Building
Rockville, MD 20850
- quarterly
- topical, research oriented

Totline
Warren Publishing
Box 2253
Alderwood Manor, WA 98036
- 6 issues
- home and school activities for infants—preschoolers

Toy Review
P.O. Box 176
Newton, MA 02160

Twinline
6421 Telegraph Avenue
Oakland, CA 94609
- quarterly newsletter
- parents of twins, professionals working with twin families

Washington Social Legislation Bulletin
CWLA Center for Government Affairs
DuPont Circle Building
1346 Connecticut Avenue, N.W.
Washington, DC 20036
- newsletter (semimonthly)
- gives information and activities of federal agencies and legislation related to a number of social welfare issues

Working Mother—McCall's
P.O. Box 10608
Des Moines, IA 50381
- monthly
- general audience of working mothers

Working Parents
441 Lexington Avenue
New York, NY 10017
- monthly
- general audience of working parents

Wordworks
Young Writers' Club
P.O. Box 216
Newburyport, MA 01950
- 10 issues
- children 8–14

Yellow Books
Washington Monitor, Inc.
499 National Press Building
Washington, DC 20045
- Congressional Yellow Book—updated four times a year
- Federal Yellow Book—updated periodically

Appendix G

Media

Agency for Instructional Television
Box A
Bloomington, IN 47401

Barr Films
3490 East Foothill Blvd.
Pasadena, CA 91107

Benchmark Films, Inc.
145 Scarborough Road
Briarcliff Manor, NY 10510

Berkeley Children's Services
1017 University Avenue
Berkeley, CA 94710

Book-Lab, Inc.
1449 37th Street
Brooklyn, NY 11218

Bowmar/Noble
4563 Colorado Blvd.
Los Angeles, CA 90039

Caedman
1995 Broadway
New York, NY 10023

Campus Film Distributors Corp.
14 Madison Avenue
P.O. Box 206
Valhalla, NY 10595

Carousel Films, Inc.
1501 Broadway
Suite 1503
New York, NY 10036

Chapel Hill Training-Outreach Project
Lincoln Center
Chapel Hill, NC 27514

Cheviot Corp.
Department M641
Box 34485
Los Angeles, CA 90034

Childcraft Education Corp.
20 Kilmer Road
Edison, NJ 08817

Childhood Resources, Inc.
5307 Lee Highway
Arlington, VA 22207

Children's Radio Theater
P.O. Box 53057
Washington, DC 20009

Children's Television Workshop
One Lincoln Plaza
New York, NY 10023

Churchill Films
662 North Robertson Blvd.
Los Angeles, CA 90069

Community Playthings
Rifton, NY 12471

CRM McGraw-Hill Films
110 15th Street
Del Mar, CA 92014

Davidson Films
850 O'Neill Avenue
Belmont, CA 94002

Day Care Consultation & Media Project
Pacific Oaks
714 West California Boulevard
Pasadena, CA 91165

Doubleday Multimedia
P.O. Box 11607
Santa Ana, CA 92705

Early Childhood
S.C. ETV
P.O. Drawer L
Columbia, SC 29250

Educational Record Center
3120 Maple Drive
Suite 124
Atlanta, GA 30305

Evelyn Green
Tidewater Child Care Association
2115 High Street
Portsmouth, VA 23704

Folkways Records
43 West 61st Street
New York, NY 10023

High/Scope Press
600 North River Street
Ypsilanti, MI 48197-2898

Home Based Training Program
Frank Porter Graham Child Dev. Program
500 NCWB Plaza
Chapel Hill, NC 27514

J. P. Lilley & Son, Inc.
2009 North Third Street
Box 3035
Harrisburg, PA 17105

JAB Press
P.O. Box 39852
Los Angeles, CA 90039

Kaplan
600 Jonestown Road
Winston-Salem, NC 27103

Learning Tree Filmstrips
934 Pearl Street
P.O. Box 1590, Dept. 100
Boulder, CO 80302

Linden International
302 Contra Costa Avenue
Department T
Tacoma, WA 98466

Macmillan Films, Inc.
34 Mac Questen Parkway South
Mt. Vernon, NY 10550

McGraw-Hill Films
Dept. 443
1221 Avenue of the Americas
New York, NY 10020

Media Five
3211 Cahuenga Blvd. West
Hollywood, CA 90068

Miss Jackie Music
10001 El Monte
Overland Park, KS 66207

Modern Talking Picture Service
2323 New Hyde Park Road
New Hyde, NY 11040

Music and Movement Unlimited
P.O. Box 639
Southington, CT 06489

National Audio Visual Center
Washington, DC 20409

Oryx Press
2214 North Central at Encanto
Phoenix, AZ 85004

Pacific Cascade Records
47534 McKenzie Highway
Vida, OR 97488

Parents' Magazine Films, Inc.
52 Vanderbilt Avenue
New York, NY 10017

Prime Time School Television
40 East Huron Street
Chicago, IL 60611

Sterling Educational Films
241 East 34th Street
New York, NY 10016

Texas Department of Community Affairs
Children and Youth Services Division
P.O. Box 13166, Capitol Station
Austin, TX 78711

Toys 'n Things Press
Resources for Child Caring, Inc.
906 North Dale Street
St. Paul, MN 55103

University of Minnesota
Audio Visual Library Service
3300 University Avenue SE
Minneapolis, MN 55414

Walt Disney Educational Media Company
500 South Buena Vista Street
Burbank, CA 91521

Weston Woods
Weston, CT 06883

Wombat Productions, Inc.
77 Tarrytown Road
White Plains, NY 10607

Women's Bureau
Department of Labor
200 Constitution Avenue
Room 53305
Washington, DC 20210

Youngheart Records
P.O. Box 27784
Los Angeles, CA 90027

Name Index

Subject Index